Lingua TOEFL® CBT

INSIDER

LinguaForum

Lingua TOEFL® CBT: INSIDER

Prior editions Copyright © 2001, 2002 by Lingua Forum, Inc.

Published by Lingua Forum, Inc.
Copyright © 2003 by Lingua Forum, Inc.
All rights reserved.

Printed with corrections, October 2002

ISBN: 89-5563-005-0 98740

TOEFL® is a registered trademark of Educational Testing Service.
This book has been neither reviewed nor endorsed by ETS.
Printed in the Republic of Korea

Reference Number: 11080150/12240150a/03250250a/10250250b

CONTENTS

Contents

Diagnostic Test 1   **1**

Introduction   **25**

    About This Book   26

    About the CBT TOEFL   26

    Concordance Table   33

Listening

    Overview of the CBT Listening Section   36

    Listening Strategies   38

Chapter 1 – General Information for Part A   **40**

Chapter 2 – Question Types for Short Conversations   **42**

    1. Implication Questions   42

    2. Meaning Questions   44

    3. Suggestion Questions   46

    4. Inference Questions   48

    5. Future Action Questions   50

    6. Comprehension Questions   52

    7. Assumption Questions   54

Mini-Test 1   **56**

Chapter 3 – Diverters for Short Conversations   **62**

    1. Similar Sounds   62

    2. Synonyms   64

    3. Conditionals (wishes, ifs, hypotheticals)   66

    4. Agreement/Disagreement   68

    5. Passives   70

    6. Degree (as ... as, nearly, over, already, almost)   72

    7. Vocabulary (idioms, multi-word verbs)   75

    8. Pronouns and Referents   78

Mini Test 2   **80**

Chapter 4 – Reviews for Part A   **86**

    Type A – 11 Questions for Part A   86

    Type B – 17 Questions for Part A   89

Chapter 5 – General Information for Part B　　94

Chapter 6 – Casual Conversations and Question Types　　96
1. Context/Comprehension　96
2. Detail/Fact　98
3. Future Action　101

Mini-Test 3　　104

Chapter 7 – Academic Discussions/Lectures and Question Types　　110
1. Main Topic　112
2. Comprehension/Detail　115
3. Inference　118
4. Negatives　120
5. Multiple-Answer　122
6. Ordering　128
7. Matching　135
8. Graphics　143

Mini-Test 4　　152

Chapter 8 – Reviews for Part B　　158
Type A – 19 Questions for Part B　158
Type B – 33 Questions for Part B　166

Structure

Overview of the CBT Structure Section　182
Types of Questions　182
Structure Strategies　184
Symbols Used in This Section　185
Patterns and Distribution of Question Types　186

Chapter 1 – Elements of Clauses　　188
Pattern 1 Subject Missing　193
Pattern 2 Verb Missing　196
Pattern 3 Subject + Verb Missing　197
Pattern 4 Subjective Complement Missing　199
Pattern 5 Object and/or Objective Complement Missing　202
Pattern 6 Incorrect Omission of Clause Elements　205

Pattern Drill for Patterns 1-6　206

Mini-Test 1　　209

Chapter 2 – Subordinate Clauses   212
Noun Clauses
Adverb Clauses
Pattern 7 Adverb Clause Missing   216
Adjective Clauses
Pattern 8 Adjective Clause Missing   220
Pattern 9 Incorrect Choice of Adjective Clause Marker   223
Pattern 10 Incorrect Inclusion/Omission of Adjective Clause Marker   226
Pattern 11 Pronoun Used Incorrectly in Place of Adjective Clause Marker   228

Pattern Drill for Patterns 7-11   229

Mini-Test 2   233

Chapter 3 – Verbals   236
Verbals
Pattern 12 Participial Phrase Missing   238
Pattern 13 Infinitive Phrase Missing   241
Pattern 14 Incorrect Choice of Verbal   242
Pattern 15 Incorrect Choice of Participle   245
Pattern 16 Incorrect Infinitive Form   247
Pattern 17 Verb Used Incorrectly in Place of Verbal   248

Pattern Drill for Patterns 12-17   249

Mini-Test 3   253

Chapter 4 – Prepositional Phrases   256
Pattern 18 Prepositional Phrase Missing   258
Pattern 19 Incorrect Choice of Preposition   260
Pattern 20 Incorrect Omission of Preposition   264
Pattern 21 Incorrect Inclusion of Preposition   267

Pattern Drill for Patterns 18-21   269

Mini-Test 4   271

Chapter 5 – Noun Phrases   274
Nouns
Pattern 22 Singular/Plural Noun   278
Pattern 23 Incorrect Plural Form   280
Pronouns
Pattern 24 Incorrect Pronoun Form   282
Pattern 25 Incorrect Choice of Pronoun   284
Pattern 26 Incorrect Inclusion of Pronoun   285
Articles
Pattern 27 Incorrect Choice of Article   286
Pattern 28 Incorrect Omission of Article   288
Pattern 29 Incorrect Inclusion of Article   289

Appositives

Pattern 30 Appositive Missing   291

Pattern Drill for Patterns 22-30   292

Mini-Test 5   297

Chapter 6 – Adjective Phrases and Comparisons   300

Pattern 31 Adjective Phrase Missing   302
Pattern 32 Comparison Missing   303
Pattern 33 Incorrect Choice of Comparison   305
Pattern 34 Incorrect Comparative/Superlative Form   306

Pattern Drill for Patterns 31-34   308

Mini-Test 6   311

Chapter 7 – Verb Phrases   314

Pattern 35 Incorrect Verb Form   317
Pattern 36 Incorrect Tense   319
Pattern 37 Active/Passive Confusion   321

Pattern Drill for Patterns 35-37   323

Mini-Test 7   325

Chapter 8 – Conjunctions and Parallelism   328

Conjunctions

Pattern 38 Conjunction Missing   331
Pattern 39 Incorrect Conjunction   333
Pattern 40 Incorrect Inclusion/Omission of Conjunction   335

Parallelism

Pattern 41 Missing Items Involving Parallel Structures   337
Pattern 42 Errors with Parallel Structures   339

Pattern Drill for Patterns 38-42   341

Mini-Test 8   343

Chapter 9 – Dangling Modifiers   346

Pattern 3 Subject + Verb Missing (Dp. Chapter 1)   348
Pattern 1 Subject Missing (Dp. Chapter 1)   348

Pattern Drill for Patterns 3 and 1   349

Mini-Test 9   351

Chapter 10 – Agreement and Word Order   354

Agreement

Pattern 43 Errors in Subject-Verb Agreement   355

Pattern 44 Errors in Pronoun-Noun Agreement   358
Word Order
Pattern 45 Missing Items Involving Word Order   359
Pattern 46 Incorrect Word Order   361
Pattern 47 Inverted Subject-Verb Word Order   363

Pattern Drill for Patterns 43-47   365

Mini-Test 10   367

Chapter 11 – Word Form   370
Pattern 48 Adjective/Adverb Confusion   372
Pattern 49 Adjective/Noun Confusion   374
Pattern 50 Noun/Verb Confusion   376
Pattern 51 Person Noun/Activity (Field) Noun Confusion   377
Pattern 52 Other Confusion   378

Pattern Drill for Patterns 48-52   381

Mini-Test 11   383

Chapter 12 – Word Choice   386
Pattern 53 Confusion of *So/Very/Too, So/Such*   387
Pattern 54 Confusion of *Another/Other, Many/Much, Few/Little, Like/Alike, Near/Nearly, No/Not/None,* and so on   389
Pattern 55 Confusion of *Make/Do*   393
Pattern 56 Confusion of Conjunction/Preposition   394

Pattern Drill for Patterns 53-56   395

Mini-Test 12   397

Chapter 13 – Miscellaneous   400
Pattern 57 Negative Word Missing   401
Pattern 58 Confusion of Cardinal/Ordinal Number   402
Pattern 59 Article Used in Place of Possessive Adjective   403
Pattern 60 Conditionals   404

Mini-Test 13   406

Reading

Overview of the CBT Reading Section   410
Reading Strategies   412

Chapter 1 – Main Idea   414
Overview   414
Strategies   415

Skill Building 417
Intensive Exercises 419
Vocabulary Review for Intensive Exercises 1.1-1.8 427

Practice Test 1 — 428

Chapter 2 – Reference and Vocabulary — 438

Reference Overview 438
Reference Strategies 439
Vocabulary-in-context Overview 440
Vocabulary-in-context Strategies 441
Skill Building 446
Intensive Exercises 451
Vocabulary Review for Intensive Exercises 2.1-2.5 456
Word Files I: TOEFL Vocabulary with Emphasis on Natural Sciences ... 457

Practice Test 2 — 458

Chapter 3 – Fact, Negative, Scanning, and Restatement Questions — 466

Overview 466
Strategies 469
Skill Building 470
Intensive Exercises 473
Vocabulary Review for Intensive Exercises 3.1-3.5 478
Word Files II: TOEFL Vocabulary with Emphasis on American History ... 479

Practice Test 3 — 480

Chapter 4 – Insertion — 490

Overview 490
Strategies 491
Skill Building 493
Intensive Exercises 496
Vocabulary Review for Intensive Exercises 4.1-4.8 504
Word Files III: TOEFL Vocabulary with Emphasis on Social Sciences and the Fine Arts ... 505

Practice Test 4 — 506

Chapter 5 – Inference — 514

Overview 514
Strategies 515
Skill Building 517
Intensive Exercises 520
Vocabulary Review for Intensive Exercises 5.1-5.5 525

Practice Test 5 — 526

Chapter 6 – Miscellaneous Overview and Purpose Questions   **536**

Overview and Strategies   536
1. Organization   536
2. Tone/Attitude/Purpose   536
3. Preceding/Following Topics   538
Skill Building   539
Intensive Exercise   545
Vocabulary Review for Intensive Exercises 6.1-6.5   550
Word Files IV: TOEFL Vocabulary with Emphasis on Biography,
         Literature, Culture, and Business   551

Practice Test 6   **552**

Writing

1. Overview of the CBT Writing Section   562
2. Step-by-Step Guide to Writing   562
3. How to Write Clearly   569
4. Essay Structure   570
5. Summary of Transitional Expressions   572
6. A Few Suggestions   573
7. Essay Ratings   574
8. Practice Scoring Writing Essays   575
9. Writing Topics   587

Complete Practice Test 1   **593**

Listening Script   **637**

Answer Key   **717**

DIAGNOSTIC TEST 1
(Simplified Version)

Listening: 15 Minutes (including listening time)
Structure: 7 Minutes
Reading: 15 Minutes
Writing: 30 Minutes

Suggested Total Time: 67 Minutes

ANSWER SHEET

Lingua TOEFL® CBT: Insider
Diagnostic Test 1

Name	
Sex	☐ male ☐ female
E-mail address	
Telephone No.	

	Number of Correct Answers	Times	= Converted Score
Listening		× 6.67	= (S1)
Structure		× 4.0	= (S2)
Reading		× 9.1	= (S3)
Writing	Score 0 ~ Score 6 (Score Level)		0 ~ 60
Your expected score will be between (S1 + S2 + S3) and (S1 + S2 + S3 + 60).			
Total Score Range	(	) ~ (	)

Cut here

Section 1: Listening	Section 2: Structure	Section 3: Reading
1 Ⓐ Ⓑ Ⓒ Ⓓ	1 Ⓐ Ⓑ Ⓒ Ⓓ	1 Ⓐ Ⓑ Ⓒ Ⓓ
2 Ⓐ Ⓑ Ⓒ Ⓓ	2 Ⓐ Ⓑ Ⓒ Ⓓ	2
3 Ⓐ Ⓑ Ⓒ Ⓓ	3 Ⓐ Ⓑ Ⓒ Ⓓ	3 Ⓐ Ⓑ Ⓒ Ⓓ
4 Ⓐ Ⓑ Ⓒ Ⓓ	4 Ⓐ Ⓑ Ⓒ Ⓓ	4 Ⓐ Ⓑ Ⓒ Ⓓ
5 Ⓐ Ⓑ Ⓒ Ⓓ	5 Ⓐ Ⓑ Ⓒ Ⓓ	5 Ⓐ Ⓑ Ⓒ Ⓓ
6 Ⓐ Ⓑ Ⓒ Ⓓ	6 Ⓐ Ⓑ Ⓒ Ⓓ	6 Ⓐ Ⓑ Ⓒ Ⓓ
7 Ⓐ Ⓑ Ⓒ Ⓓ	7 Ⓐ Ⓑ Ⓒ Ⓓ	7
8 Ⓐ Ⓑ Ⓒ Ⓓ	8 Ⓐ Ⓑ Ⓒ Ⓓ	8 Ⓐ Ⓑ Ⓒ Ⓓ
9 Spinet -	9 Ⓐ Ⓑ Ⓒ Ⓓ	9 Ⓐ Ⓑ Ⓒ Ⓓ
Giraffe piano -	10 Ⓐ Ⓑ Ⓒ Ⓓ	10 Ⓐ Ⓑ Ⓒ Ⓓ
Pyramid piano -		11 Ⓐ Ⓑ Ⓒ Ⓓ
10 Ⓐ Ⓑ Ⓒ Ⓓ		
11 *Saturday Evening Post -*		
Harper's New Monthly Magazine -		
Putnam's Monthly Magazine -		
12		
13 Ⓐ Ⓑ Ⓒ Ⓓ		
14 Ⓐ Ⓑ Ⓒ Ⓓ		
15 Ⓐ Ⓑ Ⓒ Ⓓ		

■ **Have you taken the official TOEFL Test?**

☐ Yes ──→ if any
☐ No

PBT Score	
Listening	
Structure	
Reading	
Writing	
TOTAL	

CBT Score	
Listening	
Structure	
Reading	
Writing	
TOTAL	

■ **Educational background**

☐ middle/high school ☐ undergraduate ☐ graduate

SIGNED: _____
(SIGN YOUR NAME AS IF SIGNING A BUSINESS LETTER.)

DATE: _____ / _____ / _____
MO.   DAY   YEAR

ANSWER SHEET

Lingua TOEFL® CBT: Insider
Diagnostic Test 1

Read the topic below and then make any notes that will help you plan your response.
Begin typing your response in the box at the bottom of the screen, or write your answer on
the answer sheet provided to you.

Some people believe that it harms a friendship when one borrows money from a friend. Do
you agree or disagree with this opinion? Why? Use specific reasons and details to support
your view.

Cut

Paste

Undo

Time   **LinguaForum**   ? Answer ➡
Help Confirm Next

SECTION 1
LISTENING
Suggested Time: 15 Minutes (including listening time)

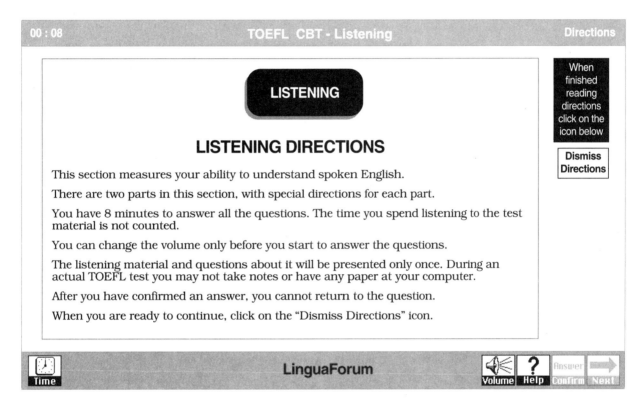

00 : 08 TOEFL CBT - Listening Directions

When finished reading directions click on the icon below

Dismiss Directions

LISTENING

LISTENING DIRECTIONS

This section measures your ability to understand spoken English.

There are two parts in this section, with special directions for each part.

You have 8 minutes to answer all the questions. The time you spend listening to the test material is not counted.

You can change the volume only before you start to answer the questions.

The listening material and questions about it will be presented only once. During an actual TOEFL test you may not take notes or have any paper at your computer.

After you have confirmed an answer, you cannot return to the question.

When you are ready to continue, click on the "Dismiss Directions" icon.

Time   LinguaForum   Volume Help Answer Confirm Next

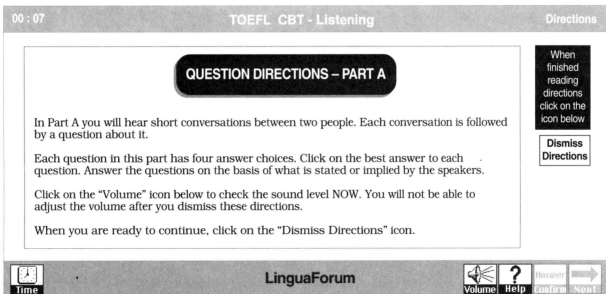

00 : 07 TOEFL CBT - Listening Directions

When finished reading directions click on the icon below

Dismiss Directions

QUESTION DIRECTIONS – PART A

In Part A you will hear short conversations between two people. Each conversation is followed by a question about it.

Each question in this part has four answer choices. Click on the best answer to each question. Answer the questions on the basis of what is stated or implied by the speakers.

Click on the "Volume" icon below to check the sound level NOW. You will not be able to adjust the volume after you dismiss these directions.

When you are ready to continue, click on the "Dismiss Directions" icon.

Time   LinguaForum   Volume Help Answer Confirm Next

Questions 1-6

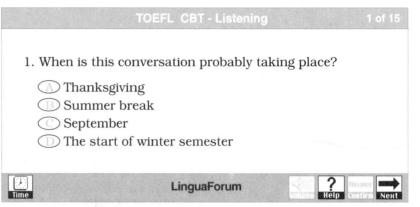

1. When is this conversation probably taking place?

(A) Thanksgiving
(B) Summer break
(C) September
(D) The start of winter semester

LinguaForum

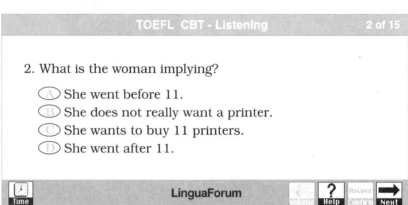

2. What is the woman implying?

(A) She went before 11.
(B) She does not really want a printer.
(C) She wants to buy 11 printers.
(D) She went after 11.

LinguaForum

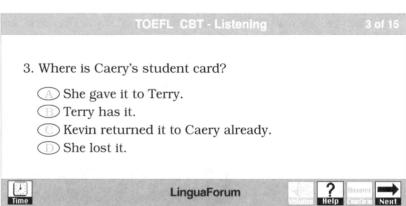

3. Where is Caery's student card?

(A) She gave it to Terry.
(B) Terry has it.
(C) Kevin returned it to Caery already.
(D) She lost it.

LinguaForum

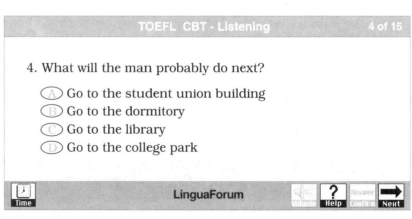

4. What will the man probably do next?

(A) Go to the student union building
(B) Go to the dormitory
(C) Go to the library
(D) Go to the college park

LinguaForum

5. What does the woman suggest to the man?

- (A) Go to the movies
- (B) Put off the paper as long as possible
- (C) Let her do some research for him
- (D) Start on his paper

Time　　　　　　LinguaForum　　　　Volume Help Confirm Next

6. What does the man mean?

- (A) He does not want to tell the woman how he did.
- (B) He did quite well.
- (C) The professor does not want to hear complaints about the exam.
- (D) It is too late to file a protest with the department.

Time　　　　　　LinguaForum　　　　Volume Help Confirm Next

SECTION 1
LISTENING

Directions

QUESTION DIRECTIONS – PART B

When finished reading directions click on the icon below

Dismiss Directions

In Part B there are several talks and conversations. Each talk or conversation is followed by several questions.

The conversations and talks are about a variety of topics. You do not need special knowledge of the topics to answer the questions correctly. You should answer each question on the basis of what is stated or implied by the speakers.

Click on the "Volume" icon below to check the sound level NOW. You will not be able to adjust the volume after you dismiss these directions.

When you are ready to continue, click on the "Dismiss Directions" icon.

Time

LinguaForum

Volume Help Confirm Next

Answer

Questions 7-9

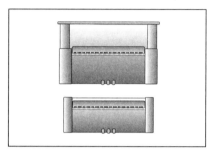

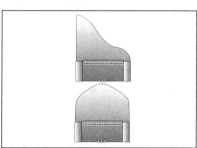

7. What is the main topic of this discussion?

   (A) The different kinds of pianos
   (B) How the grand piano revolutionized music
   (C) The American, John Isaac Hawkins
   (D) The invention of the upright piano

LinguaForum

Time   Volume Help Confirm Next

8. What makes the upright piano different than the grand piano?

   Click on 2 answers.

   [A] There is a spring-loaded hammer mechanism.
   [B] It has better sound quality than the spinet.
   [C] The strings and soundboard are vertical.
   [D] The strings begin at keyboard height.

LinguaForum

Time   Volume Help Confirm Next

9. The professor mentioned several different kinds of upright pianos. Match the name of the piano with the diagram.

Click on a piano name. Then click on the space where it belongs. Use each type only once.

Spinet
Giraffe piano
Pyramid piano

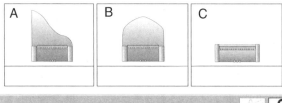

Questions 10-13

Literature

Magazines:
- *Saturday Evening Post*
- *Harper's New Monthly Magazine*
- *Putnam's Monthly Magazine*

Pulp magazines:
- *General Magazine*
- *Atlantic Monthly*

10. What is the main idea of this lecture?

(A) The earliest magazines in America were the best.
(B) 18th century magazines were printed on cheap paper.
(C) The 19th century was a very successful time for American magazines.
(D) American magazines have been published for nearly 300 years.

11. The professor mentioned several popular magazines from the 19th century. Match the magazine and its characteristics.

Click on a magazine. Then click on the space where it belongs. Use each magazine only once.

Saturday Evening Post
Harper's New Monthly Magazine
Putnam's Monthly Magazine

For a long time, the best-selling magazine in America	Best all-round magazine in American history	One of the first city magazines

12. The professor described the history of American magazines. Place the following developments into the correct chronological order.

Click on a magazine. Then click on the space where it belongs. Use each magazine only once.

Saturday Evening Post
Pulp magazines
General Magazine
Atlantic Monthly

1. [   ]   3. [   ]

2. [   ]   4. [   ]

13. What can be inferred from what the speaker said about pulp magazines?

(A) They had better paper than traditional magazines.
(B) They had low literary quality.
(C) They were published mostly in the American West.
(D) They had shocking pictures.

Questions 14-15

14. Why is Diane excited?

Ⓐ Her sister arrives at 1:30 tomorrow.
Ⓑ One of her sisters will arrive on the 30th.
Ⓒ Her sister is leaving tomorrow.
Ⓓ Her car will be fixed soon.

LinguaForum

15. What will Diane and Sarah most likely do during her trip?

Ⓐ Go out with the man
Ⓑ Go to the movies
Ⓒ Go sightseeing around the university campus
Ⓓ Go to coffee shops to talk

LinguaForum

SECTION 2
STRUCTURE
Suggested Time: 7 Minutes

STRUCTURE

STRUCTURE DIRECTIONS

When finished reading directions click on the icon below

Dismiss Directions

In this section there are two types of test questions.
In one type, you choose the word or phrase that best completes a sentence.

> Example: _____ of igneous rocks results from the two main features of these rocks – the size and the chemistry of their constituent crystals.
>
> ⊂⊃ Most of the great varieties
> ⊂⊃ Great varieties
> ⊂⊃ Great variation which
> ⊂⊃ The great variety

In the other type, you look at a sentence with four underlined words or phrases and choose the underlined word or phrase that must be changed for the sentence to be correct.

> Example: The tides <u>caused</u> by the <u>gravitational</u> <u>pull</u> of the moon and sun and
>
> <u>by the rotations</u> of the earth, moon, and sun.

You have 7 minutes to answer all of the questions.
After you have confirmed an answer, you cannot return to the question.
When you are ready to continue, click on the "Dismiss Directions" icon.

Time

LinguaForum

Help **Answer** **Confirm** **Next**

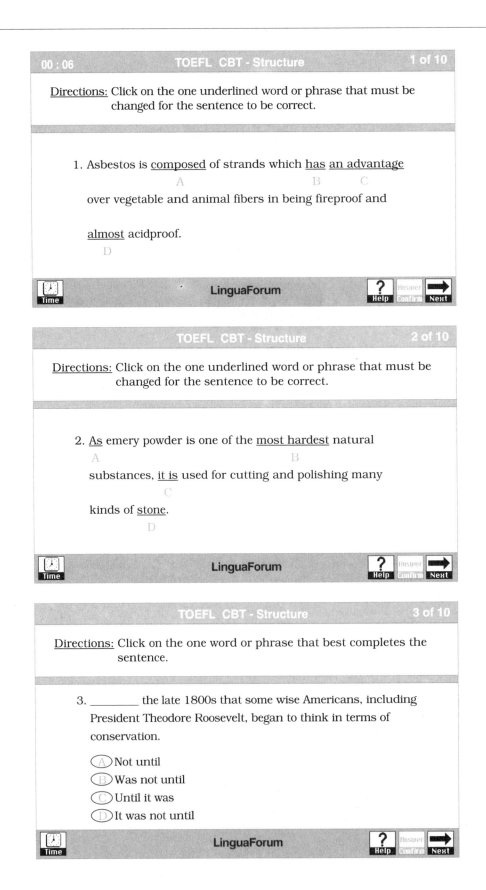

Directions: Click on the one underlined word or phrase that must be changed for the sentence to be correct.

1. Asbestos is <u>composed</u> of strands which <u>has</u> <u>an advantage</u>
                A   B   C

   over vegetable and animal fibers in being fireproof and

   <u>almost</u> acidproof.
      D

LinguaForum

Time   ? Help   Answer Confirm   Next

Directions: Click on the one underlined word or phrase that must be changed for the sentence to be correct.

2. <u>As</u> emery powder is one of the <u>most hardest</u> natural
     A   B

   substances, <u>it is</u> used for cutting and polishing many
            C

   kinds of <u>stone</u>.
          D

LinguaForum

Time   ? Help   Answer Confirm   Next

Directions: Click on the one word or phrase that best completes the sentence.

3. _____ the late 1800s that some wise Americans, including President Theodore Roosevelt, began to think in terms of conservation.

     A   Not until
     B   Was not until
     C   Until it was
     D   It was not until

LinguaForum

Time   ? Help   Answer Confirm   Next

<u>Directions:</u> Click on the one underlined word or phrase that must be changed for the sentence to be correct.

4. A skier usually <u>wearing</u> specially designed <u>clothing</u> made of
                 A   B

   <u>tightly</u> woven fabrics that are <u>resistant to</u> water and wind.
     C   D

LinguaForum

<u>Directions:</u> Click on the one word or phrase that best completes the sentence.

5. Colonial life in Virginia was best described by William Byrd, owner of Westover, _____ estate of almost 180,000 acres on the James River.

   (A) which his
   (B) an
   (C) was the
   (D) and

LinguaForum

<u>Directions:</u> Click on the one underlined word or phrase that must be changed for the sentence to be correct.

6. <u>In contrast</u> to the Middle American and Mississippian
     A

   <u>cultures</u>, Anasazi society <u>lacked of</u> a rigid class <u>structure</u>.
     B   C   D

LinguaForum

Directions: Click on the one word or phrase that best completes the sentence.

7. Autographs of famous people often have great historical significance

_____.

(A) and commercially valuable

(B) but also value commercial

(C) as well as commercial value

(D) than does commercial value

LinguaForum

Directions: Click on the one underlined word or phrase that must be changed for the sentence to be correct.

8. In the 1860s, amendments to the Constitution made <u>former</u>

                                                        A

slaves <u>freely</u> and gave <u>them</u> all the rights of citizenship,

           B   C

including the <u>right to vote</u>.

                  D

LinguaForum

Directions: Click on the one word or phrase that best completes the sentence.

9. Even the most developed Indian societies of the sixteenth century were ill equipped to resist the dynamic European cultures _____ their world.

(A) invading

(B) invaded

(C) they invaded

(D) invasion of

LinguaForum

Directions: Click on the one underlined word or phrase that must be changed for the sentence to be correct.

10. Taconite, <u>which</u> gets its <u>name</u> from the Taconic Mountains of the
      A   B

Northeastern United States, <u>is a</u> low-grade <u>so</u> important rock
                               C   D

that contains both magnetite and hematite.

LinguaForum

Time   Help   Answer Confirm   Next

SECTION 3
READING

Suggested Time: 15 Minutes

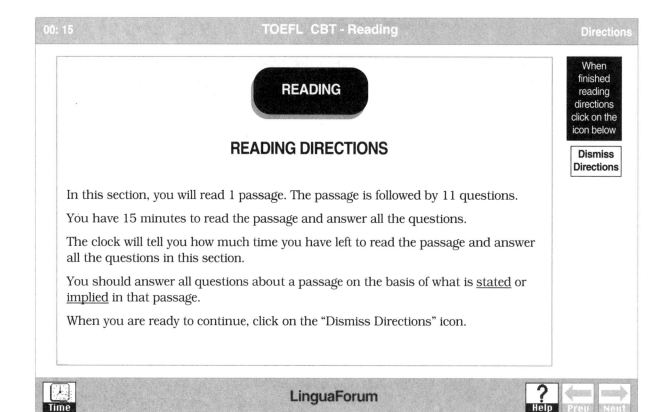

When finished reading the passage click on the icon below

Proceed

Altering the outward appearance of the body by making permanent, irreversible changes to it is widely practiced in Western as well as non-Western societies. In the West, tattooing the skin and piercing the ears are customs of long standing; inserting metal rings or other objects through the fleshy parts of the nose, brow, navel, or other parts of the body is relatively new to Westerners. They may think of these kinds of body alteration as deformation or mutilation rather than decoration, but they are not fundamentally different from ear piercing or tattooing.

For example, labrets or lip plugs, objects typically made of wood or bone that are inserted into the flesh of the lower lip, are found in many places around the world, including East Africa and South America. A small version is usually inserted in childhood, and may be increased in size as the individual matures, reflecting changes in his or her social status. Among the Kayapó of Brazil, a young man who has become a father for the first time is seen as having officially passed from boyhood to manhood. This passage is symbolized by a permanent physical change: the small plug that was inserted through the flesh of his lower lip when the new father was himself an infant is replaced by a much larger, saucerlike plate.

The insertion of the new labret is painful, although perhaps no more so than the insertion and periodic tightening of dental braces in Western society, which many Westerners consider quite bearable given the perceived aesthetic benefits of orthodontia. The benefits of the lip disc are equally worthwhile for the Kayapó.

Once a father, a Kayapó male is entitled to speak his mind on matters of concern to his village. In fact, he must, if he is to earn the respect of other villagers, for silence is not considered a virtue. Verbally assertive, mature males, and they alone, command the political respect that permits them to preside over village life. Kayapó women are not permitted to wear labrets because of their strong symbolic association with fatherhood and manhood.

Altering the outward appearance of the body by making permanent, irreversible changes to **it** is widely practiced in Western as well as non-Western societies. In the West, tattooing the skin and piercing the ears are customs of long standing; inserting metal rings or other objects through the fleshy parts of the nose, brow, navel, or other parts of the body is relatively new to Westerners. They may think of these kinds of body alteration as deformation or mutilation rather than decoration, but they are not fundamentally different from ear piercing or tattooing.

For example, labrets or lip plugs, objects typically made of wood or bone that are inserted into the flesh of the lower lip, are found in many places around the world, including East Africa and South America. A small version is usually inserted in childhood, and may be increased in size as the individual matures, reflecting changes in his or her social status. Among the Kayapó of Brazil, a young man who has become a father for the first time is seen as having officially passed from boyhood to manhood. This passage is symbolized by a permanent physical change: the small plug that was inserted through the flesh of his lower lip when the new father was himself an infant is replaced by a much larger, saucerlike plate.

The insertion of the new labret is painful, although perhaps no more so than the insertion and periodic tightening of dental braces in Western society, which many Westerners consider quite bearable given the perceived aesthetic benefits of orthodontia. The benefits of the lip disc are equally worthwhile for the Kayapó.

Once a father, a Kayapó male is entitled to speak his mind on matters of concern to his village. In fact, he must, if he is to earn the respect of other villagers, for silence is not considered a virtue. Verbally assertive, mature males, and they alone, command the political respect that permits them to preside over village life. Kayapó women are not permitted to wear labrets because of their strong symbolic association with fatherhood and manhood.

1. Which of the following is NOT the main purpose of the passage?
   (A) discuss the different reasons for practicing body alteration around the world
   (B) introduce body decoration as practiced by primitive villagers in South America
   (C) compare and contrast the body alteration practices of the Western and non-Western societies
   (D) analyze the social and cultural significance of body alteration as practiced by the Kayapó

2. Look at the word **it** in the passage. Click on the word or phrase in the **bold** text that **it** refers to.

3. All of the following are widely practiced in Western societies EXCEPT
   (A) tattooing
   (B) body piercing
   (C) manicure
   (D) ear piercing

4. The word standing in the passage is closest in meaning to
   (A) practice
   (B) value
   (C) state
   (D) volatility

5. The passage suggests that Westerners think of body alteration as
   (A) superior in aesthetic value compared to tattooing and ear piercing
   (B) incomparable with tattooing and ear piercing
   (C) not having any kind of aesthetic value
   (D) being essentially dangerous and fatal practices

LinguaForum

Altering the outward appearance of the body by making permanent, irreversible changes to it is widely practiced in Western as well as non-Western societies. In the West, tattooing the skin and piercing the ears are customs of long standing; inserting metal rings or other objects through the fleshy parts of the nose, brow, navel, or other parts of the body is relatively new to Westerners. They may think of these kinds of body alteration as deformation or mutilation rather than decoration, but they are not fundamentally different from ear piercing or tattooing.

→ For example, labrets or lip plugs, objects typically made of wood or bone that are inserted into the flesh of the lower lip, are found in many places around the world, including East Africa and South America. ■ A small version is usually inserted in childhood, and may be increased in size as the individual matures, reflecting changes in his or her social status. ■ Among the Kayapó of Brazil, a young man who has become a father for the first time is seen as having officially passed from boyhood to manhood. ■ This passage is symbolized by a permanent physical change: the small plug that was inserted through the flesh of his lower lip when the new father was himself an infant is replaced by a much larger, saucerlike plate. ■

→ The insertion of the new labret is painful, although perhaps no more so than the insertion and periodic tightening of dental braces in Western society, which many Westerners consider quite bearable given the perceived aesthetic benefits of orthodontia. ■ The benefits of the lip disc are equally worthwhile for the Kayapó. ■

Once a father, a Kayapó male is entitled to speak his mind on matters of concern to his village. In fact, he must, if he is to earn the respect of other villagers, for silence is not considered a virtue. Verbally assertive, mature males, and they alone, command the political respect that permits them to preside over village life. Kayapó women are not permitted to wear labrets because of their strong symbolic association with fatherhood and manhood.

6. The Kayapó consider a male adolescent to have attained manhood
   - (A) if the male has successfully undergone a rite of passage
   - (B) if the male is judged to be marriageable or not
   - (C) if the male has reached his legal age
   - (D) if the male has fathered a child

7. The following sentence can be added to paragraph 2 or 3.

   They vary considerably in shape and size.

   Where would it best fit in the paragraph? Click on the square [■] to add the sentence to paragraph 2 or 3. Paragraphs 2 and 3 are marked with an arrow [→].

8. The second paragraph supports which of the following statements?
   - (A) The insertion of labrets is widely practiced throughout Africa and South America.
   - (B) The labrets do not necessarily reflect the age, position and social status of the wearer.
   - (C) The labret is inserted when the male fathers his first child.
   - (D) The male changes his labret into a bigger one when he reaches manhood.

Altering the outward appearance of the body by making permanent, irreversible changes to it is widely practiced in Western as well as non-Western societies. In the West, tattooing the skin and piercing the ears are customs of long standing; inserting metal rings or other objects through the fleshy parts of the nose, brow, navel, or other parts of the body is relatively new to Westerners. They may think of these kinds of body alteration as deformation or mutilation rather than decoration, but they are not fundamentally different from ear piercing or tattooing.

For example, labrets or lip plugs, objects typically made of wood or bone that are inserted into the flesh of the lower lip, are found in many places around the world, including East Africa and South America. A small version is usually inserted in childhood, and may be increased in size as the individual matures, reflecting changes in his or her social status. Among the Kayapó of Brazil, a young man who has become a father for the first time is seen as having officially passed from boyhood to manhood. This passage is symbolized by a permanent physical change: the small plug that was inserted through the flesh of his lower lip when the new father was himself an infant is replaced by a much larger, saucerlike plate.

The insertion of the new labret is painful, although perhaps no more so than the insertion and periodic tightening of dental braces in Western society, which many Westerners consider quite bearable given the perceived aesthetic benefits of orthodontia. The benefits of the lip disc are equally worthwhile for the Kayapó.

Once a father, a Kayapó male is entitled to speak his mind on matters of concern to his village. In fact, he must, if he is to earn the respect of other villagers, for silence is not considered a virtue. Verbally assertive, mature males, and they alone, command the political respect that permits them to preside over village life. Kayapó women are not permitted to wear labrets because of their strong symbolic association with fatherhood and manhood.

9. Which of the following could best replace the word periodic in the passage?
   Ⓐ Painful
   Ⓑ Permanent
   Ⓒ Continuous
   Ⓓ Careful

10. In paragraph 3, the labret is compared to dental braces
    Ⓐ in order to help readers visualize better the appearance of the labret by introducing a familiar practice
    Ⓑ because it is the closest practice carried out in the mouth among Westerners
    Ⓒ in order to illustrate more clearly the social and aesthetic functions of the labret
    Ⓓ because it carries out a different role and function than that of dental braces

11. All of the following characterize the labret EXCEPT
    Ⓐ sexual and social status are combined in this single symbolic artifact
    Ⓑ the lip disc is worn by males whose wisdom and silence contribute to the welfare of the village
    Ⓒ the lip disc symbolizes not only fatherhood but also a male's status as a mature village leader
    Ⓓ the lip disc is worn as a social and sexual status only among men of Kayapó

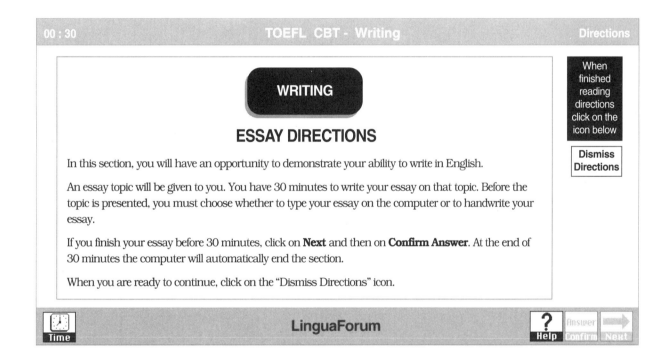

WRITING

ESSAY DIRECTIONS

In this section, you will have an opportunity to demonstrate your ability to write in English.

An essay topic will be given to you. You have 30 minutes to write your essay on that topic. Before the topic is presented, you must choose whether to type your essay on the computer or to handwrite your essay.

If you finish your essay before 30 minutes, click on **Next** and then on **Confirm Answer**. At the end of 30 minutes the computer will automatically end the section.

When you are ready to continue, click on the "Dismiss Directions" icon.

Read the topic below and then make any notes that will help you plan your response.
Begin typing your response in the box at the bottom of the screen, or write your answer on the answer sheet provided to you.

Some people believe that it harms a friendship when one borrows money from a friend. Do you agree or disagree with this opinion? Why? Use specific reasons and details to support your view.

Cut

Paste

Undo

INTRODUCTION

Introduction

About This Book

This book is for students planning on taking the TOEFL test. It is designed to provide a comprehensive understanding of TOEFL – what kind of questions to expect, what kind of answers, the various skills you will be tested on, and the "tricks" TOEFL most commonly uses.

The book covers the TOEFL by section – Listening, Structure, Reading, and Writing – providing lessons and many practice exercises to help you with every type of question you might encounter. There are diagnostic tests that let you determine your starting level of fluency, your strong points and your weak points.

Throughout the book, there are numerous strategies, helpful hints, practice problems, and other aids developed by LinguaForum to maximize your chances for success and to help you perform at your best on the TOEFL test day.

This book has been designed solely for the current Computer-Based TOEFL (CBT). In most of the world, with few exceptions, TOEFL is administered as a computer-based test. In switching to the computer-based format, ETS changed many aspects of the TOEFL test. Books designed for the old, paper-based test may provide misleading or out-of-date information, or else they may mention kinds of questions that are no longer present on the CBT. Since this book was only designed for the CBT, the information presented here is only the most relevant and the most helpful.

About the CBT TOEFL

1. What Is the TOEFL?

The Test of English as a Foreign Language is one of the tests administered by Educational Testing Service, a non-profit organization in Princeton, New Jersey. It is a test designed for students whose native language is not English, but who wish to attend a university in the United States or Canada. The test is also used by some other institutions around the world.

The test is designed to measure English ability and assign it a score, on a scale from 40 to 300. There is no "passing" grade; each school can assign its own standard. In general, better schools require higher proficiency, but check with the schools to which you are applying to confirm their requirements.

2. About the CBT

The computer:
The computer skills needed to write the TOEFL are minimal, and even if you have not used a computer before, you should be able to figure it out.

TOEFL runs on a typical MS-Windows-based operating system. You will have a regular-looking PC computer (tower, monitor, keyboard, and mouse), with certain changes made for security reasons.

Title bar: The center of this strip at the top of the screen shows which section you are working on. At left is the time remaining. The time indicator starts working when you click on the clock icon at lower left. It appears automatically in the final five minutes of each section. At the right of the title bar is the number of the item you are working on, along with the total number of items in the section.

Tool bar: Four icons (symbols or words in boxes) are usually displayed here. Use an icon ONLY when it is black. Grey icons cannot be activated. The Tool bar does NOT help answer a particular question.

 Time: The clock icon at left initiates the time remaining function on the title bar.

 Volume: Before starting work on this section, you will hear a voice at the same volume as voices in the Listening Section. You now may adjust the volume. To make it louder, click on the upward-pointing arrow. To make it lower, click on the downward-pointing arrow. During the test, you also may change volume by using the headphone switch. After you have adjusted the volume, directions for Part A will appear on the screen. To start work on this section, click on the Dismiss Directions icon.

 Help: The Help icon supplies directions for the current section and a menu of other information. Now you are almost ready to take the actual TOEFL test. A required tutorial precedes each of the test's four sections. None of the steps may be skipped. Although you may not need these tutorials, they must be completed before you take the test. Time used on tutorials is NOT deducted from your allocated time for the test.

 Confirm Answer: The Confirm Answer icon will darken. Clicking on this icon will lead you automatically to the next item.

 Next: After answering a specific question, move the pointer to the lower right part of the screen and click on the Next icon. It will be dark until you click on it. Then the icon will turn gray.

 Prev: The Reading Section has been changed. In place of an Answer Confirm icon, there is a Prev icon, for "Previous item." There is also an icon marked Next. After answering an item, click Next. To return to the previous item, click Prev. These two buttons allow you to move as far forward or backward as you wish. You may move from one item or passage to another throughout the Reading Section during your allotted time.

You will see the following computer screens:

Section 1: Listening

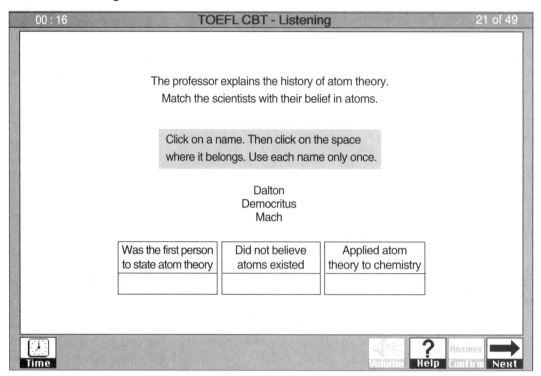

Section 2: Structure

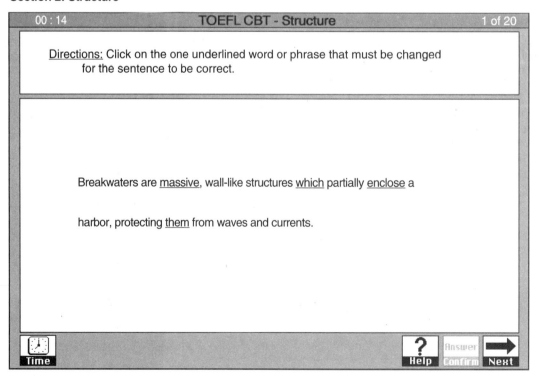

Section 3: Reading

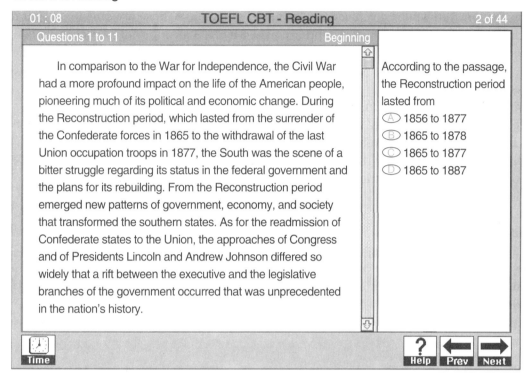

Questions 1 to 11   Beginning

In comparison to the War for Independence, the Civil War had a more profound impact on the life of the American people, pioneering much of its political and economic change. During the Reconstruction period, which lasted from the surrender of the Confederate forces in 1865 to the withdrawal of the last Union occupation troops in 1877, the South was the scene of a bitter struggle regarding its status in the federal government and the plans for its rebuilding. From the Reconstruction period emerged new patterns of government, economy, and society that transformed the southern states. As for the readmission of Confederate states to the Union, the approaches of Congress and of Presidents Lincoln and Andrew Johnson differed so widely that a rift between the executive and the legislative branches of the government occurred that was unprecedented in the nation's history.

According to the passage, the Reconstruction period lasted from
- Ⓐ 1856 to 1877
- Ⓑ 1865 to 1878
- Ⓒ 1865 to 1877
- Ⓓ 1865 to 1887

Time   ? Help   ← Prev   → Next

Section 4: Writing

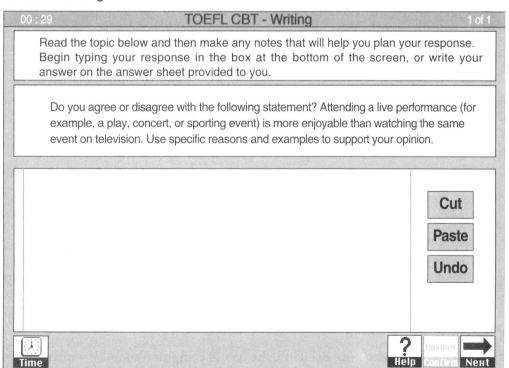

Read the topic below and then make any notes that will help you plan your response. Begin typing your response in the box at the bottom of the screen, or write your answer on the answer sheet provided to you.

Do you agree or disagree with the following statement? Attending a live performance (for example, a play, concert, or sporting event) is more enjoyable than watching the same event on television. Use specific reasons and examples to support your opinion.

Cut

Paste

Undo

Time   ? Help   Answer Confirm   → Next

The test itself:

Before the actual content part of the TOEFL, you will have to fill out registration information on the computer.

After this section, you will be given several "dummy" questions. These are questions that do NOT count towards your overall score, and are asked by ETS for internal purposes. This section is clearly labeled and is separate from the rest of the test.

The order of sections:

First comes the Listening Section. This will take between 40 minutes and an hour to complete, depending on whether you get the short 30-question version, or the longer 49/50-question test, and depending on how much time you need to answer each question.
That is immediately followed by the Structure Section. There will then be a MANDATORY 5-minute break. You must leave the testing area during this break. You will then return to finish the Reading and Writing Sections.

1) Listening:
  - 15-25 minutes of answering time, depending on the length of test
    This only refers to the time you spend answering, not to the time spent listening to the conversations and talks. Total listening section lasts 40-60 minutes.
  - 30 or 49/50 questions
  - 11 or 17 short dialogue questions, followed by 19 or 32/33 longer passage questions
  - Computer adaptive

2) Structure:
  - 15-20 minutes of reading and answering time, depending on the length of test
  - 20 or 25 questions
  - Computer adaptive

Mandatory Break

3) Reading:
  - 70-90 minutes of reading and answering time, depending on the length of test
  - 44 (4 passages) or 55 (5 passages) questions
  - Approximately 18 minutes per passage with accompanying questions
  - Computer linear

4) Writing:
  - 30 minutes total
  - Only one question
  - You must write an essay based on the topic provided. You can either write on the computer or, if you request, on the paper essay answer sheet. The test center will provide the scratch paper and writing instruments.

Computer adaptivity:

On both the Listening and Structure Sections, the test is computer-adaptive – meaning that the difficulty of the questions you face depends on how well you do. The more questions you answer correctly, the more difficult questions you get. HOWEVER, you also get many more points for answering a difficult question correctly than for an easy question. The point is this: Do not be intimidated by the idea of computer-adaptivity. Do not worry that your questions will get tougher until you are unable to answer them correctly and your score is lowered. That is not going to happen. It is always to your advantage to answer as many questions as possible.

3. How to Prepare

In some ways, TOEFL is like an arms race, with ETS versus the students and teachers. ETS writes the best test it can of English. Then the students and English teachers try their best to crack the test, to find patterns, flaws, shortcuts or other ways to boost their scores. So TOEFL revises their test, trying to eliminate those problems and make the test more "real." And the students take another whack at cracking it. And so it goes.

In its current form, TOEFL is perhaps a better gauge of English ability than it has ever been. This is not to say it is perfect or that there are still not shortcuts, but it is better. The Listening Section passages are longer, based more on realistic dialogue and less on tricks or idioms. The Structure Section still presents the same two types of questions as in the paper-based test. The Reading Section presents passages both longer and easier than those found on the paper-based test. And in the writing section, one of the writing topics in the TOEFL Bulletin by ETS may appear in your actual test.

Various books may promise you "secret" strategies and special insights "guaranteed" to raise your score dramatically. The truth is that doing well on TOEFL hinges on two basic ideas:
1) A real understanding of English, and
2) Being familiar with the TOEFL.

This book is mostly concerned with helping you understand TOEFL – preparing you for the various challenges you will face, and clearing up misconceptions about the test.

The needs of each student can vary widely, but we have made a general plan that you should follow to maximize your chances for success.

First, you should know what TOEFL is. Know the structure, duration, and types of questions so that you will not be surprised on the test day. This should be done well before you actually write the test – certainly more than a month before. If your English is solid, but you only need to familiarize yourself with TOEFL, then you will only need a few good study sessions to prepare yourself. However, if you need more extensive preparation, it will likely take time to make significant improvements.

Determining how much preparation you need should be your second step.

Second, take a diagnostic test to see where your strong points and weak points are. The result of this diagnostic test will largely influence what you do next. If listening is your weakest score, concentrate on the Listening Section. Proceed accordingly if Structure or Reading is your weakest section.

This book provides some good structural ideas to greatly improve your essay's potential in the Writing section, but on the whole, writing is a function of your other English abilities.

4. On the Test Day

What to bring to the test center:
Read ETS's TOEFL information bulletin carefully to make sure you have photo identification documents (passport, driver's license, national identification card or military identification card) required where you are testing. You will also need to bring your confirmation number and, in case you are asked for it, your voucher.

Otherwise, there is no need to bring anything. In fact, you are not allowed to enter with any sort of writing device or aid – no pencils, pens, erasers, paper, calculators or anything else.

What to expect:
You should arrive at least 30 minutes early. If you arrive late, you may be denied entry. Better safe than sorry!

The test centers are designed to be as similar to each other as possible. When you first enter, you will need to have your identification checked. Then you will be assigned a seat (and given a room and seat number).

You will need to complete a confidentiality agreement in order to take the test, promising not to pass on or reproduce the important, top-secret contents of the test. If you do not sign the agreement, you cannot take the test.

Finally, when it is time to enter the test room, you will have to sign in. In fact, you will have to provide your signature every time you enter or leave the test room. In addition, your picture will be taken and displayed at your testing station. When you sit down, make sure the correct photograph is on display.

You will not be allowed to eat or drink anything, or even chew gum.

The desk itself is simple, light brown wood veneer. Most of the space is taken up by the computer. The computer should be booted and all ready to use when you sit down.

5. Score Evaluation and Concordance Table

In the computer-adaptive TOEFL Sections – Listening and Structure – the first few questions are the most important in determining the overall level of difficulty of that section. Getting these first questions wrong would rapidly move you into a low level of difficulty and greatly lower the maximum score you could achieve. That is, getting the first three questions correct, then two wrong would probably give you a higher score than getting the first two wrong and the next three correct. Therefore it is important to spend some extra time on the first three or four questions and be extra-careful to make sure that you have answered them correctly.

In the Reading Section, your score is based on your performance on the questions, the difficulty of the questions, and on the number of question you answer correctly.

The following table shows equivalent scores and ranges on the paper-based test and the computer-based test.

● Concordance Table ●

Total Score Comparison

Paper-Based Total	Computer-Based Total
677	300
673	297
670	293
667	290
663	287
660	287
657	283
653	280
650	280
647	277
643	273
640	273
637	270
633	267
630	267
627	263
623	263
620	260
617	260
613	257
610	253
607	253
603	250
600	250
597	247
593	243
590	243
587	240
583	237
580	237
577	233
573	230
570	230
567	227
563	223
560	220
557	220
553	217
550	213
547	210
543	207
540	207
537	203
533	200
530	197
527	197
523	193
520	190
517	187
513	183
510	180
507	180
503	177
500	173
497	170
493	167
490	163
487	163
483	160
480	157
477	153
473	150
470	150
467	147
463	143
460	140
457	137
453	133
450	133

Paper-Based Total	Computer-Based Total
447	130
443	127
440	123
437	123
433	120
430	117
427	113
423	113
420	110
417	107
413	103
410	103
407	100
403	97
400	97
397	93
393	90
390	90
387	87
383	83
380	83
377	80
373	77
370	77
367	73
363	73
360	70
357	70
353	67
350	63
347	63
343	60
340	60
337	57
333	57
330	53
327	50
323	50
320	47
317	47
313	43
310	40

Range Comparison

Paper-Based Total	Computer-Based Total
660-677	287-300
640-657	273-283
620-637	260-270
600-617	250-260
580-597	237-247
560-577	220-233
540-557	207-220
520-537	190-203
500-517	173-187
480-497	157-170
460-477	140-153
440-457	123-137
420-437	110-123
400-417	97-107
380-397	83-93
360-377	70-80
340-357	60-70
320-337	47-57
310-317	40-47

Section Scaled Score Comparison

Listening		Structure / Writing		Reading	
Score-to-Score		**Score-to-Score**		**Score-to-Score**	
Paper-Based Listening Comprehension	Computer-Based Listening	Paper-Based Structure and Written Expression	Computer-Based Structure/Writing	Paper-Based Reading Comprehension	Computer-Based Reading
68	30	68	30	67	30
67	30	67	29	66	29
66	29	66	28	65	28
65	28	65	28	64	28
64	27	64	27	63	27
63	27	63	27	62	26
62	26	62	26	61	26
61	25	61	26	60	25
60	25	60	25	59	25
59	24	59	25	58	24
58	23	58	24	57	23
57	22	57	23	56	22
56	22	56	23	55	21
55	21	55	22	54	21
54	20	54	21	53	20
53	19	53	20	52	19
52	18	52	20	51	18
51	17	51	19	50	17
50	16	50	18	49	16
49	15	49	17	48	16
48	14	48	17	47	15
47	13	47	16	46	14
46	12	46	15	45	13
45	11	45	14	44	13
44	10	44	14	43	12
43	9	43	13	42	11
42	9	42	12	41	11
41	8	41	11	40	10
40	7	40	11	39	9
39	6	39	10	38	9
38	6	38	9	37	8
37	5	37	9	36	8
36	5	36	8	35	7
35	4	35	8	34	7
34	4	34	7	33	6
33	3	33	7	32	6
32	3	32	6	31	5
31	2	31	6		

Range-to-Range		Range-to-Range		Range-to-Range	
Paper-Based Listening Comprehension	Computer-Based Listening	Paper-Based Structure and Written Expression	Computer-Based Structure/Writing	Paper-Based Reading Comprehension	Computer-Based Reading
64-68	27-30	64-68	27-30	64-67	28-30
59-63	24-27	59-63	25-27	59-63	25-27
54-58	20-23	54-58	21-24	54-58	21-24
49-53	15-19	49-53	17-20	49-53	16-20
44-48	10-14	44-48	14-17	44-48	13-16
39-43	6-9	39-43	10-13	39-43	9-12
34-38	4-6	34-38	7-9	34-38	7-9
31-33	2-3	31-33	6-7	31-33	5-6

LISTENING SECTION

Listening

Overview of the CBT Listening Section

The computer-based TOEFL test has changed the listening portion of the test more than any other part. Understanding and preparing for these changes are important parts of doing well on the Listening Section.

The most talked-about change is COMPUTER ADAPTIVITY. Unlike the old test, the new listening section is not a one-size-fits-all format. The TOEFL test now changes depending on how well you do. The more questions you answer correctly, the more difficult the test becomes; the more questions you answer incorrectly, the easier the test becomes. However, you also get a lot more points for getting difficult questions correct, so it is always to your advantage to do as well as possible, even if that means facing more challenging questions.

There are now two parts in the Listening Section:

Part A is made up of short dialogues, between 2 and 4 lines long, with a single question asked.
Part B is made up of causal conversations, academic discussions, and academic lectures.

A great many questions are no longer on the TOEFL test, or are on less frequently. The old PBT tests used to contain endless idioms and plays on words, especially in Part A. Those sorts of word "tricks" have been cut down in favor of more natural, "real" understanding. The dialogues tend to be slightly longer than before, and sound more like true conversations people would actually have in an American university situation.

In spite of the rise of "real world" comprehension over tricks, most people actually find the CBT Listening Section harder than the old TOEFL. The level of English grammar and vocabulary has gotten more difficult, and the passages have grown longer.

On the plus side, however, there can be fewer questions. There are 30-question and 49/50-question versions of the Listening Section. The 30-question test features 11 Part A questions and 19 Part B questions. The 49/50-question test features 17 Part A questions and 32/33 Part B questions. On the PBT, there were usually 50 questions. If you have the longer Listening test, you will receive fewer questions in the Reading and Structure portions of the test.

In the Listening Section of this book, we have broken the question types and other ideas into 26 individual lessons. Each lesson is followed by 3-5 exercises to help you understand the concept, then a further 7-11 TOEFL-style questions for practice. There are also general review exercises after every several chapters to help reinforce the lessons, and mini-tests which are simplified versions including all the new item-types found on the actual CBT TOEFL.

● Style and Usage

The CBT TOEFL Listening Section is less formal than the Reading or Structure Sections. The Short Dialogues and Casual Conversations are, naturally, the most informal, especially when they consist of conversations between two friends. Because they are classroom situations, the

Academic Discussions are a little more formal than the Casual Conversations; however, there is still room for a certain amount of idiomatic usage and "real" dialogue. The lectures are the most formal part of the Listening Section, but even here, in an attempt at realism, the speaking style has several informalities.

The voices you hear are all fairly uniform in style, following what is commonly called a "standard American" dialect. What is the "standard American" dialect? Where is this standard dialect spoken? New York? Indiana? California? Texas? The truth is most of the voices are quite unnaturally devoid of character or regional characteristics, and sound like something you might hear on CNN or some other American news program. But this sound is considered neutral.

● Pictures

All questions on the CBT TOEFL are accompanied by pictures of the speakers. *For short dialogues and casual conversations*, these pictures are just to help you visualize the setting, and do not convey any important information you will be tested on. For example, you will not be asked about a speaker's appearance or the classroom.

However, in the academic *discussions and lectures*, you will also see pictures and graphics that relate to the material being discussed. Unlike the setting pictures, these pictures are VERY important, and are often the source of graphic questions.

● Sound

TOEFL and many books claim that you can only adjust the volume at the beginning of the exercise, but at many testing centers, you can adjust the volume manually on the headphones at any time.

● Time

You have about 15-25 minutes to answer the questions, depending on the number of questions asked. However, that time does NOT include the time when the speakers are talking. That time is ONLY the answering time. The total length of time it will take you to complete the Listening Section is probably 40-60 minutes.

● Tutorials

Like all sections of the test, the Listening Section is preceded by some tutorials. However, the Listening section's tutorial is more extensive and elaborate than the other sections, and you cannot skip it or speed it up.

Remember:
1. During the dialogue, you will be given photos and graphics to look at.
2. After the dialogue, you will be given a question and several possible answer choices. The question will be spoken aloud, too.
3. Click on the best possible answer. Then click, "Next."
4. Finally, click on "Confirm Answer." The computer will then automatically begin the next question.

Take Care

Throughout this book, we will give you extra tips called "Take Care." This features tips – things to do and traps to avoid.

LISTENING

Listening Strategies

While there are a great many suggestions and ideas for doing well on the TOEFL, we have boiled it down to 5 basic strategies to remember and follow.

Strategy 1: Know the test!

The best way to be prepared for TOEFL is to know TOEFL. There is nothing as frustrating as coming across something new and unexpected in a high-stress situation as when taking the TOEFL.

Strategy 2: Don't be misled.

The computer-based TOEFL is not the same as the paper-based version. Many of the old questions, general strategies, and tricks no longer apply. Some common misunderstandings and out-of-date information include:

1. Do not expect the old questions. Many types of questions that used to be standard on the old TOEFL are now barely used or not used at all. For example, because of the presence of pictures now, questions asking where a conversation is taking place or what a person's job is rarely appear on the test any more – the picture makes these questions too obvious.

   (Note that while Part A pictures are not very important for understanding the question, TOEFL does not use wildly wrong pictures; for example, you would not see a photo of two women when a man and a woman are talking.)

2. Do not believe you should only "listen to the last line" of the short dialogues, as many books suggest. Many of the questions, particularly Inference, Future action, and Comprehension, require information from the beginning of or the whole dialogue. In fact, many questions are designed to trick those people who over-rely on the last line.

3. Do not expect the short dialogues to be as short as they used to be. In the past, Part A Short Dialogues were dominated by brief 2-turn conversations. Now they can be 2-4 turns long, and each turn is usually longer than it used to be. This is all part of the effort to emphasize overall comprehension and realism.

4. Do not race to finish the test. If you run out of time, random guessing in the last minute or so, just to finish the test, will not help your score. In fact, it could lower your score.

5. You can no longer "look ahead" and guess at the content of the lecture from the possible answer choices given. You are not only shown one question at a time, but the question and answer choices also appear only after the dialogue is finished.

6. TOEFL and many books claim that you can only adjust the volume at the beginning of the exercise; however, at many testing centers, you can adjust the volume manually on the headphones at any time.

Strategy 3: Pace yourself.

Because of the computer adaptivity, the first 3-4 questions on the TOEFL are the most important. Take a little longer to do your best on these questions. The first few questions have the greatest effect on the overall level of difficulty of the listening section. And the more difficult the questions, the better score you can receive. So getting the best possible score depends on doing well at the very beginning most of all.

As the test goes on, however, keep an eye on the time. Because the number of questions varies from test to test, the amount of time also varies from 15 to 25 minutes. However, on the CBT, only the time you spend answering the questions counts. The time spent listening to the dialogues and lectures does not count against the amount of time you are given. All told, it will take between about 40 and 60 minutes to complete the Listening portion of the test.

Strategy 4: Use elimination.

If you are not certain of an answer, try eliminating as many wrong answers as possible. By eliminating only one or two wrong choices, you can greatly increase your odds of guessing correctly. (We will be offering tips on eliminating wrong answers throughout the Listening Section.) Remember, you can no longer skip questions or change your answers later. You must answer every question, and you only have one chance to get it right.

Strategy 5: Double-check your answer.

Always double-check your answer before clicking "Confirm." Unlike the paper-based test, you cannot go back and change any answers on the CBT. Make sure you understood the question and you are as certain as you can be of the answer.

Take Care

This is always a difficult balance – taking time to make sure you answer each question correctly, versus finishing the test in time. Again, give yourself more time to answer the first 3-4 questions, since getting them right will have the greatest effect on your score. And practice using the LinguaForum test materials.

Chapter 1 General Information for Part A

Short conversations are dialogues between 2 and 4 lines long. Usually you will hear one man and one woman speak, although on occasion you might hear two men or two women. After the dialogue, a third voice asks a question.

Person A – Dialogue
Person B – Dialogue
Narrator – Question

Person A – Dialogue
Person B – Dialogue
Person A – Dialogue
Narrator – Question

Person A – Dialogue
Person B – Dialogue
Person A – Dialogue
Person B – Dialogue
Narrator – Question

In addition, each line is longer than it used to be. At one time, Short Dialogues were dominated by an example like:

(Man)	I didn't like that movie.
(Woman)	Me neither.
(Narrator)	What does the woman mean?

Now each person's dialogue is more likely to be longer and more involved. This is also part of the effort to emphasis overall comprehension and realism.

While the dialogue is ongoing, you will see a picture of two people talking. This is only to help you visualize the conversation and does not contain useful or important information. After the dialogue, the picture will disappear and the question will appear. Then the four answer choices will appear underneath the question.

There are 7 different kinds of questions you will be asked. We will explore the question types in the order of frequency they appear on the actual TOEFL:

1. **Implication (31%)**
2. **Meaning (23%)**
3. **Suggestion (16%)**
4. **Inference (14%)**
5. **Future Action (10%)**
6. **Comprehension (3%)**
7. **Assumption (1%)**

(All percentages are approximate, but they give you a good idea of what to expect.)

If the TOEFL only required an understanding of those 7 different patterns, life would be fairly easy for the listener. Think about this:

(Man)	I think I'm going to play video games for a while.
(Woman)	If I were you, I'd be studying for your test tomorrow.
(Narrator)	What does the woman mean?

(A) The man should study for his test.

(B) She likes strawberries.

(C) Her professor is very difficult.

(D) University life is a lot of fun.

If these were your choices, then choosing the correct answer would not be very difficult (Choice A, of course). But in order to make the answers more difficult to figure out, TOEFL uses a wide variety of DIVERTERS – that is, methods for making the problems more ambiguous. Some of the methods TOEFL uses include:

1. Similar sounds
2. Synonyms
3. Conditionals (wishes, ifs, hypotheticals)
4. Agreement/Disagreement
5. Passives
6. Degree (*as ... as, nearly, over, already, almost*)
7. Vocabulary (idioms, multi-word verbs)
8. Pronouns and Referents

So instead of the first example, you are more likely to encounter a question like this:

(Man)	I think I'm going to play video games for a while.
(Woman)	If I were you, I'd be studying for your test tomorrow.
(Narrator)	What does the woman mean?

(A) The man should study for his test.

(B) She wishes she could play video games, too.

(C) The man is not good at taking tests.

(D) She has a test tomorrow.

Of the four answer choices, in addition to the one correct answer, you can expect regularly to find:

i.   One choice <u>opposite</u> to the correct answer

ii. One choice that is overly literal

iii. A choice that refers to the wrong speaker

iv. Choices that sound similar to the dialogue but have different meanings

Take **Care**

> <u>Any answer that uses the SAME words as the dialogue can usually be eliminated</u>. Of your four options, TOEFL is most likely to use the same words for an opposite or an overly literal answer. The correct answer will usually be a re-wording of the dialogue, conveying the same meaning but in DIFFERENT words. Certainly if you do not understand a dialogue and have to guess, eliminate any answer that is too similar to the dialogue.

In the next 2 chapters, we will explore the different question types for short conversations first, followed by the Diverters.

LISTENING

Chapter 2 Question Types for Short Conversations

1. Implication Questions

In this sort of question, the speaker makes his/her point INDIRECTLY. Instead of answering a question "yes" or "no," the speaker gives an opinion or adds information that in effect answers the questions.

Example

(Man)   Are you going to eat that donut?
(Woman)   I already ate too many!

The woman did not answer, "No, I will not eat that donut." But she did indicate a negative attitude towards the question. "Too" is usually used to indicate dissatisfaction. Because the woman ate a lot of donuts, she is full or tired of them, so it is logical to conclude that she does not want to eat any more.

There are a couple of different ways implication questions can be asked, such as:

What is the man implying?
What does the woman imply?

Practice 2.1
After each of the following dialogues, write what the second speaker is implying.

i.   Man: I think I may have gotten the best grade in the class.
     Woman: Oh, I did better than that.
     Implication: _____

ii. Woman: Do you want to go see that new action movie tonight?
     Man: I have a test tomorrow that I have to study for.
     Implication: _____

iii. Man: Aren't you going to take your umbrella with you?
     Woman: Thanks. I didn't realize it was raining.
     Implication: _____

TOEFL Exercise 2.1
 Listen to each short dialogue carefully, and then choose the best answer to the question.

1.   (A) She never eats lunch.
     (B) She would like to go to lunch with the man.
     (C) She thinks it is too late to eat lunch.
     (D) She is not hungry.

2.   (A) Getting a coffee would please him.
     (B) He fears he will never finish the project.
     (C) He will not take a break.
     (D) He would like to talk about the project.

3. (A) The professor is not granting more time to anyone.
    (B) She will get her paper finished on time.
    (C) He already got an extension for the paper.
    (D) The professor does not like to be bothered.

4. (A) He wants to study more.
    (B) He wants to dance but does not want to go out.
    (C) He likes the woman's idea.
    (D) He only likes to go to certain places.

5. (A) Today is Tuesday.
    (B) She does not want to see the game.
    (C) She would love to see the game.
    (D) The game is not on tonight.

6. (A) There are no homework problems for the class.
    (B) She does not like the man's idea.
    (C) They have not started the lab yet.
    (D) She thinks they should ask the professor.

7. (A) Chapter 5 is a very long chapter.
    (B) There will be 5 chapters covered by the test.
    (C) Chapter 5 is not an important part of the test.
    (D) The test will begin soon.

8. (A) The man's honesty is a problem.
    (B) She will move next weekend.
    (C) She cannot help him much longer.
    (D) It was difficult for her to help the man.

9. (A) The woman cannot enroll in the seminar.
    (B) It is unfortunate the woman is a political science major.
    (C) The seminar is already full of students.
    (D) The woman would not be interested in the course.

LISTENING

2. Meaning Questions

These questions are most reliant on the Diverters (although Diverters can be found in almost any Part A question). Meaning can be obscured by many different methods and diverters, such as idioms, negatives, conditional verbs, similar sounding words, and difficult vocabulary.

Example

(Woman)	How's your science lab coming along?
(Man)	I finally had that breakthrough I've been waiting for.

There are several multi-word verbs and idioms here that could confuse a listener. The woman asks how his lab, or experiment, is "coming along" – she is asking about his progress on his experiment. The man uses the compound word, "breakthrough," meaning a major advance or discovery. Other potential diverters here are the adverb, "finally," and the verb "waiting for." Given these diverters, you might be given possible wrong answers such as "he has finished the experiment" or "he broke four pieces of equipment."

The important part of meaning questions is to be able to understand what was said and to rephrase that in your own words.

Practice 2.2
Re-write each of the following statements in your own words.

    i. Woman: You can't rely on Jason – he's too much of a slacker.
        Meaning: _____

    ii. Man: That's easy for you to say!
        Meaning: _____

    iii. Woman: He wasn't on time for our meeting because his class ran long.
        Meaning: _____

TOEFL Exercise 2.2

 Listen to each short dialogue carefully, and then choose the best answer to the question.

  1.   (A) Bill is always one of the fairest people.
       (B) Bill won a close election.
       (C) Bill lost the election.
       (D) Bill won by a large margin.

  2.   (A) Randy is a better worker than Sandra.
       (B) Randy understands the details better than Sandra.
       (C) Randy has taken more chemistry classes than Sandra.
       (D) Randy has more free time than Sandra.

3.　(A) The wind makes painting difficult.

　　(B) They should politely ask the landlord for paint.

　　(C) There is only a little painting that needs to be done.

　　(D) Painting the house will be easy.

4.　(A) He is not interested in Jim.

　　(B) He wonders why Jim left school.

　　(C) He is curious about what Jim is doing now.

　　(D) He does not know anyone named Jim.

5.　(A) The man is the kind of person who likes to read a lot.

　　(B) There are worms and bugs in her book collection.

　　(C) The man gets bored by books easily.

　　(D) She has never been able to finish a book.

6.　(A) The professor was not interested in research about dice.

　　(B) He is not going to do the research project.

　　(C) He has to wait a while for a response.

　　(D) The professor wants to start the project immediately.

7.　(A) He thinks the position will help him pass the course.

　　(B) He will take the job.

　　(C) Dr. Adams is important in the university community.

　　(D) He cannot accept the position.

8.　(A) The prices are very affordable.

　　(B) The waiters at the restaurant are quite large.

　　(C) The restaurant is usually very busy.

　　(D) He usually takes a book with him to the restaurant.

9.　(A) The questions are too hard for her.

　　(B) She is going to go home to sleep.

　　(C) The questions are not very interesting.

　　(D) She will do the same as the man.

10.　(A) The future appears to be more hopeful.

　　(B) He cannot find some of his things.

　　(C) His grades keep getting worse.

　　(D) He needs to write a make-up exam.

11.　(A) It is beneficial for Dave to do all that work.

　　(B) Dave does not know where to put his homework.

　　(C) Dave needs the help of others, too.

　　(D) People use Dave unfairly because he lets them.

3. Suggestion Questions

A lot of questions involve one person giving the other advice or a recommendation about what to do next.

There are a number of ways people can offer advice. Some of them include:

What does the woman suggest?
I think you should ___
Let's ___
How about ___?
Why don't you ___? Why don't we ___?
Why not ___?
If I were you, I'd ___
You could always ___

This important thing here is to recognize a suggestion and not let the different ways of making suggestions confuse you.

Practice 2.3
Write what each person's suggestion really is.

   i. Man: I wouldn't take Dr. Simmon's class if I were you. It's too difficult.
      Suggestion: _____

   ii. Woman: You could always ask your professor for an extension if you're not finished yet.
      Suggestion: _____

   iii. Man: Why don't we stop to get something to eat?
      Suggestion: _____

TOEFL Exercise 2.3

 Listen to each short dialogue carefully, and then choose the best answer to the question.

1. (A) Change to a more comfortable pair of shoes
   (B) Improve the bad essay and hand it in again
   (C) Ask his professor for more time
   (D) Try harder on the next essay

2. (A) She should ask Brad if she can use his book longer.
   (B) She should understand why Brad needs his book.
   (C) She should have talked to Brad earlier.
   (D) She should be afraid of Brad.

3. (A) He should not take any seminar.
   (B) He should take the regular seminar.
   (C) He should take the easiest course.
   (D) He should take the advanced seminar.

4. (A) Book an appointment with the campus tour guide
    (B) Transfer to a smaller school
    (C) Follow him to the office
    (D) Use his book about the university

5. (A) He should telephone her parents.
    (B) He should tell his parents about the scholarship.
    (C) He should ask his parents how to apply for the scholarship.
    (D) He should not tell his parents.

6. (A) Buy a used computer
    (B) Save as much money as possible
    (C) Spend money on a good computer
    (D) Only get a new computer as a last resort

7. (A) Go to the bank for more information
    (B) Explain to the bank officials that they made a mistake
    (C) Find out the way to the bank
    (D) Do not go to the bank

8. (A) Do a little bit of grading every day
    (B) Do all the grading at once
    (C) Not do any grading
    (D) Take the night off, then start grading tomorrow

9. (A) Join the swim team
    (B) Ignore his coach
    (C) Work for the gym team for a short time
    (D) Let her join the gymnastics team instead

LISTENING

4. Inference Questions

This kind of question can be difficult, especially if you were listening for idioms or other details and were not expecting this kind of question. It asks for information NOT DIRECTLY RELATED to or explicitly stated by the dialogue, but instead SUGGESTED by the dialogue. You need to understand more than just the individual words and grammar for this type of question; you must understand the greater ideas, the whole of the conversation.

Example

(Man)   Do you think I could have more time to work on my biology experiment?

(Woman)   Now, Tim, everyone else handed in their major research projects before the deadline.

There are many things you could infer from this dialogue that were not explicitly said. The woman is most likely a professor, and the man one of her students. He is also most likely a biology major. And he already missed the deadline to hand in the project.

Take Care

> Remember, to IMPLY something is to say something indirectly, without explicitly stating it. To INFER something is to make an indirect conclusion about what someone else says or does. They are two sides of the same thing. For example, if you ask me to go to the store, and I say, "I'm watching television," I am IMPLYING I will not go, and you should INFER I will not go.

Practice 2.4

What can be inferred about the speaker from the following dialogues?

(There can be more than one inference about a dialogue.)

  i. Man: Do you want tickets to the student play? Everyone in the stage crew gets a couple of free tickets, and I don't know anyone who wants to go.

      Inference: _____

  ii. Woman: There's no way I can graduate if I don't get this chemistry paper finished by this Friday.

      Inference: _____

  iii. Man: I'm sorry but I can't let you sign out these books. The computer says you have over $5 in overdue fines.

      Inference: _____

TOEFL Exercise 2.4

 Listen to each short dialogue carefully, and then choose the best answer to the question.

1.   (A) He does not like the woman.

      (B) He does not teach many classes.

      (C) He grades students very strictly.

      (D) He is the woman's favorite professor.

2. (A) Pat will be driving.
   (B) They will be taking the train.
   (C) The man has been to Washington before.
   (D) The woman will not be traveling with the man and Pat.

3. (A) It is Saturday.
   (B) It is before noon.
   (C) The library is far from their home.
   (D) The woman wants to watch TV.

4. (A) Two friends
   (B) Employer-applicant
   (C) Teacher-student
   (D) Two office workers

5. (A) She thinks the cafeteria is too expensive.
   (B) She really did not like today's lunch either.
   (C) She does not like the cafeteria's food in general.
   (D) She has never eaten in the cafeteria.

6. (A) He has never taught before.
   (B) He teaches only seminars.
   (C) He is a philosophy professor.
   (D) He is not very popular.

7. (A) She is a short story writer.
   (B) She is really tired these days.
   (C) She is the man's boss.
   (D) She is working for the school newspaper.

8. (A) By car
   (B) By subway
   (C) By bus
   (D) By bicycle and on foot

9. (A) He has not chosen a major yet.
   (B) He is having problems with his grades.
   (C) He does not take many different courses.
   (D) He has not started university yet.

10. (A) She is busy studying.
    (B) She works in the library.
    (C) She is a psychology major.
    (D) She is a friend of the man.

5. Future Action Questions

In these TOEFL tests, future action questions are usually like the Inference questions; that is, the answer is often INDIRECTLY stated, so you must read between the lines based on the available information to determine the most likely action. Often you will hear several different possible future actions, and from the other information in the dialogue, you will be able to infer the most likely future action.

Example

(Man)   I'm going to the library because I really need to talk to Dawn before I go to class.

(Woman)   But I just saw Dawn – she said she was going to the student union building.

Several possible future actions were mentioned – going to the library, talking to Dawn, going to class, and going to the student union building. Since he wanted to go to the library in order to talk to Dawn, and Dawn is no longer there, that choice is unlikely. He indicated that talking to Dawn before class was also important. So, most likely, he will go to the student union building next, in order to talk to Dawn.

Different questions are possible, too. Sometimes you will be asked for someone's future action, but sometimes you will be asked for what someone will do <u>next</u> – in that case, being able to order events will be an important skill.

Practice 2.5
From the following dialogues, determine what the woman will most likely do next.

i. Man: Do you want to go to New York with me this weekend to visit a museum?

    Woman: I'd like to, but if I don't get this economics paper finished by Monday, I'll fail the class.

    Future Action: _____

ii. Man: I need to run home quickly and get my history textbook before class begins.

    Woman: Oh, I noticed you left it this morning, so I brought it with me for you.

    Future Action: _____

iii. Woman: I don't have time to meet with you now. I need to drive my sister to my parent's house.

    Man: That's too bad. I was hoping we could get a coffee or something to eat.

    Future Action: _____

TOEFL Exercise 2.5

 Listen to each short dialogue carefully, and then choose the best answer to the question.

1. (A) Go to Houston
    (B) Spend a weekend at the zoo
    (C) Go to Dallas
    (D) Travel with the man

2. (A) Do her math homework
    (B) Write her midterm exam
    (C) Take a break
    (D) Study for her history test

3. (A) Enroll in the major seminar
    (B) Enroll in a class with another professor
    (C) Enroll in the professor's Labor Economics course
    (D) Enroll in a lower-level class with the same professor

4. (A) Go to the library
    (B) Talk to his major advisor
    (C) Go to the student union building
    (D) Get something to eat with the woman

5. (A) Stay in the lab
    (B) Study for a test
    (C) Get some sleep
    (D) Go with the woman

6. (A) Write a new list
    (B) Do his homework
    (C) Go shopping
    (D) Make dinner

7. (A) Buy basketball tickets
    (B) Go play basketball
    (C) Have lunch with the man
    (D) Make lunch for the man

8. (A) The soccer game
    (B) A movie
    (C) A talk show
    (D) The news

9. (A) Not attend his biology class
    (B) Call the telephone company from his biology class
    (C) Go to the biology class in the afternoon
    (D) Go to the telephone company between two and four o'clock

6. Comprehension Questions

This kind of question asks you to understand the general subject of the conversation – the why's and how's. Examples of information you might be asked about include:

Why/When/Where/How did something happen?
What happened?
What is someone's problem?
How much/How many ___?

Example

(Man)   I need to talk to Professor Jenkins about my history paper – I need some advice about how to find more primary sources.

(Woman)   Well, he won't be in his office until 2:00.

This dialogue mentions why the man wants to meet his professor, the subject, the man's problem, when he can meet the professor, and where the professor will be.

Note that when writing essays in university, there can be both primary and secondary sources. Secondary sources are books and essays other people have written about a subject. Primary sources are the raw data about a subject. For example, a book about the history of the American constitution would be a secondary source, but the constitution itself is a primary source.

Practice 2.6
List some possible comprehension questions for the following dialogues.

i. Man: I can't believe how much homework Dr. Smith gave us!
   Woman: I know. Ten short questions, four long questions, and a 5-page paper. And it's all due tomorrow!
   Comprehension: _____
                  _____
                  _____

ii. Woman: Excuse me, does the number 40 bus to the university stop here?
    Man: Yes, one comes by every 15 minutes or so. And the number 140 goes by the university, too.
    Comprehension: _____
                   _____
                   _____

iii. Man: $49.95? Wow, those books are expensive.
     Woman: And that doesn't include nearly $5 in tax.
     Comprehension: _____
                    _____
                    _____

TOEFL Exercise 2.6

 Listen to each short dialogue carefully, and then choose the best answer to the question.

1. (A) 2
   (B) 16
   (C) 50
   (D) 60

2. (A) The Provost is too busy.
   (B) The Provost never meets with students.
   (C) She did not make an appointment.
   (D) She is not a university student.

3. (A) Why he will live in the new dorm
   (B) Where he will live next year
   (C) How many dormitories there are on campus
   (D) When he is planning on moving

4. (A) A method of contacting Dr. Kilmer
   (B) Who Dr. Kilmer is
   (C) The reason Dr. Kilmer is busy
   (D) When Dr. Kilmer will be in his laboratory

5. (A) $6.50
   (B) $8.50
   (C) $15
   (D) $21.50

6. (A) Turn left, and go down the road
   (B) In the Reed Building
   (C) In the same building as the music department building
   (D) In the Franklin Building

7. (A) $19
   (B) $45
   (C) $90
   (D) $180

8. (A) Submit an artistic project
   (B) Submit an essay
   (C) Submit a story
   (D) Submit a painting

9. (A) She did not work hard enough on it.
   (B) She did not use enough sources.
   (C) She did not understand the topic.
   (D) She did not do original research.

7. Assumption Questions

This kind of question is similar to the implication question: it also asks for unstated meaning. But the Assumption Question involves <u>surprise</u>, where one of the speakers discovers something unexpected to be true. This form of question is much less common.

As a rule, the emphasized part of a sentence is the assumption. When speakers emphasize something, it means they originally thought something different than the emphasized part. An example of a common sentence pattern for an assumption is:

So Bob <u>did</u> go to the new action movie after all!

Use of the emphatic ("did go," as opposed to the simple past tense, "went") stresses the verb. Tone is also important. In this example, the speaker assumed that Bob did not go to the movie. In addition, "after all" is an expression commonly used for assumptions; it shows the actual result is contrary to what a person originally thought.

There are a couple of other possible patterns for an assumption. You can emphasize the person performing the act (Bob):

So it was <u>Bob</u> who went to the new action movie after all.

This shows that the speaker assumed someone else, not Bob, had gone to the movie.

Or you can emphasize what the person did.
So Bob went to the <u>new</u> action movie after all.
So Bob went to the new <u>action</u> movie after all.

These show that the speaker assumed Bob went to a different movie than he actually did. The speaker did know Bob went to a movie, but not which one. But in the first example, the speaker thought it was an older action movie, not a new one. In the second example, the speaker thought Bob went to a different kind of movie than an action movie (maybe a romance or a comedy).

But on TOEFL, the first pattern is definitely the most common. And, fortunately, it is also the easiest to understand.

Practice 2.7
Write what the speaker had assumed.

i. Woman: So Susan and Mike did get married after all!
Assumption: _____

ii. Man: You mean you didn't go to the party?
Assumption: _____

iii. Woman: So Brian did make the football team!
Assumption: _____

TOEFL Exercise 2.7

 Listen to each short dialogue carefully, and then choose the best answer to the question.

1. (A) He liked the play.
    (B) He stayed at home.
    (C) He saw the play.
    (D) He understood the play.

2. (A) It was not an anthropology course.
    (B) Only anthropology majors could take it.
    (C) It was not a very fun class.
    (D) Only anthropology students would like it.

3. (A) She did not have tickets.
    (B) She was acting in the play.
    (C) She did not know Linda.
    (D) She did not like the theater.

4. (A) Her grades were straight A's.
    (B) She was not interested in the dual-degree program.
    (C) She was exempt from the grade requirement.
    (D) Her grades were lower than an A⁻.

5. (A) She was sleeping when he called.
    (B) She never answers her phone.
    (C) She was not home last night.
    (D) She was studying at Jen's home last night.

6. (A) Economics was part of the math department.
    (B) There was not a math requirement.
    (C) He could take any concentration.
    (D) There were no required courses.

7. (A) The man did not attempt to join the football team.
    (B) The man's name is the same as that of another student.
    (C) The football roster had an error on it.
    (D) The man had made the football team.

8. (A) It was supposed to be this week.
    (B) It was not at 3:00.
    (C) It was delayed for a week.
    (D) It was not with Dr. Harrison.

Mini-Test 1

Questions 1-6

1. What can be inferred about the woman?

(A) She is a theater major.
(B) She is not a member of the student theater club.
(C) She does not know who the man is.
(D) She was accepted into the student theater club.

LinguaForum

2. What is the woman implying?

(A) She will be there in five minutes.
(B) She will join them after taking a nap.
(C) She would rather study by herself.
(D) She needs to go to sleep.

LinguaForum

3. To whom does the calculator belong?

(A) Janet
(B) Dan
(C) The woman
(D) The man

LinguaForum

4. What will the man most likely do?

(A) Do his laundry tomorrow
(B) Put his clothes in with the woman's clothes
(C) Buy new clothes
(D) Wait until later to wash his clothes

LinguaForum

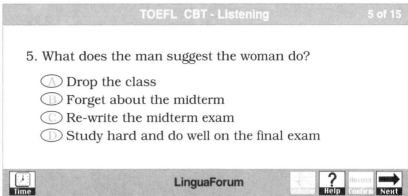

5. What does the man suggest the woman do?

- Ⓐ Drop the class
- Ⓑ Forget about the midterm
- Ⓒ Re-write the midterm exam
- Ⓓ Study hard and do well on the final exam

LinguaForum

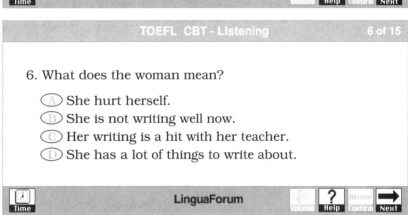

6. What does the woman mean?

- Ⓐ She hurt herself.
- Ⓑ She is not writing well now.
- Ⓒ Her writing is a hit with her teacher.
- Ⓓ She has a lot of things to write about.

LinguaForum

LISTENING

> **Business**

> **Economic Ideas in**
> - Greece
> - Rome
> - the Middle Ages

> **New Economic Ideas**
> - Mercantilism
> - Physiocracy

---

7. What is the main idea of this discussion?

    Ⓐ Free market economics
    Ⓑ Civilization before economics
    Ⓒ Why agriculture is economically more important
       than trade
    Ⓓ Economics before the free market

Time   LinguaForum   Volume | ? Help | Answer Confirm | Next

---

8. The professor mentioned several different economic
    theories. Match the economic era with the economic
    policy.

> Click on a term. Then click on the space
> where it belongs. Use each term only once.

Mercantilism
Physiocracy
Catholic Church

Against earning interest on loans	Gold and silver an index of national power	Against government interference

Time   LinguaForum   Volume | ? Help | Answer Confirm | Next

9. What was the cause of mercantilist economics?

  Ⓐ The end of the Middle Ages
  Ⓑ The rise of the nation-state
  Ⓒ The increase of gold and silver in Europe
  Ⓓ The constant warfare in 16th century Europe

LinguaForum

Questions 10-13

Agricultural Science

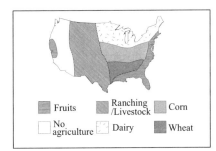

Fruits　Ranching/Livestock　Corn
No agriculture　Dairy　Wheat

New Trends in Farming
- Commercial
- Reduced in Population

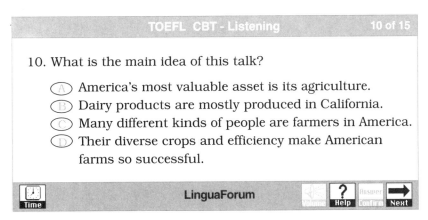

10. What is the main idea of this talk?

  Ⓐ America's most valuable asset is its agriculture.
  Ⓑ Dairy products are mostly produced in California.
  Ⓒ Many different kinds of people are farmers in America.
  Ⓓ Their diverse crops and efficiency make American farms so successful.

LinguaForum

11. The speaker mentioned many kinds of farming. Match the crop with the area where it is usually grown.

> Click on a crop. Then click on the space where it belongs. Use each crop only once.

Fruit
Cattle
Dairy

In large open places with poor soil	In colder areas, with short growing seasons	In hilly areas, not suitable for fields

12. What is responsible for the increases in farm yields in this century?

    Ⓐ More land is being cultivated.
    Ⓑ More people are working in agriculture.
    Ⓒ Machines make farming more efficient.
    Ⓓ Different crops make the land more valuable.

13. What is true of America's agricultural production?

    Ⓐ America is the world's biggest importer of agriculture.
    Ⓑ Americans consume the most food in the world.
    Ⓒ America has 2% of the world's farms.
    Ⓓ America sells more food abroad than any other country.

Questions 14-15

14. What happened to the man?

- Ⓐ He was accepted into a university.
- Ⓑ He applied to graduate school.
- Ⓒ He applied for a job interview.
- Ⓓ He made it into his school's journalism program.

Time LinguaForum Volume Help Confirm Next

15. Why was he accepted into the journalism program?

- Ⓐ He was sick one semester.
- Ⓑ He had good grades.
- Ⓒ He made a strong writing sample.
- Ⓓ He had experience working for newspapers.

Time LinguaForum Volume Help Confirm Next

LISTENING

Chapter 3 Diverters for Short Conversations

1. Similar Sounds

The most common method of diverting and confusing the listener is by using words and expressions that sound very similar (or exactly the same!) but have very different meanings. Some examples of confusing sounds might be:

going to – go into	try it – trite	reflex – reflects
your – you're	him – hymn	hate – ate
they're – there – their	new – knew – gnu	hear – here – ear
better – bitter – butter – batter		

Numbers are a common example of this problem, and they often turn up on the TOEFL exam:

fourteen – forty	fifteen – fifty	sixteen – sixty
one – won	two – to – too	four – for
eight – ate	nine – mine	

Some languages do distinguish the short *i*, "i," sound and "ee." Other languages do not have a difference between "see" and "shee." Some have a combination of other sound problems:

sit – seat – sheet	hit – heat	seaside – she sighed
haul – howl	Mary – marry – merry	

Since almost all languages have a different set of available sounds, the range of potential confusion sounds is nearly endless. Some other confusing sounds include:

ta – tha	pa – ba	fa – va
wa – va	cha – za	sh – sch

Further confusing things is the great number of ways of making sounds in English. English has 44 basic sounds, but there are over 400 ways of producing those sounds through various letter combinations.

Names are another source of potential confusion. Many names are homonyms for adjectives. "Frank" can be a name or an adjective meaning "honest and direct." Many names can also be colors – Violet and Rose are women's first names, while Green, White, Black, Gray and Brown can all be last names. Fortunately for you, TOEFL only uses traditional English-derived names, and does not include an ethnically diverse, international sampling of names.

Another major source of confusion is when sounds elide – that is, when the sound of one word slides into the next word. The most common case is when one word ends in a consonant, but the next word begins with a vowel.

Why do it? – Wide to it.	Hit in – hidden	Catch up – ketchup

Similarly, when the same sound ends one word and begins the next word, the sound is only heard one time and can be confusing:

Get two	He's sore	Thin neck
Don't talk	Bus stop	Dan never reads
Don't do it	Can't do it	

Practice 3.1
Match the word or phase with its correct meaning.

i.   bill   <u>a small medicine with a hard covering</u>
     pill   <u>to occupy to capacity</u>
     fill   <u>to cultivate the soil, farm</u>
     till   <u>a statement of money owed</u>

ii.   boy   <u>a body of water formed by an indentation in the shoreline</u>
     bay   <u>to purchase</u>
     buy   <u>to keep afloat</u>
     buoy   <u>a young man</u>

iii.   fit   <u>battle or combat</u>
     fat   <u>destiny</u>
     fate   <u>to have battled (past tense)</u>
     fete   <u>a temporary fashion</u>
     fought   <u>to lose brightness</u>
     feud   <u>hostilities between two families or clans</u>
     fight   <u>a holiday</u>
     fad   <u>overweight</u>
     fade   <u>in good physical condition</u>

TOEFL Exercise 3.1
 Listen to each short dialogue carefully, and then choose the best answer to the question.

1.   (A) The laboratory has snow in it.
    (B) The man should not have run from the lab.
    (C) The professor is being unreasonable.
    (D) Labrador Retrievers are not fast dogs.

2.   (A) She knows something bad happened.
    (B) It is a good sign that the man has not been rejected yet.
    (C) People think her nose is not attractive.
    (D) A good outcome is impossible.

3.   (A) Frank does not like the English department.
    (B) He does not like the woman's apartment.
    (C) The woman's department looks poor.
    (D) The university does not have a good English literature program.

4.   (A) He can use her carrel because she will be gone for a few hours.
    (B) He should write his paper somewhere else.
    (C) Her friend Carol is going to use the desk.
    (D) Her desk will be free for the next seven days.

5. (A) The woman's roommate likes to pet it.
   (B) It has the same name as the woman's mother.
   (C) It is the same age as her roommate's mother.
   (D) The woman's roommate recently got it.

6. (A) Where she can get some things taken to be reused
   (B) Where she could go bicycling
   (C) Where she can buy more things
   (D) Where she can park her car

7. (A) It will last a week.
   (B) It could damage his car.
   (C) It will harm his plants.
   (D) It will be too weak to do any serious damage.

8. (A) The hoses cost too much money.
   (B) He will take Rose with him to the store.
   (C) He wants to go to a different store than the one down the street.
   (D) He forgot to buy fertilizer.

9. (A) Mauritius
   (B) Morocco
   (C) Madagascar
   (D) Monaco

2. Synonyms

Synonyms are different words or phrases that have the same (or very similar) meaning. Throughout the TOEFL Listening Section, you will encounter synonyms and paraphrases. These are very important to recognize because on the test, the correct answer is very rarely the one that uses the same words as the dialogue. Usually, the correct answer will have the same meaning but use very different words.

The following is a short list of most common re-wordings you will repeatedly encounter on the TOEFL.

| need to – must | should – it's a good idea | can – have the ability |
| want – desire | I think – in my opinion | maybe – possibly |

Practice 3.2
Re-write the following sentences or phrases in your own words.

i. Man: In my opinion, our school's science department is too underfunded.
   Rewrite: _____

ii. Woman: I'm sure there's no rule that says you can't take 5 classes instead of just 4.
    Rewrite: _____

iii. Man: I took that class last year and I virtually had to move into the archives.

Rewrite: _____

TOEFL Exercise 3.2

 Listen to each short dialogue carefully, and then choose the best answer to the question.

1. (A) Her flight takes off at 1:00.
   (B) She will leave home at 1:00.
   (C) Her flight is supposed to arrive in Florida at 1:00.
   (D) Any flight at the airport will do tomorrow.

2. (A) There is no time to go shopping.
   (B) She can probably shop for only 10 minutes.
   (C) He already did the shopping.
   (D) The supermarket is close to their apartment.

3. (A) Late papers are acceptable.
   (B) He can hand the paper in late, but the professor will lower his grade.
   (C) The professor just wants him to do his best.
   (D) He cannot hand the paper in after the deadline.

4. (A) The professor told him there would be a test.
   (B) He only has six cents right now.
   (C) The test was about people's senses.
   (D) He had an unexplained feeling there would be a test.

5. (A) Tim pointed to his waist.
   (B) Tim does not do his share of work.
   (C) Tim is sensitive about his weight.
   (D) Tim never waits for others.

6. (A) The tie was white colored.
   (B) It is never right to lie.
   (C) It was a small lie that did no harm.
   (D) The tie is attractive.

7. (A) He would like Kerry to change to a pre-med major.
   (B) He would like to borrow her biology notes from Kerry.
   (C) He would like to give her his biology notes.
   (D) He would like to take Kerry to a doctor.

8. (A) How long it will take to fix her car
   (B) What the problem with her car is
   (C) How she can align the wheels
   (D) Where to find a replacement car

9. (A) He is the only person in three of his classes.
(B) Many of his courses are seminar-style this semester.
(C) He does not like seminars very much.
(D) Facts are more important in upper-level courses.

3. Conditionals (wishes, ifs, hypotheticals)

Conditionals are phrases and sentences that refer to things that are contrary to fact – to things that did not or have not happened. Wishes and "if" sentences are examples of hypothetical statements – statements that are not true, or have not actually happened.

If it rains, I will come home early.
If I lost weight, I would be much healthier.
If I had gone to the bank, I could have gotten some money.
I wish I could go to the concert tonight.

Conditionals can usually be easily recognized by the presence of an "if" or a "wish," along with modal auxiliaries like "will," "can," "would," "should," "could," and "might."

Example
(Woman)   I never would have bought this computer if I had known the student center was selling them at a discount.

From this sentence you know that:
    i.   the woman did actually buy a computer,
    ii. she did not know about the student center discount,
    iii. she did not buy her computer at the student center, and
    iv. the student center is selling computers at a discount.

Practice 3.3
Based on those following conditional sentences, write what is true or untrue.

    i. Man: If only I had studied harder, I could have gotten an A.
       Conditional: _____

       _____

    ii. Woman: I wish I had brought my textbook with me.
        Conditional: _____

    iii. Man: You're going to hurt yourself if you don't stop playing with those scissors.
         Conditional: _____

         _____

TOEFL Exercise 3.3

 Listen to each short dialogue carefully, and then choose the best answer to the question.

1. (A) She is a physics major.
    (B) She likes really easy classes.
    (C) She does not want to study physics.
    (D) She agrees with the man.

2. (A) She did not want to go to the show.
    (B) She wishes she could have met her professor instead.
    (C) She already knew that show very well.
    (D) She did not see the show.

3. (A) He thinks the coach is unfair.
    (B) He is too slow for the team.
    (C) He did not work hard enough.
    (D) He will make the team next year.

4. (A) She is playing video games too often.
    (B) It is an easy video game.
    (C) Video games are not as much fun as studying.
    (D) She will not get better unless she plays more.

5. (A) It would be better if there were more information available about their project.
    (B) He thinks they can find more information in the reference section.
    (C) It is a good idea for the library to buy more resource materials.
    (D) The library's reference area doesn't have much information.

6. (A) She does not want to study at university anymore.
    (B) Her classes all meet less than 5 hours a week.
    (C) She has never taken a course that easy.
    (D) Her major is engineering.

7. (A) Attempt to solve the problem
    (B) Go to the professor's office and talk to him
    (C) Forget about the problem
    (D) Not be egotistical

8. (A) The woman will not go to her folklore class today.
    (B) The woman is not in Dr. Thompson's class.
    (C) The woman did not sleep the previous night.
    (D) The woman needs one more day to finish the paper.

9. (A) He thinks the trustees' decision is completely unfair.
    (B) He thinks the woman is being mean.
    (C) He wants the woman not to write the letter.
    (D) He wants to write the university newspaper about the trustees' decision.

10. (A) Sam did not get to the library before it closed.
    (B) Sam used his student card to sign out the book.
    (C) Sam signed out the wrong book.
    (D) Sam did not get his book, even though the library was not closed.

4. Agreement/Disagreement

A lot of TOEFL questions involve people either agreeing or disagreeing with what someone else says. This can be done in many ways. Agreements include:

So do I.

Me, too.

I'll say.

That's for sure.

You bet.

You can say that again.

That sounds great.

*I don't either.

Neither do I. (Agree with negative statements.)

Disagreements include:

Not me.

No way.

Never.

I don't think so.

There's no way I'd ever ...

Example

Man: I love this song.
Woman: So do I.

Man: I don't think this class is very difficult.
Woman: Neither do I.

Another danger is the double negative. Sometimes people combine two negatives to produce a positive.

That's not impossible.

There's no way I would say "no."

The first choice means that something actually is possible. The second choice means that the speaker intends to say "yes."

Take Care

Sometimes an agreement can sound like a disagreement. This is particularly true when agreeing with a <u>negative</u> statement someone else makes. For example, agreeing with a positive statement, you might say, "So do I." But if you agree with a negative statement, you would say, "Neither do I."

Practice 3.4

From the following dialogues, determine if the second speaker is agreeing or disagreeing with the first speaker.

    i. Man: I loved that new comedy.
        Woman: Me, too.
        Agreement: _____

    ii. Woman: I didn't feel like going to class today, so I skipped them all.
        Man: I'd never do something like that.
        Agreement: _____

   iii. Man: I don't know the answer to question number 3.
        Woman: Neither do I.
        Agreement: _____

    iv. Woman: I'm excited about the concert tonight.
        Man: Nothing could make me miss it.
        Agreement: _____

    v. Man: Did you read John's article in the school paper? It was really good.
        Woman: I didn't think so.
        Agreement _____

    vi. Woman: I love Dr. Richard's public speaking class.
        Man: You can say that again.
        Agreement: _____

TOEFL Exercise 3.4

 Listen to each short dialogue carefully, and then choose the best answer to the question.

1.   (A) No one can help the man.
       (B) All the computers are the same.
       (C) No one can agree on which deal is the best.
       (D) None of the deals is a good value.

2.   (A) It is the best action film ever.
       (B) She agrees with the man.
       (C) She is wondering when the man will see the film.
       (D) He took a long time to see it.

3.   (A) The man should get the printer fixed.
       (B) The man should just come with her, without waiting.
       (C) The man should buy a new printer.
       (D) The woman does not know what he should do.

4. (A) He is a careless worker.
    (B) He is worried about his grades.
    (C) He is already finished the project.
    (D) He is not interested in improving the project.

5. (A) She agrees with the man.
    (B) She can think of several better teachers.
    (C) She will never forget how bad he was.
    (D) A different professor actually teaches that class.

6. (A) She should be patient.
    (B) She should take deep breaths.
    (C) She should trust Dave more.
    (D) She should not wait for Dave.

7. (A) He likes their chemistry class.
    (B) He has the same opinion as the woman.
    (C) He is doing badly in that class.
    (D) He disagrees with the woman.

8. (A) Get the book the woman wants
    (B) Get the woman to pick up his books at the library
    (C) Solve a problem for the woman's project
    (D) Be too busy to get a book for the woman

9. (A) She finds it difficult to be quiet.
    (B) She could not get a B$^+$ in physics.
    (C) She thinks he should tell his professor.
    (D) She will tell the man's professor what happened.

10. (A) It is not possible to reformat the hard drive.
    (B) The woman's idea might be a good one.
    (C) He will inspect his hard drive for problems.
    (D) It is too late for the woman's suggestion.

5. Passives

A great many English sentences can be written in either the active or the passive form.

Active	Passive
I threw the ball.	The ball was thrown by me.
You ignored the evidence.	The evidence was ignored by you.
Many factors cause inflation.	Inflation is caused by many factors.

Although academics and editors very much prefer the active form, in fact, there is no difference in meaning between the two. TOEFL will sometimes use a switch between active and passive to conceal the correct meaning – using active in the dialogue, but providing a passive answer, or vice-versa.

If a verb takes an object, it is called a transitive verb. Transitive verbs can be changed into the passive mood. Intransitive verbs cannot take an object and cannot be changed into the passive.

Active	**Passive**
I like him.	He is liked by me.
I run.	No passive. ("I was run" is impossible.)

Practice 3.5
Change the following sentences from passive to active form and active to passive form.

i. Man: Doug borrowed my book.
Change form: _____

ii. Woman: I ate spaghetti for dinner.
Change form: _____

iii. Man: David was given one last chance by his professor to improve.
Change form: _____

iv. Woman: I was surprised by your answer.
Change form: _____

TOEFL Exercise 3.5
 Listen to each short dialogue carefully, and then choose the best answer to the question.

1. (A) Dr. Phillips' project was cancelled.
(B) Dr. Phillips was worried about the project.
(C) Dr. Phillips no longer teaches astronomy.
(D) Dr. Phillips stopped the project.

2. (A) The tickets were bought by the woman.
(B) The tickets were eaten by the man's dog.
(C) The man had eight tickets to the dog show.
(D) The woman bought two tickets for the man.

3. (A) The newspaper did not publicize the poetry reading.
(B) The university did not announce the attendance.
(C) Poetry is not liked by most students.
(D) The event was announced in the newspaper.

4. (A) The Provost said they had to remove the posters.
(B) The Provost was putting up different posters.
(C) The Provost okayed the man's posters.
(D) The Provost was not told about the posters.

5. (A) She runs the student art gallery.
   (B) She is an undergraduate.
   (C) The gallery was once run by her.
   (D) The current exhibit at the gallery was made by her.

6. (A) The speakers' library does not special-order books.
   (B) The library does not have any of Dr. Riley's books.
   (C) Dr. Riley's book was partially written by the man.
   (D) The book was special-ordered by the man.

7. (A) Their team's success surprised the man.
   (B) The woman is on the school's football team.
   (C) The Saturday football game was attended by the man.
   (D) The man was surprised by the woman.

8. (A) They were needed by the man.
   (B) They were given to Jonathon by the woman.
   (C) She does not lend them to others.
   (D) The woman copied hers from Jonathon.

6. Degree (as...as, nearly, over, already, almost)

Often comparisons do not produce absolute differences. Sometimes the amount of difference is only partial – 100%, 90%, 50%, 10% or 0% are all very different conditions.

Less than words:

less than	→	A quart is less than a liter in volume.
short of	→	He is only 10 credits short of his degree requirement.
fewer	→	There are fewer than 1,000 students at our school.

"Slightly less than" words:

nearly	→	$9.95 is nearly $10.
almost	→	$9.95 is almost $10.
not quite	→	$9.95 is not quite as much as $10.

Equal quantities:

| as ... as ... | → | His desk is as big as a car. |
| the same as ... | → | One dollar is the same as 100 cents. |

Bigger than words:

more than	→	A million is more than a thousand.
over	→	At 90 kg, he is over the weight limit.
in excess of	→	The library has in excess of a million volumes.
greater than	→	A square mile is greater than a square kilometer.

You can, of course, combine these degree words. For example, to make a comparison which means the same size or larger or smaller:

| at least as ... as | → | He is at least as strong as Tim. |
| | → | He is at least as small as Tim. |

You can also compare multiple items:

David is faster than John, but not quite as fast as Sam.

Tracy's grades were as good as Kim's and even better than Don's.

Degree also can be absolute, without comparisons. It can apply to time and frequency, to how often something happens:

seldom	on occasion	frequently
rarely	sometimes	all the time
almost never	from time to time	constantly

It can also apply to size:

almost none
only
hardly
scarcely

Practice 3.6.1

With the given information, make comparison sentences using the various degree words.

i. Susan weighs 120 pounds.
Jane weighs 122 pounds.
Degree:

_____

_____

ii. There are 50 English majors at the university.
There are 55 History majors at the university.
There are 5 French majors at the university.
Degree:

_____

_____

_____

_____

iii. The number 8 bus runs every 15 minutes.
The number 50 bus runs every 10 minutes.
Degree:

_____

_____

Practice 3.6.2

Rewrite the following sentences using different frequency words.

i. Woman: I only exercised twice last month.
Frequency: _____

LISTENING

ii. Man: My biology lab keeps me busy for many hours every day.

   Frequency: _____

iii. Woman: Everyone said they would help me, but in the end, only one or two people did anything at all.

   Frequency: _____

TOEFL Exercise 3.6

 Listen to each short dialogue carefully, and then choose the best answer to the question.

1. (A) He is not as fast as the woman.
    (B) He is at least as fast as the woman.
    (C) He is nearly as fast as Megan.
    (D) He is faster than the man.

2. (A) He usually likes to study the hardest parts first.
    (B) He always has the same hard studying style as the woman.
    (C) He almost never studies as the woman does.
    (D) He does not study very much.

3. (A) The food at College Cafeteria is better than Smith Cafeteria's.
    (B) The food at Abrams Cafeteria is the best on campus.
    (C) Smith Cafeteria is the most expensive.
    (D) Abrams Cafeteria is the least expensive.

4. (A) Less well than she wanted to do
    (B) Better than she expected
    (C) Not quite well enough to pass
    (D) Guessed on too many questions

5. (A) She exercises more than the man.
    (B) She exercises every other day.
    (C) She exercises very rarely.
    (D) She never exercises.

6. (A) Nearly $2
    (B) Exactly $2
    (C) Over $2
    (D) Slightly less than $22

7. (A) Sean loses pencils very frequently.
    (B) The pencil was not very large.
    (C) He is quite forgetful.
    (D) The loss was not terribly serious.

8. (A) She has never come early to a meeting.
   (B) Everyone comes to the meetings late.
   (C) She is almost always late for the meetings.
   (D) The man is often more badly late than Becky.

9. (A) The man's salary is greater than the woman's.
   (B) The woman's salary is between the man's and Diane's.
   (C) Diane earns almost as much as the woman.
   (D) The man earns twice as much as Diane.

7. Vocabulary (idioms, multi-word verbs)

One of the most basic methods TOEFL uses to confuse the listener is vocabulary difficulty. It is difficult to listen to a word when you do not know what that word means. Most of the words and expressions you hear on the test are the sorts of things you would hear as a first-year student, and, in general, the test does feature more difficult vocabulary than it used to.

Vocabulary can be divided into three categories – difficult words, multi-word verbs, and idioms.

Difficult words:

Because English has such a large working vocabulary, just knowing the basic words can be difficult. There are also many specialized terms one hears in the university setting.

Often, there are two (or more) words with the same meaning – one with a Germanic origin, and one with a French or Latin origin. As a general rule, the more formal or scientific choice (and, therefore, the choice more likely in an academic setting) will be the French- or Latin-derived word. Think about the following examples:

to begin – to commence	speed – velocity
to hope – to anticipate	sad – despondent
to guess – to estimate	friendly – amiable

Similarly, FORM can be a difficult trick. For example, *-ing* verbs and verbs in the infinitive form are usually the same in meaning, but not always.

He stopped to eat.	→	He stopped what he was doing in order to eat.
He stopped eating.	→	He is not eating now.
Active	→	Doing many things
Activate	→	To begin doing something
Flammable	→	Able to burst into flame
Inflammable	→	Able to burst into flame

Note that, while usually adding "in-" to an adjective reverses its meaning, for "flammable," that is not the case.

Multi-word Verbs:

TOEFL is also very fond of using multi-word verbs (or compound verbs). These are often short, simple verbs that combine with prepositions to form new meanings. For example:

to break – to destroy
to break down – to collapse (physically or mentally)
to break up – to end (marriage, dating, or a nation)
to break in – to steal
to break off – to sever (a piece)
to break out – to escape

And the verb can be combined with prepositions to form a noun:

Breakaway – a stampede or sudden separation from a group
Breakthrough – a sudden advance (as in science)

Idioms:

TOEFL does not test idioms as relentlessly as it used to, but there are still many on the test. Most common are the simple, everyday idioms that people use in basic conversation.

Because the meanings of idioms bear little or no resemblance to the words' literal meanings, the listener generally must know the idiom in order to understand it. Sometimes, the context may provide clues to the meaning. Just as you should avoid answers that are too similar in wording to the original dialogue, so you should be careful of answers that are too literal.

Example
(Woman)	Did you get your lab report finished before the deadline?
(Man)	Just in the nick of time.

The man means that he finished writing his report just before it was due. The "nick" in "nick of time" has nothing to do with being cut, although TOEFL would likely have one answer with that option.

*Take*Care

Do not put a lot of energy into studying long lists of obscure or out-of-date idioms. None of the speakers on the TOEFL test will use such clunkers as "a stitch in time saves nine," "many hands make light the work," or the like. Instead, emphasize commons words and short expressions that are used idiomatically, like "hang out" or "messing around."

Practice 3.7
Write the meaning of what the person is saying.

   i. Woman: I had a great breakthrough on my experiment today.
       Meaning: _____

   ii. Man: I'm going to run for student council.
       Meaning: _____

  iii. Woman: Jane is so diligent, but everyone takes her for granted.
       Meaning: _____

  iv. Man: The provost said my essay was top-notch.
       Meaning: _____

   v. Woman: I know what Dale did was reprehensible, but you shouldn't let it get you down.
       Meaning: _____

TOEFL Exercise 3.7

 Listen to each short dialogue carefully, and then choose the best answer to the question.

1. (A) Her apartment was in perfect condition.
   (B) There was little damage to the apartment.
   (C) The apartment was in really bad condition.
   (D) Her security deposit was slightly damaged.

2. (A) Use the microfilm archives
   (B) Sign out books
   (C) Pay overdue fines
   (D) Get permission to use the checkout desk

3. (A) She could not find the back-up copy.
   (B) Mornings are always a very busy time.
   (C) The computers were not working.
   (D) It was sent to the airport.

4. (A) Take an easier science course
   (B) Enroll in a social science course
   (C) Take another year to graduate
   (D) Take a physics course

5. (A) Mike is always one of the fairest people.
   (B) Mike won a close election.
   (C) Mike lost the election.
   (D) Mike won by a large margin.

6. (A) She does not like it.
   (B) She was not allowed to take it after all.
   (C) The class has been very good.
   (D) The class is surprisingly easy.

7. (A) By bus
   (B) By train
   (C) By plane
   (D) By ferry

8. (A) Cheri needs to get a better grade.
   (B) Cheri should forget about the problems with Dr. Grant.
   (C) Cheri should take Dr. Grant's class again.
   (D) Cheri needs to complain to the school authorities.

9. (A) He was accepted into the program.
   (B) The Provost said his application was exceptional.
   (C) He is still waiting to hear how he did.
   (D) There is still a small chance he might be accepted in the future.

8. Pronouns and Referents

One of the more difficult parts of Part A – Short Dialogues is keeping track of all the actors and actions in the passages. Frequently names will only be mentioned once, and thereafter pronouns are used instead – he, she, it, you, I, him, her, me, etc.

Pronouns in English are usually governed by two ideas (not strong enough to be "rules"):
  1) A pronoun usually refers to the most recent appropriate noun.
  2) A pronoun usually refers to a dominant subject.
Unfortunately, those two ideas can contradict each other, so you have to be aware of context and other nuances.

Example

(Man)   Steve called me to say Dave was going to be late.
(Woman)   That was nice of him.

The woman here is referring to Steve, not Dave. Steve is the dominant subject in this dialogue and, more importantly, it would not make sense to say Dave was "nice" to be late.

(Man)   Steve called me to say Dave was going to be late.
(Woman)   He's never on time.

This time the "he" refers to Dave. The dialogue would not make much sense referring to Steve's lateness.

(Woman)   I need to use Steve's notes to do my homework problems.
(Man)   They're not that difficult.

In this case, "They" refers to the homework problems.

(Woman)   I need to use Steve's notes to do my homework problems.
(Man)   But I'm not finished with them.

"Them" refers to Steve's notes.

(Woman)   I need to use Steve's notes to do my homework problems.
(Man)   He said I could use them until tomorrow.

"He" is Steve and "them" is his notes.

Practice 3.8

Identify the pronouns in the following dialogues.

    i. Man: Do you have the answers to last week's quiz?
        Woman: I do, but I gave them to Eric's friend.
        What is "them"?   _____
        Who has "them"?   _____

    ii. Woman: Sue's brother Doug is supposed to be here in an hour.
        Man: I had forgotten all about that.
        What is "that"?   _____
        Who is coming?   _____

    iii. Man: Did Derek hand his paper in on time?
        Woman: No, but his professor gave him another week to finish it.

What is "it"?   _____
Who received
more time?   _____

TOEFL Exercise 3.8

 Listen to each short dialogue carefully, and then choose the best answer to the question.

1. (A) Rick
   (B) Rick's sister
   (C) The woman's sister
   (D) The man

2. (A) Jason
   (B) Jason's roommate
   (C) Terry's roommate
   (D) The woman

3. (A) The man
   (B) The man's friend
   (C) Dan's friend
   (D) Dan's brother

4. (A) Janice
   (B) Peter
   (C) The man
   (D) Naomi

5. (A) Dave
   (B) Jan
   (C) The woman
   (D) The man

6. (A) The man
   (B) The woman
   (C) David
   (D) The woman's friend

7. (A) Erica's home
   (B) Erica's friend's home
   (C) The woman's sister's home
   (D) Debby's home

8. (A) Phil's friend
   (B) Phil's sister
   (C) Phil
   (D) The man

9. (A) The woman's friend
   (B) The woman's sister
   (C) Sue's sister
   (D) Karen's friend

Mini-Test 2

Questions 1-6

1. What does the woman mean?

   Ⓐ She has a lot of free time.
   Ⓑ She has to go visit her family.
   Ⓒ She has to spend all her time studying for the next week.
   Ⓓ She has too many commitments next week to study.

LinguaForum

2. What is the man assuming about the woman?

   Ⓐ She was up late studying.
   Ⓑ She likes to go out with her friends at night.
   Ⓒ She does not have any exams this semester.
   Ⓓ She has insomnia.

LinguaForum

3. What can be inferred about the man?

   Ⓐ He cannot change his schedule.
   Ⓑ He is a junior.
   Ⓒ He is a senior.
   Ⓓ He is a graduate student.

LinguaForum

4. When does the woman have to meet Dr. Stephens?

   Ⓐ After her presentation
   Ⓑ Before her math class
   Ⓒ Before her final exam
   Ⓓ After her test

LinguaForum

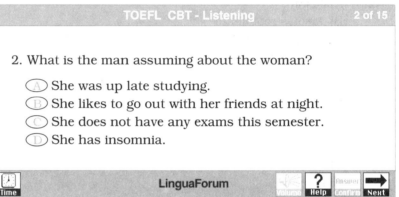
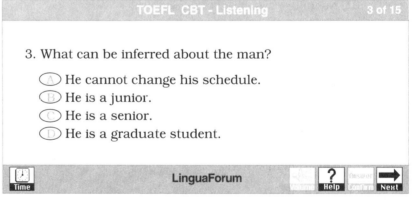
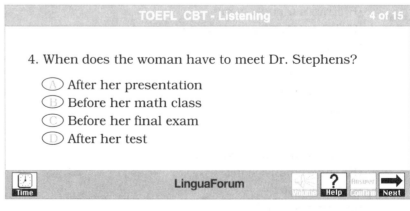

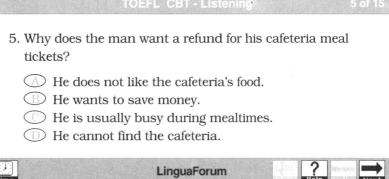

5. Why does the man want a refund for his cafeteria meal tickets?

  Ⓐ He does not like the cafeteria's food.
  Ⓑ He wants to save money.
  Ⓒ He is usually busy during mealtimes.
  Ⓓ He cannot find the cafeteria.

Time   **LinguaForum**   Volume Help Confirm Next

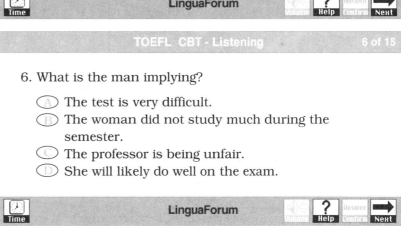

6. What is the man implying?

  Ⓐ The test is very difficult.
  Ⓑ The woman did not study much during the semester.
  Ⓒ The professor is being unfair.
  Ⓓ She will likely do well on the exam.

Time   **LinguaForum**   Volume Help Confirm Next

LISTENING

Questions 7-9

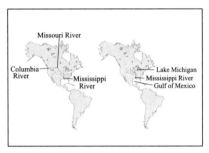

7. What is the professor's opinion of these explorers?

  Ⓐ They were the first people to ever explore North America.

  Ⓑ Lewis and Clark were the best explorers.

  Ⓒ Exploring in pairs is more efficient than going alone.

  Ⓓ They were very important in opening North America to European settlers.

LinguaForum

8. The speaker mentioned many pairs of explorers. Match the pair with the region they explored.

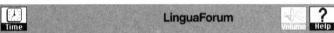

Click on a pair of names. Then click on the space where they belong. Use each pair only once.

Radisson and Groseilliers
Lewis and Clark
Marquette and Joliet

LinguaForum

9. The speaker mentioned many different explorers. Put the following explorers into the correct chronological order.

> Click on a name. Then click on the space where it belongs. Use each name only once.

Daniel Boone
Lewis and Clark
Marquette and Joliet
Radisson and Groseilliers

1. [   ]   3. [   ]

2. [   ]   4. [   ]

Questions 10-13

Urban Planning

Highways:
- Lancaster Turnpike
- National Turnpike
- Pennsylvania Turnpike

10. What is the main topic of this lecture?

(A) The car in American history
(B) The culture of roads and freeways
(C) Pivotal events in America
(D) The history of the American highway

11. The professor talked about the history of highways in the United States. Summarize by placing the following events into the correct chronological order.

Click on a sentence. Then click on the space where it belongs. Use each sentence only once.

Modern asphalt is invented.
The U.S. Interstate Highway System started.
The Lancaster Turnpike opens.
The first state highway commission started.

1. [　　　　　　]   3. [　　　　　　]

2. [　　　　　　]   4. [　　　　　　]

LinguaForum

Time   Volume   Help   Confirm   Next

12. The speaker mentioned several early roads in American history. Match the highway and its significance.

Click on a highway name. Then click on the space where it belongs. Use each highway name only once.

Lancaster Turnpike
National Turnpike
Pennsylvania Turnpike

The first public paved road	The first engineered and paved road	The first freeway

LinguaForum

Time   Volume   Help   Confirm   Next

13. What caused the renewal of road building at the end of the 19th century?

    (A) The decline of the railroad
    (B) The popularity of the bicycle
    (C) The rise of the automobile
    (D) The increase in commerce in America

LinguaForum

Time   Volume   Help   Confirm   Next

Questions 14-15

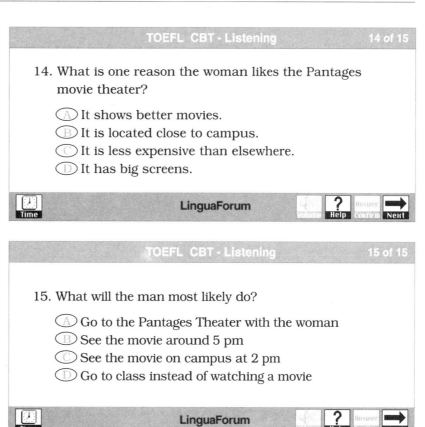

14. What is one reason the woman likes the Pantages movie theater?

   (A) It shows better movies.
   (B) It is located close to campus.
   (C) It is less expensive than elsewhere.
   (D) It has big screens.

LinguaForum

15. What will the man most likely do?

   (A) Go to the Pantages Theater with the woman
   (B) See the movie around 5 pm
   (C) See the movie on campus at 2 pm
   (D) Go to class instead of watching a movie

LinguaForum

LISTENING

Chapter 4 Reviews for Part A

The following questions are a sampling of all the various ideas introduced for Part A of the Listening Section of the TOEFL test. One test is an 11-question version of the TOEFL Short Dialogues, and the other test is a 17-question version.

Type A – 11 Questions for Part A

Questions 1-11

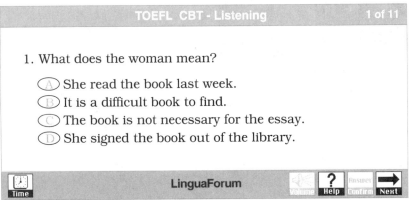

1. What does the woman mean?

   Ⓐ She read the book last week.
   Ⓑ It is a difficult book to find.
   Ⓒ The book is not necessary for the essay.
   Ⓓ She signed the book out of the library.

LinguaForum

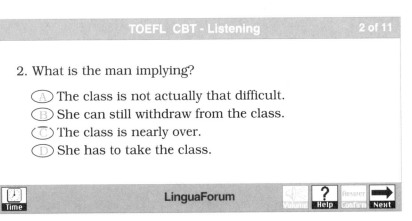

2. What is the man implying?

   Ⓐ The class is not actually that difficult.
   Ⓑ She can still withdraw from the class.
   Ⓒ The class is nearly over.
   Ⓓ She has to take the class.

LinguaForum

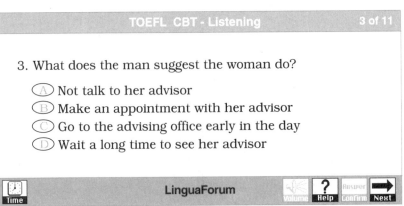

3. What does the man suggest the woman do?

   Ⓐ Not talk to her advisor
   Ⓑ Make an appointment with her advisor
   Ⓒ Go to the advising office early in the day
   Ⓓ Wait a long time to see her advisor

LinguaForum

4. What can be inferred from the conversation?

   Ⓐ The man never took a class with Dr. Robbins before.
   Ⓑ The woman plans on taking the course next semester.
   Ⓒ The man has not fulfilled his humanities requirement.
   Ⓓ Only upper-level classes count towards the humanities requirement.

LinguaForum

5. What does the woman mean?

   Ⓐ She will not play for a short time.
   Ⓑ She wants to play a few more games.
   Ⓒ Her friend Justin did hurt himself more seriously.
   Ⓓ She will never play field hockey again.

LinguaForum

6. Why does the woman want to take the bus?

   Ⓐ To go downtown
   Ⓑ To leave the city
   Ⓒ To go to the university
   Ⓓ To go to City Hall

LinguaForum

7. What is the woman implying?

   Ⓐ She did not do the research.
   Ⓑ She did not know the man wrote the report already.
   Ⓒ She does not like the man's work.
   Ⓓ She does not want to go to the movies.

LinguaForum

8. What did the woman assume about the man?

   (A) He was not taking any political science classes.
   (B) He did not work for the university newspaper.
   (C) He was busy writing an essay.
   (D) He wanted to study tomorrow.

LinguaForum

9. What is the man implying?

   (A) He does not want to do anything outdoors.
   (B) He would rather go to the beach.
   (C) He does not want to travel with the woman's friends.
   (D) He has never been camping before.

LinguaForum

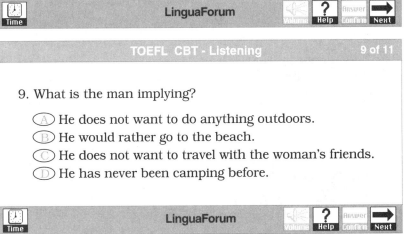

10. What does the woman mean?

   (A) There are too many people in their class.
   (B) The professor will probably not give weekly tests.
   (C) The professor was not really mad.
   (D) She is going to do whatever her professor says.

LinguaForum

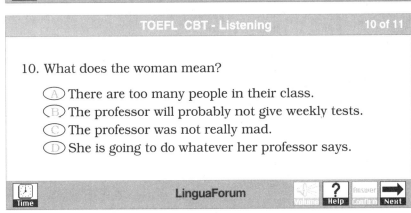

11. What will the woman most likely do next?

   (A) Meet her friend Karen
   (B) Write a test
   (C) Stay and study a while longer
   (D) Go home to sleep

LinguaForum

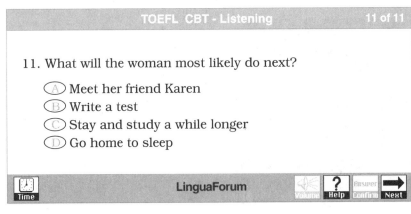

Type B – 17 Questions for Part A

Questions 1-17

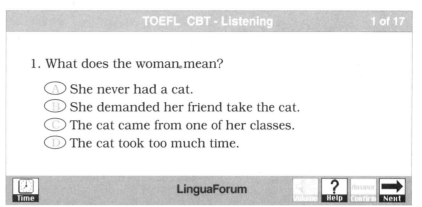

1. What does the woman mean?

  Ⓐ She never had a cat.
  Ⓑ She demanded her friend take the cat.
  Ⓒ The cat came from one of her classes.
  Ⓓ The cat took too much time.

Time   LinguaForum   Volume Help Confirm Next

2. What is the man implying?

  Ⓐ The paper needs more editors.
  Ⓑ The features are not a problem.
  Ⓒ There is not much interesting news happening.
  Ⓓ The stories are too short.

Time   LinguaForum   Volume Help Confirm Next

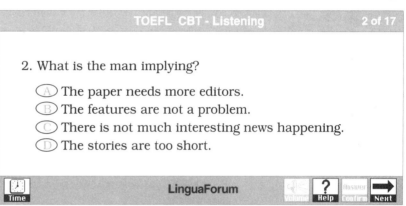

3. Who has Derrick's disk?

  Ⓐ Dale's friend
  Ⓑ Dale
  Ⓒ The woman's friend
  Ⓓ Derrick

Time   LinguaForum   Volume Help Confirm Next

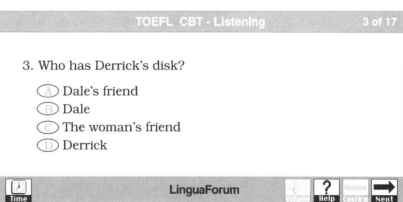

4. What will the woman most likely do next?

  Ⓐ Go to the dormitory
  Ⓑ Study by herself
  Ⓒ Go to the student union
  Ⓓ Study with the man

Time   LinguaForum   Volume Help Confirm Next

LISTENING

5. What did the woman suggest to the man?

- (A) Studying Italian
- (B) Eating at the student cafeteria
- (C) Working on their experiment right away
- (D) Going to a restaurant

Time   LinguaForum   Volume Help Confirm Next

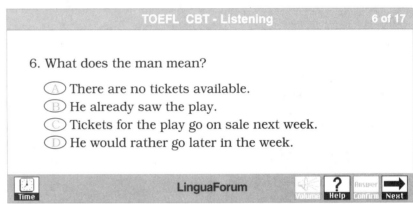

6. What does the man mean?

- (A) There are no tickets available.
- (B) He already saw the play.
- (C) Tickets for the play go on sale next week.
- (D) He would rather go later in the week.

Time   LinguaForum   Volume Help Confirm Next

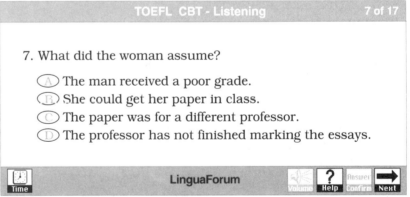

7. What did the woman assume?

- (A) The man received a poor grade.
- (B) She could get her paper in class.
- (C) The paper was for a different professor.
- (D) The professor has not finished marking the essays.

Time   LinguaForum   Volume Help Confirm Next

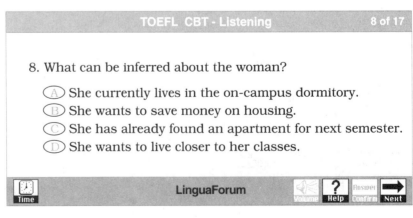

8. What can be inferred about the woman?

- (A) She currently lives in the on-campus dormitory.
- (B) She wants to save money on housing.
- (C) She has already found an apartment for next semester.
- (D) She wants to live closer to her classes.

Time   LinguaForum   Volume Help Confirm Next

9. How far away is the president's office?

    (A) 4 blocks
    (B) 5 blocks
    (C) 8 blocks
    (D) 14 blocks

LinguaForum

10. What does the woman want to know?

    (A) When the man's class will meet
    (B) Who will be teaching the history seminar
    (C) What class the man will take
    (D) Why the man is taking Dr. Fields' class

LinguaForum

11. When will the man study for economics?

    (A) After writing his essay
    (B) After meeting the woman
    (C) Before finishing his lab
    (D) Before eating lunch

LinguaForum

12. What does the man mean?

    (A) The table was covered in grease.
    (B) The table was in too poor condition to buy.
    (C) He ran to the store, but it was not open.
    (D) He can make the table look nice with some work.

LinguaForum

LISTENING

13. What is the man implying?

   (A) He will go with the woman.
   (B) He needs to work with his friends some more.
   (C) He does not drink coffee any more.
   (D) He wants to exercise for a while.

LinguaForum

14. What can be inferred about the woman?

   (A) She is a senior.
   (B) She is an economics major.
   (C) She is a graduate student.
   (D) She is a mathematics major.

LinguaForum

15. What is the total amount of time the man will use the flame?

   (A) 20 minutes
   (B) 35 minutes
   (C) 70 minutes
   (D) 100 minutes

LinguaForum

16. What is the main reason the woman thinks the student paper is much better now?

   (A) Better editing
   (B) Better design
   (C) Better writing
   (D) Better printing

LinguaForum

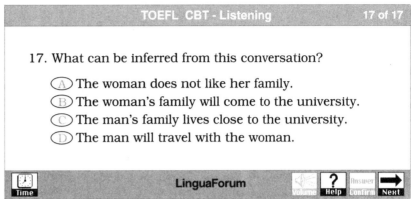

17. What can be inferred from this conversation?

   (A) The woman does not like her family.
   (B) The woman's family will come to the university.
   (C) The man's family lives close to the university.
   (D) The man will travel with the woman.

Time   **LinguaForum**   Volume   Help   Confirm   Next

LISTENING

Chapter 5 General Information for Part B

Part B is made up of a series of longer passages – a combination of longer conversations, academic discussions or seminars, and academic lectures.

Depending on your particular test, you could have either 19 or 33 Part B questions. Since there are about 2-6 questions for each listening passage, you will have between 6 and 9 listening passages total. There is no order in which to expect the conversations, seminars, and lectures. Expect to hear more than one of each type of passage.

There are few tricks like those in Part A. Instead, the questions are more based on content and overall comprehension. The passages are also longer, presenting much more information to understand and keep track of.

In the academic discussions and lectures, the CBT takes advantage of the computer and incorporates different kinds of questions such as multiple-answer questions with 2 answers, matching questions, ordering questions, and picture answers. In all of these new styles of questions, TOEFL will clearly identify what kind of question is presented. An Ordering question will always clearly be an Ordering question; a Matching question will always be clearly a Matching question.

In spite of these new types of questions, the overwhelming emphasis is on basic comprehension. Because they differ greatly, Casual Conversations and Academic Discussions and Lectures will be discussed separately.

Casual Conversations/Longer Conversations

For each of the casual conversations/longer conversations in the listening section of the TOEFL Computer-Based Test, you will see context-setting visuals as you listen to a ten- to fifteen-line conversation between two speakers. The casual conversations/longer conversations might be between two students, a student and a professor, or a student and a university administrator. After you see the visual and listen to the conversation, you will see a series of two to three questions and the four choices for each question on the computer screen.

Academic Discussions/Seminars

For each of the academic discussions/seminars which are added in the new format of the TOEFL Computer-Based Test, you will see a series of context-setting visuals as you hear a 120- to 150-second discussion (roughly 250-350 words) by two to five speakers. The academic discussions are between students and a professor. After you see the visuals and listen to the discussion, you will hear a series of three to six questions as you see each question and its answer choices on the computer screen.

Various types of questions are possible in this part of the test. Some of these types of questions may follow a discussion:

(1) A multiple choice question with one correct answer
(2) A multiple choice question with two correct answers
(3) A matching question/ordering question
(4) A question with four graphic answer choices
(5) A question and a graphic with four letters marked

Academic Lectures

1. Short Form

There are two kinds of academic lectures according to the length of lecture. For convenience's sake, they here are called the short form lecture and the long form lecture. For each of the short academic lectures in the listening section of the TOEFL Computer-Based Test, you will see a series of context-setting visuals as you hear a 120- to 150-second lecture (roughly 250-350 words) by a university professor. After you see the visuals and listen to the lecture, you will see a series of three to six questions as you see each question and its choices on the computer screen.

2. Long Form

For each of the long academic lectures, you will see a series of context-setting visuals as you hear a 150- to 250-second lecture (roughly 350-500 words) by a university professor. After you see the visuals and listen to the lecture, you will see a series of three to six questions as you see each question and its choices on the computer screen.

Various types of questions are possible in this part of the test. Some of these types of questions may follow a discussion:

(1) A multiple choice question with one correct answer
(2) A multiple choice question with two correct answers
(3) A matching question/ordering question
(4) A question with four graphic answer choices
(5) A question and a graphic with four letters marked

LISTENING

chapter 6 Casual Conversations and Question Types

Casual Conversations are, in form, basically the same as the short dialogues of Part A. The biggest difference is that Casual Conversations are longer. Where Short Dialogues were 2-4 lines long, Part B Casual Conversations are over 7 lines long – sometimes brief, but other times lasting for up to a couple of minutes. After hearing the conversation, you will hear 2-3 questions about the listening passage. Usually, you will hear one Context question, one Detail question, and one Future Action question.

The distinctive part of Casual Conversations is their straightforwardness. Unlike Part A questions, Casual Conversations do not use a lot of tricks and diverters. Unlike the other Part B questions, Casual Conversations do not use graphics or other elaborate questioning devices. Casual Conversations are mostly longer comprehension exercises.

Question Types for Casual Conversations

1. Context/Comprehension

Most Casual Conversations begin with at least one question about the general context of the dialogue – that is, the **reason** the speakers are talking. These questions might be about one of the speakers, a problem, or a special event:

What is the man/woman's problem?
What are the speakers mainly discussing?
Why is the man talking to the woman?
Why is the man/woman excited?
What is true about ___?

Practice 6.1
From the following dialogues, then write the main reason for the speaker's conversation.

i. Man: Sarah, are you all right?
    Woman: No, I'm having a hard time in my biology class.
    Man: Why's that? Is the class too difficult?
    Woman: Oh, I understand the concepts okay. But I'm having the worst time getting the labs to work.
    Question: What is the woman's problem?
    Context: _____

ii. Woman: Hi there. I got a message that you needed to see me.
    Man: Yes, Jane, thanks for coming. I've been looking at your transcript. Do you realize that you won't be able to graduate next spring?
    Woman: Really? Why's that?
    Man: You haven't fulfilled your society requirement. As you know, the university required every student to take at least 2 classes in three different categories – society, science, and the humanities. You've only taken one society course so far.
    Question: Why is the man talking to the woman?
    Context: _____

iii. Man: Did you hear that Jon made the state championships in gymnastics?

Woman: Wow, that's great news. I know he's been working really hard all year.

Man: That's for sure. He practices for hours every day. I don't know how he manages to get all his homework done.

Woman: Well, it's great that all his hard work is paying off.

Question: What is true about Jon?

Context: _____

TOEFL Exercise 6.1

 Listen to excerpts from the following Casual Conversations and answer the Context question.

Ex. 1

Why is the man meeting with the professor?

(A) To become an environmental engineering major

(B) To discuss what he missed in class last week

(C) To talk about taking a class of hers

(D) To find out how he can drop a class

Ex. 2

What can be inferred about the woman?

(A) She is talking to her undergraduate advisor.

(B) She is in a job interview.

(C) She is getting advice from a friend.

(D) She lives in Paris.

Ex. 3

What is the woman's problem?

(A) The library does not have a book she needs.

(B) She lost a library book.

(C) She does not know where Germany is.

(D) The library will not let her sign out a book.

Ex 4

Why is the woman happy?

(A) She saved a lot of money for the computer.

(B) She discovered the student union building.

(C) Her paper pleased her professor.

(D) She found her missing computer.

Ex. 5

What is the man's problem?

(A) He does not like any of his subjects.

(B) He cannot decide on a major.

(C) He does not like his major.

(D) He cannot qualify for any major.

Ex. 6

What is the woman's news?

(A) There was a fire in the chemistry building.
(B) She joined the fire department.
(C) She accidentally started a fire last night.
(D) She learned about fire in chemistry class.

Ex. 7

Why is the man excited?

(A) He is going to be a famous author.
(B) He is going to teach a class next semester.
(C) He is going to study literature.
(D) He will take a class by a famous writer.

Ex. 8

What happened to the woman?

(A) She feels moody.
(B) She is transferring to another university.
(C) She won a scholarship.
(D) She found out about a foreign study program she likes.

2. Detail/Fact

This kind of question is narrower in scope than the context question. It asks about specifics of the speakers' conversation. That might include some sort of number, such as a price or a temperature, a day, or a time. It might also ask about specifics regarding a previous Context question. Some examples of Detail questions are:

What did the man/woman say about ___?
How many ___?
Why does the woman ___?
How do the speakers describe ___?

Practice 6.2
From the following casual conversations, then list three specific details each.

i. Man: Have you seen Dave recently?
    Woman: Yeah, I just bumped into him at the library.
    Man: What's he doing there? He was supposed to meet me here in the student
              union at 3 o'clock. I've been waiting half an hour for him.
    Woman: Actually, he said he was mad at you because you didn't show up for your
              appointment. But he said you were supposed to meet at 2.
    Details: _____
              _____
              _____

ii. Woman: So I'm really interested in taking the literature honors program.

     Man: Well, it is a very difficult program. You need to take at least one upper-level course in literature, poetry, and theater and get A's just to qualify.

     Woman: I know that, and I've done it. Is there anything else I need to do?

     Man: You'll need a recommendation from a professor and a statement of purpose, about what you want to study for your honors thesis.

     Details: _____

                   _____

                   _____

iii. Man: Did you get the homework in Dr. Franklin's class?

     Woman: Sure. He told us to read chapter 4 for next class. And he wants us to hand in the 10 homework questions on page 50. Why, weren't you in class today?

     Man: No, I had an appointment with my Economics professor then.

     Woman: Oh, because the professor also announced that Wednesday's class was going to be cancelled, so you don't need to come then.

     Details: _____

                   _____

                   _____

TOEFL Exercise 6.2

Ex. 1

Why did the woman order the books on the Internet?

(A) There are no local bookstores.
(B) It is more convenient.
(C) The bookstore has a poor selection.
(D) She had a gift certificate.

Ex. 2

When does the woman NOT say her club goes biking?

(A) Sundays
(B) Weekday mornings
(C) Saturdays
(D) Weekday evenings

Ex. 3

How many compact discs does the woman have in her collection?

(A) 100
(B) Between 500 and 600
(C) Over 700
(D) 5600

LISTENING

Ex. 4

1. When will the woman come to the concert?

   (A) 8:00
   (B) 8:30
   (C) 9:00
   (D) 10:00

2. What kind of music does the man's band play?

   (A) Blues
   (B) Country
   (C) Rock
   (D) Punk

Ex. 5

What kind of roommate does the woman want?

(A) Someone who is neat and quiet
(B) Someone who is fun and likes to have a party
(C) Someone who is an early-riser and likes to have fun
(D) Someone who is fun and tidy

Ex. 6

1. When does the concert start?

   (A) 7:00
   (B) 7:20
   (C) 7:30
   (D) 8:00

2. Why is the man going to be late?

   (A) He has to meet his professor.
   (B) He has to meet with a project partner.
   (C) He has to call an old friend.
   (D) He has to have dinner.

Ex. 7

1. Why can the man not use his computer?

   (A) It was stolen.
   (B) It broke recently.
   (C) He did not keep any address files on it.
   (D) He prefers to use a book to keep information.

2. Where is the man's address book probably?

   (A) At the student center
   (B) In the library
   (C) At his friend Jack's place
   (D) At his house, on a counter

3. Future Action

There is often a question about how the speakers will solve a problem, react to a situation, or do next. These questions can be about intentions, advice, or plans. Some possible questions are:

What does the advisor suggest the student do?
What does the man offer to do for the woman?
What will the man probably do next?
What will the speakers probably do this evening?
When will the woman probably be ___?
What will the woman do to avoid this problem in the future?

Practice 6.3

From the following dialogues, write the woman's most likely future action. More than one answer is possible.

i.	Man:	Where are you going?
	Woman:	I'm on my way to the biology department. I need to buy the textbook for my biology class.
	Man:	You know that the department doesn't sell textbooks any more, right?
	Woman:	Oh, that's right. Everything is at the student bookstore now.
	Future Action:	_____

ii.	Man:	Hi there. Can I help you out?
	Woman:	Yes, I need to sign this book out, but I forgot my library card in my apartment. Do I have time to run to the dorm and get it before the library closes?
	Man:	I'm sorry, but the library is closing in just a couple of minutes.
	Woman:	But I really need this book for an essay I'm writing that's due tomorrow!
	Man:	Well, the reading room is open all night long, and you actually can sign books out from there. I'll just put the book at the desk there for you.
	Future Action:	_____

iii.	Woman:	Professor Howley, I'm having problems with my chemistry lab.
	Man:	Well, I have an appointment right now with the department chair. Maybe you could come back during my office hours at 3 today and we could talk about it then.
	Woman:	But I have a class then. Could you stick around a little later?
	Man:	No, I need to get home a little early. But I'll be in my office all day tomorrow.
	Future Action:	_____

LISTENING

TOEFL Exercise 6.3

Ex. 1
What will Dennis most likely do?

(A) Get a letter from his doctor right away
(B) Go back to the hospital for a couple of days
(C) Get a note from his doctor in a week or two
(D) Give his professor a doctor's note with his paper

Ex. 2
What will the man probably do?

(A) Pay the woman for her help
(B) Take a computer course
(C) Buy the woman lunch
(D) Give the woman some cake

Ex. 3
What will the man do?

(A) Return tomorrow morning
(B) Keep waiting
(C) Come back later in the afternoon
(D) Write the professor an email

Ex. 4
What does the man want to do?

(A) Be a law professor
(B) Be a corporate lawyer
(C) Be a medical lawyer
(D) Be involved in politics

Ex.5
What will the man probably do next?

(A) Buy a laptop
(B) Get his computer fixed
(C) Look for a used computer
(D) Save money by not getting a computer

Ex. 6
What will the man most likely do next semester?

(A) Take the professor's Civil War course
(B) Take the professor's seminar
(C) Take the professor's survey class
(D) Not take a class with that professor

Ex. 7

What does the woman want to do in the future?

(A) Be an economist for the government
(B) Earn a lot of money
(C) Publish a paper
(D) Be a university professor

Ex. 8

What does the man suggest the woman do during the vacation?

(A) Live in the cafeteria
(B) Move to the King's Court Dormitory
(C) Stay in a hotel
(D) Go visit her family

Ex. 9

What will the woman most likely do next?

(A) Ask her professor for an extension
(B) Hand in her paper
(C) Become a computer science major
(D) Get her friend to help her

Mini-Test 3

Questions 1-6

1. What does the man mean?

   (A) His stomach is really upset.
   (B) He is very tired.
   (C) He has finished all his homework.
   (D) He has a bad headache.

LinguaForum

2. What is the woman implying?

   (A) The project has a bad problem.
   (B) She does not like her professor.
   (C) She thinks she can solve the problem herself.
   (D) The project is not due for a few more days.

LinguaForum

3. Who has the smallest apartment?

   (A) Anne
   (B) John
   (C) Tony
   (D) Dave

LinguaForum

4. What will the man probably do next?

   (A) Meet his friends for dinner
   (B) Go to the department office
   (C) Get a book from the library
   (D) Get a book from his friend

LinguaForum

5. What does the man suggest?

   (A) Complain to her neighbors directly
   (B) Tell the housing office about the problem
   (C) Try going to bed later
   (D) Play some loud music

LinguaForum

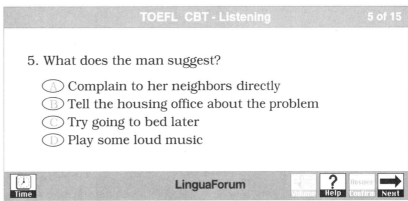

6. What does the woman mean?

   (A) She does not like the job.
   (B) She wants to change jobs.
   (C) She thinks he should work hard.
   (D) She agrees with the man.

LinguaForum

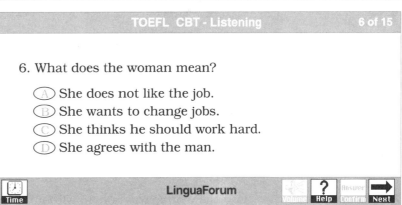

LISTENING

Questions 7-10

English Literature

Sinclair Lewis' Books:
- *Hike and the Aeroplane*
- *Main Street*
- *Arrowsmith*
- *Elmer Gantry*

7. What is the speaker's main opinion of Sinclair Lewis?

    Ⓐ He was the first American novelist of the 20th century.
    Ⓑ His writing was rough, without insight.
    Ⓒ His writing best illustrates life in America.
    Ⓓ He was the son of a doctor.

Time   **LinguaForum**   **Volume** **?Help** **Answer Confirm** **Next**

8. The lecturer described Lewis's life. Summarize by putting the following events into the correct chronological order.

    Click on a sentence. Then click on the space where it belongs. Use each sentence only once.

    He acted and wrote for the theater.
    He won a Pulitzer Prize.
    He worked for newspapers.
    He won a Nobel Prize for literature.

1. [＿＿＿＿＿]   3. [＿＿＿＿＿]

2. [＿＿＿＿＿]   4. [＿＿＿＿＿]

Time   **LinguaForum**   **Volume** **?Help** **Answer Confirm** **Next**

9. The speaker mentioned many of Sinclair Lewis's books. Match the book with what the book was about.

Click on a book title. Then click on the space where it belongs. Use each title only once.

Hike and the Aeroplane
Elmer Gantry
Arrowsmith

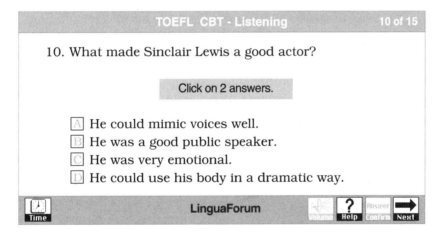

A satire on a Midwestern minister	The story of a young doctor	His first novel

10. What made Sinclair Lewis a good actor?

Click on 2 answers.

A He could mimic voices well.
B He was a good public speaker.
C He was very emotional.
D He could use his body in a dramatic way.

LISTENING

Questions 11-13

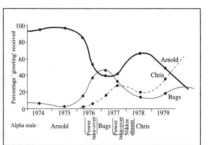

11. What is the main topic of this discussion?

    Ⓐ The story of three chimpanzees
    Ⓑ How Chris became alpha male
    Ⓒ Chimpanzee politics
    Ⓓ Balance in the animal world

Time   **LinguaForum**   Volume   Help **?**   Answer Confirm   **Next** ➡

12. The professor discussed a struggle for leadership in the chimpanzee tribe. Summarize that struggle by placing the following events into chronological order.

> Click on a sentence. Then click on the space where it belongs. Use each sentence only once.

Chris got a majority of greetings.
Bugs became alpha male.
Chris became alpha male.
Arnold received almost all greetings.

1. [＿＿＿＿＿＿＿]   3. [＿＿＿＿＿＿＿]

2. [＿＿＿＿＿＿＿]   4. [＿＿＿＿＿＿＿]

Time   **LinguaForum**   Volume   Help **?**   Answer Confirm   **Next** ➡

13. What does the professor say about chimpanzee politics?

Click on 2 answers.

A It gives their lives a logical coherence.
B It is not good for the chimpanzees.
C It enforces the hierarchy.
D It allows weaker members to participate.

LinguaForum

Volume Help Confirm Next

Questions 14-15

14. What is the man's problem?

(A) He has writer's block.
(B) He cannot go to his writing class tomorrow.
(C) He is not very creative.
(D) He needs to revise his story.

LinguaForum

Volume Help Confirm Next

15. What does the woman think is wrong with the man's story?

(A) The characters are not convincing.
(B) The plot is not interesting.
(C) The pace of the story is not smooth.
(D) There are not enough descriptions.

LinguaForum

Volume Help Confirm Next

LISTENING

Chapter 7 Academic Discussions/Lectures and Question Types

The structure of this portion of the Listening Section is a little different than the other parts. For instance, even the graphics in the academic discussions and lectures are important. The following are the elements of the CBT TOEFL academic discussions and lectures:

● Narrator Introduction

The talk begins with one or two sentences that inform the test-taker of what class the following segment will be in. This is where you find out if you will be hearing a lecture or a discussion. It may also tell you what topic the professor is talking about. For lectures, pay particular attention to the portion of the lecture that is being discussed – usually the talk is a "mini-lecture," but sometimes you might hear the beginning or end of a longer lecture.

Examples
Listen to a talk by an economics professor discussing supply and demand.
Listen to the end of a lecture given by a professor of geology.
Listen to part of a lecture in an art history class.

● Subject Chalkboard

As the narrator reveals what subject will be discussed, the subject will also appear on the screen as if it was written on a chalkboard. Throughout the lecture, this chalkboard will be used to highlight important terms and concepts that are discussed. Pay careful attention to them, as they usually reinforce information that will be included in the questions that follow.

● Picture of the Classroom

The talk begins with a picture of the general setting in order to help you get oriented. If it is a lecture, you will have a picture of a professor lecturing. If it is an academic discussion, you will get a picture of a small classroom with the professor surrounded by students.

● Graphics and Visual Aids

Lectures and discussions usually have some sort of visual aspect to them. In addition to the chalkboard, there can also be diagrams, photos, maps, and charts. These can be very useful because it is easier to remember something you hear when you have visual reinforcement, and it is likely one or more of the questions will be based on some of the graphics or visual aids.

● Subject Categories

Lecture and discussion subjects can be classified into three general categories: Physical and Life Science, Arts and Humanities, and Social Science. The difficulty level is similar to what a student encounters in the introductory courses of the first year of college. The lectures are a little more abstract and difficult than at the high school level, and require the student to do some processing of information, instead of merely rote memorization. Topics found in more advanced university courses, however, are not included in the CBT TOEFL.

Remember, this is a LISTENING test, not a test of general knowledge, and the questions are generally written in such a way as to minimize the effects of knowing the subjects well or poorly. However, if you are able to use your knowledge to help you out, do so. For example, if a question asks you what city is the capital of California, and the choices are Los Angeles, San Francisco, Sacramento, and San Diego, you can use your knowledge of geography to choose "Sacramento."

A. Physical and Life Science

These kinds of questions are now the most common type on the CBT TOEFL. Possible subjects include physics, biology, astronomy, psychology, and chemistry. The science is fairly elementary, and you should not find it difficult to understand on a technical level.

There is a fair amount of APPLIED science, too. So a lecturer is likely to talk about how a science can be used in real life to have practical effects.

B. Arts and Humanities

This is the second-most common subject type in the CBT TOEFL and includes subjects such as history, literature, music, and fine arts. Any lectures relating to the arts and humanities will exclusively be related to North America – usually the United States, but sometimes Canada or Central America. However, even if an art, music, literary, or dance style did not originate in North America, if it is prevalent in the United States, then it might be included in the CBT TOEFL. Similarly, if an artist, musician, writer, or dancer was born in North America, but spent a great portion of his or her life outside North America, he or she can also be included as a subject.

In addition, topics in the Arts and Humanities lectures and discussions tend not to be very contemporary. Topics like heavy metal music or hip-hop are highly unlikely compared to jazz or 19th century music; cutting edge artists are less likely than Impressionists or other established figures.

Lectures about U.S. history tend to focus on the time between the Revolutionary War and the Civil War, with the occasional topic from the colonial period, too. However, recent TOEFL tests have included topics as recent as President Franklin D. Roosevelt's New Deal of the 1930s.

C. Social Sciences

This is the least frequent type of lecture in the CBT TOEFL. The Social Science lecture type deals with how people function and interact, and includes subjects such as anthropology, geography, political science, urban studies and sociology. Of the different aspects of Social Science, Native American Indians and American geography are the two most common topics.

Take *Care*

One of the most difficult parts of this section is simply remembering all the information, especially with the longer dialogues. You are NOT allowed to take notes, making this all the harder. And unrealistic – can you imagine not being allowed to take notes in a university class? Of course not.

Question Types for Academic Discussions / Lectures

1. Main Topic

The first question is nearly always a general question about the topic of the listening segment. This requires a broad understanding of the whole segment. The most important part here is to choose an answer that is not too general or too specific.

Usually, it should be clear early in the lecture or discussion what the topic is. These academic listening passages are too short to change topics in the middle.

There are several ways a question can be asked, including:

1) Main topic

This kind of question requires the listener to determine what is the major subject discussed during the lecture.

2) Main idea

This question requires the listener to determine an opinion or theory about the listening passage. It is not enough to identify the topic; the listener must also understand what the speaker was saying about the topic.

3) Attitude

This is more abstract than a Main Idea question. The listener must identify the speaker's feeling towards a subject – positive, negative, content, anxious, etc.

4) Title

This is a slightly different way of asking the same question as the Main Idea, only the idea will be phrased like the title of a chapter of a book.

For example, a Main Topic of a lecture might be "Newspapers in the American Revolution." A Main Idea could be "Newspapers were necessary in developing the idea of American independence." The attitude of the professor towards newspapers could be "positive." And a possible title might be "How Newspapers Created the Idea of America."

These questions can be asked in several different ways:

What is the main subject of the lecture?
What is the talk mainly about?
What is the main idea of this discussion?
What is the speaker's attitude towards ___?

*Take*Care

Sometimes at the beginning, there might be one or two lines of MISINFORMATION – comments about a previous lecture, a different opinion, or other digressions. As usual, do not simply choose an answer based on a couple of words or phrases you remember. Look for paraphrases (not word-for-word repetition) and think about the context of what you just heard. Make sure your answer choice reflects the OVERALL listening passage.

Practice 7.1
From the following passages, write the main subject and the main idea in your own words.

i. Corn is the king of American crops. Farmers use more land for it than they do for any other crop. It provides more food for animals and people than any other crop.
Corn is a member of the grass family. It has a fibrous, woody stalk that can grow up to 20 feet high. At the top is a tassel that produces the male flowers of the plant. Farther down the stalk grow spikes that later grow into ears of corn. Each one grows out from beneath the base of a leaf, and at first it is completely wrapped in leaves. The spikes grow silky filaments, which are the female flowers.

Main subject: _____

Main idea: _____

ii. Woman: Professor Logan, why do some animals hibernate?
    Professor: Good question, Lisa. It is important to remember how all of nature is about the difficult fight for resources. When the climate becomes too cold, it is hard for many animals to find enough resources to survive. Some animals, like birds, will fly south to warmer places until better weather returns. And some animals remain active and try to eke out an existence in the cold. But many animals hide in sheltered places and hibernate.
    Man: How does hibernation differ from sleep?
    Professor: Oh, they are very different. Sleeping mammals may relax, but their way of living does not change. Hibernators, though, almost stop living. Their heart rates and breathing slow down to almost nothing. And their body temperature drops dramatically, too. But they do not freeze. If an animal's temperature drops too much and it risks freezing, it can partially awaken and move about enough to raise its temperature before going back into hibernation.
    Woman: So what kinds of animals hibernate?
    Professor: Actually, many different kinds do.

Main subject: _____

Main idea: _____

TOEFL Exercise 7.1

 Listen to the following excerpts from academic discussions and lectures, then answer the main topic / idea questions

Ex. 1
What is the main topic of this discussion?

(A) Different kinds of essays
(B) The parts of an essay
(C) How to write well
(D) Why essays are important

Ex. 2
What is the main topic of this lecture?

(A) The evolution of the horse
(B) The reasons why the horse's evolution is well documented
(C) How horses lived in the age of dinosaurs
(D) The horse's role in human history

Ex. 3
What is the main subject of this discussion?

(A) Versatile materials
(B) The nature of plastic and chalk
(C) The characteristics of cork
(D) Oak trees around the Mediterranean

Ex. 4
What is the main idea of this lecture?

(A) Transcendentalism was the most important philosophical movement of the 19th century.
(B) Transcendentalism was popular mostly in New England.
(C) Transcendentalism was a large, organized social movement.
(D) Transcendentalism played an important part in defining the American character.

Ex. 5
What is the main idea of this discussion?

(A) Cloning is too dangerous to be attempted.
(B) Cloning has some useful applications.
(C) Dinosaurs cannot be cloned.
(D) Cloning should only be used to recreate extinct animals.

Ex. 6
What is the speaker's opinion of the Mexican War?

(A) Mexico caused the war that led to the loss of Texas.
(B) The war was fought to free oppressed Americans in Texas.
(C) The war was fought so the United States could take some valuable land from Mexico.
(D) Mexico should have won the war with the United States.

Ex. 7
What is the main idea of this discussion?

(A) Niagara Falls was formed a long time ago.
(B) "Waterfalls" is an Iroquois word meaning "thunder of water."
(C) Niagara Falls is impressive because of its great height.
(D) Niagara Falls is important because of its volume of water.

Ex. 8

What is the main idea of this lecture?

(A) Cities grow quickly in America.
(B) The European and American countrysides are very different.
(C) The settling of America was disordered and chaotic.
(D) American cities developed slowly, in harmony with the landscape.

Ex. 9

What is the professor's attitude toward the Beat poets?

(A) They were rebellious and violent.
(B) They were influential and full of life.
(C) They were a minor movement.
(D) They were extremely popular.

2. Comprehension/Detail

This is the most straightforward type of question. A detail question simply asks you for numbers or facts that were given in the listening passage. A comprehension question is slightly more abstract, and asks you to understand a concept or idea mentioned in the listening passage.

Comprehension questions can ask the following:

> Why/When/Where/How did something happen?
> What happened?
> What is someone's problem ?
> How much/How many ___?

Practice 7.2

From the following listening passages, identify at least 3 specific details and write them below.

i. In the years leading up to the Civil War, America had changed greatly. It changed from primarily a rural, farming society to an industrialized one. Except briefly during the War of 1812, wholesale prices steadily declined in the first half of the 19th century, as increased efficiency and production kept prices down.

    The U.S. grew economically at an incredible pace in the 19th century, led mostly by the rise of industrialization in the North. In 1813, the sum of all manufacturing in the entire United States was less than $200 million annually. In 1859, though, it was nearly $2 billion. And of this amount, $1.3 billion was produced in the northeastern states alone. Less than 15% of manufactured goods came from the South.

    Detail: _____
    _____
    _____

ii. Man: Professor Williams, I need some help with our current unit on trees. For example, how big do trees get?

   Professor: There's a very wide range. Some species are only 10 or 12 feet, but the giant sequoia can reach over 350 feet. But the largest trees aren't necessarily the

	oldest – the bristlecone pine usually only grows to about 30 feet, but one specimen was found that was over 4500 years old.
Man:	That's impressive. How many different kinds of trees are there?
Professor:	We can classify plants into two general categories – angiosperms and gymnosperms. That's a fancy way of saying plants in which the seed is encased in a protective ovary and those with exposed seeds. Angiosperms are those trees that bear flowers, and they are the most common, with over 200,000 different species. Gymnosperms usually have cones instead of flowers, and are made up of conifers and ginkgoes. The gymnosperms are much older than angiosperms, and some gymnosperms, like the ginkgo, have been around for around 200 million years basically unchanged.

Detail: _____

_____

_____

TOEFL Exercise 7.2

 Listen to the following excerpts from academic discussions and lectures, then answer the comprehension questions.

Ex. 1

What does "Pennsylvania" mean?

(A) The nation of Penn
(B) Penn's religion
(C) The government of Penn
(D) Penn's woods

Ex. 2

Who does the speaker call the greatest science fiction author of the 19th century?

(A) Mary Shelley
(B) Jules Verne
(C) H.G. Wells
(D) Edgar Allan Poe

Ex. 3

Why does the speaker call corn a mysterious crop?

(A) It is a very new grain.
(B) Its wild ancestors are unknown.
(C) It only exists in North America.
(D) It has over 1000 different types.

Ex. 4

1. What animal, according to folklore, awakens from hibernating every February 2nd?

(A) Spider
(B) Bear
(C) Groundhog
(D) Squirrel

2. What is significant about the desert tortoise?

(A) Can hibernate in hot conditions
(B) Is the only animal to aestivate
(C) Can freeze solid in summertime
(D) Both aestivates and hibernates

Ex. 5

1. How does the speaker define "domestication"?

(A) Altering the genetic makeup of plants or animals for human benefit
(B) Raising plants and animals deliberately
(C) When organisms rely on humans for survival
(D) Farming and foraging

2. According to the speaker, why did domestication first occur?

(A) Because farming was easier than foraging
(B) Because it was more secure than foraging
(C) Because people learned that seeds become plants
(D) As a result of adapting to a changing climate

Ex. 6

Why do geologists not know what the world was like before Pangaea?

(A) There is no ocean crust older than Pangaea to examine.
(B) It was a long time ago.
(C) Pangaea was the first landmass on Earth.
(D) The colliding plates destroyed all the old evidence.

Ex. 7

What is a greenstick fracture?

(A) When an old person breaks a bone
(B) When a break is secured by a wooden splint
(C) When a bone splinters and bends instead of fully breaking
(D) When a bone is broken by a piece of wood

Ex. 8
What did Harlan Ellison prefer to call his stories?

(A) Sci-fi
(B) Magical realism
(C) Scientifiction
(D) New Wave

3. Inference

The idea of the Inference question is basically the same as in Part A; but in Part B, because the listening passages are so much longer, there is much more room for various pieces of information to be distributed which can then be added up to draw inferences.

Often the Part B inferences have to do with the basic contents of the passage – unspoken attitudes or conclusions. They are not "tricks" like those in Part A, but are much more logical and close to the original text.

Practice 7.3
Based on the following listening passages, draw inferences and write them below.

i. For much of American history, molasses was used instead of refined sugar. Until the 19th century, refined sugar was simply too expensive for most people. In fact, it was cheaper and more efficient to produce refined sugar in Europe, ship it across the ocean, and pay the high import taxes than to make it in America.

Inference about molasses: _____
Inference about sugar: _____

ii. The introduction of new, higher-resolution telescopes has revolutionized what we know about the universe. The Hubble telescope alone has been responsible for overturning many wrong theories, as well as confirming such eccentric ideas as anti-gravity and dark matter.

Inference about the Hubble: _____
Inference about anti-gravity: _____

iii. Man: I'm not sure I understand our psychology homework.
    Woman: You know it was due yesterday, don't you?
    Man: Yes, but I've been so busy working on my clinical psychology lab that I haven't had time for any of my other classes.

Inference about the man: _____
Inference about the clinical
psychology class: _____

TOEFL Exercise 7.3

 Listen to the following excerpts from academic discussions and lectures, then answer inference questions.

Ex. 1

What can be inferred from this talk?

(A) There is disagreement on the cause of the Great Depression.
(B) The Great Depression was not as serious as generally thought.
(C) The student is not good at economics.
(D) The professor does not understand the man's formulas.

Ex. 2

What can be inferred from the speaker's conclusion?

(A) People enjoy living in bigger cities.
(B) Halting city growth requires painful controls on land use.
(C) America will be less urban in the future.
(D) Megacities make America a rapidly changing nation.

Ex. 3

What can be inferred to be the major force behind the development of the primate ancestors?

(A) Brain development
(B) Geography
(C) Changes in food sources
(D) Climate change

Ex 4

What can be inferred about the skeleton?

(A) Small bones do not have any nutrient arteries.
(B) Bones are a form of soft tissue.
(C) Bones are living organs.
(D) All animals have bones.

Ex. 5

What subject is this class most likely?

(A) Economics
(B) History
(C) Biology
(D) Psychology

Ex. 6

What can be inferred from this lecture?

(A) Rubber was invented after 1850.
(B) Before the Civil War, the North and South were economically the same.
(C) Major northern cities had many publishers.
(D) The American South was more industrialized than the North before 1860.

Ex. 7

What can be inferred from this academic discussion?

(A) The American space program is the most successful in the world.
(B) Europeans have never put an astronaut into space.
(C) NASA launched the first astronaut into space.
(D) Rockets were invented in the Soviet Union.

4. Negatives

Sometimes the wrong answer is actually the right answer – that is, you will actually be asked for a wrong answer. Unfortunately, in negative questions, only one of the four answers is wrong, so these questions are just as difficult as regular questions.

The structure of the negative question is basically the same as the usual fact or comprehension question. However, instead of selecting the one true answer, you must find the one answer that is NOT true.

Typical negative questions include:

According to the talk, why did ___ NOT ___?
Which of the following is NOT true about ___?
All the following are similarities between ___ and ___ EXCEPT:
All the following are examples of ___ EXCEPT:

Practice 7.4
Based on the following passages, answer the negative questions.

i. The color spectrum is in fact a continuous shift of color, from one wavelength to the next. That we classify this spectrum into regions is arbitrary. Usually, the main colors we identify are what we call the Primary colors – red, yellow, and blue. By combining these colors in various ways, we produce the Secondary colors. For instance, red and blue combine to make purple.

Negative: What is NOT a primary color?
Answer: _____

ii. Most of the arts in American history have been highly derivative of those in Europe. Early American painting and classical music were both just attempts to imitate the popular arts of Europe. Even much of American folk music, up until the end of the 19th century, was mostly derived from Europe. In fact, with the exception of jazz music, America did not introduce many significant artistic innovations to the world before the middle of the 20th century. Even poetry and fiction mostly took their leads from the Old World.

Negative: What art form is NOT an imitation of the European arts?
Answer: _____

TOEFL Exercise 7.4

 Listen to the following excerpts from academic discussions and lectures, then answer negative questions.

Ex. 1
Which is NOT an example of an early mammal feature on some reptiles?

(A) Smaller number of bones
(B) Limbs more underneath the body
(C) Different kinds of teeth
(D) The presence of hair

Ex. 2
Which was NOT a power of the United States' original Congress?

(A) Raise taxes
(B) Postal service
(C) Indian affairs
(D) Foreign affairs

Ex. 3
1. Which is NOT a more plentiful element than uranium?

   (A) Zinc
   (B) Tin
   (C) Silver
   (D) Lead

2. Which is NOT a nation that is a major uranium producer?
   (A) South Africa
   (B) Austria
   (C) Canada
   (D) France

Ex. 4
What is NOT true about Hugo Gernsback?

(A) Wrote stories to disseminate scientific discoveries
(B) Invented the term "science fiction"
(C) Started the first science fiction magazine
(D) Invented the character "Tarzan"

Ex. 5
What is NOT a characteristic of the Virginia Creeper?

(A) It is a member of the grape family.
(B) It is found mostly in Virginia.
(C) It has small, hard-to-see flowers.
(D) It can climb up walls.

5. Multiple-Answer

This is the first example of the new type of questions now possible on the computer-based test. Sometimes you will be asked for the correct two answers, instead of just one. You will need to get both answers correct to receive credit – no points for half-answers.

Sometimes you will be given four entirely different answers. Other times, you might get two pairs of answers. For example:

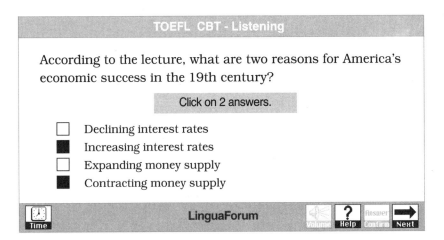

When you square on your second answer choice, the square will darken as in a normal TOEFL question. When you click on your fourth choice, the fourth square will also darken. Click on either square again to de-select it. TOEFL will always clearly tell you that you have a Multiple-Answer question, and will not let you advance to the next question without providing two answers.

Take Care

If you do not know the answer at all and have to guess, multiple answer questions actually have a LOWER chance of guessing correctly. Eliminating just one possible answer (or knowing one correct answer), however, greatly improves your odds.

Practice 7.5
Based on the following passages, answer the multiple-answer questions.

i. Many of the grains and vegetables that are a staple of our diets today came from the Native Americans. While many popular crops like rice and wheat have been internationally known for centuries, many others like corn and the tomato come to us from the highly advanced agriculture of the Native Americans, especially those of South America.

What are two crops introduced by the Native Americans?
Answer: _____
Answer: _____

ii. Man: Professor, could I talk to you about my paper? You gave me a bad grade, but I don't understand why.

Woman: Well, Sean, you did not follow the format I told you to.

Man: Format? I thought you didn't like my content.

Woman: No, the content was fine, but you did not footnote your sources properly, so it really wasn't a proper paper. And you did not double-space your paper, so it was hard for me to read and make comments.

Man: Oh, I see. Can I rewrite it and hand it in again?

Why did the man receive a poor grade on his paper?
Answer: _____
Answer: _____

iii. While jazz music had many antecedents in America, like ragtime, work songs, and spirituals, its popularity only took off after the piano was added in 1912, and larger horn sections were added in 1920. The essence of this new music was syncopation – an off-beat style of playing that is very different than classical music. Another core part of jazz is the importance of improvisation when playing.

What are the roots of jazz music?
Answer: _____
Answer: _____
Answer: _____

What additions made jazz music more popular?
Answer: _____
Answer: _____

What are the important musical aspects of jazz?
Answer: _____
Answer: _____

TOEFL Exercise 7.5

 Listen to the following excerpts from academic discussions and lectures, then answer multiple-answer questions.

Ex. 1

American History

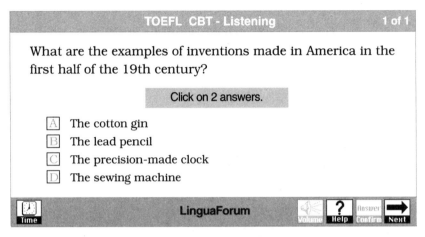

TOEFL CBT - Listening 1 of 1

What are the examples of inventions made in America in the first half of the 19th century?

Click on 2 answers.

- A   The cotton gin
- B   The lead pencil
- C   The precision-made clock
- D   The sewing machine

Time   LinguaForum   Volume Help Confirm Next

Ex. 2

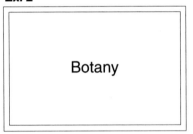

Botany

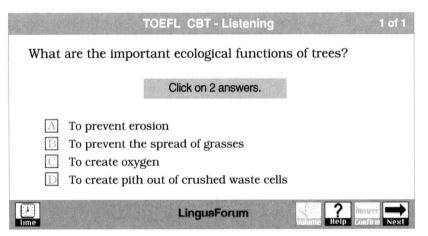

TOEFL CBT - Listening 1 of 1

What are the important ecological functions of trees?

Click on 2 answers.

- A   To prevent erosion
- B   To prevent the spread of grasses
- C   To create oxygen
- D   To create pith out of crushed waste cells

Time   LinguaForum   Volume Help Confirm Next

Ex. 3

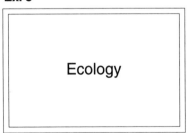

Ecology

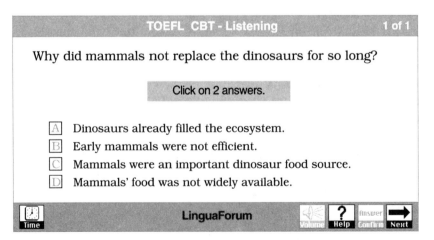

TOEFL CBT - Listening 1 of 1

Why did mammals not replace the dinosaurs for so long?

Click on 2 answers.

- A   Dinosaurs already filled the ecosystem.
- B   Early mammals were not efficient.
- C   Mammals were an important dinosaur food source.
- D   Mammals' food was not widely available.

Time   LinguaForum   Volume Help Confirm Next

Ex. 4

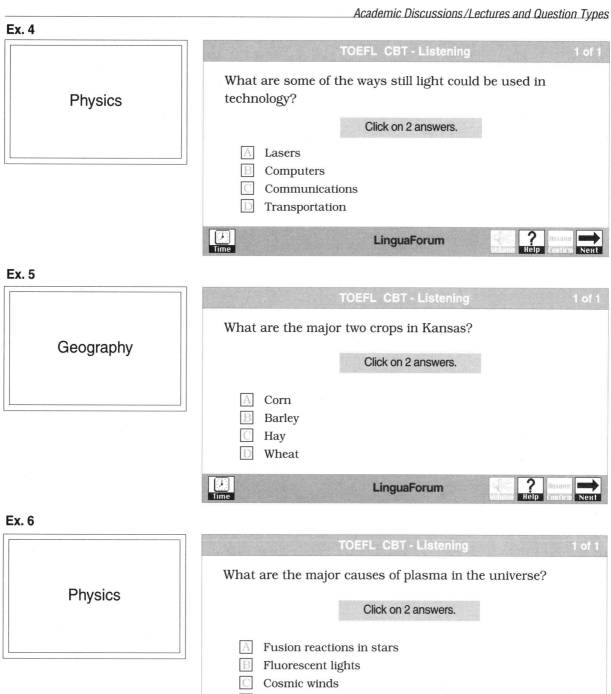

Physics

TOEFL CBT - Listening   1 of 1

What are some of the ways still light could be used in technology?

Click on 2 answers.

A Lasers
B Computers
C Communications
D Transportation

Time   LinguaForum   Volume Help Confirm Next

Ex. 5

Geography

TOEFL CBT - Listening   1 of 1

What are the major two crops in Kansas?

Click on 2 answers.

A Corn
B Barley
C Hay
D Wheat

Time   LinguaForum   Volume Help Confirm Next

Ex. 6

Physics

TOEFL CBT - Listening   1 of 1

What are the major causes of plasma in the universe?

Click on 2 answers.

A Fusion reactions in stars
B Fluorescent lights
C Cosmic winds
D Higher temperatures

Time   LinguaForum   Volume Help Confirm Next

Ex. 7

Engineering

What are two kinds of key locks?

Click on 2 answers.

A Combination locks
B Tumbler locks
C Warded locks
D Time locks

Time LinguaForum Volume Help Confirm Next

Ex. 8

Astronomy

What happened to NASA's Mars missions in 1999?

Click on 2 answers.

A Found evidence of water and life
B Collided with the Hubble telescope
C Burned up in the atmosphere
D Crashed onto the surface

Time LinguaForum Volume Help Confirm Next

Ex. 9

Biology

Which insects protect themselves by hiding?

Click on 2 answers.

A Moths
B Cockroaches
C Beetles
D Mosquitoes

Time LinguaForum Volume Help Confirm Next

Ex. 10

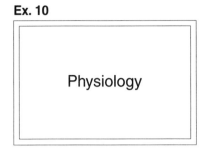

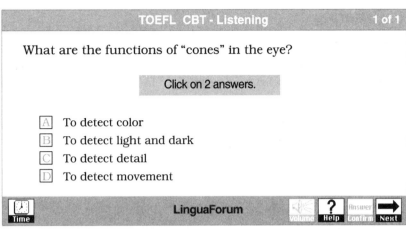

What are the functions of "cones" in the eye?

Click on 2 answers.

A To detect color
B To detect light and dark
C To detect detail
D To detect movement

LinguaForum

6. Ordering

In an Ordering question, you will be given 4-5 answers (words, phrases, or full sentences), and 4-5 empty boxes. Sometimes one of those answers will be filled in for you (usually the first or last option). You must rearrange the remaining four choices into the correct order.

There are many different kinds of orders you could be asked for. You might be asked to arrange the phrases chronologically, according to when each event happened. You might be asked to arrange them according to size, weight, or other physical characteristic. You might also be asked for a more abstract organizing scheme, like "complexity."

It helps if you can recognize a potential Ordering question while listening to the academic passage. Although not always, sometimes the speaker clearly describes an order. For example, when talking about the atmosphere, the speaker might say:

> There are four different layers in the atmosphere, going from the troposphere at the earth's surface, outwards to the stratosphere, the mesosphere, and at the edges of space, the thermosphere.
> Therefore the atmosphere could be ordered – troposphere, stratosphere, mesosphere, thermosphere – going from the earth's crust outwards.

Other times, however, the steps will not be so clearly outlined. The passage might be the history of a person or event, with different dates and stages scattered throughout the listening passage.

The first step you should take is to review the answer choices, looking for relationships you can recognize. Every sequence of events or characteristics you recognize greatly improves your chances of guessing the rest correctly.

Take Care

If you do not understand an Ordering question, it is very difficult to guess blindly. Ordering questions have three spaces to fill in, creating 1/6 odds of guessing correctly. If there are four spaces, however, that lowers the odds to 1/24 of guessing correctly.

Practice 7.6
Based on the following passages, answer the ordering questions.

i. The largest dinosaur ever to exist was the plant-eating *Brachiosaurus*. These huge dinosaurs could be over 40 feet high and nearly 100 feet long to the end of their tail. As big as the *Brachiosaurus* was, it had a brain only about the size of a large walnut. Not all plant-eaters were so big, though; the *Ankylosaurus* was only 10 to 15 feet long, but its armored shell protected it very well from predators. The largest meat-eater was the *Tyrannosaurus Rex*, or *T-Rex* as most people call it these days. The *T-Rex* had teeth that were over 6 inches long, and it stood almost 20 feet high. But the most fearsome dinosaur was not the *T-Rex*, but the *Velociraptor*. Velociraptors were only about 6 feet tall at the shoulders, but they could run very fast and could hunt in packs.

Rank the dinosaurs mentioned in this passage from largest to smallest.

_____
_____
_____
_____

ii. Man: Professor, is Bach considered a great composer because of how he
                revolutionized music?
    Woman: Not really. Bach was certainly an incredible composer, but it wasn't until
                Mozart came along that classical music started to get shaken up.
    Man: And Mozart created Romanticism?
    Woman: No, but he did introduce changes that started musicians in that direction.
                But Beethoven is generally considered to be the founder of Romanticism.
    Man: I see.
    Woman: Actually, John, you're getting a little ahead of yourself. We've just talking
                about Pergolesi and early Baroque music this month. We don't even get to
                Bach for another three weeks.

Place the composers mentioned into the correct chronological order.

_____
_____
_____
_____

iii. Our universe is overwhelmingly made of hydrogen. It may be the smallest of all the
     elements, but it is also the most common. All of the billions and trillions of stars are all
     giant nuclear reactors, running on hydrogen. As they burn, they turn much of the
     hydrogen into the slightly heavier helium. For billions of years, stars keep burning,
     continuing to turn hydrogen into helium. As a star gets older, it runs out of hydrogen to
     burn, and starts to burn the helium instead, once again changing those atoms into even
     heavier elements – from carbon to the much heavier iron atoms. Finally, once all the fuel
     is spent, the star becomes a dead star.

Place the elements mentioned in order by weight, from lightest to heaviest.

_____
_____
_____
_____

LISTENING

TOEFL Exercise 7.6

 Listen to the following excerpts from academic discussions and lectures, then answer ordering questions.

Ex. 1

American History

The speaker mentioned several events in the history of Los Angeles. Summarize by placing the following events into the correct chronological order.

Click on an expression. Then click on the space where it belongs. Use each expression only once.

Gained the nickname "Los Diablos"
Taken by the United States
Governed by Spain
Reached 50,000 in its population

1. [　　　　　　]   3. [　　　　　　]

2. [　　·　　　]   4. [　　　　　　]

Time   LinguaForum   Volume Help Confirm Next

Ex. 2

Paleontology

The professor described the evolution of the horse. Summarize by placing the following steps in the horse's evolution in the correct chronological order.

Click on an expression. Then click on the space where it belongs. Use each expression only once.

Developed modern teeth, becoming a grass eater
Reduced from 4 to 3 toes
Looked like a cross between a rabbit and a dog
Walked on a single hoofed toe

1. [　　　　　　]   3. [　　　　　　]

2. [　　　　　　]   4. [**Walked on a single hoofed toe**]

Time   LinguaForum   Volume Help Confirm Next

Ex. 3

Questions 1-3

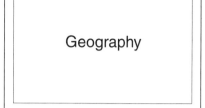

The professor mentioned the sizes of several states. Place the following states in order according to size, from smallest to largest.

Click on a state. Then click on the space where it belongs. Use each state only once.

Alaska
Hawaii
Rhode Island
Texas

1. _____   3. _____

2. _____   4. _____

Time   **LinguaForum**   Volume Help Confirm Next

LISTENING

The professor mentioned the population of several states. Place the following states in order according to population, from smallest to largest.

Click on a state. Then click on the space where it belongs. Use each state only once.

Rhode Island
Texas
Hawaii
Alaska

1. [   ]   3. [   ]

2. [   ]   4. [   ]

Time   LinguaForum   Volume Help Confirm Next

The professor mentioned the location of several states. Place the following states in order from north to south.

Click on a state. Then click on the space where it belongs. Use each state only once.

Alaska
Hawaii
Rhode Island
Texas

1. [   ]   3. [   ]

2. [   ]   4. [   ]

Time   LinguaForum   Volume Help Confirm Next

Ex. 4

Geology

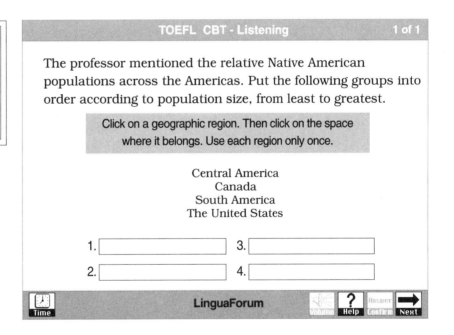

The speakers mentioned several dates in the history of Mount Vesuvius. Summarize by placing the following events into the correct chronological order.

Click on a sentence. Then click on the space where it belongs. Use each sentence only once.

An eruption buries Pompeii.
An eruption lowers the volcano several hundred feet.
An eruption raises the volcano 500 feet.
An eruption kills 18,000 people.

1. An eruption buries Pompeii.   3. [ ]
2. [ ]   4. [ ]

LinguaForum

Time   Volume   Help   Confirm   Next

LISTENING

Ex. 5

Anthropology

The professor mentioned the relative Native American populations across the Americas. Put the following groups into order according to population size, from least to greatest.

Click on a geographic region. Then click on the space where it belongs. Use each region only once.

Central America
Canada
South America
The United States

1. [ ]   3. [ ]
2. [ ]   4. [ ]

LinguaForum

Time   Volume   Help   Confirm   Next

Ex. 6

History

The speakers mentioned several events in the history of the Statue of Liberty. Summarize by placing the following events into the correct chronological order.

Click on a sentence. Then click on the space where it belongs. Use each sentence only once.

Bartholdi comes to New York to plan a memorial.
The Statue of Liberty becomes a national monument.
A memorial is proposed for the 100th anniversary of the Declaration of Independence.
The Statue of Liberty is dedicated.

1. [ ]   3. [ ]

2. [ ]   4. [ ]

Time   LinguaForum   Volume ? Help Answer Confirm Next

Ex. 7

Geography

The speaker mentioned the agricultural products of Kentucky. Summarize by placing the following crops in order, from most valuable to least.

Click on an item. Then click on the space where it belongs. Use each crop only once.

Corn
Tobacco
Wheat
Hay

1. [ ]   3. [ ]

2. [ ]   4. [ ]

Time   LinguaForum   Volume ? Help Answer Confirm Next

7. Matching

Matching questions present you with three pairs of words or sentences that must be connected. For example:

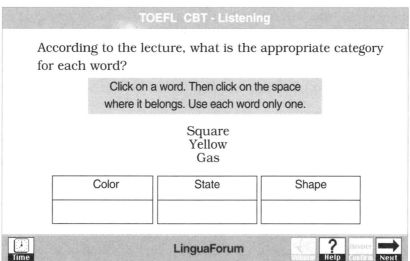

It is clear that *square, yellow,* and *gas* belong to *shape, color,* and *state* respectively. On the TOEFL, however, you will not be given three such obvious choices. Usually the three choices will be closely related. Possible matching categories include size, color, region, person or name, and purpose. You must match the correct pairs based on the information you hear or see in an academic dialogue or lecture.

If you can recognize one match, but not the other two, that greatly improves your odds of guessing correctly. You do, however, need to choose all three matches correctly to get points.

Sometimes, you might be given three choices to match to two options. You simply do not use one of the choices, and match the other two. This does not improve or hurt your odds of guessing correctly, so do not worry if you happen to get this variation.

Practice 7.7

i. Art was an integral part of the Native Americans' lives, woven into the very fabric of their culture. The Yakima Indians are famous for their tall totem poles – the trunks of massive trees, covered with faces and paint, signifying the history of each family in the tribe. The Pueblo in the American southwest used to paint massive murals on the large, exposed rocks in their desert home, even painting the faces of cliffs. The Inuit to the far north were constrained by the lack of resources of the frozen tundra; but they, too, had a rich artistic tradition, painting seal hides and sculpting animal bones. Every Native culture, no matter how different, expressed itself artistically somehow.

Beside each Native American group, write its preferred artistic medium:

Inuit: _____

Pueblo: _____

Yakima: _____

ii. The planets circling our sun vary greatly from one another in many ways. Some, like Jupiter, are gas giants – hundreds of times more massive than the Earth and much further from the sun. Venus is no giant, but it is covered with a dense, poisonous atmosphere of sulfur and other gases. Other planets, such as Mercury, have no atmosphere at all – they are simply barren round balls of rock and dust in space. Even today, with all our scientific knowledge, scientists cannot explain well the striking differences among the planets.

Beside each planet, list its characteristics.

Jupiter: _____

Venus: _____

Mercury: _____

iii. The different phases of sleep have significantly different characteristics. Phase A sleep is the shallow beginning of sleep. Brainwaves in this phase are calmer and more regular than when awake. By Phase D, the brain is deeply asleep. The brainwaves are slow and minimal. In REM sleep, however, the brain is full of activity, with brainwaves firing erratically and with much energy. This is the period in which most of our dreaming occurs.

Beside each sleep phase, write the characteristics of that phase:

Phase A: _____

Phase D: _____

REM Sleep: _____

TOEFL Exercise 7.7

Listen to the following excerpts from academic discussions and lectures, then answer matching questions.

Ex. 1

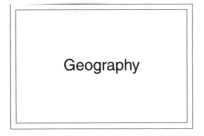

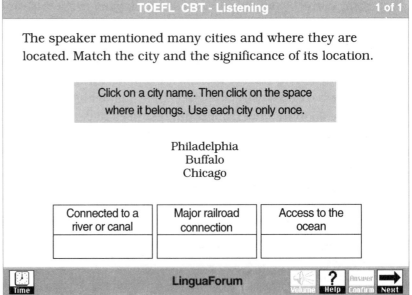

Ex. 2

Zoology

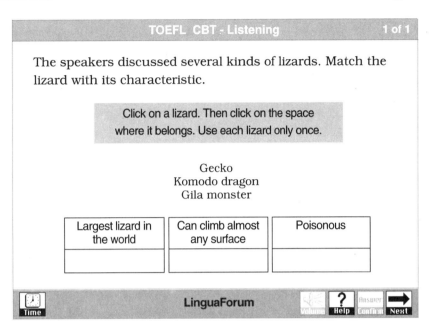

The speakers discussed several kinds of lizards. Match the lizard with its characteristic.

Click on a lizard. Then click on the space where it belongs. Use each lizard only once.

Gecko
Komodo dragon
Gila monster

Largest lizard in the world	Can climb almost any surface	Poisonous

LinguaForum

Ex. 3

U.S. Government

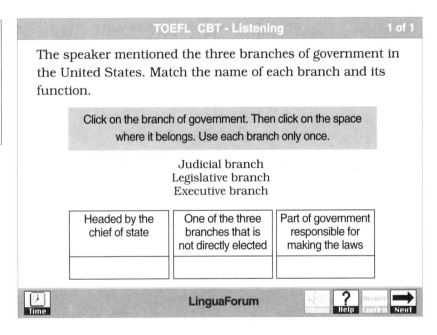

The speaker mentioned the three branches of government in the United States. Match the name of each branch and its function.

Click on the branch of government. Then click on the space where it belongs. Use each branch only once.

Judicial branch
Legislative branch
Executive branch

Headed by the chief of state	One of the three branches that is not directly elected	Part of government responsible for making the laws

LinguaForum

LISTENING

Ex. 4

American Literature

The speaker mentioned several important figures in the transcendentalist movement. Match the person's name to the significant achievement.

Click on a person's name. Then click on the space where it belongs. Use each person's name only once.

Margaret Fuller
Henry David Thoreau
Ralph Waldo Emerson

Founded the transcendentalist movement	Founded *The Dial*, the transcendentalist magazine	Wrote the important book *Walden*

LinguaForum

Time   Volume   Help   Confirm   Next

Ex. 5

American History

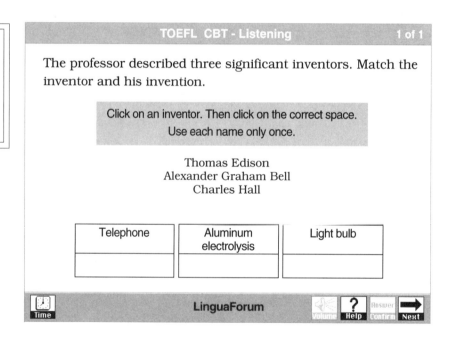

The professor described three significant inventors. Match the inventor and his invention.

Click on an inventor. Then click on the correct space. Use each name only once.

Thomas Edison
Alexander Graham Bell
Charles Hall

Telephone	Aluminum electrolysis	Light bulb

LinguaForum

Time   Volume   Help   Confirm   Next

Ex. 6

Geology

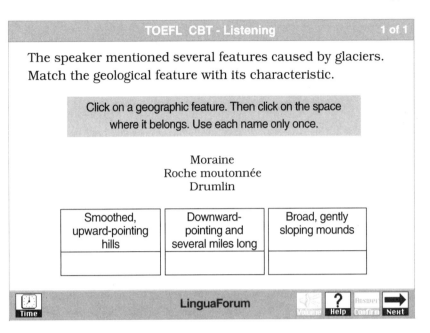

Ex. 7

Linguistics

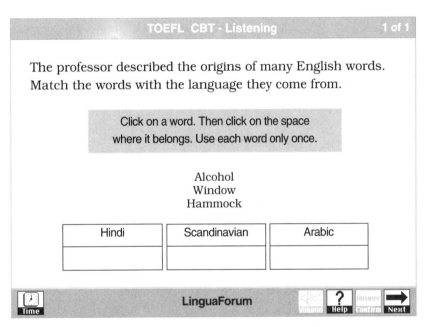

Ex. 8

Biology

The speaker mentioned several breeds of horses. Match the breed with its characteristic.

Click on a breed. Then click on the space where it belongs. Use each breed only once.

Clydesdale
Thoroughbred
Pony

The smallest type of horse	Good for hauling heavy loads	Descended from one of three Arabians

Time   **LinguaForum**   Volume   Help   Answer Confirm   Next

Ex. 9   **Questions 1-3**

American History

TOEFL CBT - Listening   1 of 3

The speakers mentioned several significant American monuments. Match the monument with what it symbolizes.

> Click on a monument. Then click on the space where it belongs. Use each monument only once.

Mount Rushmore
The Gateway Arch
The Statue of Liberty

Freedom	The greatest American presidents	The American West

Time   **LinguaForum**   Volume ? Help Answer Confirm → Next

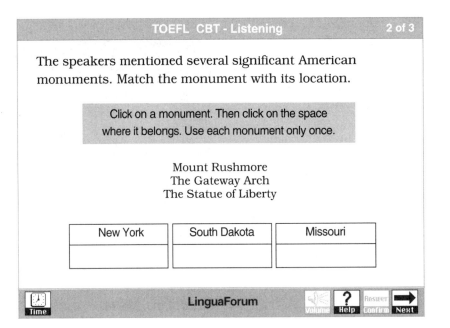

The speakers mentioned several significant American monuments. Match the monument with its location.

Click on a monument. Then click on the space where it belongs. Use each monument only once.

Mount Rushmore
The Gateway Arch
The Statue of Liberty

New York	South Dakota	Missouri

LinguaForum

Time · Volume · Help · Confirm · Next

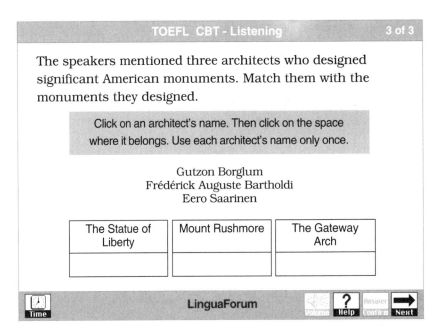

The speakers mentioned three architects who designed significant American monuments. Match them with the monuments they designed.

Click on an architect's name. Then click on the space where it belongs. Use each architect's name only once.

Gutzon Borglum
Frédérick Auguste Bartholdi
Eero Saarinen

The Statue of Liberty	Mount Rushmore	The Gateway Arch

LinguaForum

Time · Volume · Help · Confirm · Next

8. Graphics

The final type of new question that you might face on your test is the graphic question – a question which uses visual images.

TOEFL will not present you with a new graphic that you did not see during the lecture, so you do not need to worry about any surprises. But when you do see graphics during the lecture, that is a sign that you should pay extra attention to the information being presented at that time. Fortunately, it is easier to remember something with visual images to reinforce the audio, so in some ways, graphic questions can be easier than others.

1) One graphic with letters:
You must identify a particular part of a graphic.

Ex)
On this violin, there are four different strings – the E, A, D, and G strings (going from right to left). For a question, you could be given a picture of a violin and asked to identify the E-string.

2) Four graphics:
You must identify the correct picture or shape from four different choices.

Ex)
You could be given pictures of four different kinds of triangles (equilateral, isosceles, right-angled, and irregular) and be asked to identify which one is isosceles.

3) Graphic matching:
A combination of the usual graphic question and the matching question. For example, you are given three pictures and three labels that you must correctly match.

Ex)
You could be given three different pictures representing a person's brainwaves while sleeping. Then you could be asked to match each picture with the appropriate sleep phase.

TOEFL Exercise 7.8

Ex. 1

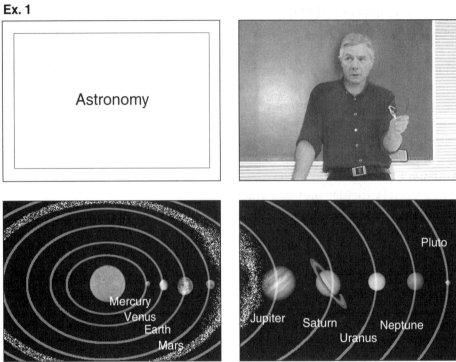

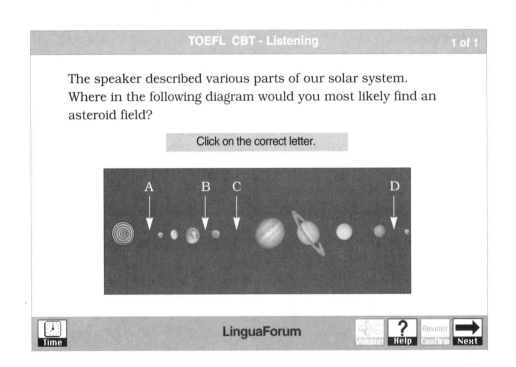

Ex. 2

Music

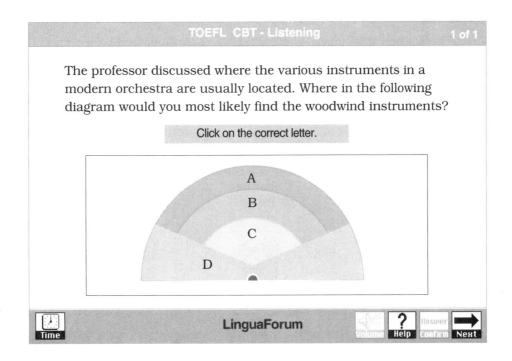

The professor discussed where the various instruments in a modern orchestra are usually located. Where in the following diagram would you most likely find the woodwind instruments?

Click on the correct letter.

Ex. 3

The speaker mentioned different facial expressions chimpanzees can have. Match the following expressions with the correct picture.

Click on an expression name. Then click on the space where it belongs. Use each expression only once.

Subservient face
Calling face
Display face

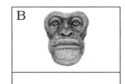

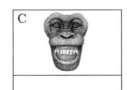

Ex. 4

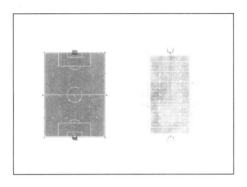

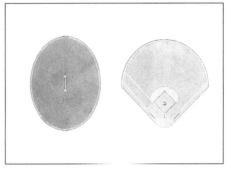

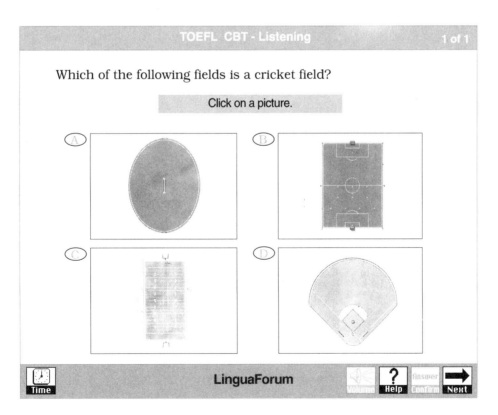

Ex. 5

Naval Architecture

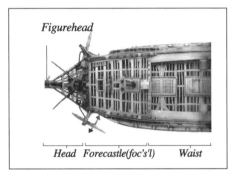

Figurehead

Head *Forecastle(foc's'l)* *Waist*

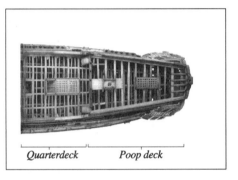

Quarterdeck *Poop deck*

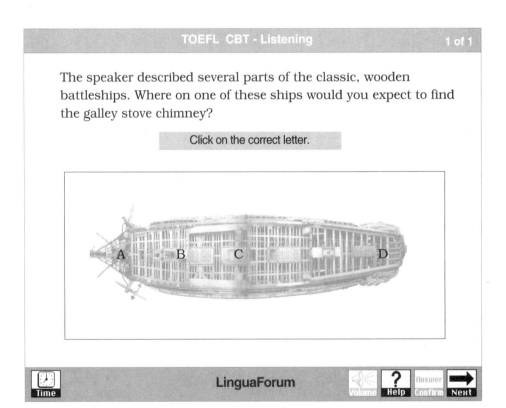

Ex. 6

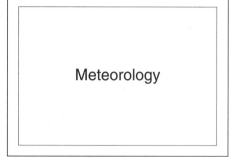

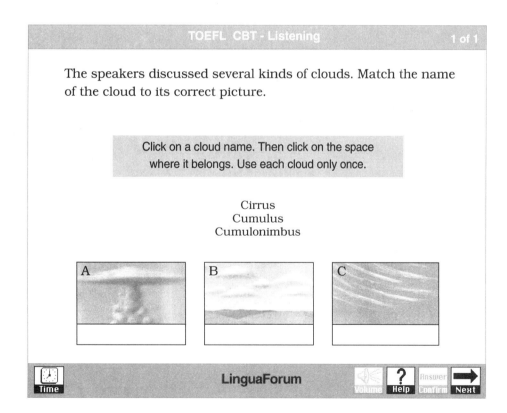

Ex. 7

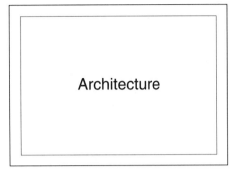

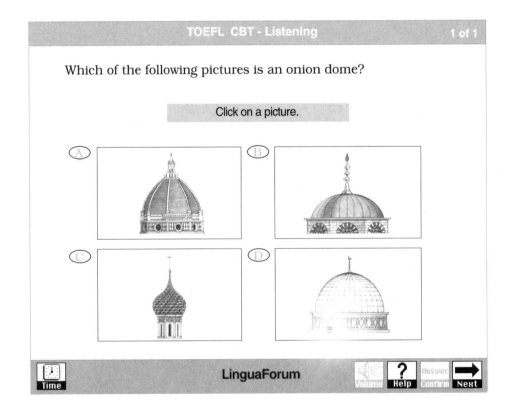

Ex. 8

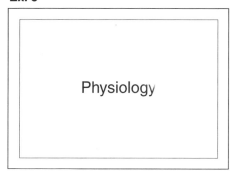

Physiology

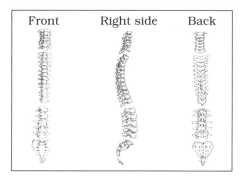

Front   Right side   Back

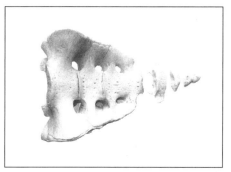

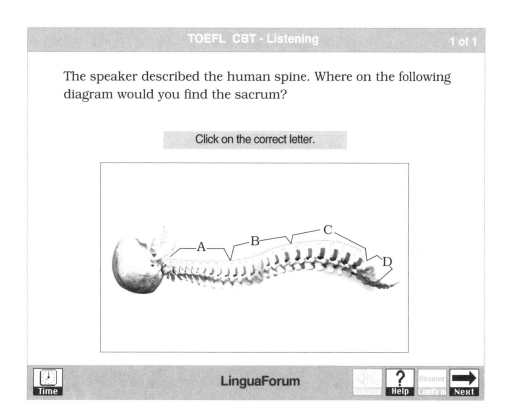

TOEFL CBT - Listening   1 of 1

The speaker described the human spine. Where on the following diagram would you find the sacrum?

Click on the correct letter.

Time   LinguaForum   Volume Help Confirm Next

Mini-Test 4

Questions 1-6

1. What does the woman mean?

  (A) She fell down.
  (B) She bought the paints at the sale.
  (C) She missed the sale.
  (D) She did not want to buy the paints there.

Time   LinguaForum   Volume Help Confirm Next

2. What is the man assuming about the woman?

  (A) She does not like to run.
  (B) She has not tried long-distance running before.
  (C) She does not look healthy.
  (D) She has never seriously exercised.

Time   LinguaForum   Volume Help Confirm Next

3. What can be inferred about the man?

  (A) He is a freshman.
  (B) He already has another major.
  (C) He is a junior.
  (D) He is not good at philosophy.

Time   LinguaForum   Volume Help Confirm Next

4. How many people came to their meeting last night?

  (A) 24
  (B) 25
  (C) 27
  (D) Over 27

Time   LinguaForum   Volume Help Confirm Next

5. Why does the man not like Dr. Fillmore?

    Ⓐ She gives too much homework.
    Ⓑ Her class is too easy.
    Ⓒ There were too many tests.
    Ⓓ He cannot understand her.

6. What is the man implying?

    Ⓐ He is going to go really late.
    Ⓑ He does not like jazz music.
    Ⓒ He cannot take her to the bar.
    Ⓓ He will not write the test tomorrow.

LISTENING

Questions 7-10

History of Science

Alchemist
↓
Paracelsus
↓
Sendivogius

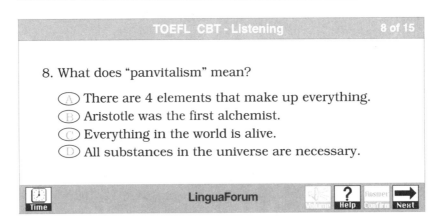

7. What is the main idea of this lecture?

    (A) Alchemy is a worthless superstition.
    (B) Alchemy was the original way people tried to understand the physical world.
    (C) Alchemy is a very old idea.
    (D) Ancient alchemy was just as useful as modern chemistry.

LinguaForum   Volume   Help   Answer Confirm   Next

Time

8. What does "panvitalism" mean?

    (A) There are 4 elements that make up everything.
    (B) Aristotle was the first alchemist.
    (C) Everything in the world is alive.
    (D) All substances in the universe are necessary.

LinguaForum   Volume   Help   Answer Confirm   Next

Time

9. Several alchemical ideas were mentioned. Match the idea and what it meant.

Click on an idea. Then click on the place where it belongs. Use each idea only once.

Elixir of Life
Philosopher's Stone
Alkahest

The substance that turns lesser minerals into gold	A universal solvent that could dissolve anything	A medicine that could heal all sickness

LinguaForum

10. The speaker mentioned how alchemy turned into modern chemistry. Summarize by placing the following events into the correct order.

Click on a sentence. Then click on the space where it belongs. Use each sentence only once.

Sendivogius realizes air is a chemical mixture.
Lavoisier discovers oxygen.
Isaac Newton conducts alchemy experiments.
Paracelsus overturns Aristotle's ideas.

1. _____   3. _____

2. _____   4. _____

LinguaForum

Questions 11-13

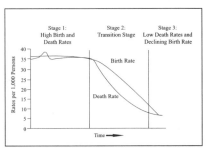

Sociology

Demographic Stage
- Initial Stage
- Transition Stage
- Mature Stage

11. What is the main topic of this lecture?

    Ⓐ European history
    Ⓑ The demographics of death
    Ⓒ The birth and date rates of modern society
    Ⓓ The demographic transition theory

LinguaForum

12. The speaker mentioned three different demographic stages. Match each phase with its characteristic.

Click on a stage. Then click on the space
where it belongs. Use each stage only once.

Mature Stage
High Potential Stage
Transition Stage

Birth rate at biological maximum	A decline in death rate	A decline in birth rate

LinguaForum

13. Why did death rates decline in Europe?

Click on 2 answers.

A Because of improved medical technology
B Because of improved sanitation
C Because of more and better food
D Because the demographic transition stage began

Time   LinguaForum   Volume Help Confirm Next

Questions 14-15

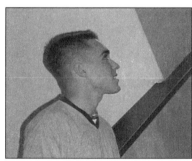

14. When is this conversation probably taking place?

A At the start of fall semester
B At the end of spring semester
C Around Thanksgiving
D During the winter break

Time   LinguaForum   Volume Help Confirm Next

15. Why did the man not go home?

A Because of his job
B Because he wanted to travel instead
C Because he had to work on his thesis
D Because he has no family

Time   LinguaForum   Volume Help Confirm Next

The following passages are a sampling of the various types of listening passages and questions from Part B of the Listening Section of the TOEFL test. One test is a 19-question version, and the other is a 33-question version.

Type A – 19 Questions for Part B

Questions 1-4

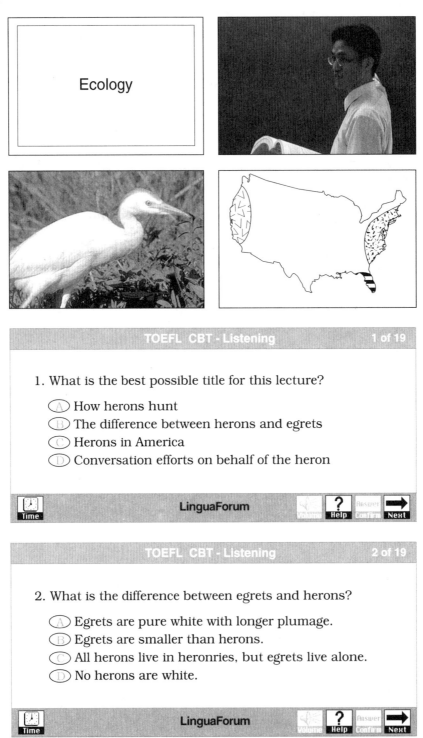

TOEFL CBT - Listening   1 of 19

1. What is the best possible title for this lecture?

   Ⓐ How herons hunt
   Ⓑ The difference between herons and egrets
   Ⓒ Herons in America
   Ⓓ Conversation efforts on behalf of the heron

LinguaForum

TOEFL CBT - Listening   2 of 19

2. What is the difference between egrets and herons?

   Ⓐ Egrets are pure white with longer plumage.
   Ⓑ Egrets are smaller than herons.
   Ⓒ All herons live in heronries, but egrets live alone.
   Ⓓ No herons are white.

LinguaForum

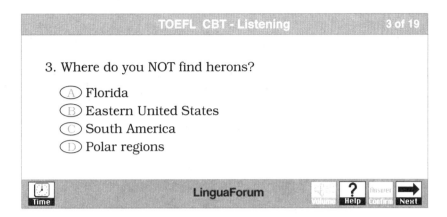

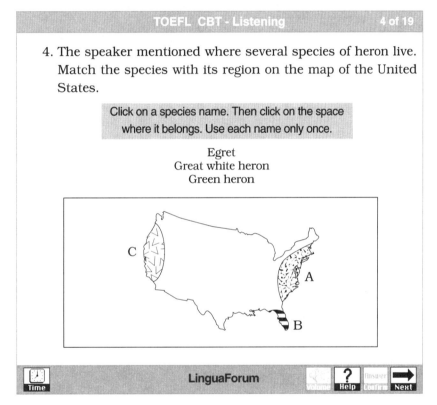

Questions 5-7

5. What is this discussion mainly about?

   (A) Hammerhead sharks
   (B) Different kinds of fishes
   (C) How tools got their names
   (D) Fishes named for human objects

Time   LinguaForum   Volume Help Confirm Next

6. The professor mentioned several types of fishes. Match the name with the kind of fish.

Click on a name. Then click on the space where it belongs. Use each name only one.

Swordfish
Hammerhead
Sawfish

Ray	Marlin	Shark

Time   LinguaForum   Volume Help Confirm Next

7. Why do researchers think hammerhead sharks have hammer-shaped heads?

Click on 2 answers.

A To use as a weapon
B To improve their eyesight
C To help steering
D To swim faster

LinguaForum

Questions 8-9

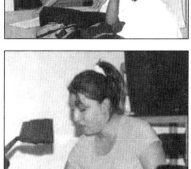

8. What can be inferred about the man?

A He is smarter than the woman.
B He is not a freshman.
C He is an English major.
D He is not interested in poetry reading any more.

LinguaForum

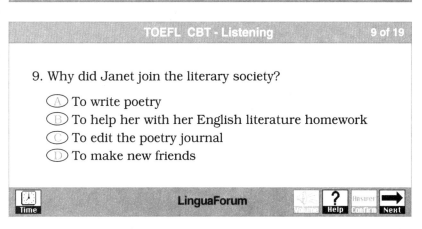

9. Why did Janet join the literary society?

A To write poetry
B To help her with her English literature homework
C To edit the poetry journal
D To make new friends

LinguaForum

LISTENING

Questions 10-13

10. What is the speaker's attitude towards the Studebakers?

    (A) They were very lucky.
    (B) They were the first vehicle makers in America.
    (C) They were relentless innovators.
    (D) Their success came from hard work.

11. Several events were mentioned in the history of the Studebaker Company. Summarize by placing the following events into the correct chronological order.

> Click on an event. Then click on the space where it belongs. Use each event only once.

Made self-propelled vehicles
Became the biggest horse-drawn vehicle maker in the world
Moved to Indiana
Received first government contract

1. [＿＿＿＿＿＿]   3. [＿＿＿＿＿＿]

2. [＿＿＿＿＿＿]   4. [＿＿＿＿＿＿]

12. Which did the speaker say was the most fortunate event in the history of Studebaker?

    (A) Receiving their first government contract
    (B) Moving to Indiana
    (C) Building gasoline cars
    (D) The rise of the railroads

LinguaForum

  Time   Volume Help Confirm Next

13. Why did Studebaker stop making wagons?

    (A) The success of their automobiles
    (B) The end of government contracts
    (C) The rise of the railroads
    (D) The decline of horses

LinguaForum

  Time   Volume Help Confirm Next

LISTENING

Questions 14-16

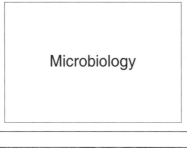

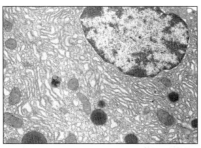

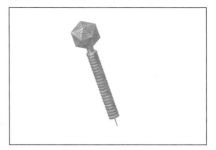

14. Why is the man talking to the woman?

    Ⓐ He is feeling sick with a virus.
    Ⓑ He did poorly on an exam.
    Ⓒ He needs help for an upcoming test.
    Ⓓ He needs to do an experiment about viruses.

Time   LinguaForum   Volume Help Confirm Next

15. What part of the virus contains the DNA?

Click on the correct part of the diagram.

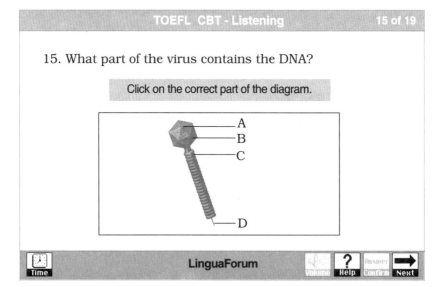

Time   LinguaForum   Volume Help Confirm Next

16. What is the purpose of the virus's protein shell?

Click on 2 answers.

- [A] Take over the infected cell
- [B] Allow the virus into the cell
- [C] Provide nutrients for the virus
- [D] Protect the virus's DNA

Time   **LinguaForum**   Volume Help Confirm Next

Questions 17-19

17. What is the woman's problem?

(A) She does not understand the lab.
(B) She is not ready for the chemistry quiz.
(C) She cannot get into Professor Atkins' course.
(D) She got wrong results on her experiment.

Time   **LinguaForum**   Volume Help Confirm Next

18. How close to the textbook does the professor say is acceptable?

(A) 0.4%
(B) 5%
(C) 10%
(D) 45%

Time   **LinguaForum**   Volume Help Confirm Next

19. What will the woman most likely do?

(A) Ask the professor for more time
(B) Hand in the experiment as it is
(C) Redo the experiment
(D) Lower her results 10%

Time   **LinguaForum**   Volume Help Confirm Next

LISTENING

Type B – 33 Questions for Part B

Questions 1-4

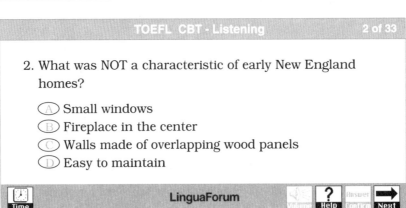

1. What is the main idea of this lecture?

   (A) American architecture is better than European.
   (B) New England is colder than Europe.
   (C) America's unique characteristics created its architecture.
   (D) American architecture is the same as other countries'.

LinguaForum   Time   Volume   Help   Confirm   Next

2. What was NOT a characteristic of early New England homes?

   (A) Small windows
   (B) Fireplace in the center
   (C) Walls made of overlapping wood panels
   (D) Easy to maintain

LinguaForum   Time   Volume   Help   Confirm   Next

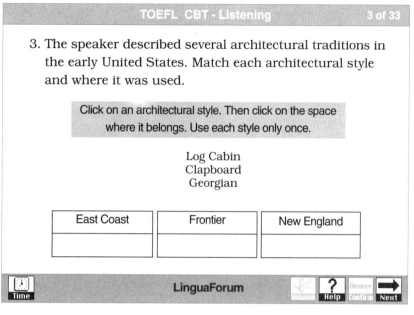

3. The speaker described several architectural traditions in the early United States. Match each architectural style and where it was used.

Click on an architectural style. Then click on the space where it belongs. Use each style only once.

Log Cabin
Clapboard
Georgian

East Coast	Frontier	New England

LinguaForum

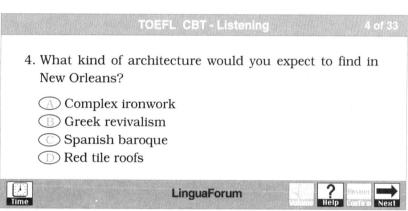

4. What kind of architecture would you expect to find in New Orleans?

(A) Complex ironwork
(B) Greek revivalism
(C) Spanish baroque
(D) Red tile roofs

LinguaForum

LISTENING

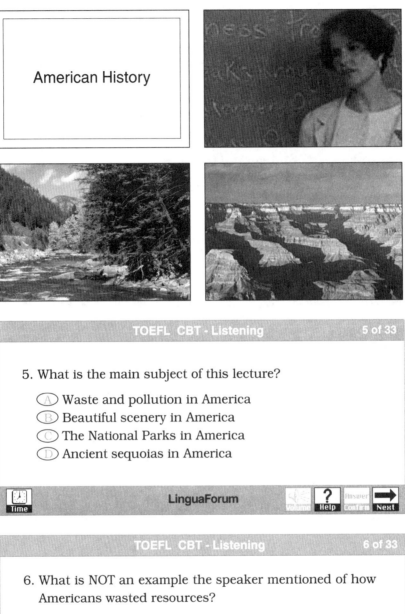

5. What is the main subject of this lecture?

    Ⓐ Waste and pollution in America
    Ⓑ Beautiful scenery in America
    Ⓒ The National Parks in America
    Ⓓ Ancient sequoias in America

LinguaForum

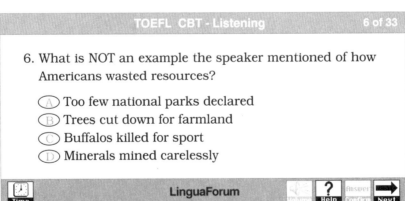

6. What is NOT an example the speaker mentioned of how Americans wasted resources?

    Ⓐ Too few national parks declared
    Ⓑ Trees cut down for farmland
    Ⓒ Buffalos killed for sport
    Ⓓ Minerals mined carelessly

LinguaForum

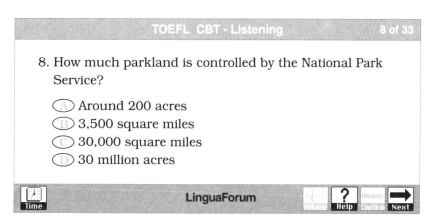

7. The speaker mentioned several national parks. Match each park with what makes it notable.

Click on a park name. Then click on the space where it belongs. Use each park name only once.

Yosemite
Grand Canyon
Yellowstone

Colorado River	First national park	Giant trees

LinguaForum

8. How much parkland is controlled by the National Park Service?

  (A) Around 200 acres
  (B) 3,500 square miles
  (C) 30,000 square miles
  (D) 30 million acres

LinguaForum

Questions 9-11

9. What is the man's problem?

Ⓐ His class is too advanced.
Ⓑ Dr. Dixon's class has too much work.
Ⓒ He never received a course syllabus.
Ⓓ He could not register for the class he wanted.

10. What can be inferred about the man?

Ⓐ He is a first year student.
Ⓑ He has taken other classes with Dr. Dixon before.
Ⓒ He is not interested in Dr. Dixon's class.
Ⓓ He is not a history major.

11. What will the man most likely do?

Ⓐ Keep taking the course
Ⓑ Petition the department to change courses
Ⓒ Stop his extracurricular activities
Ⓓ Drop the course

Questions 12-16

Biology

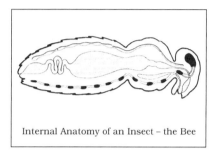

Internal Anatomy of an Insect – the Bee

12. What is the main subject of this discussion?

Ⓐ The life of insects
Ⓑ The characteristics of all insects
Ⓒ What the word "insect" means
Ⓓ The diversity of insects in the world

LinguaForum   Volume Help Confirm Next
Time

13. What is true of all insects?

Click on 2 answers.

☐ They have exoskeletons.
☐ They have sensory antennae.
☐ They have wings.
☐ They have stingers.

LinguaForum   Help Confirm Next
Time

14. What does the Latin word "insecta" mean?

    Ⓐ Six-footed
    Ⓑ Exoskeleton
    Ⓒ Chitin
    Ⓓ Segmented

LinguaForum

15. What part of an insect is the abdomen?

Click on the correct letter.

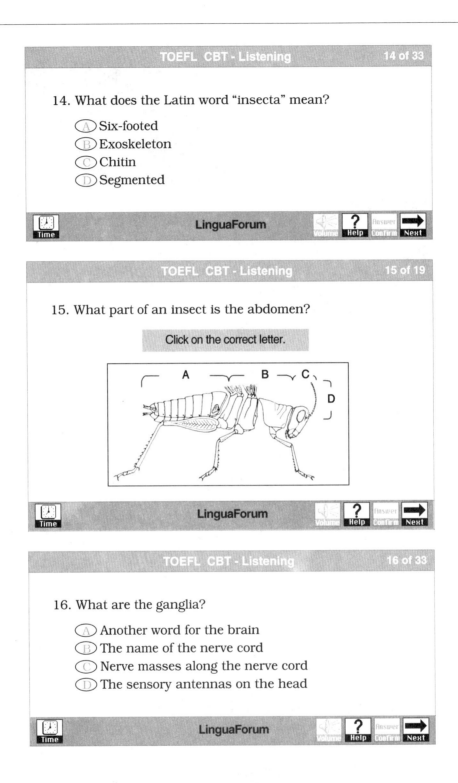

LinguaForum

16. What are the ganglia?

    Ⓐ Another word for the brain
    Ⓑ The name of the nerve cord
    Ⓒ Nerve masses along the nerve cord
    Ⓓ The sensory antennas on the head

LinguaForum

Questions 17-19

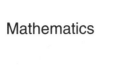 

17. What is the main subject of this lecture?

    (A) The first digital computers
    (B) How primitive peoples counted things
    (C) The history of calculating machines and ideas
    (D) The analytical engine

Time   **LinguaForum**   Volume **Help** Confirm **Next**

18. The professor mentioned several inventions in the history of calculation. Summarize by placing the following inventions into the correct chronological order.

> Click on an invention. Then click on the space where it belongs. Use each invention only once.

Algorithms
Analytical engine
Abacus
Slide rule

1. [   ]   3. [   ]

2. [   ]   4. [   ]

Time   **LinguaForum**   Volume **Help** Confirm **Next**

19. What is significant about Boolean algebra?

(A) It could be used by Babbage's calculating machines.
(B) It was invented in the Middle East.
(C) It was discovered in the 19th century.
(D) It is the foundation of modern computer programming.

Time   LinguaForum   Volume Help Confirm Next

Questions 20-22

20. What is the main reason the professor wanted to meet the man?

(A) To talk about the man's senior thesis
(B) To admit the man into graduate school
(C) To offer the man a job
(D) To warn the man he cannot graduate

Time   LinguaForum   Volume Help Confirm Next

21. What kind of job does the professor suggest to the man?

(A) Working in the admissions office
(B) Helping the professor with research
(C) Working for the school archives
(D) Writing a book for the professor

Time   LinguaForum   Volume Help Confirm Next

22. How often will the student help his professor?

(A) About 12 hours per week
(B) 10-15 hours per month
(C) 15 days next year
(D) 10 hours every day

Time   LinguaForum   Volume Help Confirm Next

Questions 23-26

Child Development

- Crying
- Gestures
- Babbling
- Words
- Pronunciation

23. What is the main subject of this lecture?

- Ⓐ The way children learn to communicate
- Ⓑ How children grow up
- Ⓒ The reason babies babble
- Ⓓ Why babies cry

Time   LinguaForum   Volume Help Confirm Next

24. Why do babies babble?

Click on 2 answers.

- Ⓐ To communicate meaning
- Ⓑ To imitate sounds they hear
- Ⓒ To understand emotions better
- Ⓓ To amuse themselves

Time   LinguaForum   Volume Help Confirm Next

25. The speakers discussed how children learn language.
Summarize by placing the following kinds of words into
the order in which children learn them.

> Click on a type of word. Then click on the space
> where it belongs. Use each type only once.

Pronouns
Verbs
Adverbs
Nouns

1. [   ]   3. [   ]

2. [   ]   4. [   ]

26. What do children need for proper pronunciation?

(A) To coordinate tongue and lips
(B) To know pronouns
(C) To have a good vocabulary
(D) To understand emotions

Questions 27-31

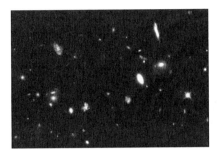

Structure of a Supergiant

27. What is the main subject of this lecture?

    (A) How stars are formed
    (B) How giant stars die
    (C) What supernovae are
    (D) Where red supergiants are formed

LinguaForum

28. The professor talked about the life of a star. Summarize by placing the following steps into the correct chronological order.

> Click on a step. Then click on the space where it belongs. Use each step only once.

Supernova
Protostar
Neutron star
Red supergiant

1. _____   3. _____

2. _____   4. _____

LinguaForum

29. Where in the following diagram of a red supergiant would you expect to find helium?

Click on the correct letter.

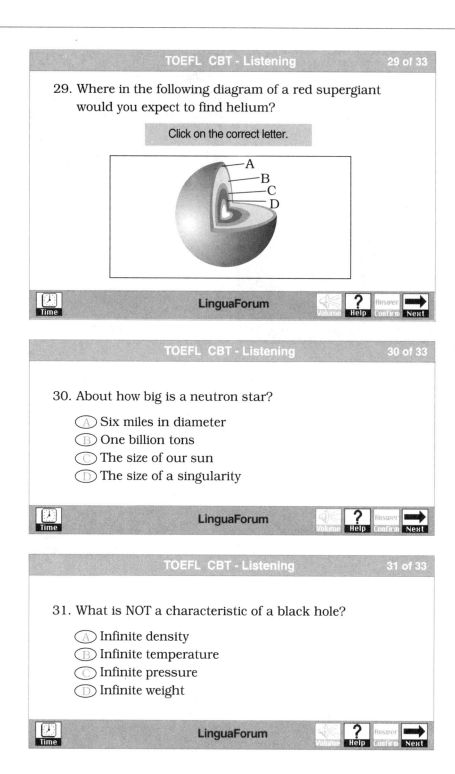

LinguaForum

30. About how big is a neutron star?

- Ⓐ Six miles in diameter
- Ⓑ One billion tons
- Ⓒ The size of our sun
- Ⓓ The size of a singularity

LinguaForum

31. What is NOT a characteristic of a black hole?

- Ⓐ Infinite density
- Ⓑ Infinite temperature
- Ⓒ Infinite pressure
- Ⓓ Infinite weight

LinguaForum

Questions 32-33

32. What is this conversation mostly about?

    Ⓐ The best places to go camping
    Ⓑ Weekend plans
    Ⓒ How to relax
    Ⓓ University life

LinguaForum

33. What will the woman most likely do?

    Ⓐ Go camping
    Ⓑ Study for a test
    Ⓒ Go dancing with friends
    Ⓓ Write her papers

LinguaForum

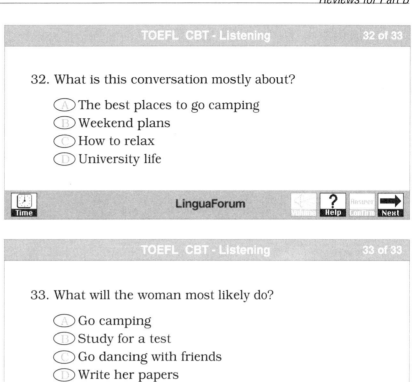

LISTENING

STRUCTURE SECTION

Structure

Overview of the CBT Structure Section

The CBT TOEFL Structure Section measures your knowledge of the structure of standard written English. In this section, the language and subject matter are more formal than the everyday language used in the Listening Section. Topics in the Structure Section often involve academic subjects including the natural sciences (such as biology or physics), the social sciences (such as sociology or psychology), or the humanities (such as literature or art). To answer these items correctly, you need not know about the subjects being discussed.

● Number of Questions

The Structure Section may involve between 20 and 25 questions. You will have 15 to 20 minutes to answer all the questions.

● Computer-adaptive Testing and Scoring

The Structure Section is computer-adaptive. Computer-adaptive testing requires you to answer every question in the order it is presented. You must answer all the questions in this section. You may not skip a question and go back. On the basis of your previous answer, the computer selects the next question from a large list of available questions. Your score on a computer-adaptive test depends on the level of difficulty of questions in relation to your overall performance at that point in the test.

Types of Questions

The Structure Section involves two types of questions.

● Type 1: Sentence-completion Questions

Each question in this category involves four words or phrases. You must select the particular word or phrase that best completes the sentence. About 40 percent of all questions are of this kind.

Here is an example of a sentence-completion question:

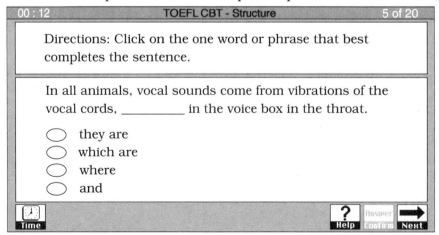

Clicking on a choice turns the oval dark. You must click on a different oval to change your answer. The correct answer is given on the screen below.

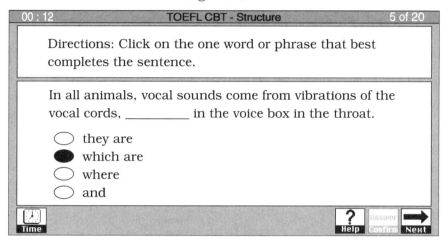

In this case, an adjective clause is needed. To answer, you therefore must click on the oval next to the second answer choice, the phrase *which are*.

After you click on **Next** and **Confirm Answer**, the next question will appear. After clicking **Confirm Answer**, you cannot change the answer you have chosen.

● Type 2: Error-identification Questions

This category of question includes four underlined words or phrases. You are asked to choose the particular underlined word or phrase that must be changed to make the sentence correct. About 60 percent of all questions are of this type. As a rule, the first 3-4 questions on TOEFL are error-identification questions.

Here is an example of an error-identification question:

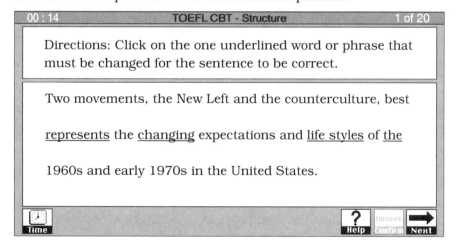

Clicking on an underlined word or phrase turns it dark. You must click on a different word or phrase to change your answer. The correct answer is given on the screen below.

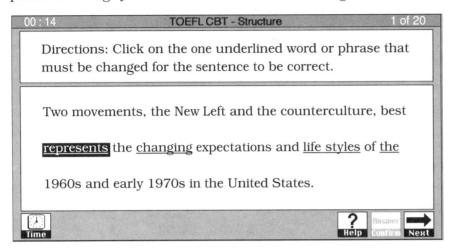

The sentence should read: "Two movements, the New Left and the counterculture, best represent the changing expectations and life styles of the 1960s and early 1970s in the United States. Therefore you should click on the word *represents*. After you click on **Next** and **Confirm Answer**, the next question will appear. You cannot go back and change your given answer after clicking **Confirm Answer.**

Structure Strategies

● How to Study for the CBT Structure

Strategy #1: Study grammar for TOEFL.

TOEFL does not test your knowledge of *all* English grammar, so you need not study unnecessary material which is *not* covered on TOEFL, such as the difference between *might* and *could*. Also, TOEFL questions may be classified according to patterns or categories. To prepare for TOEFL, study the patterns of TOEFL grammar in particular, not English grammar in general.

Strategy #2: Concentrate on difficult questions.

It pays to concentrate on studying difficult questions, because scoring of computer-adaptive depends on the level of difficulty of questions. First, find patterns classified as difficult. Then, practice questions on that level of difficulty.

● Taking the Test

Strategy #1: Use time carefully.

On the computer-adaptive TOEFL, the first 3-4 questions are the most important. Spend a little extra time on these questions to do your best. These first questions do most to determine the overall level of difficulty of the structure section. They also affect your score, because the more difficult the questions, the higher score you can make. That is why doing well on the first few questions is most important to getting the highest possible score.

Do not spend too much time, however, on the first few questions. Allocate your time carefully during the test. Also, because the number of questions differs from one test to another, the amount of time varies from 15 to 20 minutes.

Strategy #2: Eliminate wrong answers first.

When you do not know the correct answer to a question, it may help first to eliminate any answer choices that are clearly incorrect before answering. Eliminating even one or two incorrect choices can increase greatly your odds of making a correct guess.

Strategy #3: Remember, goals differ.

In questions of the sentence-completion variety, you must choose one *correct* answer to complete the sentence. In questions of the error-identification type, on the other hand, you must look for the *wrong* answer.

Symbols Used in This Section

Frequency

The symbols below indicate how often each particular pattern of questions occurs on the test. One of the following symbols appears beside each pattern title.

★☆☆☆☆ Rarely appear
★★☆☆☆ Occasionally appear
★★★☆☆ Often appear
★★★★☆ Very often appear
★★★★★ Almost always appear

Level of Difficulty

The letters below indicate the level of difficulty of questions on the test. They are presented in Notes.

D: Difficult
M: Medium
E: Easy

Example)
  M-M: Almost all of the questions are medium.
  M-E: Most questions are medium, but a few are easy.

The level of difficulty depends on factors such as the complexity of sentences and the vocabulary used in the sentences. In this book, the level of difficulty represents only the *overall* level of difficulty of questions. Accordingly, a question of this type may be difficult in some cases, even though it is classified as M-E.

Dp.

The abbreviation Dp., for "Duplicate," is used when the same pattern is involved in two different chapters.

Example)
  Dp. Chapter 1 means a pattern duplicates another pattern in Chapter 1.

Patterns and Distribution of Question Types

Patterns		Sentence-completion	Error-identification
Pattern 1	Subject Missing	O	
Pattern 2	Verb Missing	O	
Pattern 3	Subject + Verb Missing	O	
Pattern 4	Subjective Complement Missing	O	
Pattern 5	Object and/or Objective Complement Missing	O	
Pattern 6	Incorrect Omission of Clause Elements		O
Pattern 7	Adverb Clause Missing	O	
Pattern 8	Adjective Clause Missing	O	
Pattern 9	Incorrect Choice of Adjective Clause Marker		O
Pattern 10	Incorrect Inclusion/Omission of Adjective Clause Marker		O
Pattern 11	Pronoun Used Incorrectly in Place of Adjective Clause Marker		O
Pattern 12	Participial Phrase Missing	O	
Pattern 13	Infinitive Phrase Missing	O	
Pattern 14	Incorrect Choice of Verbal		O
Pattern 15	Incorrect Choice of Participle		O
Pattern 16	Incorrect Infinitive Form		O
Pattern 17	Verb Used Incorrectly in Place of Verbal		O
Pattern 18	Prepositional Phrase Missing	O	
Pattern 19	Incorrect Choice of Preposition		O
Pattern 20	Incorrect Omission of Preposition		O
Pattern 21	Incorrect Inclusion of Preposition		O
Pattern 22	Singular/Plural Noun		O
Pattern 23	Incorrect Plural Form		O
Pattern 24	Incorrect Pronoun Form		O
Pattern 25	Incorrect Choice of Pronoun		O
Pattern 26	Incorrect Inclusion of Pronoun		O
Pattern 27	Incorrect Choice of Article		O
Pattern 28	Incorrect Omission of Article		O
Pattern 29	Incorrect Inclusion of Article		O
Pattern 30	Appositive Missing	O	

Patterns		Sentence-completion	Error-identification
Pattern 31	Adjective Phrase Missing	O	
Pattern 32	Comparison Missing	O	
Pattern 33	Incorrect Choice of Comparison		O
Pattern 34	Incorrect Comparative/Superlative Form		O
Pattern 35	Incorrect Verb Form		O
Pattern 36	Incorrect Tense		O
Pattern 37	Active/Passive Confusion		O
Pattern 38	Conjunction Missing	O	
Pattern 39	Incorrect Conjunction		O
Pattern 40	Incorrect Inclusion/Omission of Conjunction		O
Pattern 41	Missing Items Involving Parallel Structures	O	
Pattern 42	Errors with Parallel Structures		O
Pattern 43	Errors in Subject-Verb Agreement		O
Pattern 44	Errors in Pronoun-Noun Agreement		O
Pattern 45	Missing Items Involving Word Order	O	
Pattern 46	Incorrect Word Order		O
Pattern 47	Inverted Subject-Verb Word Order	O	
Pattern 48	Adjective/Adverb Confusion		O
Pattern 49	Adjective/Noun Confusion		O
Pattern 50	Noun/Verb Confusion		O
Pattern 51	Person Noun/Activity (Field) Noun Confusion		O
Pattern 52	Other Confusion		O
Pattern 53	Confusion of *So/Very/Too, So/Such*		O
Pattern 54	Confusion of *Another/Other, Many/Much, Few/Little, Like/Alike, Near/Nearly, No/Not/None,* and so on		O
Pattern 55	Confusion of *Make/Do*		O
Pattern 56	Confusion of Conjunction/Preposition		O
Pattern 57	Negative Word Missing	O	
Pattern 58	Confusion of Cardinal/Ordinal Number		O
Pattern 59	Article Used in Place of Possessive Adjective		O
Pattern 60	Conditionals	O	O

STRUCTURE

Chapter 1 Elements of Clauses

What are the patterns about?

Pattern 1 Subject Missing
Pattern 2 Verb Missing
Pattern 3 Subject + Verb Missing
Pattern 4 Subjective Complement Missing
Pattern 5 Object and/or Objective Complement Missing
Pattern 6 Incorrect Omission of Clause Elements

About 30-40 percent of the sentence completion-type questions on TOEFL require you to supply missing clause elements, including subjects, verbs, objects, and complements. You need a basic knowledge of sentence structure to answer such questions on TOEFL.

1. Sentences

Sentence construction is based on units smaller than the sentence itself. These smaller units include those known by the terms – *clause, phrase,* and *word.*

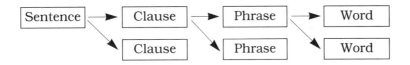

All sentences consist of one or more clauses. A simple sentence consists of one independent, main clause.

> You look healthy.

A compound sentence is made up of two or more independent clauses connected by a coordinating conjunction such as *and, but,* or *or.*

> Carol lives in Chicago, but she was born in Miami.

A complex sentence is made up of an independent clause and a dependent, or subordinate, clause.

> I have read that he is an important executive.
> Bill visited us while you were away.
> Joan walked to her office, which is next to the train station.

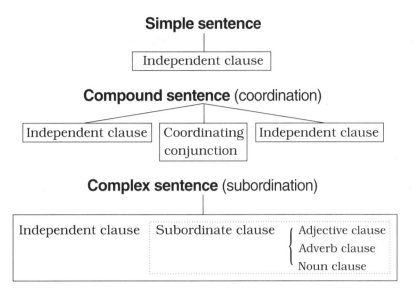

All three kinds of subordinate clauses occur in TOEFL and are discussed in Chapter 2. This chapter, however, emphasizes basic elements of independent clauses.

2. Independent (Main) Clauses

Independent clauses consist of at least one subject and one finite verb, and can function as a main clause.

> Betty made some fresh coffee.

Every sentence must have at least one independent clause.

There are two categories for components of clauses: functional and formal. The first category is a "functional" category based on the components' functions in clauses. The functional category involves the "basic elements" of clauses, namely subject, verb, complement, and object.

(1) Basic elements of clauses

Basic Elements	Subject		*The gerbil* is popular as a pet.
	Verb		She *felt* some pain in her arm.
	Complement	Subjective Complement	A wave is *a disturbance in the water.*
		Objective Complement	A visit to the mountains did me *good.*
	Object	Direct Object	Water covers *most of the earth.*
		Indirect Object	My wife bought *me* a new armchair.

cf) An adverbial may be an element of a clause. Components such as an adverb phrase, adverb clause, or prepositional phrase may serve as adverbials in clauses.

> The weather has been very hot *just recently.*
> Martin is working *in a garage.*
> Julia telephoned *while you were out.*

(2) Clause types

The main verb does most to determine what form the rest of the structure will have. Different categories of verbs require different complementation to complete the verb's meaning, or sometimes no complementation at all. Examples of five clause types are given below.

SV	The moon is rising.
	S V
SVC	The city seems quiet.
	S V C
SVO	That book fascinated me.
	S V O
SVOO	I must send my family an invitation.
	S V O O
SVOC	Most buyers have found it fairly useful.
	S V O C

3. Phrases

The second, "formal" category is based on form. In this category are verb phrases, noun phrases, adjective phrases, adverb phrases, and prepositional phrases.

Phrases may serve as structural elements of clauses.

[Phrases as elements of clauses]

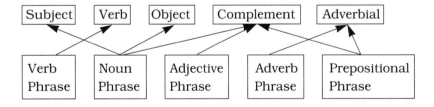

(1) Verb phrases (see Chapter 7)

Verb phrases involve a main verb which either constitutes the entire verb phrase or follows an auxiliary. The verb phrases serve as the verb elements in a clause and are the most important part of the clause.

> Bob *plays* the trumpet.
> The game *has been canceled.*

(2) Noun phrases (see Chapter 5)

Noun phrases are made up of a noun and elements which either modify the noun or complement some other element of the phrase. Noun phrases may serve as subjects, objects, or complements of the clause.

> *My father* enjoys watching football.
> The park contains *some magnificent redwood trees.*
> He became *a famous surgeon.*

(3) Adjective phrases (see Chapter 6)

Adjective phrases include an adjective, optionally preceded and followed by modifying elements. Adjective phrases may function as complements and modifiers.

> The novel was *extremely long.*
> Most people consider those cars *extravagant indeed.*
> She has a hat *familiar to me.*

(4) Adverb phrases

Adverb phrases are similar to adjective phrases in their structure, except that they have an adverb instead of an adjective. Adverb phrases may serve as adverbials.

> He would *never* have done such a thing.
> I see them *quite frequently.*

Adverb phrases are not common in TOEFL, and so are not given an independent chapter in this book. However, infinitive phrases, participial phrases, and prepositional phrases, which function as adverb phrases, are covered in other chapters.

(5) Prepositional phrases (see Chapter 4)

Prepositional phrases may be defined as prepositions followed by their objects, which in most cases are noun phrases. Prepositional phrases may serve as adjective or adverb phrases.

> The rise *of the United States* challenged the power *of the British Empire.*
> It is *of no importance.*
> There used to be a lake *on the island.*

cf) Gerund, infinitive, and participial phrases may serve as clause elements (such as subjects, objects, and complements) like noun phrases, or function like adjective or adverb phrases. Such phrases may be considered clauses because their internal structure includes the same functional elements found in finite clauses.

> *Knowing* [V] *the value of silence* [O], I did not reply.
> *I* [S] *know* [V] *the value of silence* [O].

Moreover, the phrases act in the manner of subordinate clauses. For example, the following infinitive structure acts like a noun clause, a kind of subordinate clause.

> *For him to do nothing in this situation* is out of the question.
> *That he should do nothing in this situation* is out of the question.

This is why gerund, infinitive, and participial phrases differ from other phrases such as noun phrases and verb phrases. This book, however, treats gerund, infinitive, and participial phrases as phrases, not clauses.

4. Words

A phrase consists of one or more words. Words may be classified among the following parts of speech.

Noun – *Jane, desk, water*
Adjective – *new, happy, good*
(Article – *a, the*)
Verb – *visit, search, seem*
Adverb – *really, quickly, completely*
Pronoun – *he, they, who*
Preposition – *of, at, in, without*
Conjunction – *and, that, when*
Interjection – *oh, ah, ugh*

[Tree Diagram for Sentence and Clause Elements]

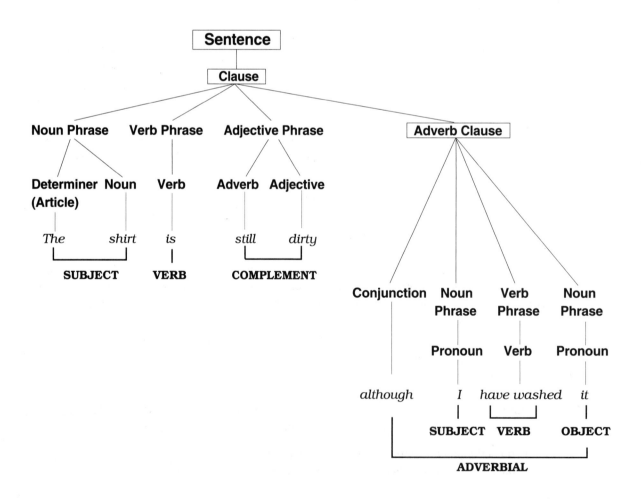

 **Pattern 1** **Subject Missing** ★★★☆☆

This pattern involves supplying missing subjects.

Every clause must have a subject.

Subjects

1. Form

The subject may consist of a noun phrase (including gerund or infinitive phrase) or a noun clause, as follows.

Noun phrase	*Several ducks* are floating on the pond.
Infinitive phrase	At that time, *to split the atom* was considered impossible.
Gerund phrase	*Walking along a deserted beach* is relaxing.
Noun clause	*That actions have consequences* seems undeniable.

2. Position

The subject usually precedes the verb and occurs at the beginning of the clause.

> *The truck* appears to be in good repair.

In many cases, the subject follows a prepositional phrase, participial phrase, or adverb clause.

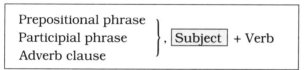

Prepositional phrase
Participial phrase   }, Subject + Verb
Adverb clause

> <u>After a successful interview</u>, *Bill* got the job.
> <u>Reading the newspaper</u>, *Bob* saw an advertisement.
> <u>When her brother came to visit her</u>, *Alice* was out of town.

A modifier may occur after the noun phrase functioning as the subject. The modifier is usually an adjective clause, participial phrase, adjective phrase, prepositional phrase, or appositive phrase. The modifier, however, may be considered part of a larger noun phrase (see Chapter 5).

Subject + Modifier {
Adjective clause
Participial phrase
Adjective phrase   } + Verb
Prepositional phrase
Appositive phrase
}

> *The students* <u>who took part in the contest</u> are seniors.
> *His latest book*, <u>focusing on the history of aircraft</u>, took two years to write.
> *The person* <u>responsible for office supplies</u> is Jill.
> *The desk* <u>in the corner</u> is mine.
> *Anna*, <u>my best friend</u>, wants to study in France.

A phrase or clause may occur both before the subject and after the head noun.

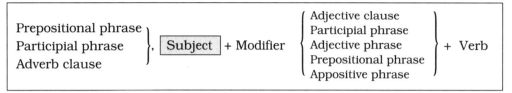

<u>In humans</u>, *the visual sense*, <u>which supplies most information to the brain</u>, is very important.

Notes

1. Level of Difficulty: E-M
   Although this kind of question is usually easy, it may be difficult if part of the subject is absent.
2. You may be asked to provide a whole noun phrase or part of such a phrase.
3. After checking to see whether or not the clause has a subject, choose the suitable form for the subject.

Examples

P1-1

_____ enabled engineers to solve in just a few minutes many kinds of problems previously considered too long and complex to permit solution.

(A) Computers are used
(B) The use of computers
(C) Since to use computers
(D) That computers used

[Explanation]

The subject in this case is missing. Choice (A) is incorrect, because the clause includes double verbs, *enabled* and *are used*. Choice (C) is incorrect because it would make the sentence an adverb clause, whereas all sentences include at least one independent clause. Choice (D) is incorrect because the conjunction *That* creates a noun clause, but not a complete one. Therefore the correct answer must be Choice (B), the noun phrase.

P1-2

Understandably in view of how much commerce occurs online, _____ on the World Wide Web has become an increasingly popular marketing strategy.

(A) are placed, sites
(B) sites are placed
(C) by placing sites
(D) placing sites

[Explanation]

The main clause requires a subject. Choices (A) and (B) have a redundant verb, *are placed*, and therefore are incorrect. Because the prepositional phrase, *by placing sites,* cannot serve as a subject, Choice (C) is incorrect. Choice (D), the gerund phrase, is therefore the correct answer.

P1-3

At each stage of the manufacture of a good, _____ value added to the good at the stage of manufacture is counted as part of GNP.

(A) which the
(B) only the
(C) with only its
(D) only to

[Explanation]

A portion of the subject is missing. The subject should be the phrase preceding the verb *is*, because the prepositional phrase starting with *At* cannot serve as a subject. Moreover, the participial phrase, *added to the good at the stage of manufacture*, modifies the subject, so that a noun phrase or clause functioning as a subject should be placed in the blank. Although the word *which* in Choice (A) forms an adjective clause, it is not correct because every sentence requires at least one independent clause. Choice (C), the prepositional phrase, cannot be a subject. Choice (D), the infinitive, is incorrect because the past participle *added* cannot follow the infinitive. Choice (B) is therefore the only correct answer.

P1-4

_____ their way to the same areas year after year is still a mystery to scientists.

(A) All birds to find
(B) Birds find
(C) How birds find
(D) Although birds find

[Explanation]

The main clause lacks a subject. Choice (A) is incorrect because the subject does not agree with the singular verb *is*. Choices (B) and (D) cannot be a subject. Therefore Choice (C), a noun clause, is correct.

Supplementary Exercise

Exercise 1.1
Underline the complete subject in the following sentences.

ex) <u>Bill and his sister</u> went to the same university.

1. To eat too much is not good for your health.
2. During the conference the board of directors considered its decision.
3. Nowadays recycling products such as bottles, plastics, and paper is encouraged.
4. Deep in our minds lie half-forgotten memories.
5. What he had written surprised me.

Pattern 2 Verb Missing

Questions of this kind involve supplying missing verbs.

All clauses require a verb. A verb phrase including a finite verb* may serve as a verb, one of the elements of a clause. A verbal such as a gerund, infinitive, or participle may not serve as a verb.

> He *was writing* it carefully. (correct)
> He *writing* it carefully. (incorrect)

* A finite verb has tense contrast (such as *has, had*) and agrees with the subject in number and person (as in *run, runs*).

Notes

1. Level of Difficulty: E-E
2. The missing verb may be a single verb, or a verb-adverb or auxiliary-verb combination. The answer may consist of a verb and its object.
3. In most questions of this kind, choices include a verbal or an adjective clause marker + verb as a diverter. Remember that every sentence must include at least one independent clause.
4. Because passive and active verbs both may occur in choices, be careful when selecting a finite verb. The missing verb is probably active if the blank precedes a noun phrase.

Examples

P2-1

The term "dinosaur," coined by the English zoologist Sir Richard Owen, _____ terrible lizard.

(A) literally means
(B) literally meaning
(C) which literally mean
(D) it means

[Explanation]

In this question, the verb is being tested. The word *coined* is not a finite verb, but instead a past participle modifying *dinosaur*. Choice (B) is incorrect because the participle, *meaning*, cannot be the verb of the main clause. Choice (C) creates an adjective clause. The subject *it* in Choice (D) is redundant. Therefore Choice (A) is the correct answer.

P2-2

Humans and other organisms _____ that respond selectively to stimuli in the environment.

(A) to have receptors
(B) which have receptors
(C) receptors they have
(D) have receptors

[Explanation]

The main clause lacks a verb. The infinitive, Choice (A), cannot act as a verb. Choice (B) forms an adjective clause and is inappropriate. The verb *have* in Choice (C) cannot be the verb of the main clause, because it is in an adjective clause. Therefore Choice (D) is correct.

Pattern 3 Subject + Verb Missing

In this pattern, both subject and verb are missing and must be supplied.

Every clause requires a subject and verb.

SV	The sun is setting.
SVC	The restaurant looks busy.
SVO	That poem delighted me.
SVOO	I must tell my friends the news.
SVOC	Most users have found it very valuable.

Sometimes a clause begins with *it* or *there*.

1. Sentences Beginning with *It*

(1) *It* + Verb + Extraposed subject

It is a pity <u>to give up so soon</u>.
It surprised me <u>to hear her say that</u>.
It is certain <u>that she has the highest grades</u>.
It does not matter <u>how tall or short you are</u>.

(2) *It* + *Be* ···*That:* for emphasis

It was Clark Gable that/who played the role of Rhett Butler in the movie *Gone with the Wind*.
It was in 1941 that/when the Japanese attacked Pearl Harbor.

(3) *It* + *Take* + Time phrase + Infinitive

It takes a long time to learn how to write well.

2. Sentences Beginning with *There*

> ***There* + *Be* + Indefinite noun phrase** (*a* /*many* /*much* /*some* /*no* + noun)

There are a couple of reasons for her to refuse the offer.

Notes

1. Level of Difficulty: E-M
   This kind of question is not difficult in itself, but dangling modifiers (see Chapter 9) may make it more difficult.
2. Missing subject + verb + object also belongs to this pattern but is usually mentioned in questions involving dangling modifiers.
3. In some cases, a noun phrase, an appositive phrase, precedes the blank, so in that case be careful not to choose a verb alone.

STRUCTURE

Examples

P3-1

_____ in the 1930s by a research team headed by an American chemist, Wallace H. Carothers, working for E. I. du Pont de Nemours & Company.

(A) That nylons were developed
(B) Nylons were developed
(C) Nylons developed
(D) Developing nylons

[Explanation]

A subject and a verb are both missing in this case. Choice (A) is incorrect because it forms a noun clause, and the sentence lacks a main clause. Choice (C) is incorrect because it still has no verb. Choice (D) is incorrect because it has only a gerund phrase to serve as a subject. Therefore Choice (B) is the only correct answer.

P3-2

In every country and in every time, _____ rhymes and jingles sung or said to children to amuse or quiet them.

(A) there have been
(B) they are
(C) the
(D) when the

[Explanation]

This question involves a missing subject and verb. Choice (B) is incorrect because it makes the sentence awkward. That is, the pronoun _they_ in Choice (B) cannot refer to _rhymes and jingles_. Choices (C) and (D) are both incorrect because they lack a verb. Choice (A) is therefore the only correct answer.

P3-3

_____ that _Homo erectus_ used wood for fire at least 750,000 years ago.

(A) To believe
(B) It is believed
(C) The belief
(D) Believing

[Explanation]

The main clause lacks a subject and verb. Only Choice (B) completes the sentence.

Pattern 4 Subjective Complement Missing ★★★☆☆

Questions of this kind involve supplying missing subjective complements.

Complements

A complement explains or describes the referent of the clause element to which it applies. A subjective complement applies to the subject, whereas the objective complement applies to the object. As mentioned earlier, the verb determines clause types, such as SVC, SVO, and SVOC. Linking verbs such as *appear, be, become,* and *hear* precede a subjective complement. Certain transitive verbs such as *consider, choose, find,* and *make* precede an object and objective complement.

Type SVC: The county became *an incorporated city.* [Subjective Complement]
Type SVOC: People consider Picasso *a genius.* [Objective Complement]

1. Form

As a rule, the complement is a noun phrase (including gerund and infinitive phrase) or adjective phrase (including participial phrase), but it may be a noun clause as well.

Noun phrase	A classmate of mine became *a famous singer.*
	Alice made Sally and Janice *her partners.*
Adjective phrase	This soup tastes *really delicious.*
	We find it *very funny.*
Noun clause	The point is *that we should waste no time.*

cf) Prepositional phrases can function as complements, as adjective phrases do.

She was *out of breath.*

2. Position

In most cases, the subjective complement follows the subject and verb, and the objective complement follows the object.

His family calls him *Arnie.* [*Arnie* is an objective complement]
He is called *Arnie* by his family. [*Arnie* is a subjective complement.]

In the passive clause, the objective complement becomes the subjective complement. Be careful not to add a preposition before the subjective complement in the passive clause.

Pattern 4 involves subjective complements, as in this case. Objective complements are covered in Pattern 5, because TOEFL often requires one to supply a missing object and objective complement at the same time.

Notes

1. Level of Difficulty: E-M
   This category of question is basically easy but may be complicated by the necessity of completing both a complement and the phrase modifying it.
2. Whole noun phrases that operate as complements occur most often on the test, and adjective phrases or noun clauses less frequently.
3. You may be asked to provide part of a noun phrase, a determiner like *a* or *the*, or a partial expression (that is, without a determiner).
4. If a blank follows the verb *be* or some other verb such as *appear,* check first for a missing complement.

Examples

P4-1

Casting is _____ by which a piece of sculpture is reproduced through the use of a mold.

(A) to process
(B) processed
(C) in the process of
(D) the process

[Explanation]

Here, the subjective complement is missing. Choices (A) and (B) are both incorrect because they lack the noun phrase to which the adjective clause refers. Choice (C) has incorrect double prepositions. Therefore, only Choice (D) is the correct answer, because it may serve as a complement.

P4-2

An organism's behavior is _____ for its survival and the successful production of offspring.

(A) vital importance
(B) a vitally important
(C) vitally important
(D) it vitally important

[Explanation]

In this sentence, a complement of the verb is missing. Choice (A) is incorrect because it has an awkward meaning, *An organism's behavior = vital importance*. Choice (B) creates an incomplete noun phrase. The word *it* in Choice (D) is not necessary. Therefore Choice (C) is correct.

P4-3

During most of our planet's history, its climate appears _____ than it is at the present time.

(A) warm
(B) to be warm
(C) to have been warmer
(D) have been warmer

[Explanation]

The main clause lacks a complement of the verb *appears*. This question is also related to a comparative construction. The verb *appears* takes an infinitive as its complement, and so Choices (B) and (C) are possible answers. But only Choice (C) is correct, because the comparative form *warmer* is compatible with *than* following the blank.

P4-4

One of the greatest benefits of glass is _____ it lets in light and provides protection at the same time.

(A) what
(B) that
(C) not
(D) then

[Explanation]

The complement should follow the verb *be*. Choices (A) and (B) can introduce the clause beginning with *it*. Choice (A), however, is not appropriate because the clause already has a subject, *it*, and an object, *protection*. That is, a conjunction, not a relative pronoun, is needed in the blank. Therefore Choice (B) is correct.

P4-5

In 1936 Eugene O'Neill became _____ the Nobel Prize in literature.

(A) who the first American dramatist
(B) the first American dramatist won
(C) the first American dramatist to win
(D) as the first American dramatist winning

[Explanation]

This question involves the complement. Neither Choice (A) nor (D) can be the complement of the verb *became*. Neither can Choice (B), an independent clause, be the complement. Only Choice (C) can be the complement; and the infinitive *to win* modifies the noun phrase, *the first American dramatist*. Therefore Choice (C) is the correct answer.

Supplementary Exercise

Exercise 1.2
Underline the complete verb in the following sentences.

ex) The course <u>can be taken</u> only by advanced students.

1. The requirements for the course have changed since last year.
2. Obsolete equipment caused trouble for researchers.
3. The dancers leap into the air, spin rapidly, and race around the stage.
4. A little more evidence might have proven his thesis to be correct.
5. Pets must be fed and groomed by their owners.

Exercise 1.3
Identify the subjective complement in the following sentences.

ex) After working hard all day, he looks <u>really exhausted</u>.

1. Bob appeared ill when he was in class today.
2. What we need to know is whether the program will run or not.
3. He appears to have been healthy before he had that accident.
4. "Yesterday" is one of his most famous songs.
5. My only goal is to provide for my family.

STRUCTURE

Pattern 5 — Object and/or Objective Complement Missing ★★★☆☆

This pattern involves supplying missing object and/or objective complement.

Transitive verbs require objects. Certain transitive verbs such as *give, provide*, and *send* may have two objects: that is, an indirect and a direct object. Certain transitive verbs such as *consider, choose, find*, and *make* precede an object and objective complement.

> **Type SVO:** They selected *a chairman.*
> **Type SVOO:** We sent *them an e-mail.*
> **Type SVOC:** They named *their daughter* Felicia.

Objects

1. Form

As a rule, the object, like the subject, is a noun phrase (including infinitive phrase and gerund phrase) or a noun clause.

Noun phrase	I ate *a doughnut and coffee* for breakfast today.
Infinitive phrase	Sally wants *to have a happy marriage.*
Gerund phrase	Would you mind *turning on the stove?*
Noun clause	He believes *that there is a nest of birds nearby.*

cf) When objects such as *that*-clauses or infinitive phrases are extraposed, *it* may take the place of the objects.

> We consider *it* fair <u>to give them the same opportunities.</u>
> I found *it* necessary <u>that we should perform the operation immediately.</u>

2. Position

In most cases, the object follows the subject and verb. The indirect object usually precedes the direct object if both objects are present.

> Bob can play *the trombone.*
> He gave *me his card.*

Notes

1. Level of Difficulty: E-M
2. Test questions may deal with entire or partial phrases.
3. Questions often involve objects and/or objective complements of the verb *make*. The verb *make* follows the patterns below:

> *make* + Object (Noun phrase) + Objective complement (Noun phrase)
> *make* + Object (Noun phrase) + Objective complement (Adjective phrase)
> *make* + *it* + Adjective phrase + Infinitive phrase
> *make* + *it* + Adjective phrase + *that*-clause

> The hawk's eyes *make* <u>it a successful hunter.</u>
> Airlines *made* <u>the rapid delivery of mail</u> possible.
> Computers *made* <u>it</u> possible <u>to carry out complex calculations rapidly.</u>
> The new law *makes* <u>it</u> possible <u>that everyone may have equal rights.</u>

Examples

P5-1

When a person's skin is cut or scraped, his blood soon produces _____ to cover the wound.

(A) a protective layer of tissue
(B) a layer of tissue and protective
(C) is a protective layer of tissue
(D) a layer of tissue is protective

[Explanation]

Here, the object of a verb is missing. Choice (B) is incomplete. Neither Choice (C) nor (D) can be the object, because both contain a finite verb. Choice (A) is therefore the correct answer.

P5-2

Throughout the rest of the 16th century, the European fishing fleets continued _____ almost annual visits to the eastern shores of Canada.

(A) make
(B) made it
(C) to make
(D) for making

[Explanation]

The verb *continued* needs an object. It takes an infinitive or gerund as its object, and therefore Choice (C) is the correct answer.

P5-3

Sir Isaac Newton showed _____ was the only celestial body that orbited the earth.

(A) and the moon
(B) for the moon
(C) the moon which
(D) that the moon

[Explanation]

The verb *showed* needs an object. Choice (A) is incorrect because a clause beginning with the conjunction *and* cannot be an object. The word *for* in Choice (B) can be either a preposition or a conjunction, but neither of them can be an object of the verb. Therefore, the correct answer is Choice (D), the noun clause beginning with the conjunction *that*.

P5-4

Computers have made vast amounts of information _____ everyone who can afford it, whether via CD-ROMs or by accessing the so-called Information Highway.

(A) available to
(B) is available to
(C) availability
(D) and available

[Explanation]

In this sentence, the verb *make* needs an objective complement. Therefore Choice (A) is appropriate.

P5-5

The invention of the power-driven lathe and saw made _____ to cut many identical furniture parts quickly and easily.

(A) it is possible
(B) it possible
(C) the possible
(D) its possibility

[Explanation]

In this case, the object and objective complement of the verb *made* are missing. The correct pattern is *make* + *it* + adjective phrase + infinitive. Therefore Choice (B) is the correct answer.

Supplementary Exercise

Exercise 1.4
Identify the object (O) of a verb, or the objective complement (OC) in the following sentences.

ex) We have to have <u>our rugs</u> <u>cleaned</u>.
            O   OC

1. I wonder if we can visit there this summer.
2. The author's book has both strengths and weaknesses.
3. I really must speak with you when you have an opportunity.
4. We do consider it right.
5. Do not leave children unattended.
6. The committee awarded the author a Pulitzer Prize.
7. The doctor urged me to avoid alcohol and exercise regularly.
8. The trainer made her dog jump through a hoop.
9. She disregarded what he said.
10. I prefer being outdoors on a beautiful day like this.

Incorrect Omission of Clause Elements

This pattern involves identifying incorrectly omitted clause elements.

A sentence is incorrect if it lacks one of the basic elements of the clause: a required subject, verb, complement or object.

> Bill started telling a story but did not bring it to a conclusion. (correct)
> Bill started telling a story but did not bring to a conclusion. (incorrect)

Notes

1. Level of Difficulty: D-M
2. If more than two words are underlined, check to see that all elements are present.

Examples

P6-1

<u>Rain of</u> no benefit if it <u>quickly runs</u> off steeply sloping land or sinks <u>deep</u> in <u>porous soil</u>.
   A   B   C   D

[Explanation]

The main clause beginning with the word *Rain* lacks a verb. The missing verb is likely to be the verb *is*. Therefoe the correct answer is Choice (A).

Correction: Rain is of

P6-2

The <u>hatching</u> bird breaks <u>out of</u> the shell by <u>chipping with</u> a sharp spine, <u>called</u> the "egg
        A   B   C   D
tooth," near the tip of the bill.

[Explanation]

The verb *chipping* lacks its object. The missing object is likely to be the pronoun *it*, which refers to *the shell*.

Correction: chipping it with

Supplementary Exercise

Exercise 1.5
Supply incorrectly omitted elements of clauses.

1. The road so long that you can't see the end of it.
2. Put the ice cream in the freezer so that won't melt.
3. I think very dangerous to play that sport.
4. Gold looks like pyrite, which a compound of iron.
5. A hundred years ago, travel was much slower than is today.

1. The buoyant force of a gas is _____ in weight between equal volumes of the gas and air, measured under the same conditions.

   (A) different from
   (B) the difference
   (C) that the difference
   (D) a different

2. Television presents many animated cartoon programs for children and _____ in educational programming and advertising.

   (A) using animation techniques
   (B) animation techniques use
   (C) uses animation techniques
   (D) animation techniques which use

3. Some plants are able to absorb selenium compounds from certain kinds of soil in sufficient quantity to make _____.

   (A) they are poisonous
   (B) them a poisonous
   (C) poisonous
   (D) them poisonous

4. When a bowler knocks down all the pins, _____ the lane clear and resets the pins.

   (A) a sweeper bar brushes
   (B) a sweeper bar that brush
   (C) brushes a sweeper bar
   (D) a sweeper bar and brush

5. A private enterprise is _____ by an individual or firm under private rather than governmental initiative.

   (A) a business, which carries on
   (B) that a business carried on
   (C) carried on a business
   (D) a business carried on

6. When a camel that has been without water for a time is permitted to drink again, _____ takes only the amount that has been lost.

   (A) it
   (B) but it
   (C) which
   (D) as

7. Since the sun and the earth are embedded in the Galaxy, it is difficult for us to obtain _____ of the Galaxy.

   (A) an overall view
   (B) view an overall
   (C) the view is overall
   (D) for the overall view

8. The earth's atmosphere is _____ for animals to breathe easily and for plants to soak up the carbon dioxide they need for growth.

   (A) so dense that
   (B) dense enough
   (C) too densely
   (D) enough density

9. In the first years of the 20th century, _____ that atoms of the same element exist in different sizes and weights.

   (A) when scientist discovered
   (B) scientists discovered
   (C) scientists who discovered
   (D) scientists discovery

10. The Calvert Cliffs _____ about 30 miles along Chesapeake Bay in southern Maryland.

    (A) where it extends
    (B) extending
    (C) extend
    (D) which extend

11. <u>Powerful</u> enzymes from the <u>digestive</u> glands in the starfish's arms <u>enable to</u> digest and
        A   B   C

    absorb <u>its</u> prey.
         D

12. In skin diving, the diver carries _____ with him and receives none from above the water surface.

    (A) not to supply air
    (B) for air to be supplied
    (C) and air is not supplied
    (D) no air supply

13. _____ that the surface of Venus is too hot – an average of 800° F. – for liquid water to exist there.

    (A) The knowledge
    (B) If they know
    (C) It is known
    (D) Known as

14. The term "shaman," borrowed from the vocabulary of a Siberian group, the Evenks, _____ as one who is excited or moved.

    (A) to be translated into
    (B) translate
    (C) can translate it
    (D) can be translated

15. Formed inside a volcano, _____ relatively quickly on reaching the surface, especially if the surface is the sea bed, to make extrusive rocks.

    (A) and lava cool
    (B) where lava cools
    (C) cool lava is
    (D) lava cools

16. While seismographs can record the shocks that sometimes precede an earthquake, scientists have not yet learned _____ when a temblor will occur.

    (A) that predicting
    (B) to predict how
    (C) how to predict
    (D) what to predict

17. _____ industries, once thought essential, which have become unimportant with the introduction of machines and new methods of production.

    (A) The
    (B) There are
    (C) Because the
    (D) Of the

18. The lemon tree _____ and has fruit in all stages of development most of the year.

    (A) flowers continuously
    (B) which flowers continuously
    (C) flowering continuously
    (D) in flower

19. The ancient astronomers thought that the positions of celestial bodies revealed _____ on Earth.

    (A) were going to happen
    (B) what was going to happen
    (C) that it was going to happen
    (D) to be going to happen

20. _____ needed by a grown man each day amount to a mass no larger than a grain of rice.

    (A) All vitamins which
    (B) Of all the vitamins
    (C) Because all vitamins are
    (D) All the vitamins

Mini-Test 1

1. <u>Until</u> a little more than a century ago, no one <u>knew</u> how to
     A   B

   <u>analyze it</u> an <u>organic</u> substance such as meat.
     C   D

LinguaForum

2. In basketball, play begins <u>when</u> the referee <u>tosses</u> up the ball
                           A   B

   <u>between</u> two opposing players, <u>which</u> stand with one or both
     C   D

   feet on or inside the center circle.

LinguaForum

3. Callisto, <u>the outermost</u> Galilean moon, is a <u>little</u> smaller <u>as</u>
               A   B   C

   Mercury, with a <u>diameter</u> of 3,000 miles.
                     D

LinguaForum

4. Silver is not affected by water or pure air, _____ 22 times
   its volume of oxygen when melted.

   (A) it can absorb
   (B) but it can absorb
   (C) to absorb it
   (D) which absorb

LinguaForum

5. <u>Because</u> gold <u>resists</u> corrosion, it is employed in electrical
    A   B

contacts <u>where</u> great <u>reliable</u> is desired.
       C   D

LinguaForum

Time   Help Confirm Next

6. When one end of a very small tube is put into a glass of water,
_____ in the tube to a little above its level in the glass.

- (A) in the water
- (B) and the water rises
- (C) the water which rises
- (D) the water rises

LinguaForum

Time   Help Confirm Next

7. <u>Since late</u> 1950s California law has <u>enforced</u> the <u>use</u> of
    A   B   C

antipollution <u>devices</u> on cars, trucks, and buses.
           D

LinguaForum

Time   Help Confirm Next

8. Birds land by setting their wings at the proper angle _____,
then throwing the body backward and the legs forward.

- (A) to reduce speed
- (B) reduced speed
- (C) speed is reduced to
- (D) reducing speed

LinguaForum

Time   Help Confirm Next

9. <u>A</u> sparrow hawk hovering a hundred or more <u>feet</u> above a field
   A   B

   can spot a grasshopper and <u>dropping</u> <u>directly</u> on it, keeping it
                                       C   D

   in focus all the way to the ground.

LinguaForum

Time   ? Help Answer Confirm Next

10. _____ people may take in several times their weight in
    food each year, their weight rarely fluctuates much.

    (A) Many
    (B) Although
    (C) Even
    (D) Instead of

LinguaForum

Time   ? Help Answer Confirm Next

STRUCTURE

Chapter 2 Subordinate Clauses

What are the patterns about?

Noun Clause
Adverb Clause
Pattern 7 Adverb Clause Missing
Adjective Clause
Pattern 8 Adjective Clause Missing
Pattern 9 Incorrect Choice of Adjective Clause Marker
Pattern 10 Incorrect Inclusion / Omission of Adjective Clause Marker
Pattern 11 Pronoun Used Incorrectly in Place of Adjective Clause Marker

TOEFL tests always include questions about subordinate clauses: that is, adverb, adjective, and noun clauses. These questions may take the form of sentence completion or error identification. Questions about adjective clauses occur most frequently of these three types.

As described in the previous chapter, subordinate clauses have three types. According to their potential functions, we divide subordinate clauses into the following major categories: noun, adverb, and adjective.

Noun Clauses

Noun clauses have functions approximately like those of noun phrases: subject, object, complement, and prepositional object.

Subject	*That we need better organization* has become clear.
Object	I wonder *if you can assist me.*
Complement	The question is *who will be our candidate.*
Prepositional object	The future depends on *what we do today.*

Noun clauses begin with noun clause markers such as *that, wh*-words, *if*, or *whether*.

> I saw *that he had a deep suntan.*
> *How well you perform* depends on how hard you work. [*wh*-interrogative clauses]
> He tasted *what I bought.* [nominal relative clause*]
> They did not say *whether or not they will return today.*

*Nominal relative clauses, like *wh*-interrogative clauses, are introduced by a *wh*-element. In effect, a nominal relative clause is a noun phrase modified by a relative clause. The only difference is that the *wh*-element in a nominal relative clause merges with its antecedent (the phrase to which the *wh*-element refers).

> She understood *what I said.*
> She understood *that which I said.*

Some noun clauses introduced by *wh*-words may be reduced to *wh*-word + infinitive.

> In a command economy, the government tells industries *what they should produce.* [Noun clause]
> → In a command economy, the government tells industries *what to produce.* [Infinitive Phrase]

The noun clause marker or the whole noun clause may be missing in TOEFL questions. Most questions involve a noun clause used as an object of a verb or preposition.

Questions involving noun clauses are not treated as a separate pattern, because a noun clause may serve as a subject (Pattern 1), complement (Pattern 4), object (Pattern 5), or prepositional object (Pattern 18).

Adverb Clauses

Adverb clauses function as adverbials and include an adverb clause marker (subordinating conjunction) together with at least a subject and verb.

> The demand for electricity increases *when hot weather encourages use of air conditioning.*

The clause may precede or follow the main clause. A comma is used to separate the main clause from the adverb clause when the adverb clause comes first.

> *When hot weather encourages use of air conditioning,* the demand for electricity increases.

Adjective Clauses

Adjective clauses may join two sentences. The adjective clause in the resulting joined sentence describes or modifies a noun in another clause within the sentence. Thus, the adjective clause is also a subordinate clause like an adverb clause or noun clause.

1. How an adjective clause is made

> The vase was very old. Ms. Wilson bought it.
> ➔ The vase *which Ms. Wilson bought* was very old.

In the joined sentence, the adjective clause marker replaces *it*, the object of the verb, *bought*. Notice that including the pronoun *it* in the joined sentence is an error.

> The vase which Ms. Wilson bought *it* was very old. (incorrect)

As all clauses do, an adjective clause must include a subject and verb. Sometimes the adjective clause marker is the subject.

> I found a book. It is 100 years old.
> ➔ I found a book *which is 100 years old.*

In the joined sentence, the adjective clause marker *which* replaces *it*, the subject of the second sentence, and the marker itself serves as the subject of the adjective clause.

2. Restrictive or nonrestrictive

Adjective clauses may be either restrictive or nonrestrictive. Restrictive clauses supply information that is required to identify the noun.

> Weeds *that appear in gardens* should be removed before other plants suffer. **[Restrictive]**

Nonrestrictive clauses provide additional information. These clauses are set apart by commas, whereas restrictive clauses are not.

My house, *which is very small*, needs repairs. **[Nonrestrictive]**

Which, who, and *whom* may be used in restrictive or nonrestrictive clauses. *That,* on the other hand, may be used only in restrictive clauses.

3. Relative Pronouns

Adjective clauses may start with the following relative pronouns.

Relative Pronoun	Use	Example
Who	Subject (referring to people)	I know a man *who* reads five languages.
Whom	Object (referring to people)	She is the woman *whom* I mentioned. He is the man with *whom* I work.
Whose	Possessive (referring to people/things)	I have a son *whose* wife is a doctor. Is the cup *whose* rim is yellow yours?
Which	Subject/Object (referring to people)	I bought a book *which* is 1,000 pages long. This is the book *which* I borrowed. That is the canvas on *which* I will paint.
That	Subject/Object (referring to people/things)	He wears a hat *that* is made of wool. The person *that* I met was his teacher.

4. Relative Adverbs

Adjective clauses also may begin with the following relative adverbs.

Relative Adverb	Use	Example
When	Modifying a Noun of Time	I don't know the time *when* he finishes work.
Where	Modifying a Noun of Place	This is the office *where* he works.

Remember

An adjective clause introduced by a relative adverb may modify a noun, but the relative adverb does not serve as a subject or object in the clause in the manner of a relative pronoun. Instead, it serves as an adverbial.

5. Reduced Adjective Clauses

Some adjective clauses may be reduced to phrases without changing their meaning. The adjective clauses may be reduced to phrases only when *who, which,* or *that* is the subject of the clause.

(1) Adjective clause marker + *be*-verb

In this case, the adjective clause marker and *be*-verb are omitted.

The ideas *which were presented in that article* are original.

→ The ideas *presented in that article* are original.

   [Past Participial Phrases] (see Chapter 3)

Bob is the person *who is responsible for computer repair.*

→ Bob is the person *responsible for computer repair.*

   [Adjective Phrases] (see Chapter 6)

The clothes *that are in that locker* are mine.

→ The clothes *in that locker* are mine.

   [Prepositional Phrases] (see Chapter 4)

One application of computers is cryptology, *which is the study of codes.*

→ One application of computers is cryptology, *the study of codes.*

   [Appositive Phrases] (see Chapter 5)

(2) Adjective clause marker + non-*be* verb

When the adjective clause lacks a *be*-verb, the marker is omitted, and the main verb takes the *-ing* form.

The issues *that concern us most* involve our families.

→ The issues *concerning us most* involve our families.

   [Present Participial Phrases] (see Chapter 3)

Remember

1. All clauses, whether independent or dependent, have subjects and finite verbs of their own.
2. Subordinate clauses must be joined to independent clauses.

 **Adverb Clause Missing**

The missing elements in questions of this kind are adverb clause markers (subordinating conjunctions) or whole adverb clauses (or reduced adverb clauses) including the markers.

1. Adverb Clause Markers (Subordinating Conjunctions)

(1) The following table lists the most commonly used adverb clause markers.

Time	Cause	Contrast	Condition	Comparison
when	because	although	if	as
while	since	though	unless	than
after	as	even though	only if	
before		whereas		
since		while		
until				
as				
as soon as				

(2) Words that end with *-ever (however, whatever, whenever, wherever)* may act as adverb clause markers.

> They eat at that restaurant *whenever they are in New York.*

2. Reduced Adverb Clauses

An adverb clause may be reduced when the subject of the main clause is the same thing or person as the subject of the adverb clause.

(1) Adverb clause marker + Subject + *be*-verb

The adverb clause marker remains in the reduced form, but the *be*-verb and subject are omitted.

> How many of us would go to the moon *if we were given the opportunity?*
> ➔ How many of us would go to the moon *if given the opportunity?*
> **[Adverb clause marker + Past participial phrase]**

> *Although it is old,* the story is still popular.
> ➔ *Although old,* the story is still popular.
> **[Adverb clause marker + Adjective phrase]**

> *While I was in New York, I saw the Empire State Building.*
> ➔ *While in New York, I saw the Empire State Building.*
> **[Adverb clause marker + Prepositional phrase]**

> *While he was a boy,* he built model airplanes.
> ➔ *While a boy,* he built model airplanes.
> **[Adverb clause marker + Noun phrase]**

(2) Adverb clause marker + Subject + non-*be* verb

When the adverb clause lacks a *be*-verb, the subject is omitted, and the main verb takes the *-ing* form.

> *Before I left the office,* I turned off the lights.
> → *Before leaving the office,* I turned off the lights.
> **[Adverb clause marker + Present participial phrase]**

Frequently used subordinating conjunctions in reduced clauses of this kind include *after, although, before, if, though, until, unless, when,* and *while.* Reduced adverb clauses never occur after *because.*

> *Because I was expecting a visitor,* I stayed at home.
> → *Because expecting a visitor,* I stayed at home. (incorrect)

Remember

> Present participles (*-ing*) are used to reduce adverb clauses containing active verbs, whereas past participles (*-ed*) are used to reduce adverb clauses containing passive verbs.

cf) Sometimes, the subordinating conjunction and subject may both be omitted. When that happens, adverb clauses are reduced to participial phrases without adverb clause markers.

> *When they fly through airless space,* spaceships do not encounter air resistance.
> →*Flying through airless space,* spaceships do not encounter air resistance.
> **[Participial Phrase] (see Chapter 3)**

For convenience, this chapter will cover participial phrases with an adverb clause marker. Chapter 3 covers participial phrases without the adverb clause marker.

3. Prepositions with the Same Meaning as Conjunctions

Conjunctions occur before clauses, while prepositions are used before noun phrases.

Conjunctions	Prepositions
though/although	despite/in spite of
because	because of/due to/on account of/owing to
while/when	during

> *Though* <u>she has a paper due tomorrow</u>, she is playing tennis.
> *Despite* <u>the high price</u>, he bought a new computer.

> I often saw Jack *while* <u>he was at my university</u>.
> *During* <u>the spring break</u> we went to Cape Cod.

1. Level of Difficulty: M-E
2. In questions where a conjunction is the correct answer, prepositions listed above may be used as distractors.
3. If conjunctions occur in choices, check to see if the expression following a blank is a clause or a phrase.

Examples

P7-1

_____ Robert Frost sold his first poem in 1894, he was not able to earn a living as a poet until more than 20 years later.

(A) For
(B) In spite of
(C) Nevertheless
(D) Although

[Explanation]

In this question, there are two clauses without any connective word, so a conjunction should be inserted in the blank. Choice (A), *For*, is either a preposition or conjunction. If it is a preposition, then it is incorrect because a preposition cannot introduce a clause. Although it is a conjunction, it is incorrect because the clause introduced by the conjunction *for* cannot occur at the beginning of the sentence. Also, the sentence is awkward when *for* is used. Choice (B) is incorrect because it is a preposition. Choice (C) is incorrect because a conjunctive adverb cannot take the place of a conjunction. Therefore Choice (D) is the correct answer.

P7-2

_____ only one figure to the right of the decimal point, we say "tenths" when we read the decimal.

(A) We have
(B) If there is
(C) Having been
(D) When there are

[Explanation]

In this question, the sentence has already an independent clause. Choice (A) is incorrect because two clauses are joined without any conjunction. Choice (C) is incorrect because *we* cannot be *only one figure.* Choice (D) is incorrect because the verb *are* does not agree in number with the subject *only one figure.* Therefore, Choice (B) is the correct answer.

P7-3

_____, emery is spread on some kind of surface to form emery paper, emery cloth, or emery sticks.

(A) Using to polish metals
(B) To polish metals it is used
(C) It is used to polish metals
(D) When used to polish metals

[Explanation]

In this question, the sentence already has an independent clause, so Choices (B) and (C) are incorrect. Choice (A) is incorrect because *emery is used*, not *use*. In other words, since the adverb clause *when emery is used to polish metals* is reduced, Choice (A) is incorrect, and Choice (D) therefore is correct.

STRUCTURE

Supplementary Exercise

Exercise 2.1
Underline adverb clauses in the following sentences.

1. Although his arm was broken, he made his way home.
2. After the author finished the last chapter, the book was ready for publication.
3. I was surprised when I saw her in a restaurant.
4. He did not stop working until the sun went down.
5. If the problem is not corrected, it will only get worse.
6. Alan thought about the project while he had lunch.
7. I studied English before I studied abroad.
8. Whenever I hear a song, I think of that singer.
9. The ship changed its course because it had to help another ship in trouble nearby.
10. You've lost a lot of weight since we last met, and I didn't recognize you at first.

Exercise 2.2
Change reduced adverb clauses to clauses that contain subjects and verbs.

1. Although very tired, Bill finished his work.
2. When working, I forget about time.
3. While a postman, he wrote many poems.
4. Elisabeth worked on the project until finishing it.
5. Before leaving for work, he ate breakfast.

 **Adjective Clause Missing**

Questions in this category involve supplying a missing adjective clause marker or adjective clause marker (+ subject) + verb.

1. Preposition + Relative Pronoun

A preposition may precede a relative pronoun.

> The singer was good. We listened to him last night.
> ➔ The singer _to whom_ _we listened last night_ was good.

The verb *listened* requires the preposition *to*. Therefore, the preposition must precede *whom*. However, the preposition may follow the verb in the adjective clause.

> The singer _whom_ _we listened to last night_ was good.

Remember

Only *whom* or *which* may be used if the preposition occurs at the beginning of the adjective clause. *That, where, when,* and *who* may never follow a preposition at the beginning of an adjective clause.

2. Quantifier + *of* + Relative Pronoun

An adjective clause may include an expression of quantity. Only *whom, which,* and *whose* are used in this pattern.

> all, both, each,
> a few, half, many,   } + *of* + Relative Pronoun
> most, none, several,
> some, two ...

> We met with two lawyers, *both of whom* we have known for a long time.
> The Johnsons own three cassette players, *one of which* is out of order.
> They met five authors, *none of whose works* was familiar to them.

3. Omitted Relative Pronoun

The relative pronouns *which, that,* and *whom* may be omitted when they are used as objects of the verb in an adjective clause.

> The book *that I wanted* was sitting on the desk.
> ➔ The book *I wanted* was sitting on the desk.

Notes

1. Level of Difficulty: M-D
2. Questions involving a preposition/quantifier or omitted relative pronoun are often difficult.
3. Although only the adjective clause marker can be missing, in most cases the missing items are the marker + the subject (if one exists) + the verb.

Examples

P8-1

Harvard College, _____ its history to 1636, had as its primary purpose the training of Latin school graduates for the ministry.

(A) traces
(B) it traces
(C) traced
(D) which traces

[Explanation]

In this question, the main clause already has a subject and verb. The expression, ~ *its history to 1636*, functions as a modifier. Choices (A) and (B) are incorrect because they create another independent clause. Choice (C) is either a past verb or past participle. If it is a past verb, then it is incorrect for the same reason that Choices (A) and (B) are incorrect. Although it is a past participle, it is incorrect because a past participle cannot have an object. Therefore, Choice (D), part of an adjective clause, is correct.

P8-2

Until motorcars and airplanes were invented, the camel was the only means _____ to cross the hot deserts.

(A) were
(B) had men
(C) that men
(D) men had

[Explanation]

In this question, the main clause has a subject, verb, and complement. The noun phrase *the only means* is a complement of the main clause. Choice (A) is incorrect because it creates a main clause. Choice (B) is incorrect because it has the wrong word order. Choice (C) lacks a verb of the adjective clause. Therefore, Choice (D), an adjective clause functioning as a modifier, is correct.

P8-3

Kansas is named for the Kansa tribe of Sioux Indians _____ once lived along the Kansas River.

(A) where
(B) who
(C) they
(D) which

[Explanation]

In this question, the main clause has all necessary elements. A subordinate clause may follow the main clause. Choices (A) and (D) are incorrect because the antecedent, to which the adjective clause marker refers, is not a place or thing. Choice (C) is incorrect because two clauses are joined without any connective word. Therefore, Choice (B) is correct.

P8-4

Nerves, unlike telephone wires _____, generate their own self-amplified electrical signals, the nerve impulses.

(A) compare them
(B) they are compared
(C) to which they are compared
(D) when they compared

[Explanation]

The main clause already has a subject and verb. In the blank a modifier must be inserted to modify the noun phrase, *telephone wires*, which functions as object of the preposition, *unlike*. Therefore Choice (A) is incorrect. Choice (B) is not correct because it lacks a preposition, *to*. Choice (D) is incorrect because the clause is incomplete. Accordingly, Choice (C) is correct.

P8-5

There are approximately 900 species of ribbon worms, _____ are marine.

(A) most
(B) most of which
(C) which most
(D) of which

[Explanation]

Choice (A) is incorrect because two independent clauses are connected without any conjunction. Choice (C) is incorrect because the relative pronoun *which* refers to nothing. Choice (D) is incomplete. Therefore the correct answer is Choice (B).

Supplementary Exercise

Exercise 2.3
Complete the sentences with relative pronouns or relative adverbs.

1. One can still see holes _____ foundations for ancient buildings were dug.
2. Farming requires soil _____ may or may not be fertile.
3. Jobs _____ require a master's degree are very common today.
4. This is a problem to _____ there is no easy solution.
5. The woman to _____ you spoke yesterday is our business manager.
6. Rick, _____ family is very poor, received a scholarship on the basis of need.
7. Mount Vesuvius is a volcano _____ has a long history of eruptions.
8. Jack is the man _____ delivers our newspaper in the morning.
9. The chairman of our department, _____ is from India, specializes in linguistics.
10. Walter, _____ major is English, wants to become a novelist.

Pattern 9 Incorrect Choice of Adjective Clause Marker ★★★☆☆

Questions of this kind involve identifying one relative pronoun used incorrectly in place of another.

1. *Who / Whom / Whose*

Who is the only relative pronoun that has case: the nominative *who*, objective *whom*, and possessive *whose*.

(1) *Who*

Who serves as a subject pronoun.

> The man *who* arrived yesterday is our new accountant.

(2) *Whom*

Whom serves as an object pronoun, the object of a verb or preposition.

> The man *whom* I met yesterday is our new accountant. (an object of a verb)
> He is the man with *whom* I am working. (an object of a preposition)

(3) *Whose*

Whose indicates possession.

> This is the man *whose novel* won a prize.
> I work for a company *whose founder* was born 200 years ago.

Whose precedes a person or a thing and has the same meaning as other possessive pronouns used as adjectives: *his, her, its,* and *their*. Like *his, her, its,* and *their, whose* is used with a noun.

> I know the woman. *Her house* was robbed.
> ➔ I know the woman *whose house* was robbed.

Remember

Whose + person or thing can serve as a subject or object in an adjective clause, whereas *who* or *whom* itself may serve as a subject or object.

2. *Who (Whom) / Which; Which / That; Which / What*

(1) *Who/ Whom*

Who and *whom* apply to persons.

> I saw the woman *who* won a prize for literature.
> She is the best author *whom* I've ever known.

(2) *Which*

Which applies to things.

> The school *which* he attends is the best in the state.

Remember

Who or *whom* applies to a person, whereas *which* applies to a thing.

(3) That

- *That* may apply to persons or things.

  The musician *that* you met yesterday is famous for his first album.
  Did you find the information *that* you needed?

- *That* never follows a preposition at the beginning of an adjective clause.

  A mountain range, from *that* many rivers flow, dominates western North America. (incorrect)

- In many cases, the relative pronoun *that* has a limiting or restrictive influence in a sentence. *That* cannot begin an adjective clause (a so-called nonrestrictive clause) when commas occur around the clause. In other words, *that* can be used only in restrictive clauses.

  The Philippine Islands, *that* previously were Spanish territory, came under U.S. rule. (incorrect)

Remember

Which may follow a preposition, but *that* may not.

(4) What

In general, *what* refers to something that has a certain nature or quality. The antecedent of *what* – *the thing which*, or *that which* – is always implied, never expressed.

  Here is *what* you wanted.

Remember

Because *which* or *that* creates an adjective clause, it may follow a noun. *What* may not follow a noun, because it creates a noun clause, not an adjective clause.

Notes

1. Level of Difficulty: M-D
2. Most questions of this kind involve *what* used in place of *which/that*, *who/whom* used in place of *whose*, or *who* used in place of *which/that*.
3. A noun phrase occurring before *what* means that it is likely to be the correct answer, because a clause introduced by *what* is a noun clause, not an adjective clause.

Examples

P9-1

Certain fishes <u>who eggs</u> are food for <u>hundreds of</u> enemies <u>lay</u> millions <u>at a time</u>.
                     A   B   C   D

[Explanation]
The relative pronoun *who* in Choice (A) is incorrectly used for *whose*.
Correction: whose eggs

P9-2

Common screws for cabinet and carpenter work are made by automatic machines much like
  A   B   C

those who make nails.
      D

[Explanation]

The relative pronoun *who* is incorrectly used for *which* or *that*, because *those* in this context refers to things, *automatic machines.*

Correction: which (*OR* that)

P9-3

Under normal circumstances, the concentration of the ozone what absorbs the ultraviolet
                      A   B   C

light is constant.
     D

[Explanation]

The relative pronoun *what* is incorrectly used for *which* or *that* because *what* cannot introduce an adjective clause.

Correction: which (*OR* that)

P9-4

Electric cells produce current by a chemical action in that parts of one chemical take
           A   B

the place of parts of another chemical.
   C   D

[Explanation]

The relative pronoun *that* is incorrectly used for *which* because *that* cannot follow a preposition.

Correction: in which

Supplementary Exercise

Exercise 2.4

Reduce the relative clauses in the following sentences.

ex) My father gave me a book which was written by a British novelist.
    → My father gave me a book written by a British novelist.

1. William is the man who was named to replace our former chairman.
2. The blue car that is parked outside is Andrew's.
3. The girl who is absent today is Lisa.
4. Martin, who is fluent in three languages, works as a foreign correspondent.
5. We bought a house that cost 100,000 dollars.

STRUCTURE

Incorrect Inclusion/Omission of Adjective Clause Marker

In questions of this kind, an adjective clause marker is included or omitted incorrectly.

1. Incorrect Inclusion

In most cases, an adjective clause marker is inserted incorrectly before a finite verb in a main clause, noun clause, or adverb clause.

> The fishermen *who* were able to fill their boat with fish despite bad weather. (incorrect)

In this case, *were* is a finite verb of the main clause, and therefore there is no need for the adjective clause marker *who*.

2. Incorrect Omission

An adjective clause marker that serves as a subject of the clause may not be omitted.

> Do not ignore people *who need* your help. (correct)
> Do not ignore people *need* your help. (incorrect)

> The drawings *which are reproduced* in that book are beautiful. (correct)
> The drawings *are reproduced* in that book are beautiful. (incorrect)

We can identify the error here as incorrect omission of an adjective clause marker (Pattern 10) or as verb used incorrectly in place of verbal (Pattern 17), because the following sentence is also correct.

> The drawings *reproduced* in that book are beautiful. (correct)

Remember
1. Every sentence must have at least one independent clause.
2. Two phrases or clauses may be joined by any connective words, including relative pronouns and conjunctions.

Notes
1. Level of Difficulty: M-D
2. Check to see if an independent clause has a finite verb or not.

Examples

P10-1

Man from the beginning of recorded history <u>who has</u> constructed barriers <u>across</u> rivers and
             A   B

other water <u>courses</u> <u>to store</u> or divert water.
     C   D

[Explanation]
The relative pronoun *who* in Choice (A) is incorrectly included because the verb *has* is a finite verb of the independent clause beginning with *Man*.
Correction: has

P10-2

Eskimos and <u>explorers</u> in the Arctic regions <u>sometimes build</u> igloos, or huts, of snow blocks,
                A   B

<u>can</u> be kept surprisingly warm <u>in even</u> the coldest weather.
  C   D

[Explanation]

In front of *can*, an adjective clause marker is omitted. The verbal phrase *can be kept* is not a finite verb of the independent clause, which already has the subject *Eskimos and explorers* and the verb *build*. The phrase, *can be kept*, functions as a verb in an adjective clause modifying the noun phrase *snow blocks*.

Correction: which can

Supplementary Exercise

Exercise 2.5
Correct the following sentences.

1. The date on that the U.S. Declaration of Independence allegedly was signed was July 4, 1776.
2. An executive which cannot delegate authority will overwork himself.
3. The whale's brain, that is larger than a human's, also must control a vastly greater body than a human's.
4. The Cascade Mountains, what are popular with tourists, include several famous and beautiful volcanoes.
5. The woman who computer broke down by accident came near crying.
6. The town had a house who was three centuries old.
7. Difficulties do not kill us, usually make us stronger.
8. The American hot dog which has been popular for approximately a century.
9. My professor, who books are known for beautiful illustrations, has never written a bestseller.
10. I have three brothers, all of them are very tall.

STRUCTURE

 **Pattern 11   Pronoun Used Incorrectly in Place of Adjective Clause Marker** ★★☆☆☆

In questions of this kind, a pronoun is incorrectly used as an adjective clause marker. That is, other pronouns (*it, its, them, those*) are substituted incorrectly for relative pronouns (*which, whom, whose*).

Pronouns, such as *them* or *it*, cannot serve as connective words, unlike relative pronouns. That is, they cannot be used in place of the relative pronouns.

> I attended a number of classes. Most of them were very helpful.
> → I attended a number of classes, most of *which* were very helpful. (correct)
> → I attended a number of classes, most of *them* were very useful. (incorrect)

In this case, the second clause lacks a connective word and therefore is incorrect.

Notes

1. Level of Difficulty: D-M
2. Note that relative pronouns can function both as pronouns and as conjunctions, whereas other pronouns cannot serve as connective words.
3. This kind of question usually involves quantity word + *of* + relative pronoun. When you see *them* in ⋯ *of them* underlined, check to see if the word after it is a finite verb or a verbal.

Examples

P11-1

Paints <u>are made of</u> various <u>basic</u> ingredients, some of <u>them</u> are natural <u>while others</u> are
          A   B   C   D
synthetically manufactured.

[Explanation]
The pronoun *them* is used incorrectly for *which*, because the clause starting with *some* has no connective word. Therefore, *them* should be changed to a relative pronoun which can function as a connective word.
Correction: which

P11-2

<u>Some</u> parasites are <u>helpful</u> to man by <u>reducing</u> the insect population <u>it</u> would attack his crops.
  A   B   C   D

[Explanation]
The pronoun *it* should be the relative pronoun *which*, because the two clauses are joined without any connective word.
Correction: which

1. Today nearly all states mail absentee ballots to qualified voters _____ business keeps them outside their precinct, county, or state on election day.

   (A) that
   (B) whose
   (C) have
   (D) their

2. A tissue culture is a piece of human or animal tissue <u>who</u> is kept <u>alive</u> in a <u>nourishing</u>
                                          A   B   C

   solution <u>so</u> that new cells will grow.
           D

3. _____ children are not born with the knowledge of any particular language, it is necessary that they be exposed to the language in order to learn it.

   (A) Since
   (B) Why
   (C) Because of
   (D) Nevertheless

4. Usually carnivorous animals eat herbivorous animals, _____ their energy from the plants they eat.

   (A) get
   (B) which get
   (C) which they get
   (D) that getting

5. Many people in different times and different places <u>have attempted</u> to put <u>into</u> words <u>which</u>
                                                A   B   C

   life <u>is</u> all about.
         D

6. Bell peppers are usually harvested _____, before they lose their dark green color.

   (A) firm and crisp
   (B) they are firm and crisp
   (C) their firm and crisp
   (D) when firm and crisp

7. The orange tree is believed to be a native of southern China or Burma, _____ it was cultivated as early as 1000 or 1500 B.C.

   (A) which
   (B) who
   (C) where
   (D) that

STRUCTURE

8. Tim Berners-Lee, the <u>physics</u> <u>researcher first</u> conceived the Web in 1989, compared the
                               A   B

<u>difference</u> between the Internet and the Web <u>to</u> the difference between the brain and the mind.
    C   D

9. _____ for buildings and bridges down through water or quicksand, they use caissons.

(A) The foundations engineers put
(B) When engineers put foundations
(C) Engineers put foundations
(D) To put foundations engineers

10. A baseball team's standing depends upon its "percentage," which is determined by dividing the number of games _____ by the number it has played.

(A) the team which has won
(B) the team has won
(C) and the team has won
(D) has the team won

11. <u>When</u> cell division does occur, the parent <u>splits into</u> two daughter cells, each of <u>whom</u> has the
   A   B   C

same <u>parts the</u> parent had.
        D

12. Arizona receives very little rain _____ the high Pacific coast mountains block moisture-laden clouds from the ocean.

(A) due to
(B) because
(C) despite
(D) so that

13. <u>During</u> the Revolutionary War many Indian tribes <u>fought for</u> the British, <u>when</u> posed as
   A   B   C

<u>defenders</u> of Indian land against the colonists.
    D

14. Hang gliders consist of a simple frame _____ is stretched to form the wings.

(A) whose material is rigid or flexible
(B) across rigid or flexible material
(C) across which rigid or flexible material
(D) which rigid or flexible material across

15. Plumbing <u>which is</u> the <u>installation</u> and maintenance of pipes and fixtures <u>for</u> carrying and
              A   B   C
<u>using</u> water, liquids, and gases.
  D

16. All fungi are nonmotile throughout their life cycle, _____ may be carried
great distances by the wind.

(A) despite spores
(B) except for spores
(C) spores
(D) although spores

17. Embroidery is <u>best learned</u> by practicing basic stitches <u>on</u> a small piece of fabric <u>who</u> has
                      A   B   C
been marked with <u>a simple</u> pattern.
          D

18. A morpheme is a root word or a part of a word _____ a meaning.

(A) carries
(B) which it carries
(C) and carrying
(D) that carries

19. When a person sees a star through a telescope, the star is not <u>precisely</u> in the <u>direction</u>
                                                                A   B
toward <u>that</u> the telescope is <u>pointing</u>.
        C   D

20. _____, the more volatile liquid will vaporize and pass off at a lower
boiling point.

(A) The more heat a mixture of two liquids
(B) If a mixture of two liquids is heated
(C) There is a mixture of two liquids heated
(D) That a mixture of two liquids is heated

21. Parents are <u>the first</u> people with <u>which</u> a child <u>has contact</u>, and for many years he
                  A   B   C
depends on them <u>to satisfy</u> his needs.
                  D

22. _____ many drugs originally came from plants or animals, most drugs today are
created synthetically in the laboratories of pharmaceutical chemists.

(A) With
(B) Despite
(C) Though
(D) Whether

23. The moon is the only body in the universe, other than the earth, whom surface features
                                                      A   B
have been mapped in detail.
  C   D

24. When Americans and Canadians use the name "elk," they usually mean the big deer what
     A   B   C
the Shawnee Indians called wapiti.
                          D

25. A solution containing more than one percent gelatin is stiff _____.

    (A) to cool it
    (B) when cooled
    (C) it is cooled
    (D) when to cool

26. Each of the solar planets has special characteristics, some of them are well known.
           A   B   C   D

27. The synthesis of an amino acid or a vitamin requires a series of chemical reactions,
    _____ is catalyzed by a particular enzyme.

    (A) each
    (B) each of which
    (C) each of
    (D) they each

28. White light from the Sun is made up of all the visible wavelengths of radiation, which can
    be seen _____ by using a prism.

    (A) they are separated
    (B) by separating
    (C) when they are separated
    (D) because the separation

29. The American Plains Indians had a ceremonial dance what imitated the courtship dance of
                                  A   B   C
the prairie chickens.
      D

30. Through President Theodore Roosevelt, _____ in his poetry, Edwin Arlington
    Robinson got a position in the New York Customs House, which he held for several years.

    (A) who became interested
    (B) became interested
    (C) whose interest
    (D) had interest

Mini-Test 2

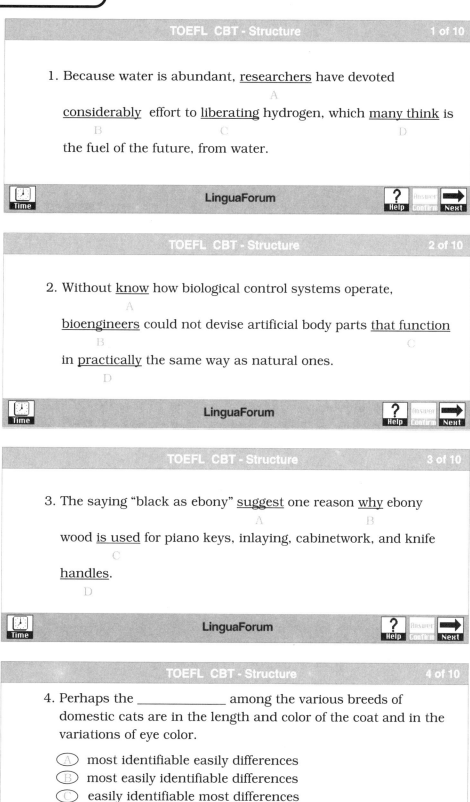

1. Because water is abundant, <u>researchers</u> have devoted
                                        A

   <u>considerably</u> effort to <u>liberating</u> hydrogen, which <u>many think</u> is
       B   C   D

   the fuel of the future, from water.

Time   LinguaForum   **Help Confirm Next**

2. Without <u>know</u> how biological control systems operate,
              A

   <u>bioengineers</u> could not devise artificial body parts <u>that function</u>
       B   C

   in <u>practically</u> the same way as natural ones.
         D

Time   LinguaForum   **Help Confirm Next**

3. The saying "black as ebony" <u>suggest</u> one reason <u>why</u> ebony
                                    A   B

   wood <u>is used</u> for piano keys, inlaying, cabinetwork, and knife
           C

   <u>handles</u>.
       D

Time   LinguaForum   **Help Confirm Next**

4. Perhaps the _____ among the various breeds of
   domestic cats are in the length and color of the coat and in the
   variations of eye color.

   (A) most identifiable easily differences
   (B) most easily identifiable differences
   (C) easily identifiable most differences
   (D) identifiable differences most easily

Time   LinguaForum   **Help Confirm Next**

5. The Swiss psychologist Carl Jung defined <u>extroverts</u> as people
                                                 A

   <u>whose</u> interests are <u>directed</u> toward the world around them and
    B   C

   toward <u>another</u> people.
           D

LinguaForum

---

6. Early philosophers studied aspects of the natural and human
   world _____ separate sciences such as astronomy,
   physics, psychology, and sociology.

   (A)   and later became
   (B)   that they later became
   (C)   when they became
   (D)   that later became

LinguaForum

---

7. <u>The state</u> of Hawaii <u>a</u> chain of <u>rugged</u> islands, coral reefs, and
    A   B   C

   <u>rocky</u> shoals located in the North Pacific Ocean.
    D

LinguaForum

---

8. Montreal, on the St. Lawrence, some 800 miles from the
   Atlantic, is not only the largest city in Canada _____
   world's largest inland ports.

   (A)   is also one of the
   (B)   one of the
   (C)   but also one of the
   (D)   but one of its

LinguaForum

9. Rainfall may be measured by catching <u>of it</u> in any flat-bottomed
                                          A

vessel with <u>perpendicular</u> sides, <u>placed</u> <u>exactly</u> level.
              B   C   D

10. When a debtor opposes a petition to force him into bankruptcy,
    the court appoints a referee to investigate the case, arrive at a
    settlement, and _____ over the arrangements.

    Ⓐ presiding
    Ⓑ preside
    Ⓒ presides
    Ⓓ its presiding

STRUCTURE

Chapter 3 Verbals

What are the patterns about?

Pattern 12 Participial Phrase Missing
Pattern 13 Infinitive Phrase Missing
Pattern 14 Incorrect Choice of Verbal
Pattern 15 Incorrect Choice of Participle
Pattern 16 Incorrect Infinitive Form
Pattern 17 Verb Used Incorrectly in Place of Verbal

Verbals are often involved in TOEFL questions. Both types of questions in the Structure Section test the use of verbals.

Verbals involve gerunds, infinitives, and participles. Although derived from verbs, verbals serve as adjectives, adverbs, or nouns. The verbals may take objects, complements, and modifiers to form phrases, including gerund, infinitive, and participial phrases. These phrases may function as noun, adjective, or adverb phrases.

1. Function

(1) Gerund and infinitive phrases may function as clause elements, as noun phrases do.

Subject	*Getting all As* is my goal.
	To do nothing in this situation is out of the question.
Object	She likes *to sing.*
	He enjoys *playing basketball.*
Complement	The best plan is *to write a sympathetic letter to her.*
	His first job was *repairing computers.*

Gerund and infinitive phrases serving as clause elements in this manner are covered in Chapter 1.

cf) Gerund phrases, but not infinitive phrases, may serve as prepositional objects.

> We are thinking of *hiring someone to cut down a tree.*

Pattern 18 in Chapter 4 discusses this structure.

(2) Infinitive and participial phrases may function as a modifier, as adjective phrases do.

> This is a good way *to find a new job.*
> The woman *wearing a gray dress* is my mother.
> A book *written by my professor* was published this month.

(3) Infinitive and participial phrases serve as an adverbial, as adverb phrases do.

> She studied hard *to get an A.*
> I came home *to find all the windows open.*
> *Not wanting to spend too much money,* they stayed at an inexpensive hotel.
> *Having been asked to help,* we could hardly say no.

2. Verbals have "Verb Nature."

Verbals never act as verbs, yet they retain the properties of verbs.

(1) Having understood subjects

<u>I</u> want *to help him.*

I want <u>you</u> *to help him.*

The text is too difficult <u>*for me*</u> *to comprehend.*

<u>The man</u> *driving the bus* is my uncle.

Her mother doesn't like <u>*her*</u> *seeing that young man.*

Feeling tired, <u>Susan</u> went to bed early.

(2) Having objects or complements

I've decided *to study <u>African literature</u> in college.*

My hobby is *collecting <u>model airplanes</u>.*

People *using <u>the park</u>* should pay for its upkeep.

Seeing <u>that his argument was correct</u>, I decided to vote for him.

He supposed the stranger *to be <u>friendly</u>.*

(3) Modified by modifiers like adverbs or prepositional phrases

What I want is for him *to return <u>soon</u>.*

Getting <u>well</u> is all you need to do.

She watched her puppy *playing <u>on the rug</u>.*

(4) Tense of verbals

I consider him *to be* the best person for the job. (The tense of *to be* – Present)

I was glad *to have made* you happy. (The tense of *to have made* – Past perfect)

He is proud of *being* able to help other people. (The tense of *being* – Present)

We regret *having made* such a big mistake. (The tense of *having made* – Past)

They sat on the beach *watching* the tide come in. (The tense of *watching* – Past continuous)

Having read the magazine, I put it back on the shelf. (The tense of *having read* – Past perfect)

The perfect form (*having/ to have* + past participle) indicates that the action of the verbals occurred before that of the principal verb.

cf) **Verbal nouns** are close to nouns, with little of their verb nature. They are modified by articles, possessives, and adjectives. However, they do not take their objects, although they are transitive verbs. Besides, they are not modified by adverbs.

The *writing* of the book was difficult. (verbal noun)
Writing the book was difficult. (gerund)

The *writing* the book was difficult. (incorrect)
Writing of the book was difficult. (incorrect)

Likewise, **participial adjectives** (one-word participles) are close to adjectives, with little of their verb nature. They usually follow the pattern: *the/a* + one-word participle + noun.

He told an *exciting* story. (participial adjective)
The *excited* crowd began to cheer. (participial adjective)
The man *drinking* coffee is my brother. (participle)
Things *made* well may last for centuries. (participle)

STRUCTURE

 **Pattern 12 Participial Phrase Missing**

Questions in this category require you to supply missing participial phrases.

Participial phrases consist of a participle and its objects and modifiers. Most participial phrases are used to reduce clauses (see Chapter 2).

1. Participial Phrases as Reduced Adjective Clauses

Only when the clause includes *that*, *which*, or *who* as its subject may an adjective clause be reduced to a phrase.

(1) Present participles

Present participles reduce adjective clauses that contain active verbs.

The general *who led the rebellion* was Pompey.
➔ The general *leading the rebellion* was Pompey.

Here, the participial phrase, *leading the rebellion*, modifies the noun *general*.

(2) Past participles

Past participles reduce adjective clauses that contain passive verbs.

The War between the States, *which was begun in 1861*, lasted four years.
➔ The War between the States, *begun in 1861*, lasted four years.

In this case, the participial phrase, *begun in 1881*, describes the noun phrase, *The War between the States*.

2. Participial Phrases as Reduced Adverb Clauses

Adverb clauses may be reduced to participial phrases. As Chapter 2 mentioned, the adverb clause marker usually remains in the reduced form, but in some cases the marker may be omitted. This pattern covers the participial phrase without the marker.

(1) Present participles

Present participles reduce adverb clauses containing *active* verbs.

When astronauts fly outside the atmosphere, they are exposed to harsh radiation.
➔ *Flying outside the atmosphere*, astronauts are exposed to harsh radiation.

(2) Past participles

Past participles reduce adverb clauses that contain passive verbs.

Although it was damaged, the house was still standing.
➔ *Damaged*, the house was still standing.

cf) Absolute phrases

When the subject of an adverb clause differs from that of a main clause, the unlike subject must precede the participial phrase. The participial phrase is known as an absolute phrase when it includes an overt subject but is not introduced by a conjunction.

He will visit relatives in Montreal, *if time permits*.
➔ He will visit relatives in Montreal, *time permitting*.

Notes

1. Level of Difficulty: M-D
2. Usually, the participle is absent from structure items of this kind, although an entire participial phrase or other part of the phrase may be missing.
3. Choices often include finite verbs, infinitives, or other participles, to distract you.
4. The process of elimination, or POE, helps here. For example, first try eliminating a finite verb if the verb already occurs in the clause. Then, the relationship between the modified word and the participle will allow you to eliminate the other participle or an infinitive. At last, you will have the correct answer.

Examples

P12-1

Many historians believe that Newark may originally have been New Ark or New Work, _____ to the fresh start of the community.

(A) referring
(B) referred
(C) refers
(D) it refers

[Explanation]

Here, the main clause is complete. The expression, ~ *to the fresh start of the community*, may function as a modifier. Choice (B) may be the past verb or past participle, but both are incorrect. If it is a verb, then it is incorrect because a verb cannot come in the blank without any connective word. Although it is a past participle, it is incorrect because *New Ark or New York refers to the fresh start* ⋯ , not *is referred to* ⋯ . Choices (C) and (D) are not correct because they contain a verb, *refers*. Choice (A) is therefore the correct answer. The participle is reduced from the adjective clause *which refers to the fresh start of the community*.

P12-2

The first organization _____ for the purpose of improving the condition of black people in the United States was the National Association for the Advancement of Colored People.

(A) forming
(B) formed
(C) that formed
(D) its formation

[Explanation]

In this question, the main clause already has a subject and verb. The expression, ~ *for the purpose of improving the condition of black people in the United States*, modifies the subject. Choices (A) and (C) have an active verb and thus are incorrect, and the noun phrase, Choice (D), cannot follow another noun phrase without any connective word. The past participle, Choice (B), is correct because the participle can modify the subject.

STRUCTURE

P12-3

_____, the Pueblo tribes included representatives of four different language groups: Uto-Aztecan, Tano-Kiowa, Zuni, and Keresan.

(A) Share basically the same culture
(B) That basically the same culture was shared
(C) There was basically the same culture
(D) Sharing basically the same culture

[Explanation]

In this case, the main clause already has a subject and verb. In the blank, an adverbial or modifier can occur. Choice (A) is incorrect because the finite verb *share* cannot occur at the beginning of a sentence. Choice (B) is incorrect because it creates a noun clause, and Choice (C) is incorrect because two independent clauses may not be joined without a connective word. Therefore, by elimination, Choice (D), the participial phrase, is the correct answer. The participial phrase may function as an adverbial.

P12-4

In a combination defense, two or three players guard certain zones, _____ playing man-to-man defense.

(A) while the others
(B) and the others
(C) the others
(D) which the others

[Explanation]

In this question, the main clause is complete. Choices (A) and (B) are incorrect because the conjunction *while* or *and* is not needed. Choice (D) is incorrect because the adjective clause is incomplete. Therefore, by elimination, Choice (C) is the correct answer. In this case, the phrase beginning with *the others* is an absolute phrase.

Supplementary Exercise

Exercise 3.1
Complete the sentence with the correct forms of verbs in parentheses.

1. The man _____ (wear) a gray hat is my brother.
2. This is a song _____ (compose) by Mozart.
3. The man fell down on the floor, _____ (exhaust) from the heat and humidity.
4. _____ (Enrage) at the birds in her garden, Martha threw rocks at them.
5. Bob was listening to the music with his eyes _____ (close).

attern 13 · Infinitive Phrase Missing ★★★☆☆

Questions of this kind involve supplying missing infinitive phrases.

Infinitive phrases may consist of an infinitive and its objects and modifiers. Most infinitive phrases may serve as noun, adjective, or adverb phrases,

Notes

1. Level of Difficulty: M-M
2. This pattern applies only to infinitive phrases used as adjective or adverb phrases. Infinitive phrases used as noun phrases are treated in Chapter 1.
3. In such questions, the infinitive alone is usually absent, but sometimes the infinitive phrase is the missing element.
4. Noun phrases, finite verbs, or relative clauses may serve as distractors.

Examples

P13-1

Delaware was the first of the 13 original colonies _____ the federal Constitution in 1787.

(A) ratified
(B) which they ratified
(C) to ratify
(D) to their ratification

[Explanation]

In this case, a modifier is needed. Choice (A) may be the past verb or past participle, but neither is correct, because the main clause has the verb *was*, and a past participle cannot have *the federal Constitution* as an object. Choice (B) is incorrect because the subject *they* in the adjective clause, *which they ratified the federal Constitution*, is redundant. Choice (C), the infinitive, can modify the noun phrase and thus is correct.

P13-2

Bride-service occurs when a son-in-law works for his father-in-law _____ for the loss of his daughter's service.

(A) compensation from him
(B) to compensate him
(C) compensate
(D) he compensates

[Explanation]

In this question, the adverb clause has a subject, verb, and prepositional object. An adverbial or modifier can occur in the blank. The noun phrase, Choice (A), cannot follow another noun phrase without any connective word. Choices (C) and (D) have a verb and therefore are incorrect. Choice (B) is correct because the infinitive functions as an adverbial, which shows a purpose.

Pattern 14 Incorrect Choice of Verbal

Any verbals – gerunds, infinitives, or participles – may be used in error when another of them is needed. For example, an infinitive may be used incorrectly in place of a gerund, or a participle in place of an infinitive. Questions of this kind also may involve an infinitive used in place of a bare infinitive.

1. Gerunds

(1) Verb + Gerund
Gerunds, not infinitives, follow some verbs.

acknowledge	complete	dislike	practice	resent
admit	consider	enjoy	put off	resist
anticipate	delay	mind	quit	risk
appreciate	deny	miss	recall	suggest
avoid	discuss	postpone	recollect	understand

He admitted *lying* about his school record.
She practiced *playing* the violin for 5 years.
I postponed *taking* that course until next year.

(2) Preposition + Gerund
Only gerunds, not infinitives, can function as objects of prepositions.

The criminal was afraid of *being caught* by the police.
The audience should refrain from *talking* during the movie.

The table below shows how the word *to* in the phrases acts as a preposition and therefore is followed by a gerund.

be accustomed to *-ing*	be addicted to *-ing*
be devoted to *-ing*	be opposed to *-ing*
be used to *-ing*	look forward to *-ing*
object to *-ing*	prefer ··· to *-ing*
with a view to *-ing*	

2. Infinitives

(1) Verb + Infinitive
Infinitives, not gerunds, follow some verbs.

afford	claim	hesitate	plan	threaten
agree	consent	hope	prepare	volunteer
appear	decide	intend	pretend	wait
arrange	demand	learn	promise	want
ask	deserve	manage	refuse	wish
attempt	determine	mean	seek	
care	expect	need	struggle	
choose	fail	offer	swear	

I did not mean *to startle* you.
I want *to hear* another opinion.
I refuse *to give* them any help.

(2) Verb + Object + Infinitive

Some verbs have the pattern, verb + object + infinitive.

allow	encourage	instruct	permit	teach
ask	expect	intend	persuade	tell
beg	forbid	invite	promise	urge
cause	force	mean	remind	want
dare	get	order	require	warn

My parents encouraged me *to go* to graduate school.
They forced the thief *to return* the stolen money.
The ticket agent told me *to wait* for the next train.

(3) Bare Infinitive (Base Form)

- **Verb (*have, let, make*) + Object + Bare infinitive**

  Mrs. Davis had her sons *rearrange* the furniture.
  My doctor won't let me *drink* alcohol.
  Aging makes people *forget* what they did when young.

- **Verb (*help*) + Object + Infinitive/Bare infinitive**

  Therapy helps patients *overcome* illness.
  Therapy helps patients *to overcome* illness.

Notes

1. Level of Difficulty: M-E

Examples

P14-1

An all-star game has <u>no effect</u> <u>on</u> standings, but fans enjoy <u>to see</u> the top stars <u>compete</u>
                 A   B   C   D
against one another.

[Explanation]
The infinitive *to see* is incorrectly used for the gerund *seeing* because the verb *enjoy* has the gerund as its object.
Correction: seeing

P14-2

Frigate birds <u>soar majestically</u> along the coast, forcing <u>other</u> seabirds <u>regurgitating</u> fish
                     A   B   C
<u>in midair</u> or catching prey from the surface.
   D

STRUCTURE

[Explanation]

The word *regurgitating* is incorrectly used for the infinitive *to regurgitate* because the verb *force* follows the pattern, *force* + object + infinitive.

Correction: to regurgitate

P14-3

When landscapes and distant objects are photographed, telephoto lenses can be used in
A   B   C

order to make the scenes and faraway objects to seem closer to the camera.
                                                        D

[Explanation]

To seem is incorrectly used for the base form of the verb *seem* because the verb *make* follows the pattern *make* + object + bare infinitive.

Correction: seem

Supplementary Exercise

Exercise 3.2
Choose the correct form of the verb in parentheses.

1. The company admitted (receiving/to receive) our letter.
2. The announcer agreed (repeating/to repeat) the message.
3. Carl has decided (applying/to apply) to college in Canada.
4. The cat carefully avoided (making/to make) any noise.
5. I was considering (going/to go) to England until I fell ill.

Exercise 3.3
Choose the correct form of the verb in parentheses.

1. The (boring/bored) audience left before the speech was over.
2. Children (entering/entered) a new school may encounter problems.
3. Suggestions (making/made) earlier in the meeting were discussed.
4. The (losing/lost) ship was thought to have sunk near Hawaii.
5. The windows (overlooking/overlooked) the garden receive plenty of light.

 **Incorrect Choice of Participle** ★★★☆☆

In questions of this kind, past participles are used incorrectly for present participles, and vice versa. Questions of this kind involve both participial adjectives and participial phrases.

The main difference between a present participle (*-ing*) and a past participle (*-ed*) is between active and passive forms.

1. Participial Adjectives (one-word participle)

(1) Present participles

Present participles indicate that the nouns they modify perform the action.

> Yesterday I had a *tiring* day at work.
> The *crashing* waves broke on the shore.

(2) Past participles

Past participles indicate that the nouns they modify receive action from the verb.

> John saved the *finished* document on diskette.
> Although the *damaged* book was stained, we could read it.

BE CAREFUL especially when using verbs such as *amaze, bore, excite, horrify, interest, please, puzzle, shock, startle*, and *terrify* in participle form.

Which is correct, *the interesting story* or *the interested story*?

> The story interests someone. (correct)
> The story is interested in someone. (incorrect)

The noun *story* is the performer, not the receiver, of the action, *interest*. Therefore **the interesting story** is a correct expression.

2. Participial Phrases

(1) Present participial phrases

Present participles may replace active verbs.

- **Transitive verbs**
  When transitive verbs are replaced by present participles, an object follows the participles in most cases.

  > A canal *connecting* the river with Lake Erie was first proposed in the late eighteenth century.

- **Intransitive verbs**
  When intransitive verbs are replaced by present participles, an object does not follow them.

  > Animals *living* in beach sands are inconspicuous but very numerous.

(2) Past participial phrases

Because past participles replace passive verbs, a prepositional phrase, not an object, usually follows them. Transitive verbs can be past participles, because only these verbs take the passive form.

> I did not understand the explanation *provided* by the instructor.

Notes

1. Level of Difficulty: M-D
2. In many questions of this kind, the past participle is incorrectly substituted for the present participle, which modifies a noun.
3. Examine the relationship between the participle and the modified word. If the modified word is the subject of the action (that is, active), then it must be the present participle. If the modified word is the object of the action (that is, passive), then it must be the past participle.
4. Note that the present participle may take an object when it is a transitive verb, but the past participle may be followed by the prepositional phrase beginning with *by*. Intransitive verbs can take the form of a present participle without any accompanying object.

Examples

P15-1

<u>Despite</u> its <u>fat body</u>, the pig <u>can move</u> with <u>amazed</u> speed.
   A   B   C   D

[Explanation]

The past participle *amazed* is substituted incorrectly for the present participle *amazing*, because *speed* is the subject of the action *amaze*, not the object.

Correction: amazing

P15-2

Downhill racing <u>consists of</u> skiing down <u>from</u> the top to the bottom of a <u>prescribing</u> course by
                   A   B   C

the shortest and fastest route <u>possible</u>.
                             D

[Explanation]

The present participle *prescribing* is incorrectly used in place of the past participle *prescribed* because *the course* does not *prescribe* something, but *is prescribed* by someone.

Correction: prescribed

P15-3

Because of the hydrogen bonds <u>held</u> the water molecules <u>together</u>, <u>water has</u> a high surface
                                  A   B   C

tension and a high <u>specific heat</u>.
                     D

[Explanation]

The past participle *held* is incorrectly used for the present participle *holding* because it precedes an object, *the water molecules*.

Correction: holding

 **Pattern 16** **Incorrect Infinitive Form**

This type of question involves an incorrect infinitive form.

An infinitive assumes the form of *to* + base form of a verb. Incorrect infinitive forms such as *to conducting* may be used in place of the correct form, *to conduct*.

cf) The word *to* in the following expressions must not be confused with the *to* in the infinitive. The verb/adjective (participle) + preposition must be followed by the gerund.

> Henry <u>confessed to</u> *stealing* the jewels.
> They are <u>accustomed to</u> *sleeping* late.

Notes

1. Level of Difficulty: E-E
2. Be careful not to choose the preposition *to* + *-ing* (gerund) as an answer.

Examples

P16-1

Although tilting trains have been <u>in use</u> since the 1960s, only <u>recent technological</u>
                                A   B

developments have been able <u>to preventing</u> passenger discomfort <u>caused</u> by cornering at high
                                  C   D

speeds.

[Explanation]
  The correct form of the infinitive is *to* + base form of a verb, so (C) is incorrect.
  Correction: to prevent

P16-2

In the <u>hot, dry</u> climate of Egypt, a <u>roof device</u> called the mulguf <u>is commonly</u> used
        A   B   C

<u>to deflection</u> breezes into the house for ventilation.
    D

[Explanation]
  The correct form of the infinitive is *to* + base form of a verb, so Choice (D) is incorrect.
  Correction: to deflect

Supplementary Exercise

Exercise 3.4
Correct any mistakes in the following sentences.

1. An encourage letter from a friend gave her new hope.
2. Who is responsible for wash the dishes after the party?
3. The man was asked to serve as president accepted.
4. After put away their tools, the workers went home.
5. The rain looked like a curtain move across the field.

 **Verb Used Incorrectly in Place of Verbal**

This type of question uses a verb incorrectly when a verbal is required. For example, a verb may be used incorrectly in place of a participle, gerund, or infinitive.

Notes

1. Level of Difficulty: M-E
2. Most questions of this kind involve a verb used in place of a participle or a verb used in place of a gerund.
3. When the underlined verb follows a preposition, it is always the correct answer.

Examples

P17-1

Until 1909 the largest part of the income of the United States government was derived from
A   B   C

customs, or tariff, duties were imposed on goods imported into the country.
                           D

[Explanation]
The finite verb *were imposed* is incorrectly used for the past participle *imposed*.
Correction: imposed (*OR* which were imposed)

P17-2

Insects produce songs and respond to appropriate songs without ever have heard a song
                                 A   B   C

before.
 D

[Explanation]
The verb *have* is incorrectly used for the gerund *having* because it is the object of the preposition *without*.
Correction: having

P17-3

Because green light is refracted more than red light by the atmosphere, green is the last
    A   B   C

disappear.
 D

[Explanation]
The verb *disappear* is incorrectly used for the infinitive *to disappear*, which modifies the noun *the last*.
Correction: to disappear

1. _____ only through the exchange of bodily fluids, AIDS first appeared in the United States among intravenous drug users and the homosexual population of the major cities.

   (A) Transmitted
   (B) The transmission
   (C) Transmitting it
   (D) Is transmitted

2. Doctors believe <u>that</u> <u>during</u> adolescence, hormones <u>are produced</u> by the adrenal glands
                    A   B   C
   increase the <u>activity</u> of the oil glands.
                D

3. In <u>the early</u> 1920s the <u>outstanding</u> jazz bands in Chicago <u>were</u> Oliver's Creole Jazz Band,
        A   B   C
   <u>featured</u> Armstrong on second cornet, and the white New Orleans Rhythm Kings.
      D

4. In 1866 John Swett, <u>superintendent</u> of public instruction, <u>succeeded in</u> having the California
                           A   B
   legislature <u>to organize</u> a statewide system of <u>public education</u>.
            C   D

5. An apple <u>falls</u> from <u>the limb</u> of a tree 16 <u>feet</u> above the ground strikes the ground <u>in</u>
            A   B   C   D
   one second.

6. Forests are commonly found where the climate is humid and not too cold for trees
   _____.

   (A) grow
   (B) that grows
   (C) to grow
   (D) are grown

7. Biologists <u>traditionally</u> divide symbiosis into different <u>categories</u> according to whether the
                  A   B
   organisms <u>involve</u> benefit or suffer <u>from</u> the relationship.
             C   D

8. Many railroads, trucking companies, and bus lines work together, _____ doing the part of the transportation job that it is best equipped to do.

   (A) each is
   (B) each of
   (C) each
   (D) and each

STRUCTURE

9. The Curtis Institute of Music, found in 1924, is one of the world's leading conservatories.
                                  A   B   C   D

10. Planktonic animals are those that float on the surface of the sea, drifts with the currents.
                         A   B   C   D

11. There is a huge variety of matter because particles can arrange themselves in countless
    A   B
    ways, in one substance or by mix with others.
                            C   D

12. Cotton is comfortable wear because it absorbs and releases moisture quickly.
                        A   B   C   D

13. Enzymes break down the carbohydrates into carbon dioxide and water, _____
    energy for their own use.

    (A) and getting
    (B) which they get
    (C) get
    (D) thereby getting

14. Stratigraphers attempt reconstructing the history of the earth by studying the sequences of
                                      A   B   C
    rock layers.
      D

15. The earth is unique in the solar system in having an atmosphere capable of support any life.
    A   B   C   D

16. Railroads were among the first industries _____ collective bargaining between
    management and employees as a general practice.

    (A) adopt
    (B) to adopt
    (C) they adopted
    (D) adopted

17. Some marine organisms that are exposed to the air at low tide have a coating of wax that
    A   B
    helps keep them from dry out.
                        C   D

18. When the first federal census was taken in 1790, there were fewer than 4 million people
                        A   B   C
    lived in the 13 states.
      D

19. Butterflies <u>rest</u> with their wings <u>hold</u> upright <u>over</u> their backs, and moths with their wings
                A   B   C

    <u>outspread</u>.
      D

20. _____ of pink Georgia marble, Buckingham Memorial Fountain stands in the center of a formal garden in Grant Park overlooking Lake Michigan.

(A) It was built
(B) Building
(C) Built
(D) When built

21. <u>Was restored</u> about 1930, Fort Frederick is the <u>main attraction</u> of Fort Frederick State
      A   B

    Park, <u>one</u> of two dozen Maryland state <u>parks</u>.
        C   D

22. Ordinary soda water is water with flavoring and carbon dioxide gas _____ in it under pressure.

(A) dissolving
(B) dissolves
(C) to dissolve
(D) dissolved

23. The sea surface has <u>been rising</u> and falling <u>in the</u> rhythmic pattern <u>has known</u> as the tides
                          A   B   C

    for <u>billions</u> of years.
       D

24. _____ on time, temperature, and other factors, peat may become compressed into coal, petroleum, or natural gas.

(A) In depending
(B) Depending
(C) It depends
(D) Have depended

25. <u>If</u> a person breathes air <u>contained</u> only a little carbon monoxide, more and more
    A   B

    hemoglobin combines <u>with</u> the carbon monoxide <u>and cannot</u> carry oxygen.
                            C   D

26. <u>Despite</u> the development of <u>atomic missiles</u>, tanks have continued <u>to being</u> an important
     A   B   C

    weapon for <u>field armies</u>.
            D

STRUCTURE

27. If <u>there were no</u> Panama Canal, a ship <u>goes</u> from San Francisco to New York City would

          A   B

have to <u>sail</u> down <u>around the tip</u> of South America.

           C   D

28. _____ than its ancestors, *Homo erectus* became better able to adapt to different situations through the medium of culture.

(A) It had larger brains
(B) To have large brains
(C) Having larger brains
(D) Large brains have

29. Contour lines enable the <u>map reader</u> <u>estimated</u> the elevation of <u>any point</u> <u>within</u> a narrow

                              A   B   C   D

limit.

30. Maine is <u>the first</u> place in the United States <u>to see</u> the dawn; <u>it</u> has a sense of <u>to be</u> at the

             A   B   C   D

edge of the United States.

Mini-Test 3

1. In <u>most</u> parts of the United States there <u>are</u> many organizations
      A   B

   <u>to which</u> persons <u>interesting</u> in cats may belong.
     C   D

LinguaForum

2. Kepler's laws described the positions and motions of the planets

   with great <u>accurately</u>, <u>but they</u> did not explain <u>what</u> caused the
            A   B   C

   planets <u>to follow</u> those paths.
        D

LinguaForum

3. People feel excitement, pleasure, <u>angry</u>, and <u>all the</u> other
                              A   B

   emotional states in a way <u>that is</u> very different <u>from their</u>
                         C   D

   intellectual responses.

LinguaForum

4. _____ to isolate from low-priced essential oils certain
   constituents which by chemical treatment can be converted
   into other substances.

   Ⓐ Even though it is possible
   Ⓑ It is possible
   Ⓒ Possible for
   Ⓓ The possibility

LinguaForum

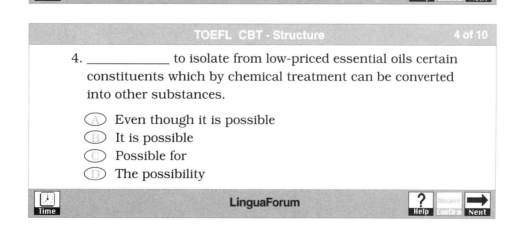

5. A <u>mother rabbit</u> provides a nest by scraping <u>out</u> a hollow in the
      A   B

grass or <u>moving</u> into <u>a</u> old woodchuck hole.
       C   D

Time   Help Confirm Next

6. In American English, phonograms are sometimes hard to
    match with the sounds _____.

    (A)   which stand for
    (B)   stand for
    (C)   and stand for
    (D)   they stand for

Time   Help Confirm Next

7. In addition to <u>regulating</u> the <u>amount</u> of water in the body, the
                A   B

kidneys <u>control</u> the concentration of many <u>substance</u> in the
        C   D

blood.

Time   Help Confirm Next

8. Since radioactive particles are too small to be seen by the most
    powerful microscope, radioactivity _____ by its effects.

    (A)   should detect and measure
    (B)   must be detected and measured
    (C)   detection and measurement
    (D)   detected and measured

Time   Help Confirm Next

9. There <u>is</u> at least 200 <u>separate</u> Indian languages in North
　　　A　　　　　　　　B

America, <u>each</u> with <u>its own</u> grammar and vocabulary.
　　　　　C　　　　　D

10. If a region does not provide some means of _____ the
winds that blow over it, it cannot have any rain.

(A) cool
(B) cooling
(C) to cool
(D) cool and

STRUCTURE

Chapter 4 Prepositional Phrases

What are the patterns about?

Pattern 18 Prepositional Phrase Missing
Pattern 19 Incorrect Choice of Preposition
Pattern 20 Incorrect Omission of Preposition
Pattern 21 Incorrect Inclusion of Preposition

TOEFL may include questions that require providing a missing prepositional phrase or identifying incorrect use of prepositions.

Prepositional Phrases

1. Form

PREPOSITIONAL PHRASE	
Preposition	Object
on	the desk
by	writing a letter
from	what we saw
in terms of	cost

- Object of a preposition

Noun phrase	Virginia is famous for *its historic rivers.*
Gerund phrase	John Steinbeck is well known for *writing about the troubles of poor people.*
Noun clause	Most of *what scholars know about Shakespeare* is based on very few documents.

A preposition may not have as an object a subject pronoun, infinitive phrase, or *that*-clause.

He was happy at { *she.* / *to see her.* / *that she noticed him.* } (incorrect)

cf) A *that*-clause may follow a preposition, such as *in* or *except.*

Calcium is important in our diet, *in that* it is essential for healthy bones and skin.
Granite and diorite look much alike, *except that* granite sparkles slightly in the sunlight.

2. Function

(1) As modifiers

A prepositional phrase may serve as a postmodifier in a noun phrase in the manner of an adjective phrase.

The people [in the store] were buying groceries.

Here, the prepositional phrase, *in the store*, is actually a reduced adjective clause. (See Chapter 2.)

The people *who were in the store* were buying groceries.

(2) As adverbials

A prepositional phrase may serve as an adverbial in a clause as an adverb phrase does.

The people were buying groceries [in the store].
[At noon], we took a break for lunch.

cf) In some cases, prepositional phrases may serve as complements in the manner of adjective phrases:

She is [out of patience]. (=She is impatient.)

Such prepositional phrases may be coordinated with adjective phrases that serve as complements:

She is [out of patience] and [very angry.]

Prepositions

Prepositions are necessary elements of prepositional phrases and usually indicate the relationship between their objects and other words in a sentence. They express relationships involving time, place, direction, purpose, agent, and instrument.

The class starts *at* one o'clock.
The class meets *in* Wilson Hall.
The professor walked *into* Wilson Hall.
He went *to* Wilson Hall *for* a class.
The class was taught *by* a professor.
The class started *with* a short quiz.
An English poet was the subject *of* the class.
The poet's work was much *like* Shakespeare's.
The poet was also known *as* a playwright.

Some prepositions, called compound prepositions, include more than one word.

according to	due to	in contrast to	on account of
as a result of	except for	in favor of	out of
because of	in addition to	in spite of	regardless of
by means of	in case of	instead of	

In spite of poverty, he earned a college degree.
They did not get much benefit *out of* it.

 **Pattern 18** **Prepositional Phrase Missing** ★★★☆☆

Questions of this kind involve missing prepositional phrases.

Notes

1. Level of Difficulty: M-E
2. The correct answer in questions of this kind may be an entire prepositional phrase or part of such a phrase: in other words, a preposition or prepositional object.
3. Most TOEFL questions in this category involve prepositional phrases functioning as adverb phrases.
4. As a rule, a prepositional phrase may not serve as the subject of a sentence. If the blank precedes the subject, then a prepositional phrase is probably the right answer.

Examples

P18-1

_____ the novel or the drama, the essay does not aim primarily to create characters and through them to tell a story.

(A) Whereas
(B) For
(C) Otherwise
(D) Unlike

[Explanation]

The expression, ~ *the novel or the drama*, may function as an adverbial or modifier, because the sentence has a complete main clause. In the blank, a preposition can be used, not a conjunction, because the expression *the novel or the drama* is a noun phrase. So the preposition *Unlike*, Choice (D), should occupy the blank. Choice (B), *For*, can be used as a preposition but does not make sense in this sentence.

P18-2

In 1762, _____, Mozart traveled throughout Europe with his father and talented sister, performing for kings and queens.

(A) was six years old
(B) at the age of six
(C) age six
(D) when six years

[Explanation]

The sentence has a complete main clause, so a clause or phrase functioning as an adverbial or modifier can come in the blank. Choice (A) is incorrect because it contains a finite verb. Choice (C) is incorrect because it does not make sense. Choice (D) is incorrect because it creates an incomplete adverb clause. Therefore, by elimination, Choice (B), a prepositional phrase, is the correct answer.

P18-3

The honey guides are noted for their habit of _____ animals and human beings to bee trees, presumably so that they will break down the tree for the honey.

(A) lead
(B) to lead
(C) the lead
(D) leading

[Explanation]

In this sentence, the preposition *of* requires an object. Choices (A) and (B) are not correct because the base form of a verb or an infinitive form cannot function as an object of a preposition. Choice (C) is incorrect because it cannot be joined to a following noun phrase without any connective word. Only Choice (D) can be the object of the preposition, because the gerund can have its own object, *animals and human beings.*

Supplementary Exercise

Exercise 4.1

Fill in the blanks with appropriate prepositions.

1. He had lived in London _____ 1970 _____ 1985 before he moved to Paris.
2. He was born _____ the fourth of July.
3. Police blamed high unemployment _____ the sudden rise in crime.
4. Mr. Allan will substitute _____ the English teacher who is out of town.
5. I usually drink tea instead _____ coffee.
6. We participated _____ an anti-war campaign.
7. His boss said she was not satisfied _____ his performance.
8. Detectives have succeeded _____ finding the missing persons.
9. The garden shop was filled _____ all kinds of plants.
10. He lived in Boston _____ 1995 and 1998.

 **attern 19** **Incorrect Choice of Preposition** ★★★☆☆

Questions of this kind involve incorrect choice of prepositions. This type of error can be difficult to identify, because preposition use is very complicated.

1. Common Prepositions Used on TOEFL

(1) *In/On/At*

in + Year Month	*on* + Day Date	*at* + Time

in 1952, *in* June, *on* Tuesday, *on* May 15th, *at* 12:00

(2) *From ··· to*

This dance was popular *from* about 1920 *to* 1930.

Do not use other words, such as *for* or *to*, in place of *from*.

(3) *Between ··· and*

Power is shared *between* the king *and* the parliament.
Europeans saw the tension *between* Germany *and* Britain intensify.

Do not use other words like *besides* in place of *between*.

(4) *About*

About is placed before numbers or amounts to indicate that they are approximate.
In this case, the word *about* is called a prepositional adverb.

We drove *about* three hours.

Do not use other words like *among* in place of *about*.

(5) *By*

- *By* serves to indicate the person or thing (that is, the agent) performing the action of the verb in a passive form.

  He was trained *by* a master craftsman.
  The criminal was identified *by* a witness to the crime.

- *By* serves to indicate the amount by which something increases or decreases.

  Our budget was reduced *by* more than 20 percent.
  My rent went up *by* half when I moved to the city.

(6) *Between/Among*

- We use *between* with two people or things that we see as individual or separate.

  There was a disagreement *between* John and Jane.
  It is hard to decide *between* chicken and fish for dinner.

- We use *among* when somebody or something is in a group or a mass of people or things which we do not see separately.

  She stood *among* many other contestants.
  Among her baggage was a medicine chest.

cf) You do not say that you are *among* two people or things. You say that you are *between* them.

  Margaret divided the money *between* the two children.

  You do not say that you are *between* several people or things. You say that you are *among* them.

  Margaret divided the money *among* the three children.

(7) *Since/During/Until*

- *Since* means beginning at a specific, previous time or event and continuing until the present, or until some specified later time or event. In most cases, *since* is used with the perfect tense.

  We have been married *since* 1995.

- *During* indicates that something happens repeatedly or continuously over a given period. In most cases, *during* is used with the simple past and past perfect tenses.

  I lived in Seattle *during* the 1990s.

- *Until* indicates that an activity, event, or situation stops at a particular point or time.

  We start work at nine in the morning and work *until* 5 p.m.

  Until is often used in the pair *from ··· until.*

  We work *from* nine in the morning *until* 5 p.m.

  Never use *during* in place of *from* or *until* in the pair *from ··· until ···.*

2. Verb + Preposition Combinations

Some commonly used verb + preposition combinations are listed below.

account for	belong to	differ from	search for
accuse of	benefit from	divide into	stare at
adjust to	concentrate on	object to	strive for
apologize for	consist of	participate in	substitute for
approve of	count on	refer to	succeed in
attach to	deal with	rely on	
begin with	depend on	respond to	
believe in	devote to	result from (in)	

STRUCTURE

Writing *differs from* speech in many ways.

Water can *substitute for* milk in this recipe.

Some other verb + preposition combinations take two objects.

blame A for B	prevent A from B
compare A with/to B	regard A as B
excuse A for B	remind A of B
mistake A for B	supply A with B
prepare A for B	thank A for B

He *mistook* their car *for* ours.

That music *reminds* me *of* childhood.

3. Adjective (Past Participle) + Preposition Combinations

Some adjectives, many of which occur with the verb *be*, are usually followed by prepositions.

absent from	concerned with	familiar with	opposed to
accustomed to	conscious of	famous for	proud of
acquainted with	contrary to	filled with	related to
afraid of	convinced of	fond of	responsible for
annoyed with	credited with	free of	satisfied with
associated with	dependent on	independent of	scared of
aware of	different from	interested in	similar to
based on	disappointed with	known for (as)	suitable for
bored with	distinguished from	made of	surprised at/by
capable of	equal to	native to	
characteristic of	equipped with	necessary for	
composed of	exposed to	next to	

She *was fond of* baked potatoes.

Virginia *is famous for* its apples.

Notes

1. Level of Difficulty: M-E
2. Many preposition questions involve verb + preposition combinations or adjective + preposition combinations.
3. Examine the verb or adjective before, or the noun after, an underlined preposition.

Examples

P19-1

Burns range <u>to</u> minor <u>annoyances</u> to serious injuries that <u>can cause</u> permanent crippling or .
       A   B   C

<u>even death</u>.
   D

[Explanation]

  To is incorrectly substituted for *from* because the correct expression is *from ⋯ to*.

  Correction: from

P19-2

<u>A</u> university differs <u>with</u> a college <u>in that</u> it is usually larger, has a broader curriculum, and
A   B   C

<u>offers</u> graduate and professional degrees in addition to undergraduate degrees.
  D

[Explanation]

  The preposition *with* is incorrectly used for *from*, because the verb *differ* follows the pattern, *⋯ differs from ⋯*.

  Correction: from

P19-3

Religious beliefs <u>are frequently</u> associated <u>as</u> myths, <u>timeless</u> stories <u>that</u> describe the origin
              A   B   C   D

of something.

[Explanation]

  Here, an adjective (past participle) + preposition combination is asked. The participle *associated* must be paired with the preposition *with*.

  Correction: with

Supplementary Exercise

Exercise 4.2

Correct any mistakes involving prepositions in the following sentences where necessary.

1. We did not attend the debate among Miller and Brown.
2. A typical house cat may weigh for 3 to 6 kilograms.
3. There was no one from our company between the many people at the trade fair.
4. Humorist Will Rogers was known as his comic tales about life in the American West.
5. Modern civilization relies heavily in petroleum for energy.
6. The business benefited from its convenient location.
7. I did not visit her because I was afraid of upsetting her.
8. He weighs among 70 kilograms.
9. I have been living in Seoul since 1997.
10. The original story, to which the film is based, has a happy ending.

 **Incorrect Omission of Preposition** ★★★☆☆

In questions of this kind, a preposition is omitted when one is required.

A preposition is incorrectly omitted where required, as follows:

1. In Compound Prepositions

> We all got satisfaction *out of* it. (correct)
> We all got satisfaction *out* it. (incorrect)

2. In Verb + Preposition

> The answer to a question *depends on* how the question is asked. (correct)
> The answer to a question *depends* how the question is asked. (incorrect)

> For centuries, the Aleuts have *lived along* the shores of the Arctic Ocean. (correct)
> For centuries, the Aleuts have *lived* the shores of the Arctic Ocean. (incorrect)

3. In Adjective (Past Participle) + Preposition

> He worked on engineering problems *associated with* aircraft. (correct)
> He worked on engineering problems *associated* aircraft. (incorrect)

4. In Preposition + Relative Pronoun

When an adjective clause is used as the object of a preposition, the preposition must follow the verb or precede the relative pronoun. On TOEFL, questions may omit a preposition preceding the relative pronoun.

> The building *which* he works *in* is very tall. (correct)
> The building *in which* he works is very tall. (correct)
> The building *which* he works is very tall. (incorrect)

Errors of this kind are closely related to the use or misuse of relative pronouns, but this pattern covers the error because a preposition is incorrectly omitted where required.

5. In Other Expressions

> *hundreds (thousands, millions ···) of* + Noun
> *part of* + Noun

> There are *hundreds of* species of ants. (correct)
> There are *hundreds* species of ants. (incorrect)

> Calculus is an important *part of* mathematics. (correct)
> Calculus is an important *part* mathematics. (incorrect)

Notes

1. Level of Difficulty: D-M
2. Words on either side are underlined when a preposition is omitted.
3. It is very hard to identify omitted prepositions before an adjective clause. When noun + adjective clause markers are underlined, check to see if a preposition is required between them.

Examples

P20-1

In pantomime, <u>actors</u> use gestures <u>instead words</u> <u>to convey</u> ideas.
A   B   C   D

[Explanation]

In this sentence, the preposition *of*, part of the compound preposition *instead of*, is incorrectly omitted.

Correction: instead of words

P20-2

Artificial kidneys <u>consist a</u> number of permeable filmy <u>membranes</u> encased in a cartridge
                          A   B

<u>that is</u> immersed in <u>appropriate</u> cleansing solutions.
    C   D

[Explanation]

The preposition *of*, part of the verb + preposition combination *consist of*, is incorrectly omitted.

Correction: consist of a

P20-3

In 1913, with the opening of the <u>controversial</u> Armory Show in New York City, the American
                                  A

public had <u>its</u> first glimpse of <u>what</u> was to become <u>known</u> "modern" art.
           B   C   D

[Explanation]

The preposition *as*, part of the past participle + preposition combination *known as*, is incorrectly omitted.

Correction: known as

P20-4

The red or Norway pine <u>is a</u> beautiful tree, <u>having</u> reddish-brown <u>bark which</u> it gains <u>its</u>
                       A   B   C   D

common name.

[Explanation]

A preposition is incorrectly omitted between *bark* and *which* in Choice (C). The adjective clause means that *it gains its common name from reddish-brown bark*, so the preposition *from* should come before *which*.

Correction: bark from which

STRUCTURE

P20-5

<u>Football</u> is the <u>chief</u> sport in <u>most</u> colleges and universities and in <u>thousands secondary</u>
   A   B   C   D

schools in the United States.

[Explanation]

The preposition *of* is incorrectly omitted after *thousands*.

Correction: thousands of secondary

Supplementary Exercise

Exercise 4.3

Correct any mistakes in the following sentences.

1. An award was presented the player who scored the most points.
2. A skilled artist can produce many different kinds effects with a brush.
3. The rate which a chemical reaction proceeds depends partly on temperature.
4. We are planning of a visit to France next month.
5. Four rocky planets, Mercury, Venus, Earth and Mars, orbit relatively close the sun.
6. There were fewer than 50 of tigers in the whole country.
7. She has many faults, but we're all very fond her.
8. His hard work accounts his success.
9. We are dependent the sun for energy.
10. The town which the college is located is very pretty.

 **Pattern 21** **Incorrect Inclusion of Preposition** ★★★☆☆

In questions of this kind, a preposition is used when not needed.

1. Between Transitive Verbs and Objects

An unneeded preposition is sometimes inserted between a transitive verb and its object.

> Mary published her novels. (correct)
> Mary published *of* her novels. (incorrect)

> John considered his options, not knowing which was best. (correct)
> John considered his options, not knowing *of* which was best. (incorrect)

2. Before Objective Complements

A preposition may be inserted before an objective complement when not needed.

> Zoologists call cats *Felidae*. (correct)
> Zoologists call cats *as Felidae*. (incorrect)

A verb such as *appoint, call, choose, declare, elect,* or *name* may take an objective complement immediately following its object, with no preposition. Although the sentence becomes passive, the preposition need not be used in front of the objective complement.

> Certain properties of food are called "nutrition." (correct)
> Certain properties of food are called *as* "nutrition." (incorrect)

3. Between Modifier and Modified

The preposition *of* may be inserted incorrectly where it is not needed, as follows.

(1) Noun + Participle phrase

> The man wearing the blue suit is my father. (correct)
> The man *of* wearing the blue suit is my father. (incorrect)

> The tools used in ancient construction have been discovered. (correct)
> The tools *of* used in ancient construction have been discovered. (incorrect)

(2) Adjective (Number) + Noun

> The price of gasoline rose 10 percent last year. (correct)
> The price of gasoline rose 10 *of* percent last year. (incorrect)

(3) Quantifier + Nonspecific noun

> Few Roman emperors had peaceful reigns. (correct)
> Few *of* Roman emperors had peaceful reigns. (incorrect)

Expressions of quantity follow the patterns listed below:

all, most, some/any	+ *of* +	Specific plural countable noun or non-countable noun
many, (a) few, both, several, two	+ *of* +	Specific plural countable noun
much, (a) little	+ *of* +	Specific non-countable noun

> all of the chickens
> all of my furniture

few of those chairs

a little of the money

cf) *Of* is optional in the structure *all, both (of)* + Specific noun.

    all / both those chickens (correct)

    all / both of those chickens (correct)

When a noun is nonspecific, *of* does not follow the quantifiers.

all, most, some / any *many, (a) few, several, two* } + Nonspecific noun *much, (a) little*

    all chickens (correct)

    few chairs (correct)

    all of chickens (incorrect)

    few of chairs (incorrect)

Notes

1. Level of Difficulty: M-D
2. Check to see if a preposition is necessary when two or more words including a preposition (*of, by, as*) are underlined.

Examples

P21-1

A basic piece of evidence supporting of the particle view of light is that light travels in straight
  A   B   C   D
lines.

[Explanation]

The preposition *of* in Choice (B) is incorrectly included because the participle form of a transitive verb, *supporting*, takes an object without any preposition.

Correction: the particle

P21-2

When several of roots become fleshy, as in the sweet potato, they are called clustered, or
             A   B   C   D
fascicled roots.

[Explanation]

The preposition *of* in Choice (A) is incorrectly included because the quantifier *several* modifies nouns directly, *several roots*, or follows the pattern *several, few, both, one* + *of* + specific plural countable noun, *several of those roots*.

Correction: roots

1. <u>Among</u> 15 miles southeast of Cumberland, the Potomac River <u>is formed</u> by the <u>junction</u> of
   A   B   C
   <u>its</u> North and South Branches.
   D

2. Soccer <u>is a</u> team sport <u>which</u> players attempt <u>to score</u> goals by passing the ball down the
            A   B   C
   field past <u>opposing defenders</u>, and kicking the ball into the goal net.
                        D

3. _____ George Washington's first term, the basic structure of the U.S. government was
   put into place.

   (A) While
   (B) Since
   (C) During
   (D) As

4. A piano is <u>tuned</u> by increasing or decreasing <u>of the</u> tension of the strings <u>so that</u> they vibrate
                A   B   C
   at <u>a certain</u> pitch.
          D

5. <u>By</u> various <u>methods</u> including carbon dating, a procedure <u>in which</u> the relative
   A   B   C
   <u>amounts different</u> forms of carbon are measured, the age of the microfossils can be determined.
          D

6. <u>During</u> primitive times until <u>the early</u> 1800s, the only way <u>to move</u> loads overland was by
   A   B   C
   using the <u>physical strength</u> of men and animals.
                      D

7. The Indians had <u>lived America</u> for <u>many</u> centuries <u>when</u> the white men <u>first</u> came
                          A   B   C   D
   from Europe.

8. _____ size and location in the middle of the continent, Minnesota has changeable
   weather.

   (A) On account
   (B) Because of its
   (C) Since it
   (D) While its

9. Heat travels <u>in</u> a warm object to a cold one, so one way <u>to cool</u> an <u>enclosed</u> space might be to
                 A   B   C
   put <u>a cold</u> stone in it.
          D

10. The preteen is <u>extremely</u> <u>interested</u> in, and influenced <u>in</u>, peers, <u>better</u> known as
                         A   B   C   D
    "the gang."

11. George Orwell's *Nineteen Eighty-four* is a grim picture of _____ might be like if totalitarianism triumphs throughout the world.

    (A) a society
    (B) which society
    (C) those societies
    (D) what society

12. Blueprinting, which came into use about 1876, made it possible to get copies within a
               A   B   C
    few of minutes.
      D

13. Carbohydrates are composed mainly with the basic elements of most organic
                A   B   C
    molecules: carbon, hydrogen, and oxygen.
      D

14. In striving to an epigrammatic conciseness, Emily Dickinson stripped her language of
            A   B   C
    superfluous words.
      D

15. Photosynthesis is the most fundamental activity of a plant, for which all else depends.
      A   B   C   D

16. The word "robot" today is applied any of countless mechanical devices which relieve
                            A   B   C
    humans of dangerous or monotonous chores.
                           D

17. _____, the number below the line is the denominator, and the number above the line is the numerator.

    (A) In a common fraction
    (B) A common fraction is
    (C) When a common fraction
    (D) There is a common fraction

18. Glass with a rough or textured surface is produced by rolling molten glass among two
    A   B   C
    rollers with rough patterns on their surfaces.
                         D

19. Apollo 17 was launched in December 7, 1972, with Navy officers Eugene A. Cernan and
                A   B   C
    Ronald E. Evans and civilian geologist Harrison H. Schmitt aboard.
                                              D

20. When Venus was named after the Roman goddess of love and beauty, scholars were
                        A
    unaware the nightmarish conditions that exist at its surface.
      B   C   D

Mini-Test 4

1. Kingston, Ontario <u>is</u> a leading French center of government and
   A

   trade until <u>it</u> fell <u>into</u> the <u>hands</u> of the British in 1758 during
   B   C   D

   the French and Indian War.

LinguaForum

2. <u>Determined</u> to help <u>other</u> peoples become democratic and <u>order</u>,
   A   B   C

   Woodrow Wilson became the greatest military <u>interventionist</u> in
                                                D

   U.S. history.

LinguaForum

3. Among Baltimore's many parks <u>are</u> Federal Hill Park, <u>so</u> named
                                 A   B

   <u>because</u> a great celebration there marked Maryland's <u>entrance</u>
   C   D

   into the Union in 1788.

LinguaForum

4. It is true that the closer a star is to the earth, _____
   radiation energy will actually reach the earth.

   (A) more than its
   (B) most of its
   (C) while its
   (D) the more of its

LinguaForum

STRUCTURE

5. Today Florida <u>ranks</u> first in grapefruit and oranges, <u>growing</u>
               A   B

about three <u>fourth</u> of the United States <u>crop</u>.
               C   D

LinguaForum

6. _____ in small communities, they based their government and social organization upon loyalty to the family and to the tribe.

  (A) Most Indians who lived
  (B) Since most Indians lived
  (C) While most Indians living
  (D) There were Indians living

LinguaForum

7. <u>Biologists</u> today, <u>whose</u> specialize in classification, or taxonomy,
     A   B

<u>systematically</u> arrange living organisms by lines of descent,
       C

from <u>the earliest</u> forms of life.
         D

LinguaForum

8. Jetliners fly at high altitudes, _____ at 26,000–36,000 ft, where they can use fuel efficiently and usually avoid bad weather.

  (A) typically cruising
  (B) typically cruise
  (C) they cruise
  (D) but their cruise

LinguaForum

9. Pearl Buck's deep interest in children <u>led</u> her <u>to establish</u> the
                                         A   B
   Pearl S. Buck Foundation of Philadelphia, <u>which it</u> has aided in
                                                    C
   the <u>adoption</u> of Amerasian children.
           D

10. By the end of the Triassic period, dinosaurs dominated Pangaea,
    possibly contributing to _____ of many other reptiles.

    Ⓐ extinct
    Ⓑ the extinction
    Ⓒ become extinct
    Ⓓ and be extinct

STRUCTURE

What are the patterns about?

Nouns
 Pattern 22 Singular/Plural Noun
 Pattern 23 Incorrect Plural Form
Pronouns
 Pattern 24 Incorrect Pronoun Form
 Pattern 25 Incorrect Choice of Pronoun
 Pattern 26 Incorrect Inclusion of Pronoun
Articles
 Pattern 27 Incorrect Choice of Article
 Pattern 28 Incorrect Omission of Article
 Pattern 29 Incorrect Inclusion of Article
Appositives
 Pattern 30 Appositive Missing

Many TOEFL questions require supplying missing noun phrases functioning as clause elements, or missing parts of the noun phrases. TOEFL also requires identifying errors in the use of nouns, pronouns, and articles.

Noun Phrases

1. Form

<table>
<tr><th colspan="4">NOUN PHRASE</th></tr>
<tr><th colspan="3">NOUN PHRASE</th><th></th></tr>
<tr><th>(Determiner)</th><th>(Premodifier)</th><th>Head</th><th>(Postmodifier)</th></tr>
<tr><td>Article
Possessive
Demonstrative</td><td>(Adverb) Adjective
Noun</td><td>Noun</td><td>Adjective clause
Participial phrase
Prepositional phrase
Adjective phrase
Appositive phrase</td></tr>
</table>

Post modifiers, like adjective clauses or participial phrases, may be considered components of a larger noun phrase.

Examples of noun phrases

1. a good dinner
   [article + adjective + noun]
2. Ann's dress
   [possessive + noun]
3. a clothes dryer
   [article + noun + noun]

4. those young men <u>who are playing soccer</u>

[demonstrative + adjective + noun+ adjective clause]

5. the girls <u>drinking coffee</u>

[article + noun + participial phrase]

6. the very large book <u>on the shelf</u>

[article + adverb + adjective + noun + prepositional phrase]

7. the only person <u>suitable for the position</u>

[article + adjective + noun + adjective phrase]

8. Mrs. Betty Jones, <u>the manager of the department</u>

[noun phrase, appositive phrase]

2. Function

Noun phrases may serve as subjects, objects, complements, or prepositional objects in clauses.

Subject	[The music] was too loud to be tolerable.
Object	I remember [his grandmother] well.
Complement	The novel became [a television series].
Prepositional object	I met her at [a little restaurant].

These noun phrases are covered in Pattern 1, Pattern 5, Pattern 4, and Pattern 18.

3. Components

(1) Nouns

Nouns are heads of noun phrases and therefore are necessary elements of noun phrases. A noun by itself may be a noun phrase.

[The *girl*] sang.

[The young *girl*] sang.

[*Girls* in white dresses] sang.

[*Girls*] like to sing.

(2) Pronouns

Most pronouns function as noun phrases rather than as nouns. Possessive forms or demonstratives function as determiners, components of noun phrases.

Ann gave [*us*] a gift.

[*His* voice] reminded me of [*my* brother's].

[*This* new magazine] is very thick.

(3) Articles

Articles act as determiners, components of noun phrases.

[*The* tall girl] is my sister.

She bought [*a* book].

(4) Appositives

An appositive phrase may be defined as a noun phrase that rephrases or explains another noun phrase.

STRUCTURE

[Anna, *my youngest sister*], was here this afternoon.
[Plankton, *very small marine organisms*,] support other life in the ocean.

cf) Other postmodifiers except for appositive phrases are covered in separate chapters.

As mentioned above, nouns, pronouns, articles, and appositives are components of noun phrases. This is the reason why they are treated in this chapter.

Nouns

Nouns are names of persons, things, and places. The two types of nouns are proper nouns and common nouns.

1. Proper Nouns

Proper nouns refer to specific persons, places, or things. Most of them are unique. (Examples are *Mark Twain* and *Grand Canyon*.) Proper nouns are never the focus of TOEFL questions.

2. Common Nouns

Common nouns refer to people, places, or things but are not the names of particular individuals or locations. (Examples are *cat*, *bravery*, *arm*, *apple*, and *coffee*.) Common nouns occur in two categories: countable nouns and non-countable nouns.

(1) Countable nouns

Countable nouns name things that it is possible to count. Countable nouns may be either singular or plural.

> I bought *a bag*.
> Mary bought *three bags*.

(2) Non-countable nouns

Non-countable nouns identify things that cannot be counted in the ordinary sense because they exist in collective form.

> They bought *furniture*.

Non-countable nouns ordinarily do not follow *a* or *an*, though they often follow *some* and *the*.

> I bought *a* salt. (incorrect)
> May I borrow *some* salt? (correct)

Non-countable nouns normally precede singular verbs.

> *Coal* is mined there.

Almost all TOEFL tests include at least one question that involves identifying errors in nouns. Most questions of this kind involve using the singular form in place of the plural, or vice versa. Some questions may involve identifying errors in plural forms of nouns.

Pronouns

A pronoun is a word that substitutes for a noun or another pronoun to avoid needless repetition.

Pronouns are usually classified as follows:

1. Personal Pronouns: *I, your, he, she, him, her, its, ours*

A personal pronoun applies to persons.

2. Reflexive Pronouns: *myself, himself, itself, themselves*

A reflexive pronoun reflects the action of the verb back to its subject.

3. Demonstrative Pronouns: *that, this, these, those*

A demonstrative pronoun indicates something or someone. Its chief function is to indicate to whom or what one refers.

4. Relative Pronouns: *who, whom, what, which*

A relative pronoun refers to a noun or a pronoun while serving as a conjunction in a sentence.

5. Indefinite Pronouns: *all, anybody, both, each, every, one, some, none*

An indefinite pronoun is indeterminate. It does not replace a specific noun. An indefinite pronoun may be an adjective or pronoun.

Questions related to pronouns occur only as questions of the error-identification kind. In most cases, such questions require you to identify errors in the use of the pronoun form.

Articles

Articles introduce nouns. Indefinite articles are *a* and *an*. The definite article is *the*.

1. Indefinite Article: *a /an*

An indefinite article indicates one person or thing, any one person or thing, or a certain person or thing. The indefinite article is used with singular, countable indefinite nouns and refers to things that are new to either the listener or the speaker.

This is what happens to *a* person whose kidneys start to fail.
I ate *a* banana for breakfast.

2. Definite Article: *the*

The definite article *the* indicates a definite person or object. *The* is applied to singular nouns, plural nouns, and uncountable nouns.

The man with gray hair is my father.
The ducks in the pond are feeding.
The water in the pot is boiling.

Although article usage is governed by many rules with numerous exceptions, TOEFL concentrates on testing fundamental knowledge, and most questions are simple.

 **Singular/Plural Noun**

Questions of this kind involve using the singular form in place of the plural, or vice versa.

Determiners before the underlined noun are essential to answering this pattern of question.

Determiners Used with Singular Nouns	Determiners Used with Plural Nouns
a /an	one of
one	other
another	many
each	few
every	a few
this	several
that	two, three, ten ···
	both
	a couple of
	a series of
	a number of
	numerous
	various
	a variety of
	dozens of
	hundreds of
	thousands of
	these
	those

Notes

1. Level of Difficulty: M-D
2. TOEFL questions involve singular nouns in place of plural nouns more frequently than plural nouns in place of singular nouns.
3. First, look at the determiner modifying the underlined noun.
4. Any countable singular noun which is underlined but not modified by a determiner (for example, *washing* *machine*), may be incorrectly used for a plural noun, because a determiner should precede a singular noun.

Examples

P22-1

Florida is one of <u>the most</u> popular vacation <u>region</u> in the country <u>and a</u> leading <u>producer</u> of
　　　　　　　　　A　　　　　　　　　　　　　B　　　　　　　　　　C　　　　　　　D
citrus fruits and vegetables.

[Explanation]

The correct pattern is *one of the* + superlative adjective + plural noun. Choice (B) is the correct answer because *region* (singular noun) is incorrect.

Correction: regions

P22-2

It is <u>physiologically</u> normal <u>for</u> an individual, 15 to 20 minutes <u>after eating</u> a meal, to have a
      A   B   C

high blood sugar <u>contents</u>.
               D

[Explanation]

In this sentence, the plural noun *contents* is incorrectly used for the singular noun *content*, for the determiner *a* is used.

Correction: content

P22-3

<u>Except for</u> such primitive egg-laying <u>mammal</u> as the duckbill <u>and</u> the echidna, mammalian
   A   B   C

embryos <u>develop</u> within the mother's uterus.
          D

[Explanation]

A countable singular noun cannot be used without any determiner, so the noun *mammal* should be pluralized. Choice (B) is the correct answer because *mammal* (singular noun) is incorrect.

Correction: mammals

STRUCTURE

Supplementary Exercise

Exercise 5.1

Correct any mistakes involving nouns in the following sentences.

1. Russia is the largest of all the nation in area, but not in population.
2. Both my brother moved to Seoul after they finished college.
3. The ice cream had melted in only a few minute.
4. The artist had two exhibition of paintings last year.
5. We have faced a lot of environmental problem.
6. Quartz is one of the most abundant mineral on Earth.
7. Dogs include such different breed as collies, Chindos, and Corgis.
8. Every items must be recorded.
9. There were ten families on our street, and each families had two child.
10. He has a special pills that he must take daily.

 **attern 23** **Incorrect Plural Form**

This pattern is related to plural forms of nouns.

Plural Forms of Nouns

1. Noun + -s / -es

chairs, friends, songs, toys, classes, watches

2. Irregular Plural Nouns

child − *children*	foot − *feet*	goose − *geese*
man − *men*	tooth − *teeth*	woman − *women*

3. Non-countable Nouns

A non-countable noun like *time, furniture* or *information* cannot occur in plural form. But determiners including *little, much*, and *a lot of* occur in front of non-countable nouns.

Determiners Used with Non-countable Nouns
much
little
a little
a great deal (amount) of
some*
a lot of*

* The expressions *some* and *a lot of* are also used with plural countable nouns.

4. Compound Nouns

In compound nouns, only the second noun takes the plural form.

telephone *poles*, tour *buses*, soup *pots*, guard *dogs*

5. Number Expression + Noun + Noun

When a number expression is combined with a noun serving as a modifier, the noun is singular and a hyphen is required.

We live in a two-*story* house.
She has a ninety-*year*-old grandmother.

Notes

1. Level of Difficulty: M-E
2. It is *always* wrong to put a plural noun after a determiner that modifies only non-countable nouns.

Examples

P23-1

Pollen grains <u>have provided</u> much <u>informations</u> <u>on</u> the origin and geologic history of
                    A   B   C

<u>terrestrial</u> plant life.
     D

[Explanation]
   The determiner *much* before the noun, *informations*, indicates that the noun is non-countable and
   therefore cannot be pluralized. Choice (B) is the correct answer because *informations* (plural) is
   incorrect.
   Correction: information

P23-2

Miniaturized <u>televisions</u> sets are <u>small enough</u> to <u>be held</u> in the hand <u>while being</u> watched.
                   A   B   C   D

[Explanation]
   The plural form of the compound noun *television set* is *television sets*, not *televisions sets*.
   Correction: television

Supplementary Exercise

Exercise 5.2
Supply the correct form of the underlined pronoun. Some are correct.

1. The man bought flowers and brought them home to <u>him</u> wife.
2. Despite <u>its</u> great age, the book is still worth reading.
3. Mary returned refreshed from <u>she</u> vacation.
4. Her grade was higher than <u>me</u>.
5. He was late because <u>him</u> car would not start.
6. All musicians have <u>theirs</u> favorite composers.
7. Many sick people actually think that <u>their</u> are healthy.
8. People in Canada as well as <u>them</u> in the U.S. speak English.
9. I hope to find the man who left <u>his</u> business card here.
10. The mountain was so beautiful that <u>it</u> became a favorite vacation spot.

 **Incorrect Pronoun Form**

Questions of this kind involve incorrect pronoun forms, such as an object form or a subject form in place of a possessive form, or a possessive pronoun used instead of a possessive adjective.

The form of a personal pronoun depends on how it functions in a sentence. The following table contains all personal pronouns in all genders, persons, numbers, and cases.

		Subject Pronoun	Possessive Adjective	Object Pronoun	Possessive Pronoun
First Person	Singular	I	my	me	mine
	Plural	we	our	us	ours
Second Person	Singular	you	your	you	yours
	Plural	you	your	you	yours
Third Person*	Singular/Feminine	she	her	her	hers
	Singular/Masculine	he	his	him	his
	Singular/Neuter	it	its*	it	—
	Plural/All Genders	they	their	them	theirs

* TOEFL questions deal only with third person pronouns, never first or second person.

* Never confuse "its" with "it's," a contraction of "it is."

1. Subject Pronouns

A subject pronoun serves as the subject of a clause.

He is not as old as *she* is.

2. Object Pronouns

An object pronoun serves as an object of a verb and an object of a preposition.

I like *you* as much as I do *them*.
She often talks with *me*.

3. Possessive Adjectives

A possessive adjective serves as an adjective to modify a noun and shows possession.

Bill and Sally love *their* new baby very much.

4. Possessive Pronouns

A possessive pronoun serves as a subject, the object of a verb, or the object of a preposition. Unlike possessive adjectives, a possessive pronoun may stand by itself, with no following noun to modify.

If you need a calculator, you can use *mine*.

Remember

Unlike subject, object, and possessive pronouns, *only* possessive adjectives may serve as adjectives. In other words, a possessive adjective may be followed by a noun.

Notes

1. Level of Difficulty: E-M
2. Most questions involve possessive adjectives: *it – its, hers – her, he – his, she – her.*
3. If a pronoun is underlined, first see that a noun follows the pronoun.

Examples

P24-1

<u>Every</u> sizable mass of liquid <u>tends to</u> flatten out, with <u>it</u> upper surface <u>as low as</u> possible.
  A   B   C   D

[Explanation]
> The pronoun *it* should be changed to the possessive form *its* to modify the noun phrase *upper surface*.
> Therefore, Choice (C) is the correct answer.
> Correction: its

P24-2

Like <u>he</u> fellow Regionalists, Thomas Benton <u>believed that</u> the <u>rural</u> areas of the South and
    A   B   C
Midwest <u>were</u> the source and strength of American art.
          D

[Explanation]
> The pronoun *he* should be the possessive form *his*. Choice (A) therefore is the correct answer.
> Correction: his

P24-3

Jane Addams <u>became</u> one of the most <u>deeply loved</u> and famous <u>Americans</u> of <u>hers</u> time.
              A   B   C   D

[Explanation]
> The pronoun *hers* should be the possessive form *her*. Therefore Choice (D) is the correct answer.
> Correction: her

Supplementary Exercise

Exercise 5.3
Underline any redundant pronoun.

1. Crowded on the window ledge, the birds they cheeped for food.
2. Any famous person who expects it privacy will probably be disappointed.
3. Bill and Sue they have both applied to the same university.
4. This plan it is sure to succeed.
5. Mr. Anderson, the housing director, he said there was one room left vacant.
6. The paper you wrote it is too short.
7. The woman who she wrote the novel is giving a talk tonight.
8. Sinclair Lewis, who wrote the novel *Main Street*, he also wrote *Babbitt*.
9. The most important thing right now it is to get well.
10. He talks too much, which it annoys me.

In questions of this kind, the incorrect type of pronoun is used, such as a personal pronoun used when a demonstrative pronoun is required.

Demonstrative Pronoun *those*

The demonstrative pronoun *those* can be followed by a phrase or clause that modifies it.

> The doctor spoke with *those* <u>on his staff</u>.
> The author thanked *those* <u>who bought his book</u>.

cf) The personal pronoun *them* cannot be modified by a phrase or clause.

> The doctor spoke with *them* <u>on his staff</u>. (incorrect)
> The author thanked *them* <u>who bought his book</u>. (incorrect)

Remember

The pronoun *those*, but not *them*, may precede a phrase, or a clause that modifies it.

Notes

1. Level of Difficulty: M-D
2. Commonly asked pairs include *those – them*.
3. If you see the pronoun *them* underlined, check to see if a phrase or clause modifies it.

Examples

P25-1

Many animals undertake migrations similar to <u>them</u> of birds; that is, they move
                                              A

<u>at regular</u> intervals <u>from</u> a breeding place to <u>another</u> location.
   B   C   D

[Explanation]
   The pronoun *them* is wrongly used for *those*. The phrase *of birds* cannot modify the pronoun *them*.
   Correction: those

P25-2

The biological control <u>systems that</u> regulate populations and societies of organisms are
                             A

<u>not as</u> clear-cut as <u>them</u> that control <u>specific</u> body functions.
   B   C   D

[Explanation]
   In this question, the pronoun *them* is incorrectly substituted for the pronoun *those* because *them* cannot be modified by a clause.
   Correction: those

Pattern 26   Incorrect Inclusion of Pronoun ★★☆☆☆

Questions of this kind involve the needless use of pronouns. For example, a personal pronoun may occur as a subject or object in a sentence where a noun subject or object exists already; or else may be used unnecessarily in an adjective clause.

1. Redundant Subject Pronoun

Skiers from all over the world *they* come to Colorado's mountains. (incorrect)
A unicycle is a cycle which *it* has only one wheel. (incorrect)

2. Redundant Object Pronoun

People sometimes call sharks *them* "wolves of the sea." (incorrect)
He has a skill that he knows how to use *it*. (incorrect)
Paul's photo had already been shown *it* to the policeman. (incorrect)

Notes

1. Level of Difficulty: E-D
2. In many independent clauses, a noun subject is repeated by a pronoun. Difficulty may occur, however, in an adjective clause where another pronoun repeats the relative pronoun used as a subject or object.
3. When two parts of the sentence, including a pronoun, are underlined, see if the sentence contains another subject or object.

Examples

P26-1

The term "genealogy" it is derived from the Greek words for "family" and "theory."
A   B   C   D

[Explanation]
In this sentence, the pronoun *it* is redundant, because the subject is the noun phrase *the term "genealogy."*
Correction: is

P26-2

Brittle stars, which they are also known as serpent stars, look like starfish with particularly
                A   B   C   D
skinny arms.

[Explanation]
The pronoun *they* in Choice (A) is redundant, because the relative pronoun *which* is the subject of the clause.
Correction: which

P26-3

Walking is something that almost any normal, healthy person can do it.
A   B   C   D

[Explanation]
The pronoun *it* in Choice (D) is redundant, because the relative pronoun *that* is an object of the verb *do*.
Correction: do

Pattern 27 Incorrect Choice of Article ★★★★☆

Questions of this kind involve an incorrectly used article such as *a* used instead of *an* (or vice versa), or *a* or *an* used instead of *the* (or vice versa).

1. Indefinite Article: *a/an*

(1) The indefinite article *a* precedes words starting with a consonant.

> *a* bird, *a* cup

(2) *An* precedes words starting with a vowel.

> *an* exit, *an* apple

a	one, universal, university, uniform, union, unique, unit, usage, useful, usual, utility, walk, yacht, yawn, yard, year, yellow, yolk
an	heir, honest, honor, hour, umbrella, ugly, unusual, X-ray, FBI agent, MA

Remember

Pronunciation, not the initial spelling (letter) of individual words, determines whether *a* or *an* is used.

2. Definite Article: *the*

The definite article *the* precedes the expressions mentioned below.

| (1) **Ordinal number** | *the* first |
| | *the* fourth year |

(2) Superlative forms
the most important factor
the longest river

(3) Decades, Centuries
the 1960s
the sixties
the twentieth century

(4) Quantifier + *of* + *the* + Noun
most of *the* pencils
many of *the* children
some of *the* time
all of *the* population
a few of *the* papers

(5) Time and position
the present, *the* past, *the* future,
the back, *the* beginning, *the* bottom, *the* center, *the* end,
the front, *the* middle, *the* rear, *the* side, *the* surface, *the* top

(6) Official names of cities, states or provinces, and nations
the United States of America
the state of Texas
the city of Baltimore

(7) Miscellaneous
the rate of, *the* rest of

Notes

1. Level of Difficulty: E-M
2. A frequent error is to use *a* in place of *an*. Another common error is to use *a* or *an* in place of *the*.
3. When you see the article *a* underlined, see if the word after it starts with a vowel or consonant. Then check to see if the expression begins with an ordinal number, an adjective in superlative form, et cetera.

Examples

P27-1

Cheese was <u>a</u> important item in the diet of the Vikings, <u>who from</u> about the 8th to the 10th
          A   B
century <u>sailed</u> the seas <u>on</u> long voyages.
          C   D

[Explanation]

In this question, the article *a* is incorrectly used for *an*, because the article occurs before the word *important*, which begins with a vowel sound. Therefore the correct answer is Choice (A).
Correction: an

P27-2

A <u>nuclear</u> family is <u>an</u> unit <u>consisting of</u> a father, a mother, and unmarried <u>children</u>.
  A   B   C   D

[Explanation]

The indefinite article *an* is incorrectly substituted for the indefinite article *a*. The word *unit* begins with a consonant sound. The correct answer therefore is Choice (B).
Correction: a

P27-3

Rhynia major, now extinct, <u>is</u> an example of <u>an</u> earliest known <u>vascular</u> plants,
                               A   B   C
<u>dating back</u> some 400 million years.
   D

[Explanation]

A superlative form, *earliest*, requires the definite article *the*. Therefore the correct answer is Choice (B).
Correction: the

 **Pattern 28** **Incorrect Omission of Article** ★★★☆☆

Questions in this category deal with incorrectly omitted articles. TOEFL tests your understanding of articles by omitting the necessary articles.

1. Indefinite Article

The indefinite article *a/an* must precede every singular (non-definite) countable noun. In other words, a singular countable noun without an article is incorrect.

> They do not eat pork in Saudi Arabia because they consider *a* pig *an* unclean animal. (correct)
> They do not eat pork in Saudi Arabia because they consider *a* pig unclean animal. (incorrect)

2. Definite Article

The definite article *the* must be used in the expressions (*the center, most of the pencils, the city of Baltimore,* and so on) mentioned in Pattern 27.

> Lake Superior is one of *the* five Great Lakes in North America. (correct)
> Lake Superior is one of five Great Lakes in North America. (incorrect)

Notes

1. Level of Difficulty: D-M
2. You may find it difficult to identify an incorrectly omitted indefinite article when a singular countable noun has a long modifier before it, or when it is unclear whether or not the noun is countable.
3. The two words on either side of the omitted article will be underlined in questions of this kind.

Examples

P28-1

In ski jumping the <u>jumper</u> slides <u>down prepared</u> track and <u>then leaps</u> into space from a <u>takeoff</u>
                      A   B   C   D
platform.

[Explanation]
> The indefinite article *a* should be inserted before the noun phrase *prepared track*, because the noun *track* is a singular countable noun. The correct answer is Choice (B).
> Correction: down a prepared

P28-2

All but <u>forgotten</u> by the public in his <u>later years</u>, Herman Melville in modern times is
          A   B
regarded <u>as</u> one of <u>great</u> writers in American literature.
          C   D

[Explanation]
> The definite article *the* should not be omitted from the expression *one of the* + plural noun. Therefore the correct answer is Choice (D).
> Correction: the great

Pattern**29**   Incorrect Inclusion of Article   ★★★☆☆

In questions of this kind, an article is incorrectly included when it is not required.

No article is used in the following cases:

1. Before Plural Countable Nouns (not specified by a modifier)

Major events can often be anticipated. (correct)
A major events can often be anticipated. (incorrect)

2. Before Non-countable Nouns (not specified by a modifier)

Hydrogen is a highly flammable gas. (correct)
The hydrogen is a highly flammable gas. (incorrect)

3. After Possessive Form of a Noun or Pronoun

Canada's history is long and complex. (correct)
Canada's the history is long and complex. (incorrect)

Governments usually act in *their national* interest. (correct)
Governments usually act in *their the national* interest. (incorrect)

Notes

1. Level of Difficulty: M-D
2. When phrases including articles are underlined, see whether or not the article is required.

Examples

> **P29-1**
>
> The Hudson River <u>originates</u> in <u>a small</u> postglacial lakes in the Adirondack Mountains <u>near</u>
>   A   B   C
> Mount Marcy, <u>the highest</u> point in New York.
>   D

[Explanation]
The indefinite article *a* in (B) is incorrectly included because the following noun is plural, *lakes*.
Correction: small

> **P29-2**
>
> <u>Provincetown</u>, at the north end of the peninsula of Cape Cod, <u>is</u> famous <u>for</u> its art schools,
>   A   B   C
> <u>the exhibits</u>, galleries, and shops.
>   D

[Explanation]
The definite article *the* in Choice (D) is not needed. Therefore Choice (D) is the correct answer.
Correction: exhibits

STRUCTURE

P29-3

The gold will not react with common acids, but it is attacked by a three-to-one mixture of
   A   B   C   D
hydrochloric and nitric acids.

[Explanation]

The definite article *the* is not needed because *gold* is a non-countable (material) noun.

Correction: Gold

Supplementary Exercise

Exercise 5.4
Correct any mistakes involving articles in these sentences.

1. A state of Virginia, in the United States, is called the "Old Dominion."
2. An university education is one of the necessities for the position these days.
3. The Wright Brothers made their famous flight in an early twentieth century.
4. A hour passed before we received his reply.
5. A tallest building in Manhattan is the Empire State Building.
6. Newfoundland is an large island in eastern Canada.
7. He spent many years in a unpleasant job.
8. A egg is said to provide a complete diet.
9. A first lesson is about author Harold Wright.
10. Be sure to wear a overcoat.

Exercise 5.5
Cross out unneeded articles or insert articles which are needed.

1. The secretary finished her the work for the day.
2. His most famous book was first that he wrote.
3. Tokyo has one of highest population densities in the world.
4. It is reward for your effort.
5. I put a new cartridges in the printers.
6. A juggler must keep several objects in the air at time.
7. Don Quixote is character in a novel by Cervantes.
8. He arrived at the theater in middle of the performance.
9. Few of people who can draw actually do so.
10. The borough of Manhattan, in New York City, is built on large island.

 **Pattern 30** ## Appositive Missing

Questions of this kind involve supplying missing appositives.

Appositives

1. In most cases, appositives immediately follow the noun that they rephrase. Sometimes, however, they immediately precede the noun.

    > Abraham Lincoln, *a lawyer from Illinois*, became president of the United States.
    > *A lawyer from Illinois*, Abraham Lincoln became president of the United States.

2. Appositives are in fact reduced adjective clauses. (See also Chapter 2.)

    > Mercury, *which is the only liquid metal*, has the symbol Hg. (adjective clause)
    > Mercury, *the only liquid metal*, has the symbol Hg. (appositive)

3. Although appositives are usually separated from the rest of the sentence by commas, short appositives are not.

    > *Novelist Sinclair Lewis* won a Nobel Prize.

Notes

1. Level of Difficulty: M-E
2. All or part of an appositive phrase may be absent.
3. If commas surround the blank, first check to see if an appositive is absent.

Examples

P30-1

Fossils, _____, are usually found in sedimentary rocks.

(A) and organisms that once lived on earth remain
(B) once lived on earth the remains of organisms
(C) the remains of organisms that once lived on earth
(D) which the remains of organisms that once lived on earth

[Explanation]
In this case, the clause has a subject and verb. A modifier may occupy the blank. Choices (A) and (B) are incorrect because they create double verbs. Choice (D) is incorrect because the adjective clause is incomplete. If the verb *are* were inserted after the relative pronoun *which*, then it would be a correct answer. Choice (C), an appositive phrase, is therefore the correct answer.

P30-2

The Caldecott Medal was named in honor of Randolph Caldecott, _____ 19th-century English illustrator of children's books.

(A) who a
(B) was the
(C) a
(D) in the

[Explanation]
In this question, the phrase after the comma may be a modifier which renames *Randolph Caldecott*. Choice (A) is not correct because the adjective clause is incomplete; *who was a* would be a correct answer to this question. Choice (B) is incorrect because the clause has double verbs. Choice (D) is incorrect because the prepositional phrase beginning with *in* has an awkward meaning. Choice (C) is therefore the correct answer.

STRUCTURE

Pattern Drill for Patterns 22-30

1. The name "football" <u>has been</u> applied <u>to</u> several different <u>game</u>, <u>including</u> soccer and rugby.
                 A   B   C   D

2. <u>In the</u> 1940s the American <u>painter</u> Jackson Pollock departed from <u>him</u> earlier naturalistic
     A   B   C
   style and <u>began to paint</u> in a semiabstract expressionistic style.
             D

3. <u>Many</u> water birds have to run <u>over surface</u> of the water with wings <u>flapping</u> until they gain
      A   B   C
   enough speed to <u>lift themselves</u>.
              D

4. Orangutans <u>prefer</u> trees, <u>where</u> they travel easily at five to six miles <u>a</u> hour by <u>swinging</u>
               A   B   C   D
   along on the branches.

5. <u>Except</u> for a few <u>venture</u> into <u>other</u> settings, William Faulkner wrote <u>about his</u> hometown of
    A   B   C   D
   Oxford, in Lafayette County, Mississippi.

6. The United Nations was <u>formed</u> by the <u>victorious</u> nations of World War II <u>to keep</u> the peace
                       A   B   C
   <u>they</u> efforts had won.
    D

7. Ancient <u>heaps</u> of discarded mollusk shells <u>have been</u> found in coastal areas <u>throughout</u> the
           A   B   C
   world, including <u>them</u> of China, Japan, Peru, Brazil, and Denmark.
                D

8. <u>To aid</u> motorists traveling in foreign <u>country</u>, an international system of road signs using
     A   B
   symbols, <u>rather than</u> word explanations, <u>was adopted</u>.
             C   D

9. <u>Almost</u> every society <u>has developed</u> <u>a</u> distinct legal system, usually closely related to <u>it</u>
    A   B   C   D
   customs.

10. Noam Chomsky's work <u>virtually</u> defined the methods of linguistic <u>analysis</u> used in <u>a second</u>
                           A   B   C
    half of the <u>20th</u> century.
            D

11. <u>Although</u> wheat is the most famous of Canada's <u>the farm</u> products, <u>its sales</u> make up only
      A   B   C

    about 15 to 20 percent of the total farm <u>cash income</u>.
                                         D

12. Incas were <u>ignorant</u> of writing, <u>but they</u> kept records by means of <u>a</u> intricate system of
              A   B   C

    <u>knotted</u> cords.
      D

13. Human <u>speech</u> is only one small part of the <u>communicative inventory</u> of chirps, snorts,
          A   B

    whistles, gestures, and <u>barks which</u> we find <u>in rest</u> of the animal kingdom.
                            C   D

14. <u>More</u> than a thousand enzymes that exist <u>in nature</u> are <u>usually named</u> for <u>theirs</u> substrates,
      A   B   C   D

    with -*ase* as a suffix.

15. *The Black Crook*, _____ in 1866, was the most successful musical
    performance in the United States up to that time.

    (A) was an extravaganza produced
    (B) an extravaganza was produced
    (C) to produce an extravaganza
    (D) an extravaganza produced

16. The <u>upland region</u> of the Ozark Mountains <u>rises</u> <u>like</u> an island <u>in midst</u> of the Middle
           A   B   C   D
    Western plains.

17. <u>Balloon</u> pilot in the U.S. must be <u>at least</u> sixteen years <u>old</u> and <u>be licensed by</u> the Federal
      A   B   C   D
    Aviation Administration.

18. About 6 mm <u>long</u>, the potato beetle is yellow <u>with</u> three black <u>stripe</u> on <u>its</u> wing covers.
              A   B   C   D

19. Most of <u>familiar</u> spiders in the United States <u>have</u> bodies about <u>half an</u> inch <u>long</u>.
           A   B   C   D

20. When <u>an</u> well is <u>sunk deep</u> in the earth, water sometimes flows up <u>naturally</u>, <u>as it does</u>
          A   B   C   D
    from a spring.

STRUCTURE

21. The <u>distinction</u> <u>between</u> sex, which is biological, and gender, which <u>is</u> cultural, is an
        A   B   C

    important <u>ones</u>.
               D

22. Electrons <u>revolve around</u> the central nucleus in <u>a series</u> of orbits that <u>reflect</u> differences in
                     A   B   C

    <u>them</u> energy levels.
     D

23. Gulls <u>usually fly</u> with their bills <u>on a line</u> with the body, <u>while</u> terns carry <u>their</u> pointed
              A   B   C   D

    downward.

24. <u>Since</u> water is <u>much heavier</u> than air, marine organisms <u>are under</u> much more pressure
       A   B   C

    than <u>them</u> on land.
          D

25. Many <u>kinds</u> of frogs and toads have long, <u>sticky</u> tongues that <u>their</u> use <u>for catching</u> food.
          A   B   C   D

26. Jessamyn West is best <u>remembered for</u> *Friendly Persuasion*, <u>which</u> gathered stories that
                          A   B

    reflect <u>hers</u> Quaker <u>heritage</u>.
          C   D

27. As a protest against <u>slavery</u>, Henry David Thoreau, writer and <u>the naturalist</u>, actually
                      A   B

    <u>went to prison</u> rather than pay taxes to a government that allowed <u>it</u>.
       C   D

28. <u>An</u> American cartoonist, Walt Disney, <u>made</u> the world <u>love</u> an ugly duck and dozens of
     A   B   C

    other animal <u>character</u>.
               D

29. Louis Pasteur <u>was</u> the <u>first</u> person <u>to use them</u> scientific principles in <u>making</u> vaccines.
              A   B   C   D

30. Sympathetic nerves <u>usually prepare</u> the body for such emergencies as <u>a temperature</u>
                    A   B

    extremes, <u>lack of</u> water, or <u>physical</u> harm.
             C   D

31. A movie <u>consists of</u> a rapid series of still <u>picture</u> <u>flashed</u> on the screen with about 1 / 60 of a
                A   B   C
    second of <u>complete</u> darkness after each one.
                  D

32. <u>The body</u> of a starfish <u>consists of</u> a central disk from <u>which radiate</u> a number of <u>arm</u>.
     A   B   C   D

33. As a means of <u>defraying</u> the increasing expenses of government, taxes on income have
                    A
    <u>become</u> an important part of the fiscal system of <u>practically</u> every modern <u>nations</u>.
     B   C   D

34. <u>The</u> first textbooks in the United States were <u>modeled after</u> catechisms, short <u>book</u>
    A   B   C
    covering religious principles <u>written</u> in question-and-answer format.
                               D

35. Most professional designers <u>specialize in</u> a <u>particular</u> field <u>such as</u> dresses, <u>furnitures</u>,
                                  A   B   C   D
    automobiles, or books.

36. <u>While</u> Illinois is shedding its <u>the smokestack</u> industries, <u>it</u> is attracting foreign <u>direct</u>
    A   B   C   D
    investment in its place.

37. A <u>smooth</u> surface, <u>such as</u> the side of a cliff, <u>it reflects</u> sound waves, and we hear the
        A   B   C
    reflection <u>as an echo</u>.
               D

38. There are several <u>type</u> of influenza, <u>caused</u> by different viruses that <u>are present</u> in
                     A   B   C
    secretions and <u>other discharges</u> from the nose and mouth of an infected person.
                      D

39. Heather is a small evergreen shrub, <u>sometimes rising</u> only <u>a few</u> inches above the ground,
                                         A   B
    but often growing to <u>a height</u> of three <u>foot</u> or more.
                    C   D

40. Genetic characteristics are determined by DNA, _____ giant molecule in the cell
    nucleus composed of two long, twisted chains of nucleotides.

    (A) a
    (B) is a
    (C) that the
    (D) for the

41. Instead of valves, the trombone has movable slide that can be pushed away from or drawn
       A   B   C   D

    toward the player.

42. When the Spaniards conquered Peru in 16th century, they found the Incas using llamas
                     A   B   C

    as beasts of burden.
      D

43. Times Square was named for the old Times Tower, which it stands on the southern triangle
                  A   B   C   D

    at 42d Street.

44. One of the greatest fiction writer in American literature, Nathaniel Hawthorne is
            A   B   C

    best-known for *The Scarlet Letter* and *The House of the Seven Gables.*
      D

45. From year to year the Earth's climate varies, gradually bringing about many dramatic
          A   B   C

    change.
      D

46. Rather than avoiding references to mass culture, pop artist accepted and used them:
               A   B   C

    soft-drink bottles, gas stations, comic strips, billboards, airplanes, and hamburgers.
                                      D

47. Noam Chomsky set out his theory of transformational grammar in *Syntactic Structures*,
    _____ that revolutionized the development of theoretical linguistics.

    (A) is a book
    (B) so a book
    (C) a book in
    (D) a book

48. In he day James Fenimore Cooper was best known as the author of the *Leatherstocking*
       A   B   C

    Tales, five novels of frontier life.
             D

49. When the moon is at it maximum distance from the earth, the moon is smallest in the sky.
      A   B   C   D

50. Many of the world's most important and predictable winds they have been given their own
       A   B   C   D

    names.

Mini-Test 5

1. Legal monopolies are created how the government grants patents
      A   B   C

   or copyrights to inventors, authors, and others.
              D

LinguaForum

2. In the course of its development, most insects pass through a
              A   B

   complete metamorphosis that is controlled by the interaction of
               C

   at least three hormones.
      D

LinguaForum

3. The Allegheny Plateau covers the entire eastern part of Ohio
               A   B   C

   and extensive into West Virginia and Pennsylvania.
        D

LinguaForum

4. The moon is much smaller than the earth, with a diameter of
   only 2155 miles _____ with the earth's 7,900 miles.

   (A) is compared
   (B) comparing
   (C) compared
   (D) to compare

LinguaForum

5. Because <u>emotion</u> moves us <u>to do</u> the things we do, <u>and some</u>
            A   B   C

psychologists <u>have compared</u> it to the mainspring of a watch.
            D

LinguaForum

6. Early in the 19th century, _____ disagreed on
whether lowly forms of life could spring from dead matter or
whether they all had to evolve from previously existing life.

(A) when biologists
(B) biologists
(C) for biologists
(D) biologists who

LinguaForum

7. September was the seventh month of the <u>Roman calendar</u>,
                                        A

which <u>begins</u> <u>with</u> March, <u>but</u> is the ninth month of the
       B   C   D

present-day calendar.

LinguaForum

8. The brain is _____ of the central nervous system and
the control center for all the body's voluntary and involuntary
activities.

(A) that is the major organ
(B) as a major organ
(C) the major organ
(D) where a major organ

LinguaForum

9. Andrew Carnegie believed <u>that</u> it was the <u>solemn</u> duty of a rich
                                          A   B

man <u>to redistribute</u> his wealth in the <u>interest public</u>.
        C   D

LinguaForum

Time   Help   Confirm   Next

10. Venus is the second planet in order of distance from the sun,
and it comes _____ the earth than does any other
planet.

(A) closely
(B) close to
(C) the closer
(D) closer to

LinguaForum

Time   Help   Confirm   Next

STRUCTURE

Chapter 6 Adjective Phrases and Comparisons

What are the patterns about?

Pattern 31 Adjective Phrase Missing
Pattern 32 Comparison Missing
Pattern 33 Incorrect Choice of Comparison
Pattern 34 Incorrect Comparative / Superlative Form

TOEFL may include questions that involve supplying a missing adjective phrase serving as a modifier, but more frequently includes questions that require supplying missing expressions involving comparisons, or identifying incorrect use of comparisons.

Adjective Phrases

1. Form

Adjective phrases include an adjective, optionally preceded and followed by modifying elements.

ADJECTIVE PHRASE		
(premodifier)	Adjective	(postmodifier)
incredibly	cold	
	pleasant	enough
too	hot	to be enjoyable

2. Function

Adjective phrases may function as complements and modifiers.

(1) As complements
Subjective complement

> The essay was [very funny].
> He appears [very ill].

Objective complement

> Most people consider that hotel [luxurious indeed].
> She made the garden [beautiful].

(2) As modifiers
Premodifier

> He bought some [very expensive] furniture.

Postmodifier

> She told a story [familiar to everyone].
> Bill is the person [responsible for computer repair].

Adjective phrases that serve as complements are described in Patterns 4 and 5 of Chapter 1, which discuss clause elements. Pattern 31 involves only adjective phrases that serve as modifiers.

Comparisons

When most adjectives and a few adverbs are involved, three types of comparison are possible.

1. Equative Degree

The equative degree represents equality.

> His car is *as big as* mine.

2. Comparative Degree

The comparative degree compares unequal things.

> He is *older than* I am.

3. Superlative Degree

The superlative degree compares three or more unequal things and shows that something has a special quality.

> She is *the tallest girl* in our school.

 **Pattern 31** **Adjective Phrase Missing** ★★☆☆☆

In questions of this kind, adjective phrases modifying a noun are missing.

In most cases, adjective phrases that postmodify a noun are actually reduced adjective clauses. (See Chapter 2.) To reduce an adjective clause to an adjective phrase, delete an adjective clause marker (such as *which* or *who*) and the verb *be*.

> He has a name *which is familiar to me.* [Adjective clause]
> He has a name *familiar to me.* [Adjective phrase]
>
> Bill is the person *who is responsible for computer repair.* [Adjective clause]
> Bill is the person *responsible for computer repair.* [Adjective phrase]

cf) Adjective phrases functioning as premodifiers of noun phrases are usually tested in error-identification type (see Pattern 48).

> He bought some [very expensive] furniture. (correct)
> He bought some [very expensively] furniture. (incorrect)

Notes

1. Level of Difficulty: M-E
2. If a blank follows a noun phrase, then a full or reduced adjective clause (adjective phrase, appositive phrase, participial phrase, or prepositional phrase) may complete the missing section of the sentence. If the correct answer is an adjective phrase, then an incomplete adjective clause may be presented as a distractor.

   Position of an adjective phrase serving as a postmodifier:

S + [Adjective phrase] + V
S + V + C + [Adjective phrase]
S + V + O + [Adjective phrase]

Example

> **P31**
>
> The human hand, _____ delicate manipulation as well as powerful gripping actions, is an extremely versatile tool.
>
> (A) is capable of
> (B) capable of
> (C) has capability to
> (D) it is capable

[Explanation]
In this question, the noun phrase before the verb *is*, *The human hand ~ actions*, is a subject of the clause, and so a phrase to postmodify the noun *hand* may come in the blank. Therefore Choice (B) is the correct answer.

 **Comparison Missing**

In questions of this kind, expressions involving comparisons are missing.

1. Equative

The following rule usually governs this type of comparison.

> Subject + Verb + *as* + Adjective (+ Noun) + *as* + Noun/Pronoun (+ Verb)

Jack is *as tall as* Bill (is).
Mary has *as much money as* John (does).

Sometimes *so* instead of *as* may precede the adjective in negative comparisons.

He is *not* { *as* / *so* } *talkative as* his brother.

2. Comparative

The following rule usually governs this type of comparison.

> Subject + Verb + { Adjective + *-er* (+ Noun) / *more/less* + Adjective } + *than* + Noun/Pronoun (+ Verb)

Yesterday was *colder than* today (is).
A car has *fewer seats than* a bus (does).
That computer is *less expensive than* this one (is).

Intensifiers like *much, very much,* or *far* may premodify the comparative.

The test was <u>(very) much</u> *easier than* I expected.
He sings <u>far</u> *better than* he used to.

cf) Double Comparative

> *The* + Comparative + Subject + Verb, *the* + Comparative + Subject + Verb

The first comparative represents cause, whereas the second comparative represents result.

The longer you practice, *the more successful* you will be.
The higher he climbed, *the farther* he could see.

3. Superlative

The following rule usually governs this type of comparison.

> Subject + Verb + *the* + { Adjective + *-est* / *most/least* + Adjective } + { *in* + Singular countable noun / *of* + Plural countable noun / Adjective clause }

Jill is *the youngest child* <u>in the family</u>.
This cloth is *the most durable* <u>of all</u>.
He is *the most articulate person* <u>I know</u>.

The intensifier *far* or *by far* may premodify the superlative.

That was <u>by far</u> *the best story* that I have read in years.

Notes

1. Level of Difficulty: M-E-D
2. TOEFL questions often involve missing comparatives or superlatives among comparisons.
3. Missing superlatives (and sometimes missing comparatives) are often involved with word order questions (see Chapter 10).
4. When expressions in choices include comparisons, check to see if clues such as *more, less, than, as, of all,* or *one of* are present in the sentence.

Examples

P32-1

Decimals are easier to write and to print _____ .

(A) common fractions
(B) than are common fractions
(C) than fractions are common
(D) common as fractions

[Explanation]

The expression that contains comparisons is missing. The comparative *easier* must accompany *than,* so Choices (A) and (D) are not correct. Choices (B) and (C) are paired with the comparative form *easier,* but Choice (C) is incorrect because it is illogical. Therefore Choice (B) is appropriate.

P32-2

The gorilla is the _____ to humans with the exception of the chimpanzee.

(A) relative that living closest
(B) living relative is closest
(C) closest living relative
(D) closest living relative that

[Explanation]

The superlative degree follows the pattern *the* + ⋯ *-est/most* ⋯ + noun. Therefore Choice (C) is the correct answer.

P32-3

The larger the area of a lens, _____ it gathers and focuses upon a point in the image.

(A) the most light
(B) as does the light
(C) more than
(D) the more light

[Explanation]

This question involves a double comparative construction. The double comparative follows the pattern: *the* + comparative (+ subject + verb), *the* + comparative (+ subject + verb). Therefore Choice (D) is correct.

Pattern 33 Incorrect Choice of Comparison ★★☆☆☆

In questions of this kind, one of the three forms of comparisons is used incorrectly in place of another.

John has _more_ CDs than Janet. (correct)
John has _much_ CDs than Janet. (incorrect)

Mammals have _fewer_ legs than insects. (correct)
Mammals have _few_ legs than insects. (incorrect)

She works _far better than_ she used to. (correct)
She works _far better as_ she used to. (incorrect)

Notes

1. Level of Difficulty: M-E
2. Many questions involve using the equative adjective form in place of the comparative form. _As_ may be used in place of _than_, or vice versa.
3. If you see an adjective underlined, look first to see if words like _as_ or _than_ follow or precede the adjective. The comparative form ... _-er_ or _more_ ... must accompany _than_, and the equative form must include _as_ ... with _as_. This is how you can tell from the question when one degree structure should be substituted for another.

Examples

P33-1

Ozone depletion <u>results</u> <u>when</u> ozone destruction occurs <u>at</u> a <u>fast rate</u> than ozone
                        A   B   C   D
production.

[Explanation]
The equative form _fast_ in Choice (D) is incorrectly used because _than_ must accompany the comparative form _faster._
Correction: faster rate

P33-2

Just as more sugar <u>will dissolve</u> in hot tea <u>as</u> in cold, <u>mineral components</u> in the magma
                           A   B   C
become <u>less soluble</u> as the magma cools.
              D

[Explanation]
The word _as_ is incorrectly used for _than_ because the comparative form _more_ modifies the noun _sugar._ Therefore Choice (B) is the correct answer.
Correction: than

STRUCTURE

Pattern 34 — Incorrect Comparative /Superlative Form

Questions of this kind involve incorrect forms of comparatives or superlatives, such as *more bigger* or *most smallest*.

Regular Form

The following table summarizes general rules for the comparative and superlative forms of adjectives.

	Equative	Comparative	Superlative
one-syllable adjectives, and two-syllable adjectives ending in -y	base form	adjective + *-er* + *than*	*the* + adjective + *-est*
	big happy	bigger than happier than	the biggest the happiest
most two- and three-syllable adjectives	base form	*more* + adjective + *than*	*the* + *most* + adjective
	costly expensive	more costly than more expensive than	the most costly the most expensive

Irregular Form

Some adjectives use irregular forms for the comparative and superlative.

bad	worse	worst
good	better	best
little	less	least
many	more	most
much	more	most

Remember

The suffix *-er* means *more*. That is why they can never be used together.
The suffix *-est* means *most*. That is why they can never be used together.

Notes

1. Level of Difficulty: E-E
2. The error most often encountered is *most + -est*.
3. If underlined, *most + -est* or *more + -er* is probably the correct answer.

Examples

P34-1

William Lloyd Garrison was <u>one</u> of the <u>most earliest</u> <u>leaders</u> of the antislavery <u>movement</u> in
                     A   B   C   D

the United States.

[Explanation]
The phrase *most earliest* is not correct, so Choice (B) is the answer.
Correction: earliest

P34-2

Penguins' bones are <u>more heavier</u> than <u>those of</u> other <u>birds</u> <u>to reduce</u> buoyancy and make
                      A   B   C   D

diving easier.

[Explanation]

More heavier is incorrect, because the word *more* would be redundant, so Choice (A) is the correct
answer.

Correction: heavier

Supplementary Exercise

Exercise 6.1
Complete the sentences with the correct form of the adjectives and adverbs in parentheses.

1. Bill felt _____ (bad) than anyone else about losing the tournament.
2. He paints portraits _____ (well) as Goya.
3. The _____ (much) you practice writing, the better you will do it.
4. Jack is the _____ (tall) man that I know.
5. A new computer is much _____ (powerful) than an earlier one.
6. Henry is the _____ (smart) of the two boys.
7. Carla studies _____ (easily) than her brothers.
8. You have _____ (few) math courses as I.
9. Last month was _____ (rainy) as this month.
10. Hawaii is _____ (far) from California than Nevada.

Exercise 6.2
Correct any errors involving comparisons in the following sentences.

1. The shorter the book, the quick it is to read.
2. Toni runs fast than any other girl on the team.
3. This new computer is lesser expensive than the previous model.
4. Their new apartment is as large than any other apartment in the building.
5. New Jersey is the more densely populated state in the United States.
6. The weather today is more better than yesterday.
7. This diamond is probably the most famousest in the world.
8. This summer will certainly be much hotter as last summer.
9. The longer we stayed, the best the concert became.
10. Heather's grades are no high this year than they were last year.

STRUCTURE

1. Steel, which is refined from iron, _____ cast iron, particularly in structural strength.

    (A) is more durable
    (B) than durable
    (C) is more durable than
    (D) more durable than is

2. The <u>common</u> plants and animals <u>we know</u> are <u>much</u> <u>more larger</u> than viruses and microbes.
         A   B   C   D

3. When a horse eats more grain _____, it turns the extra grain into fat and stores the fat in tissues.

    (A) used
    (B) than it can use
    (C) as its use
    (D) that can use it

4. <u>Light</u> travels <u>as</u> slowly in water than <u>in</u> air; the speed is <u>even</u> less in glass.
      A   B   C   D

5. If a man is to remain alive and comfortable, he must lose heat to his surroundings about as fast _____ he generates it.

    (A) so
    (B) as
    (C) since
    (D) once

6. <u>Because</u> it is <u>heated</u> from within, a homeotherm is <u>warm</u> at the core of <u>its body</u> than at the
      A   B   C   D
   periphery.

7. _____ the temperature of the star, the more energy it gives off, and the more this energy is concentrated in high-frequency radiation.

    (A) When the high
    (B) Of the high
    (C) The highest
    (D) The higher

8. An average <u>planetary</u> nebula <u>has a</u> diameter of slightly <u>little</u> than half a light-year and a
                    A   B   C
   mass only 20 percent <u>that of</u> the sun.
                            D

9. One of _____ in library training in the United States was Melvil Dewey, who established the first training program for librarians in 1887.

   (A) the earliest pioneer is
   (B) earlier pioneers
   (C) pioneered early
   (D) the earliest pioneers

10. Although Conrad Marca-Relli is classed with the abstract expressionists, he is _____ strident than most of them in his technique.

    (A) far less than
    (B) very
    (C) much less
    (D) least

11. The story of the Vikings or Norsemen is _____ by Americans than that of the Celts.

    (A) more likely to be known
    (B) to be known
    (C) be likely to know
    (D) know more

12. The paired kidneys are located _____ as a person's elbows if he holds his arms at his sides.

    (A) high
    (B) about as high
    (C) even higher
    (D) much higher than

13. A nuclear reactor is a unit constructed to enclose all the equipment and material _____ to produce and control the process of nuclear fission.

    (A) necessarily
    (B) is necessary
    (C) necessary
    (D) which necessary

14. A large oyster may filter _____ a barrel of water through its body in a day.

    (A) much as
    (B) than
    (C) more than
    (D) most

15. A <u>world globe</u> shows <u>that</u> there is twice as <u>much land</u> in the Northern Hemisphere
           A   B   C

    <u>than</u> south of the equator.
      D

16. Carbon <u>provides</u> the framework <u>for</u> <u>many</u> compounds than <u>any other</u> element.
          A   B   C   D

17. Since the Pacific Ocean is predominantly rimmed by subduction zones, earthquakes
_____ in the Pacific Ocean than they are in the Atlantic Ocean.

   (A) more common
   (B) are far more common
   (C) much more common
   (D) by far the most common

18. Air temperatures are warmer in summer and colder in winter over the continents
_____ over the oceans at the same latitude.

   (A) than they are
   (B) than do they
   (C) in that they do
   (D) they are

19. Alexander Hamilton <u>was one</u> of the <u>most youngest</u> and most brilliant <u>founders</u> <u>of the</u> United
                               A   B   C   D
States.

20. Animals that live in hot climates <u>characteristically</u> have <u>exposed</u> surface areas <u>large</u> than
                                            A   B   C
animals <u>that live</u> in the cold.
                 D

Mini-Test 6

1. Ants, honeybees, and wasps are <u>called social</u> insects <u>because</u>
                               A   B

they live together <u>highly</u> <u>organized</u> societies.
                   C   D

LinguaForum

2. Grizzlies and polar bears are short <u>tempered</u> and savage, <u>but</u>
                                    A   B

most bears are peaceable <u>animal</u> if they and their <u>young</u> are not
                              C   D

disturbed.

LinguaForum

3. The <u>reliability</u> of a <u>measuring</u> instrument or of a test <u>refers</u> to
      A   B   C

how <u>consistent</u> it measures something.
       D

LinguaForum

4. _____ provided by geology, biochemistry, and the study
of fossils suggests that early living forms must have resembled
certain one-celled plants and animals that exist today.

     (A) Evident
     (B) Evidence
     (C) Evidence is
     (D) Although evidently

LinguaForum

STRUCTURE

5. A fossil may be the preserved remains of an organism itself, <u>an</u>
                                                            A

impression of it in rock, or preserved traces <u>were left</u> by an
                                                      B

organism <u>while</u> it was <u>alive</u>.
        C   D

LinguaForum

6. The dinosaurs were _____ large group of reptiles that were
the dominant land vertebrates for most of the Mesozoic era.

(A) as
(B) a
(C) whether
(D) among

LinguaForum

7. In 1987 the Reagan Administration <u>negotiated</u> a free trade
                                        A

<u>treaty</u> with Canada, <u>what</u> opened up the borders <u>beginning</u>
  B   C   D
January 1, 1989.

LinguaForum

8. Most building codes in the United States require concrete
foundations and do not permit buildings _____ on
wood piling alone.

(A) which set
(B) setting
(C) to be set
(D) are set

LinguaForum

9. If a <u>pitch</u> throws <u>four balls</u> to any one batter, the batter is <u>given</u>
        A   B   C

a walk to first base; that is, he goes to first without <u>having</u> to hit
                                            D

and run.

LinguaForum

10. _____ the earth's atmosphere, it is heated by
friction and appears as a glowing streak of light called a meteor.

   Ⓐ There is a meteoroid entering
   Ⓑ A meteoroid which enters
   Ⓒ A meteoroid enters
   Ⓓ If a meteoroid enters

LinguaForum

STRUCTURE

Chapter 7 Verb Phrases

What are the patterns about?

Pattern 35 Incorrect Verb Form
Pattern 36 Incorrect Tense
Pattern 37 Active/Passive Confusion

TOEFL includes many questions about verb phrases. The questions may require supplying missing verb phrases or identifying errors in verb form, tense, and voice.

Verb Phrases

1. Form

VERB PHRASE	
auxiliary	**main verb**
	eat
can	eat
was	eating
has been	eaten
	eating

2. Function

Verb phrases function as the verb element in a clause: that is, as the central and indispensable element. It is impossible to formulate a clause without a verb phrase.

> Julie [works] at an office downtown.
> The bus [will arrive] in ten minutes.

Questions involving missing verb phrases are discussed in Pattern 2.

cf) In this book, a verb phrase means a single verb or an auxiliary + verb combination that serves as a verb element in a clause. Do not mistake a VERB PHRASE for a PREDICATE (verb and combinations of object, complement, and adverbial).

Subject	Predicate
She	can play the flute.
Julie	works at an office downtown.
The bus	will arrive in ten minutes.

3. Components

(1) Auxiliary (Helping) verbs

Auxiliary verbs, also known as helping verbs, include the auxiliary and modal auxiliary.

- **Auxiliary:** *be, do, have*

  The house *was* built last year.
  I *do* not believe it.
  We *have* had a good time.

- **Modal auxiliary:** *can, could, may, might, must, shall, should, will, would*

  A modal expresses attitude, mood, or feeling. Modals are always followed by the base form of a verb.

  Bob *can read* Russian. (correct)
  Bob *can reads* Russian. (incorrect)

  Double modals may not be used.

  Bob *will can* read Russian. (incorrect)
  Bob *will be able to* read Russian. (correct)

(2) Main verbs

Main verbs may be classified as follows:

- **Transitive verbs**

  The action of a transitive verb is directed to a receiver. An object must follow the verb.

- **Intransitive verbs**

  An intransitive verb does not direct its action to a receiver. An intransitive verb may indicate a state or condition and may include a linking verb which connects the subject of a sentence to a complement (such as *appear, be, become, feel, get, look, prove, remain, seem, sound, taste, turn*). Linking verbs, however, are often placed in a third category called copular verbs.

As a rule, the main verbs largely determine clause types such as SVO or SVOC, as mentioned in Chapter 1.

Intransitive	1) SV	The door *opens*.
Verb	2) SVC	He *appears* happy.
	3) SVO	They *grow* their own food.
Transitive	4) SVOO	Lois *gave* Bob a smile.
Verb	5) SVOC	They *made* Bill the new president.

Some verbs may require different clause types.

Her husband *is running*. [SV]
Her husband *is running* a business. [SVO]

Tense

Verbs use 12 tenses to indicate the time of an action, possession, or state of being.

	Present	**Past**	**Future**
Simple Tense	She *watches* television.	She *watched* television.	She *will watch* television.
Continuous Tense	She *is watching* television.	She *was watching* television when I returned.	She *will be watching* television by the time I return.
Perfect Tense	She *has already watched* television.	She *had already watched* television when I returned.	She *will have* already *watched* television by the time I return.
Perfect Progressive	She *has been watching* television for an hour.	She *had been watching* television for an hour when I returned.	She *will have been watching* television for an hour by the time I return.

Voice

Voice indicates the relationship between the subject and verb in a sentence.

1. Active Voice

A verb is in active voice when the subject performs the action.

Thomas Edison *invented* the incandescent light bulb.

2. Passive Voice

A verb is in passive voice if the subject is acted upon.

The incandescent light bulb *was invented* by Thomas Edison.

 **Incorrect Verb Form**

Questions of this kind involve identifying errors in verb forms. Errors in verb form occur where one form is used when another is required. For example, a participle form may be used in place of a present or past form, a present form instead of a base form, or a present or past form in place of a participle form.

Verbs exhibit five forms: base, present, past, present participle, and past participle. Five forms of certain verbs are shown below:

Base Form	Present Form	Past Form	Present Participle	Past Participle
be	am/is/are	was/were	being	been
have	have (has)	had	having	had
speak	speak(s)	spoke	speaking	spoken
go	go(es)	went	going	gone

1. Base Form

> modal + base form

    should keep (correct)
    should kept (incorrect)

2. Present Participle

Continuous Tense

> *be* + present participle

    is speaking (correct)
    is speak (incorrect)

3. Past Participle

Perfect Tense

> *have* + past participle

    have given (correct)
    have give (incorrect)
    have giving (incorrect)

Passive

> *be* + past participle

    is trusted (correct)   are driven (correct)   to be found (correct)
    is trust (incorrect)   are drove (incorrect)   to be find (incorrect)

4. Present / Past Form

The present and past form can be a finite verb, which has a tense and inflects, or agrees with its subject. In turn, the finite verb can function as a verb (*am/are/is, was/were, works, runs*), the basic element of the clause.

    She *runs* a mile every morning.
    Mammoths *lived* in what is now Siberia.

Notes

1. Level of Difficulty: M-E
2. Note the following patterns: modal auxiliary + base form, *have* + past participle (in perfect tense), *be* + past participle (in passive), and *be* + present participle (in continuous tense).
3. Remember that present or past form may serve as a verb in a clause, but the present/past participle *(going/gone)* may NEVER serve as a verb in a clause.

Examples

P35-1

<u>A</u> spectroscope can <u>told</u> astronomers <u>whether</u> a star is moving toward or <u>away from</u> the earth
A   B   C   D
by means of the Doppler effect.

[Explanation]
> The past participle form *told* should be *tell*, base form. The correct pattern is modal + base form.
> Correction: tell

P35-2

When a plane <u>flies</u> east or west around the world, <u>its passengers</u> find on <u>their</u> return that
               A   B   C
they have <u>gain</u> or lost a day.
         D

[Explanation]
> The verb form *gain* is incorrectly substituted for the past participle form *gained*. The present perfect form is *have* + past participle.
> Correction: gained

P35-3

The Range and Township grid system is <u>use</u> mainly on maps of <u>central</u> and western North
                                       A   B
America <u>to locate</u> and describe <u>tracts</u> of land.
        C   D

[Explanation]
> The verb form *use* should be *used*, past participle form. The correct passive pattern is therefore *be* + past participle.
> Correction: used

P35-4

<u>A</u> legend <u>says that</u> Hanson Crockett, a sea captain from Maine, first <u>putting</u> a hole <u>in</u> a
A   B   C   D
doughnut.

[Explanation]
> The present participle *putting* in (C) cannot be a verb, so it should be the simple past form *put*.
> Correction: put

 **Incorrect Tense**

Questions of this kind involve verb tenses. For example, past tense may be used in place of present perfect tense, or vice versa.

Tense-related errors on TOEFL usually involve the simple past or present perfect tense.

1. Commonly Asked Tenses

(1) Simple past tense

The past tense is appropriate when the action occurred or existed entirely in the past.

> I *went* to Japan last week.
> He *visited* relatives in England.

(2) Present perfect tense

The present perfect tense occurs only when the action started in the past and continues.

> I *have been* a teacher for two years.
> She *has written* stories since she was very young.

2. Sequence of Tenses

(1) The verb tense used in a sentence must be consistent with the time element of the entire sentence. In many cases, words or expressions that serve as *time indicators* determine the time element of a sentence.

Time Indicator	Example
Past Tense Indicators	*in 1995, in January, three years ago, last week, once, in those days*
Present Perfect Tense Indicators	*since 1995, already, for ten years*

(2) The verb in a subordinate clause must agree with the principal verb. In other words, principal verbs in the present tense may have subordinate verbs in any tense; but **principal verbs in the past-time tense must be followed by subordinate verbs signifying past time.**

> Ben *told* me that he *was* feeling ill.
> She *worked* at a pizza restaurant when she *was* a student.
> The Huns *were* outstanding warriors whose accomplishments *astonished* the Romans.

(3) Verbs in clauses linked by coordinating or correlative conjunctions must be parallel in tense.

> Bill *enjoyed* the book and *recommended* it to his friends.
> She not only *wrote* the text but also *illustrated* it.

Notes

1. Level of Difficulty: M-E
2. Most TOEFL questions involving verb tenses may use tenses that do not agree with the time frame in the rest of a sentence.
3. Checking time indicators is very important to answering this type of question.

Examples

P36-1

On May 20–21, 1927, Charles Lindbergh <u>has flown</u> a small <u>silvery monoplane</u>, the Spirit of
$\qquad\qquad\qquad\qquad\qquad\qquad\qquad\qquad$ A $\qquad\qquad\qquad\qquad$ B

St. Louis, <u>nonstop</u> <u>from</u> New York City to Paris.
$\qquad\qquad$ C $\qquad$ D

[Explanation]

The tense of the verb, *has flown,* does not agree with the time marker, *on May 20–21, 1927,* indicating the past.

Correction: flew

P36-2

The earth's magnetic field was <u>probably</u> <u>initiated by</u> the sun's magnetic field when the earth
$\qquad\qquad\qquad\qquad\qquad\qquad\qquad$ A $\qquad\qquad$ B

<u>is</u> still a <u>swirling ball</u> of dust and gas, billions of years ago.
C $\qquad\qquad$ D

[Explanation]

The present tense verb *is* of choice (C) is incorrect because it does not agree with the principal verb *was* and is not consistent with the time indicator, *billons of years ago.*

Correction: was

P36-3

Television <u>played</u> a <u>major role</u> in the life of Americans since 1950, <u>affecting</u> everything from
$\qquad\qquad$ A $\qquad\qquad$ B $\qquad\qquad\qquad\qquad\qquad\qquad\qquad\qquad$ C

the conduct of politics <u>to</u> eating patterns.
$\qquad\qquad\qquad\qquad\qquad$ D

[Explanation]

The past tense *played* is incorrect because it does not agree with the time indicator *since 1950,* representing the present perfect tense.

Correction: has played

Supplementary Exercise

Exercise 7.1

Insert the correct form if the underlined verb is incorrect.

1. He cannot <u>get</u> to work because his car will not start.
2. He was delighted to be <u>grant</u> a scholarship.
3. Our director, who <u>reaching</u> age 65 next year, intends to retire.
4. That tree has <u>stood</u> there since my grandparents were little.
5. Having read the book, I was greatly <u>disappointed</u>.
6. She is the best singer I have ever <u>meet</u>.
7. We must <u>to look</u> there for fresh fruit.
8. The author was <u>misunderstand</u> when his book was published.
9. Regulations <u>requiring</u> that each office should submit a report.
10. Joan was <u>listen</u> to music when the telephone rang.

 **Active / Passive Confusion**

In questions of this type, active verb forms are used where passive forms are required, and vice versa.

1. Active

The subject is the doer of the action and occurs before the verb. The object of the action occurs following the verb.

> Bill *threw* the ball.

2. Passive

The subject of the sentence is the receiver of the action (originally the direct or indirect object of the verb), and the doer of the action either occurs after the verb or is omitted. This is why only transitive verbs, which accompany an object, can be used in the passive voice.

> The ball *was thrown* by Bill.
> The ball *was thrown*.

Remember

As a rule, a passive verb may not have an object immediately after it.

Notes

1. Level of Difficulty: M-D
2. A passive verb may be also used incorrectly in place of an active verb in an adjective clause. In this case, you should check the relationship between the verb and the word (the antecedent) to which the relative pronoun refers.
3. Check to see if the object follows the verb when an active or passive verb is underlined.

Examples

P37-1

<u>In</u> marathon dancing, <u>if</u> the dancers' knees touched the floor, they <u>eliminated</u> <u>from</u> the
A   B   C   D
contest.

[Explanation]
This question involves active/passive confusion. *Eliminated* should be changed to the passive form *were eliminated*, because *they* is the object of the action *eliminate*, not a subject.
Correction: were eliminated

P37-2

The United States completed <u>its</u> southeastern <u>expansion</u> in 1819, <u>when</u> Spain <u>was given</u> up
                          A   B   C   D
East Florida.

[Explanation]
In this question, the passive verb, *was given*, is used in place of the active verb, *gave*. However, the sentence contains a direct object, *East Florida*. Direct objects come after active verbs, not passive verbs.
Correction: gave

Supplementary Exercise

Exercise 7.2
Supply the correct tense using the verb in parentheses.

1. I _____ (own) this house since 1975.
2. Janet was making breakfast when her sister _____ (call).
3. At one time, Mr. Brown _____ (manage) this business.
4. Maria _____ (have) dinner with her parents last night.
5. He _____ (visit) the Empire State Building in New York City three years ago.

Exercise 7.3
Supply the correct tense if the underlined verb is incorrect.

1. I finished work for the day, locked my filing cabinet, and <u>go</u> home.
2. When I saw an ambulance outside, I <u>knew</u> something was wrong.
3. The readout showed only five zeroes, which <u>puzzle</u> Bill.
4. They were pleased when their plan <u>works</u> out.
5. Al told Bob that Ellen <u>had found</u> a job.

Exercise 7.4
Correct any mistakes involving active or passive in the following sentences. Some are correct.

1. Insects consume huge amounts of crops every year.
2. This announcement should print in the newspaper.
3. The courier was delivered a package to our office.
4. We attended the game which had been postponed because of rain.
5. On the fishing trip, we found that the fishing laws allowed only a few fish to catch.
6. Three students sent home because of illness.
7. Light traffic was allowed us to arrive ahead of time.
8. This is a fragrance which extracts from flowers.
9. The bird swallowed a fish which it had just caught.
10. The company has passenger airplanes which are carried lots of people.

1. First words have <u>reported</u> as appearing in <u>normal</u> children <u>from</u> as young as 4 months to as
     A   B   C
old as 18 months, or <u>even older</u>.
       D

2. The word "utopia" was first <u>use</u> by the <u>Englishman</u> Sir Thomas More in <u>his</u> book *Utopia*,
         A   B   C
published <u>in</u> Latin in 1516.
    D

3. Until <u>a few</u> centuries ago areas of the world were almost <u>cutting</u> off one from another <u>due to</u>
   A   B   C
the <u>difficulties</u> of transportation.
   D

4. <u>Since</u> the first McDonald's restaurant opened <u>in the 1950s</u>, fast-food chains have <u>grow</u> into
 A   B   C
a multibillion-dollar <u>industry</u>.
     D

5. Herds of bison, or American buffalo, once moved <u>southward</u> for 200 to 400 miles <u>as</u> winter
               A   B
<u>draws</u> near and started north again with <u>the return</u> of mild weather.
 C   D

6. Minnesota's "sky-blue waters," dense <u>forests</u>, and <u>pleasant</u> summer weather have
            A   B
<u>been made</u> it <u>a</u> resort state.
 C D

7. <u>When</u> the Revolutionary War <u>broken out</u> at Lexington and Concord, April 19, 1775,
 A   B
<u>few colonists</u> desired <u>independence</u>.
 C   D

8. <u>In the</u> course of <u>their</u> evolution humans, like all animals, have been continually <u>face</u> with
 A   B   C
the problem of <u>adapting to</u> their environment.
     D

9. Digestion is <u>the process</u> which <u>is changed</u> food into <u>soluble</u> products <u>that</u> can be used by the
    A   B   C   D
body.

10. In 1894, the <u>control</u> and development of the modern Olympic Games was <u>entrust</u> to the
    A   B
I.O.C., <u>with</u> headquarters <u>to be established</u> in Switzerland.
   C   D

11. Thomas Benton <u>has emerged</u> <u>as</u> the <u>spokesman</u> for the American Regionalist <u>painters</u>
                               A   B   C   D

    about 1929.

12. It is possible to see through <u>transparent substances</u> more or less <u>clearly</u> because light can
                                       A   B

    <u>passes</u> through <u>them</u> without being scattered or stopped.
      C   D

13. Algonquin Indians had lived in <u>what is</u> now Connecticut <u>for two</u> centuries before English
                                        A   B

    <u>settlers</u> first <u>arriving</u> in 1635.
      C   D

14. <u>It</u> is thought <u>that</u>, <u>between</u> 350 and 250 million years ago, South America and Africa <u>are</u>
   A   B   C   D
    joined together.

15. The science of mineralogy <u>is</u> concerned <u>with</u> the natural substances called minerals, which
                                 A   B

    <u>making</u> up the rocks, clays, sand, and <u>similar</u> materials of the earth.
      C   D

16. The <u>present</u> development of Arkansas' <u>natural resources</u> began in 1887 when John C.
       A   B
    Banner <u>discovers</u> bauxite ore <u>near</u> Little Rock.
             C   D

17. <u>According to</u> the fossil record, ferns first <u>to appear</u> almost 400 million years ago, and <u>they</u>
     A   B   C
    are still <u>relatively abundant</u>.
                D

18. <u>Botanists</u> have traditionally <u>divide</u> the angiosperms <u>into</u> two <u>groups</u>: the monocotyledons
     A   B   C   D
    and the dicotyledons.

19. Since the <u>extinction</u> of the dinosaurs 65 <u>million</u> years ago, mammals <u>were</u> the dominant
               A   B   C
    vertebrates <u>on</u> Earth, including terrestrial, aerial, and aquatic forms.
              D

20. Greek sculpture rose to its highest <u>achievement</u> in <u>the 5th</u> century B.C., when the spirit of
                                  A   B
    Greece <u>itself</u> <u>is</u> at its height.
            C D

Mini-Test 7

1. Homeostasis, the <u>maintain</u> of a <u>constant</u> internal environment,
       A   B
<u>is</u> the result of a variety of <u>processes</u> within the animal body.
C   D

2. Deserts have also <u>be</u> defined <u>as</u> places without
                     A   B
<u>enough vegetation</u> to support a human <u>population</u>.
         C   D

3. The Civil Rights Movement inspired many <u>other</u> minority
                                           A
groups <u>to organizing</u> to seek recognition and rights, and <u>they</u>
          B   C
achieved <u>considerable</u> success.
             D

4. Silent trade is a specialized form of barter _____ no
   verbal communication takes place.

   (A) in which
   (B) where there is
   (C) which has
   (D) whose

STRUCTURE

5. Henry Louis Gehrig <u>was</u> one of the <u>few men</u> in baseball history
　　　　　　　　　　　　A　　　　　　　　B

<u>to hit</u> four <u>home run</u> in one game.
　C　　　　　D

6. A fat molecule consists of three molecules of fatty acid
_____ to one glycerol molecule.

(A) which joined
(B) joined
(C) joins
(D) joining

7. Molecules of air <u>scatters</u> the shorter wavelengths of light more
　　　　　　　　　A

<u>than</u> the longer wavelengths, which is <u>the reason that</u> the sky
　B　　　　　　　　　　　　　　　　　　　　C

appears blue <u>in color</u>.
　　　　　　D

8. As a result of the Women's Movement, which began in the
1960s, _____ many women in the legal and medical
professions by the 1990s.

(A) when
(B) there were
(C) was
(D) for

9. The Maya practiced agriculture, built <u>a great</u> stone buildings
                                          A

and pyramid temples, and made <u>use of</u> a form of hieroglyphic
                               B

writing <u>that</u> has now <u>largely</u> been deciphered.
        C   D

10. Father Louis Hennepin, _____, was the first
white man to view the falls of the Niagara River in 1678.

- (A) and the priest to accompany La Salle
- (B) the priest, accompanied La Salle
- (C) the priest who accompanied La Salle
- (D) accompanied La Salle

STRUCTURE

Chapter (8) Conjunctions and Parallelism

What are the patterns about?

Conjunctions
Pattern 38 Conjunction Missing
Pattern 39 Incorrect Conjunction
Pattern 40 Incorrect Inclusion/Omission of Conjunction
Parallelism
Pattern 41 Missing Items Involving Parallel Structures
Pattern 42 Errors with Parallel Structures

Both types of questions in the Structure Section involve conjunctions. Among the most frequently mentioned items are Parallel structures, which also are tested in both types of questions.

Conjunctions

Conjunctions are words and expressions that are used to connect words, phrases, or clauses.

1. Coordinating Conjunctions

Coordinating conjunctions link equivalent structures: single words, phrases, or clauses.

> Steven Spielberg *and* George Lucas are famous directors.
> You can have dinner now *or* postpone it.
> I enjoy traveling, *but* my husband prefers to stay at home.
> She must have passed the test, *for* she looks happy.
> It is late, *so* I should go home now.

2. Correlative Conjunctions (Paired Conjunctions)

Correlative conjunctions occur in two paired parts and connect equivalent structures: that is, single words, phrases, or clauses.

> Sue speaks *both* French *and* German fluently.
> *Either* he *or* I must approve the purchase.
> *Neither* he *nor* I have authority to decide.
> This newspaper is sold *not only* in the U.S., *but also* in Canada.

3. Subordinating Conjunctions

Subordinating conjunctions join dependent clauses to independent clauses (adverb clauses or noun clauses).

(1) Adverb clause markers

> *When* school is finished, I want to work abroad.
> I like his music *because* it is so cheerful.
> *Though* it is a holiday, I will go to the office today.

(2) Noun clause markers

> The point is *that* no one will benefit.
> *Whether* she leaves or stays is undecided.
> I asked her *if* she had visited Seoul.

All the conjunctions mentioned above involve the linking of units, but coordinating or correlative conjunctions involve coordination, whereas subordinating conjunctions involve subordination. Chapter 2 discusses subordination using subordinating conjunctions.

Coordination and Parallelism

Coordination involves a relation between two or more units parallel in structure. These units may be whole clauses but in many cases are smaller units such as noun phrases or verb phrases.

1. Coordination of Clauses

(1) Independent clauses

> [Autumn arrived], and [the harvest began].

(2) Dependent clauses

> The doctors believe [that her condition is improving], and [(that) she will soon get well].

2. Coordination of Infinitive, Gerund, and Participial Phrases

(1) Infinitive phrases

> I have asked him [to visit us in person] or [(to) write a letter].

(2) Gerund phrases

> Bill enjoys [fishing in the lake] and [hiking in the woods].

(3) Participial phrases

> Insurance paid to rebuild homes [damaged by wind] or [wrecked by heavy rain].

3. Coordination of Predicates

> Bill [fried an egg] and [made coffee].
> Anna [is busy] but [will soon be finished].

In most cases, shared auxiliaries in conjoined predicates are omitted:

> By now, they must have [finished work] and ((must) have) [gone home].

4. Coordination of Verb Phrases

(1) Verb phrases

All my ancestors [were born,] [lived,] [died,] and [were buried] in this town.

(2) Portions of verb phrases

The city [can] and [must] recover from its present crisis.

Coordination of main verbs, with shared auxiliary, occurs often:

We have [copied] and [filed] the reports.
Mary is [admired] and [respected] by the man.

5. Coordination of Noun Phrases

(1) Noun phrases

He asked me to mail [two letters,] [a package of books,] and [a postcard].
The car was repaired by [Allan,] [Tom,] and [my brother].

(2) Portions of noun phrases

My [brothers] and [sisters] all have blond hair.
I found the [dishes] and [glasses] stored in the cabinet.

6. Coordination of Adjective Phrases and Adjectives

The novel was [long] and [very boring].
My dog is [very healthy,] [very strong,] and [ready to enter the dog show].
His [calm] and [confident] manner reassured everyone.

7. Coordination of Adverb Phrases

She wrote her report [quickly] but [quite accurately].

8. Coordination of Prepositional Phrases and Prepositions

He voted [for the first proposal] but [against the second proposal].
He climed [up] and [over] the wall.

Remember

Elements linked by coordinating or correlative conjunctions require a similar or parallel grammatical form.

Coordination and Ellipsis

In many cases, when *and, or,* or *but* coordinates clauses, a second clause is reduced by an ellipsis.

[One author has written a novel,] and [the other △ a collection of essays].
[My mother lived to age 90,] and [my father △ to 95].
[Tom has looked more relaxed,] and [Jane △ more cheerful,] since they moved to the country.

 **Conjunction Missing**

This kind of questions involves missing coordinating and correlative conjunctions. Questions may ask about coordinating conjunctions only or the conjunction (+ subject) + verb combination.

1. Coordinating Conjunctions

The following table is a list of coordinating conjunctions.

Conjunction	Use	Example
and	addition	We played the piano *and* went shopping.
but	contrast	I like tea, *but* my wife prefers coffee.
yet		He was badly injured, *yet* he survived.
or	alternative	You can order fried fish *or* chicken for dinner.
for*	reason	He must be sick, *for* he did not come to work today.
so	result	I don't think it's important, *so* I'll ignore it.

*For is used to link clauses, not individual words or phrases.

He must be sick, *for* did not come to work today. (incorrect)

2. Correlative Conjunctions

The following table is a list of correlative conjunctions.

Conjunction	Use	Example
both ··· and	addition	*Both* Harry *and* Sue got an A on the test.
not only ··· but also		I bought *not only* gloves, *but also* a scarf.
either ··· or	alternative	*Either* you win *or* you lose.
neither ··· nor	negative alternative	She *neither* drinks *nor* smokes.
not ··· but	exclusion/ inclusion	A prairie dog is actually *not* a dog, *but* a rodent.

Notes

1. Level of Difficulty: M-E
2. When a coordinating conjunction is the correct answer, adjective clauses or participial phrases may occur as distractors.
3. Read the whole sentence after inserting all choices into the blank.
4. If choices include correlative conjunctions, then check to see if another part of the conjunctions occurs in the given sentence, such as *either ··· or* or *both ··· and.*

Examples

P38-1

The male elk is about five feet in height at the shoulders _____ may weigh from 600 to 800 pounds.

(A) it
(B) although
(C) also
(D) and

[Explanation]

In this question, a conjunction is missing. Choice (A) is incorrect because two clauses cannot be joined without a connective word. Choice (B) is incorrect because it forms an adverb clause without a subject. Choice (C) is incorrect because the conjunctive adverb, *also*, cannot connect two phrases. Therefore, Choice (D) is correct.

P38-2

Skates are similar to rays in appearance and feeding habits, _____ a whip-like tail and stinging spines.

(A) which they lack
(B) lack
(C) they lack
(D) but they lack

[Explanation]

Choice (A) is incorrect because the adjective clause introduced by *which* is incorrect. Choice (B) is incorrect because two main clauses cannot occur without any connective word. Choice (C) is incorrect because two clauses are joined without any connective word. Therefore, Choice (D) is correct.

P38-3

Most of the earth's deserts are strung along the Tropic of Cancer and the Tropic of Capricorn between 20° and 35° in _____ north and south latitudes.

(A) both
(B) which both
(C) both of
(D) the both

[Explanation]

In this question, a correlative conjunction is missing. The correlative conjunction *both* follows the pattern *both ··· and* (as in *both dictionaries and encyclopedias*), and *both (of)* specific plural nouns (*both of my sisters* or *both my sisters*). Therefore the correct answer is Choice (A).

Pattern 39   Incorrect Conjunction   ★★★☆☆

Questions in this category involve incorrectly used conjunctions, such as incorrect correlative conjunctions, incorrect coordinating conjunctions, coordinating conjunctions used in place of subordinating conjunctions, or conjunctive adverbs used in place of coordinating conjunctions.

Conjunctive Adverbs

(1) The following table is a list of frequently used conjunctive adverbs.

Addition	Contrast	Effect	Condition	Time
also besides moreover furthermore in addition	however instead nevertheless	therefore thus consequently	otherwise	then meanwhile

(2) The conjunctive adverbs mentioned above cannot take the place of any conjunction.

> The lungs absorb oxygen *and* expel carbon dioxide. (correct)
> The lungs absorb oxygen *also* expel carbon dioxide. (incorrect)

(3) Semicolons should be used with conjunctive adverbs.

> Porous materials absorb sound; *therefore*, they are used to line recording studios.

Notes

1. Level of Difficulty: M-E
2. Many of the questions involve the pairs *both … and, neither … nor, not … but,* and *not only … but also.*

Examples

P39-1

A first-degree burn is one that reddens the skin for does not produce blisters.
     A   B   C   D

[Explanation]

In this question, the coordinating conjunction *for* is incorrectly used for the conjunction *but*. The conjunction *for* is used to introduce a clause explaining why you made the statement in the main clause. Furthermore, *for* cannot connect phrases, but clauses.
Correction: but

P39-2

An allergy is <u>an</u> abnormal reaction to substances <u>that</u> are neither harmful <u>or</u> infectious to
                 A   B   C

<u>most people</u>.
  D

[Explanation]

This question involves the incorrect use of the correlative conjunction *neither* ··· *nor*.

Correction: nor

P39-3

<u>Despite</u> lack of <u>written records</u>, sociologists and anthropologists <u>generally</u> agree <u>but</u> the first
  A   B   C   D

social unit was the family headed by a parent.

[Explanation]

In this question, the coordinating conjunction *but* is incorrectly used for the subordinating conjunction *that*, which introduces a noun clause.

Correction: that

P39-4

Grasslands are <u>some</u> of <u>the most</u> valuable <u>places</u> on earth, both ecologically <u>also</u>
                 A   B   C   D

economically.

[Explanation]

In this question, the conjunctive adverb *also* is incorrectly used for the conjunction *and*.

Correction: and

Supplementary Exercise

Exercise 8.1
Insert conjunctions in the blanks.

1. The floodwaters receded overnight, _____ now the town must clear away debris.
2. Mary plays _____ the piano but also the violin.
3. _____ Bob nor I am skilled with computers.
4. I visited _____ Japan and Russia last year.
5. Hiking _____ swimming are both attractions of this resort.

Pattern 40 Incorrect Inclusion/Omission of Conjunction

★★☆☆☆

In questions of this kind, a conjunction is incorrectly used when not needed, or else a conjunction is incorrectly omitted when it is necessary.

1. Incorrect Inclusion

(1) A main clause can have no conjunction when an adverb clause precedes or follows the main clause.

> When he fell, I laughed. (correct)
> When he fell, *and* I laughed. (incorrect)

(2) No conjunction is needed before the subject of a main clause, even if it is accompanied by a phrase.

> Looking at her watch, Wanda saw that she was late for class. (correct)
> Looking at her watch, *and* Wanda saw that she was late for class. (incorrect)

2. Incorrect Omission

Two main clauses can be connected only with a conjunction.

> Max needed a new car, *but* he could not afford to buy it. (correct)
> Max needed a new car, he could not afford to buy it. (incorrect)

Notes

1. Level of Difficulty: M-E
2. Questions involve incorrectly included conjunctions more often than incorrectly omitted conjunctions.
3. If a conjunction and a subject are both underlined, check to see if the conjunction is required or not.

Examples

P40-1

When two <u>protons</u> fuse, <u>but one</u> of the particles <u>loses</u> its <u>positive</u> charge and becomes a
　　　　　　　A　　　　　　B　　　　　　　　　C　　　　D
neutron.

[Explanation]

In this question, the conjunction *but* is incorrectly included. Because an adverb clause precedes the main clause, the conjunction is not needed.

Correction: one

STRUCTURE

P40-2

In *This Side of Paradise*, a novel of student life at Princeton, <u>and F. Scott Fitzgerald</u> wrote <u>of</u>
A   B

the <u>great current</u> American <u>phenomenon</u>, the petting party.
  C   D

[Explanation]

In this question, the conjunction *and* is incorrectly included where it is not needed. *F. Scott Fitzgerald* is a subject of a main clause, and therefore no conjunction is needed before the subject.

Correction: F. Scott Fitzgerald

P40-3

The I.O.C. as a whole meets annually, <u>a</u> meeting can <u>be convened</u> at any time that <u>one-third</u>
          A   B   C

of the members <u>request</u>.
      D

[Explanation]

In this question, a conjunction is incorrectly omitted. Two main clauses cannot be joined without any conjunction, so the conjunction *and* or *but* should be inserted before the second clause beginning with the subject *a meeting*.

Correction: and a (*OR* but a)

Supplementary Exercise

Exercise 8.2
Insert a correction if an underlined word is used incorrectly.

1. He did the job both quickly <u>also</u> quietly.
2. Garnet is not only an attractive mineral <u>and also</u> important as an abrasive.
3. A binary computer can register either 1 <u>nor</u> 0, but nothing inbetween.
4. Some computers are not digital <u>and</u> analog in nature.
5. The car was so big <u>but</u> it could not fit through the door.

Exercise 8.3
Correct any mistakes in the following sentences.

1. He sent her a book in the mail, it never arrived.
2. Whoever can solve this problem and will get an award.
3. Although the job paid well, but it was also difficult.
4. We lived in a town that had no fire department and no bank.
5. To forecast economic trends, and economists use sophisticated computer models.

 **Missing Items Involving Parallel Structures**

Questions of this kind require supplying items in parallel structures.

1. Parallel Structure with Coordinating Conjunctions

A, B, and /or C (elements in series)

The elements of a deed are *motive, means*, and *opportunity.*

Bill is *patient, experienced*, and *calm.*

This task must be completed *quickly, accurately*, and *efficiently.*

The maid *changed the bed, cleaned the bathroom*, and *vacuumed the carpet.*

The duties of the government are *to make laws, to maintain the courts*, and *to provide for national defense.*

Editorial work includes *writing articles, proofreading text*, and *selecting illustrations.*

A and /or B

What I want is *to be a doctor* or *to become an author.*

Bill works *slowly* but *methodically.*

Children enjoy *flying kites* and *climbing trees.*

The medicine must be *stirred* in water and *diluted* before it is drunk.

He is considered *a man of dignity* but *a man of boldness* too.

Nouns in parallel structure must be parallel in their meaning as well as their form.

Astrophysics is based on the sciences of *physics, mathematics*, and <u>*astronomy*</u>. (correct)

Astrophysics is based on the sciences of *physics, mathematics*, and <u>*astronomers*</u>. (incorrect)

2. Parallel Structure with Correlative Conjunctions

You should either *get a job* or *go to graduate school.*

I want to be both *healthy* and *successful.*

A greedy man knows neither *happiness* nor *security.*

Volcanoes not only *produce ash* but also *expel molten rock.*

He was thinking not *about work* but *about vacation.*

3. Parallel Structure with Comparisons

To produce is as important as *to consume.*

Playing tennis is more fun than *watching it on TV.*

The two things being compared must also have parallel meanings.

The temperature on the mountain top is lower than *that at sea level.* (correct)

The temperature on the mountain top is lower than *at sea level.* (incorrect)

The population of New York is greater than *that of Seattle.* (correct)

The population of New York is greater than *Seattle.* (incorrect)

Notes

1. Level of Difficulty: M-E

2. As a rule, questions involve elements in a series.

Example

P41

The lyrics of Emily Dickinson are short, compressed, rhymed, and metrical; whereas Walt Whitman's lines, in free verse, are loose, unrhymed _____.

(A) or diffusion
(B) are somewhat diffused
(C) and a diffuse style
(D) and somewhat diffuse

[Explanation]

In this case, Choices (A) and (C) are incorrect because the elements in the series are not parallel, and Choice (B) is incorrect because it has an unnecessary finite verb. Choice (D) is correct because the elements *loose, unrhymed,* and *somewhat diffuse* are parallel.

Supplementary Exercise

Exercise 8.4
Change the words in parentheses into correct, parallel forms.

1. I made every effort to buy the book or (borrow) it from a public library.
2. Watching performances on TV and (attend) live performances are both rewarding.
3. The windows rattled in their frames, and the building (tremble) during the earthquake.
4. Many ecologists think we should protect the global environment by reducing "greenhouse gas" emissions, (plant) as many trees as possible, and halting the destruction of forests.
5. Eric opened the door, walked in, and (look) around.

Exercise 8.5
Change the following sentences into correct, parallel forms.

1. Not all parents raise their children wisely and careful.
2. He likes to swim, jog, and fencing.
3. Medicines can protect us from debilitation, disease, and dead.
4. He does his job quietly, quickly, and efficient.
5. The owl opened its eyes, looked around, and to spread its wings.
6. Her husband is kind, soft-spoken, and patience.
7. The article is very long, detailed, and boredom.
8. The building was planned, constructed, and equipment to serve many different uses.
9. I think that violent motion pictures do viewers more damage than beneficial.
10. Attending a live concert is better than watch one on television.

attern42 Errors with Parallel Structures ★★★★★

Questions of this kind require identifying errors in parallel structure.

Notes

1. Level of Difficulty: M-E
2. Questions usually involve elements in a series.
3. In most cases, questions involve a noun used in place of an adjective and vice versa, or else a noun used instead of a verb and vice versa.

Examples

P42-1

<u>In the early</u> 1900s, the United States Weather Bureau <u>measured</u> wind velocity, temperature,
     A   B

and <u>humid</u> with instrument <u>carrying</u> kites.
     C   D

[Explanation]

In this sentence, the elements *wind velocity*, *temperature*, and *humid* in the series joined with *and* are not parallel. Choice (C) is the correct answer because the adjective *humid* is incorrectly used for *humidity*.

Correction: humidity

P42-2

In North America, 1.8 trillion <u>liters of</u> fresh water are <u>used daily</u>, primarily for domestic,
                                   A   B

<u>industry</u>, and agricultural <u>purposes</u>.
   C   D

[Explanation]

In this case, the words in the series *domestic*, *industry*, and *agricultural* are not parallel. The words *domestic* and *agricultural* are adjectives, whereas *industry* is a noun. Choice (C) is the correct answer, because the adjective *industrial* should be used in place of the noun *industry*.

Correction: industrial

P42-3

Fishes obtain <u>oxygen</u> <u>dissolved</u> in water and <u>releasing</u> carbon dioxide <u>through</u> paired gills.
                   A   B   C   D

[Explanation]

The words *obtain* and *releasing*, joined by *and*, are not parallel. Therefore Choice (C) is the correct answer.

Correction: release

P42-4

Automobiles and trucks <u>have</u> batteries to start the engine and <u>supplying</u> current <u>for</u> the
                               A   B   C

ignition and the <u>lights</u>.
                  D

[Explanation]

The words *to start* and *supplying*, joined by the conjunction *and*, are not parallel. Therefore Choice (B) should be the infinitive form, *to supply*.

Correction: to supply

P42-5

<u>Modern</u> paints not only beautify, but also <u>protection</u> surfaces <u>from</u> <u>decay</u> and corrosion.
  A   B   C   D

[Explanation]

The elements *beautify* and *protection*, linked by the correlative conjunction pair *not only ··· but also*, are not parallel. Therefore Choice (B) should be the verb *protect*.

Correction: protect

P42-6

Catching a snail should <u>be easier</u> than <u>to take</u> hold of any <u>other</u> animal, <u>since</u> the snail is the
                                  A   B   C   D

slowest of all land animals.

[Explanation]

The elements compared, *Catching a snail* and *to take hold of any other animal*, are not parallel. Therefore Choice (B) should be the gerund *taking*.

Correction: taking

Pattern Drill for Patterns 38-42

1. Arsenic <u>is a</u> naturally occurring element that is <u>usually present</u> in both surface water <u>or</u>
        A   B   C
   groundwater <u>in minute</u> concentrations.
               D

2. Each of the <u>billions of</u> cells in the human body is close <u>enough to</u> a capillary to exchange
             A   B
   materials, energy, and <u>inform</u> with <u>it</u>.
                   C   D

3. <u>Many</u> important problems in chemistry, <u>biological</u>, and medicine <u>are</u> concerned <u>with</u> the
     A   B   C   D
   acidity or alkalinity of a solution.

4. Quills are <u>usually made</u> from goose or turkey feathers, and are noted <u>for</u> <u>their</u> flexibility and
           A   B   C
   <u>able</u> to produce fine lines.
     D

5. Born to parents who had been slaves <u>until</u> the Civil War, <u>but Mary M. Bethune</u> became
                                   A   B
   president of the college <u>bearing</u> her name and an adviser to President Franklin D. Roosevelt.
    C   D

6. The Indians <u>along</u> the Eastern seaboard of North America <u>helped</u> the early English <u>colonists</u>
              A   B   C
   establish settlements, raise crops, and <u>adjustment</u> to living in a wilderness.
                                  D

7. Adolf Dehn's lithographs are popular for the richness of their tones _____ for their
   wide range of subject matter.

   (A) as well
   (B) also
   (C) as well as
   (D) so well as

8. <u>Almost all</u> the great new <u>discoveries</u> in <u>medical science</u> have been originated, tested, and
      A   B   C
   <u>perfect</u> by physiological methods.
     D

9. Each year with great regularity birds return to their homes, court their mates, build their
   nests, lay eggs, _____.

   (A) when they rear the young
   (B) or rearing their young
   (C) and rear their young
   (D) to rear their young

10. New York is mountainous <u>in its</u> eastern part, level or <u>hill</u> in the center and west, and <u>rolling</u>
                                A   B   C
   in the <u>southern section</u>.
            D

11. The oceans <u>are</u> a <u>vast reservoir</u> of the heat, <u>moist</u>, and carbon dioxide <u>needed</u> by the
             A   B   C   D
    atmosphere.

12. Upper Paleolithic peoples <u>lived</u> not only in caves and rock shelters, <u>or also</u> in <u>structures built</u>
                                A   B   C
    out in <u>the open</u>.
           D

13. Most aquatic animals are able to get their oxygen directly from the water, _____
    have to breathe air.

    (A) which some
    (B) but some
    (C) some
    (D) or in some

14. An <u>antibiotic</u> must <u>make contact</u> with the infecting organisms <u>before it</u> can destroy them or
            A   B   C
    <u>checking</u> their growth.
      D

15. Religion <u>involves</u> beliefs, rituals, and <u>emotional</u> that often contribute to social coherence,
              A   B
    <u>especially</u> in technologically <u>simpler</u> societies.
      C   D

16. When we want <u>to measure</u> very small <u>amounts</u> of things, we use <u>neither</u> small units of
                 A   B   C
    measure or fractional part of <u>larger</u> units.
                D

17. <u>Between</u> the ages of 5 and 8, <u>most children</u> are open, energetic, and <u>easily</u> to <u>get along with</u>.
      A   B   C   D

18. <u>The wild</u> reindeer of North America, <u>or</u> caribou, <u>lacks</u> the symmetry and <u>graceful</u> of a true
      A   B   C   D
    deer.

19. Jazz was developed by African-Americans and influenced by _____ European harmonic
    structure and African rhythmic complexity.

    (A) both
    (B) either
    (C) whether
    (D) instead

20. <u>Risking</u> fines, <u>imprison</u>, and even death, some of the white people were <u>active</u> in the
      A   B   C
    movement to abolish <u>slavery</u> in the United States.
                      D

Mini-Test 8

1. <u>As early as</u> 1821 the Boston School Committee <u>established</u> the
   A   B
   English Classical School, which <u>was first</u> public <u>secondary</u>
                                       C   D
   school in the United States.

2. Rabies is most commonly <u>transmit</u> by dogs, <u>but</u> it may also be
                              A   B
   spread by other mammals, <u>including</u> cats, bats, <u>foxes</u>, and
                               C   D
   skunks.

3. <u>The teeth</u> of human beings <u>help</u> to form the sounds of speech
   A   B
   and <u>determining</u> the <u>facial</u> expression.
          C   D

4. Skis are usually _____ and vary in length from
   about three feet to more than seven feet.

   (A) wide about three inches
   (B) about wide three inches
   (C) about three inches wide
   (D) three inches about wide

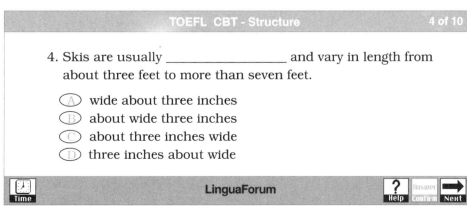

STRUCTURE

5. <u>Because of</u> its small size and the intense solar radiation it
     A

<u>receives</u>, it is not <u>surprising</u> that Mercury has <u>virtual</u> no
     B   C   D

atmosphere.

LinguaForum

6. Dow Jones & Company, _____, began computing
a daily industrial average in 1897, using a list of 12 stocks and
dividing their total price by 12.

(A) published a financial news
(B) was a financial news publisher
(C) a financial news publisher which
(D) a financial news publisher

LinguaForum

7. Opium poppies, with <u>them</u> fragile flowers of red or white or
                 A

purple, <u>thrive in</u> a hot climate <u>but cannot</u> endure <u>heavy</u> rain.
       B   C   D

LinguaForum

8. The Smithsonian Institution, established in 1846, _____ for
scientific knowledge in the United States.

(A) is a center
(B) a center
(C) being a center
(D) as a center

LinguaForum

9. <u>Most</u> tornadoes have wind speeds of about 110 mph, <u>which</u> can
    A   B

damage roofs, <u>uproot</u> trees, and fill the air <u>of</u> lethal debris.
                C   D

LinguaForum

Time | Help | Confirm | Next

10. In addition to using balloons for dialogue, comic strips may
contain _____ within or below the panels.

(A) a written narrative
(B) a narrative is written
(C) write a narrative
(D) a narrative in which

LinguaForum

Time | Help | Confirm | Next

STRUCTURE

Chapter 9 Dangling Modifiers

What are the patterns about?

Pattern 3 Subject + Verb Missing (Dp. Chapter 1)
Pattern 1 Subject Missing (Dp. Chapter 1)

TOEFL questions involving dangling modifiers require you to supply missing subjects and verbs in sentences that begin with modifiers. In some cases, you may be asked to provide a missing subject.

Dangling Modifiers

1. A dangling modifier is a phrase that comes at the beginning of a sentence but does not refer to the subject. That is, if the implied subject in the introductory phrase actually differs from the subject of the main clause, then the modifying phrase is *a dangling modifier*, because the phrase "dangles," with nothing in the sentence to modify.

> *Fearing an epidemic*, <u>quarantine</u> was imposed by authorities. (incorrect)

The introductory phrase, *Fearing an epidemic*, is a dangling modifier because it has no logical connection with the subject *quarantine*. The implied subject of the present participial phrase should be a person, the doer of the action, thus:

> *Fearing an epidemic*, <u>authorities</u> imposed quarantine. (correct)

2. Dangling modifiers may occur in the following structures:

(1) Present participial phrases

> *Entering the building*, <u>a statue</u> can be seen at the end of the hall. (incorrect)
> *Entering the building*, <u>one</u> can see a statue at the end of the hall. (correct)

(2) Past participial phrases

> *Based on new information*, <u>the committee</u> made a new decision. (incorrect)
> *Based on new information*, <u>a new decision</u> was made by the committee. (correct)

(3) Appositive phrases

> *The largest U.S. president*, <u>William Howard Taft's weight</u> was more than 150 kilograms. (incorrect)
> *The largest U.S. president*, <u>William Howard Taft</u> weighed more than 150 kilograms. (correct)

(4) Adjective phrases

> *Snowy in winter*, <u>skiers</u> enjoy Vermont. (incorrect)
> *Snowy in winter*, <u>Vermont</u> is enjoyed by skiers. (correct)

(5) Prepositional phrases

> *After a hearty lunch*, <u>a nap</u> seemed unusually attractive to him. (incorrect)
> *After a hearty lunch*, <u>he</u> thought a nap seemed unusually attractive. (correct)

cf) Absolute phrases

The subject of an absolute phrase is independent of the main subject.

> <u>The clock</u> *having struck eight*, <u>we</u> left the house.

This absolute phrase has its own subject, *The clock*, and therefore the phrase does not dangle.

Remember

The present participle indicates that the action is active, and therefore the doer of the action should be the subject of the main clause. Because the past participle is passive, however, the object of the action should be the subject of the main clause.

Supplementary Exercise

Exercise 9
Correct the following sentences if they are incorrect.

1. Set on fire by a welding torch, the ship burned at its pier.
2. Ignoring all objections, the committee's decision was made.
3. Studying for a law degree, he had no time for entertainment.
4. Launched from Earth, landing on the moon was the goal of a manned mission in 1969.
5. Delayed by strong winds, the aircraft arrived an hour late.
6. Struggling with an unfamiliar instrument, the composition was difficult for the violinist.
7. Hidden among the mountains in Colorado, the ranch was hard to find.
8. Deeply in love with a young woman, the young man's behavior became very strange.
9. Long and narrow, earthquakes often rock the nation of Chile.
10. Actually not an island at all, Rhode Island has the smallest area of any state in the U.S.

Pattern3/1 Subject + Verb Missing
Subject Missing (when only related to Dangling Modifiers)

Notes

1. Level of Difficulty: D-M
2. As a rule, TOEFL questions in this category involve missing subject + verb (+ object) of the clause accompanied by participial phrases, or appositives.
3. Most answer choices are long.
4. Consider the relationship between the subject and modifying phrase. In other words, you must decide to which subject the modifier correctly refers.

Examples

P3

Trying to capitalize on the native liking for wampum, _____ into the Northeast.

(A) tubular glass beads which white traders introduced
(B) tubular glass beads were introduced white traders
(C) and white traders introduced tubular glass beads
(D) white traders introduced tubular glass beads

[Explanation]

This question involves a dangling modifier. At the beginning of the sentence is a modifier, that is, a present participial phrase, but the subject and verb of the sentence are missing. Also, the choices are very long. Choice (A) is incorrect because no verb is present. Choice (B) is incorrect because the subject, *tubular glass beads*, is inconsistent with the subject of the phrase *trying to capitalize*. In other words, it is *white traders* who tried to capitalize, not *tubular glass beads*. The conjunction *and* in Choice (C) is not needed. Therefore Choice (D) is the correct answer.

P1

Built on a cliff or treetop to command a wide view, _____ is made of dead branches and lined with grass and leaves.

(A) the nest of the bald eagle
(B) the bald eagle nests
(C) where the bald eagle's nest
(D) in the nest of the bald eagle

[Explanation]

In this question, the subject is missing. At the beginning of the sentence is a past participle and therefore the object of the action *built* should be a subject of the sentence. Choice (B) is incorrect because its subject, *the bald eagle*, is a doer of the action *built*. Besides, it has the redundant verb *nests*. Choice (C) is incorrect because it creates an adverb clause. Choice (D) is incorrect because it is a prepositional phrase. The correct answer, therefore, is Choice (A).

Pattern Drill for Patterns 3 and 1

1. Once exposed at the earth's surface, _____ during which they slowly disintegrate and decompose as a result of their interaction with water, ice, and air.

   (A) all rocks weathered undergo
   (B) all rocks undergo weathering
   (C) weathering all rocks undergo
   (D) all rocks undergoing, weathering

2. Orbiting between Earth and Mercury, _____.

   (A) the surface temperatures of Venus are high enough to melt lead
   (B) with surface temperatures high enough to melt lead Venus
   (C) Venus has surface temperatures high enough to melt lead
   (D) the surface temperatures of Venus high enough to melt lead

3. Designed in a Neo-Italian Renaissance style, _____ for the industrialist Andrew Carnegie, its builder and original owner.

   (A) the name of Carnegie Hall
   (B) Carnegie Hall was named
   (C) naming Carnegie Hall
   (D) Carnegie Hall named

4. Peering at fuzzy patches of light on photos, _____.

   (A) and investigating the structure of galaxies
   (B) the structure of galaxies was investigated by astronomers
   (C) are the structure of galaxies astronomers investigate
   (D) astronomers investigated the structure of galaxies

5. Originally called New Amsterdam, _____ after the city came under British rule.

   (A) its present name was acquired and New York
   (B) acquiring its present name, New York
   (C) New York acquired its present name
   (D) New York's present name

6. Seeing in Alaska a great strategic resource, _____ from Russia in the 19th century.

   (A) the United States purchased Alaska
   (B) the purchase of Alaska, the United States
   (C) the United States which purchased Alaska
   (D) Alaska was purchased by the United States

7. Once referred to as the Great American Desert, _____ is now one of the chief farming states in the nation.

   (A) Nebraska's land
   (B) Nebraska
   (C) while Nebraska
   (D) Nebraska had

8. An American painter who was prominent in the second generation of Abstract Expressionists, _____ while in a hospital after being wounded in World War II.

(A) the paintings of Sam Francis began
(B) began painting and Sam Francis
(C) Sam Francis began painting
(D) Sam Francis who began painting,

9. Aware that proteins consisted of amino acids strung out in polypeptide chains, _____ in hemoglobin and myoglobin.

(A) the sequence of the amino acids was determined by biophysicists
(B) biophysicists determined the sequence of the amino acids
(C) biophysicists who determined the sequence of the amino acids
(D) and the sequence of the amino acids determined by biophysicists

10. By persuading about 100 Chicagoans to pledge $50 annually for five years, _____ to launch *Poetry: A Magazine of Verse* in 1912.

(A) so a lot of money was raised by Harriet Monroe
(B) Harriet Monroe who raised money
(C) Harriet Monroe raised money
(D) all the money Harriet Monroe raised

Mini-Test 9

1. A <u>specialized</u> field of topical geography, known as urban
     A
   geography, <u>is</u> devoted <u>for</u> analyzing the <u>distribution</u> of cities and
              B   C   D
   of things within cities.

 LinguaForum

2. Most birds <u>lay</u> their <u>egg</u> in a burrow or nest of some kind, <u>where</u>
                A   B   C
   they can incubate them with the <u>warmth</u> of their own bodies.
                                      D

 LinguaForum

3. <u>Farming</u>, which had been the <u>dominance</u> occupation of Americans
     A   B
   <u>through</u> the 19th century, provided jobs for fewer and fewer
     C
   people, <u>yet</u> production increased throughout the 20th century.
             D

 LinguaForum

4. While teeth help people to speak clearly and give shape to the
   face, _____ the chewing of food.

   (A) their main function is
   (B) so is their main function
   (C) mainly functioning
   (D) they function

 LinguaForum

5. <u>Some</u> <u>computerized</u> systems can even "decide" what kind of,
    A   B

and how <u>much</u> of, a drug should be administered to <u>critically</u> ill
       C   D

patient.

LinguaForum

6. Plants have _____ to develop or use helpful
adaptations than animals, except in small details of roots,
leaves, stems, flowers, and seeds.

   (A) chances
   (B) very few chances
   (C) far fewer chances
   (D) the fewer chances

LinguaForum

7. A rocket <u>moves</u> in <u>accordance with</u> Isaac Newton's third law of
           A   B

motion, <u>which says</u> that for every action there is an equal and
         C

opposite <u>reactions</u>.
         D

LinguaForum

8. _____ the biological clock within an organism is a
single master rhythm or a myriad of associated rhythms is not
yet known.

   (A) Though in
   (B) All
   (C) What
   (D) Whether

LinguaForum

9. To save time, ensure <u>an</u> accurate count, and <u>prevention</u> illegal
                         A   B

marking of ballots, <u>many</u> places use <u>voting machines</u>.
                     C   D

10. For many years Edwin Arlington Robinson summered at the
    MacDowell Colony, in Peterborough, N.H., where
    _____ was written.

    (A) his finest much of poetry
    (B) his finest poetry much of
    (C) much finest of his poetry
    (D) much of his finest poetry

STRUCTURE

Chapter 10 Agreement and Word Order

What are the patterns about?

Agreement
Pattern 43 Errors in Subject-Verb Agreement
Pattern 44 Errors in Pronoun-Noun Agreement
Word Order
Pattern 45 Missing Items Involving Word Order
Pattern 46 Incorrect Word Order
Pattern 47 Inverted Subject-Verb Word Order

Errors in agreement – both subject-verb and pronoun-noun – are included on TOEFL. Many questions involve word order.

Agreement

Agreement means consistency between two parts of a sentence.

1. Subject-Verb Agreement

Subjects and verbs must agree in number.

> <u>Carl</u> *has* two sisters.
> <u>They</u> *work* for a marketing company.

2. Pronoun-Noun Agreement

Pronouns must agree in number, person, and gender with the nouns (so-called referents) to which they refer.

> <u>John</u> attended a meeting while *his* wife Mary shopped at a mall.
> <u>My brother and his wife</u> will visit us tomorrow, and we will have dinner with *them*.
> Like the wolf, <u>the coyote</u> is known for *its* distinctive cry.

Word Order

1. Standard Word Order

> Subject + Verb + Object and/or Complement

> Tom runs every day.
> He is a stockbroker.
> Mary likes coffee.
> He made me upset.

2. Inversion

Inversion means changing the normal word order by putting the verb in front of the subject. Usually an auxiliary verb is put in front of the subject, and the rest of the verb phrase is put after the subject. If no other auxiliary is used, a form of *do* is used, unless the verb is *be*.

> Never <u>have</u> I experienced such pain.
> Not only <u>are</u> <u>birds</u> beautiful, but they also catch harmful insects.
> Little <u>did</u> I realize the danger I faced.

# Pattern 43 Errors in Subject-Verb Agreement ★★★☆☆

Questions of this kind require you to identify errors in subject and verb agreement.

Subjects and verbs must agree in number.

> Singular Subject – Singular Verb
> Plural Subject – Plural Verb

Special Rules for Subject-Verb Agreement

1. Singular Subjects

(1) Gerunds, Infinitives, or Noun clauses

<u>Painting a picture</u> *requires* much preparation before the artist even picks up a brush.
<u>To be a great artist</u> *is* her goal.
<u>How people interact with each other</u> *is* the basis of sociology.

(2) Some indefinite pronouns

anybody	everybody	nobody	somebody	each + Noun
anyone	everyone	no one	someone	every + Noun
anything	everything	nothing	something	

<u>Everyone</u> *has* a favorite food.
<u>Each country</u> *protects* its borders.

(3) Some nouns ending in -s
- the names of fields of study: *economics, mathematics, biophysics, statistics, dynamics*
- the names of countries, states, or lands: *the United States, the Netherlands, the Antilles*
- the names of certain illnesses: *diabetes, measles, mumps, rabies*
- miscellaneous: *news*

  <u>Mathematics</u> *is* Susan's major subject.
  <u>The United States</u> *is* located in North America.

2. Plural Subjects

(1) Subjects joined by *and*
Two subjects linked by *and* are considered plural, and a plural verb therefore must follow them.

  <u>Bass and trout</u> *make* good sport fishes.
  <u>Eggs and milk</u> *are* rich in calcium.

(2) Some pronouns

> both, few, many, several

  Of all the nations, *few* <u>are</u> as small as Luxembourg.

STRUCTURE

3. Quantifier + *of* + Noun + Verb

The verb agrees with the noun, not the quantifier.

> *All, Any, Half, Most, None, Some* } + *of* + Singular Noun + Singular Verb
> + Plural Noun + Plural Verb

> Most of <u>the book</u> *was* a lot of boring talk.
> Most of <u>the married men and women</u> in the city *have* separate jobs.

4. Relative Pronoun + Verb

The verb agrees with the noun (antecedent) to which the relative pronoun refers.

> Singular Antecedent + Relative Pronoun + Singular Verb
> Plural Antecedent + Relative Pronoun + Plural Verb

> <u>The war</u> that *was* started in 1861 ...
> <u>The finalists</u> who *were* chosen ...

5. *There* + Verb + Subject

The verb agrees with the subject it precedes.

> *There* + Singular Verb + Singular Subject
> *There* + Plural Verb + Plural Subject

> There was <u>a brief silence</u> ...
> There were <u>a few obstacles</u> ...

6. *A/The number of* + Noun + Verb

> *A number of* + plural noun + plural verb
> *The number of* + plural noun + singular verb

> <u>A number of</u> rules *govern* the game of baseball.
> <u>The number of</u> cat species *is* about 40.

7. *(Either)* A *or* B
Neither A *nor* B } + Verb
Not only A *but also* B

The verb agrees with the part that is closer to the verb in the sentence.

> Either the acrobats or <u>the singer</u> *is* scheduled to appear next.
> Either the singer or <u>the acrobats</u> *are* scheduled to appear next.

Remember

Phrases and clauses located between the subject and verb do not affect the number of the subject. Because these phrases and clauses modify the subject noun, they are part of the subject but have no effect on the verb.

<u>All officials</u> chosen by popular vote *are* responsible to the voters.

<u>A substance</u> that encourages growth of plants *is* called a "fertilizer."

Notes

1. Level of Difficulty: M-E
2. Note that the subject should agree with the verb, even though the modifying phrase or clause is long.
3. When you see a verb underlined, first check to see that it agrees with the subject.

Examples

P43-1

Solar radiation <u>reaching</u> the Earth's surface in higher latitudes <u>are</u> less intense <u>than</u> it is in
           A   B   C

lower latitude <u>equatorial</u> regions.
               D

[Explanation]

In this question, the plural verb *are* is incorrectly used for the singular verb *is*, because the subject, *Solar radiation*, is singular. The phrase *reaching the Earth's surface in higher latitudes* modifies the subject. Therefore the subject of the sentence is not *higher latitudes*, but *Solar radiation*.
Correction: is

P43-2

Florida's warm, <u>sunny</u> climate is <u>the chief</u> reason <u>why</u> so many people <u>vacations</u> in the state.
                A   B   C   D

[Explanation]

In this question, the singular verb *vacations* is incorrectly used for the plural verb *vacation*.
Correction: vacation

STRUCTURE

 **Pattern44** **Errors in Pronoun-Noun Agreement** ★★★☆☆

Questions of this kind require you to identify errors in pronoun and noun agreement.

1. Pronouns must agree in gender, person, and number with the nouns to which they refer.

> The double bass is bigger and heavier than the cello, and *it* makes a much deeper sound.
> Beavers use twigs and other plant material to build *their* nests.
> Andrea is concerned about *her* grades.

2. Besides, the demonstrative adjectives (*this, that, these,* and *those*) must agree in number with the nouns they modify. *This* and *that* must be used to modify singular nouns; *these* and *those* are used to modify plural nouns.

> *This* portrait of the author is the original.
> *These* books are from the architecture library.

Notes

1. Level of Difficulty: M-D
   Difficulty may arise when it is hard to discern to which noun a pronoun refers.
2. When a (singular) noun is underlined, rather than a (plural) pronoun, there may be difficulty in detecting the error and answering the question.
3. Commonly used pairs in questions are *its-his, their-its, them-it, this (that)-these (those)*.
4. When a pronoun is underlined, first see whether the noun that it refers to is singular or plural; then check its gender. When the demonstratives, *this (these)* and *that (those)*, are underlined, see whether the nouns following them are singular or plural.

Examples

P44-1

The Northern Hemisphere <u>contains</u> seven <u>tenths</u> of the earth's land and a <u>vast majority</u> of
                    A   B   C

<u>their</u> people.
D

[Explanation]
In this question, the pronoun *their* does not agree in number with the noun *earth*, to which it refers.
Correction: its

P44-2

Banks often require the <u>owner</u> of checking accounts <u>to keep</u> a minimum balance in their
                       A   B

accounts, <u>and charge</u> a fee <u>if</u> the balance falls below the minimum.
            C   D

[Explanation]
The singular noun *owner* should be plural, because the pronoun that refers to the noun is *their*.
Correction: owners

Pattern 45 **Missing Items Involving Word Order** ★★★☆☆

Questions of this kind require you to supply missing items involving word order.

Most Frequently Asked Word Orders

1. Comparison Construction

(1) *the* + **Superlative adjective /adverb + Noun**

> the most popular sport

(2) Comparative adjective /adverb + *than*

> more powerful than

2. *Such*

(1) *such* A *as* B (A *such as* B)

> *such* crops *as* barley, wheat, or corn
> crops *such as* barley, wheat, or corn

(2) *such a* (+ **Adjective) + Noun**

> *such* a (beautiful) thing

3. *Enough*

(1) Adjective + *enough* (+ **Infinitive)**

> big *enough* (to see)

(2) *enough* + **Noun**

> *enough* time

4. (Adverb) + Adjective + Noun

> an extremely effective plan
> several million dollars
> special measures

5. *Too* + Adjective + Infinitive

> *too* heavy to lift

Notes

1. Level of Difficulty: E-M
2. All answer choices contain almost identical words arranged in four different sequences.
3. The most frequently asked questions involve expressions including the superlative form.

Examples

P45-1

_____ of an exchange rate is a bilateral exchange rate, such as the dollar price of yen or of Deutsche marks, or of sterling.

(A) The conventional concept most
(B) The concept most conventional
(C) The most conventional concept
(D) Most conventional the concept

[Explanation]

The correct word order of the expressions involving superlatives is _the_ + superlative adjective + noun. Therefore the correct answer is Choice (C).

P45-2

Two-dimensional designing includes _____ drawing, painting, and producing surface patterns on fabrics, rugs, and wallpaper and in advertising layouts.

(A) activities as such
(B) such activities as
(C) such as activities
(D) as activities such

[Explanation]

Items involving _such_, which is used to introduce examples of something, follow the pattern _such_ A _as_ B, or A _such as_ B. Therefore the correct word order is Choice (B).

Supplementary Exercise

Exercise 10.1

Correct any mistakes in the following sentences.

1. A biologist get information about the migration of birds by tracking them on radar.
2. The house which face the sea has a beautiful view.
3. Qualifications for this job becomes more restrictive every year.
4. There was too many wild animals for the forest to support.
5. The origin of words are often fascinating.
6. Each of the stories require 20 minutes to read.
7. The console for the CD player and CDs are made of hickory wood.
8. A laser beam, which engineers use for precise work, guide the digging of tunnels.
9. None of our software can help people who lacks computer skills.
10. Very broad, colorful ties was popular in the United States 30 years ago.

 **Incorrect Word Order** ★★★★☆

Questions of this kind require you to identify two words switched incorrectly.

Most Frequently Switched Word Orders

1. Adjective (Number) + Noun

professional soldiers, one hundred dollars

2. Adverb + Adjective

unusually tired

3. Preposition + Relative Pronoun

the office *in which* she works

4. *Be* + Past Participle

The robber *is caught* by a policeman.

5. Adverb + Participle

quickly made suggestions

6. Adverb + Preposition / Adverb Clause Marker

immediately before, long after

7. *Almost* + Adverb, Adjective, or Quantifier

almost completely, almost inadequate, almost none

8. Multiple Numbers *(half, twice, three times)* + *as ··· as ···*

Fresh fruit costs *twice as* much *as* canned fruit.

STRUCTURE

Notes

1. Level of Difficulty: M-E
2. The incorrect word order most often encountered is noun + adjective.
3. In questions of this type, more than two words are always underlined.

Examples

P46-1

The <u>wild</u> blue phlox, or <u>sweet</u> William, <u>grows in</u> the spring in <u>woods moist</u> from Canada to
   A   B   C   D
the Gulf coast.

[Explanation]
Woods moist in Choice (D) should be *moist* (adjective) *woods* (noun).
Correction: moist woods

P46-2

Acne is <u>a</u> condition <u>which in</u> the sebaceous glands become overactive and <u>inflamed</u>, causing
      A   B   C

a <u>breakout</u> of pimples on the skin.
   D

[Explanation]

The correct word order is preposition + relative pronoun (*in which*), not relative pronoun + preposition (*which in*).

Correction: in which

P46-3

The United States is <u>nearly</u> <u>as twice</u> wide <u>from</u> east to west as <u>it is</u> from north to south.
               A   B   C   D

[Explanation]

The correct word order is *twice as ⋯ as*, not *as twice ⋯ as.*

Correction: twice as

Supplementary Exercise

Exercise 10.2

Correct any mistakes involving word order.

1. Apartment owners in this neighborhood seldom charge rents high.
2. Only in rare cases have white whales actually been seen.
3. It is not enough warm for trees to bloom.
4. Not until next week the new rules will go into effect.
5. Pain can make an illness seem than worse it really is.
6. Microchips are a recent very development.
7. Rarely Bill drinks alcohol.
8. The town which in we live is very small.
9. At the end of the hall stands a statue of a Civil War general.
10. Not until you've taken Biology 101 you should try to take higher courses.

 **Inverted Subject-Verb Word Order** ★★☆☆☆

Questions in this category involve supplying missing inverted subject and verb.

Subject and verb are inverted in the following cases:

1. With Negative Words and Related Expressions

not until	never	nor	nowhere	rarely	scarcely
not only	neither	no sooner	seldom	hardly	little

Never before <u>had</u> <u>I</u> seen such a large dog.
Not only <u>did</u> <u>the book</u> become a bestseller, but it also remained in print for many years.
Not until 1969 <u>did</u> <u>the United States</u> land astronauts on the moon.
The president is not attending the conference, *nor* <u>is</u> <u>the vice-president</u>.

2. With Expressions Starting with *Only:* only after, only recently, only when, only once, only during, only if, only in, only until

Only in rare cases <u>will</u> <u>you</u> see him here.
Only once <u>did</u> <u>she</u> ever lose her temper.

cf) When a negative word(s) or *only* occurs in a subordinate clause, the subject and verb of the subordinate clause are not inverted. Instead, the subject and the verb of the main clause are inverted.

Not until Vincent Van Gogh died <u>were</u> <u>collectors</u> able to appreciate his work fully.
Only after everyone has spoken <u>is</u> <u>the vote</u> taken.

3. With Place Expressions

In front of the courthouse <u>stands</u> <u>an old cannon</u>.
On the list <u>were</u> <u>the names of five suspects</u>.

Note that in this kind of inversion the main verb, not the auxiliary *do*, is put in front of the subject.

In a faraway land <u>lives</u> <u>this beautiful bird</u>. (correct)
In a faraway land <u>does</u> <u>this beautiful bird</u> live. (incorrect)

The subject and verb are inverted only when place expressions are necessary to complete a sentence.

In the city <u>are</u> <u>many tall buildings</u>. (*In the city* is necessary.)
In the city <u>the children</u> <u>walked</u> for many hours. (*In the city* is optional.)

Inversion is used when the subject is other than a personal pronoun.

Into the water <u>splashed</u> <u>the swimmer</u>. (Subject = *the swimmer*)
Into the water <u>he</u> <u>splashed</u>. (Subject = *he*)

4. In Comparison Clauses

In comparison clauses, inversion of subject and verb is optional.

I use more money *than* <u>do</u> <u>my friends</u>.
I use more money *than* <u>my friends</u> <u>do</u>.

Jill does as much work *as* <u>does</u> <u>anyone else</u>.
Jill does as much work *as* <u>anyone else</u> <u>does</u>.

Inversion is used when the subject is other than a personal pronoun.

Ray worked longer *than* <u>did</u> <u>his brother</u>. (Subject = *his brother*)
Ray worked longer *than* <u>he</u> <u>did</u>. (Subject = *he*)

5. With *So* + Adjective /Participle

So strong <u>was</u> <u>he</u> that he could bend a steel rod in his hands.
So weathered <u>was</u> <u>the wood</u> that it crumbled when touched.

6. In Conditional Sentences where *if* is omitted

If he had met you, he would have liked you.
➔ <u>Had</u> <u>he</u> met you, he would have liked you.

Notes

1. Level of Difficulty: D-M
2. This type of question occurs as the sentence completion type.
3. When the expressions mentioned above precede a blank, use the inverted subject and verb.

Examples

P47-1

Not only _____ at a comparatively high temperature, but it also absorbs a lot of heat when it melts.

(A) ice which melts
(B) ice melts
(C) does ice melt
(D) to melt ice

[Explanation]
The clause beginning with the negative words *Not only* has the inverted subject + verb. Therefore the correct word order is Choice (C), *does ice melt*.

P47-2

Within each ovary _____ which will eventually develop into seeds.

(A) are one or more ovules
(B) one or more ovules in
(C) and one or more ovules
(D) one or more ovules

[Explanation]
The prepositional phrase *Within each ovary* cannot be a subject, and the subject and verb of the clause beginning with the expression of place are inverted, so Choice (A) is correct.

1. Not until the middle of the 19th century _____ to celebrate Independence Day become general in the United States.

   (A) the custom of shooting off fireworks
   (B) the custom that shot off fireworks
   (C) did the custom of shooting off fireworks
   (D) and the custom of shooting off fireworks

2. <u>For</u> many years the ideas of Henry David Thoreau <u>was</u> known to scholars and
   　A　　　　　　　　　　　　　　　　　　　　　　　　　B
   to <u>thinkers</u> but <u>not to</u> the general public.
   　　　C　　　　　　D

3. Jazz, adapted <u>as</u> bebop, <u>popular became</u> among African American <u>musicians</u> in the 1950s
   　　　　　　　A　　　　　　B　　　　　　　　　　　　　　C
   and had <u>an impact</u> on the development of American popular music.
   　　　　　　D

4. The Industrial Revolution, <u>which</u> began <u>in</u> England about 1770, <u>spread</u> to continental
   　　　　　　　　　　　　　　　A　　　　　B　　　　　　　　　　　C
   Europe and to the United States within a <u>time short</u>.
   　　　　　　　　　　　　　　　　　　　　　　D

5. Jaundice is a yellow <u>discoloring</u> of the skin and eyeballs that <u>results from</u> an
   　　　　　　　　　　　A　　　　　　　　　　　　　　　　　　　B
   <u>amount excess</u> of bile pigment <u>in the</u> bloodstream.
   　　C　　　　　　　　　　　　D

6. A biologist <u>try to</u> find laws and <u>principles</u> <u>that</u> apply to <u>all life</u> – plant and animal.
   　　　　　　A　　　　　　　　　B　　　C　　　　　　D

7. Marmosets' long, curved claws enable <u>it</u> <u>to grasp</u> the bark of trees and to run along the tree
   　　　　　　　　　　　　　　　　　　A　　B
   limbs <u>as</u> cats or squirrels <u>do</u>.
   　　C　　　　　　　　　D

8. <u>Before long</u> the white man <u>came to</u> North America, the region <u>that is</u> now Georgia was
   　　　A　　　　　　　　　　B　　　　　　　　　　　　　　C
   <u>occupied</u> by the peace-loving Cherokee and Creek Indians.
   　D

9. <u>Although</u> most cats are night hunters, a few <u>is</u> more active during <u>the day</u>, <u>like</u> the cheetah.
   　A　　　　　　　　　　　　　　　　　B　　　　　　　　　C　　D

10. So important _____ that bee-pollinated flowers often have conspicuous patterns of guide lines to ensure that the insect is directed to the nectar.

    (A) bees have visual cues
    (B) visual cues to bees
    (C) visual cues to bees are
    (D) are visual cues to bees

11. <u>A total</u>, or "perfect," vacuum would <u>be</u> a space <u>from which</u> all matter <u>have been</u> removed.
       A   B   C   D

12. High-carbon steel is excellent for such products as wire and springs, which must be

    _____.

    (A) but tough not brittle
    (B) not tough brittle but
    (C) tough but not brittle
    (D) brittle not but tough

13. A rodent <u>to native</u> South America, the chinchilla <u>furnishes</u> one of the most expensive and
                A   B

    <u>beautiful furs</u> <u>used for</u> fashionable garments.
        C   D

14. Snowflakes have a <u>characteristic</u> <u>six-sided</u> symmetry which <u>reflect</u> the internal hexagonal
                      A   B   C

    <u>bonding</u> of the water molecules of ice.
      D

15. Cartoons are <u>closely</u> related to caricatures, <u>which in</u> a person, a type of person, or an action
                 A   B

    is <u>depicted</u> with <u>exaggerated</u> or distorted features.
       C   D

16. One of _____ between Indians and whites took place in 1636 in
    Connecticut when colonists attacked the principal village of the Pequots.

    (A) the violent earliest clashes
    (B) the earliest clashes violent
    (C) earliest violent the clashes
    (D) the earliest violent clashes

17. Pittsburgh's <u>growth early</u> as <u>a major</u> industrial center <u>was spurred</u> by exploitation of the
              A   B   C

    area's vast <u>resources</u> of coal.
           D

18. Brown sugar is prepared by <u>boiling</u> cane syrup in <u>a such</u> way that <u>very small</u> crystals
                      A   B   C

    <u>are formed</u>.
      D

19. The most remarkable fact about the <u>sense of smell</u> is the <u>small excessively</u> amount of
                               A   B

    substance <u>needed to</u> stimulate the nerve endings <u>in the</u> nasal passages.
             C   D

20. Brown bears fear and <u>avoid</u> man, but <u>when</u> wounded or surprised <u>at close</u> quarters, <u>it</u> will
                  A   B   C   D

    fight furiously.

Mini-Test 10

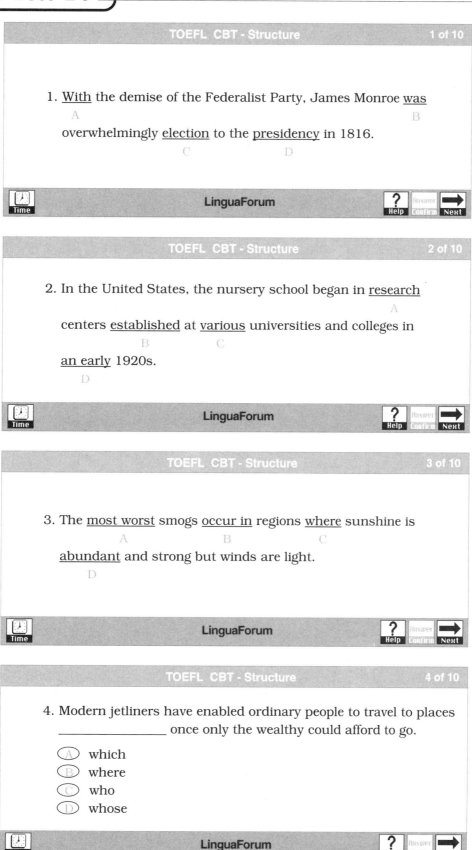

1. <u>With</u> the demise of the Federalist Party, James Monroe <u>was</u>
   　A　　　　　　　　　　　　　　　　　　　　　　　　　B
   overwhelmingly <u>election</u> to the <u>presidency</u> in 1816.
   　　　　　　　　C　　　　　　　D

LinguaForum

2. In the United States, the nursery school began in <u>research</u>
   　　　　　　　　　　　　　　　　　　　　　　　　　A
   centers <u>established</u> at <u>various</u> universities and colleges in
   　　　　　B　　　　　　C
   <u>an early</u> 1920s.
   　　D

LinguaForum

3. The <u>most worst</u> smogs <u>occur in</u> regions <u>where</u> sunshine is
   　　　A　　　　　　B　　　　　　C
   <u>abundant</u> and strong but winds are light.
   　　D

LinguaForum

4. Modern jetliners have enabled ordinary people to travel to places
   _____ once only the wealthy could afford to go.
   - Ⓐ which
   - Ⓑ where
   - Ⓒ who
   - Ⓓ whose

LinguaForum

STRUCTURE

5. Languages differ <u>from</u> one another not only in the sounds they
                    A

use, but also in the order in <u>which</u> <u>theirs</u> sounds may be
                              B   C

<u>arranged</u>.
D

6. Believing that diseases were caused by evil spirits,
   _____ to remove the evil influence.

   (A) the charms and magic the Indians used
   (B) did the Indians use charms and magic
   (C) the Indians who used charms and magic
   (D) the Indians used charms and magic

7. George Lucas <u>who produced</u> *Star Wars*, which captured the
                A

public's imagination with <u>its</u> combination of science fiction,
                          B

morality play, and <u>extraordinary</u> special <u>effects</u>.
                   C   D

8. Fats in foods are high in calories _____ may result in artery-
   clogging deposits that can cause heart disease.

   (A) while
   (B) and
   (C) also
   (D) what

9. The <u>fragrant plants</u> that <u>belong to</u> the mint family are valued for
          A   B

their <u>much</u> flavors and perfumes, <u>produced</u> from oil in glands on
       C   D

the leaves.

10. Pianos have two pedals that control the vibration of the strings
    for _____.

    (A) musical effects are special
    (B) special musical effects
    (C) which are special musical effects
    (D) musical effects specially

STRUCTURE

Chapter (11) Word Form

What are the patterns about?

Pattern 48 Adjective/Adverb Confusion
Pattern 49 Adjective/Noun Confusion
Pattern 50 Noun/Verb Confusion
Pattern 51 Person Noun/Activity (Field) Noun Confusion
Pattern 52 Other Confusion

Questions involving word forms are the most commonly asked error-identification type questions on TOEFL. In most cases, errors in this category involve one part of speech used in place of another. Nouns, verbs, adjectives, and adverbs are the parts of speech usually involved. As a rule, word form problems involve words with the same root, such as *eager – eagerly* or *decision – decisive*.

Words

1. Category of a Word

The category of a word – noun, verb, et cetra – determines its distribution.

> Betty will *abandon* the race. (correct)
> Betty will *abandonment* the race. (incorrect)
>
> George abandoned the *investigation*. (correct)
> George abandoned the *investigate*. (incorrect)

2. Suffixes

Suffixes help to identify parts of speech, nouns, adjectives, adverbs, verbs, and so on.

(1) Noun suffixes

Suffix	Example
-tion	composition, location
-sion	commission, permission
-ment	installment, government
-ness	goodness, happiness
-ence	conscience, existence
-ance	appearance, forbearance
-ity	reality, activity
-al	denial, arrival
-ery	discovery, trickery
-ism	individualism, capitalism
-tude	attitude, amplitude
-th	wealth, stealth
-logy	biology, geology
-ship	censorship, comradeship
-cracy	autocracy, democracy
-dom	kingdom, wisdom
-hood	adulthood, brotherhood

(2) Adjective suffixes

Suffix	Example
-ous	prosperous, generous
-able	profitable, desirable
-ible	tangible, credible
-ish	selfish, reddish
-ant	resistant, defiant
-ive	aggressive, passive
-ate	deliberate, compassionate
-ful	hopeful, stressful
-less	pointless, tactless
-al	commercial, normal
-y	happy, cloudy
-ic	magnetic, economic
-ical	statistical, electrical

(3) Adverb suffixes

Suffix	Example
-ly	quickly, truly

(4) Verb suffixes

Suffix	Example
-ize	magnetize, legitimize
-en	strengthen, lessen
-ate	infiltrate, administrate
-ify	verify, signify
-er	cover, chatter

(5) Person noun suffixes

Suffix	Example
-er	discoverer
-or	author
-ist	pianist
-ent	president
-ee	employee
-ic	critic
-ian	statistician
-ant	informant

 **Adjective/Adverb Confusion**

This pattern of questions involves an adverb used in place of an adjective, or vice versa.

1. Adjectives

(1) Adjectives often precede the nouns which they modify.

> She is a *famous* person.

(2) Adjectives may follow the nouns which they modify.

> Mary is the person *responsible* for office supplies.

In this situation, most adjective phrases result from reduced adjective clauses.

> Mary is the person *who is responsible* for office supplies.

(3) Adjectives also serve as subjective complements or objective complements.

> My dog is *friendly*.
> In winter, hands get *cold* easily.
> His visit made me very *happy*.

2. Adverbs

(1) Adverbs may modify other adverbs, adverb clause markers, adjectives, participles, prepositions, verbs, or entire sentences. As a rule, they precede the words which they modify.

> He *eagerly* agreed to run for office.
> The plane took off in *rapidly* deteriorating weather.
> She lives in a *brightly* painted house.
> He had to leave on *extremely* short notice.
> The letter arrived *shortly* after you left.
> Children grow up *unbelievably* quickly.
> *Generally*, food is inexpensive here.

(2) Most adverbs are formed by adding the suffix *-ly* to an adjective.

> easily, happily, truly, quickly, finally, historically

(3) Certain adverbs may be identical to adjectives.

> early, hard, long, late, high, low, deep, wide, fast

cf) Some adjectives may have the form *-ly*, noun + *-ly*.

> daily, weekly, monthly, yearly, lovely, friendly, costly, worldly, orderly, elderly

(4) Irregular adverb form

> good → well

Remember

Adjectives modify nouns, whereas adverbs modify verbs, other adverbs, adjectives, or participles.

Notes

1. Level of Difficulty: M-E
2. Check the preceding and following words first when you see adjectives or adverbs underlined. It is not easy to detect the error if the words modified by adjectives or adverbs have an identical noun/verb form, such as *end* (noun)/*end* (verb), *add* (noun)/*add* (verb).
3. Word order is an important clue and will help you increase your chance of selecting the correct answer (adjective + noun, adverb + adjective, adverb + adjective + noun).

Examples

P48-1

<u>An armistice</u>, or truce, <u>differs from</u> a surrender or peace treaty <u>in that</u> it does not <u>legal</u> end a
    A   B   C   D
war.

[Explanation]

The adjective *legal* is incorrect because *end* is not a noun, but a verb. So the adverb *legally*, which modifies the verb, is correct.
Correction: legally

P48-2

Ammonia is an <u>invisible</u> gas under <u>ordinarily</u> conditions, <u>a compound</u> of one nitrogen atom
                A   B   C
and three hydrogen <u>atoms</u>.
                         D

[Explanation]

The adverb *ordinarily* is incorrectly substituted for the adjective that modifies the noun *conditions*.
Correction: ordinary

STRUCTURE

 **attern 49** **Adjective / Noun Confusion** ★★★★☆

This pattern of questions involves an adjective used in place of a noun, or vice versa.

1. Adjectives

(1) Adjectives precede or follow the nouns which they modify, and nouns may not replace the adjectives.

> She is a *famous* person. (correct)
> She is a *fame* person. (incorrect)

> Mary is the person *responsible* for office supplies. (correct)
> Mary is the person *responsibility* for office supplies. (incorrect)

(2) Adjectives serve as complements, and nouns may not replace the adjectives.

> Natural resources are *abundant* in the region. (correct)
> Natural resources are *abundance* in the region. (incorrect)

> His visit made me *happy*. (correct)
> His visit made me *happiness*. (incorrect)

2. Nouns

Nouns may serve as subjects or objects, but adjectives may not.

> The *value* of a gemstone depends on its size and quality. (correct)
> The *valuable* of a gemstone depends on its size and quality. (incorrect)

> His paintings are known for their *intensity* of color. (correct)
> His paintings are known for their *intense* of color. (incorrect)

Notes

1. Level of Difficulty: M-M
2. In such questions as these, adjective/noun pairs with similar (and therefore easily confused) forms are often asked: *hot – heat, basic – basis, hungry – hunger, wealthy – wealth, abundant – abundance, various – variety*.
3. Questions most commonly involve an adjective incorrectly used in place of a noun in *the (a) + noun + of*, or a noun incorrectly used in place of an adjective in *adjective + noun*.

Examples

> **P49-1**
>
> Volcanoes are <u>the end</u> product of the ascent of <u>heat</u> magma <u>from</u> the interior of the
>   A   B   C
> earth toward <u>its</u> surface.
>   D

[Explanation]
The noun *heat* is incorrectly substituted for *hot*, which can modify the noun *magma*.
Correction: hot

P49-2

A passport <u>contains</u> a <u>descriptive</u> of the <u>bearer</u> and an identifying photograph <u>that meets</u>
            A   B   C   D
rigid specifications.

[Explanation]

The adjective *descriptive* is incorrectly substituted for the noun *description*. A noun, which is an object of the verb, is needed after the article *a*.

Correction: description

Supplementary Exercise

Exercise 11.1
Correct the underlined words in the following sentences.

1. A huge mural <u>adornment</u> the room.
2. A glacier sometimes can move <u>quick</u>.
3. Lightning can be a <u>dangerous</u> during storms.
4. If you want to be a good <u>candid</u> for employment, you should dress well.
5. Whales and dogs <u>representation</u> two different kinds of mammals.
6. A volcano can erupt <u>unexpected</u>.
7. The <u>taste</u> meal was welcome.
8. Parents must <u>guardian</u> their children against <u>hazard</u> influences.
9. One <u>vitality</u> branch of medicine is surgery, which <u>involvement</u> the removal of diseased organs and tissues.
10. Sandy <u>usual</u> wore a bright yellow dress.

Exercise 11.2
Correct the underlined words in the following sentences.

1. Land is more expensive in <u>heavy</u> populated zones.
2. Views <u>different</u> on how the ocean liner actually sank, but most <u>scholarships</u> believe that it was lost in a storm.
3. Job <u>loser</u> among young people is one possible source of crime.
4. The fields of <u>literary</u> and music interested <u>philosophy</u> Theodore A. Langerman.
5. I felt great <u>satisfy</u> hearing that I passed the exam.
6. His <u>appoint</u> to the committee made his friends <u>intense</u> happy.
7. After many <u>yearly</u> of hard work, the project was finished, but much <u>laborious</u> remained to be done.
8. Kimchi is usually spicy, but some <u>blandly</u> varieties exist.
9. The newest addition to the museum's collection <u>completion</u> what its founder started.
10. The song she sang for us is <u>differ</u> from what she sang on stage.

STRUCTURE

 **Pattern 50** **Noun / Verb Confusion**

This pattern of questions involves a verb used in place of a noun, or vice versa.

1. Nouns

(1) Nouns, but not verbs, may serve as subjects or objects and be modified by adjectives.

The orchestra gave fine *performances*. (correct)
The orchestra gave fine *perform*. (incorrect)

(2) Nouns, but not verbs, may occur following determiners such as *the* or *a*.

In the early 1900s, immigrants from Europe increased the *population* of the Midwest. (correct)
In the early 1900s, immigrants from Europe increased the *populate* of the Midwest. (incorrect)

2. Verbs

Verbs, but not nouns, may function as finite verbs of clauses.

Geologists *characterize* an eruption as a release of gas, ash, or molten rock from underground. (correct)
Geologists *character* an eruption as a release of gas, ash, or molten rock from underground. (incorrect)

Notes

1. Level of Difficulty: M-M
2. Questions usually involve easily confused verb/noun pairs such as *renew – renewal, populate – population, characterize – character.*
3. Look to see if an underlined verb or underlined noun is a main verb, a subject, or an object of a verb or a preposition, or if an adjective modifies it.

Examples

> **P50-1**
>
> The <u>discover</u> of gold at Orofino Creek in northern Idaho in 1860 <u>triggered</u> a gold rush,
>   A   B
> <u>but Idaho</u> remained <u>mostly</u> frontier and Indian territory.
>   C   D

[Explanation]
The verb *discover* is incorrectly substituted for the noun *discovery*. A noun is needed after the article *the*.
Correction: discovery

> **P50-2**
>
> A drama <u>in which</u> the actors <u>song</u> all or most of the dialogue, <u>accompanied</u> by an orchestra,
>   A   B   C
> is <u>an</u> opera.
>   D

[Explanation]
The noun *song* is incorrectly substituted for the verb *sing*, which functions as a verb in the adjective clause.
Correction: sing

Pattern 51 Person Noun/Activity (Field) Noun Confusion

★★☆☆☆

This pattern of questions involves a noun of activity or field used in place of a person noun, or vice versa: *philosophy – philosopher, composition – composer.*

Nouns representing particular fields of activity or actions have endings such as *-logy, -ness,* or *-tion.* Nouns representing a person practicing a given activity have endings such as *-er, -or,* or *-ist.*

Person Noun	Activity (Field) Noun	Person Noun	Activity (Field) Noun
adviser	advice	geologist	geology
architect	architecture	inventor	invention
astronomer	astronomy	manager	management
athlete	athletics	musician	music
biologist	biology	observer	observation
chemist	chemistry	painter	paint, painting
composer	composition	philosopher	philosophy
critic	criticism	photographer	photography
debtor	debt	physicist	physics
editor	editing	poet	poem, poetry
educator	education	refugee	refuge
electrician	electricity	sculptor	sculpture
geographer	geography	surgeon	surgery

STRUCTURE

Notes

1. Level of Difficulty: D-M
   The need to understand the entire sentence correctly makes this kind of question very difficult. This type of question differs from others in that it cannot be answered by examining the structure of the given phrase or sentence.
2. If a noun that refers to an activity or person is underlined, first look at the appositive, if one exists, that renames the noun. Then reread the sentence to understand its meaning correctly.

Examples

P51-1

T.S. Eliot's <u>poet</u> *The Waste Land* is <u>an immediate</u> reflection of the disillusionment which
           A   B

<u>many</u> artists felt after World War I, when life <u>seemed</u> meaningless and trivial.
  C   D

[Explanation]
   Poet is incorrectly substituted for *poem* because its appositive, *The Waste Land,* is not a poet but a poem.
   Correction: poem

P51-2

<u>Most</u> liverworts are <u>so</u> small that they are <u>noticeable</u> only to a keen <u>observation</u>.
  A   B   C   D

[Explanation]
   Observation is incorrectly substituted for *observer,* because the object of *be noticeable to* must be a person.
   Correction: observer

 **Other Confusion**

Questions of this kind involve confusion between a noun and gerund, a noun and participle, a noun and adverb, a verb and adjective, a verb and adverb, and so on.

1. Gerunds / Nouns

Gerunds are equivalent to nouns in that they may be used as objects of prepositions, but gerunds differ from nouns in that they require an object themselves.

> Barry Goldwater was known for *opposing* new government programs. (correct)
> Barry Goldwater was known for *opposition* new government programs. (incorrect)

2. Participles / Nouns

Participles serve as modifiers or are used in a passive or continuous mode, whereas nouns are basic elements of a sentence.

> When a car's wheels are *aligned* correctly, tires wear evenly. (correct)
> When a car's wheels are *alignment* correctly, tires wear evenly. (incorrect)

> The backup generator prevents accidental *loss* of power. (correct)
> The backup generator prevents accidental *lost* of power. (incorrect)

3. Adverbs / Nouns

Adverbs are modifiers, while nouns serve as basic elements of clauses.

> Animals with two heads are *rarely* seen. (correct)
> Animals with two heads are *rarity* seen. (incorrect)

> The plant's response shows its *sensitivity* to light. (correct)
> The plant's response shows its *sensitively* to light. (incorrect)

4. Verbs / Adjectives

Verbs may not modify nouns, while adjectives may not be used as verbs, basic elements of clauses.

> *Various* stringed instruments are played with bows. (correct)
> *Vary* stringed instruments are played with bows. (incorrect)

> The height of waves *depends* partly on wind velocity. (correct)
> The height of waves *dependent* partly on wind velocity. (incorrect)

Notes

1. Level of Difficulty: M-M
2. If a noun immediately following a preposition is underlined, check to see if another noun (that is, the object of a gerund) follows the noun.

Examples

P52-1

The Department of the Army <u>is responsible</u> for <u>provision</u> support for the national and
                                    A   B

<u>international</u> policies and the security of the United States <u>by means</u> of land forces.
   C   D

[Explanation]

The noun _provision_ is incorrectly substituted for the gerund _providing_, because only the gerund can take the object _support_.
Correction: providing

P52-2

The New Deal ended a period of laissez-faire government <u>with</u> an <u>emphasized</u> on
                                                      A   B

individualism, <u>which</u> had been practiced by Herbert Hoover and the Republican <u>leaders</u> of
               C   D

the 1920s.

[Explanation]

The past participle _emphasized_ is incorrectly used of the noun _emphasis_.
Correction: emphasis

P52-3

Eclipses happen <u>irregularity</u> <u>because</u> the plane of the moon's orbit around the earth <u>is</u>
                          A   B   C

slightly <u>different from</u> the plane of the earth's orbit around the sun.
               D

[Explanation]

The noun _irregularity_ is incorrectly substituted for the adverb _irregularly_, which modifies the verb _happen_.
Correction: irregularly

P52-4

<u>Laboratory apparatus</u> that must <u>resistant</u> heat and chemical action <u>is usually</u> made
                A   B   C

<u>of an alloy</u> of platinum and iridium.
   D

[Explanation]

The adjective _resistant_ is incorrectly substituted for the verb _resist_.
Correction: resist

P52-5

Some animals slowly down or stop reproduction when their habitat becomes too crowded.
  A   B   C   D

[Explanation]

The adverb *slowly* is incorrectly substituted for the verb *slow*.

Correction: slow

Supplementary Exercise

Exercise 11.3
Correct the underlined words in the following sentences.

1. Metal implants sometimes replacement weak bones.
2. To represent 20th-century art, we chose a selected of illustrations.
3. This computer is more versatile than the previously model.
4. Illness may make a person more vulnerability to other diseases.
5. The ship was construction in only six weeks.
6. I cannot say whether or not the budget is sufficiency.
7. The U.S. was division into two nations during the War Between the States.
8. We owe you a tremendously debt for helping us so much.
9. They decided against establishment the organization.
10. It was quite pleasing to meet her and talk to her in personal.

Exercise 11.4
Correct any mistakes in the following sentences.

1. Puppies and kittens pleasant people.
2. Regularly, well-balanced meals and a low-fat diet help to keep one health.
3. Johann Sebastian Bach is the most fame of all European music.
4. We have a solemnly obligation to preserve resources for future generations.
5. Countries ruled tightly by authoritarian governments are sometimes called dictators.
6. Downloading is the transfer of a filed from the Internet to an individual computer.
7. The American War Between the States represented a boldly attempt at Southern independence.
8. One founder of modern physicist was the German scientist Ernst Mach.
9. Computers did much to relieve the difficult of calculation.
10. We could not understand the instruct for the camera.

1. A pint of milk each day <u>offers</u> more than the daily <u>require</u> of <u>essential</u> amino acids for women
                        A   B   C
   and practically all of <u>those needed</u> by men.
                          D

2. <u>Among</u> the many <u>annually</u> awards for children's literature, <u>the most</u> prestigious are the John
   A   B   C
   Newberry and the Caldecott medals, <u>administered</u> by the American Library Association.
                                      D

3. <u>Natural vegetation</u> and animal life <u>various</u> from place <u>to place</u> according to temperature,
   A   B   C
   rainfall, soil, land surface, and <u>other</u> conditions.
                                     D

4. The earliest <u>inhabitations</u> of western North America in general were <u>apparently</u> rather
                A   B
   unspecialized hunters and gatherers, with big-game hunting <u>important</u> only <u>in</u> marginal
                                                               C   D
   areas.

5. <u>Not until</u> the 20th century did engineers <u>full</u> understand the principles of flying that birds
   A   B
   have <u>been using</u> for millions of <u>years.</u>
        C   D

6. Polo <u>was once</u> played only <u>by the</u> wealthy because of the <u>expensive</u> of <u>maintaining</u> stables of
          A   B   C   D
   polo ponies.

7. <u>Before</u> the Spanish <u>conquer</u> of Mexico and Central America, the Maya possessed <u>one of the</u>
   A   B   C
   greatest <u>civilizations</u> of the Western Hemisphere.
            D

8. Ecology <u>emphasizes</u> the dependence of every form of life on <u>other</u> living things and on the
            A   B
   <u>naturally</u> resources in <u>its</u> environment.
   C   D

9. A group <u>which</u> is <u>held</u> together <u>more or less</u> <u>permanent</u> is often called a society.
           A   B   C   D

10. <u>Not</u> all parts of the world <u>have</u> <u>abundance</u> water with the qualities <u>desired.</u>
    A   B   C   D

STRUCTURE

11. <u>Geologists</u> can reconstruct the ancient geography and environment of a region <u>by studying</u>
        A   B

the <u>distribute</u> of <u>its</u> sedimentary rocks.
     C   D

12. A <u>three-dimensional</u> relief model, or molded-relief map, <u>is</u> a striking way of <u>portrayal</u>
         A   B   C

difference <u>in elevation</u>.
       D

13. Andy Warhol received sudden <u>notorious</u> in 1962, <u>when</u> <u>he</u> exhibited <u>paintings</u> of Campbell's
                       A   B   C   D

soup cans, Coca-Cola bottles, and wooden replicas of Brillo soap pad boxes.

14. The field of ethics <u>is</u> a branch of <u>philosopher</u> that deals with <u>human actions</u> from the moral
           A   B   C

point of view – <u>as</u> right or wrong, good or bad.
          D

15. Orthodontists <u>are dentists</u> trained <u>to correct</u> malocclusion by <u>moving</u> the teeth into <u>properly</u>
              A   B   C   D

position.

16. Charles William Beebe earned his <u>famous</u> chiefly as the <u>explorer</u> who plunged more than
                              A   B

3,000 feet into the ocean in a metal globe in order <u>to study</u> sea life never before <u>observed</u>.
                                         C   D

17. Idaho <u>was acquired</u> by the United States in 1803 under the Louisiana treaty, <u>but</u> its
           A   B

boundaries were not <u>settlement</u> <u>until</u> the Oregon treaty of 1846.
                C   D

18. In the United States, <u>several states</u> attempted <u>to levy</u> an income tax <u>before</u> 1900, but its
                         A   B   C

first <u>successfully</u> use was in Wisconsin in 1911.
       D

19. Although 70-80 percent of the people <u>who</u> are struck survive, around 100 people are
                                   A

<u>killed directly</u> by forked lightning every <u>yearly</u> in the United States <u>alone</u>.
     B   C   D

20. <u>The rate</u> of interest <u>that</u> banks charge <u>dependent on</u> the type <u>and length</u> of the loan.
         A   B   C   D

Mini-Test 11

1. Ordinary stars are <u>so</u> hot that <u>almost</u> of their energy is emitted
                A   B

in visible light, <u>with little</u> energy emitted <u>at</u> radio frequencies.
           C   D

2. Sweating is the only means <u>which by</u> man can survive <u>for long</u>
                      A   B

in a place <u>where</u> air temperature <u>exceeds</u> body temperature.
         C   D

3. Robert Frost <u>acquiring</u> his <u>poetic</u> persona of a New England
                A   B

rural sage <u>during</u> the years he and his family <u>spent</u> at Derry.
         C   D

4. Radio telescopes receive waves and signals sent by stars too
distant _____ with any telescope that uses light.

- Ⓐ detect
- Ⓑ to be detected
- Ⓒ which are detected
- Ⓓ to detect it

5. A tendon, or sinew, <u>is</u> a cord of <u>tissue that</u> attaches <u>the end</u> of a
                     A   B   C

muscle <u>with</u> a bone.
       D

LinguaForum

Time   ? Help   Answer Confirm   Next

6. The European rabbit is an exceedingly prolific animal _____ main breeding season runs from February to October.

(A) its
(B) whose
(C) due to
(D) which

LinguaForum

Time   ? Help   Answer Confirm   Next

7. <u>Amnesty</u> is the act of pardoning <u>individual</u> <u>for</u> their <u>violations</u> of
    A   B   C   D

the law.

LinguaForum

Time   ? Help   Answer Confirm   Next

8. If Brooklyn were not one of the five boroughs of New York City, it would be _____ in the United States.

(A) the largest city fourth
(B) the largest fourth city
(C) the fourth largest city
(D) the city fourth largest

LinguaForum

Time   ? Help   Answer Confirm   Next

9. The science that <u>deals with</u> the ways in which plants and
                    A

animals <u>depend</u> on one another and on the <u>physical settings</u> in
         B   C

which they live is called <u>ecologist</u>.
                           D

10. In a highly competitive industry such as apparel manufacturing,
_____ single producer sells in large enough quantities to
influence price significantly.

(A) never
(B) no
(C) nor
(D) not

STRUCTURE

Chapter 12 Word Choice

What are the patterns about?

Pattern 53 Confusion of *So/Very/Too, So/Such*

Pattern 54 Confusion of *Another/Other, Many/Much, Few/Little, Like/Alike, Near/Nearly, No/Not/None,* and so on

Pattern 55 Confusion of *Make/Do*

Pattern 56 Confusion of Conjunction/Preposition

Errors in word choice involve using one word incorrectly in place of another. In many cases, the two words are similar in function or meaning.

Confusion of *So / Very / Too, So / Such* ★★★☆☆

In this pattern of question, *very* or *too* is used in place of *so*, and *so* is used in place of *such*, or vice versa.

The words *so*, *too*, and *such* may be used as follows:

---

1. *So*

(1) *so* + Adjective/Adverb + *that*
: cause-and-result

He was *so* nervous *that* he could not sleep.
He walks *so* slowly *that* he takes an hour to get home.

(2) *so* + *many (few)/ much (little)* + Noun + *that*
: cause-and-result

They have *so* many children *that* they need a bigger home.
They had *so* little money *that* they could barely buy enough food.

2. *Too*

too + Adjective + Infinitive
: indicates an excessive or unacceptable degree

She is *too* short to play on the basketball team.

cf) *Very* means to a high degree or great extent, but not impossibly or undesirably so.

John is *very* responsible.
She always thinks *very* carefully.

3. *Such*

(1) *such* A *as* B (A *such as* B)
: serves to introduce examples of something

Strategic minerals include *such* metals *as* titanium and uranium.
Predators include animals *such as* hawks, wolves, and sharks.

(2) *such* + (a) + Adjective + Noun + *that*
: cause-and-result

He had *such* a severe injury *that* he could not walk.
They were *such* strong athletes *that* they both won medals.

Remember
Too or *very* cannot replace *so* or *such* in the cause-and-result pattern represented by *so/such ⋯ that*. Also, *so* cannot replace *such* in *such as ⋯* or *such ⋯ as*.

Notes
1. Level of Difficulty: D-M
2. Most questions involve *very* or *too* used in place of *so*.
3. Check to see if a cause-and-result clause is present, when *very* or *too* is underlined.

Examples

P53-1

During the Middle Ages, ginger was <u>too</u> scarce and valuable that a pound <u>of it</u> was <u>worth</u> a
  A   B   C   D
whole sheep.

[Explanation]

In this question, *too* is incorrectly used in a cause-and-result clause.

Correction: so

P53-2

Limulus, a bottom dweller <u>that</u> feeds upon <u>so</u> small animals as annelids and clams,
                                     A   B

<u>is common</u> in the shallow waters <u>along</u> the East Coast of the United States.
    C   D

[Explanation]

In this question, *so* is incorrectly substituted for *such* in the expression *such ··· as*.

Correction: such

Supplementary Exercise

Exercise 12.1
Correct any mistakes in the following sentences.

1. Bill was so small to play football, so he played baseball instead.
2. The tool had too many applications that it became very popular.
3. Ecosystems involve so different animals as bears and bees.
4. Earth's gravitation is too strong that only fast-moving objects can escape it.
5. This food is very fattening that I have to avoid it.

Exercise 12.2
Insert a correction if an underlined word is used incorrectly.

1. He was surprised to find that he had several <u>other</u> uncles than those he knew.
2. Whales, <u>alike</u> mammals on land, must have air to breathe.
3. Global productivity today is perhaps 10 times as <u>much</u> as it was in 1945.
4. His sister has much education, but he has only <u>a few</u>.
5. The project will be easier if you use <u>another</u> method.
6. The two of you must be kind to each <u>another</u>.
7. The movie is <u>near</u> over, so I think they will be home soon.
8. Her pets give her <u>many</u> pleasure.
9. There is <u>none</u> excuse for such behavior.
10. <u>Mostly</u> cats exhibit the same basic body pattern, though they differ greatly in size.

Confusion of *Another / Other, Many / Much, Few / Little, Like / Alike, Near / Nearly, No / Not / None,* and so on ★★★★☆

This pattern involves confusion between words having similar meanings.

1. *Another/Other*

Another, meaning "one more" or "an additional or extra one," may occur as an adjective before a singular noun. *Other* means an additional member of a group or set and may be used to modify either plural or non-countable nouns.

> *another* + Singular noun
> *other* + Plural noun, Non-countable noun

> Their new baby means *another* mouth to feed.
> *Other* members of my family are my mother, father, and sister.
> There is *other* fruit besides apples in the box.

Another and *other* are also used in the following expressions:

> *each other, one another,*
> *-er/more ⋯ than any other* + Singular noun

cf) *Others* means several more besides one mentioned already. *Others* serves as a pronoun.

> Some people like tea, but *others* prefer coffee.

Never use *others* in place of *other.*

> *Others* courses are offered next year. (incorrect)

2. *Many/Much*

Many and *much* have similar meanings, but *many* applies to plural countable nouns, whereas *much* occurs before non-countable nouns.

> *many* + Plural countable noun
> *much* + Non-countable noun

> *Many* people in the U.S. watch television eight hours each day.
> *Much* of the U.S. population watches television eight hours each day.

3. *(A) Few/(A) Little*

(A) few and *(a) little* have the same meaning, but *(a) few* is used with plural countable nouns, and *(a) little* occurs before non-countable nouns.

> *(a) few* + Plural countable noun
> *(a) little* + Non-countable noun

> We have only *a few* problems left to solve.
> We have *little* work left to do.

4. *Like/Alike*

Like, a preposition, must precede an object. The adjective *alike*, on the other hand, indicates similarity between two or more nouns and, in most cases, follows them. Besides, *alike* can be used as an adverb, meaning "equally."

> She looks exactly *like* her sister.
> Identical twins look exactly *alike*.
> The plan was opposed by parents and students *alike*.

5. *Near/Nearly*

Near serves as an adjective, meaning "close to," but *nearly* serves as an adverb, meaning "almost."

> I want to live in a house *near* the seashore.
> Their house rents for *nearly* a thousand dollars a month.

6. *No/Not/None*

The adjective *no* modifies nouns and indicates the absence of something, whereas the word *not* is an adverb negating verbs, adjectives, infinitives, and so on. *None*, a pronoun meaning *not any* or *not one*, occurs when the noun it replaces has already been used.

> There is *no* reason to feel uneasy.
> This is *not* the product I ordered.
> *None* of the products I ordered arrived.

7. *Every/All*

Every occurs before singular countable nouns, while *all* precedes plural countable nouns.

> *every* + singular noun
> *all* + plural noun

> *Every* man volunteered for duty.
> *All* mammals have hair.

8. *Most/Mostly/Almost*

Most may be used as an adjective or a pronoun, and means "the majority." The adverb *mostly* means "mainly, principally, or usually." *Almost* serves as an adverb that means "not yet or completely, but close to completion."

> *Most* students say that they enjoy that course.
> Bob has heard *most* of the CDs in our collection.
> On weekends, I *mostly* sleep.
> Bob has heard *almost* all of the CDs in our collection.

9. *Late/Lately*

Late may function as an adjective or an adverb. As an adjective, *late* usually means "after the customary time" or "near the close of a period in history or a person's life or career." The adjective *late* also may mean that a person is deceased. The adverb *late* means "after the anticipated time." The adverb *lately* means "recently."

> I had a *late* breakfast.
> In the *late* 1970s, economic growth slowed.
> The *late Mr.* Wilson was buried last week.
> Bill arrived *late* for an interview.
> We have *lately* received many telephone calls.

10. *Hard/Hardly*

Hard may serve as an adjective or an adverb. As a rule, the adverb *hard* follows the verb it modifies. *Hardly,* an adverb, means "barely" or "scarcely" and usually precedes the verb it modifies.

Quartz, a *hard* mineral, forms beautiful crystals.
When the wind blows *hard,* it can damage houses.
Students can *hardly* make good grades unless they study.

11. *Beside/Besides*

Beside is a preposition and means "next to." *Besides* is a conjunctive adverb and means "also" or "in addition to."

There is a little restaurant *beside* the hotel.
Major surgery is hard on the patient; *besides,* it can be a tremendous expense.

12. *Ago/Before*

Ago describes a time before the present, whereas *before* describes a time earlier than some other moment.

The war began almost 150 years *ago.*
The war began *before* the presidency of Andrew Johnson.

Notes

1. Level of Difficulty: M-E
2. The pairs most commonly asked are *other – another, many – much.*
3. If the aforementioned words are underlined, first check the words following them.

Examples

P54-1

Marine biology is the scientific study of the plants, animals, and another organisms that live
  A   B   C   D
in the ocean.

[Explanation]
In this question, *another* is used to describe *organisms*. However, *another* is used only with singular countable nouns. The word *other* should be used in place of *another*.
Correction: other

P54-2

Cotton accepts much dyes, is usually washable, and can be ironed at relatively high
        A   B   C   D
temperatures.

[Explanation]
In this question, *much* is used to modify the plural countable noun *dyes*. However, *much* is used only with non-countable nouns. So, *many* should be used in place of *much*.
Correction: many

STRUCTURE

P54-3

The object of the game of golf <u>is</u> to hit the ball into <u>each hole</u> in turn, and <u>to complete</u> the
                         A   B   C

round using as <u>little</u> strokes as possible.
          D

[Explanation]

In this question, the word *little* is incorrectly substituted for *few* because the noun *strokes* is countable.

Correction: few

P54-4

<u>Alike</u> energy from any <u>other</u> source, <u>nuclear</u> energy can be used to <u>do work</u>.
 A   B   C   D

[Explanation]

In this question, the word *Alike* should be changed to the preposition *Like*.

Correction: Like

P54-5

The Himalayan Mountains are <u>near</u> <u>twice</u> as high as the Alps, even though <u>both chains</u> of
                                A B   C

mountains <u>were formed</u> by the collision of two continents.
              D

[Explanation]

In this question, the word *near* should be changed to the adverb *nearly*, meaning "almost."

Correction: nearly

P54-6

Sharks have <u>none</u> swim bladder and must swim <u>perpetually</u> to keep from <u>sinking</u> to
                  A   B   C

<u>the bottom</u>.
    D

[Explanation]

In this question, the word *none* should be changed to the adjective *no*.

Correction: no

Pattern 55 Confusion of *Make / Do* ★☆☆☆☆

In this pattern, *make* and *do* may be incorrectly used in place of each other. Questions of this kind have rarely appeared on recent TOEFL tests.

In its broadest sense, the verb *make* means *to construct, create,* or *produce,* whereas the verb *do* means *to act, execute, complete,* or *perform.* These verbs also occur in various set expressions:

1. *Make*

make advances	make an offer
make an agreement	make a plan
make an announcement	make a point
make an attempt	make a prediction
make a comparison	make a profit
make a contribution	make a promise
make a decision	make a reference to
make a discovery	make a sound/noise
make a distinction	make a suggestion
make a forecast	make up
make an investment	be made up of

2. *Do*

do an assignment	do the laundry
do business with	do one's duty
do homework	do research
do a job (errand, chore)	do someone a favor

Example

P55

Charles Darwin, <u>best</u> known for <u>proposing</u> the <u>modern theory</u> of evolution, also <u>did</u> important

               A   B   C   D

contributions to marine biology.

[Explanation]
The correct expression is *made contributions*, not *did contributions.*
Correction: made

Supplementary Exercise

Exercise 12.3
Insert a correction if an underlined word is used incorrectly.

1. Mr. Jones was elected president <u>although</u> his lack of experience.
2. He became interested in biology <u>while</u> his years in college.
3. He cleaned the floor <u>during</u> the business was closed.
4. <u>Because</u> delays in shipping, the company lost money.
5. John is going fishing <u>despite</u> the fact that he has a heart problem.

STRUCTURE

In questions of this kind, conjunctions are incorrectly used in place of prepositions, or vice versa.

1. Conjunctions

Conjunctions such as *because, although, when,* or *while* are used before clauses.

> *Because* she became overheated, she went to hospital.
> *Though* she never watches television, she has a TV set in her home.
> My brother was promoted five times *while* he was in the army.

2. Prepositions

Prepositions such as *because of, due to, on account of, in spite of, despite,* or *during* occur before noun phrases.

> *Despite* the differences between us, we are good friends.
> *Because of* a leg injury, I cannot play basketball.
> *During* the winter, many animals hibernate.

Notes

1. Level of Difficulty: M-M
2. The most commonly asked pairs are *although – despite (in spite of)* and *when (while) – during.*
3. If you see prepositions or conjunctions underlined, check to see if they precede a clause or a phrase.

Examples

P56-1

<u>While</u> flight the nighthawk holds <u>its</u> mouth <u>open</u> and uses it like a trap <u>to catch</u> flying
  A   B   C   D
insects.

[Explanation]

In this question, the conjunction *while* is incorrectly substituted for the preposition *during* because the noun *flight* follows the word.

Correction: During

P56-2

<u>Despite</u> it is <u>commonly</u> called a "lead" pencil, a pencil contains <u>no lead</u> and is not a
  A   B   C
<u>true pencil</u>.
    D

[Explanation]

In this question, the preposition *Despite* is incorrectly substituted for the conjunction *Although,* because the expression beginning with *it* is a clause, not a phrase.

Correction: Although

1. <u>Powdered</u> cinchona bark became <u>very</u> popular in Europe for the treatment of malaria that
     A   B

  the <u>demand</u> was <u>enormous</u>.
        C   D

2. Not until 1888 <u>did the</u> state of Rhode Island remove <u>property</u> restrictions and grant the vote
               A   B

  to <u>every</u> male citizens <u>over</u> age 21.
     C   D

3. <u>When atoms</u> approach other atoms closely, the negative charges of their electrons <u>repel</u> each
     A   B

  <u>another</u> and tend to prevent contact <u>between</u> the atoms.
     C   D

4. There are <u>little</u> bonds <u>between</u> the particles in a gas, <u>allowing</u> for expansion <u>in</u> every
           A   B   C   D
  direction.

5. A magnet can attract <u>or repel</u> <u>other</u> magnet or a piece of soft iron <u>without</u> touching <u>it</u>.
                      A   B   C   D

6. <u>It</u> is <u>thought</u> that as <u>much</u> as 70,000 to 200,000 glaciers <u>exist</u> throughout the world.
  A   B   C   D

7. <u>Though</u> the great number of <u>gestures</u>, it is clear that most of the gesturing that people
     A   B

  engage in <u>when they</u> communicate <u>is coordinated</u> with speech.
           C   D

8. <u>Comets vary</u> in appearance <u>from small</u> stellar images to huge tailed objects <u>too</u> bright that
     A   B   C

  they can <u>be seen</u> in daytime near the sun.
         D

9. <u>Although</u> pineapple plants need <u>few</u> water and <u>only fair</u> soil, the land has to be <u>heavily</u>
     A   B   C   D
  fertilized.

10. <u>From</u> southeast Massachusetts the peninsula of Cape Cod <u>extends</u> into the Atlantic <u>alike</u>
     A   B   C

  an arm of land with a <u>bent</u> elbow.
               D

STRUCTURE

11. Silver is <u>not affected</u> by water or <u>pure air</u>, but it can absorb 22 times <u>its</u> volume of oxygen
            A   B   C

    <u>during</u> melted.
       D

12. <u>Not</u> one even <u>ventured</u> into the Antarctic area <u>until</u> the 18th century, when whalers braved
      A   B   C

    the fierce winds and <u>rough</u> waters.
                      D

13. Hair and fur can <u>harbor</u> <u>a wide</u> range <u>of</u> ticks, mites, fleas, lice, and <u>another</u> small
                     A   B   C   D

    creatures.

14. Religion, <u>alike</u> laws and judges, <u>provides</u> individuals <u>with</u> rules or guidelines for <u>behavior</u>.
            A   B   C   D

15. <u>Early</u> man <u>no doubt</u> learned <u>much</u> of his dance movements and patterns from the birds
     A   B   C

    and animals <u>around him</u>.
               D

16. In the grasshopper and many <u>other</u> insects, the nitrogenous wastes <u>are eliminated</u> in the
                                   A   B

    form of <u>near</u> dry crystals of uric acid, <u>an adaptation</u> that promotes water conservation.
               C   D

17. <u>Not</u> of the Indian cultures <u>in the</u> Americas <u>developed</u> a system of <u>private</u> land ownership.
     A   B   C   D

18. <u>While</u> the latter part of the 18th century a new phase of botany <u>began to be</u> developed,
     A   B

    which dealt <u>with</u> the structure and development of plants and <u>their</u> organs.
              C   D

19. The <u>planetary</u> nebulae were <u>such</u> named because, <u>when they</u> are observed through a small
         A   B   C

    telescope, they <u>resemble</u> planets.
               D

20. Although <u>much</u> animals are <u>green</u>, <u>no</u> true animal contains <u>grains</u> of chlorophyll.
           A   B C   D

Mini-Test 12

1. A baby deer is <u>invisible almost</u> in the forest <u>because</u> <u>its</u> spotted
                 A   B C

   coat <u>looks like</u> patches of sunlight in the brown leaves.
         D

LinguaForum

2. Ants and bees <u>instinctively</u> cooperate <u>in a</u> manner that clearly
                       A   B

   <u>indicates</u> a <u>degree social</u> organization.
     C   D

LinguaForum

3. Galileo devised <u>a simple</u> thermometer and <u>inspired</u> <u>its pupil</u>,
                 A   B C

   Evangelista Torricelli, <u>to invent</u> the barometer.
                    D

LinguaForum

4. A major marketing center of the Pacific Northwest, Seattle ranks
   with Portland _____ of the region's leading ports.

   - (A) where one
   - (B) as is
   - (C) as one
   - (D) is one

LinguaForum

STRUCTURE

5. <u>While</u> the 19th and early 20th centuries, the American
     A

   capitalist system <u>experienced</u> major economic <u>difficulties</u>
           B   C

   approximately <u>every</u> twenty years.
           D

LinguaForum

6. A culture must have _____ to change in order to
   adapt to new circumstances or to altered perceptions of existing
   circumstances.

   (A) been capable of
   (B) the capacity for
   (C) the capacity
   (D) of the capacity

LinguaForum

7. <u>More than</u> a century ago, physicists learned <u>identifying</u>
     A   B

   elements by the <u>colored</u> lines <u>they</u> give in a spectrum.
               C   D

LinguaForum

8. Beginning in 1833, _____ the government to begin
   depositing government money in selected state banks that were
   quickly called "pet banks."

   (A) Jackson ordered
   (B) Jackson's order
   (C) when Jackson ordered
   (D) for Jackson to order

LinguaForum

9. <u>Under</u> normal circumstances, <u>positively</u> charged particles like
       A   B

protons have a very strong <u>tend</u> to repel <u>one another</u>.
                       C   D

LinguaForum

Time | Help | Answer Confirm | Next

10. The virus that causes AIDS _____ in 1983; it is
    called HIV, or human immuno-deficiency virus.

    (A) identified
    (B) identifying
    (C) was identified
    (D) and identifies

LinguaForum

Time | Help | Answer Confirm | Next

STRUCTURE

Chapter (13) Miscellaneous

What are the patterns about?

Pattern 57 Negative Word Missing
Pattern 58 Confusion of Cardinal/Ordinal Number
Pattern 59 Article Used in Place of Possessive Adjective
Pattern 60 Conditionals

 **attern57** **Negative Word Missing**

In this pattern, negative words are missing.

Negative words most often tested in this pattern are as follows:

1. *No*

No is an adjective that modifies nouns and indicates that something is absent.

> *No* time is left.
> We have *no* opportunity to ask. (= We do not have any opportunity to ask.)

2. *Not*

The word *not* is an adverb that negates verbs, adjectives, infinitives, and so on.

> I usually do *not* have breakfast.
> Tell them *not* to be late for dinner.

3. *None*

None is a pronoun meaning *not one* or *not any*.

> *None* of them appears to understand.
> It is *none* of my doing.

cf) Errors in choice of the negative words are covered in Pattern 54 of Chapter 12.

Notes

1. Level of Difficulty: M-E
2. As a rule, adjectives tested in this pattern follow the nouns they modify.
3. The missing negative most frequently asked involves *no* used as an adjective.
4. Be sure first to check the words preceding and following the blank if you see modifiers such as adverbs, adjectives, and negative words in choices.

Example

> **P57**
>
> In northeastern South America is the huge Surinam toad, which has _____ tongue and spends its life in the water.
>
> (A) not
> (B) nor
> (C) no
> (D) without

[Explanation]

> The negative word is missing in this sentence. The word *tongue* that comes after the blank is a noun, so the adjective *no*, Choice (C), is the correct answer. Choice (D) is incorrect because it creates a prepositional phrase, not a noun phrase, which functions as an object of the verb *has*.

STRUCTURE

Pattern 58 Confusion of Cardinal/Ordinal Number ★★☆☆☆

In this pattern, ordinal and cardinal numbers may be incorrectly used in place of each other.

Cardinal/Ordinal Number

The two kinds of numbers are *cardinal* and *ordinal*.

Cardinal	Ordinal
one	first
two	second
three	third
four	fourth
twelve	twelfth
twenty-two	twenty-second

Ordinal numbers indicate the position something occupies in an ordered set of things. In most cases, ordinal numbers follow the definite article, *the,* or the possessive.

> *The first* book on the reading list is short.
> *The twentieth* century was a time of rapid change.
> This ocean is *the fourth* largest body of water in the world.
> *His third* job involved running a paper factory.

Example

> ### P58
>
> Slavery was revived in the <u>fifteen</u> century <u>when</u> Europeans <u>first</u> came into close and
>   A   B   C
>
> continued <u>contact with</u> Africans.
>   D

[Explanation]
  The correct pattern is *the* + ordinal + *century.* Therefore *fifteen* should be *fifteenth.*
  Correction: fifteenth

Supplementary Exercise

Exercise 13
Supply the correct negative words.

1. _____ task is less pleasant than this one.
2. _____ of the athletes finished the race.
3. There is _____ thermostat in this room.
4. It is _____ a practical plan.
5. They had _____ excuse at all, _____ even ignorance.

Pattern 59

Article Used in Place of Possessive Adjective

★☆☆☆☆

In this pattern, articles are incorrectly used in place of possessive adjectives. Questions of this kind have rarely appeared on recent TOEFL tests.

As a rule, articles are incorrectly substituted for possessive adjectives, part of the following expressions:

> *in* + one's + *20s (30s, 40s ···) /lifetime*

> Bill retired while still *in his forties*.
> The composer wrote many operas *in his lifetime*.

> *on* + one's + *own*

> We can't do everything *on our own*.

Example

P59

<u>It</u> is <u>unusual</u> for a novelist's first book to <u>be published</u> while the writer is still in <u>the</u> twenties.
A   B   C   D

[Explanation]
The correct pattern is *in* one's *twenties*. Therefore the article *the* should be the possessive *his or her*.
Correction: his or her

 **Conditionals**

Questions of this kind involve supplying missing conditionals and identifying incorrect conditionals.
Questions of this kind have rarely appeared on recent TOEFL tests.

The two kinds of conditionals are *real* and *unreal.*

1. Real Conditionals

Real conditionals apply to possible situations.

$$If + \text{Subject} + \text{Present}, \quad \ldots \left\{ \begin{array}{l} will \\ can \\ may \end{array} \right\} + \text{Base form of verb}$$

> If I *see* him, I *will tell* him you are here.
> (It is possible that I will see him.)

2. Unreal Conditionals

Unreal conditionals apply to impossible or unreal situations.

(1) Present unreal

$$If + \text{Subject} + \text{Past}, \quad \ldots \left\{ \begin{array}{l} would \\ could \\ should \\ might \end{array} \right\} + \text{Base form of verb}$$

> If he *worked* harder, he *could succeed.*
> (He doesn't work hard.)

> If he *were* rich, he *would go* to Europe to study.
> (He is not rich.)

For all persons, the correct form of the verb *be* is *were.*

(2) Past unreal

$$If + \text{Subject} + \text{Past perfect}, \quad \ldots \left\{ \begin{array}{l} would \\ could \\ should \\ might \end{array} \right\} + have + \text{Past participle}$$

> If he *had worked* harder, he *would have succeeded.*
> (He didn't work hard.)

Examples

P60-1

If New York were a country, _____ the ninth largest economy in the world.

(A) be
(B) it is
(C) it would be
(D) would it be

[Explanation]

This sentence indicates a present unreal condition. Therefore a verb in the main clause should be *would* + base form. The correct answer is Choice (C).

P60-2

If the camel <u>has</u> to go <u>without</u> food for <u>a period</u> of time, the fat in the hump could nourish it
          A   B   C
for <u>several days</u>.
      D

[Explanation]

This sentence indicates a present unreal condition. Therefore the verb has in the *if*-clause should be the past form, *had*.
Correction: had

Mini-Test 13

1. *Miacis* is believed by <u>many</u> to be the common <u>ancestor</u> of all
                   A   B

   <u>land-dwelled</u> carnivores, including dogs <u>as well as</u> cats.
        C   D

LinguaForum

2. <u>In</u> the 19th century several famous American <u>historian</u> wrote
   A   B

   histories of the United States <u>assuming</u> the young nation was
                                   C

   <u>particularly blessed.</u>
         D

LinguaForum

3. In 1765 Samuel Adams was elected <u>to</u> the Massachusetts
                              A

   <u>colonial</u> assembly and <u>become</u> the <u>leader</u> of opposition to the
     B   C   D

   British government.

LinguaForum

4. The New Deal was _____ the problems created by the
   Depression by having the federal government take action and
   intervene in the business cycle.

     (A)   to solve a major effort
     (B)   as a major effort solved
     (C)   a major effort to solve
     (D)   a major effort and solution

LinguaForum

5. The Statue of Liberty is <u>very</u> large <u>that</u> <u>as many as</u> twelve
                                    A   B   C

people can <u>stand inside</u> the torch.
                  D

---

6. Meteoroids are small chunks of stone or stone and iron,
_____ are fragments of asteroids or comets.

- Ⓐ which some
- Ⓑ they
- Ⓒ some of them
- Ⓓ some of which

---

7. Key West, which is <u>the southernmost</u> city in the United States,
                              A

<u>spread</u> over a small island, four <u>miles</u> long and <u>less than</u> two
    B   C   D

miles wide.

---

8. Not only _____ more air faster than other mammals, but
they also are better at absorbing and storing the oxygen in the air.

- Ⓐ that marine mammals do breathe
- Ⓑ while marine mammals breathe
- Ⓒ marine mammals breathe
- Ⓓ do marine mammals breathe

STRUCTURE

9. Watercolors are <u>equally</u> suitable for <u>making</u> a <u>quickly</u> sketch
                A   B   C

with <u>a few strokes</u> or a detailed, highly finished painting.
      D

LinguaForum

10. _____ liquid water cools, the molecules not only move
more slowly, but they also pack more closely together and take
up less space.

(A) That
(B) In
(C) When
(D) Nevertheless

LinguaForum

READING SECTION

Reading

Overview of the CBT Reading Section

This section consists of four to five reading passages, each accompanied by an average of eleven questions referring to those passages, depending on the types of tests.

The test is timed, and you will be given 70 minutes (4 passages with 44 questions) or 90 minutes (5 passages with 55 questions) to complete this section. An average amount of time assigned for each passage and eleven accompanying questions is about eighteen minutes.

	Listening	**Structure**	**Reading**	**Writing**
Type 1	49/50 questions	20 questions	44 questions	1 question
	25 min.	15 min.	70 min.	30 min.
Type 2	30 questions	25 questions	55 questions	1 question
	15 min.	19 min.	90 min.	30 min.

(Table 1: Types of tests)

Each passage consists of about 280 to 350 words usually divided into two to five paragraphs. Passages cover a wide variety of topics from subjects including, but not limited to, natural sciences and technology, North American history & culture, social sciences, biography and arts. Passages are similar in style and topic to those found in textbooks used in North American universities and colleges.

Natural sciences and technology	North American history and culture	Social sciences	Arts	Biography
40%	20%	10%	15%	15%

(Table 2: Approximate distribution of subjects)

● Should you guess?

The CBT Reading Section is not computer-adaptive but linear, which means that the items on any given test do not change based on your performance on prior questions during the test. Your score is based on your performance on the questions presented, the difficulty of the questions presented, and on the number of questions you answer. On the other hand, the Listening and Structure Sections are computer-adaptive.

Within the CBT Reading Section, you may skip a question, move on to others and return later to answer a question you have left blank. You can also change your previous answer choice. To choose a different answer, click on a different oval in the multiple-choice questions.

Compare with the Listening and Structure Sections in which you are not allowed to skip a question and to go back later after you have confirmed the answer choice and moved on to other questions.

Remember, though, that it will cost you precious time to skip a question and return to it later. Moreover, you may have trouble remembering which questions you have left blank.

Thus, it is strongly recommended to answer all the questions about one reading passage before moving on.

When you need to guess the answer, try to use the process of elimination. Your chances of choosing the correct answer will get higher if you eliminate more answer choices as incorrect before guessing.

● Types of Questions Represented in the CBT Reading Section

We strongly recommend that you familiarize yourself with the main types of questions. According to the methods of answering, two types of questions appear on the test. You may sometimes encounter answer choices consisting of drawings.

Types of Questions
(1) Multiple-choice questions
　　Click on an oval and the oval darkens to show which answer you have chosen.
(2) "Click-on" questions
　　Click on a black square, any part of the word, phrase, sentence, or paragraph in the passage as directed by each question.

Representation
(1) Multiple-choice questions only
　　Main idea (main topic, best title) questions
　　Fact/Negative type questions
　　Inference questions
　　Purpose questions
　　Organization, Tone/Attitude/Purpose, Preceding/Following Topic questions
(2) "Click-on" questions only
　　Insertion questions (sentence addition question)
　　Scanning questions
(3) Both Multiple-choice and "Click on" questions
　　Reference/Vocabulary questions

● How to Begin the CBT Reading Section

(1) The very first screen of the Reading Section is "Directions."
　　On the upper right side of the computer screen, you will see the icon Dismiss Directions. Click on the Dismiss Directions icon to view the very first passage.

(2) You should first read the entire passage. You will see only the part of the passage on the first screen. It is because the actual passage is too long to fit on the first screen at one time. Use the scroll bar to view the rest of the passage. You cannot see the first question about that passage without viewing the entire passage, regardless of whether you actually read it or not.

　　On the upper right side of the computer screen, you will see the icon Proceed. Click on the Proceed icon. Then the questions about the passage will be presented. There will be just one question per screen. When you click on an oval before each answer choice, the oval darkens.

To choose a different answer, just click on a different oval. Then the newly selected oval will darken to show which answer you have chosen. Do not spend too much time on any one question. Keep in mind that an average amount of time per passage and 11 questions is about eighteen minutes. You may leave a tough question blank and return later to answer it.

At the bottom of the right side of the Reading screen, you will see the icons Help, Prev, Next. Click on Next to move on to the next question. There is no Confirm Answer icon because the Reading Section is not computer-adaptive.

(3) To answer the "Click-on" questions, you can click on any part of the passage as stated by the question-specific directions. You will have ample opportunity to become familiar with the wording of questions or directions by working through Intensive Exercises and Practice Tests provided in this book.

Click on the word, phrase or sentence in the **bold** typed section of the passage as you think proper. When you need to click on a sentence in the passage, you may click on any part of the sentence. Then, the whole sentence will be highlighted. Likewise, click on any part of the word or phrase in the passage as directed by the questions. The relevant part of the passage is marked with an arrow (➔).

Click on the black square [■] between the sentences in the insertion (i.e. sentence addition) question. An insertion question requires you to click on a black square to insert the excerpted sentence, given in the question part, into the passage. When you click on a black square where you think the excerpted sentence should be added, the excerpted sentence will appear in the passage in a dark box, replacing a black square [■]. You may click on another square to change your answer.

Reading Strategies

Strategy 1: Getting ready for the Test

1. Know the test beforehand and practice! Before taking the test, you are advised to familiarize yourself with the types of questions appearing on the CBT Reading Section and exercise with the practice tests regularly until you find yourself comfortable approaching them.

2. You will find the whole package of reading questions divided into just six categories in this book. Knowing all six categories is not an overwhelming task. Moreover, knowing what is going to be tested beforehand will greatly relieve you psychologically and enable you to use the test time more efficiently.

3. Practice computer skills needed to navigate through the passage and to answer questions. Know what the icons such as Prev or Next represent and when to click them.

Strategy 2: How to do best during the Test

1. Pacing yourself is important.
   On average, about eighteen minutes are allotted to each passage and eleven associated questions. Passages vary in length or degree of difficulty. However, do not spend too much time on any one set of passages/questions.

2. Apply the required reading skill properly.

   You are not supposed to read the whole passage whenever you are faced with a question. For overview items, read the whole passage cursorily. For questions focusing on details, scan the relevant part of the passage looking for the information needed to answer that particular question. You should practice locating the relevant part using key expressions. In some questions, the relevant paragraphs are marked with arrows.

3. You may leave some questions unanswered and return later.

   Unlike the Listening and Structure Sections, you may move forward or backward among questions as you wish within the CBT Reading Section. Be sure to come back to the questions you left unanswered before you move on to the Writing Section. You should guess even if you are not sure of the correct answer, because your score is not penalized for the questions answered incorrectly.

Strategy 3: How to score high in the CBT Reading Section

This book provides ample test tips in each chapter as to how to approach each category of questions. Please refer to individual chapters for detailed test tips.

Take Care

Test Day Checklist

Don't forget to bring your photo-bearing Identification Document:
Valid passport, or valid driver's license, or a National Identity Card bearing a recognizable photograph.

Testing normally begins at 9:00 a.m. or 1:30 p.m. (twice a day).
Be sure to arrive at the test center thirty minutes early (by 8:30 a.m. or 1:00 p.m.) to ensure proper check in. Your identification will be checked before you are assigned a seat in the test room. The test starts with the tutorial. The test lasts up to 4 hours.

Dismissal is at 1:00 p.m. or 5:30 p.m. (You may leave early.)
During the entire test, there will be one mandatory five-minute break after the structure section is finished. Then the test will resume with the reading section. You must leave the room during this break.

Chapter 1 Main Idea

Frequency of appearance per passage with 11 questions: one
Standard Multiple-Choice
Difficulty Range: Medium to Difficult

Overview

1. What is the question about?

The main idea (main topic, best title) questions ask you to identify the most important idea (thought) in the passage, or the author's reason for writing the passage. To put it simply, the main idea is what the passage is about as a whole.

The main idea is sometimes explicitly stated in a single sentence. However, in many cases, you have to decide upon a main idea from a collection of individual ideas (thoughts) scattered throughout the passage. Thus, practicing how to construct a main idea from individual ideas is very important.

Main topic questions may be asked where a single, dominating main idea is not readily identifiable. These questions ask you to identify the main subject of the entire passage. Answer choices usually consist of nouns or noun phrases instead of full sentences.

Main idea and main topic questions are sometimes reformulated to ask the best title for the entire passage. Although less frequently asked, another type of question asks you about a single paragraph's main topic.

2. What terms should I know?

Main Idea: *the author's message or the important thought of the passage*
It may be stated directly in a topic sentence, often appearing near the beginning or end of the passage. In such a case, read the first and last sentences of the passage to identify the main idea of the passage. In many cases, the main idea does not appear as a single sentence. Also, it is not stated directly but suggested by key expressions. The main idea directs both the writer and the reader through the discussion of the main topic.

Main Topic: *the subject of the passage*
In other words, the topic of a passage is what the passage is mainly about. It is the passage's most talked-about subject and usually stated in a few words or a phrase.

Best Title: *the name of a piece of writing*
The best title is generally the restatement of the main idea or topic of the passage in the form of a heading placed at the top of the passage.

Supporting Sentences: *the details in the passage*
Supporting sentences consist of detail sentences that explain, illustrate, develop, or otherwise support the main topic or idea.

3. How is the question worded?

Passage Main Idea

What does the passage mainly discuss?

The passage is primarily concerned with ...

What is the passage mainly about?

The passage supports which of the following generalizations?

The passage focuses on which of the following aspects of ____?

Which of the following is the main topic of the passage?

With what is the passage mainly concerned?

Which of the following aspects of ____ does the passage mainly discuss?

What is the main idea of the passage?

What is the subject of the passage?

Why did the author write the passage?

Which of the following would be the best title?

Paragraph Main Idea

Which of the following is the main point the author makes about ____?

What aspect of ____ does paragraph __ mainly discuss?

What is paragraph __ mainly about?

With what topic is paragraph __ mainly concerned?

Paragraph __ is marked with an arrow [➡].

Strategies

1. Key points to remember

Skimming the passage is useful to get a general idea of a passage quickly. Skimming involves looking through the passage to have an idea of a passage's topic, main idea, overall organization, or other overview items such as purpose and tone.

When you take the TOEFL, begin each passage by skimming it. Pay attention to the first and the last sentence of each paragraph. Skim the rest of the passage with the focus on key expressions. You should be able to distinguish between main ideas and specific details.

Take notice that a passage's central idea and details may be arranged differently to correspond to different ways of developing the central idea. However, usual locations are as follows:

(1) Main idea at the beginning

In this case, a topic sentence comes first. Then follow clarifying, limiting, supporting, or other detail sentences.

(2) Main idea at the end

In some passages, the central idea (the topic sentence) may appear at the end, after supporting sentences set the stage for the appearance of a main idea statement.

(3) Main idea in the middle

In another type of the passage, details come first and are summed up in a topic sentence occurring in the middle, which is supported further with more details and examples. The main idea of the passage appears in the middle.

Topic sentence Supporting sentences	General statement or Introduction Detail sentences **Topic sentence**	General statement or Introduction **Topic sentence** Detail sentences
(main idea at the begining)	(main idea at the end)	(main idea in the middle)

2. Test tips

To answer questions on the CBT about the topic and the main idea of a passage, proceed as follows:

(1) Read the first several sentences until you find the topic sentence or main idea sentence.

(2) Read the last several sentences to get an idea of concluding remarks and the rephrased main idea.

(3) Skim the rest of the passage surrounding the key words to verify the topic and the main idea of the passage.

(4) Read the first question (usually involving the topic or main idea) about the passage.

(5) Read the answer choices. Eliminate answer choices that are too broadly or too narrowly formulated. They are most likely to be wrong answers. The more choices you can eliminate, the better your chances are for answering correctly. Choose the best answer from the remaining ones.

Skill Building

Skill Building: Selecting a topic sentence

Guide : *A topic sentence in a paragraph alerts readers to the main point of the paragraph by stating the central idea and expressing the writer's attitude towards it. The central idea (the topic sentence) may come at the beginning, in the middle or at the end of the paragraph. Other sentences in the paragraph usually function as supporting ones with specific details bolstering the central idea.*

Directions : *Read the following paragraphs. Underline the sentence that best qualifies as the topic sentence for each paragraph.*

* Remark: Questions in the following format do not appear on the actual CBT reading.

1. Animals learn not only by trial and error, but also by conditioning, which involves a system of rewards or punishments. If you have a dog, you and your parents probably trained it in this way. A Russian scientist named Pavlov once conducted a famous experiment in conditioning. Pavlov rang a bell every time he offered food to a group of dogs. The dogs would begin to salivate when they were fed. After repeating this action many times, Pavlov continued to ring the bell, but without feeding the dogs. He discovered that the dogs still began to salivate every time he rang the bell.

[Explanation]

The first sentence is the topic sentence with the main idea. The rest of the paragraph bolsters the main idea by giving a detailed description of the experiments conducted by Pavlov.

2. Look at the Atacama Desert of South America. It is found near the thirtieth parallel south of the equator. Similarly, the Sahara and the Rub'al-Khali deserts of northern Africa and nearby Saudi Arabia are 30° north of the equator, while the Kalahari Desert of southern Africa is about 30° south of it. The Gobi Desert of central Asia lies a little farther than 30° north, at about 45°, while the Great Sandy and Gibson deserts of Australia fall back into the pattern, lying 30° south of the equator. This pattern is no coincidence. All the hot deserts are found about the same distance north or south of the equator.

[Explanation]

The last sentence is the topic sentence with the main idea. The rest of the paragraph leads to the main idea by giving specific and diverse examples of the deserts in the world and their locations.

VOCABULARY

1
reward: something given in exchange for good behavior
conduct: to organize and direct (a particular activity)
salivate: to produce saliva (the natural, watery liquid in the mouth)

2
parallel: being the same distance apart along all their length
equator: an imaginary line that goes around the middle of the earth and that is an equal distance from the North Pole and the South Pole
coincidence: an occasion when two or more

things happen at the same time

3. Andrew Jackson may have been a headstrong, stubborn general, and cruel to Native Americans. However, he was very popular with the American people. His great popularity helped get him elected president in 1828, and President Jackson brought his frontier ways to Washington, D.C. He had grown up in the Carolina backwoods and had lived much of his life as a soldier. Some people saw him as a "self-made man" who had succeeded because of his own toughness and efforts. He was not born rich or had any special advantages.

[Explanation]

The topic sentence with the main point is in the middle of the paragraph. The rest of the paragraph supports the main idea by giving specific and various descriptions of Andrew Jackson.

4. The Progressives of the early decades of the 20th century wanted to clean up and reform government and to use government to advance human welfare. They were opposed to the abuse of power by political machines and monopolies. They wanted to apply scientific management to government just as it was being applied to business and to use it to solve urban problems. Many Progressives had an aversion to party politics.

[Explanation]

The first sentence is the topic sentence with the main idea. The rest of the paragraph bolsters the main idea by giving several examples of viewpoints taken by progressives.

5. As one of its last acts during the reconstruction era, Congress passed a Civil Rights Act in 1876 to provide equal accommodation in public places like hotels. No enforcement provisions were included, however, and without federal enforcement provisions, the Act was a failure. This failure discouraged Congress from making further attempts to secure civil rights by legislation. When the Civil Rights Movement got Congress to act in the 1960s, enforcement measures were included in the Civil Rights Act.

[Explanation]

The topic sentence is located in the middle of the paragraph. The main point that the author tries to make is that the Civil Rights Act of 1876 was a failure because it contained no provision for enforcement.

VOCABULARY

3 **stubborn**: opposed to change or suggestion
frontier: (in the past in the US) a border between developed land where white people lived and land where Indians lived or land that was wild
tough (n. toughness): difficult to do or deal with, likely to be violent or to contain violence

4 **progressive**: in favor of new ideas, modern methods and change
abuse: the use of something in an unsuitable or wrong way
monopoly: complete control of the supply of particular goods or services
aversion: a feeling of strong dislike to do something

5 **reconstruction**: the activity of building again something that has been damaged or destroyed
accommodation: a place to live, work or stay in
enforce (n. enforcement): to make sure that people obey a particular law or rule
measure: an official action that is done in order to achieve a particular aim

Intensive Exercises

Exercise 1.1

Joseph Pulitzer, who began with a St. Louis newspaper and moved to New York, introduced the idea of the "yellow press," which was named for the "yellow kid" in his colored comic page in the New York World. Yellow journalism is based on sensationalism and exposures in order to sell papers. Papers battling for more readers and more advertising struggled to outdo each other in reporting scandals.

The public bought the papers suggesting an aspect of the American character different from the clean cowboy image of frontier legend. William Randolph Hearst in the San Francisco *Examiner* was another noted practitioner of yellow journalism. Both he and Joseph Pulitzer built large publishing empires.

Editors' competition for readers led to emotional reporting on the international situation in Cuba in the 1890s. The press had a major role in bringing the United States into the Spanish-American War.

1. Which of the following best summarizes the author's main idea?
   - (A) The first newspaper ever founded was a St. Louis newspaper.
   - (B) Yellow journalism is developed to sell more papers.
   - (C) The press had a very important role in the United States.
   - (D) The press relied on scandals to compete for readers.

 Time

LinguaForum

 Help Prev Next

READING

[Explanation]

1. Choice (A) is too specific and not mentioned in the passage (irrelevant). Choice (C) is too broadly formulated. Choice (D) is too specific and just supports the author's main point. The correct choice should mention the key expression of the passage, that is, "yellow journalism."

VOCABULARY

sensationalism: a way of getting people's interest by using shocking words or by presenting facts and events as worse or more shocking than they really are

exposure: the fact of being discussed or mentioned on television, in newspapers, etc.
outdo: to do more or better than somebody else
legend: a story from ancient times about people

and events, that may or may not be true
practitioner: a person who regularly does a particular activity, especially one that requires skill

Exercise 1.2

The American economic system had worked for Hoover, and he was committed to preserving that system as he knew it. He had explained his views on the American system and "rugged individualism" during the 1928 campaign, saying the system demanded "economic justice as well as political and social justice" and was "no system of laissez-faire." He also extolled liberalism as "a force truly of the spirit, a force proceeding from the deep realization that economic freedom cannot be sacrificed if political freedom is to be preserved."

By thus tying economic freedom to political freedom, when faced with the recession, Hoover firmly believed he could not act to control or infringe the freedom enjoyed by business and business interests. Yet he believed in economic and political justice and that the government was "an umpire instead of a player in the economic game." He believed that the government could have a role in economic activity, but only as an insurer of fair play.

1. Which of the following is the main point the author makes about Hoover?
   - (A) Hoover supported economic freedom at the cost of economic justice.
   - (B) Hoover held contradictory beliefs as to the role of the government.
   - (C) Hoover recommended extensive government involvement in the economic system.
   - (D) Hoover consistently extolled the economic system of laissez-faire.

 Time

LinguaForum

 Help **Prev** **Next**

[Explanation]

1. The passage indicates that although Hoover believed in economic justice and the role of government as an umpire, he nonetheless extolled liberalism, rugged individualism and economic freedom as well. In this regard, Hoover was a man of contradictions. Choice (A) is inaccurate. Choices (C) and (D) represent only one side of Hoover's policy.

VOCABULARY

rugged: strong or powerful; not delicate
laissez-faire: the policy of allowing private businesses to develop without government control
extol: to praise highly

liberalism: liberal opinions and beliefs, especially in politics
umpire: a person who controls a game and makes sure that the rules are followed

contradictory: containing or showing a contradiction
contradiction: a lack of agreement between facts, opinions, actions, etc

Exercise 1.3

The full recognition of the place of the artist is most important to the future of our country and our civilization. In a free society, art is not a weapon and it does not belong to the sphere of polemics and ideology. Artists are not engineers of the soul.

It may be different elsewhere. But in the democratic society, the highest duty of the writer, the composer, the artist is to remain true to himself and to let the chips fall where they may. Furthermore, if art is to nourish the roots of our culture, society must set the artist free to follow his vision wherever it takes him.

By doing so, we may look forward to a great future for America – a future in which our country will match its economic strength with our moral restraint, its wealth with our wisdom, its power with our purpose.

1. What aspect of the artists does the passage mainly discuss?
   - (A) The roles of artists as social engineers
   - (B) The high aesthetic standards of artists in the democratic society
   - (C) Polemics among the writer, the composer and the artist
   - (D) The importance of the artist's fidelity

LinguaForum

READING

[Explanation]

1. In the middle of the passage, we find the topic sentence: "But in the democratic society, the highest duty of the writer, the composer, the artist is to remain true to himself and to let the chips fall where they may." Its main point is that artists should keep their true characters, instead of pretending to be soul-engineers. Choice (A) contradicts the information in the passage. Answer choices (B) and (C) are too broad.

VocaBULARY

recognition: the acceptance of something as true
nourish: to provide (people or animals) with food in order to make them grow and keep them healthy
polemics: the practice or skill of arguing strongly

for or against something
let the chips fall where they may: let what happens happen regardless of outcome
restraint: determined control over behavior in

order to prevent the strong expression of emotion or any violent action

Exercise 1.4

The accumulating evidence indicates that acid rain is one of the most serious worldwide pollution problems confronting us today. The potential consequences of its effects on biological systems are immense: lowered crop yields, decreased timber production, the need for greater amounts of increasingly expensive fertilizer to compensate for nutrient leaking, the loss of important freshwater fishing areas, and, possibly, of the eastern forests as well. The monetary and social costs of allowing the conditions that create acid rain to continue (or even to increase) are potentially very great, as are the costs of available processes to remove the sulfur and nitrogen oxides at the source, before they enter the air.

Scientists from many fields are presently engaged in research to gain a greater understanding of the causes and effects of acid rain and the likely consequences of proposed solutions. Although scientists can provide information on which decisions can be based, the choices that lie ahead are essentially social and economic, to be made through political processes.

1. What is the main idea of the passage?
   - (A) Acid rain does less damage than originally thought by the environmentalists.
   - (B) Scientists have the ultimate authority to decide which issue should be addressed.
   - (C) Solutions to the problem of acid rain are not entirely based on scientific data but also on value judgment.
   - (D) Cost-benefit analysis is highly recommended before scientists embark on the costly research on acid rain.

 LinguaForum

[Explanation]

1. Pay attention to the last sentence of the passage, which states that "Although scientists can provide information on which decisions can be based, the choices that lie ahead are essentially social and economic, to be made through political processes." The author placed his main point at the end of the passage. Choice (A) is too specific. Choice (B) or (D) is irrelevant.

Vocabulary

potential: possible but not yet achieved
immense: extremely large; great in size or degree

yield: a profit or an amount produced
fertilizer: a natural or chemical substance that is

spread on land in order to make plants grow well
sulfur, nitrogen: chemical elements

Exercise 1.5

Westerners, having been introduced to the music of their own cultural tradition as part of the childhood enculturation process, usually find Western music most appealing. Conversely, they may find Asian music unappealing, because it separates tones from one another differently from Western music. In the fixed set of tones (or scale) on which Western music is based, each tone is separated from its nearest neighbor according to how many more or fewer vibrations it comprises. Divided from one another in this way, the tones on which Western music is based make up an octave, a set of eight primary tones. To the Western ear, music based on the octave sounds "correct" and pleasing.

But in Japan, where the set of tones on which traditional music is based does not conform to the octave, Western music may sound unmusical. The two very different kinds of music are, however, equally pleasing to listeners in the context of their own cultures.

1. Which of the follwing is the main point the author makes about music?

  (A) An octave is a universal feature of different kinds of music.

  (B) Music is an important part of social life, often accompanying social events.

  (C) Different kinds of music are equally appealing in the context of listeners' cultural backgrounds.

  (D) Music sounds "correct" when the set of tones conforms to a set of eight primary tones.

 LinguaForum

READING

[Explanation]

1. The last sentence ("The two very different kinds of music are, however, equally pleasing to listeners in the context of their own cultures") summarizes the author's main point. Other sentences in the passage support the main point as specific examples.

VOCABULARY

conversely: from a different and opposite way of looking at something
vibration: a continuous shaking movement

comprise: to consist of or to be made up of
conform: to operate according to a rule

octave: the difference between the first and last notes in a series of eight notes on a musical scale

Exercise 1.6

It has already been noted that, because physical and chemical conditions change from place to place, different parts of the ocean harbor very distinct communities. For convenience, marine biologists categorize communities according to where and how the organisms live. Perhaps the simplest classification relates to the lifestyle of the organism: whether it lives on the bottom or up in the water column. Benthic organisms, or the benthos, are those that live on or buried in the bottom. Some benthic organisms are sessile, or attached to one place; others move around. Pelagic organisms, on the other hand, live up in the water column, away from the bottom.

Pelagic organisms are further subdivided according to how well they can swim. Some marine organisms swim only weakly or not at all. These organisms, called plankton, are at the mercy of the currents and are carried from place to place. The term "plankton" comes from the Greek word for "drifters." Planktonic algae and other autotrophs are collectively called the phytoplankton and are the most important primary producers in many marine ecosystems. The animal plankton is called the zooplankton.

1. What aspect of the marine environment does the passage mainly discuss?
   (A) Characteristics of different parts of the ocean
   (B) The simplest classification of organisms
   (C) Subdivision of the organisms according to how well they can swim
   (D) Classification of marine organisms according to their lifestyles

 Time　　　**LinguaForum**　　　 **Help** **Prev** **Next**

[Explanation]

1. Refer to the first paragraph ("For convenience, marine biologists categorize communities according to where and how the organisms live. Perhaps the simplest classification relates to the lifestyle of the organism") as well as the first sentence of the second paragraph. Choices (A) and (B) are too broad. Choice (C) applies only to paragraph 2, and is too specific.

VOCABULARY

harbor: to protect by giving them a place to hide
benthic organism, pelagic organism: types of organisms living in the ocean

sessile: attached to one place
plankton: the very small forms of plant and animal life that live in seas, rivers, lakes, etc.

algae: very simple plants that grow in or near water and do not have ordinary leaves or roots

Exercise 1.7

Farmers conserve or add to the fertility of the soil by keeping some land fallow each season. Fallow land is plowed but is not seeded during a growing season. Farmers also help keep the soil fertile by growing a fallow crop. A fallow crop is one that nourishes the soil, such as soybeans.

Extensive irrigation systems and complex farm machinery also help to increase the region's agricultural production. Nearly all farmers in the United States and Canada use tractors rather than animals for plowing. However, owners of smaller farms often find it too costly to buy equipment such as combines. Combines are harvest machines used for reaping and threshing grain. These machines are very costly and are best suited for very large farms. As more-complex and more-expensive machinery is developed, it is harder for owners of small farms to compete with the owners of large farms. Therefore, the number of large farms in the United States and Canada is steadily increasing, while the number of small farms is decreasing.

1. What aspect of farming does the passage mainly discuss?
   - (A) Ways to increase agricultural production and side effects
   - (B) Competition between owners of large farms and those of small farms
   - (C) Hardship of installing costly equipments on small farms
   - (D) A competitive advantage in the agriculture of the United States and Canada

 Time LinguaForum   **Help** **Prev** **Next**

[Explanation]

1. Refer to the first sentence of the first paragraph: "Farmers conserve or add to the fertility of the soil by keeping some land fallow each season." And also look at the first sentence of the second paragraph: "Extensive irrigation systems and complex farm machinery also help to increase the region's agricultural production." Choice (B) or (C) is too narrow, related only to the side effects of utilizing costly machines. Choice (D) is too broad and irrelevant.

VOCA BULARY

conserve: to keep and protect from waste, loss, or damage; preserve

fallow: not used for growing crops, especially so that the quality of the land will improve

fertile: able to produce a large number of high-quality crops

irrigate: to supply with water so that crops and plants will grow or grow better

thresh: to remove the seeds of crop plants by hitting, using either a machine or a hand tool

Exercise 1.8

Large, slow-moving bodies of heated or cooled air are called air masses. Air masses form over North America and affect our weather. There are seven major air masses in North America: three in the north, and four in the south. Northern air masses are usually cooler high pressure systems, while southern air masses are warm, low pressure systems. Air pressure is the weight of the air pressing down on the earth, and air pressure systems are the ways different parts of the air press down on the earth.

Air masses can also be wet or dry, depending on whether they form over very dry land, such as the desert, or wet areas, such as the oceans. The wet Tropical Atlantic air mass forms over the warm currents of the Gulf Stream, and travels up the eastern coast of the United States.

The three northern and four southern air masses tend to meet over an area covering the parts of North America that the most number of people live in. This is known as the zone of mixing or the temperate zone. Most of the United States is in the temperate zone. Because the number of hot and cold air masses is almost the same, they tend to balance each other out, and the temperate zone has warm summers, cold winters, and moderate spring and fall temperatures.

1. Which of the following would be the best title?
   - (A) The Causes of Different Types of Climate
   - (B) How Air Masses Affect Weather and Climate
   - (C) How Clouds are Formed in the Temperate Zone
   - (D) Where in North America Air Masses Tend to Meet Each Other

LinguaForum

[Explanation]

1. Choice (A) is too broad. Choice (C) is irrelevant (not mentioned in the passage), and Choice (D) applies only to the 3rd paragraph. The phrase "air mass" is the key expression mentioned throughout the passage. Thus, the answer choice that contains the expression "air mass" is most likely to be the correct answer.

VOCABULARY

tropical: of or characteristic of the tropics
tropics: the hottest area of the earth, the area on either side of the equator reaching to 23.5 degrees to the north and south

current: a movement of water or air
zone: an area, esp. one that has different characteristics from the ones around it or is used for different purposes

temperate: not extreme; within a middle range
moderate: not extreme

Vocabulary Review for Intensive Exercises 1.1-1.8

1. Sometimes small firms can _____ multinational business when it comes to customer care.

    (A) outdo
    (B) overdose
    (C) outlook
    (D) outside

2. Her documentary film has been subject to a lot of media _____ recently.

    (A) public
    (B) extension
    (C) exposure
    (D) upset

3. A less _____ vehicle would never have finished the trip.

    (A) inert
    (B) reversible
    (C) rugged
    (D) presumptuous

4. His public appearance is directly in _____ to his private life.

    (A) contradiction
    (B) conversion
    (C) conviction
    (D) diversion

5. The young movie star demanded _____ of his privacy.

    (A) retribution
    (B) resent
    (C) rage
    (D) recognition

6. Breast feeding _____ a baby and provides natural immunity.

    (A) notes
    (B) nourishes
    (C) neutralizes
    (D) notifies

7. A competent salesman is eager to talk with _____ customers.

    (A) popular
    (B) plain
    (C) potential
    (D) proficient

8. Whales are _____ animals that can grow as long as sixty feet.

    (A) immense
    (B) immediate
    (C) imaginary
    (D) impartial

9. Shelly refused to _____ to the traditional woman's role.

    (A) conform
    (B) catch
    (C) cause
    (D) confuse

10. Bob feels _____ to his stepfather.

    (A) attended
    (B) attached
    (C) approved
    (D) appreciated

11. In order to _____ natural gas, they installed extra insulation.

    (A) consent
    (B) contact
    (C) contract
    (D) conserve

12. The disease only _____ young children.

    (A) affords
    (B) applauds
    (C) affects
    (D) achieves

Practice Test 1

Questions 1-11

Modern European and American artists were slow to discover native North American art, when compared with the relatively early interest which African objects had stimulated in Cubist art circles. In this case, it was notably the émigré European Surrealists such as Max Ernst who saw in native American art the sources of renewal and deeper vision that they held to be representative of the "primeval" world. These artists were especially attracted to the art of the Northwest coast because it was largely literary, and their intuitive acceptance of these works was in many ways more broadly based than the anthropologists' recognition of their particular aesthetic principles.

Other modern artists, such as American John Sloan, were responsible for the greater acceptance of native American painting in wider American art circles. By 1920, Sloan had learned about the native painters of San Ildefonso and arranged an exhibition of their works at the Society of Independent Artists in New York. Other shows of modern Indian painting were organized during the next years. Finally, after a dramatic turn-around in Federal policy, a government-funded Indian Art School known as the Studio was opened in Santa Fe in 1932. In the emerging Pan-Indian painting tradition nobody could fail to recognize art.

➜ ■ Gradual efforts to foster interest in the native American art increased. ■ With the goal of stimulating the public's interest, the Denver Museum in 1925 exhibited for the first time native American Art as works of art and not as anthropological specimens. ■ Other milestones include an exhibition organized in 1939 for the Golden Gate Exhibition in San Francisco, also known as the San Francisco World's Fair, and another one in 1941 at the Museum of Modern Art in New York. ■

➜ **During the 40s and 50s, interest declined but the early 60s witnessed a major renaissance. ■ Since then, the recognition of North American native art has become universal. ■ Major shows, numerous art books, and journals have resulted from the revival of Indian art, but most of all the development of a market for tribal crafts, with prices proving them to be art, attest to the successful transformation. ■**

---

1. The main topic of the passage is
   - (A) the influence of native American art on modern European art
   - (B) the diffusion of native American art in European and American art circles
   - (C) the history of the development of native American art
   - (D) the gradual acceptance of native American art in the general public

2. Look at the word **their** in the passage. Click on the word or phrase in the **bold** text that **their** refers to.

3. According to the passage, native North American art influenced all of the following EXCEPT
   - (A) John Sloan
   - (B) Max Ernst
   - (C) African art
   - (D) modern European artists

4. The passage implies that

(A) European artists were more enthusiastic about native North American art than their American counterparts

(B) North American native art has been recognized universally since the 1940s

(C) native American art was accepted earlier than African art among modern artists

(D) European artists were more active in introducing modern Indian paintings to Americans

5. Native American art was exhibited in the following places EXCEPT

(A) the Museum of Modern Art

(B) the Studio

(C) the Society of Independent Artists

(D) the Denver Museum

6. The San Francisco World's Fair took place in

(A) 1930

(B) 1932

(C) 1939

(D) 1941

7. For most European artists, native North American art was

(A) merely anthropological specimens

(B) representative of the ancient world

(C) aesthetically of the best quality

(D) commercially unviable

8. Which of the following is closest in meaning to foster in the passage?

(A) fray

(B) fund

(C) exploit

(D) stimulate

9. European artists were most interested in native American art of the

(A) Northwest coast

(B) Northeast coast

(C) East coast

(D) West coast

10. Look at the word renaissance in the passage. Click on the word or phrase in the **bold** text that best replaces renaissance.

11. The following sentence can be added to paragraph 3 or 4.

From its collection came many of the art works shown during the 1931 Exposition of Indian Tribal Art, held in New York.

Where would it best fit in the paragraph? Click on the square [■] to add the sentence to paragraph 3 or 4. Paragraphs 3 and 4 are marked with an arrow [➡].

VOCABULARY

stimulate: to encourage something to grow, develop, or become active

primeval: from the earliest period of the history of the world, very ancient

literary: connected with literature

intuitive: (of ideas) obtained by using your feelings rather than by considering the facts

aesthetic: relating to the enjoyment or study of beauty, or (of an object or work of art) showing great beauty

exhibition: a collection of things shown publicly

specimen: something shown or examined as an example; a typical example

universal: existing everywhere or involving

everyone

attest: (of a person) to state with authority that something is true, or (of a situation or event) to show that something is likely to be true

Questions 12-22

The pragmatism of Americans was one of the outstanding traits noted by foreign visitors. In Europe, where class consciousness prevailed, Alexis de Tocqueville remarked that people occupy themselves with "arrogant and sterile researches of abstract truths, while Americans, due to the social conditions and institutions of democracy, busy themselves to seek immediate and useful practical results of the sciences."

One of the most striking examples of the connection between pure research and innovation was in the work of Joseph Henry, a Princeton physicist. His research in electromagnetism provided the basis for Samuel F. B. Morse's invention of the telegraph and for electrical motors later on.

→ It would be difficult to exaggerate the importance of science and technology in changing the ways people live. ■ To cite but a few examples: improved transportation and a spreading market economy combined with innovations in canning and refrigeration to provide people with a more healthy and varied diet. ■ Fruit and vegetables, available only during harvest season, could be shipped in much of the year. ■ Scientific breeding of cattle helped make meat and milk more abundant.

→ Technological advances also helped improve living conditions: houses were larger, better heated and better illuminated. ■ Although working-class residences had few creature comforts, the affluent were able to afford indoor plumbing, central heating, gas lighting, bathtubs, iceboxes, and sewing machines. ■ Even the lower classes were able to afford new coal-burning cast-iron cooking stoves that facilitated the preparation of more varied meals and improved heating. ■ The first sewer systems began to help rid city streets of human and animal waste, while underground water lines enabled fire companies to use hydrants rather than bucket brigades. ■ Machine-made clothes fit better and were cheaper than homespun; newspapers and magazines were more abundant and affordable, as were clocks and watches. ■ Invention often brought about completely new enterprises, the steamboat and the railroad being the most spectacular, without which the pace of development would have been slowed immeasurably. ■

12. The passage mainly discusses
    (A) the pragmatism of Americans as opposed to the idealism of Europeans
    (B) early technological advances in America
    (C) the history of science and technology in early America
    (D) advances in pure research and innovation

13. The word noted in the passage is closest in meaning to
    (A) elected
    (B) classified
    (C) cherished
    (D) observed

14. Look at the word occupy in the passage. Click on the word or phrase in the **bold** text that is closest in meaning to occupy.

15. The author cites the work of Joseph Henry in order to

    (A) illustrate how the US was technologically advanced compared to Europe
    (B) illustrate the increasing importance of university research in America
    (C) show how the result of pure research was put to practical use
    (D) demonstrate how practical research was dependent on pure research

16. Look at the word His in the passage. Click on the word or phrase in the **bold** text that His refers to.

17. The passage cites all of the following innovations EXCEPT

    (A) washing machines
    (B) indoor plumbing
    (C) central heating
    (D) scientific breeding of cows

18. The following sentence can be added to paragraph 3 or 4.

    All aspects of life – the social, cultural, economic, and political – were and are shaped by it.

    Where would it best fit in the paragraph? Click on the square [■] to add the sentence to paragraph 3 or 4.
    Paragraphs 3 and 4 are marked with an arrow [➜].

19. The passage suggests that improvements brought about by technological advances were

    (A) affordable
    (B) expensive
    (C) common
    (D) rare

20. Look at the word working-class in the passage. Click on the word or phrase in the **bold** text that is OPPOSITE in meaning to working-class.

21. The phrase creature comforts in the passage refers to

    (A) small comforts
    (B) comforts for children
    (C) advances in urban living
    (D) improvements in living conditions

22. According to the passage, the lower classes and the affluent both enjoyed

    (A) refrigeration
    (B) indoor plumbing
    (C) cooking stoves
    (D) gas lighting

VOCABULARY

pragmatism: thinking about solving problems in a practical and sensible way rather than by having fixed ideas and theories
prevail: to exist and be accepted among a large number of people, or to get a position of control and influence
abstract: existing as an idea, feeling, or quality, not as a material object
exaggerate: to make something seem larger; more important, better, or worse than it really is
abundant: more than enough; a lot
illuminate: to put light in or on something
hydrant: a pipe in the street that water can be pumped from in order to put out fires or to clean the streets
spectacular: exciting and interesting because of being large or extreme

Questions 23-33

→ As long as people have been communicating with words, they have manipulated language to create pleasurable or meaningful works of art. ■ In Western societies, art in the form of words – poetry, fiction, essays – is usually read from a printed page, and thus experienced silently. ■ But in nonliterate societies, art in the form of words is oral art, spoken or sometimes sung aloud. ■ Even in some small-scale societies whose language is now written, art in the form of words is still primarily oral. ■

→ In traditional settings, oral art consists of stories, songs, poems, riddles, sayings, and other traditional verbal expressions collectively referred to as folklore. ■ Often, the verbal expressions of disparate cultures exhibit remarkable similarities. ■ For instance, the "trickster" – a playful folk figure often portrayed as a young, small, or weak cultural outsider who regularly outwits older, larger or more powerful characters thanks to his cleverness and humor – appears in the oral art of cultures all over the world. ■ The formal study of folklore grew out of nineteenth century scholars' interest in the verbal art of European peasants. ■

The audience for a Western book consists of an unrelated group of individuals separately reading something composed by an author they have in most cases never met. The audience for a work of oral art, in contrast, consists of socially linked individuals who not only listen together to a work of oral art, but may also become an important part of it. The oral artist becomes a performer. He or she is in direct, continuing contact with individuals who, by their instant reaction to the performance, stimulate and sometimes even guide the artist into composing what they wish to hear. The audience for a work of art may consist of members of a particular group, perhaps a lineage or age set or people of a certain social rank, and the theme, content, and purpose of the oral narrative to which they listen may change to fit the social context in which it is recited. The words may also change from recitation to recitation as the mood of the audience changes. And a story told to children will be told differently to adults.

23. Which of the following would be the best title for the passage?
- (A) Narrative Forms in Nonliterate Societies
- (B) Arts in Nonliterate Societies
- (C) The Art of Oral Narrative
- (D) Forms of Verbal Expressions

24. Look at the word they in the passage. Click on the word or phrase in the **bold** text that they refers to.

25. In Western societies, written works of art are
- (A) experienced individually rather than collectively
- (B) experienced in the privacy of one's room
- (C) expressed internally rather than externally
- (D) kept and maintained privately rather than publicly

26. Which of the following is true about oral art?

   (A) It is art practiced among people of low intelligence.

   (B) It is an art form that is primarily performed in literate societies.

   (C) It is art practiced among societies that do not have schools.

   (D) It is still practiced among small-scale societies.

27. The word disparate in the passage could best be replaced by

   (A) difficult
   (B) different
   (C) individual
   (D) specific

28. The following sentence can be added to paragraph 1 or 2.

Later, when ethnographers began collecting data from traditional societies outside Europe, the term came to be applied to their oral literature as well.

Where would it best fit in the paragraph? Click on the square [■] to add the sentence to paragraph 1 or 2. Paragraphs 1 and 2 are marked with an arrow [➡].

29. The passage suggests which of the following is true about the figure of the trickster?

   (A) The trickster belonged to the main stream of traditional societies.

   (B) The trickster was usually an orphan who sought happiness and freedom.

   (C) The trickster was a character who shed light on social injustices.

   (D) The figure of the trickster was exclusively enjoyed by European peasants.

30. Look at the word linked in the passage. Click on the word or phrase in the **bold** text that is OPPOSITE in meaning to linked.

31. Click on the sentence that mentions the origin of the study of folklore.

Scroll the passage to see all of the paragraphs.

32. According to the passage, all of the following describe oral narratives EXCEPT

   (A) adaptable
   (B) spontaneous
   (C) flexible
   (D) predictable

33. It can be inferred from the passage that

   (A) due to the performable nature of oral narratives, performers were considered as professional actors

   (B) due to the flexibility of its contents, there remains no single accurate version of an oral narrative

   (C) contrary to the demands of the audience, performers had to keep their performances fairly predictable

   (D) because of the popularity of oral narratives, performers belong to a particularly well-paid social rank

VOCABULARY

manipulate: to influence or control someone to your advantage, often without their knowing it
oral: spoken; not written
verbal: spoken rather than written
outwit: to obtain an advantage over someone by

being more intelligent
peasant: a member of a low social class of small farmers or farm workers
instant: happening immediately
lineage: the series of families that someone is

descended from
recite: to say (a piece of writing) aloud from memory, or to state in public (a list of things)

Birds have some significant advantages over reptiles, including the ability to fly. They are endotherms, or homeotherms, also known as "warm-blooded." This has allowed them to live in a wide variety of environments, unlike reptiles. **Their bodies are covered with waterproof feathers that help conserve body heat. Water-proofing is provided by oil from a gland above the base of the tail. The birds preen by rubbing the oil into their feathers with their beaks. Flight is made easier by their light, hollow bones. Furthermore, their eggs are more resistant to water loss than those of reptiles.**

→ Seabirds are those birds that spend a significant part of their lives at sea. ■ They nest on land but feed at least partially at sea and have webbed feet to aid them in the water. Seabirds descend from several different groups of land birds. ■ As a result, they differ widely in their flying skills, feeding mechanisms, and ability to live away from the land. Although comprising only about 3% of the estimated 8,600 species of birds, seabirds are distributed from pole to pole, and their impact on marine life is significant. Most are predators of fish, squid, and bottom invertebrates, but some feed on plankton. ■ They need a lot of food to supply the energy required to maintain their body temperatures. ■

→ The shape of a seabird's beak is related to the kind of food it eats and the bird's feeding style. ■ Penguins have strong heavy beaks, a characteristic of seabirds that feed on fish and large plankton like krill. Penguins are the seabirds most fully adapted for life at sea. They are flightless, with wings modified into stubby "flippers" that come alive underwater. ■ **On land it is another story: they are clumsy and awkward. The tubenoses comprise a large group of seabirds with distinctive tube-like nostrils and heavy beaks that are usually curved at the tip. They spend months and even years on the open sea. ■ In tubenoses such as petrels, the beak is relatively short, heavy, and hooked – an ideal shape for holding and tearing prey that are too big to be swallowed whole. ■ Such a beak is best suited for shallow feeding because its size and shape interfere with fast pursuit underwater. ■ Boobies, terns and other plunge divers have a straight and narrow beak for feeding on fish that are swallowed whole. Skimmers are the only birds with a lower part of the beak that is longer than the upper, which permits feeding while flying.**

34. The author is mainly concerned with
 (A) an introduction to birds as a species
 (B) the feeding patterns of seabirds
 (C) a general overview of seabirds
 (D) the differences between seabirds and reptiles

35. How are birds different from reptiles?
 (A) The eggs of birds have a better chance of survival than those of reptiles.
 (B) Reptiles are very sensitive to weather and freeze to death easily.
 (C) Reptiles more easily adapt to their present environments than birds.
 (D) Reptiles have heavy bones that make quick movements impossible.

36. Look at the word their in the passage. Click on the word or phrase in the **bold** text that their refers to.

37. Seabirds differ widely among themselves because they

   (A) live away from the land
   (B) prey on different animals
   (C) are developed from various groups of land birds
   (D) share the same evolutionary history

38. The word comprising in the passage is closest in meaning to

   (A) reforming
   (B) compromising
   (C) combining
   (D) constituting

39. The following sentence can be added to paragraph 2 or 3.

   Whatever they feed on, seabirds have amazing appetites.

   Where would it best fit in the paragraph? Click on the square [■] to add the sentence to paragraph 2 or 3.
   Paragraphs 2 and 3 are marked with an arrow [➡].

40. Look at the word clumsy in the passage. Click on the word or phrase in the **bold** text that is closest in meaning to clumsy.

41. Look at the word curved in the passage. Click on the word or phrase in the **bold** text that is closest in meaning to curved.

42. According to the passage, the beaks of the seabirds

   (A) are an example of how form follows function
   (B) have adapted to the demands of the environment
   (C) are examples of how function follows form
   (D) are the only means through which birds may be differentiated

43. Click on the sentence that mentions what seabirds feed on.

   Scroll the passage to see all of the paragraphs.

44. What does the author mean by the statement its size and shape interfere with fast pursuit underwater?

   (A) Its size and shape allows fast pursuit in the shallow water.
   (B) Its size and shape does not allow fast enough pursuit under the water.
   (C) It enjoys pursuing its prey fast in spite of its shape and size.
   (D) Its size and shape interrupt fast pursuit wherever it occurs.

READING

Questions 45-55

→ The author of two of the most popular books in eighteenth-century America, and the most persuasive rhetorician of the cause for independence that it has ever known, Thomas Paine was born in England in 1737 and did not come to America until he was thirty-seven years old. ■ Paine's early years prepared him to be a supporter of the Revolution. The discrepancy between his high intelligence and the limitations imposed upon him by poverty and class made him long for a new social order. ■

→ **When Paine arrived in Philadelphia with a letter of introduction from Benjamin Franklin, he already had had a remarkably full life. ■ Until he was thirteen he went to grammar school, and then was apprenticed in his father's corset shop; at nineteen he ran away from home to go to sea. ■** From 1757 to 1774 he was a corsetmaker, a tobacconist and grocer, a schoolteacher and an exciseman, a government employee who taxed goods. ■ **During his employment as an exciseman, Paine already demonstrated his courage to challenge the establishment. He defied the government by attempting to organize the excisemen and to demand a raise in income. ■ Franklin was right in recognizing Paine's genius, for like Franklin himself, he was a remarkable man, self-taught, outstanding and curious about everything, from natural sciences to the philosophy of law. ■**

In Philadelphia, he established himself as a journalist and he made his way quickly in that city, first as an abolitionist, speaking against slavery, and then as the anonymous author of *Common Sense*, the first pamphlet published in America to urge immediate independence from Britain. **Paine was obviously the right man in the right place at the right time. Relations with the mother country were at their worst. *Common Sense* sold almost half a million copies and its authorship could not be kept a secret for long. Paine enlisted in the Revolutionary Army and served as an aide-de-camp in battles in New York, New Jersey and Pennsylvania. He followed his triumph of *Common Sense* with the first of sixteen pamphlets entitled *Crisis*. The first *Crisis* paper was read to Washington's troops at Trenton and boosted the spirits of the Revolutionary soldiers. It undoubtedly raised the morale of the soldiers and ultimately brought about the much sought-after independence from England.**

45. The passage is most likely to appear in
  Ⓐ a journal of American politicians
  Ⓑ an anthology of early American literature
  Ⓒ an introduction to Benjamin Franklin
  Ⓓ a tourist guide to New England

46. Look at the word **he** in the passage. Click on the word or phrase in the **bold** text that refers to **he**.

47. The passage explains which of the following terms?
  Ⓐ Corsetmaker
  Ⓑ Exciseman
  Ⓒ Tobacconist
  Ⓓ Pamphleteer

48. Paine sought a new social order due to

    Ⓐ his intelligence

    Ⓑ his hatred towards the British monarchy

    Ⓒ the inability to improve his life because of class and poverty

    Ⓓ his desire to seek a better life in the New World

49. Look at the word outstanding in the passage. Click on the word or phrase in the **bold** text that is closest in meaning to outstanding.

50. The incident during his employment as an exciseman suggests all of the following EXCEPT that

    Ⓐ Paine tried to correct the inequities of society

    Ⓑ Paine sought to challenge authority

    Ⓒ Paine was not content to remain passive in the face of injustice

    Ⓓ Paine argued for maintaining the status quo in eighteenth-century America

51. The following sentence can be added to paragraph 1 or 2.

His effort to organize excisemen and make Parliament raise their salary was unprecedented.

Where would it best fit in the paragraph? Click on the square [■] to add the sentence to paragraph 1 or 2. Paragraphs 1 and 2 are marked with an arrow [➜].

52. The author of *Common Sense* was at first

    Ⓐ Benjamin Franklin

    Ⓑ Thomas Paine

    Ⓒ unknown

    Ⓓ British

53. Look at the word raised in the passage. Click on the word or phrase in the **bold** text that best replaces raised.

54. The passage implies that before Paine

    Ⓐ many had desired to seek independence from England

    Ⓑ no one had written a document arguing for the independence of the colonies from England

    Ⓒ no had proposed the need for independence from England

    Ⓓ many had opposed the idea of independence from England

55. Click on the sentence which explains the term "abolitionist" in the passage.

Scroll the passage to see all of the paragraphs.

VOCABULARY

rhetorician: a person who makes formal speeches in public or is good at public speaking; an orator

discrepancy: a difference between two or more things that should be the same

apprentice: to make somebody an apprentice (somebody who works for an expert to learn a particular skill or job)

defy: to refuse to obey or to do something in the usual or expected way

anonymous: (of a person) with a name that is not known or not made public

urge: to strongly advise someone to do something or to ask that something be done

enlist: to join or to make somebody join the armed forces

morale: the amount of confidence and enthusiasm, etc. that a person or a group has at a particular time

Chapter 2 Reference and Vocabulary

> *Reference:*
> *Frequency of appearance per passage with 11 questions: one*
> *Standard Multiple-Choice or Click on the passage item*
> *Difficulty Range: Easy to Medium*

Reference Overview

1. What is the question about?

In reference questions, you are supposed to identify what the highlighted word such as it or they refers to. Mostly, reference questions on the CBT ask you to find and click on the referents (usually word or phrase) in the **bold** text. Sometimes, you are asked to identify the referent of a specified term or phrase such as this concept.

2. What terms should I know?

Reference words: *words such as pronouns that refer back or forward to other words in the sentence or paragraph*
A reference word is given in the question in the form of a highlighted word such as it.

Referents: *word(s) that pronouns or other such words* (reference words) *refer to*
You are asked to find the referents either directly on the passage or among the answer choices.
Pay attention to the position of referents in the following examples.
Referents usually come before the reference words. (See example 1.)
However, especially within the identical sentence, the reference words may be located before referents. (See example 2-1, 2-2.)
Generally speaking, referents are located in the nearby sentences from the reference words.
Occasionally, the referent may be the whole sentence. (See example 3.)

Examples

1. Many people go to City Hall to see the Christmas trees. They are very beautiful.
                                                Referent   Reference word

2-1. In order to ensure his desire to build a canal across Panama, President Theodore
                 Reference word   Referent
    Roosevelt drafted and signed the Clayton-Bulwer Treaty.

2-2. When they reach their destination, the Khans live in black tents of goathair cloth
        Reference word   Referent
    woven by the women.

3. When an organism grows or replaces old or damaged tissues, the chromosomes are
                              Referent
    duplicated and another complete set of genes is passed on unchanged to the

    "daughter cell." This process is known as mitosis.
                            Reference words

3. Pronouns as reference words and their possible referents

As the following table shows, the form of pronouns varies depending on their number and case.

Reference words and possible referents				
Subject Pronouns	Object Pronouns	Possessive Adjectives	Possessive Pronouns	Reflexive Pronouns
I	me	my	mine	myself
we	us	our	ours	ourselves
you	you	your	yours	yourself(selves)
he	him	his → (*singular male*)	his	himself
she	her	her → (*singular female*)	hers	herself
it	it	its → (*singular thing, place, idea, etc.*)	___	itself
they	them	their → (*plural persons, things, places, ideas, etc.*)	theirs	themselves
Demonstrative pronouns				
this, that → (*singular thing, action, idea, etc.*)		these, those → (*plural things, actions, ideas, etc.*)		

4. How is the question worded?

Multiple-Choice Type:

The word ▨ in the passage refers to ...

Click-on-the-word Type:

Look at the word ▨ in the passage.

Click on the word or phrase in the **bold** text that ▨ refers to.

Reference Strategies

1. Key points to remember

Usually, the referent is located before the reference word in the passage, often very close to it. However, the referent (noun) may be located after the reference word, especially in the context of the identical sentence.

Look for the noun(s) that corresponds with the reference word in terms of gender, number and case. Always verify the meaning of the sentence substituted with the referent in place of reference words (pronouns or other words); that is, check that the substituted sentence has acquired an originally intended meaning.

2. Test tips

(1) Read the highlighted pronouns or other words in the **bold**-typed sentences. Check whether the reference word(s) is in the singular or plural form.

(2) Locate singular or plural nouns in the **bold**-typed sentences. Sometimes the referent may be a phrase or a sentence. You will find examples of such cases in the following **Skill Building Section for Reference.**

(3) Mentally cross out the reference word(s) and replace it with the answer and check whether the restated sentence has the meaning identical to the original one. Another checkpoint will be: ask yourself whether the answer correctly replaces the reference word(s) in terms of gender, number, and case.

(4) If you are unable to decide immediately which answer is correct in the multiple-choice, substitute all four choices in place of the reference word. Check the structure (grammar) and the meaning of the sentence to determine the answer.

Vocabulary-in-context:
Frequency of appearance per passage with 11 questions: three or more
Standard Multiple-Choice or Click on the passage item
Degree of Difficulty: Easy to Medium

Vocabulary-in-context Overview

1. What is the question about?

Vocabulary questions test your knowledge of word(s) and phrase in the context of the passage. You may understand "the context" simply as surrounding words. Words usually have more than one meaning. Therefore, use the context to your advantage.

On average, three or more vocabulary questions are likely to appear per passage in the form of either "Click on the word that is closest in meaning to ▨ in the passage" or "standard multiple-choice." Usually, the "click on the word" type is easier to solve than "standard multiple-choice" type.

In many cases, words have several different meanings. The meaning of word(s) or phrase(s) on the CBT TOEFL is the meaning that makes sense in the context of a particular paragraph in which it appears. Therefore, its precise meaning will be determined by the general context of the passage or the specific context in which it is used.

* Remark: Please refer to the section **Skill Building 2** for context clues.

2. How is the question worded?

Multiple-Choice Type:
The word ▨ in the passage is closest in meaning to ...
The phrase ▨ in the passage is closest in meaning to ...
Look at the word ▨ in the passage. By which of the following could the word ▨ best be replaced?
Which of the following terms is defined in the passage?

Click-on-the-word Type:
Look at the word ▨ in the passage. Click on the word or phrase in the **bold** text that is closest in meaning to ▨ .

Vocabulary-in-context Strategies

1. Key points to remember

Words may have several meanings. Often words with multiple meanings are tested on the CBT. Words surrounding an unfamiliar word usually give you some clues to the meaning of words you do not know.

To figure out the meaning of words in context, you should learn to take advantage of different kinds of context clues: structural clues, the role of punctuation, and the meaning of surrounding words in the identical sentence or paragraph.

The context in which an unfamiliar word occurs suggests which meaning is correct. Try to guess the plausible meaning of an unfamiliar word by using your understanding of the contents (topics) in the passage as well as your background knowledge.

You may assume that words are related to the topic of the passage. For example, words from a passage on biology may have meanings that fit into biological issues under discussion. Expand your vocabulary. Learning prefixes and suffixes will help you guess the meaning of words you do not know. Prefixes or suffixes are added at the beginning or end of a root word to change its meaning.

However, it is not always possible to guess the meanings of unfamiliar words using the context. Therefore, expand your vocabulary by reading extensively on a variety of topics. It is highly advised to learn beforehand American terms that appear frequently in CBT subjects such as American history or American studies.

2. Test tips

It is possible, although not in every case, to guess the meaning of an unfamiliar word. When doing so, you should rely on the context in order to enhance the chances of being correct. You are advised to familiarize yourself with the reasoning process called "an educated guess." An educated guess is more efficient than a purely random guess. Structural clues provide some tips useful for an educated guess.

Structural clues from the context are valuable when you guess the meanings of unfamiliar words. These clues may consist of nearby words, phrases, or grammatical structures that point to relations among the parts of a sentence.

Structural clues help you guess the meaning of unfamiliar words by relating them to other words whose meanings are familiar to you. Learn the following types of useful clues suggesting the meanings of words you do not know.

(1) Appositive

An appositive is a noun or phrase that usually follows a noun, separated by commas. An appositive adds a further explanation to the preceding noun(s). In other words, the meaning of an unfamiliar word is identified by an appositive.

Examples

1. There is some disagreement as to precisely what constitutes **symbiosis**, living together.
   → From the structural clue of an appositive, we know that the "symbiosis" means "living together."
2. Thermal power stations are designed to pass as much energy as possible from the fuel to the **turbines**, machines with blades turned by the movement of the steam.

READING

➔ The meaning of turbines is given by an appositive, a group of nouns after the comma. Turbines are machines with blades that are turned by the movement of the steam.

3. The **cranium**, the part of the skull surrounding the brain, is made up of many bones. When a baby is born, there are spaces between some of these bones, but as a child gets older, the bones of the cranium grow together and these spaces are closed.
    ➔ In this sentence, commas are clues to make you guess the meaning of the word "cranium." A noun group set off by commas is an appositive of "cranium."

4. Blood relatives are related to each other by **consanguinity**, a relationship based on the tie between parents and children.
    ➔ The word "consanguinity" is defined by its appositive.

(2) Examples, list, or series

The meaning of a word is sometimes identified by examples. Examples are often introduced by the following signal words: *as, or, such as, like, for instance, for example.*

Examples

1. He was born with a huge **inheritance** such as land and valuable possessions received from his grandparents.
    ➔ The phrase following "such as" gives the examples as well as the meaning of the word "inheritance."

2. Moreover, subtle messages about **emotions** and intentions are conveyed: Is the speaker happy, sad, enthusiastic, tired, or in some other emotional state?
    ➔ You can infer the meaning of "emotions" from a list of adjectives describing emotional states.

3. Since such a huge group is too big to be socially practical, the group is usually reduced to a small circle of paternal and maternal relatives, or other **descendant** groups.
    ➔ The meaning of "descendant" could be gathered from the preceding words such as "paternal" and "maternal relatives." You may guess that "descendant" involves "blood relatives."

(3) Punctuation

Punctuation clues can help you understand the meanings of unfamiliar words. Punctuation marks are sometimes used to set off word(s) in order to identify, rename, or define another word.

Punctuation marks used in this way	
Comma	,
Dash	—
Double quotation mark	" "
Colon	:
Semicolon	;

Examples

1. You cannot catch **non-communicable** diseases; they are not contagious. However, they can be passed from parent to child through genes: for example, **hemophilia**, a disease in which the blood does not clot correctly, is a hereditary disease.
    ➔ The word "non-communicable" and the phrase "not contagious" are similar in meanings, set off by the semicolon. The word "hemophilia" is also defined in the sentence following the colon, set off by commas.

2. Peddlers added **bulkier goods** to their stock – pots and pans, hats, shoes, even books.

➔ The meaning of "bulkier goods" is identified by examples, set off by a dash.

3. In the 1920s, most Americans lived better than ever before. But the decade of the 1930s was just the opposite – a time of great economic **hardship** and widespread poverty. This period of hardship and poverty became known as the "Great Depression."

➔ A dash (–) is used to give details to the expression "the opposite." The word "opposite" together with the preceding sentence allows readers to guess the meaning of "hardship."

4. For example, **planktonic** organisms – those that drift in the water – face much different conditions than **benthic** organisms – those that live on the bottom – or **nekton** – organisms that swim.

➔ Dashes (–) are used to define the terms.

(4) Adjective Clauses

Adjective clauses modifying the head noun(s) may provide helpful context clues.

Examples

1. Such actions made him look like a **judicious sage**, whose wise image was confirmed later by other incidents.

➔ "A judicious sage" is modified by the adjective clause. You may guess that "a judicious sage" means "a wise person."

2. Unlike the **carnivores**, which are meat eaters, and the several orders of herbivores, we are **omnivores**, eating a wide variety of fruits, vegetables, and other animals.

➔ "The carnivores" is modified by the adjective clause "which are meat eaters."

(5) Contrasting Structures

Specific contexts such as contrasting structures in which an unfamiliar word occurs may disclose the meaning of word(s) you do not know.

Examples

1. Divorce is legally **permissible** in most societies, although in some it is **prohibited** by religion.

➔ From the contrasting structure of the sentence signaled by "although," you can guess that "prohibited" is opposed to "permissible."

2. Does life exist on Mars? Possibly. Mars is dry, cold, and less **favorable** than the earth for the support of life, but not implacably **hostile**.

➔ The structure of the sentence "Mars is dry, ~ but not implacably hostile." gives you clues about the meaning of "hostile." "Hostile" means "not favorable." The author intends to say that Mars is not that hostile although less favorable than the earth for life.

(6) Word-form Analysis (Prefix, Root, Suffix)

Word parts can help you understand the meanings of unfamiliar words. Many English words are made up of parts of Greek, and Latin words. It is possible to use these parts as clues. If you know the meanings of some of these word parts, you can vastly increase the chances to guess the meaning of an unfamiliar word correctly.

Keep in mind that learning the meaning of those word parts greatly improves your chance of finding the right answer to the vocabulary question. Practice using both context clues and word parts.

Examples

1. Sometimes species evolve together, forming a special relationship called **symbiosis**. In a symbiotic relationship, two species live together in a way that is beneficial to both.
   → The prefix "sym-" ("syn-") means "together, happening at the same time" in Greek. The prefix "bio-" means "life." Other examples are "sympathy" (feeling together), "syndicate" (a group of people that join together to share the costs of doing business), and "synthesis" (the act of combining different ideas).

2. **Binary** fission is the division of one cell into two equal cells.
   → The prefix "bi-" means "two." Other examples are "bicycle," "biannual," "bilingual," and "bimonthly." In this sentence, you may guess the meaning of the word "binary" based on the clue from the surrounding words such as "two equal cells."

Word Parts: Enrich Your Vocabulary Power.

Your knowledge of prefixes, roots, and suffixes will help you guess the meanings of unfamiliar words.

Prefixes, Roots, Suffixes		
Prefix	**Meaning**	**Examples**
ante-	before	antedate, antecedent, antebellum
anti-	against	antibody, antipathy, antifreeze
bene-	well	beneficiary, beneficial, benefit
circum-	around	circumference, circumscribe, circumcise
con-, com-, co-, col-, cor-	together, with	confront, conjunction, conceive combine, compound, compassionate coincide, cooperate, coalesce collaborate, collective, collapse correspond, correlate, corrupt
de-	from, off, away	defend, degrade, deduce, detect, depart
dis-	not	disappear, dishonest, disagree
en-, em-	make	embolden, empathy, enslave, enlighten
e-, ex-	out, from	evade, evaporate, evacuate except, exhibit, exhaust, exhale
im-	not	imbalance, immoral, impatient
mal-	bad	malignant, malfunction, malice
para-	beside	paralegal, paramilitary, parasite
pre-	before	precede, predict, prepare, preempt
pro-	advancing	proceed, promote, provide, prospect
re-	back, again	recover, remind, repeat, retrieve
sub-	under	subconscious, substandard, subway
trans-	across	transfer, transverse, transmit

Root	Meaning	Examples
aqua-, aque-, aqui-	water	aquamarine, aquatic, aqueous, aqueduct, aquifer
audi-	hear	audible, audience, auditorium
bio-	life	biography, biodegradable, biological
ego-	self	egoism, egomania, egocentric
frag-, frac-	break	fragile, fragment, fracture, fraction
gen-	birth, race	generate, genetic, genuine
geo-	earth	geographic, geologic, geothermal
herbi-	plants	herbicide, herbivore, herb
hetero-	different	heterophobia, heterogeneous, heterodox
homo-	alike	homonym, homogeneous, homophile
hydro-	water	hydroelectric, hydrogen, hydroponics
lingua-	tongue	linguist, linguistic, lingual
lumin-	light	luminary, luminescence, luminous
manu-	hand	manufacture, manual, manuscript
mort-	death	mortal, mortify, mortality
omni-	all	omnivorous, omnipresent, omniscient
pater-, patri-	father	patrimony, paternity, patriarch
phil-	love	philanthropic, philharmonic, philologist
pseudo-	false	pseudocarp, pseudopod, pseudonym
tele-	distance	telephone, telephoto, telescope
thermo-	heat, hot	thermal, thermometer, thermonuclear
vis-	see	visage, vision, visual
-graph	writing	photograph, monograph, lithograph
-pathy	feelings	apathy, antipathy, sympathy
-phobia	fear	Anglophobia, aquaphobia, acrophobia
-vene	come	convene, intervene, prevent

Suffix	Meaning	Examples
-ee	affected person	payee, addressee, employee, examinee
-hood	quality, condition status, rank	falsehood, likelihood, childhood fatherhood
-ia	disease	malaria, phobia, dementia
-ive (forming a noun)	condition	native, captive, fugitive
-ive (forming an adjective)	showing a certain quality	positive, distinctive, permissive
-en	cause become	darken, sharpen, lighten heighten, lengthen, shorten

READING

Skill Building 1: Reference

Directions : *Look at the underlined word or phrase in **bold** type in the following sentences. Find the referent that the word or phrase refers to.*

1. Airships had hydrogen in them for lift and engines for thrust. **They** had no wings.
   (A) Airships
   (B) engines
   (C) wings

2. The Wright brothers had worked on gliders for four years. They made two hundred different wings and watched **them** move in the wind.
   (A) brothers
   (B) years
   (C) wings

3. Actions like running or picking something up require thinking. We do **these things** on purpose.
   (A) Actions like running or picking something up
   (B) picking something up
   (C) thinking

4. We also do not have to command our hearts to beat because the brain and the nervous system do **it** for us.
   (A) the brain
   (B) the nervous system
   (C) to command our hearts to beat

5. New Yorkers love parades and there is one in some parts of the city most months of the year. Two of **these** are the St. Patrick's Day parade and Macy's Thanksgiving Day parade.
   (A) parts
   (B) parades
   (C) months

6. There are many show caves which people can visit without getting dirty and wet. People widen the passages and make floors and stairs. They put artificial light in **them** to show the stairs.
   (A) floors
   (B) people
   (C) passages

7. Many may not achieve reproductive success, but those whose physical characteristics enable them to do well in the new environment will usually reproduce, so that **their** genes will show up more frequently in subsequent generations.
   (A) physical characteristics
   (B) those whose physical characteristics enable them to do well in the new environment
   (C) subsequent generations

8. As children learn words and the meanings of words, they learn about their culture. They also acquire tools that enable **them** to think about the world – to interpret their experiences, establish and maintain relationships, and convey information. To become fluent in another language is not merely a matter of reading and conversing in that language but of actually being able to think in that language. Similarly, when young children learn the language of their culture, they acquire a thinking tool.
   (A) children
   (B) words
   (C) meanings

9. Dada represented a complete liberation of the creative impulse, and it was therefore able to embrace the most astonishing contradictions – above all the contradiction that, in spite of **their** destructive intentions, the Dada artists returned to certain essentials of art, and their art has proved as enduring as any art of the twentieth century.
   (A) contradictions
   (B) Dada artists
   (C) essentials of art

10. Overall, intellectual gains, measured by the difference between successive test scores, were greater for those students who had been identified as "bloomers" than **they** were for those not identified.
    (A) intellectual gains
    (B) test scores
    (C) students

READING

VOCABULARY

1 **thrust**: the force produced by an engine that pushes in one direction
4 **command**: to give an order or orders with authority
nerve (adj. nervous): a group of long, thin fibers in the body, esp. in the brain, which send and receive messages that control how the body reacts to signals it receives

6 **passage**: a usually long and narrow part of a building with rooms on one or both sides, or an enclosed path that connects places
artificial: made by people, often as a copy of something natural
7 **reproduce**: to produce a copy of something, or to show or do something again

subsequent: happening after something else
8 **convey**: to take or carry someone or something to a particular place
10 **successive**: following immediately one after the other

Skill Building 2: Vocabulary

Directions : *Pay attention to the context clues that are helpful to figure out the meaning of the word. Choose the word that is closest in meaning to the underlined word in **bold** type.*

1. She has a **nagging** cough that worries her parents.
   (A) annoying
   (B) exhaustive
   (C) concurrent

[Explanation]
   The context clue is "worries." Choice (B) can be eliminated, because "exhaustive" means "thorough," "complete," or "extensive." None of those synonyms is clearly associated with "worry." Likewise, Choice (C) can be eliminated, because "concurrent" means "simultaneous" or "at the same time," and therefore has no connection with "worry." The only possible answer is therefore Choice (A). Also, the verb "to nag" means to annoy a person with repeated demands. Because "nagging" is worrisome, Choice (A) is again the correct answer.

2. We spent a relaxed evening with **congenial** friends.
   (A) serious
   (B) pleasant
   (C) congenital

[Explanation]
   The context clue is "relaxed." Because one would not be relaxed in serious company, Choice (A) is inappropriate and may be eliminated. Although "congenital" appears similar to "congenial," the two words actually have different meanings. "Genial" means "friendly," whereas "genital" means "related to reproduction." Therefore "congenial" (friendly or agreeable) does not mean the same thing as "congenital" (inherited through reproduction). Thus, Choice (C) also can be eliminated, leaving Choice (B) as the only suitable answer.

3. He was delighted to inherit an **immense** fortune.
   (A) immaterial
   (B) obvious
   (C) huge

[Explanation]
   The context clue is "delighted." Because "delight" means great happiness, one may infer that the cause of that happiness is also great. For this reason, Choice (C), "huge," meaning "great," is the best answer. Choice (A), "immaterial," meaning "non-material," is inappropriate, because a "fortune" is practically by definition a material gain; that is, property and/or money. Choice (B), "obvious," would be redundant in context, because if a person knows he has inherited a fortune, then its existence is obvious in any case.

4. I grew up happily under the **benevolent** influence of my uncle.
   (A) impulsive
   (B) helpful
   (C) superfluous

[Explanation]

The context clue is "happily." Because the prefix "bene-" means something helpful, friendly, or leading to happiness, Choice (B) is the best answer. Choice (A) may be eliminated because an impulsive person is quick to act, and immediate actions do not always have pleasing results. "Superfluous" means "useless or unnecessary," and thus is not associated with "happiness." Choice (C) also may be eliminated, then, leaving Choice (B) as the only possible answer.

5. Those kids are not **appropriately** dressed for the cold.
   (A) properly
   (B) inherently
   (C) apparently

[Explanation]

The context clue is "not appropriately dressed for the cold." We may infer from context that the underlined word "appropriately" means "correctly." The only word in this list that means "correctly" is "properly." Therefore, Choice (A) must be correct. Choice (C) is a distracting word, meaning the way something appears, and may be eliminated. Choice (B), meaning "by nature," may be eliminated also, because if children by nature were suited to cold weather, then they would not have to be dressed in a certain way for it. By process of elimination, then, Choice (A) is the correct answer. Note also that "appropriately" and "properly" both contain the syllable "-*prop*-," indicating "correctness." This is yet another reason why Choice (A) is correct.

READING

VOCA<small>BULARY</small>

nag: annoy a person by making continual criticisms or suggestions

exhaustive: detailed and complete (exhausting: making someone very tired)

concurrent: happening at the same time

congenial: producing a feeling of comfort or satisfaction

congenital: existing at or from birth

immense: extremely large; great in size or degree

immaterial: not likely to make a difference

obvious: easily seen, recognized, or understood

impulsive: acting suddenly without any consideration of the results

generous: willing to give help or support more than usual or expected

superfluous: more than is needed; extra and not necessary

appropriate(ly): correct or right for a particular

occasion

apparently: according to the way something appears; in fact

inherent: existing as a natural and permanent quality of something or someone

deliberately: on purpose

6. She has been **<u>deliberately</u>** ignoring him all day to upset him.
   (A) ideally
   (B) perennially
   (C) intentionally

[Explanation]

   The context clue is "ignoring ~ to upset him." Because upsetting someone is usually an undesirable situation (that is, not ideal or perfect), Choice (A), "ideally," is inappropriate and should be eliminated. Choice (B), "perennially," meaning "always," is likewise inappropriate, because there is no indication that this behavior occurs all the time. Choice (C) thus becomes the only suitable answer. Also, "deliberate" and "intentional" have the identical meanings of "planned," and for this reason also, Choice (C) is correct.

7. His ruthless accumulation of wealth stands as a **<u>paradigm</u>** of greed in the business world.
   (A) parade
   (B) etiquette
   (C) example

[Explanation]

   The context clue is "~ ruthless ~ greed." Because "greed" and "ruthlessness" are personal traits expressed in behavior, the best answer in this case is a word that describes or represents such behavior. Choice (A), "parade," may be eliminated, because a parade – a public celebration of something – does not represent personal behavior and qualities. "Parade" here is a distracting word, because it happens to have the same first four letters as "paradigm" but in fact has a very different meaning. "Etiquette," Choice (B), means "correct, polite, formal behavior," to which "ruthlessness and greed" do not belong; therefore Choice (B) is incorrect and may be eliminated. Choice (C) then becomes the only correct answer.

8. The Coast Guard, searching for drug smugglers, spotted a fast boat but then lost their **<u>quarry</u>** in the fog.
   (A) target
   (B) raid
   (C) status

[Explanation]

   The context clue is "~ spotted a fast boat but then lost their quarry in the fog." Clearly, the "quarry" is something the Coast Guard is trying to catch. That definition matches neither Choice (B) nor Choice (C), thus making Choice (A) the only appropriate answer.

VOCABULARY

6
ideal: not likely to be real, but perfect in imagination
perennially: happening again and again; continuing for a long time
intentionally: done with intention
7
parade: a large number of people marching in a formal way as a way of celebration

paradigm: a very clear or typical example used as a model
etiquette: a set of rules or customs that control accepted particular social groups
8
quarry: a person, animal, or group being hunted or looked for

raid: a planned attack that is done suddenly and unexpectedly
status: position in a social group; the position of respect and importance

Intensive Exercises

Exercise 2.1

Many plants can **propagate** themselves by vegetative reproduction. **In this process**, part of a plant separates, takes root, and grows into a new plant. Vegetative reproduction is a type of asexual reproduction; it involves only one parent and there is no fusion of gametes (sex cells). Plants use various structures to reproduce vegetatively. Some plants use underground storage organs. Such organs include rhizomes (horizontal, underground stems), the branches of which produce new plants; bulbs (swollen leaf bases) and corms (swollen stems), which produce daughter bulbs or corms that separate from the parent; and stem tubers (thickened underground stems) and root tubers (swollen adventitious roots), which also separate from the parent. Other propagative structures include runners, creeping horizontal stems that take root and produce new plants; bulbils, small bulbs that develop on the stem or in the place of flowers, and then drop off and grow into new plants; and adventitious buds, miniature plants that form on leaf margins before dropping to the ground and growing into mature plants.

1. Look at the word **propagate** in the passage.
   Click on the word or phrase in the **bold** text that is closest in meaning to propagate.

2. The phrase **this process** refers to all of the following EXCEPT
   - (A) vegetative reproduction
   - (B) asexual reproduction
   - (C) unilateral reproduction
   - (D) bisexual reproduction

3. The word **adventitious** in the passage is closest in meaning to
   - (A) accidental
   - (B) visible
   - (C) aquatic
   - (D) adventurous

 Time

LinguaForum

 Help **Prev** **Next**

READING

[Explanation]

1. In the context of this passage, "propagate" means "reproduce." The word "propagate" means "to produce (a new plant) from a parent plant." No other words in the bold text have the same meaning as the word "propagate."

2. The phrase "this process" refers to the preceding phrase, "vegetative reproduction." The term is rephrased as "asexual reproduction" and followed by the definition in the 3rd sentence of the passage. Because the process involves only one parent, one may characterize it as "unilateral."

3. One can find a clue in the sentence containing the word "adventitious," which is "~ buds, miniature plants that form on leaf margins before dropping to the ground and growing into mature plants."

VOCABULARY

vegetative: relating to plant life
fusion: the process of joining two or more things
corm: the small round underground part of some

plants

propagate (adj. propagative): to produce new plants from a parent plant

adventitious: happening accidentally; not planned
margin: the border of space
mature: well-developed

Exercise 2.2

People born in the United States and Canada can generally expect to live long and relatively healthy lives. At present, about 11 percent of the region's population is over 65 years of age.

Most people in the United States and Canada generally enjoy good health. Public sanitation services, which include food inspection and garbage removal, are supervised by local governments to help keep the environment healthy. The people of the region have become more educated about disease prevention and health maintenance.

The region's health-care systems have contributed in several ways to people's improved health. There are large numbers of hospitals and clinics in the region. There are also large numbers of doctors, nurses, and hospital workers to care for the health needs of the region's people. The latest medicines and treatments are generally available because most people live fairly close to large medical facilities.

In general, many diseases are either prevented or successfully treated because of the health care provided within the United States and Canada. **People are generally immunized, or given medicines to protect them from certain sicknesses. The survival rate of infants in the region is high – 990 out of 1,000 live births. This is partly due to the attempts to immunize infants against certain diseases.**

1. The word supervised in the passage is closest in meaning to
   (A) suspected
   (B) surrounded
   (C) overseen
   (D) enforced

2. Look at the word facilities in the passage. Click on the word or phrase in the **bold** text that is closest in meaning to facilities.

3. Look at the word This in the passage. Click on the word, phrase or sentence in the **bold** text that This refers to.

  LinguaForum

[Explanation]

1. The word "supervise" means "oversee."
2. Pay attention to the whole expression "medical facilities." "Facilities" are places, especially buildings, where a particular activity happens. "Medical facilities" would be "hospitals and clinics."
3. "This" indicates the preceding sentence. Remember that pronouns sometimes point to the entire sentence.

VOCABULARY

sanitation: the equipment and systems that keep places clean

inspect (n. inspection): to officially visit a school, factory, etc. in order to check that rules are being

obeyed and that standards are acceptable

supervise: to be in charge of somebody/something and make sure that everything is done correctly, safely, etc.

immunize: to protect a person or an animal from a disease

infant: the period of being a baby

Exercise 2.3

It is not known how religion first began, although archaeology provides some clues about when. Some archaeologists interpret materials found at sites dating as far back as 70,000 years ago as evidence of religious belief. Later, some 30,000 years ago, the Upper Palaeolithic Cro-Magnon people of western Europe seem to have been expressing religious feelings when they carved and painted bones, stones, and the walls of caves. The survival of these gatherers and hunters required that females reproduce abundantly and that hunting be successful. Both fertility and successful hunting are prominent themes in Cro-Magnon art. **Statuettes called "Venus figurines" represent women with pregnant bellies and huge breasts; cave paintings include apparently pregnant animals and others with spears lodged in their bodies. Perhaps the hunters believed they could influence events by creating the image of a pregnant woman or animal or by portraying the killing of an animal, thus prompting life to imitate art.** This requires a belief in agencies beyond the merely human.

1. Look at the word clues in the passage. Click on the word or phrase in the **bold** text that is closest in meaning to clues.

2. The word fertility in the passage could best be replaced by
   (A) fervor
   (B) felicity
   (C) onslaught
   (D) reproduction

3. Look at the word Statuette in the passage. Click on the word or phrase in the **bold** text that is closest in meaning to Statuette.

4. The word agencies in the passage could best be replaced by
   (A) organizations
   (B) institutions
   (C) forces
   (D) autonomies

 Time   LinguaForum   **Help** **Prev** **Next**

READING

[Explanation]

1. The word "clues" provide information that helps you to find an answer to the problem. In the context of the passage, "clues" is similar in meaning to "evidence."

2. Look at the preceding phrase, "that females reproduce abundantly and that hunting be successful." You may guess that "fertility" in "Both fertility and successful hunting" is related to the part of the previous sentence, "reproduce abundantly."

3. Look at the preceding phrase: Statuettes called "Venus figurines." "Statuettes" are similar to "figurines."

4. In the context of this passage, the expression "agencies" in the phrase "agencies beyond the merely human" means "supernatural forces."

VOCABULARY

Palaeolithic: from or connected with the early part of the Stone Age
abundantly: in large quantities

prominent: important or well known
portray: to show somebody/something in a picture
prompt: to make somebody decide to do

something
imitate: to copy
agency: a force

Exercise 2.4

El Niño is also **blamed** for many **subsidiary** effects. Crop and livestock losses were enormous, bringing **hardship** to farmers, especially in poorer countries, and in some places famine. In financial terms **they** amounted to hundreds of millions of dollars, and financial markets were affected widely as prices rose because of reduced supply. The fisheries crash in Peru and Chile had similar effects: much of the catch was processed into animal food and farmers as far away as Ireland faced higher feed price. Fires, often lit by farmers using the opportunity to clear land, raged out of control in drought-stricken Indonesia and the Amazon basin. Thousands of square miles of rainforest were **demolished**. The fires in Indonesia were so outrageous that much of southeastern Asia endured months of haze and air pollution, and an accompanying increase in respiratory ailments. The thick smoke was even responsible for several plane crashes. Mass coral bleaching occurred on many reefs around the world.

1. Look at the word **blamed** in the passage. Click on the word or phrase in the **bold** text that is closest in meaning to **blamed**.

2. Look at the word **subsidiary** in the passage. Click on the word or phrase in the **bold** text that is closest in meaning to **subsidiary**.

3. The word **hardship** in the passage could best be replaced by
   Ⓐ hunger
   Ⓑ drought
   Ⓒ suffering
   Ⓓ contention

4. Look at the word **they** in the passage. Click on the word or phrase in the **bold** text that the word **they** refers to.

5. The word **demolished** in the passage could best be replaced by
   Ⓐ demanded
   Ⓑ drenched
   Ⓒ eliminated
   Ⓓ dehydrated

 Time   **LinguaForum**   **Help** **Prev** **Next**

[Explanation]
1. Look for the phrase structured like "~ blamed for ~." "Responsible" in "~ even responsible for ~" is similar in meaning to "blamed."
2. "Subsidiary" means to be "secondary." "Secondary or side effects" is similar in meaning to "accompanying effects."
3. "Hardship" is a very comprehensive expression in terms of its meaning. Therefore, such words as "hunger" or "drought" are examples of hardship. But they are not identical in scope.
4. Looking at the entire passage, one may guess that "they" refers to losses or something like that. Read "Crop and livestock losses were enormous ~" in connection with "they amounted to hundreds of millions of dollars."
5. The word "demolish" means "eliminate."

VOCABULARY

subsidiary: connected with something but less important than it

demolish: to pull or knock down a building
outrageous: very shocking and unacceptable

respiratory: connected with breathing
ailment: an illness that is not very serious

Exercise 2.5

Of all mishaps, however, the massive oil spills that result from the sinking or collision of supertankers are the most devastating to the marine environment. The 1978 grounding of a supertanker, the Amoco Cadiz, poured 230,000 tons of crude oil along the coasts of Brittany, in northwestern France. In 1989 more than 35,000 tons of crude oil were spilled by the Exxon Valdez, damaging the unspoiled coasts of southern Alaska, the home of whales, sea otters, salmon, fish-eating bald eagles, and other wildlife. **Accidents have prompted tighter restrictions, such as having double hulls, on the construction and operation of tankers.**

Most of the components of oil are insoluble in water and float on the surface. **They can be seen in most harbors as thin, iridescent slicks on the surface or as black deposits on sandy and rocky beaches. You would expect large areas of the ocean to be covered with the oil that has accumulated over the years. Fortunately, some of its lighter components evaporate, and bacteria ultimately break the oil down.** Oil is said to be almost completely biodegradable because, though very slowly, it is broken down, or decomposed, by bacteria. Different marine communities, however, have different sensitivities to oil. For instance, it lasts much longer in salt marshes and mangrove forests.

1. Look at the word mishaps in the passage. Click on the word or phrase in the **bold** text that is closest in meaning to mishaps.

2. Look at the word devastating in the passage. Click on the word or phrase in the **bold** text that is closest in meaning to devastating.

3. The word prompted in the passage could best be replaced by
   (A) procrastinated
   (B) issued
   (C) approved
   (D) precipitated

4. Look at the word its in the passage. Click on the word or phrase in the **bold** text that its refers to.

 LinguaForum

READING

[Explanation]

1. From the sentence that states "Of all mishaps, the massive oil spills ~," we can guess that the massive oil spills are mishaps. Therefore, "mishap" is similar in meaning to "accidents."

2. Oil spills damage the environment. "Devastating" is similar in meaning to "damaging."

3. In the context of the passage, "prompt" should be something that hastens the happening of something. "Precipitate" is similar in meaning to "prompt." All other three choices are not accepted meanings of the word "prompt."

4. The second paragraph discusses oil. Some components of oil may evaporate, and bacteria may break the oil down. "Its" is the possessive case of "it," which refers to a singular noun.

VOCABULARY

iridescent: showing many bright colors that seem to change in different lights

slick: an area of oil that is floating on the surface of the sea

biodegradable: able to decay naturally and without

harming the environment

decompose: to destroy by breaking it into smaller parts

marsh: an area of low land that is always soft and wet

mangrove: a tropical tree that grows in mud or at the edge of rivers and sends roots down from its branches

Vocabulary Review for Intensive Exercises 2.1-2.5

1. The movie displayed a perfect _____ of tradition and modern trends.

   - Ⓐ fission
   - Ⓑ fusion
   - Ⓒ reel
   - Ⓓ press

2. Plants are _____ to other places by dispersed seeds.

   - Ⓐ declared
   - Ⓑ referred
   - Ⓒ propagated
   - Ⓓ sacked

3. Public health officials regularly _____ the premises.

   - Ⓐ inspect
   - Ⓑ elect
   - Ⓒ notify
   - Ⓓ invest

4. Her job is to _____ children playing on a beach.

   - Ⓐ outweigh
   - Ⓑ bewilder
   - Ⓒ supervise
   - Ⓓ affect

5. The prosecutor presented _____ evidence to prove his guilt.

   - Ⓐ inverse
   - Ⓑ opague
   - Ⓒ presumptuous
   - Ⓓ abundant

6. She was the most _____ in the fashion industry.

   - Ⓐ prominent
   - Ⓑ ornamental
   - Ⓒ peremptory
   - Ⓓ redundant

7. Most of the city was _____ by the earthquake.

   - Ⓐ denigrated
   - Ⓑ denounced
   - Ⓒ demolished
   - Ⓓ dejected

8. He is prone to play the most _____ pranks on his little brother.

   - Ⓐ reflexive
   - Ⓑ outrageous
   - Ⓒ remote
   - Ⓓ opportune

9. You can get a discount fare on the Internet, but a few _____ apply.

   - Ⓐ advice
   - Ⓑ restrictions
   - Ⓒ commissions
   - Ⓓ notice

10. Certain kinds of chemical substances never _____.

   - Ⓐ decompose
   - Ⓑ fake
   - Ⓒ dredge
   - Ⓓ tirade

Word Files I: TOEFL Vocabulary with Emphasis on Natural Sciences

adapt: v. to change something; to modify

cellular: adj. connected with the cells

classify: v. to divide into groups according to type

collaborate: v. to work together

collide: v. to crash into each other

conspicuous: adj. easy to notice; obvious

convert: v. to change one form to another

culture: n. the growing of plants or animals in an artificial environment

debris: n. broken pieces

ecology: n. the study of the relationship of organisms to their environment

erupt: v. to explode; to break out suddenly

exhaust: v. to use something completely; to make you feel very tired

exposure: n. a situation with no protection from something harmful

extinct: adj. no longer existing

fauna: n. all the animals living in a particular area or period of time

feature: n. an important characteristic

flora: n. all the plants living in a particular area or period of time

formula: n. a particular method of doing something

fossil fuels: n. fuels such as gas, coal, and oil from under the ground

genetic: adj. connected with genes

hemisphere: n. half of a sphere

hereditary: adj. given to child by its parents

heterogeneous: adj. of different parts

homogeneous: adj. of identical parts

humus: n. a substance made of dead leaves and plants added to soil

immune: adj. protected from a particular disease

magnitude: n. the size of something

mangrove: n. a tropical tree that sends roots down from its branches

mantle: n. a layer of something that covers a surface

marine: adj. connected with the sea

mold: v. to shape into a particular form

molecule: n. the smallest unit consisting of a group of atoms

offspring: n. the young of an animal or plant

particle: n. a very small piece of matter

perennial: adj. (of plants) living for many years

perpendicular: adj. standing straight up

petroleum: n. mineral oil from under the ground

plankton: n. small forms of life living in seas

pollinate: v. to put pollen into a flower to make seeds

precipitation: n. rain or snow

prey: n. a creature hunted and killed for food by another animal

primate: n. mammals such as humans, monkeys and apes

property: n. a quality of something

radiation: n. heat or light in waves

rainforest: n. a forest in a hot area that receives a lot of rain

reflect: v. to send back light or heat

reinforcement: n. the act of making something stronger

reproduce: v. to produce young

rung: n. one of the bars that forms a step in a ladder

scavenge: v. (of animals) to feed on decaying flesh

sediment: n. (geology) sand, stones, or mud carried by water or wind and left on the bottom of a river, lake, or sea

sequence: n. the order in which things follow each other

species: n. animals or plants with similar characteristics

specimen: n. an example

speculate: v. to make guesses

sporadic: adj. not continuous or regular

stratify: v. to arrange something in layers

succulent: adj. (of fruit) containing a lot of juice

synthetic: adj. relating to products made from artificial substances

thermal: adj. connected with preserving heat

trait: n. a characteristic

tropics: n. the hottest area of the earth

vibrate: v. to cause to shake

wane: v. to appear slightly smaller each day after being full

READING

Practice Test 2

Questions 1-11

One of the important differences between subsocial and eusocial honey bees is that the latter survive the winter. Eusocial or "truly social" bees are characterized by cooperation in caring for the young and a division of labor, with sterile individuals working on behalf of reproductive ones. The colony of subsocial or presocial bees is not permanent, there is no division of labor, and all females are fertile.

→ In the spring, when the nectar supplies are at their peak, so many young may be raised that the group separates into two colonies. ■ The new colony is always founded by the old queen, who leaves the hive, taking about half of the workers with her. They stay together in a swarm, for a few days, gathered around the queen, after which the swarm will settle in some suitable hollow tree or other shelter found by its scouts. ■ As the old queen is preparing to leave the hive, the new queens are getting ready to emerge. ■ As these signals are exchanged, the workers remain motionless. ■ During this period, ovarian development begins in some of the workers, a few of which lay eggs. The unfertilized eggs develop into male or drones.

→ After the old queen leaves the hive, a new young queen emerges, and any other developing queens are destroyed. ■ The young queen then goes on her nuptial flight, exuding a pheromone that entices the drones of neighboring colonies. The queen exerts influence on her subject by means of pheromones. ■ The influence of one of the pheromones inhibits ovarian development in the worker bees and prevents them from becoming queens or from producing rival queens. ■ She mates only on this one occasion, although she may mate with more than one male and then returns to the hive to settle down to a life devoted to egg production. ■

During her nuptial flight, the queen receives enough sperm to last her entire life, which may be five to seven years. The drones' only contribution to the life of the hive is their participation in the nuptial flight. Since they are unable to feed themselves, they become an increasing liability to the social group. As nectar supplies decrease in the fall, they are stung to death by their sisters or are driven out.

1. The purpose of the passage is to introduce
   - (A) the queen bee and describe her function within the eusocial community
   - (B) eusocial and subsocial bees and compare their survival techniques
   - (C) eusocial bees and explain the ways they survive the winter period
   - (D) the annual life cycle of bees and describe the ways they form their community

2. Look at the word latter in the passage. Click on the word or phrase in the **bold** text that latter refers to.

3. Subsocial bees are called presocial because
   - (A) female bees are not as developed as eusocial ones
   - (B) they do not cooperate as eusocial bees do
   - (C) they cooperate especially in caring for the young
   - (D) female bees do all the work while male bees do nothing

4. Subsocial bees are "not permanent," meaning that they

- (A) do not survive the winter, unlike the eusocial bees
- (B) wander aimlessly from place to place
- (C) migrate frequently to warmer places
- (D) like to travel and discover new places

5. The word founded in the passage is closest in meaning to

- (A) structured
- (B) discovered
- (C) established
- (D) designed

6. What happens when the old queen bee leaves for the new hive?

- (A) Workers lay fertilized eggs that later become workers themselves.
- (B) Workers remain motionless and some begin ovarian development.
- (C) New queens emerge and fight among themselves to become the ruler.
- (D) Neighboring drones are enticed by the queen bee and follow her to the new colony.

7. The following sentence can be added to paragraph 2 or 3.

These two events are synchronized by sound signals transmitted through the comb.

Where would it best fit in the paragraph? Click on the square [■] to add the sentence to paragraph 2 or 3. Paragraphs 2 and 3 are marked with an arrow [➡].

8. The queen bee is able to do all of the following EXCEPT

- (A) laying fertilized eggs
- (B) attracting drones
- (C) founding a new colony
- (D) working continuously

9. Which of the following could best replace the word entices in the passage?

- (A) Attracts
- (B) Commands
- (C) Enslaves
- (D) Confuses

10. The main responsibility of the drone consists in

- (A) creating a new hive with the queen bee
- (B) helping the queen bee attract neighboring bees
- (C) feeding the new queen bee during her mating period
- (D) injecting the queen bee with sperms which fertilize the eggs

11. Drones become a liability to the colony because

- (A) workers were unable to provide food to drones
- (B) they do not assist female bees in reproducing for the colony
- (C) they cannot obtain subsistence for themselves
- (D) they interrupt the queen bee from finding food

VOCABULARY

sterile: (of a person or animal) unable to produce young, or (of land) unable to produce plants or crops
colony: a group of animals, insects, or plants of the same type that live together
nectar: a sweet liquid produced by flowers and

collected by bees
synchronize: to cause something to happen in a planned way at exact times
drone: a male bee that does not work and only lives in order to reproduce
exude: to produce from the inside and spread out

slowly
inhibit: to take an action that makes something less likely to happen, or that discourages someone from doing something
liability: the responsibility of a person, business, or organization to pay or give up something of value

Questions 12-22

Although population growth and the need to feed more people cannot explain the origin of the food-producing way of life, they do have a lot to do with **its** subsequent spread. As already noted, domestication inevitably leads to higher yields, and higher yields make it possible to feed more people. In addition, farmers have available a variety of foods that are soft enough to be fed to infants, which food foragers usually do not. Hence, farmers do not need to nurse their children so intensively, nor for so many years. In humans, prolonged nursing, so long as it involves frequent stimulation of the nipple by the infant, has a dampening effect on ovulation. As a result, women in food-foraging societies are less likely to become fertile as soon after childbirth as they are in food-producing societies. Coupled with this, too many children to care for at once interferes with the foraging activities of women in hunter-gatherer societies. However, among farmers, numerous children are frequently seen as assets, to help out with the many household chores.

➜ Paradoxically, while domestication increases productivity, so does it increase instability. ■ This is so because those varieties with the highest yields become the focus of human attention, while other varieties are less valued and ultimately ignored. ■ As a result, farmers become dependent on a rather narrow range of resources, compared with the wide range utilized by food foragers. ■ The dependence upon fewer varieties means that when a crop fails, farmers have less to fall back on than do food foragers. ■ Furthermore, the likelihood of failure is increased by the common farming practice of planting crops together in one locality, so that a disease contracted by one plant can easily spread to others. ■ Moreover, by relying on seeds from the most productive plants of a species to establish next year's crop, farmers favor genetic uniformity over diversity. ■ The result is that if some virus, bacterium or fungus is able to destroy one plant, it will likely destroy them all. ■ This is what happened in the famous Irish potato famine of 1845-46, which sent waves of Irish immigrants to the United States. ■

12. The passage primarily deals with
    (A) advantages and disadvantages of farming
    (B) hunter-gatherer societies contrasted with farmer societies
    (C) the development of farming and its effects on human living
    (D) a variety of foods produced by farmers

13. Look at the word **its** in the passage. Click on the word or phrase in the **bold** text that **its** refers to.

14. The origin of the food-producing way of life
    (A) is solely due to gradual population growth
    (B) is not affected by a sudden increase of population
    (C) is not related to a desire to feed more people
    (D) cannot be explained definitely by the author

15. The main purpose of the first paragraph is to

    (A) explain the causes of the spread of food production among humans

    (B) explain the origins of food production among humans

    (C) discuss the concept of family between hunter-gatherer and farming societies

    (D) compare the roles of children in hunter-gatherer and farming societies

16. The word prolonged in the passage is closest in meaning to

    (A) ample
    (B) extended
    (C) generous
    (D) preliminary

17. All of the following characterize foraging societies EXCEPT

    (A) women are more fertile and give birth to more babies than women in farming societies

    (B) women ovulate less than women in farming societies due to prolonged nursing

    (C) women have to extend nursing due to the lack of soft foods for infants

    (D) children are not appreciated because they interfere with the need to find food

18. The word assets in the passage could best be replaced by

    (A) gifts
    (B) resources
    (C) strengths
    (D) advantages

19. According to paragraph 2, productivity could lead to

    (A) instable food foraging
    (B) a variety of seeds
    (C) conflict among farmers
    (D) food shortage

20. The following sentence can be added to paragraph 2.

Modern agriculture, for example, relies on about 20 crops, versus the more than 100 species regarded as edible by the Bushmen of Africa's Kalahari Desert.

Where would it best fit in the paragraph? Click on the square [■] to add the sentence to paragraph 2.
Paragraph 2 is marked with an arrow [➜].

21. Click on the sentence that first mentions the result of prolonged nursing on women.

Scroll the entire passage to see all of the paragraphs.

22. It can be inferred from the passage that the Irish

    (A) had longed to migrate to the United States for a long time

    (B) had depended on potatoes as their main subsistence

    (C) were accustomed to their potato famine

    (D) were famous for a variety of potato dishes

READING

VOCABULARY

domesticate: to grow plants for human use
yield: a profit or an amount produced
forage: to go searching, esp. for food
dampen: to make something less strong

fertile: able to produce a large number of high-quality crops
ultimately: finally; in the end
utilize: to make use of something

contract: to catch or become ill with a disease
favor: to prefer
famine: an extreme lack of food in a region, causing suffering and death

Questions 23-33

Carbon dioxide, a normal component of the atmosphere, provides a warming effect on the earth's surface, a phenomenon known as the greenhouse effect. As sunlight strikes the planet, most of the solar energy, about 70%, is absorbed by the earth. Of the absorbed energy, some is radiated back as infrared radiation. Carbon dioxide traps part of this heat energy, like the glass of a greenhouse, and warms the earth. **It has been estimated that without the greenhouse effect the earth would be about 10 degrees Celsius colder.**

Living organisms, both in the sea and on land, contribute to the greenhouse gas in the atmosphere. Producers, mostly phytoplankton, in the open sea, remove carbon dioxide from the atmosphere through photosynthesis; both producers and consumers return it through respiration. Humans have been increasing the amount of carbon dioxide in the atmosphere by burning enormous amounts of fossil fuels. These fuels, oil and coal, are nothing but the fossilized remains of ancient forests. People release their energy and turn them into carbon dioxide when driving cars and running power plants. Humans also cut down the tropical rain forests that consume a great deal of carbon dioxide, burn them, and release even more carbon dioxide in the process!

→ Carbon dioxide has increased by 25% since 1850, and the planet may be warming up – an effect known as global warming. ■ How warm it will get and what the consequences will be are highly debatable. ■ Warming will cause more water to evaporate from the oceans, increasing rain, hurricanes, and other storms. ■ Some areas will be wetter, other drier. Scientists fear that the polar ice caps will begin to melt and that sea level will rise and flood coastal lands. ■ How far up and how fast sea level would rise is something scientists don't agree on. Projections from computer models vary from a rise of 0.3 to 1.5 m by 2030. ■ This may seem like a small change, but some nations have started planning for the consequences of rising waters. ■ Large portions of Florida and the Netherlands would be flooded, and island-group nations such as the Maldives may disappear altogether. ■

23. What is the best title for the passage?
  (A) Our Warming Earth
  (B) Dangers of Pollution
  (C) The Future of the Earth
  (D) Past, Present and Future of the Earth

24. According to the passage, carbon dioxide is
  (A) neutral as to nature and to human health
  (B) a naturally existing component of air on earth
  (C) produced by photosynthesis
  (D) increasing the amount of infrared radiation

25. According to the passage, which of the following is true?
  (A) Carbon dioxide absorbs heat from the sun and produces infrared radiation.
  (B) Carbon dioxide is produced as well as consumed by humans.
  (C) The degree of global warming is proportional to the number of greenhouses.
  (D) Carbon dioxide is acting like glass and creates the greenhouse effect.

26. The word traps in the passage is closest in meaning to

    Ⓐ releases
    Ⓑ limits
    Ⓒ catches
    Ⓓ reflects

27. Look at the word it in the passage. Click on the word or phrase in the **bold** text that it refers to.

28. Which of the following does NOT produce carbon dioxide?

    Ⓐ Cars
    Ⓑ Power plants
    Ⓒ Tropical forests
    Ⓓ Burning fossil fuels

29. Click on the sentence in the passage that gives examples of fossil fuels.

Scroll the passage to see all of the sentences.

30. Which of the following could best replace the word running in the passage?

    Ⓐ Operating
    Ⓑ Organizing
    Ⓒ Damaging
    Ⓓ Releasing

31. According to the passage, global warming is

    Ⓐ the result of increasing consumption of carbon dioxide
    Ⓑ the depletion of carbon dioxide due to burning of fuels

    Ⓒ the decrease in the level of infrared radiation
    Ⓓ the decrease in the level of carbon dioxide and the increase in its consumption

32. The following sentence can be added to paragraph 3.

But some predict a rise of 1.5 degrees Celsius to 4.5 degrees Celsius in the next century.

Where would it best fit in the paragraph? Click on the square [■] to add the sentence to paragraph 3.
Paragraph 3 is marked with an arrow [➡].

33. The passage implies all of the following EXCEPT that global warming will

    Ⓐ raise the sea level and create disasters such as the partial sinking of countries
    Ⓑ eventually bring about the end of living organisms on earth as we know them
    Ⓒ cause an unbalanced and unpredictable weather pattern that will be harmful
    Ⓓ melt ice caps which will contribute to the increase of sea level

READING

VOCABULARY

carbon dioxide: the gas produced when animal or vegetable matter is burned, or when animals breathe out
component: one of the parts of a system, process, or machine
phenomenon: anything that is or can be experienced or felt, esp. something that is noticed

because it is unusual or new
radiate: to send out heat or light
respiration: the act of breathing
fossil: part of a plant or animal, or its shape, that has been preserved in rock or earth for a very long period
remains: the parts of ancient objects and buildings

that have survived and are discovered in the present day
evaporate: to cause a liquid to change to a gas

Questions 34-44

→ Advances in transportation during the early 1900s in America were quite startling. Wilbur and Orville Wright of Dayton, Ohio, built and flew the first airplane at Kitty Hawk, North Carolina in 1903. ■ But the use of planes advanced slowly until the outbreak of World War I, after which the Europeans quickly developed the plane as a military weapon. ■ When America entered the war, it still had no combat planes – American pilots fought in British or French aircraft. ■ An American aircraft industry developed during the war but foundered in the postwar demobilization. ■ Under the Kelly Act of 1925, however, the government began to subsidize the industry through airmail contracts. ■

→ A psychological boost to aviation came in 1927 with the solo flight of Charles A. Lindbergh, Jr., from New York to Paris in thirty-three hours and thirty minutes. ■ The deed, which won him a prize of $25,000, was dramatic. ■ The parade down Broadway in his honor surpassed even the celebration of the Armistice. ■

By far the most significant economic and social development of the time was the automobile. The first motor car had been manufactured for sale in 1895, but the founding of the Ford Motor Company in 1903 revolutionized the industry. Ford's reliable Model T came out in 1908 at a price of $850, which dropped to $290 in 1924. Ford vowed "to democratize the automobile. When I'm through, everybody will be able to afford one, and about everyone will have one."

He was right. In 1916, the total number of cars manufactured passed 1 million; by 1920 more than 8 million were registered, and in 1923 more than 23 million. The production of automobiles consumed large amounts of the nation's steel, rubber, glass, and textile output, among other materials. It quickened the movement for good roads, financed in large part from a gasoline tax, speeded transportation, encouraged the expansion of suburbs, and sparked real-estate booms in California and Florida. By virtue of its size and importance, the automobile industry became the salient example of mass production.

34. What is the best title for this passage?
   (A) Airplanes, Automobiles and Cars
   (B) Planes, Trains and Cars
   (C) Airplanes, Automobiles and their economic impact
   (D) Revolution in Air transportation

35. Which of the following statements is true?
   (A) America invented the airplane and quickly developed it into a commercial industry.
   (B) America invented the airplane but Europe was first to develop it into an industry.
   (C) America showed the possibility of flying but Europe was first to invent a functioning plane.
   (D) America showed hope for the invention of the plane but was defeated by the Europeans.

36. It can be inferred that planes were in the beginning mass-produced mainly for

    (A) commercial reasons
    (B) military reasons
    (C) transportation reasons
    (D) scientific reasons

37. The following sentence can be added to paragraph 1 or 2.

    The Air Commerce Act of 1926 started a program of federal aid to air transport and navigation, including aid in establishing airports.

    Where would it best fit in the paragraph? Click on the square [■] to add the sentence to paragraph 1 or 2. Paragraphs 1 and 2 are marked with an arrow [→].

38. The word subsidize in the passage is closest in meaning to

    (A) encourage
    (B) support
    (C) fortify
    (D) enlarge

39. Look at the word him in the passage. Click on the word or phrase in the **bold** text that him refers to.

40. All of the following are true EXCEPT

    (A) Lindbergh was the first American to cross the Atlantic by plane
    (B) Lindbergh's accomplishment fueled the aviation industry throughout the world
    (C) Lindbergh's monumental solo flight from Paris to New York took place in 1927
    (D) Lindbergh's accomplishment won him both fame and money

41. The word deed in the passage could best be replaced by

    (A) record
    (B) achievement
    (C) demise
    (D) recognition

42. By stating that he would "democratize the automobile," Ford meant that he would

    (A) be open about his creation of a new car and allow the world to see it
    (B) create a highly mobile society through the introduction of automobiles
    (C) build a prototypical automobile for future manufacturers
    (D) not make the automobile a luxury item but make it affordable for everyone

43. Click on the sentence that states the date when the first car was manufactured.

    Scroll the passage to see all of the paragraphs.

44. The automobile industry became significant for all of the following reasons EXCEPT that it

    (A) organized under one company various different businesses
    (B) brought about major improvements in road and transportation facilities
    (C) stimulated other industries such as steel, rubber, glass, textiles, etc.
    (D) provided the model of mass production for future industries

VOCABULARY

startle: to surprise someone suddenly in a way that slightly shocks or frightens them
founder: to fail because of a particular problem or difficulty
subsidize: to pay part of the cost of something

aviation: the activity of flying aircraft, or of designing, producing, and maintaining them
surpass: to better or do more than something else
revolutionize: to produce a very great or complete change in something

register: to record (someone's name or ownership of property) on an official list
salient: most noticeable or important

| **Frequency of appearance per passage with 11 questions: three or more**
| **Standard Multiple Choice or Click on the passage item**
| **Difficulty Range: Easy to Medium**

Overview

1. What is the question about?

Fact Questions

Factual questions test your understanding of explicitly stated facts and other details mentioned in the passage. You should be able to comprehend details and other supporting ideas: plain facts, reasons, examples, comparisons, and further explanation. Authors provide details to support important (main) ideas.

Factual questions often start with one of the "wh" words: *who, what, when, why, where,* or *how much.* However, on the CBT, factual questions became even more diversely and specifically formulated. For example, factual questions are more often composed as open-ended questions such as "All of the following are true EXCEPT..." Sometimes, the wording of the question is very specific: for example, "The author mentions ___ in the passage as examples of items that ..."

Factual questions often begin with the phrase "According to the passage, ..." or "According to the author, ..." It signals that the information needed to answer the question is explicitly stated somewhere in the passage.

You should scan a passage for the specific information you need. Scanning can be done using key expressions given in the question because the relevant part in the passage contains the identical key expressions.

Variation 1: Negative Questions

These questions ask you to determine which one of the four answer choices is NOT discussed (mentioned) in the passage. These questions are stated with negatives such as NOT, EXCEPT, and LEAST (~ LEAST likely to ~).

Scan the passage to locate the relevant information in the passage. The answer choice that is NOT consistent with the passage is the answer choice.

Negative questions often take more time to solve than plain fact questions because you have to find out three correct choices so that you have one answer left that is NOT mentioned in the passage.

Approach negative questions as if they were true/false questions and mark all of the choices with true/false as you proceed. Then, click the oval of the answer choice marked with "false." Generally, you will see at least one negative type question per passage.

Variation 2: Scanning Questions

Scanning questions in the form of "click on the passage" are new items on the CBT. The question requires you to look for statements in the passage about specific points.

In other words, you are supposed to find and click on the sentence or paragraph in the passage where certain particular details are located. Details are specific information such as facts, statistics, examples, reasons, or illustrations. Such details are in the passage to bolster the author's main point.

As in the case of multiple-choice questions, identify key expressions in the wording of questions and then apply scanning methods to locate the relevant part quickly. Scroll down the whole passage to see all of the paragraphs if you are asked to click on the paragraph. More than one paragraph may discuss the point about which the question is asking. Therefore, be careful not to make a hasty determination.

When you are asked to click on the sentence in the designated paragraph, the relevant paragraph is marked with an arrow (➡). You should focus on the paragraph headed by an arrow (➡) only.

Then, click on the sentence or paragraph of your choice. You may click anywhere in the chosen sentence or paragraph to get the whole sentence or paragraph highlighted automatically.

Variation 3: Restatement Questions

You are supposed to find the answer choice that has the same meaning as the statement given in the question. Understand exactly what the author intends to mean. You should find similar expressions in the answer choices, starting from the wording of the base statement given in the question. However, if you see the identical expressions in the answer choices, be careful not to be tricked by distractors. The idea of the statement as a whole, not the fragment of expressions, is important.

2. How is the question worded?

Fact Questions
According to
According to the passage, ...

According to the passage, what is ...?

According to the passage, what was the importance of _____ mentioned in paragraph __?
  Paragraph __ is marked with an arrow [➡].

According to paragraph __, which of the following statements about _____ is true?
  Paragraph __ is marked with an arrow [➡].

According to paragraph __, which of the following is true about _____?

Comprehension
It is clear the author has a high opinion of ...

The author supports which of the following statements about _____?

It is significant that _____ because ...

Which of the following statements about _____ is supported by the passage?

It is most likely that ...

Mention
Which of the following does the author mention as _____?

Which of the following is mentioned as _____?

The author mentions _____ as an example of ...

Which of the following is _____ that is mentioned in the passage?

The author mentions _____ in the passage as examples of items that ...

The author mentions that ...

Which of the following differences between _____ and _____ is mentioned in the passage?

Which/Why

Which of the following is true about ____?

For which of the following reasons does ____?

Which of the following is true of ____?

What is ____ that the author discusses in paragraph __?

Why were ____?

Why is ____?

Miscellaneous

The ____ described in paragraph 1 is ...

    Paragraph 1 is marked with an arrow [➜].

Paragraph __ is mainly a description of ...

    Paragraph __ is marked with an arrow [➜].

The author uses ____ in paragraph __ as an example of ...

The author indicates that ...

The author believes that ...

In the passage, ____ is being compared to ...

Variation 1: Negative Questions

EXCEPT

All of the following are mentioned in the passage as ____ EXCEPT ...

According to the passage, all of the following ____ EXCEPT ...

The passage mentions all of the following ____ EXCEPT ...

All of the following ____ EXCEPT ...

All of the following are reasons why ____ EXCEPT ...

All of the following are part of ____ EXCEPT ...

____ has all of the following characteristics EXCEPT ...

The passage supports all of the following statements about ____ EXCEPT ...

The following are mentioned as ____ EXCEPT ...

NOT

Which of the following is NOT mentioned as ____?

LEAST

Which of the following is LEAST likely to be true about ____?

Variation 2: Scanning Questions

Click on the sentence in paragraph 1 that explains ____.

    Paragraph 1 is marked with an arrow [➜].

Click on the paragraph that explains ____.

    Scroll the passage to see all of the paragraphs.

Look at the four sentences in **bold** text in the passage.

    Click on the sentence that mentions/in which the author ____.

    Scroll the passage to see all of the **bold** sentences.

Click on the sentence in the passage that discusses/states ____.

Click on the sentence in paragraph __ that mentions ____.

Variation 3: Restatement Questions

What does the author mean by the statement ▨▨▨▨▨▨▨▨▨▨▨▨▨?

* Remark: Please refer to the section **Skill Building: Restatement.**

Strategies

1. Key points to remember

For fact questions, you may want to scan the passage searching for key expressions related to the specific information. By doing so, you can manage the test time more efficiently.

Scanning is a kind of selective reading to locate the specific information you need, while skimming is reading the entire passage quickly without skipping around to get an idea about the whole passage. Skimming is suitable for approaching questions asking main ideas or other overview items.

Keep in mind that correct answer choices for fact questions seldom use exactly the same words as found in the passage; they usually use synonyms or rephrased groups of words. Thus, do not pick up the answer choice just based on the identical key expressions found both in the passage and the answer choice.

The order of presenting detail questions about the passage generally follows the order in which ideas are presented in the passage. In addition, the part of the passage related to the specific detail question will show up on the left side of the computer screen. Focus mostly on the relevant part of the passage so that you save time in locating the specific information you need.

2. Test tips

To answer fact questions, you need to focus on the relevant part and identify the specific information necessary to answer the question. In case you do not remember from the first reading where to look for the specific information, try the following scanning procedure.

(1) Identify one or two key expressions as you read the question.

(2) Scan the passage looking for the identical key words or equivalent expressions.

(3) Don't reread the entire passage word by word to find a correct answer choice.

(4) When you find the identical key words in the passage, read the whole sentence in which they appear. You may have to read the surrounding sentences as well.

(5) Remind yourself whether you are supposed to answer simple fact questions or negative type fact questions. If the question has more specific directions, you have to bear them in mind when scanning the passage to find the relevant (related) part.

Skill Building

Skill Building: Restatement

Directions: *Read the following statements. Choose the restatement that has the same meaning as the underlined statement.*

1. What does the author mean by the statement
   <u>Picasso decided to experiment with ways of showing human features based on African styles of representation</u>?
   (A) Picasso tried African styles to represent human features.
   (B) Picasso used new styles to show features of Africans.
   (C) African artists learned much about painting human faces from Picasso.

[Explanation]
   "Try" means "experiment."

2. What does the author mean by the statement
   <u>If you look at the outline of the house, you will notice that it is wider than it is tall</u>?
   (A) The house's outline is taller than it is wide.
   (B) The width of the house's outline is greater than its height.
   (C) The house is less wide than it is tall.

[Explanation]
   "Width" corresponds to "wide," and "height" to "tall."

3. What does the author mean by the statement
   <u>Little was known about cell division at the time, and no one could grasp the broad implications of Mendel's findings</u>?
   (A) No one could appreciate Mendel's findings, because so little was known about cell division then.
   (B) So little was known about Mendel that no one knew what he was talking about.
   (C) Mendel's findings were so broad that no one could comprehend cell division at that time.

[Explanation]
   "Appreciate" means "grasp the broad implications."

4. What does the author mean by the statement
   In a symbiotic relationship, two species live together in a way that is beneficial to both?
   (A) In a beneficial relationship, two species always live together.
   (B) The mutually beneficial coexistence of two species is a symbiotic relationship.
   (C) A symbiotic relationship is whenever two species live together.

[Explanation]
   "Mutually beneficial" means to be "beneficial to both." The other two choices are not similar in meaning to the statement in the question.

5. What does the author mean by the statement
   Nearly half of all the world's species of animals and two-thirds of the world's flowering plants are found in the tropical rainforests?
   (A) Almost half of all animals and more than half the flowering plants are found in tropical rainforests.
   (B) Most animals and plants live freely in tropical rainforests.
   (C) The Amazon rainforests are home to half the species on Earth.

[Explanation]
   "Almost" means to be "nearly," and "two-thirds" is "more than half." Be careful not to add any extra knowledge, as is shown by "the Amazon rainforests" in Choice (C).

6. What does the author mean by the statement
   An undetermined but significant portion of male-female differences is a product of the ways in which males and females are treated?
   (A) Other people's behavior leads to many differences between males and females.
   (B) Males and females treat other people in significantly different ways.
   (C) Females require significantly different treatment from males.

[Explanation]
   The phrase "the ways in which males and females are treated" is rephrased as "other people's behavior."

7. What does the author mean by the statement
   As the economic focus shifted from the farm environment to the factory and office, the family became less involved in the children's lives?
   (A) Fewer children were employed in factories and offices than on farms.
   (B) The shift toward factory and office work reduced the family's involvement in the children's lives.
   (C) Children had a greater impact on the environment as the economic focus shifted from the farm to the factory and office.

[Explanation]
   The clause "the family became less involved in the children's lives" is restated as "reduced the involvement with the children's lives within the family."

READING

8. What does the author mean by the statement
   The Internet will allow people to bypass the formalized hierarchy devoted to controlling the
   flow of information?
   (A) The Internet will allow people to use more informal information than ever before.
   (B) Using the Internet will become a formal occasion as more information is needed.
   (C) It will become easier and quicker to obtain information through the Internet.

[Explanation]
   The phrase "bypass the formalized hierarchy" is paraphrased as "easier and quicker to obtain."

9. What does the author mean by the statement
   Globalization involves interdependence at the grass-roots level that aims to enhance
   people's access to the basic resources they need to live a life?
   (A) Globalization will make edible grasses much easier to grow and provide more food.
   (B) Global interdependence aims to make essential resources more readily available to
       people.
   (C) People in a global world will be expected to depend upon each other more than ever.

[Explanation]
   You have to know the meaning of "grass-roots" to comprehend the whole sentence correctly. The
   context provides a clue to its meaning. It means "ordinary people in society." Additionally, "enhance
   people's access to ~ resources" is restated as "make resources readily available to people."

10. What does the author mean by the statement
    Those in positions of authority often use the power of their positions improperly to restrict
    resources and censor information?
    (A) People in positions of authority often abuse their power.
    (B) Censoring information is necessary to maintain a position of authority.
    (C) People in positions of power tend to have highly restricted authority.

[Explanation]
   "Use the power of their positions improperly to restrict ~ and censor ~" is equivalent to "abuse their
   power."

VOCABULARY

1 **representation**: the act of presenting somebody or something in a particular way
feature: a noticeable or important characteristic or part
3 **cell**: the smallest basic unit of a plant or animal
appreciate: to increase in value
4 **symbiosis (adj. symbiotic)**: the relationship between two different living creatures that live close together and depend on each other in particular ways, each getting particular benefits from the other

beneficial: tending to help; having a good effect
5 **tropical**: characteristic of the tropics
rainforest: a thick forest in tropical parts of the world that have a lot of rain
6 **portion**: a part or share of something larger
7 **impact**: the strong effect or influence that something has on a situation or person
8 **bypass**: to avoid (something) by going around it
formalize: to make (something) official

hierarchy: a system in which people or things are put at various levels or ranks according to their importance
9 **global**: relating to the whole world
10 **restrict**: to limit the size, amount or range of something
censor: to remove parts of (something to be read, seen, or heard) because it is offensive or considered morally wrong, or because it is secret

Intensive Exercises

Exercise 3.1

The continuous movement of the Earth's crustal plates can squeeze, stretch, or break rock strata, deforming them and producing faults and folds. A fault is a fracture in a rock along which there is movement of one side relative to the other. The movement can be vertical, horizontal, or oblique (vertical and horizontal). Faults develop when rocks are subjected to compression or tension. They tend to occur in hard, rigid rocks, which are more likely to break than bend.

The smallest faults occur in single mineral crystals and are microscopically small, while the largest – the Great Rift Valley in Africa, which formed between 5 million and 100,000 years ago – is more than 6,000 miles long. A fold is a bend in a rock layer caused by compression. Folds occur in elastic rocks, which tend to bend rather than break. The two main types of folds are upholds and downholds. Folds vary in size from a few millimeters long to folded mountain ranges hundreds of miles long, such as the Himalayas and the Alps, which are repeatedly folding.

1. Which of the following best describes faults and folds?
   - (A) The movements of the Earth
   - (B) The gap between two continents
   - (C) Crack in the oldest rocks of the earth's crust
   - (D) Deformation of rigid rocks as well as elastic rocks

2. Which of the following is NOT mentioned among factors causing the formation of faults?
   - (A) Stretching of the rigid rock strata
   - (B) Squeezing of elastic rocks
   - (C) Compression of hard rocks
   - (D) Movement of the Earth's rigid rock layer

LinguaForum

[Explanation]

1. Scan the passage for key words such as "faults" and "folds." Refer to the last sentence in the 1st paragraph, which is "They (faults) tend to occur in hard, rigid rocks, which are more likely to break than bend." In the middle of the 2nd paragraph, it is stated that folds occur in elastic rocks.

2. The negative type question requires you to identify one false choice that usually contradicts the facts in the passage. All of the other three choices will correctly restate the facts mentioned in the passage. In this question, three choices discuss or mention rigid or hard rocks. Thus, the answer choice mentioning different types of rocks is likely to be the answer. Also, it is explicitly stated in the passage that folds, not faults, occur in elastic rocks.

VOCABULARY

crust: a hard, outer covering, as on a loaf of bread or a pastry

fault: a place where there is a break that is longer than usual in the layers of rock in the earth's crust

fold: a curve or bend in the line of the layers of rock in the earth's crust

oblique: having a sloping direction, angle, or position

compress (n. compression): to press or squeeze something together or into a smaller space

Exercise 3.2

Carnivorous (insectivorous) plants feed on insects and other small animals in addition to producing food in their leaves by photosynthesis. The nutrients absorbed from trapped insects allow carnivorous plants to thrive in acid, boggy soils that lack essential minerals, especially nitrates, where most other plants could not survive. All carnivorous plants have some leaves modified as traps. Many use bright colors and scented nectar to attract prey, and most use enzymes to digest the prey. There are three types of traps. Pitcher plants, such as the monkey cup and cobra lily, have leaves modified as pitcher-shaped pitfall traps, half-filled with water. Once lured inside the mouth of the trap, insects lose their footing on the slippery surface, fall into the liquid, and either decompose or are digested. Venus flytraps use a spring-trap mechanism; when an insect touches trigger hairs on the inner surfaces of the leaves, the two lobes of the trap snap shut.

1. What does the author mean by the statement The nutrients absorbed from trapped insects allow carnivorous plants to thrive in acid, boggy soils that lack essential minerals, especially nitrates, where most other plants could not survive?

(A) Carnivorous plants could survive without essential minerals, especially nitrates, thriving on the acid topsoil.

(B) The nitrates in acid, boggy soils protect insects from being trapped by carnivorous plants.

(C) The nutrients from trapped insects supplement minerals lacking in acid soils where carnivorous plants may live.

(D) Insects allow carnivorous plants to survive in the boggy soils because they help enrich the soil so that plants could best thrive.

2. Click on the sentence that suggests why insects so easily slide into the inside of carnivorous plants.

 LinguaForum

[Explanation]

1. This question tests your ability to paraphrase the statement. Look for the sentence that correctly restates the basic elements of the statement in the question. Also, verify the overall meaning of the paraphrased statement to make sure it does not distort what the author originally meant. In the question, "The nutrients absorbed from trapped insects allow ~" is restated as "The nutrients from trapped insects supplement ~." "Acid, boggy soils that lack ~" is restated as "lacking minerals in acid soils."

2. This is a "scan and click question," which is new on the CBT. In order to find the reason why insects easily slide into carnivorous plants, you need to scan the passage looking for the sentence that describes why the insects got trapped. Expressions such as "slippery surface" or "fall into" will be clues found in the passage.

VOCABULARY

carnivore (adj. carnivorous): any animal that eats meat
photosynthesis: the process by which green plants turn carbon dioxide and water into food

using energy from sunlight
enzyme: a substance, usually produced by plants and animals, which helps a chemical change happen

lure: to persuade or trick somebody to go somewhere or to do something by promising them a reward
lobe: a part of an organ in the body

Exercise 3.3

The northeastern part of the United States has many waterfalls. Waterfalls can be used to produce power to run machines. It was partly for this reason that the first water-powered cotton mill was built in Rhode Island in 1793. Other factories were also set up where waterpower was available. This was the beginning of industrialization in the region.

Industrialization is the setting-up of manufacturing that uses machinery. The abundant coal deposits in Pennsylvania and Ohio helped lay the base for industry in the Midwest. An industry is any business that produces goods or provides services. The many rivers in the region were used to transport goods from factories to port cities.

A growing demand for cotton by the textile industry in the Northeast made cotton production highly profitable. Cotton became the South's major cash crop. Swamps were drained and pine forests cleared for more cotton plantations. Slave labor became more important than ever before, and the number of slaves in the South increased.

1. According to the passage, where was the first water-powered cotton mill built?
   - Ⓐ In Pennsylvania
   - Ⓑ In the Northwest
   - Ⓒ In Rhode Island
   - Ⓓ In North America

2. What does the author mean by the statement The abundant coal deposits in Pennsylvania and Ohio helped lay the base for industry in the Midwest?
   - Ⓐ There are more coal deposits in Pennsylvania and Ohio than in the Midwest.
   - Ⓑ The main industry in the Midwest was construction until coal was discovered in Pennsylvania and Ohio.
   - Ⓒ No coal deposits in Pennsylvania and Ohio helped increase the base for industry in the Midwest.
   - Ⓓ The Midwest's industry was positively influenced by coal located in Pennsylvania and Ohio.

3. All of the following contributed to industrialization in America EXCEPT
   - Ⓐ swamps
   - Ⓑ slave labor
   - Ⓒ rivers
   - Ⓓ waterfalls

 Time   **LinguaForum**   **Help** **Prev** **Next**

[Explanation]

1. The passage states that "the first water-powered cotton mill was built in Rhode Island in 1793."
2. "Abundant" means "more than enough." "Lay the base" means that something became the foundation or most important part. A lot of coal deposits in Pennsylvania and Ohio became the foundation of industry in the Midwest.
3. The passage discusses swamps that were drained and pine forests that were cleared for more cotton plantations. Slave labor indirectly contributed to the textile industry by working on cotton plantations.

VOCABULARY

industrialize (n. industrialization): if a country or an area is industrialized, industries (the production of goods) are developed there

deposit: a layer of a substance that has formed naturally underground

drain: to make something empty or dry by

removing all the liquid from it

plantation: a large area of land that is planted with trees to produce wood

Exercise 3.4

Architecture, like art, in colonial times in the United States and Canada was greatly influenced by European styles. The English settlers modeled their farmhouses and other buildings after English styles. The Swedes in Delaware introduced the log cabin. The French influenced architecture in Quebec and Louisiana. Roman or Greek styles were also often copied. In the Southwest settlers combined Indian and Spanish elements in adobe buildings.

One of the most important contributions to world architecture, the skyscraper, was developed in the United States. After a great fire destroyed much of Chicago in 1871, the city became a center of skyscraper designs during its rebuilding. Building upward meant that only a small piece of land had to be used to house many people or businesses.

During the late 1800's Frank Lloyd Wright of the United States introduced a new, clean-cut look to architecture. He emphasized the use of wood and of other materials as they appear in nature. Wright designed his low, horizontal prairie style houses to seem to grow out of the ground and to blend with the openness of the Midwest prairie.

1. Which of the following were NOT influenced by European architecture styles?
   - (A) Adobes
   - (B) Terraces
   - (C) Farmhouses
   - (D) Log cabins

2. According to the passage, when did Chicago become a center of skyscraper designs?
   - (A) After Frank Lloyd Wright visited the city
   - (B) After land prices increased in the city
   - (C) After other countries began to build them
   - (D) After a fire burned much of the city

3. What does the author mean by the statement Wright designed his low, horizontal prairie style houses to seem to grow out of the ground and to blend with the openness of the Midwest prairie?
   - (A) Wright's houses had many windows and no roofs so that people could enjoy the openness of the Midwest prairie.
   - (B) Wright's houses did not cost very much to design because they were made with materials from the Midwest.
   - (C) Wright's flat houses looked as if they were natural parts of the prairies in the Midwest.
   - (D) Wright designed most of his houses in the Midwest because he enjoyed the environment there.

[Explanation]
1. Terraces were only part of Frank Lloyd Wright's houses.
2. The passage states that "After a great fire destroyed much of Chicago in 1871, the city became a center of skyscraper designs during its rebuilding."
3. "Horizontal" means parallel to the earth's surface. "Prairie style" means the style appropriate for the environment of the prairie.

VOCABULARY

colonial: connected with or belonging to a country that controls another country
adobe: mud that is dried in the sun, mixed with

straw and used as a building material
prairie: a flat wide area of land without many trees and originally covered with grass

blend: to combine with something in an attractive way

Exercise 3.5

One of the most enduring legacies of the Roosevelt years was his energetic support for the conservation movement. Concern for protecting the environment grew with the rising awareness that exploitation of natural resources was despoiling the frontier. As early as 1872, Yellowstone National Park had been set aside as a public reserve (the National Park Service would be created in 1916 after other parks had been added). In 1881 Congress had created a Division of Forestry in the Department of Agriculture, and Roosevelt's appointment of Gifford Pinchot, one of the country's first scientific foresters, as chief brought vigorous administration of forests on public lands. The president strove to halt the unchecked destruction of the nation's natural resources and wonders by providing a barrier of federal regulation and protection. To do so, Roosevelt added fifty federal wildlife refuges, approved five new national parks, and initiated the system of designating national monuments such as the Grand Canyon. He also used the Forest Reserve Act (1891) to exclude from settlement or harvest some 172 million acres of timberland. Lumber barons were irate, but Roosevelt held firm. As he bristled, "I hate a man who would skin the land."

1. According to the passage, what was despoiling the frontier?
   - Ⓐ Visitors at Yellowstone National Park
   - Ⓑ Laws passed by Gifford Pinchot
   - Ⓒ Destruction of wildlife refuges
   - Ⓓ Exploitation of natural resources

2. What does the author mean by the statement The president strove to halt the unchecked destruction of the nation's natural resources and wonders by providing a barrier of federal regulation and protection?
   - Ⓐ The president checked to see if natural resources were being destroyed.
   - Ⓑ The president could not protect nature because of the government's laws.
   - Ⓒ The president passed laws to protect America's natural environment.
   - Ⓓ The president wanted to continue to protect natural resources and wonders without federal regulation.

3. All of the following are true EXCEPT
   - Ⓐ Roosevelt cared about conserving America's forests
   - Ⓑ Roosevelt helped create the Department of Agriculture
   - Ⓒ Roosevelt saved some timberland under the Forest Reserve Act
   - Ⓓ Roosevelt started the system of naming national monuments

  LinguaForum

READING

[Explanation]

1. The passage states that "Concern for protecting the environment grew with the rising awareness that exploitation of natural resources was despoiling the frontier."

2. "Strove to halt the unchecked destruction" means that Roosevelt tried to stop destruction that was proceeding unopposed.

3. Roosevelt helped create the Division of Forestry in the already existing Department of Agriculture.

VOCABULARY

legacy: a situation that exists now because of events, actions, etc.
exploitation: the use of land, oil, minerals, etc.

refuge: shelter or protection from danger, trouble, etc.
irate: very angry

bristle: to suddenly become very annoyed or offended at what somebody says or does
skin: to take the skin off

Vocabulary Review for Intensive Exercises 3.1-3.5

1. The _____ of the earth is its outer layer.
   - (A) crust
   - (B) core
   - (C) diameter
   - (D) radius

2. She tried a new hairstyle with an _____ hair band.
   - (A) outpouring
   - (B) overt
   - (C) eligible
   - (D) elastic

3. The _____ of easy money made him quit his job.
   - (A) attire
   - (B) lure
   - (C) emergency
   - (D) enigma

4. He was _____ to a big fraudulent scheme.
   - (A) prey
   - (B) pressure
   - (C) priority
   - (D) prompt

5. This state is _____ with natural resources.
   - (A) rarely
   - (B) stubborn
   - (C) approximate
   - (D) abundant

6. She washed the spoiled milk down the _____.
   - (A) plumber
   - (B) drain
   - (C) plug
   - (D) dump

7. The first _____ of the state of Utah were Mormons.
   - (A) settlers
   - (B) residence
   - (C) relatives
   - (D) confidants

8. Prince William attempted to _____ in with the other students.
   - (A) fix
   - (B) blend
   - (C) compete
   - (D) combine

9. She filed a lawsuit to stop the _____ of child labor.
   - (A) expertise
   - (B) extinction
   - (C) exploitation
   - (D) extravagance

10. The San Francisco Bay area is a _____ for some rare species of birds.
    - (A) refuge
    - (B) refund
    - (C) relic
    - (D) reparation

Word Files II: TOEFL Vocabulary with Emphasis on American History

accustom: v. to familiarize with something

advocate: n. a supporter

agriculture: n. the practice of farming

alliance: n. an agreement to work together

allocate: v. to give as a share

amendment: n. a change made to a law

assault: n. a violent attack

assume: v. to accept as true without proof

boycott: v. to refuse to buy

cease: v. to stop

charge: v. to accuse of a crime

civil rights: n. the rights every person has

collapse: n. a sudden failure of something

colony: n. a country controlled by a more powerful country

compliance: n. obeying rules

confederate: a. allied

confiscate: v. to officially take something away

congregation: n. assembly

consensus: n. wide agreement

conservative: adj. opposing change

controversy: n. public discussion and argument

coordinate: v. to make work together

declare: v. to say something officially; proclaim

delegate: n. a person chosen by a group to represent them; deputy

depression: n. a period when there is little economic activity

disrupt: v. to prevent from continuing as usual

doctrine: n. belief, theory

enact: v. to make a law

enterprise: n. a business plan

eradicate: v. to get rid of

extort (n. extortion): v. to obtain by force

federal: a. connected with the central government

grass roots: pl. n. the ordinary people

hardship: n. a situation that is difficult

halt: v. to stop

immigration: n. the process by which people come in to a foreign country

inflation: n. a continuing rise in prices

inhabitant: n. a person living in a place

initiative: n. a new attempt

integrate: v. to combine something

launch: v. to send out

legitimate (n. legitimacy): adj. valid

lenient: adj. not as strict as expected

mandate: n. an official order

manipulate: v. to control someone

manufacture: v. to produce

morale: n. the amount of confidence

negotiate: v. to try to reach an agreement

panic: n. a sudden feeling of anxiety

persuade: v. to cause to believe something

pioneer: n. the first visitor in an area

pledge: n. a serious promise

ploy: n. a trick

plunder: v. to steal goods forcefully

prejudice: n. an unreasonable opinion

propaganda: n. a methodical spread of information

rally: v. to return to a better condition

ratify: v. to agree in writing to do something

recession: n. depression in the economy

reconcile (n. reconciliation): v. to harmonize

reparation: n. payment for damage

resolution: n. the act of solving a problem

restore: v. to bring back into existence

resume: v. to start again after a pause

revitalize: v. to put new energy into something

segregate: v. to separate people into groups

separate: v. to divide into different groups

settlement: n. an official agreement

sovereignty: n. the authority to rule

strategy: n. a plan for achieving something

subsidy: n. money given as part of the cost of something to encourage it to happen

suffrage: n. the right to vote in an election

survey: v. to look at; to measure

tariff: n. a tax on goods entering or leaving a country

territory: n. land that belongs to a particular country

tolerate: v. to put up with

treaty: n. a formal agreement

vigorous: adj. very active; full of energy

welfare: n. physical and mental health and happiness

READING

Practice Test 3

Questions 1-11

While many of America's most talented writers and artists dealt directly with the human suffering and social tensions provoked by the Great Depression, the more popular cultural outlets such as radio programs and movies provided patrons with a welcome "escape" from the decade's grim realities.

→ By the 1930s, radio had become a major source of family entertainment. More than 10 million families owned it. ■ Millions of housewives listened to formulaic radio "soap operas" during the day. ■ The shows lasted fifteen minutes and derived their name from their sponsors, the soap manufacturers. ■ The recipe for a successful soap opera, according to one writer, was to provide "twelve minutes of dialogue, add predicament, villainy, and female suffering in equal measure, throw in a dash of nobility, sprinkle with tears, season with organ music, flavor with a rich announcer sauce, and serve five times a week." ■ The soap operas provided struggling people with distractions as well as a sense of comparative well-being. ■

→ Late afternoon radio programs were directed at children home from school. ■ In the evening after supper, families would gather around the radio to listen to newscasts, comedies such as *Amos n' Andy* and adventure dramas such as *Superman*, *Jack Armstrong*, *The Lone Ranger*, *Dick Tracy* and *The Green Hornet* and "big band" musical programs. ■ Franklin Roosevelt was the first president to take full advantage of the popularity of radio broadcasting. ■ He hosted sixteen "fireside chats" to generate public support for his New Deal initiatives. ■

In the late 1920s, what had been "silent" films were transformed by the introduction of sound. The "talkies" made the movie industry by far the most popular form of entertainment during the 1930s – much more sought-after than today.

Films of the 1930s rarely dealt with the hard times of the depression or with racial and ethnic tensions. Exceptions were the film version of *The Grapes of Wrath* and classic documentaries by Pare Lorenz entitled *The River* and *The Plow That Broke the Plains*. Much more common were movies intended for pure entertainment that transported viewers into the realm of adventure, spectacle and fantasy.

1. The passage discusses mainly
   - (A) the history of entertainment in the United States
   - (B) the introduction of sound into film during the Great Depression
   - (C) the role of radio and movies in the era of the Great Depression
   - (D) the popularity of radio in the era of the Great Depression

2. Look at the word *it* in the passage. Click on the word or phrase in the **bold** text that *it* refers to.

3. The radio programs popular among housewives were called "soap operas" because
   - (A) they introduced housewives to various types of soaps and detergents available in the market
   - (B) they introduced housewives to different methods of cleaning
   - (C) the daily melodramas were sponsored by soap manufacturers
   - (D) they introduced various commercials

4. Look at the word flavor in the passage. Click on the word or phrase in the **bold** text that is closest in meaning to flavor.

5. Listeners of the soap operas experienced all of the following EXCEPT

   - Ⓐ comfort
   - Ⓑ relief
   - Ⓒ distraction
   - Ⓓ disturbance

6. The passage mentions all of the following radio programs EXCEPT

   - Ⓐ *Superman*
   - Ⓑ *The Lone Ranger*
   - Ⓒ *Spiderman*
   - Ⓓ fireside chats

7. Look at the word popular in the passage. Click on the word or phrase in the **bold** text that is closest in meaning to popular.

8. The following sentence can be added to paragraph 2 or 3.

   Fans could also listen to baseball and football games or boxing matches.

   Where would it best fit in the paragraph? Click on the square [■] to add the sentence to paragraph 2 or 3.
   Paragraphs 2 and 3 are marked with an arrow [➜].

9. Movies in the 1930s were called "talkies" because

   - Ⓐ characters other than human beings talked
   - Ⓑ actors did nothing but talk
   - Ⓒ for the first time, sound was incorporated into films
   - Ⓓ people talked mostly about films

10. Click on the paragraph that explains why the films became so popular in the 1930s.

    Scroll the passage to see all of the paragraphs.

11. Movies of the 1930s

    - Ⓐ were mostly social documentaries depicting the lives of common folk
    - Ⓑ were much more popular than radio programs among housewives
    - Ⓒ were intended to distract the public from the hard times of the depression
    - Ⓓ tried to alert the general public to economic and racial problems

READING

Questions 12-22

From time to time, especially near the coast, the sea surface becomes bright red literally overnight. This phenomenon, called a red tide, has occurred for thousands of years. The Old Testament may contain the earliest known reference to a red tide when it describes the waters of the Nile turning to blood. The Red Sea is named after the red tides that often occur there. The term "red tide" is here to stay, but it is somewhat confusing. For one thing, red tides have nothing to do with the tide. They are massive blooms of phytoplankton. **At the peak of a red tide there may be thousands, even tens or hundreds of thousands, of cells in a single drop! Furthermore, red tides are not always red. The sea may instead turn orange, brown or bright green. In fact, the name "red tide" is applied to harmful phytoplankton blooms even if they discolor the water only slightly. In recent years the term "brown tide" has been used in some places for blooms of a particular type of phytoplankton called chrysophytes.**

➔ Red tides occur all over the world. Only around 6% of all phytoplankton species are known to cause red tides. ■ About half of red tide organisms are dinoflagellates, but many other organisms including cyanobacteria, diatoms, chrysophytes, and several other groups can cause red tides. These exceptional phytoplankton blooms are often nothing more than oceanographic oddities, but sometimes they cause serious problems. ■ Such harmful algal blooms or HABs are receiving increasing attention from both scientists and society at large. Of course, what is harmful depends on your point of view. If you are on a beach vacation, a foul brown foam may be nothing more than an annoying reason to cut the vacation short. ■ Some blooms are more than just a nuisance. ■ **They are deadly. About a third of red tide organisms produce poisons, some of which are among the most powerful toxins known. ■ Under normal circumstances, there are too few of the organisms around to worry about, but when they bloom they can cause serious problems. ■ Mussels, clams, crabs, and other shellfish often tolerate the toxins by storing them away in the digestive gland, kidney, liver, or other tissues. ■ People who eat the shellfish may suffer nausea, diarrhea, vomiting, numbness and tingling, loss of balance and memory, slurred speech, shooting pains, and paralysis. The most severe cases are fatal. ■ Swimming or boating in affected water can cause sore throats, eye irritation, and skin complaints. There is even proof that some of the toxins are carcinogenic. ■**

12. What would be the best title for the passage?
- Ⓐ Red Poison
- Ⓑ Deadly Seas
- Ⓒ Harmful Algal Blooms
- Ⓓ Red Pigments

13. The word literally in the passage is closest in meaning to
- Ⓐ figuratively
- Ⓑ amazingly
- Ⓒ lively
- Ⓓ really

14. The earliest reference to a red tide has been found in
- Ⓐ the Old Testament
- Ⓑ the HABs
- Ⓒ the Red Sea
- Ⓓ the Nile

15. Which of the following is true of a red tide?

Click on 2 answers.

- [A] It can be observed in only designated places.
- [B] It is a recently discovered phenomenon.
- [C] It is caused by massive blooms of phytoplankton.
- [D] Its color may also be orange, green or brown.

16. Look at the word they in the passage. Click on the word or phrase in the **bold** text that they refers to.

17. It can be inferred from the passage that the term "red tide" is

- Ⓐ derived from the unique color of high tides
- Ⓑ customarily used to describe blooms of phytoplankton
- Ⓒ recently coined by marine biology experts
- Ⓓ recently replacing the term "brown tide"

18. Algal blooms are more than just a nuisance because of

- Ⓐ a cancelled vacation
- Ⓑ a negative economic impact
- Ⓒ deadly poisons
- Ⓓ the discoloration of the ocean water

19. The following sentence can be added to paragraph 2.

To the motel owner depending on your business, however, it is a disaster.

Where would it best fit in the paragraph? Click on the square [■] to add the sentence to paragraph 2. Paragraph 2 is marked with an arrow [➡].

20. Look at the word deadly in the passage. Click on the word or phrase in the **bold** text that is closest in meaning to deadly.

21. Marine life forms are not affected by toxins because

- Ⓐ they have learned to avoid the season of HABs
- Ⓑ their bodies have adapted to tolerate the toxins
- Ⓒ their bodies have created a safety device to reject such deadly substances
- Ⓓ they have learned not to eat the deadly phytoplankton

22. Toxins produced by the algal blooms are sometimes fatal because they

- Ⓐ are polluting the ocean water
- Ⓑ may be commercially unprofitable
- Ⓒ will soon become extinguished
- Ⓓ are carcinogenic

VOCABULARY

phytoplankton: tiny plant particles floating in bodies of water
chrysophyte: any algae of the phylum chrysophyta, comprising the yellow-green algae, golden-brown algae, and diatoms
dinoflagellate: any of numerous chiefly marine plankton of the phylum Pyrrophyta
cyanobacteria: blue-green algae

diatom: any of numerous microscopic, unicellular, marine or freshwater algae
nuisance: something or someone that annoys you or causes trouble for you
gland: an organ of the body that produces chemicals that influence various bodily activities, such as growth and sexual desire, and that have an important effect on the organism's health

tissue: a group of related cells that forms larger parts of animals and plants
nausea: a feeling of illness in the stomach that makes you think you are going to vomit
diarrhea: a condition in which a person's solid waste is too watery and is excreted too frequently

Questions 23-33

A two-dimensional technique which may be regarded as intermediate between painting and mosaic is that commonly referred to as sand painting. Dry painting is a more appropriate term since besides red, yellow and white sands, such materials as corn meal, pollen, pulverized flower petals, and charcoal, separately or in mixtures, are strewn on a background of usually tan-colored sand. Paintings varying in size from 1 to 24 feet across were made exclusively for ceremonial purposes by the Navajo as well as by inhabitants of the Pueblos, of southern California, and occasionally also of the Plains. Dry painting is an extremely impermanent art form: no fixatives are used, and the painting had to be destroyed for religious reasons immediately after use.

Very little is consequently known about dry paintings from the Pueblo area, where traditional religion is scrupulously concealed from outside view, and from the Plains, where little attention has been paid to it, except that it originated in the Southwest. Navajo dry painting, first recorded in 1885, was made permanent by White observers who copied the originals on paper or cardboard, and later by Navajos who did the same in spite of traditional prohibitions against the making of fixed representations of the sacred designs.

An insurmountable problem in the study and appreciation of Navajo dry painting is that none of the sources permanently available for inspection is original. **The paintings themselves represent the communal effort of four to six men working under the supervision of the ritual specialist. Besides being in a different medium, copies by Navajos often exhibit color changes, while copies by Whites display many stylistic conventionalizations and idiosyncracies of their collectors. Since 1958, permanent versions of dry paintings on boards have been produced for the tourist market. Made by more than 500 Navajo men and women, especially from the Sheep Spring area in New Mexico, they are hardly representative of the original art form.**

23. The passage focuses on which of the following aspects of dry painting?
    - (A) Its different types
    - (B) Its history and development
    - (C) Its religious significance
    - (D) Its place in the history of art

24. The passage preceding this one would most probably have discussed
    - (A) the different types of native American Indian art
    - (B) the geographical background of native American Indians
    - (C) the history and development of painting and mosaics in native American Indian art
    - (D) the history and development of painting in native American Indian art

25. The ingredients used for dry painting include all of the following EXCEPT
    - (A) pebbles
    - (B) white sand
    - (C) pollen
    - (D) charcoal

26. According to the passage, the subject matter of Indian dry painting consisted of

(A) nature
(B) tribal history
(C) sacred images
(D) mythic figures

27. The second paragraph implies that

(A) Indians and Whites were constantly fighting
(B) there was contact between Whites and Indians despite mutual hostility
(C) the Navajo Indians tried to sell their tribal art to Whites in exchange for goods
(D) the Navajo Indians were the only ones who dared to break tradition

28. It can be inferred from the passage that studies of dry painting are

(A) not available to art historians
(B) exactly about its original form
(C) representative of studies about folk art
(D) at best an approximation

29. Look at the word permanent in the passage. Click on the word or phrase in the **bold** text that is closest in meaning to permanent.

30. According to the passage, dry painting was an impermanent art form because

(A) paintings were so small in size
(B) little attention had been paid to it
(C) it originated in the Southwest
(D) it had to be destroyed after use

31. Look at the word exhibit in the passage. Click on the word or phrase in the **bold** text that is closest in meaning to exhibit.

32. Which of the following does the word they in the passage refer to?

(A) Men and women
(B) Permanent versions
(C) Navajos
(D) Collectors

33. The last paragraph suggests that

(A) it is difficult to reproduce the color of natural materials such as sand in artificial painting
(B) Navajos preferred painting to dry painting
(C) Whites respected the original dry paintings
(D) techniques of dry painting were transmitted from one generation to the other

READING

VOCABULARY

pulverize: to press or crush something until it becomes powder or a soft mass
ceremonial: relating to or used in a ceremony
fixative: a substance that is used to prevent colors or smells from changing or becoming weaker, for example in photography or art

scrupulous: extremely careful to do what is right or moral
sacred: holy and deserving respect
insurmountable: (esp. of a problem or a difficulty) so great that it cannot be dealt with successfully
communal: belonging to or used by all members

of a group
ritual: a set of actions or words performed in a regular way, esp. as part of a religious ceremony
idiosyncrasy: a strange or unusual habit, way of behaving, or feature

Questions 34-44

Scientists don't always agree on the best way to do science. In the past there were serious disputes over which methods of scientific reasoning were acceptable. Some people thought that the only truly scientific form of thinking was induction, in which one starts with a number of separate observations and then arrives at general principles. Others believed that scientists should use deduction, and reason from general principles to specific conclusions. Most scientists now agree that both ways of thinking are indispensable.

→ **When using induction, a scientist starts by making a series of individual observations. Ideally, he or she has no goal or hunch about the outcome and is completely objective. ■ The combination of these observations suggests a general conclusion. ■ For example, suppose a particular marine biologist examined a sailfish, a shark, and a tuna and found that they all had gills. Because sailfish, sharks, and tuna are all fishes, he might draw the general conclusion, *All fishes have gills*. This is an example of induction. ■** The step from isolated observations to a general statement depends on the number and quality of the observations. ■ If the biologist had stopped after examining the sailfish, which happens to have a bill, he might use induction to make the false conclusion *All fishes have bills*. ■ Even after examining all three fishes, he might have concluded *All marine animals have gills* instead of just *All fishes have gills*. This is where deduction comes into play. ■

→ In deductive reasoning, scientists start with a general statement about nature and predict what the specific consequences would be if the general statement is true. ■ They might arrive at the general statement by hunch or intuition, but usually the statement is the result of induction, that is, based on observations. ■ Suppose one marine biologist used induction to make the general statement *All marine animals have gills*. He might then reason that if all marine animals have gills and whales are marine animals, then whales must have gills. ■ The biologist has used a general statement about all marine animals to make a statement about a particular kind of marine animal. ■

34. What is the best title for the passage?
  - (A) Science and Marine Biology
  - (B) Observations of Marine Animals
  - (C) Two Ways of Scientific Thinking
  - (D) Theory and Practice

35. According to the passage, scientists consider induction and deduction as being
  - (A) contradictory to each other
  - (B) indistinguishable from each other
  - (C) both needed in reasoning
  - (D) invalid ways of thinking

36. Why does the author give an example of three fishes in the 2nd paragraph?
  - (A) To show how induction may lead to a false conclusion
  - (B) To assert that deduction is superior to induction
  - (C) To demonstrate how induction is applied to marine biology
  - (D) To illustrate that all marine animals have gills

37. The word ideally in the passage is closest in meaning to

(A) practically
(B) hopefully
(C) completely
(D) really

38. Look at the word he in the passage. Click on the word or phrase in the **bold** text that he refers to.

39. It is implied in the passage that

(A) the inductive method is never reliable
(B) deductive reasoning is final and credible
(C) deductive reasoning is always correct
(D) the inductive method is limited

40. The following sentence can be added to paragraph 2 or 3.

However, the scientist must be careful in making inductions.

Where would it best fit in the paragraph? Click on the square [■] to add the sentence to paragraph 2 or 3.
Paragraphs 2 and 3 are marked with an arrow [➜].

41. All of the following affect the accuracy of the inductive method EXCEPT

(A) number of observations
(B) quality of observations
(C) examination
(D) intuition

42. Which of the following could best replace the word isolated in the passage?

(A) Ignored
(B) Separated
(C) Private
(D) Excluded

43. According to the passage, which of the following is an example of inductive reasoning?

(A) Sailfish, sharks and tunas have gills. They are all fishes.
(B) Some marine animals have bills. All fishes have bills.
(C) Sailfish, sharks and tunas have gills. All sea animals have gills.
(D) Sailfish, sharks and tunas have gills. Only fishes have gills.

44. Click on the sentence that explains how deductive reasoning works.

Scroll the entire passage to see all of the paragraphs.

V OCA BULARY

reason: to use your power to think and understand
dispute: an argument or disagreement
deduction: the process of learning something by considering a general set of facts and thinking about how something specific relates to them
indispensable: too important not to have
hunch: an idea that is based on feeling and for

which there is no proof
objective: not influenced by personal beliefs or feelings; fair or real
gill: the organ through which fish and other water creatures breathe
marine: of or near the sea

intuition: an ability to understand or know something without needing to think about it or use reason to discover it
induction: a method of discovering general rules and principles from particular facts and examples

Questions 45-55

Although not all rituals are religious in nature, those which are play a crucial role in religious activity. Religious ritual is the means through which persons relate to the sacred; it is religion in action. Not only is ritual the means by which the social bonds of a group are reinforced and tensions relieved; it is also one way that many important events are celebrated and crises, such as death, made less socially disruptive and less difficult for individuals to bear. Anthropologists have classified several different types of rituals, among them rites of passage, which pertain to stages in the life cycle of the individual, and rites of intensification, which take place during a crisis in the life of the group, serving to bind individuals together.

→ **In one of anthropology's classic works, Arnold Van Gennep analyzed the rites of passage that help individuals through the crucial crises of their lives, such as birth, puberty, marriage, parenthood, advancement to a higher class, occupational specialization and death. ■ He found it useful to divide ceremonies for all of these life crises into three stages: separation, transition and incorporation. ■ Van Gennep described the male initiation rites of Australian aborigines. ■ When the time for the initiation is decided by the elders, the boys are taken from the village, while the women cry and make a ritual show of resistance; the elders sing and dance while the initiates act as though they are dead. ■ The climax of the ritual is a bodily operation, such as circumcision or the knocking of a tooth. ■**

→ The novice may be shown secret ceremonies and receive some instruction during this, but the most significant element is his complete removal from society. ■ The initiate must learn the tribal lore that all adult men are expected to know; he is given, in effect, a "cram course." ■ The trauma of the occasion is a pedagogical technique that ensures that he will learn and remember everything. ■ In a non-literate society the perpetuation of cultural traditions requires no less, and so effective teaching methods are necessary. ■

45. The main subject of the passage is
   (A) the role that religious rituals play in the rite of passage
   (B) the origin and evolution of rituals in primitive societies
   (C) the nature of rituals and the characteristics of non-religious rituals
   (D) the differences between rituals practiced in primitive and non-primitive societies

46. The phrase relate to in the passage is closest in meaning to
   (A) approach
   (B) believe
   (C) take advantage of
   (D) symbolize

47. Rituals carry out all of the following functions EXCEPT
   (A) release tension
   (B) control crisis
   (C) discourage religion
   (D) celebrate birth

48. Which of the following is an example of the rites of passage?

- (A) Social bond
- (B) Initiation
- (C) Sacrifice
- (D) Mass

49. Which of the following could best replace the word disruptive in the passage?

- (A) Cumulative
- (B) Dangerous
- (C) Selfish
- (D) Disastrous

50. Look at the word they in the passage. Click on the word or phrase in the **bold** text to which they refers.

51. All of the following characterize a rite of passage EXCEPT

- (A) it is religious in nature but is optional
- (B) it applies to individuals rather than to groups
- (C) it is composed of three stages: separation, transition and incorporation
- (D) it has been observed and documented by scientists

52. The following sentence can be added to paragraph 2 or 3.

The individual would first be ritually removed from the society as a whole, then isolated for a period, and finally incorporated back into society in his or her new status.

Where would it best fit in the paragraph? Click on the square [■] to add the sentence to paragraph 2 or 3. Paragraphs 2 and 3 are marked with an arrow [➔].

53. The passage suggests that female aborigines

- (A) are very much opposed to the rites of passage and cry as a sign of objection
- (B) can only cry at seeing their children undergo a cruel and painful experience
- (C) are not against the rites of passage but must participate in the ritual by pretending to object to it
- (D) hope to end the cruel practice by continuously mounting their show of resistance

54. Click on the sentence that shows the example of a primitive tribe that undertakes the male initiation rites.

Scroll the entire passage to see all of the paragraphs.

55. The Australian aborigines who undergo the rites of passage pretend to be dead because

- (A) they need to learn and experience what death is like
- (B) they need to express complete submission to the older members of the tribe
- (C) they need to learn survival tactics that will help them while hunting in the wilderness
- (D) they need to perform symbolically their transition from adolescence to manhood

Chapter 4 Insertion

Frequency of appearance per passage with 11 questions: one or none
Click on the passage item
Difficulty Range: Medium to Difficult

Overview

1. What is the question about?

Insertion questions test your ability to recognize coherence and unity between the sentences in the passage. The question provides you with the sentence that should be added to the passage (called "the excerpted sentence" hereafter). The passage presents four or more black squares [■], spread over one or more paragraphs.

You must be able to decide where the excerpted sentence should be added to fill the gap in the flow of ideas. After adding the sentence to the passage, read the adjacent sentences and the excerpted sentence together as a whole to verify the coherence and unity of ideas.

The sentence preceding the excerpted sentence usually contains some clues or references that logically or structurally connect adjacent sentences. The sentence following the excerpted sentence continues the flow of information from the excerpted sentence.

Click on the black square [■] to which you decided the excerpted sentence belongs. If all three sentences (the preceding, the excerpted, and the following sentence) flow logically with coherence, you have correctly identified the insertion position marked by the black square [■].

2. What terms should I know?

Insertion: *adding a sentence to achieve coherence of the passage*
Adding a sentence enables the paragraph as a whole to acquire a coherent idea.

Coherence: *the quality of agreement and unity among the parts of a piece of writing*
Insertion questions test your skill at recognizing the unity and coherence of the ideas developed in one or more paragraphs.

If a passage is coherent, there is a logical connection among sentences within the paragraph or passage. Parts of a passage fit together as a block of ideas in a well-composed piece of writing. Coherence is achieved by using transitional words (connectors) properly in the process of developing ideas. For example, "nevertheless" is used to signal that the author is about to contradict what he just mentioned.

On the other hand, incorrect answer spots (black squares) would disrupt the close-knit paragraph that otherwise stands well in terms of structure and the flow of ideas.

3. How is the question worded?

The following sentence can be added to paragraph __.
<——————————— Excerpted Sentence in **bold** type ——————————>
Where would it best fit in the paragraph?
Click on the square [■] to add the sentence to paragraph __.
　　Paragraph __ is marked with an arrow [➜].

Strategies

1. Key points to remember

The author uses certain devices to ensure the coherence of the passage. These devices are generally found in the excerpted sentence given in the question.

A few examples of such devices are: transitional words, reference words (pronouns), demonstratives, expressions with identical meanings, repetition of identical words.

Examples

(1) Transitional words

- In small animals, oxygen – which is essential in the release of energy through respiration – can easily move from the water to reach all the tissues. ***However***, in the larger and relatively more active animals, obtaining enough oxygen from the water is a potential problem.
- A language may make extensive use of kinds of utterances that are not found at all in English and which an English-speaking linguist may not, therefore, even think of requesting. ***Furthermore***, certain speakers may pretend not to be able to say certain things considered by their culture to be impolite, taboo, or inappropriate for mentioning to outsiders.
- They believed in dealing with the controversy by discussion and compromise. ***As a result***, administration leaders introduced a new tariff bill granting the president additional authority to execute the revenue laws.
- Inferences may be made on the basis of a broad background of previous experience with the subject matter or with no experience at all. ***For example***, the inferences a good mechanic can make about the internal condition of a motor by listening to it are often startlingly accurate.

Logical Relations in the Passage
"And" relation: complementary relationship among the different ideas *additionally, also, as a matter of fact, besides, for example, for instance, furthermore, in addition, in other words, likewise, that is*
"But" relation: contrasting relationship among the different ideas *despite, however, in spite of, nevertheless, nonetheless, on the other hand, rather*
"Because" relation: cause and effect relationship between the different ideas *accordingly, as a result, consequently, for this/that reason, hence, on account of, therefore, correspondingly*
"Sequence" relation: relationship where there is an order among a set of actions or events *afterwards, at last, finally, at the same time, in sum, in the end, in the meantime, meanwhile, next, subsequently*

(2) Reference words (pronouns)

- Slave marriages had no legal status, but ***slave owners*** generally seem to have accepted marriage as a stabilizing influence on the plantation. Sometimes ***they*** performed marriages themselves or had a minister celebrate a formal wedding with all the trimmings.
- The Americans focused their contempt on the ***Indians***. In the mining culture it was not a crime to work ***them*** to death.

READING

(3) Demonstratives

- **_Two layers of cells_** form the body wall. One of **_these_**, the ectoderm, is external, whereas the other, the endoderm, lines the gut.
- At Tenochtitlan, with a total area of about 20 square miles, a huge temple and two lavish palaces stood in the central plaza, also called **_the Sacred Precinct_**. Surrounding **_this area_** were other ceremonial buildings belonging to each lineage.
- Both the Coercive Acts and the Tea Act would be repealed; **_Parliament would pledge never to tax the colonies_**. Instead of implementing **_this proposal_** promptly, Parliament delayed until March 1778.
- Kennedy and his wife Jackie exuded charisma, which inspired people and created **_a surge of purpose and confidence in the nation_**. In spite of **_this new spirit_** in the White House, Kennedy had little success in getting Congress to pass major domestic legislation that he suggested as part of his New Frontier, including a number of reforms in housing and medical care.

(4) Expressions with identical meanings

- The New Deal was a bold plan that gave hope to most Americans. But it did not immediately end **_the Great Depression_**. **_Hard times_** continued through the 1930s.
- Rural poverty was widespread in the postwar period. Because it was not as concentrated, **_rural_** poverty was not as obvious as **_urban_** poverty. Yet in absolute numbers there were more poor people **_in the country_** than **_in the cities_**.

(5) Repetition of identical words

- Malcolm X once described his life as a chronology of **_changes_**. One of the remarkable **_changes_** in his life took place in prison.
- They cannot sell (or buy) land, but their **_permission_** must be asked by outsiders to enter the territory. To refuse such **_permission_**, though, would be unthinkable.

2. Test tips

(1) Read the excerpted sentence and pay attention to structural clues or signaling devices.
(2) Starting from the sentence immediately preceding the first black square [■], scan adjacent sentences to locate the identical key word(s) or referents depending on transitional devices embedded in the excerpted sentence.
(3) Click on the black square [■] in the most plausible position to add the excerpted sentence, depending on clues.
(4) Read the sentences preceding and following the answer square to verify whether the three sentences (the preceding, the excerpted, and the following sentences) as a chunk have acquired a satisfying coherence.

Skill Building

Skill Building: Rearranging sentences

Guide : *First, identify the topic sentence. Keep in mind that the topic sentence does not usually start with connectors or pronouns. After choosing a topic sentence, pay attention to connectors, transitional words, or reference words such as pronouns to determine the logical order among supporting sentences.*

Directions : *Decide the best order in which to arrange the sentences to form a well-organized paragraph.*

* Remark: Questions in the following format do not appear on the actual CBT reading.

1.
(1) Soon most cities were surrounded by large, middle-class communities.
(2) Yet, the suburbs gave more people a chance to own their own homes than ever before.
(3) However, the homes in the suburbs were often in "housing developments" where every house looked like every other house.
(4) Most of the new houses built after World War II were built not in large cities but in the surrounding areas, or suburbs.

[Explanation]
   Topic sentence ➔ the identical key word such as "surrounded" ➔ details ➔ conclusion

2.
(1) As a result, instead of land or material help, the freed slaves more often got advice and moral platitudes.
(2) But even dedicated abolitionists shrank from endorsing measures of land reform that might have given the freed slaves more self-support and independence.
(3) A few northerners argued that what the ex-slaves needed most was their own land.
(4) They thought citizenship and legal rights were one thing, wholesale confiscation of property and land redistribution quite another.

[Explanation]
   Topic sentence ➔ a transitional word such as "but" ➔ the reference word "They" and the referent "dedicated abolitionists" ➔ conclusion

3.
(1) Later tools continued to be made by chipping and flaking stone.
(2) Early harvesting tools were made of wood or bone with serrated flints inserted.
(3) But during the Neolithic period, stone was too hard to be chipped.
(4) Thus, it was ground and polished for tools.

[Explanation]
   Topic sentence ➔ contrasting words such as "Early harvesting tools" and "Later tools" ➔ a transitional word "but," as well as connecting word "stone" ➔ the referent "stone" in the preceding sentence and the reference word "it" in the following sentence

4.
(1) They have inherited this from their primate ancestors.
(2) However, they have developed it in their distinctively human way such as group living.
(3) Among humans, reliance on the group for survival is a basic characteristic.
(4) Moreover, unlike primate ancestors, group living by humans requires the participation of adults of both sexes.

[Explanation]
Topic sentence ➔ the referent "humans" in the preceding sentence and the reference pronoun "They" in the following sentence ➔ the transitional word "However" and the reference word "they" ➔ "Moreover" signaling a further explanation, and the phrase "group living" linking two sentences

5.
(1) About one-third of this solar energy is reflected back into space as light.
(2) Some of this absorbed heat energy serves to evaporate the waters of the oceans.
(3) Life here on earth depends on the flow of energy from the thermonuclear reactions taking place at the heart of the sun.
(4) Much of the remaining two-thirds is absorbed by the earth and converted to heat.

[Explanation]
Topic sentence ➔ phrases such as "the flow of energy ~ at the heart of the sun" and "this solar energy" connecting two sentences ➔ words such as "one-third" and "two-thirds" connecting two sentences ➔ the word "absorbed" and the phrase "this absorbed heat" in the adjacent sentences

6.
(1) These sanctions can be positive or negative, formal or informal.
(2) But when conformity cannot be achieved voluntarily, other mechanisms of social control are used to convey and enforce norms and expectations.
(3) Socialization brings about conformity, and, ideally, conformity is voluntary.
(4) Such mechanisms are known as sanctions.

[Explanation]
Topic sentence ➔ the repetition of the word "conformity" ➔ the phrase "mechanisms of social control" and the phrase "Such mechanisms" ➔ the repetition of words "sanctions" and "These sanctions"

7.
(1) The New Deal saw the farm problem as one of overproduction.
(2) The cash for the benefits was obtained by a tax on the processors of agricultural goods.
(3) In the Agricultural Adjustment Act they introduced the principle of subsidies to cut production.
(4) The subsidy principle established by the AAA set cash benefits to be paid to farmers who voluntarily did not grow certain products.

[Explanation]
Topic sentence ➔ the word "overproduction" and the phrase "to cut production" ➔ the expression "the Agricultural Adjustment Act" and the acronym "the AAA" ➔ the phrase "cash benefits" and the phrase "The cash for the benefits"

8.

(1) To them the teachings of the Buddha provided support for their less competitive view of society.

(2) In the 1960s members of the counterculture became interested in eastern religions.

(3) Eastern gurus developed large followings.

(4) For instance, the Unification Church founded by the Reverend Sun-Myung Moon from Korea grew rapidly.

[Explanation]

Topic sentence ➔ the phrase "eastern religions" and the phrase "the teachings of the Buddha" ➔ the word "teachings" and the phrase "Eastern gurus" ➔ the phrase "Eastern gurus" and the phrase "the Reverend Sun-Myung Moon"

READING

VOCABULARY

surround: to be around something on all sides

community: all the people who live in a particular area, or a group of people who are considered as a unit because of their shared interests, background, or nationality

suburbs: an area outside a city but near it and consisting mainly of homes, sometimes also having stores and small businesses

material: connected with money, possessions, etc. rather than with the needs of the mind

platitude: a statement that has been repeated so often that it is meaningless

abolitionist: a person who supports an end to something

endorse: to make a public statement of your approval or support for something or someone

wholesale: the activity of selling goods, usually in large amounts, to businesses which then sell them to the public

confiscate: to officially take private property away from someone, usually by legal authority

chip: to cut or break small pieces off something

with a tool

flake: a small, thin piece, esp. of a layer on a surface

serrated: having a series of sharp points on the edge like a saw

flint: a very hard gray or black stone

insert: to put something in something else

Neolithic: of the later part of the Stone Age

polish: to make something smooth and shiny by rubbing it with a piece of fabric

primate: any animal that belongs to the group of mammals that includes human beings, apes and monkeys

distinctive: having a quality or characteristic that makes something different and easily noticed

survive: to continue to live, esp. despite some dangerous or threatening event

participate: to take part in or become involved in an activity

reflect: to send back (light, heat, or sound) from a surface

absorb: (of a substance or object) to take in (a

liquid, gas, or chemical) and make a part of itself

evaporate: to disappear, esp. by gradually becoming less and less

thermonuclear: connected with nuclear reactions that only happen at very high temperatures

convert: to change or make something change from one form, purpose, system, etc. to another

sanction: punishment for not behaving in a particular way

conformity: behavior or actions that follow the accepted rules of society

norm: standards of behavior that are accepted within a society

benefit: money provided by the government to people who need financial help

obtain: to get something by a planned effort

subsidy: money given as part of something to encourage it to happen

counterculture: a way of life opposed to those accepted by most of society

guru: a Hindu religious teacher or leader

Intensive Exercises

Exercise 4.1

The electrons of an atom have differing amounts of energy. Electrons closer to the nucleus have less energy than those farther from the nucleus and thus are at a lower energy level. ■ An electron tends to occupy the lowest available energy level, but with an input of energy, it can be boosted to a higher energy level. ■

The chemical behavior of an atom is determined by the number and arrangement of its electrons. ■ An atom is most stable when all of its electrons are at their lowest possible energy levels and those energy levels are completely filled with electrons. ■

The first energy level can hold two electrons; the second energy level can hold eight electrons, and so can the third energy level of the small atoms of greatest interest in biology. ■ Chemical reactions between atoms result from the tendency of atoms to reach the most stable electron arrangement possible. ■

1. The following sentence can be added to the passage.

   On the other hand, when the electron returns to a lower energy level, energy is released.

   Where would it best fit in the passage?
   Click on the square [■] to add the sentence to the passage.

 LinguaForum

[Explanation]

1. Contrast is the transitional device that connects the excerpted sentence with the preceding sentence. The two sentences are related by the contrast between "a higher energy level" in the preceding sentence and "On the other hand, ~ a lower energy level, ~ " in the excerpted sentence.

VOCABULARY

electron: a very small piece of matter with a negative electric charge, found in all atoms
atom: the smallest part of a chemical element that can take part in a chemical reaction

nucleus: the central part of an atom, that contains most of its mass and that carries a positive electric charge
chemical: produced by or using processes which

involve changes to atoms or molecules
tendency: if somebody/something has a particular tendency, they are likely to behave or act in a particular way

Exercise 4.2

TOEFL CBT - Reading

Fossils are the remains of plants and animals that have been preserved in rock. ■

A fossil may be the preserved remains of an organism itself, and impression of it in rock, or preserved traces (known as trace fossils) left by an organism while it was alive, such as organic carbon outlines, fossilized footprints, or droppings. ■ Most dead organisms soon rot away or are eaten by scavengers. For fossilization to occur, rapid burial by sediment is necessary. ■ The organism decays, but the harder parts – bones, teeth, and shells, for example – may be preserved and hardened by minerals from the surrounding sediment. ■ Fossilization may also occur even when the hard parts of an organism are dissolved away to leave an impression called a mold. ■

The study of fossils (paleontology) not only can show how living things have evolved, but can also help reveal the Earth's geological history – for example, by aiding in the dating of rock strata. ■

1. The following sentence can be added to the passage.

   The mold is filled by minerals, thereby creating a cast of the organism.

   Where would it best fit in the passage?
   Click on the square [■] to add the sentence to the passage.

LinguaForum

READING

[Explanation]

1. Repetition of words ("The mold") is the device that connects the excerpted sentence with the previous sentence. The two sentences are related by the phrase "The mold."

VOCABULARY

remains: the body of a dead person or animal
preserve: to make sure that something is kept
sediment: the solid material that settles at the

bottom of a liquid
decay: to be destroyed gradually by natural processes

dissolve: to mix with a liquid and become part of it
stratum (pl. strata): a single layer of something

Exercise 4.3

The El Niño ocean current was blamed for 1,000 deaths and billions of dollars worth of damage to buildings and crops around the world. ■ The weather in the United States is affected by many factors. ■ The wind that blows over each part of the country is affected by altitude and by bodies of water. Wind patterns are also affected by temperature changes elsewhere. ■

Normally, a temperature change in the ocean near South America would not cause much change in weather patterns in the United States. However, in 1982, the El Niño ocean current near the equator was especially large. ■ The sheer size of the 1982 El Niño current made it strong enough to change weather conditions around the world.

■ Scientists believe that the El Niño begins when the trade winds that normally blow from east to west slow down and actually change direction. ■ The winds then blow warm water toward South America, where the normal weather patterns are changed for a time. ■

1. The following sentence can be added to the passage.

It covered 8,000 square miles.

Where would it best fit in the passage?
Click on the square [■] to add the sentence to the passage.

 Time   **LinguaForum**   **Help** **Prev** **Next**

[Explanation]

1. "It" is the device that connects the excerpted sentence with the previous sentence. The two sentences are related by the referent "the El Niño ocean current" in the preceding sentence and the referring pronoun "It" in the excerpted sentence.

VOCABULARY

current: a movement of water or air
altitude: the height above sea level
sheer: used to emphasize the size, degree or

amount of something
trade wind: a strong wind that blows all the time towards the equator and then to the west

pattern: the regular way in which something happens or is done

Exercise 4.4

By the 1960s the "baby-boomers" were maturing. Now young adults, they differed from their elders in that they had experienced neither economic depression nor a major war. They also had grown up amid the homogenizing effects of a flourishing consumer culture and television. ■

Moreover, they viewed the cold war primarily as a battle of words and gestures without immediate consequences for them. Record numbers of these young people were attending American colleges and universities during the 1960s. ■ At the same time, many universities had become gigantic institutions dependent on research contracts from huge corporations and the federal government. ■ As universities grew more bureaucratic and hierarchical, they unknowingly invited resistance from a generation of students wary of involvement in what Eisenhower had labeled the "military-industrial complex." ■

The success of the Greensboro sit-ins in 1960 not only precipitated a decade of civil rights activism, but also signaled an end to the supposed apathy that had enveloped college campuses and social life during the 1950s. ■ Although most immediately concerned with the rights and status of African Americans, the sit-ins, marches, protests, principles, and sacrifices associated with the civil rights movement provided the model and inspiration for other groups that demanded justice, freedom, and equality as well. ■

1. The following sentence can be added to the passage.

   For instance, the college enrollment quadrupled between 1945 and 1970.

   Where would it best fit in the passage?
   Click on the square [■] to add the sentence to the passage.

 LinguaForum

[Explanation]

1. "For instance" is a transitional phrase that connects the excerpted sentence with the previous sentence. The two sentences are related by the contrast between "Record numbers of ~ during the 1960s" in the preceding sentence and " ~ enrollment quadrupled between 1945 ~ " in the excerpted sentence.

VOCABULARY

hierarchy: a system in which people or things are put at various levels or ranks according to their importance

precipitate: to make something happen suddenly

or sooner than expected

apathy: lack of interest, or the attitude of not caring resulting from it

inspire (n. inspiration): to fill with confidence and

eagerness so that they feel they can achieve something difficult or special

Exercise 4.5

The effect of oil spills on exposed rocky shores is less devastating than it may appear at first sight. ■ Initially there is mortality among many attached inhabitants. ■ Rocky shore communities do recover, though recovery is dependent on factors such as the amount of oil, wave action, and temperature. ■ Degradation, or breakdown, by bacteria takes place, but it is very slow, especially in cold water. ■ Spills are degraded more quickly by bacteria if an oil-soluble fertilizer is added to the water or sprayed on rocks and sediment. ■ Experience has shown that recovery begins within months and that an apparent near-normal condition may occur as early as one or two years after the spill. ■ Higher oil concentrations in sediments and isolated pockets, however, have been found to remain for 15 years or longer.

1. The following sentence can be added to the passage.

   But wave action and tides help clean away the oil.

   Where would it best fit in the passage?
   Click on the square [■] to add the sentence to the passage.

 LinguaForum

[Explanation]

1. "But" is the transitional device that connects the excerpted sentence with the previous sentence. The two sentences are related by the contrast between "Initially there ~ mortality among many inhabitants" in the preceding sentence and "but, ~ help clean away the oil" in the excerpted sentence.

VOCABULARY

expose: to create a situation or a condition that makes someone likely to be harmed
mortality: the condition of being mortal (having to die)

degrade: to cause someone to seem to be worth less and lose the respect of others

apparent: able to be seen or understood
isolate: to separate something from other things, or to keep something separate

Exercise 4.6

TOEFL CBT - Reading

The wave model of light would lead you to predict that the brighter the light – that is, the stronger, or more intense, the beam – the greater the force with which the electrons would be dislodged. ■ But as we have already seen, whether or not light can eject the electrons of a particular metal depends not on the brightness of the light but on its wavelength. ■

According to the particle model of light resurrected by Albert Einstein in 1905, light is composed of particles of energy called photons. ■ The energy of a photon is not the same for all kinds of light but is, in fact, inversely proportional to the wavelength – the longer the wavelength, the lower the energy. ■

The wave model of light permits physicists to describe certain aspects of its behavior mathematically, and the photon model permits another set of mathematical calculations and predictions. ■ These two models are no longer regarded as opposed to one another; rather, they are complementary, in the sense that both – or a totally new model – are required for a complete description of the phenomenon we know as light. ■

1. The following sentence can be added to the passage.

   Photons of violet light, for example, have almost twice the energy of photons of red light, the longest visible wavelength.

   Where would it best fit in the passage?
   Click on the square [■] to add the sentence to the passage.

 LinguaForum

[Explanation]

1. The phrase "for example" in the excerpted sentence is the main transitional device that connects that sentence with the previous sentence. As additional clues, both sentences contain the phrases "the energy of a photon" and "the wavelength."

VOCABULARY

---

dislodge: to remove (esp. a person or people) by force from a position
resurrect: to bring (someone) back to life, or bring (something) back into use or existence after it

disappeared
inverse (adv. inversely): changing in an opposite direction in relation to something else, esp. an amount

complement (adj. complementary): to add to something in a way that improves it or makes it more attractive

Exercise 4.7

Mammals have fewer, but larger, skull bones than the fishes and reptiles, an example of the fact that "simpler" and "more primitive" may have quite opposite meanings. ■ In the mammals, as in some other vertebrates, a bony platform or partition has developed that separates nasal and food passages far back in the throat, preventing food from entering the lungs. ■ The lower mammalian jaw, unlike that of reptiles, consists of a single bone. Moreover, mammals, unlike snakes or lizards, cannot move the upper jaw in relation to the brain case. ■ Mammals must either feed on organisms smaller than themselves or tear the food into pieces small enough to be swallowed. ■

In many respects, humans are among the least specialized of the mammals. ■ Unlike the carnivores, which are meat eaters, and the several orders of herbivores, we are omnivores, eating a wide variety of fruits, vegetables, and other animals. ■ Our hands closely resemble those of a primitive reptile, in contrast to the highly specialized forelimbs developed by, for example, whales, bats, and horses. ■ We cannot see as well as an owl monkey. ■ Our sense of smell is much less keen than a dog's, and our sense of taste far less sensitive than that of an enormous variety of other animals. Many animals can run faster, swim more powerfully, and climb trees with more agility. ■

1. The following sentence can be added to paragraph 1.

   As a result, mammals lack the ability of snakes to swallow food items larger than themselves.

   Where would it best fit in the paragraph?
   Click on the square [■] to add the sentence to paragraph 1.

2. The following sentence can be added to paragraph 2.

   Nevertheless, few can do all three.

   Where would it best fit in the paragraph?
   Click on the square [■] to add the sentence to paragraph 2.

 Time   LinguaForum   **Help** **Prev** **Next**

[Explanation]

1. "As a result" is the transitional device that connects the excerpted sentence with the previous sentence. Both sentences contain the identical key words "mammals" and "snakes."

2. The phrase "all three" in the excerpted sentence refers to "run faster, swim more powerfully, and climb trees with more agility" in the preceding sentence.

VOCABULARY

vertebrate: any animal with a backbone, including all mammals, birds, fish, reptiles and amphibians
partition: the division of something into smaller

parts, or something that divides a space
passage: an enclosed path that connects places
variety: the characteristic of frequently changing, or

of including many different types or things
agile (n. agility): able to move about quickly and easily

Exercise 4.8

No two languages are ever sufficiently similar to be considered as representing the same reality. ■ The worlds in which different societies live are distinct worlds, not merely the same world with different labels attached. ■ These assumptions underlie the linguistic relativity hypothesis advanced by linguist Edward Sapir in his highly influential book, *Language: An introduction to the Study of Speech.* ■

Sapir argued that languages are so different that it is nearly impossible to make translations in which words produce approximately the same effects in the speaker of language X as in the speaker of language Y. ■ Today, most social scientists reject this position and argue that, although considerable work may be required, it is possible for people to discover one. ■

As children learn words and the meanings of words, they learn about their culture. ■ To become fluent in another language is not merely a matter of reading and conversing in that language but of actually being able to think in that language. ■ Similarly, when young children learn the language of their culture, they acquire a thinking tool.

1. The following sentence can be added to the passage.

   They also acquire tools that enable them to think about the world – to interpret their experiences, establish and maintain relationships, and convey information.

   Where would it best fit in the passage?
   Click on the square [■] to add the sentence to the passage.

 Time

LinguaForum

 Help **Prev** **Next**

READING

[Explanation]

1. "They" is the transitional device that points to the proper place to add the excerpted sentence. Pay attention to plural nouns in the sentences preceding black squares. The word "also" indicates that the excerpted sentence provides a further explanation to the previous sentence.

Voca<small>BULARY</small>

distinct: clearly separate and different
relativity: (specialized) a theory in physics describing motion and the relationships between

space, time, and energy
hypothesis: an explanation for something that is based on known facts but has not yet been proven

approximate (adv. approximately): to come near in quality, amount, or value
adequate: enough for a particular purpose

Vocabulary Review for Intensive Exercises 4.1-4.8

1. These two people will form the _____ of a new management team.

   (A) atom
   (B) electron
   (C) proton
   (D) nucleus

2. I have a _____ to talk too much when I am nervous.

   (A) taste
   (B) tendency
   (C) trend
   (D) transition

3. He was anxious to _____ his reputation.

   (A) preserve
   (B) procrastinate
   (C) persevere
   (D) proclaim

4. Heat gently until the sugar _____.

   (A) evaporates
   (B) disappears
   (C) digests
   (D) dissolves

5. The plane made a dive to a lower _____.

   (A) latitude
   (B) longitude
   (C) distance
   (D) altitude

6. The murders all seem to follow a similar _____.

   (A) pageant
   (B) patent
   (C) pattern
   (D) pedigree

7. His resignation _____ a leadership crisis.

   (A) pledged
   (B) precipitated
   (C) plucked
   (D) prefabricated

8. The article said that children _____ to smoke are more likely to be sick.

   (A) contagious
   (B) exposed
   (C) immune
   (D) prerogative

9. By and large, your ability to cope with change varies _____ with age.

   (A) inversely
   (B) single-handedly
   (C) headlong
   (D) fortunately

10. The sorority club offers a _____ of educational and recreational activities for female college students.

   (A) scale
   (B) value
   (C) result
   (D) variety

11. A top-rated football player combines speed with _____.

   (A) complexity
   (B) agility
   (C) display
   (D) argument

12. Several _____ for global warming have been recently suggested.

   (A) principals
   (B) priorities
   (C) privileges
   (D) hypotheses

Word Files III: TOEFL Vocabulary with Emphasis on Social Sciences and the Fine Arts

abstract: adj. (of art) not representing people or things in a realistic way

affect: v. to have an influence on

agent: n. a force producing an effect

ambiguous: adj. not clearly stated

assimilation: n. a process of becoming similar to others

assign: v. to have a particular task done

association: n. an official group

barter: n. exchange of goods and services without the use of money

celebrate: v. to recognize a special day

census: n. the process of officially counting something

charisma: n. a powerful personal quality

compromise: n. an agreement

conventional: adj. of the usual practices

demography: n. the change in births, deaths, etc. over a period of time

disparate: adj. different from each other

distort: v. to twist facts, ideas, etc. so that they are no longer correct or true

diversity: n. the state of being different

dwelling: n. a house where a person lives

eligible: adj. satisfying the requirements

enterprise: n. a company; the ability to think of new projects

ethnic: adj. connected with a nation or race that shares a cultural tradition

exhibit: v. to show publicly for amusement

expansion: n. an act of increasing something in size or amount

fabricate: v. to manufacture goods from various different materials

figure: n. a shape or form

gender: n. learned aspect of maleness or femaleness

global: adj. relating to the whole world

guardian: n. a person who protects something

heritage: n. features belonging to the culture of a particular society

hierarchy: n. a system in which people are put at various levels of importance

identity: n. the characteristics that distinguish people from others

innovation: n. the introduction of new things, ideas or ways of doing something

means: n. a way of achieving something

minority: n. the smaller part of something

motto: n. a sentence expressing one's aims

nomads: n. a group of people traveling to find grazing land for animals

norm: n. an informal rule for behavior

option: n. one thing that one can choose from a set of possibilities

paradigm: n. an example used as a model

passion: n. a very strong feeling

phenomenon: n. a fact or an event in nature or society

preserve: n. to keep a particular quality

prestige: n. status; respect

primitive: adj. belonging to an early stage

privilege: n. a special right or advantage

projection: n. an estimate

proliferate: v. to increase in number

prototype: n. the first design of something

publicity: n. activity to get attention

random: adj. happening by chance

raw material: n. material in natural state

reconstruct: v. to build or create again

recruit: v. to find new people to join an organization

regulate: v. to control something by rules

resolution: n. the act of solving a problem

restore: v. to return something to an earlier condition

revolt: v. to refuse to be controlled

ritual: n. any act done regularly

sanction: n. an official order that limits trade or contact; official permission

scale: n. a set of musical notes

sculpture: n. the art of creating objects out of materials such as wood, metal, etc.

status: n. the legal position of a person

stigma: n. feelings of disapproval about particular ways of behaving

stimulus: n. something causing a reaction

strategy: n. a plan for reaching a goal

superficial: adj. on the surface only

survey: n. an investigation of opinions

trait: n. a particular quality

transact: v. to buy or sell things

urban: adj. connected with a town or city

READING

Practice Test 4

Questions 1-11

One of the most famous architects in history, the American Frank Lloyd Wright is remembered both for his non-traditional approach to architecture and for emphasizing the dictum , "Form follows function." That motto is the basis of "functionalism," which gave rise to many a famous edifice, such as Wright's own design for the Guggenheim Museum in New York City. One of the world's most famous art museums, the Guggenheim Museum is built around a great helical gallery several stories in height. The gallery consists of a broad ramp along which works of art are displayed. Thus, the building's form – a structure built around a broad, helical ramp – complements its function, which is to display a large number of exhibits within a limited space and in an easily accessible setting. It has become one of the landmarks of New York City.

→ Wright was born in Richland Center, Wisconsin, in 1869. At age 15, Frank Lloyd Wright entered the University of Wisconsin, where he studied engineering. ■ From the university, he went on to work as personal draftsman for Louis H. Sullivan, a distinguished architect who invented the skyscraper. ■ From him, Wright adopted the principle that form should follow function. Sullivan assigned Wright much of the work of designing houses. ■ Soon, however, a conflict arose between Wright and Sullivan. Wright had expensive tastes and designed houses for private clients in his free time to cover his bills. ■ Sullivan objected to Wright's work outside Sullivan's firm. Wright then left Sullivan's employ and started his own architectural practice. ■

→ Wright specialized in designing houses, some of which are among his most celebrated works. A famed example is Falling Water, built as a home at Bear Run, Pennsylvania. ■ Wright designed his own home, Taliesin, which was constructed on his grandfather's farm in Wisconsin. The name Taliesin is Welsh and means "shining brow." ■ Wright's other famous works include the Johnson Wax Company Building in Racine, Wisconsin, and the Larkin Building in Buffalo, New York. ■ He also designed Japan's earthquake-resistant Imperial Hotel, in 1916. ■ Built according to a cantilever design and set to "float" on underlying sediment, it survived the great earthquake which destroyed most of Tokyo in 1923. ■ His books include *Autobiography, The Living City,* and *A Testament.* Wright was awarded the Gold Medal of the American Institute of Architects in 1949. He died in 1959 in Phoenix, Arizona.

1. This passage is concerned primarily with Frank Lloyd Wright's
   - (A) conflict with Louis H. Sullivan
   - (B) life and career
   - (C) design for the earthquake-resistant Imperial Hotel
   - (D) attachment to the state of Wisconsin

2. Look at the word dictum in the passage. Click on the word in the **bold** text which is closest in meaning to dictum .

3. The basis of functionalism is the principle that

     Ⓐ everything should have more than one function

     Ⓑ everything should have only one function

     Ⓒ everything in a building should function

     Ⓓ function determines form

4. According to the passage, a broad, helical ramp is the basis of Wright's design for the

     Ⓐ Imperial Hotel

     Ⓑ Guggenheim Museum

     Ⓒ Larkin Building

     Ⓓ Johnson Wax Company Building

5. According to the passage, a conflict arose between Wright and Sullivan because Sullivan

     Ⓐ thought Wright was trying to claim credit for inventing the skyscraper

     Ⓑ objected to Wright designing homes for Wright's own clients

     Ⓒ did not believe that form should follow function

     Ⓓ found out that Wright had been commissioned to design Falling Water

6. According to the passage, Wright did NOT design

     Ⓐ the Imperial Hotel

     Ⓑ the Guggenheim Museum

     Ⓒ Taliesin

     Ⓓ the Empire State Building

7. The following sentence can be added to paragraph 2 or 3.

A low, wide structure, Falling Water was designed to grow, so to speak, out of a cliff beside a stream.

Where would it best fit in the paragraph? Click on the square [■] to add the sentence to paragraph 2 or 3. Paragraphs 2 and 3 are marked with an arrow [→].

8. The word **it** in the passage most likely refers to

     Ⓐ sediment

     Ⓑ cantilever design

     Ⓒ earthquake

     Ⓓ Imperial Hotel

9. It is possible to infer from the passage that Frank Lloyd Wright

     Ⓐ enjoyed living in luxury and was honored for his work

     Ⓑ had no background in engineering

     Ⓒ wrote the famous novel *Native Son*

     Ⓓ spent little time in Wisconsin

10. It is most likely that this passage is part of

     Ⓐ a history of Wisconsin

     Ⓑ a biographical directory of architects

     Ⓒ a history of skyscrapers

     Ⓓ a travel guide to Pennsylvania

11. Click on the sentence that mentions where the origin of the word "Taliesin" is described.

Scroll the passage to see all of the paragraphs.

VOCABULARY

dictum: a statement that expresses something that people believe is always true or should be followed
edifice: a large impressive building
helical: a shape of a continuous, curving line that forms circles around a center point
complement: to add to something in a way that improves it or makes it more attractive

exhibit: an object or a work of art put in a public place, for example a museum, so that people can see it
invert (adj. inverted): to put something upside down or in the opposite order or position
celebrated: famous for having good qualities
cantilever: a long piece of metal or wood that

sticks out from a wall to support the end of a bridge or other structure
award: to give something valuable, such as money or a prize following an official decision
institute: an organization whose purpose is to advance the study of a particular subject

Questions 12-22

The most mysterious portion of the ocean is its deepest part, known as the benthic environment: the bottom of the sea and the waters immediately above it. Although much has been learned about the benthic realm with the development of remote exploration technologies, scientists are only beginning to understand the processes at work in this darkest and deepest layer of the ocean. Expensive, time-consuming, and sometimes dangerous, exploration of the benthic regime proceeds slowly.

Among the features of the benthic environment are the abyssal plains, vast level areas of the seabed covered in fine sediment eroded from the continents and deposited gradually on the ocean floor. Immediately off the eastern coast of the United States, for example, the Hatteras Abyssal Plain lies at the bottom of the North Atlantic Ocean. The sediments of this abyssal plain originated from the North American landmass and were carried to the sea by rivers such as the Hudson, Delaware, and James Rivers. From the mouths of the rivers, mud, clay, and silt flowed through canyons to the abyssal plains.

→ ■ The deep ocean is of importance particularly to climatologists, or scientists who study the world's climate. ■ **Sediments from the benthic environment are of great value to climatology because they provide a lengthy record of climatic conditions. Analysis of organisms' remains accumulated in the sediment may give climatologists some idea of temperatures in centuries past, before historical records were compiled. ■ The military also has taken a keen interest in the benthic environment, because the bottom of the sea has supplied an ideal place to install listening devices which monitor noise from ships and submarines. ■ A microphone on the ocean floor can tell military intelligence, for example, when a hostile submarine is leaving port at the start of a lengthy patrol. ■**

→ Because the benthic environment is the site of shipwrecks and many other artifacts, archeologists and historians are profoundly interested in it. ■ In exceptional cases, a sunken ship may be preserved almost intact for thousands of years. This is not to say, however, that the benthic environment is completely inactive. Even at tremendous depths, organisms are at work. ■ When the wreck of the British liner *Titanic*, sunk in 1912, was rediscovered and photographed on the floor of the North Atlantic in the 1980s, it was found to be covered in "rusticles," red-brown, icicle-like formations produced by the action of bacteria on the iron of the hull. ■

12. This passage is concerned primarily with
   (A) the environment at and just above the bottom of the sea
   (B) preservation of artifacts discovered at the bottom of the ocean
   (C) varieties of sediment deposited at the bottom of the sea
   (D) the formation of the Hatteras Abyssal Plain

13. Look at the word accumulated in the passage.
   Click on the word in the **bold** text which is closest in meaning to accumulated.

14. According to paragraph 1, exploration of the benthic environment is

   Ⓐ expensive, time-consuming, and sometimes dangerous

   Ⓑ unlikely to yield any significant discoveries

   Ⓒ focused primarily on the wreck of the British liner *Titanic*

   Ⓓ the key to understanding Venus and Mars

15. According to the passage, the Hatteras Abyssal Plain is NOT

   Ⓐ located off the western coast of the United States

   Ⓑ located beneath the North Atlantic Ocean

   Ⓒ a vast level area

   Ⓓ filled with sediment eroded from the North American landmass

16. Look at the word abyssal in the passage. Click on the word in the **bold** text which is closest in meaning to abyssal .

17. According to the passage, rivers which contribute sediment to the Hatteras Abyssal Plain include

   Ⓐ the Rhine, Loire, and Seine

   Ⓑ the Yalu, Volga, and Yenisei

   Ⓒ the Mississippi and Nile

   Ⓓ the Hudson, Delaware, and James

18. The following sentence can be added to paragraph 3 or 4.

Researchers in many different disciplines are involved in studies of the benthic environment.

Where would it best fit in the paragraph? Click on the square [■] to add the sentence to paragraph 3 or 4. Paragraphs 3 and 4 are marked with an arrow [➡].

19. It is implied in the passage that

   Ⓐ the benthic environment is unaffected by changes in world climate

   Ⓑ surface vessels and submarines emit considerable noise

   Ⓒ microphones on the ocean floor are of great value to climatologists

   Ⓓ submarines are extremely sensitive to changes in climate

20. The word intact in the passage is closest in meaning to

   Ⓐ untouched

   Ⓑ spoiled

   Ⓒ intake

   Ⓓ intangible

21. The word it in the passage most likely refers to

   Ⓐ the wreck of the British liner *Titanic*

   Ⓑ the floor of the North Atlantic

   Ⓒ the action of bacteria on the iron of the hull

   Ⓓ a matrix composed of dead bacteria and their secretions

22. Click on the sentence where the author mentions why archeologists and historians are interested in the benthic environment.

Scroll the passage to see all of the paragraphs.

VOCABULARY

benthic: relating to or happening on the bottom under a body of water

submersible: capable of being immersed in water

regime: a particular area or environment

alien: strange and frightening; different from what you are used to

abyssal: relating to the great depths of the oceans

sediment: sand, stones, mud, etc. carried by water

or wind and left, for example, on the bottom of a lake, river, etc.

silt: a sedimentary material consisting of very fine particles intermediate in size between sand and clay

preserve: to keep a particular quality, feature, etc.

monitor: to watch and check something over a period of time in order to see how it develops, so that you can make any necessary changes

artifact: an object that is made by a person, especially something of historical or cultural interest

hull: the main, bottom part of a ship, that goes in the water

matrix: a mold (container) in which something is shaped

To an engineer, soil includes all unconsolidated sediment that overlies bedrock. To an Earth scientist, however, it is defined as loose material at the Earth's surface that is capable of supporting plants and their root systems. The thin veneer of material that separates bedrock from the atmosphere not only consists of unconsolidated sediment, plant life, and a variety of microorganisms that depend on plant life, but also contains pore spaces that contain trapped air and water. Soils are therefore a venue in which all the Earth's systems come together and interact.

Most of the Earth's surface has a layer of unconsolidated sediment consisting of rock and mineral fragments produced by weathering of the underlying bedrock. However, processes operating within this sediment may cause it to develop a layered structure capable of supporting life. The layered sequence as a whole is known as a soil profile, and it is this profile that dictates the use of the soil for agricultural purposes. The degree of layering depends on a number of factors, but the most important are climate, the length of time that soil-forming processes have been operative, and the action of microorganisms.

→ Soils are best developed in regions with warm climates and abundant rainfall. These favorable conditions occur in tropical regions and at mid-latitudes where microorganisms flourish. ■ The topography and the nature of the underlying bedrock also influence the development of soil layers and are important in explaining the variation of soil quality within the same climate belt. ■

→ A mature soil is one in which soil-forming processes have been operating for a considerable amount of time. ■ The uppermost layer is referred to as the O horizon. This layer is only a few centimeters thick and is rich in decaying organic matter. ■ Beneath the O horizon is the A horizon, where plant roots, microorganisms, and burrowing animals live. ■ Dead plant material is broken down by microorganisms, and the vigorous organic activity results in the formation of humus, which is also known as topsoil. Other than organic material, the A horizon consists mostly of clays and stable minerals such as quartz. ■ This layer constitutes a "zone of leaching" because percolating groundwater dissolves soluble material and generally transports the material downward. ■

23. The primary purpose of the passage is to

(A) introduce the soil profiles of planet Earth

(B) introduce the different kinds of soil found on Earth

(C) introduce the Earth's surface and its structures

(D) introduce the different life forms that live in and outside of the soil

24. According to Earth scientists, what determines soil is

(A) its composition of different minerals and microorganisms

(B) its essential ability to sustain life

(C) its role as barrier between the earth and the atmosphere

(D) its role in providing a livable surface on which all forms of life live and interact

25. Look at the word it in the passage. Click on the word or phrase in the **bold** text to which it refers.

26. According to the passage, a mature soil contains all of the following EXCEPT

(A) organic matter
(B) microorganisms
(C) clays
(D) chemicals

27. The ability to maintain life is determined by

(A) the interaction of animals and plants on the surface of the Earth
(B) the unconsolidated sediment that is the uppermost surface
(C) the layered structure that is the result of processes within the unconsolidated sediment
(D) processes occurring on the surface of the unconsolidated sediment

28. Which of the following could best replace the word dictates in the passage?

(A) Constitutes
(B) Determines
(C) Defies
(D) Transforms

29. Successful farming depends on

(A) abundant knowledge of geography
(B) keen interest in chemistry and geology
(C) deep underlying bedrock of the soil
(D) precise knowledge of soil profile

30. All of the following determine the layering of soil EXCEPT

(A) rainfall
(B) venue
(C) microorganisms
(D) climate

31. The word that best replaces decaying in the passage is

(A) decomposing
(B) primary
(C) nutritious
(D) beneficial

32. All of the following are characteristics of topsoil EXCEPT that

(A) it is known also as the A horizon
(B) it is only a few centimeters thick and is rich in putrefying organic materials
(C) it is full of microorganisms busy breaking down dead plants
(D) it is where plants and burrowing animals live

33. The following sentence can be added to paragraph 3 or 4.

A mature soil has a number of characteristic layers.

Where would it best fit in the paragraph? Click on the square [■] to add the sentence to paragraph 3 or 4. Paragraphs 3 and 4 are marked with an arrow [→].

READING

VOCABULARY

unconsolidated: not yet consolidated; not forming a solid mass
venue: the place of an incident or process
abundant: existing in large quantities; more than enough
topography: the physical features of an area of land, especially the position of its rivers, mountains, etc.; the study of these features

decay: to be destroyed gradually by natural processes
burrow: to make a hole or a tunnel in the ground by digging
humus: a substance made from dead leaves and plants, added to soil to help plants grow
quartz: a hard mineral, often in crystal form, that forms a large part of many soils

leach: to remove a substance from a material, esp. from earth, by the process of water moving through the material, or to remove parts of a material using water
percolate: (of a liquid, gas, etc.) to move gradually through a surface that has very small holes or spaces in it

Questions 34-44

→ The revival of emotional piety during the early 1800s represented a widespread tendency throughout the Western world which accentuated the stirring of the spirit over the dry logic of reason and the allure of material gain. ■ By the 1780s, a revolt was brewing in Europe against the stasis of the Enlightened thinkers. ■ Were there not, after all, more things in this world than reason and logic could box up and explain: moods, impressions, and feelings; mysterious, unknown, and half-seen things? ■ Americans also took readily to the romantics' emphasis on individualism, idealizing now the virtues of common people, now the idea of original or creative genius in the artist, the author, or the great personality. ■

→ Where the Enlightened thinkers of the eighteenth century had scorned the Middle Ages, the romantics now looked back to the period with fascination. ■ America, lacking a feudal history, nonetheless had an eager audience for the novels of Sir Walter Scott and copied the Gothic style in architecture. ■ In contrast to well-ordered classical scenes, romantic artists such as Thomas Cole and Thomas Doughty preferred wild and misty landscapes. ■

The German philosopher Immanuel Kant gave the worldwide romantic movement a summary definition in the title of his *Critique of Pure Reason*, an influential book that emphasized the limits of human science and reason in explaining the universe. People have innate conceptions of conscience and beauty, the romantics believed, and religious impulses too strong to be dismissed as illusions. In those areas in which science could neither prove nor disprove concepts, people were justified in having faith. The impact of such ideas elevated intuitive knowledge at the expense of rational knowledge.

---

34. With what topic is paragraph 1 mainly concerned?
    - (A) The limit of romanticism
    - (B) Advocates of romanticism in America
    - (C) Introduction of romanticism in America
    - (D) Different types of romanticism

35. The word accentuated in the passage is closest in meaning to
    - (A) increased
    - (B) emphasized
    - (C) evaluated
    - (D) respected

36. Look at the word stirring in the passage. Click on the word or phrase in the **bold** text that is OPPOSITE in meaning to stirring.

37. The following sentence can be added to paragraph 1 or 2.

 Another great victory of heart over head was the romantic movement in thought, literature, and the arts.

 Where would it best fit in the paragraph? Click on the square [■] to add the sentence to paragraph 1 or 2. Paragraphs 1 and 2 are marked with an arrow [➜].

38. The word brewing in the passage is closest in meaning to

 Ⓐ criticizing
 Ⓑ disclosed
 Ⓒ boisterous
 Ⓓ imminent

39. According to the passage, the Enlightened thinkers

 Ⓐ thought that an orderly world was desirable
 Ⓑ thought highly of invisible things
 Ⓒ favored American arts, culture and emotions
 Ⓓ preferred individualism to collectivism

40. According to the passage, romanticists respected all of the following EXCEPT

 Ⓐ moods
 Ⓑ mysteries
 Ⓒ the head
 Ⓓ impressions

41. Click on the sentence that mentions the attitudes of the Enlightened thinkers about the Middle Ages.

 Scroll the passage to see all of the paragraphs.

42. It is implied in the passage that the Enlightened thinkers

 Ⓐ were received favorably
 Ⓑ linked the Ancient Ages to the Middle Ages
 Ⓒ didn't favor the Gothic style in architecture
 Ⓓ created the new style in art

43. The word innate in the passage is closest in meaning to

 Ⓐ complex
 Ⓑ various
 Ⓒ inborn
 Ⓓ educated

44. Look at the phrase such ideas in the passage. Click on the word, phrase or sentence in the **bold** text that such ideas refers to.

VOCABULARY

piety: a strong belief in God or a religion, shown by your worship and dutiful behavior
allure: the quality of being attractive
revolt: a protest against authority
fascination: a very strong attraction that makes something very interesting
feudal: relating to the social system of Western Europe in the Middle Ages or any society that is organized rigidly according to rank
Gothic: of or like a style of building common in Europe between the 12th and the 16th centuries
impulse: a sudden strong wish or need to do something, without stopping to think about the results
dismiss: to reject as a matter of consideration
intuitive: obtained by using your feelings rather than by considering the facts
rational: able to think clearly and make decisions based on reason rather than emotions

Chapter 5 Inference

Frequency of appearance per passage with 11 questions: one or more
Standard Multiple-Choice
Difficulty Range: Medium to Difficult

Overview

1. What is the question about?

Not all details are stated explicitly in the passage. The passage you read suggests more than it says on its face. Moreover, language conveys messages beyond the actual meaning of words. Authors expect you to figure out hidden ideas, assumptions, or other undisclosed details on your own.

Inference is a process to follow the author's reasoning in order to understand less explicit aspects of the passage and draw a conclusion from the passage.

On the CBT, it means that you have to rely on available information or facts explicitly given in the passage. In other words, answer the questions on the basis of information provided in the passage. In some cases, inferences can be made from a single sentence; in others, they must be based on one or more paragraphs or even on the entire passage.

Drawing inferences sometimes requires making predictions. That is, you must determine what the author would probably say, based on the statements in the passage; or you may have to identify which statement the author would agree with.

2. What terms should I know?

Inference: the process of finding out what is not explicitly stated from information explicitly stated in the passage

To make an inference, you must figure out ideas that are not stated directly by the author.

Examples
1. I *inferred* from the evidence that his wife was guilty of the crime as charged by the prosecutor.
2. It can be *inferred* that railroad dining cars came into use after 1900.
3. AT&T used to have a monopoly on telephone services in the United States. You can *infer* that there is currently more than one telephone service-company in the United States.

Implication: something that is suggested or indirectly stated

The author may imply or suggest what he or she does not state directly by mentioning certain details. When the author tries to imply something, you must guess or deduce the meaning based on what the author apparently tells you.

Examples
1. In his article, the author *implied* that being an American is a great privilege.
2. Normal speech depends on repeating what one hears. This hypothesis *implies* that children who are born deaf or nearly so find it almost impossible to speak naturally.
3. The languages of Middle Eastern camel-herding people contain many terms denoting various kinds of camels and the harnesses and saddles that accompany camel herding as a way of life. Likewise, the vocabularies of North Americans, whose ancestors depended heavily on fishing, contain a large number of terms for fish and fishing equipment. These observations *imply* that creating terms to distinguish among different types of equipment used for one's livelihood was a useful linguistic adaptation to life in most societies.

4. All children acquire their first language before the age of four. This statement **implies** that all six-year-old children speak at least one language.

5. Kinship terms are important. Anthropologists can **infer** from kinship terms how societies classify relatives and allocate social positions. Kinship terms may **imply** the relative importance or unimportance of the father's or mother's side of the family.

3. How is the question worded?

Imply

The author implies that ...

The author implies that ... because _____

The author states that _____ to imply that ...

By stating _____, the author implies that ...

What does the author imply by stating in the passage that _____?

Infer

It can be inferred that ...

It can be inferred from the passage that ...

What can be inferred from the passage about _____?

Which of the following statements can be inferred about _____?

From the first sentence in the passage, it can be inferred that ...

It can be inferred from paragraph __ that ...

It can be inferred from the passage that _____ for which of the following reasons?

Support/Suggest

The passage supports which of the following conclusions?

With which of the following conclusions would the author probably agree?

Which of the following statements about _____ is suggested by the passage?

Strategies

1. Key points to remember

Several inferences may be drawn from the passage. Some inferences are obvious and easy; others may be not obvious and, therefore, may be difficult to make. However, the most important skill is to distinguish between "what can be inferred" and "what cannot be inferred from the passage no matter what."

You are supposed to draw some conclusions about what is intended by the author but not directly stated in the passage. Because answers to inference questions are not explicitly provided in the passage, you must "read between the lines."

Occasionally, you may be called upon to use common sense, especially in cases of finding an assumption or a presumption. A presumption is something that is thought to be true or probable. Yet, you are not supposed to apply any specialized specific knowledge that is not provided in the passage.

When you are asked to make a prediction, rely on your understanding of the author's factual statements, message, reasons, and logic. Certain expressions offer clues that help you understand the author's viewpoints about diverse topics.

2. Test tips

(1) Read the question carefully and be certain about what is being asked.

(2) Read the answer choices to see what kinds of answers you have available.

(3) Scan the passage looking for information needed to figure out hidden ideas.

(4) Make a reasonable guess based on the information in the passage.

(5) Be careful about the inferences you make. Always double-check whether your inferences are supported by the passage.

Skill Building

Skill Building: Drawing inferences

Guide : *These questions require you to activate the reasoning process called "inference." You have to form an opinion based on available information or facts in the paragraph. In the following drills, you are supposed to find hidden information validly drawn from given sentences.*

Directions : *Read the statements and choose one valid inference that can be made from the information given in the statements.*

* Remark: Questions in the following format do not appear on the actual CBT reading.

1. In recent years, airplanes have become more and more important as a means of transportation in the region.
   (A) The region has been accessible by various means of transportation.
   (B) Ships used to be the most efficient method of transportation in the region.
   (C) Airplanes have made it possible for the region to develop tourism.

[Explanation]

Airplanes have increased in importance as a means of transportation in the region recently compared with other means of transportation. Therefore, we can guess that there have been other available means of transportation as well in the region.

2. Even where there is a healthy publishing industry, some writers and publishers are subjected to censorship by government agencies.
   (A) Government tries to force upon writers what will be written and published.
   (B) To publish whatever material writers find truthful is solely within their discretion.
   (C) People do not always get all the facts in an unbiased way.

[Explanation]

Materials subjected to censorship may not always present plain facts as the author originally intends. It means that people in the countries practicing censorship have been exposed to biased information.

3. In response to increasing use of machines, a movement known as romanticism developed in the regions in the late 1700s and 1800s. This style of painting tries to show feelings and emotions. The paintings of romantic artists ranged from scenes of imagined nightmares to lofty, peaceful landscapes.
   (A) The 1700s and 1800s saw a flowering of painting showing details of the natural world.
   (B) Artists in the 1700s and 1800s created newer trends in response to industrialization.
   (C) In the eighteenth and nineteenth century, artists began to stress the importance of human reason.

[Explanation]

Society's increasing use of machines means the industrialization of the society. Artists in the 1700s and 1800s triggered a new movement emphasizing human feelings and emotions in paintings.

4. The pink orchids have developed a symbiotic relationship with a species of fungus that grows with the plant's roots. The fungus helps the orchid by increasing the amount of water and nutrients it can take in. The orchid, in turn, serves the fungus by supplying it with carbohydrates.

  (A) In a symbiotic relationship, two species live together in a way that is beneficial to one, but not to both.

  (B) The symbiotic relationship is a way of living that may be beneficial to both.

  (C) The orchids will perish without the fungus.

[Explanation]
   Using the example for symbiosis, we can conclude that the relationship may benefit both.

5. Automobiles were not the only machines Americans spent their money on. In the 1950s American homes were suddenly full of gadgets designed to make life easier – everything from high-powered washing machines to electric carving knives. Americans bought many appliances. The 1950s were good times for most Americans.

  (A) In the 1950s Americans families spent most of their time watching TV at home.

  (B) In the 1950s designer gadgets became a "status symbol."

  (C) The use of electricity increased during the 1950s.

[Explanation]
   Using the examples of high-powered washing machines and electric carving knives, we can conclude that American homes consumed more electricity in the 1950s than before because of many newly developed appliances.

6. Throughout World War II, black soldiers served strictly in all-black units. During and after the war, a leader of the civil rights movement named Randolph protested this injustice. In early 1948, Randolph met with President Truman, and asked him to integrate the armed forces. At the same time, he urged young black men to refuse to join the armed forces.

  (A) Young black men were not allowed to fight for their country during World War II.

  (B) African-Americans in the armed forces were segregated as recently as the 1940s.

  (C) It was illegal that young black men refused to join the armed forces.

[Explanation]
   Using the first sentence, we can infer that blacks and whites did not fight side by side during World War II.

7. Tribespeople are horticulturalists whose method of subsistence provides food more abundantly than gathering and hunting. So tribes can be populous, and their settlements can be more concentrated. It takes many hands to clear a forest for planting or to move a herd of camels from one graze area to another.

  (A) Gathering and hunting provided abundantly for a herd of camels.

  (B) People did not have to live in large groups for horticulture.

  (C) The tribespeople, as horticulturalists, lived in villages.

[Explanation]
   The second sentence states that tribespeople settled down for horticulture.

8. Various forms of expressive culture may function as learning tools through which information is transmitted. Aesop's fables incorporate moral lessons important at that time. Likewise, for literate Indians, the lessons of a long epic poem have long been transmitted in written form. On the other hand, they have been passed along mostly by word of mouth in rural Indian villages.

   (A) People in rural Indian villages are mostly illiterate.

   (B) Oral storytellers never recited Aesop's fables.

   (C) Aesop's fables contain more moral lessons than an Indian epic poem.

[Explanation]

The third sentence contrasts "transmission of an epic poem in written form among literate Indians" with "passed along by word of mouth in rural Indian villages."

9. Food production by and large requires more hard work than hunting and gathering. It's not necessarily a more secure means of subsistence. Food production requires people to eat more of the foods that food foragers eat only when they have no other choice. Therefore, it is likely that food production came about as a consequence of a chance convergence of separate natural events and cultural developments.

   (A) Food production generally provides more leisure time than food foraging.

   (B) People embarked on a new way of life voluntarily.

   (C) People probably did not become food producers through choice.

[Explanation]

Pay attention to the phrases such as "hard work," "not necessarily a more secure," and "requires people to eat more of ~ food foragers eat only when they have no other choice." The last sentence specifically mentions the theory explaining probable causes for a new way of life.

VOCABULARY

efficient: working or operating in a way that gets the results you want without any waste

censorship: the act or policy of censoring books, etc.

discretion: the freedom or power to decide what would be done in a particular situation

romanticism: a style and movement in art, music and literature in the late 18th and early 19th century, in which strong feelings, imagination and a return to nature were more important than reason, order and intellectual ideas

lofty: (of buildings, mountains, etc.) very high and impressive

fungus: a plant without leaves, flowers, or color that lives on other plants or on decaying matter

gadget: a small tool or device that does something useful

integrate: to combine two or more things so that they work together

segregate: to separate people of different races, religions or sexes and treat them differently

horticulture: the activity of growing plants

subsistence: what a person needs to stay alive

settle (n. settlement): to live in a place permanently

graze: (of animals) to eat grass

transmit: to send or give something

incorporate: to include something within something else

epic: a book or movie that contains a lot of action, dealing with a historical subject

subsistence: what a person needs in order to stay alive

converge (n. convergence): to move toward the same point and come closer together

Intensive Exercises

Exercise 5.1

Once the rock is broken into smaller pieces by the forces of weathering, it may be eroded (moved away from the parent rock) by water, glaciers, and wind. The constant waves of big lakes and oceans can not only weather the rocky shore by breaking or rubbing away at rocks, but also move rocks and sand away from the waterside. The action of water on sand can lead to beaches being washed away and re-formed someplace else. And the running water of a stream or river can form a deep canyon.

The Grand Canyon was created by the weathering and eroding action of a river. Over millions of years, the water of the Colorado River picked up tiny pieces of rock and carried them along. Just as sandpaper wears wood smooth, those tiny rocks scoured out the walls of the Grand Canyon, breaking down the mighty rock into tiny pieces, which the river swept away. These pieces were then deposited further downstream, in places where the river slows down. The process is still going on today.

Erosion can change the land in other ways, too. For example, the Mississippi River, like the Colorado, carries large amounts of tiny rocks and soil in its waters and deposits them downstream as sediment. The Mississippi deposits its sediment where it empties into the Gulf of Mexico. The sediment built up this way at the mouth of a river is called a delta. Deposited sediment forms soil rich in nutrients.

1. Which of the following does the passage imply?
   (A) The action of water on rocks can have a powerful eroding effect.
   (B) Only rocks are carried by water to be deposited far from their source.
   (C) Rocks may form bedrock at the mouth of a river.
   (D) Glaciers probably formed the valleys in the Grand Canyon.

2. The author states that deposited sediment forms soil rich in nutrients to imply that
   (A) deltas are tourist attractions
   (B) the Mississippi River carries large amounts of soil
   (C) the area around the Gulf of Mexico is the world's largest delta
   (D) deltas are often fertile farming areas

   LinguaForum

[Explanation]
1. Since the last sentence of paragraph 1 states that "the running water can form a deep canyon," it may be concluded that the action of water can have a powerful eroding effect.
2. It may be concluded that soil rich in nutrients forms fertile farming land. None of the other choices can be logically derived from the statement "deposited sediment forms soil rich in nutrients."

VOCABULARY

erode: to weaken or damage something by taking away parts of it gradually
scour: to search a place or thing very carefully

deposit: a layer of a substance
nutrient: any substance that plants or animals need in order to live and grow

fertile: (of land) able to produce a large number of high-quality crops

Exercise 5.2

In the new, more permissive atmosphere, men were again allowed to study history, which had been under a ban for two centuries. The effect was electric. To those austere and antiseptic minds, conditioned to the requirements of a technically advanced authoritarianism, the rediscovery of man's history was intoxicating. It generated an intellectual excitement that dominated the whole twenty-third century. Scholars were entranced by the variety of human experience, shocked by the violence and barbarism, saddened by the stupidities, and exalted by the achievements of their forebears. And as they searched that history, excitedly, sadly, lovingly, they returned increasingly to the twentieth century as a moment of curious and critical importance in the long pageant.

1. Which of the following does the passage imply?
   - (A) Scholars did not study history during the 21st and 22nd centuries.
   - (B) Scholars found it easy to begin studying man's history again.
   - (C) Scholars did not enjoy studying history during the 23rd century.
   - (D) Scholars advanced technology dramatically during the 23rd century.

2. The author implies that
   - (A) humans in the 23rd century will not be interested in the past at all
   - (B) the intelligence of humans varies proportionally with the progress of technology
   - (C) the twentieth century will bring intellectual excitement to the future
   - (D) as the centuries advanced, human intelligence deteriorated as a whole

 Time

LinguaForum

 Help **Prev** **Next**

READING

[Explanation]

1. According to the passage, men in the 23rd century were again allowed to study history, which had been under a ban for two centuries.

2. The author states that the rediscovery of human history generated an intellectual excitement that dominated the whole twenty-third century. Choices (A) and (D) contradict the facts mentioned in the passage. Choice (B) is related to the phrase "technically advanced authoritarianism" in the passage. But the passage does not establish a link between human intelligence and the progress of technology.

VOCABULARY

austere: plain and without decoration, comforts, or anything extra
antiseptic: a chemical used to prevent infection from an injury, esp. by killing bacteria
authoritarian (n. authoritarianism): demanding

total obedience to those in positions of authority
barbarian (n. barbarism): a person who has no experience of the habits and culture of modern life, and whose behavior you therefore consider strange or offensive

forebear: an ancestor (any member of your family from long ago)
pageant: a show, celebration, or parade in which people wear special clothing

Exercise 5.3

The water molecule as a whole is neutral in charge, having an equal number of electrons with negative charges and protons with positive ones. However, the molecule is polar. Because of the very strong attraction of the oxygen nucleus for electrons, the shared electrons of the covalent bonds spend more time around the oxygen nucleus than they do around the hydrogen nuclei.

Moreover, the oxygen atom has four additional electrons in its outer energy level. These electrons are paired in two orbitals that are not involved in covalent bonding to hydrogen. Each of these orbitals is a weakly negative zone. Thus, the water molecule, in terms of its polarity, is four-cornered, with two positively charged "corners" and two negatively charged ones.

1. The very strong attraction of the oxygen nucleus of the water molecule for electrons implies that
   (A) the water molecule as a whole is negatively charged
   (B) the oxygen atom has less electrons than the hydrogen atom
   (C) the region near each hydrogen nucleus is a weakly positive zone
   (D) the water molecule's four corners are polar zones with no charges

2. It can be inferred from the passage that
   (A) the oxygen atom has electrons not used in covalent bond to hydrogen
   (B) the hydrogen atom has electrons not used in covalent bond to oxygen
   (C) the water molecule has more electrons than protons and therefore is negatively charged
   (D) the shared electrons of the bond are equal in distance from oxygen and hydrogen

 Time   **LinguaForum**   **Help** **Prev** **Next**

[Explanation]
1. Since the author states that the shared electrons with negative charges spend more time around the oxygen nucleus than they do around the hydrogen nuclei, it can be inferred that the region near the hydrogen nucleus is positively charged.
2. The passage states that the oxygen atom has four additional electrons in its outer energy level paired in two orbitals not involved in the bonding.

VOCABULARY

molecule: the smallest unit into which a substance can be divided without chemical change, usually a group of two or more atoms
covalent bonding: one of the types in which the

chemical compounds are produced
orbit (adj. orbital): the curved path through which objects in space move around a planet
polarity: the quality in an object that produces

opposite magnetic or electric charges
charge: the amount of electricity that an electrical device stores or carries

Exercise 5.4

As the twentieth century advanced, the easy faith in progress and reform expressed by Social Gospelers and other liberals fell victim to a series of frustrations and disasters: the Great War, the failure of the League of Nations, the failure of Prohibition, the Great Depression, the rise of fascist dictators and continuing world crises.

New currents in science and social thought also challenged the belief in a rational universe. Darwin's biology portrayed humans as more akin to apes than to angels. And Darwin's contemporary, Karl Marx, portrayed people as creatures of economic self-interest. In capitalist society, Marx argued, freedom was an illusion: people were actually driven by impersonal economic forces. In Freud's psychology people were also driven, but by needs arising from the depths of the unconscious.

1. The author implies that

   (A) Social Gospelers should have preached faith in reform more enthusiastically

   (B) fascist dictators were not very liberal

   (C) liberals caused frustrations to the reform-minded

   (D) no liberals existed before the 20th century

2. It is implied in the passage that

   (A) humans were more rational than animals

   (B) Darwin, Marx, and Freud suggested that humans were driven by forces beyond control

   (C) Marx said that humans were freed by economic self-interest

   (D) Darwin, Marx, and Freud said that humans were naturally unkind

 Time

LinguaForum

Help *Prev* *Next*

READING

[Explanation]

1. The rise of fascist dictators is listed as a reason why liberals began to lose faith. We can therefore infer that fascist dictators were conservative, and not liberal.

2. The passage states that new currents in science and social thought also challenged the belief in a rational universe. The author quotes Darwin, Marx, and Freud as representing new thoughts. It can be concluded that Darwin, Marx, and Freud claimed human beings were not in control of their fate.

VOCABULARY

frustration: disappointment or discouragement, or a discouraging situation

prohibition: In the US, Prohibition was the period from 1920 to 1933 when the production and sale of alcohol was illegal.

prohibit: to forbid something by law

portray: to represent or describe someone or something in writing or in a movie

illusion: an idea or belief that is not true, or something that is not what it seems to be

Exercise 5.5

Slaves were victims. There was no question about that. But to stop with so obvious a perception would be to miss an important story of endurance and achievement. If ever there was a melting pot in American history, the most effective may have been that in which Africans from a variety of ethnic, linguistic, and tribal origins fused into a new community and a new culture as African Americans.

Members of the slave community were bound together in helping and protecting one another, which in turn created a sense of cohesion and pride. Slave culture incorporated many African survivals, especially in areas where whites were few. Among the Gullah blacks of the South Carolina and Georgia coast, a researcher found as late as the 1940s more than 4,000 words still in use from the languages of twenty-one African tribes.

But the important point, as another researcher put it, was not survivals that served "as quaint reminders of an exotic culture sufficiently alive to render the slaves picturesquely different but little more." The point was one of transformations in a living culture. Elements of African cultures thus "have continued to exist as dynamic, living, creative parts of life in the United States," and have interacted with other cultures with which they came in contact.

1. It can be inferred from the passage that slaves were
   - (A) a homogeneous group lacking ethnic diversity from the beginning
   - (B) incorporated into the community where whites were few
   - (C) active in keeping their cultures alive in the United States
   - (D) loners refusing to be integrated into the melting pot in American history

2. The cultures of African Americans were very likely to be
   - (A) merely picturesque without being creative
   - (B) diverse but not yet incorporating
   - (C) once exotic but now fully integrated
   - (D) interactive yet distinct

 Time   **LinguaForum**   **Help Prev Next**

[Explanation]

1. The passage states that "Members of the slave community were bound together in helping and protecting one another, which in turn created a sense of cohesion and pride. Slave culture incorporated many African survivals, especially in areas where whites were few."

2. Refer to the last sentence of the passage. It says that "Elements of African cultures thus 'have continued to exist as dynamic, living, creative parts of life in the United States,' and have interacted with other cultures with which they came in contact."

VOCABULARY

endurance: the physical or mental strength to continue doing something for a long time
cohesion: the state of sticking together

incorporate: to include something within something else
quaint: attractive because of being unusual and

esp. old-fashioned
exotic: unusual and specially interesting because of coming from a distant country

Vocabulary Review for Intensive Exercises 5.1-5.5

1. A natural feature of a physical object is
   _____ by the effect of weather.

   - Ⓐ evolved
   - Ⓑ eroded
   - Ⓒ emanated
   - Ⓓ embarked

2. A thick _____ of mud accumulated on the
   floor of river.

   - Ⓐ depot
   - Ⓑ department
   - Ⓒ dig
   - Ⓓ deposit

3. Monks and nuns are supposed to lead a(n)
   _____ life.

   - Ⓐ austere
   - Ⓑ prodigal
   - Ⓒ gratuitous
   - Ⓓ presumptuous

4. Our community held a _____ of Great
   Pioneers.

   - Ⓐ awareness
   - Ⓑ enrollment
   - Ⓒ pageant
   - Ⓓ passage

5. The spacecraft launched last week went into
   _____.

   - Ⓐ vertigo
   - Ⓑ orbit
   - Ⓒ summit
   - Ⓓ opposite

6. Protons have a positive electric _____.

   - Ⓐ level
   - Ⓑ resistance
   - Ⓒ quantity
   - Ⓓ charge

7. A conflict of opinions finally made him quit
   in _____.

   - Ⓐ reservation
   - Ⓑ appointment
   - Ⓒ frustration
   - Ⓓ exemption

8. The book _____ him as an unduly
   misinterpreted politician.

   - Ⓐ resembled
   - Ⓑ relocated
   - Ⓒ commuted
   - Ⓓ portrayed

9. Practice enhances an athlete's strength and
   _____.

   - Ⓐ endurance
   - Ⓑ stock
   - Ⓒ procrastination
   - Ⓓ rigidity

10. A chemical reaction takes place whenever
    bonds between atoms lose _____.

    - Ⓐ conference
    - Ⓑ radiation
    - Ⓒ cohesion
    - Ⓓ transfusion

READING

Practice Test 5

Questions 1-11

The middle of the 19th century saw the beginning of a truly independent American literature. This exciting period, especially the years 1850-55, has been called the American Renaissance. More masterpieces were written at this time than in any other equal span of years in American history. New England was the center of intellectual activity in these years, and Ralph Waldo Emerson was the most prominent writer.

→ ■ Emerson began his career as a clergyman. ■ Thus he became an independent essayist and lecturer, a lay preacher to Americans. ■ He preached one message – that the individual human being, because he is God's creature, has a spark of divinity in him which gives him great power. ■ "Trust yourself," Emerson said in his essay, *Self-Reliance* (1841). He believed it made no difference what one's work is or where one lives. ■ Emerson himself lived in the village of Concord. There, as oracle and as prophet, he wrote the stirring prose that inspired an entire nation. ■

→ One person who took Emerson's teaching to heart and lived by it was his Concord neighbor Henry David Thoreau. ■ Thoreau lived a life of independence. He was a student of wildlife and the great outdoors. ■ He was also a student of literature, who himself wrote fresh, vigorous prose. His great works include *Walden, or Life in the Woods* (1854), an account of his two-year sojourn at Walden Pond. "I went to the woods," he wrote, "because I wished to live deliberately" – that is, to decide what is important in life and then to pursue it. ■

The simplicity of Thoreau's life holds a strong appeal for modern readers. They are impressed too by his essay *Civil Disobedience* (1849), which converted Emersonian self-reliance into a workable formula opposing the power of government. He advocated passive resistance, including, if necessary, going to jail, as he himself did. Mahatma Gandhi, who was jailed so many times in his fight to free India from British rule, was strongly influenced by the ideas contained in this essay of Thoreau's.

---

1. What is the author's main point in the passage?
   - (A) The flowering of American literature
   - (B) The style of American literature
   - (C) Masterpieces in the middle of the 19th century
   - (D) American writers

2. Look at the word exciting in the passage. Click on the word or phrase in the **bold** text that is closest in meaning to exciting .

3. It can be inferred from the passage that
   - (A) American readers had read primarily the works of foreign writers before the middle of the 19th century
   - (B) American writers had criticized foreign literature before the middle of the 19th century
   - (C) American literature had been dependent on foreign literature before the middle of the 19th century
   - (D) American literature had been influenced by the European Renaissance before the middle of the 19th century

4. According to the passage, a truly independent American literature

  Ⓐ dealt with black Americans
  Ⓑ described the events of the Revolutionary War
  Ⓒ was written during the Revolutionary War
  Ⓓ was begun in the middle of the 19th century

5. The following sentence can be added to paragraph 2 or 3.

  He came to feel, however, that he could better do his work outside the church.

  Where would it best fit in the paragraph? Click on the square [▇] to add the sentence to paragraph 2 or 3.
  Paragraphs 2 and 3 are marked with an arrow [➡].

6. The word lay in the passage is closest in meaning to

  Ⓐ passive
  Ⓑ lazy
  Ⓒ untrained
  Ⓓ shy

7. Which of the following is NOT true about Emerson?

  Ⓐ Emerson wrote masterpieces.
  Ⓑ At first, Emerson was a clergyman.
  Ⓒ Emerson had an influence on Thoreau.
  Ⓓ Emerson envied Thoreau.

8. Which of the following could best replace the word sojourn in the passage?
  Ⓐ Stay
  Ⓑ Travel
  Ⓒ Solitude
  Ⓓ Writing

9. The word appeal in the passage is closest in meaning to

  Ⓐ criticism
  Ⓑ attraction
  Ⓒ shock
  Ⓓ difference

10. Look at the word his in the passage. Click on the word or phrase in the **bold** text that his refers to.

11. According to the passage, Henry David Thoreau

  Ⓐ wrote *Self-Reliance* and *Walden, or Life in the Woods*
  Ⓑ taught young people at Walden Pond
  Ⓒ wrote *Walden, or Life in the Woods* and *Civil Disobedience*
  Ⓓ was influenced by Mahatma Gandhi

ᐯOCA_BULARY

span: to include a large area or a lot of things
prominent: famous
lay: not in an official position in the Church
preach: to give a religious talk in a public place, especially in a church during a service
oracle: (in ancient Greece) a soothsayer or

medium
vigorous: very active, determined or full of energy
sojourn: a temporary stay in a place away from your home
disobedience: failure or refusal to obey
convert: to change or make something change

from one form, purpose, system, etc. to another
advocate: to speak in support of an idea or course of action

Questions 12-22

→ ■ Most sharks are harmless – at least to humans. Nevertheless, 25 species of sharks are known to have attacked humans, and at least 12 more are suspected of doing so. ■ Three are particularly dangerous: the great white, tiger, and bull sharks. ■ Even so, shark attacks are rare. ■ The chances of being attacked by a shark are lower than those of being hit by lightning.

→ ■ A U.S. naval officer was killed by massive bites while swimming in the Virgin Islands in 1963, an abalone diver in southern California was last seen protruding from the mouth of a shark, parts of arms and legs were found in the stomach of a tiger shark caught after a man had been mortally wounded in Australia, and a series of attacks by tiger sharks occurred in Hawaii. ■

Great white sharks typically inflict a massive wound on their prey (such as seals and sea lions) and then release it. The sharks wait until the bleeding prey is too weak to resist. White shark attacks on humans wearing wet suits may be cases of mistaken identity. Sometimes people are able to escape when sharks release them after the first bite. It has been discovered that before attacking, the small but dangerous gray reef shark performs a distinct aggressive display.

How can you decrease the risk of an attack? First, do not swim, dive, or surf in an area known to be frequented by dangerous sharks. Sea lion colonies and coastal garbage dumps attract them. Blood and feces also attract sharks. Avoid night swims. Sharks should not be provoked in any way. Even resting nurse sharks can turn and bite. Leave the water if fish suddenly appear in large numbers and behave erratically, which may be an indication that sharks are around. If you see a large shark, get out of the water with as little splashing as possible.

Actually, humans threaten the survival of sharks more than they threaten them. They reproduce slowly, and their numbers are already being depleted by over-fishing in many areas. This attitude toward sharks may be short-sighted. When large sharks were netted off South Africa, for example, the number of species of small sharks, which are eaten by large sharks, increased. As an apparent result, the number of bluefish, a commercially important species, decreased. Others practice shark hunting for sport. A magnificent predator, the shark may soon be exterminated by human

12. The passage focuses on which of the following aspects of sharks?
- (A) How to eliminate them to avoid the loss of human life
- (B) How to decrease the risk of shark attacks
- (C) How to avoid harmful encounters between sharks and humans
- (D) How to prevent the extinction of shark species

13. According to the passage, which of the following is NOT true about sharks?
- (A) Most sharks do not attack humans.
- (B) Sharks attack humans sometimes by accident.
- (C) Sharks usually retreat when provoked.
- (D) Most sharks are active at night.

14. The word mortally in the passage could best be replaced by
- (A) recently
- (B) suddenly
- (C) fatally
- (D) unfortunately

15. What does the author mean by the statement White shark attacks on humans wearing wet suits may be cases of mistaken identity?

    Ⓐ White shark attacks humans only in case they wear wet suits.

    Ⓑ Perhaps white sharks attack people in wet suits by accident.

    Ⓒ White sharks always mistake humans for something else.

    Ⓓ Humans are vulnerable to attack in case white sharks are mistakenly identified.

16. Look at the word them in the passage. Click on the word or phrase in the **bold** text that them refers to.

17. The following sentence can be added to paragraph 1 or 2.

    Many shark attacks, however, have been documented over the years.

    Where would it best fit in the paragraph? Click on the square [▪] to add the sentence to paragraph 1 or 2. Paragraphs 1 and 2 are marked with an arrow [➡].

18. Which of the following is closest in meaning to the word erratically in the passage?

    Ⓐ Erroneously
    Ⓑ Instantaneously
    Ⓒ Massively
    Ⓓ Unpredictably

19. Look at the word depleted in the passage. Click on the word or phrase in the **bold** text that is closest in meaning to depleted.

20. Which of the following can be inferred from the passage?

    Ⓐ The survival of sharks is not an issue at all.

    Ⓑ Small sharks are endangered species due to shark hunting.

    Ⓒ Small sharks feed on bluefish.

    Ⓓ Sharks are hunted for no reason.

21. All of the following are causes threatening the survival of sharks EXCEPT

    Ⓐ slow reproduction
    Ⓑ over-fishing
    Ⓒ shark-hunting for sport
    Ⓓ big blue fish preying on small sharks

22. It is implied in the passage that the author

    Ⓐ is only interested in the safety of humans

    Ⓑ would like to protect sharks at the expense of human lives

    Ⓒ encourages shark hunting to protect humans

    Ⓓ would like to protect both humans and sharks

READING

VOCABULARY

massive: extremely large or serious
protrude: to stick out from something
wound: to injure part of the body
inflict: to force someone or something to experience something unpleasant

frequent: to often visit a particular place
feces: solid waste excreted from the bodies of animals and people
erratic (adv. erratically): changing suddenly and unexpectedly; not following any regular pattern

deplete: to reduce supplies or energy in size or amount
exterminate: to kill all the animals in a particular place or of a particular type

Questions 23-33

→ Writer F. Scott Fitzgerald dubbed the era after World War I the "Jazz Age" because young people were willing to experiment with new forms of recreation and sexuality. ■ The new jazz music bubbling up in New Orleans, Kansas City, Memphis, New York City, and Chicago blended African and European musical traditions into a distinctive sound characterized by improvisation, "blue notes," and polyrhythms. ■ The syncopated rhythms of jazz were immensely popular among rebellious young adults and helped spawn carefree new dance steps that shocked guardians of morality. ■

→ Much of the shock to old-timers during the Jazz Age came from the revolution in manners and morals, evinced first among young people, and especially on the college campuses. ■ In *This Side of Paradise*, a novel of student life at Princeton, F. Scott Fitzgerald wrote of "the great current American phenomenon, the "petting party." ■ From such novels and from magazine pieces, the heartland learned about the wild parties, bathtub gin, promiscuity, speakeasies, roadhouses, "shimmy dancers," and the new uses to which automobiles were put on secluded lovers' lanes. ■

Writers also informed the nation about the "new woman" eager to exercise new freedom. These independent females discarded corsets, sported bobbed hair, heavy makeup, and skirts above the ankles; they smoked cigarettes and drank beer, drove automobiles, and in general defied old Victorian expectations for womanly behavior.

Sex came to be discussed with a new frankness during the 1920s. Much of the talk derived from a spreading awareness of Dr. Sigmund Freud, the father of psychoanalysis. When in 1909, he visited Clark University, he was surprised to find himself so well known "even in prudish America." By the 1920s and 30s, his ideas had begun to percolate into the popular awareness, and the talk spread in society and literature about libido, inhibitions, Oedipus complexes, transference, sublimation, and repression.

Fashion also reflected the rebellion against prudishness and a loosening of inhibitions. By 1927 women's skirts were at the knees, and the "flapper" – with her bobbed hair, rolled stockings, cigarettes, lipstick and sensuous dancing – was providing a shocking model of the new feminism. The name derived from the way fashionable women allowed their galoshes to "flap" about their ankles.

23. The main subject of the passage is
   (A) the origins and radical influence of jazz music on America
   (B) the cultural atmosphere of the 1920s in America
   (C) the cultural revolution in America inspired by jazz music
   (D) the feminist movement inspired by jazz music in America

24. The "Jazz Age" is described as all of the following EXCEPT
   (A) amoral
   (B) exorbitant
   (C) rebellious
   (D) shocking

25. The word spawn in the passage is closest in meaning to
   (A) create
   (B) imitate
   (C) spread
   (D) fix

26. The following sentence can be added to paragraph 1 or 2.

   None of the Victorian mothers, he said, "had any idea how casually their daughters were accustomed to be kissed."

   Where would it best fit in the paragraph? Click on the square [■] to add the sentence to paragraph 1 or 2. Paragraphs 1 and 2 are marked with an arrow [→].

27. Which of the following is true?

   (A) The Jazz Age is noted for its introduction of a new genre to America and to the rest of the world.
   (B) The Jazz Age is responsible for the moral degeneration of the 1920s in America.
   (C) The Jazz Age consisted partly of a sexual revolution which fostered the feminist movement.
   (D) The Jazz Age brought about new dance forms that led to rebellion among young people.

28. The word defied in the passage is closest in meaning to

   (A) defined
   (B) challenged
   (C) obeyed
   (D) triumphed

29. Look at the word they in the passage. Click on the word or phrase in the **bold** text that they refers to.

30. The "new woman" defied Victorian standards through

   (A) criminal behavior
   (B) public protests
   (C) private politics
   (D) radical fashion

31. Click on the sentence that mentions the cities in which jazz music was most popular.

   Scroll the entire passage to see all of the paragraphs.

32. Dr. Freud was shocked to find himself well known in America because

   (A) he did not think that Americans were interested in psychoanalysis
   (B) he did not believe that he had become so influential and popular
   (C) he did not believe that Americans, being so conservative, would talk about sexual matters
   (D) he did not understand how Americans had accepted his radical ideas

33. It can be inferred from the passage that before the Jazz Age

   (A) it was unacceptable for women to show their legs and their knees in public
   (B) it was illegal to drink and dance as was done during the Jazz Age
   (C) it was indecent for women and men to be seen together in public
   (D) it was tolerable for women to speak publicly about matters of sex

---

VOCABULARY

dub: to give somebody or something a particular name, often in a humorous or critical way
syncopated: in syncopated rhythm the strong beats are made weak and the weak beats are made strong
spawn: to cause something to develop
gyrate (n. gyration): to move around in circles

secluded: quiet and private; not used or disturbed by other people
discard: to get rid of something that you no longer want or need
defy: to refuse to obey or to do something in the usual or expected way
prudish: very easily shocked by things connected

with sex
percolate: to move gradually through a surface that has very small holes or spaces in it
transference: the process of moving something from one place, person or use to another

Questions 34-44

There were many religious colonies in America during the 19th century, such as the Shaker communities and the Rappites, but the most important communitarians were the Mormons. A remarkable Vermont farm boy, Joseph Smith, founded the religion in western New York in 1820s. Smith saw visions; he claimed to have discovered and translated an ancient text, the Book of Mormon, written in hieroglyphics on plates of gold, which described the adventures of a tribe of Israelites that had populated America from biblical times until their destruction in a great war in A.D. 400.

➡ With a small band of followers, Smith established a community in Ohio in 1831. ■ The Mormons' dedication and economic efficiency attracted large numbers of converts, but their unorthodox religious views and their exclusivism, a product of their sense of being a chosen people, caused resentment among unbelievers. ■ The Mormons were forced to move first to Missouri and then back to Illinois, where in 1839 they founded the town of Nauvoo. Nauvoo flourished, but once again the Mormons ran into local trouble. ■ They quarreled among themselves, especially after Smith secretly authorized polygamy and a number of other unusual rites for members of the "Holy Order," the top leaders of the church. ■ Smith, envisaging the group as a semi-independent state within the Union, announced that he was a candidate for the presidency of the United States. ■ Rumors spread that the Mormons intended to take over the entire Northwest for their "empire," and once again, they were forced out.

➡ Under a new leader, Brigham Young, they established themselves on the shores of Great Salt Lake. ■ At last, they established their Zion and began making their impact on American history. Irrigation made the desert flourish, precious water wisely being treated as a community asset. ■ Hard, cooperative, intelligently directed effort spelled growth and prosperity. ■ In time, the communal Mormon settlement broke down, but the religion has remained, along with a distinctive Mormon culture that has been a major force in the shaping of the West. The Mormon church is still by far the most powerful single influence in Utah and is a thriving organization in many other parts of the United States and in Europe. ■

34. The main purpose of the passage is
   - (A) to compare and contrast the Mormons to the Shakers and Rappites
   - (B) to analyze the disappearance of the Mormons
   - (C) to evaluate the influence of the Mormons in the United States and in Europe
   - (D) to discuss the history of the Mormons and their basic beliefs

35. Look at the word their in the passage. Click on the word or phrase in the **bold** text that their refers to.

36. The passage that precedes this one most likely discusses
   - (A) religious reformation in 19th century America
   - (B) religious foundations in early American history
   - (C) the beginning of religious communities in 19th century America
   - (D) the significance of religious communities in 19th century America

37. Joseph Smith's objective in establishing the Mormon community consisted of

Ⓐ carrying out orders from God received in his vision

Ⓑ resurrecting the forgotten Israelite tribe that had once populated America

Ⓒ practicing faithfully the orders that he translated in his vision from the Book of Mormon

Ⓓ reforming the cultural and spiritual chaos that the nation was experiencing

38. According to the passage, which of the following could be true EXCEPT that

Ⓐ they were different from ordinary people

Ⓑ they were the kind of people that God prefers

Ⓒ all men are created equal

Ⓓ they were the best of mankind

39. All of the following describe the Mormons EXCEPT

Ⓐ devout

Ⓑ industrious

Ⓒ elitist

Ⓓ militant

40. The word spread in the passage is closest in meaning to

Ⓐ extended

Ⓑ covered

Ⓒ grew

Ⓓ circulated

41. The passage suggests that Mormons

Ⓐ did not believe that the world was soon coming to an end

Ⓑ did not believe that sexual intercourse was sinful

Ⓒ did not faithfully carry out the orders that God had sent

Ⓓ did not believe in peace and sought to harm others

42. The word asset in the passage is closest in meaning to

Ⓐ gift

Ⓑ compensation

Ⓒ wealth

Ⓓ emergency

43. The following sentence can be added to paragraph 2 or 3.

In 1847, they marched westward, pressing through the mountains until they reached the desolate wilderness on the shores of Great Salt Lake.

Where would it best fit in the paragraph? Click on the square [■] to add the sentence to paragraph 2 or 3. Paragraphs 2 and 3 are marked with an arrow [➡].

44. All of the following are places in which the Mormons settled down EXCEPT

Ⓐ Ohio

Ⓑ Illinois

Ⓒ Vermont

Ⓓ Utah

VOCA_{BULARY}

hieroglyphic: a picture or symbol of an object, representing a word, syllable or sound, esp. as used in ancient Egyptian and other writing systems
efficiency: the quality of doing something well with no waste of time or money
convert: a person who has changed their religion, beliefs or opinions

unorthodox: different from what is usual or accepted
resentment: a feeling of anger or unhappiness about something that you think is unfair
authorize: to give official permission for something, or for somebody to do something
polygamy: the custom of having more than one

wife at the same time
envisage: to imagine what will happen in the future
spell: to have something as a result
prosperity: the state of being successful, esp. financially

Questions 45-55

Insect societies are among the most ancient of all societies and, along with modern human societies, are among the most complex. Social insects include termites and hymenopterans (ants, wasps, and bees). As with other animals, the social insects evolved from forms that were originally solitary. Among bees, true sociality appears to have evolved on at least eight distinct occasions, and among wasps four times.

→ A honey-bee society usually has a population of 30,000 to 40,000 workers and one adult queen. ■ Each worker, always a diploid female, begins life as a fertilized egg deposited by the queen in a separate wax cell. Drones, or male bees, develop from unfertilized eggs and are therefore haploid. ■ The fertilized egg hatches to produce a white larva that is fed almost continuously by the nurse workers; each larval bee eats about 1,300 meals a day. ■ **After the larva has grown until it fills the cell, a matter of about six days, the nurses cover the cell with a wax lid, sealing it in. It pupates for about 12 days, after which the adult bee emerges.** ■

→ The newly emerged adult worker rests for a day or two and then begins successive phases of employment. ■ She is first a nurse, bringing honey and pollen from storage cells to the queen, drones, and larvae. This occupation usually lasts about a week. ■ Then she begins to produce wax, which is exuded from the abdomen, passed forward by the hind legs to the front legs, chewed thoroughly, and then used to enlarge the comb. ■ During this stage of employment as a houseworking bee, she may also remove sick or dead comrades from the hive, clean emptied cells for reuse, or serve as a guard at the hive entrance. ■ It is only in the third and final phase of her existence that the worker bee forages for nectar and pollen. At about six weeks of age, she dies. ■

45. According to the passage, insects were originally
- (A) social
- (B) complex
- (C) solitary
- (D) ancient

46. All of the following describe social insects EXCEPT
- (A) bees took less time than wasps to evolve into social insects
- (B) they include termites, ants, bees and wasps
- (C) through eight different phases, bees developed sociality
- (D) along with modern human societies, they are the most ancient and the most complex

47. The word distinct in the passage is closest in meaning to
- (A) continuous
- (B) separate
- (C) general
- (D) corresponding

48. The second paragraph suggests that in honey-bee societies
    (A) division of labor is equally distributed among male and female bees
    (B) both drones and female workers have a short life span
    (C) reproduction occurs continuously and quickly for fear of extinction
    (D) male workers do not play a major function in maintaining and governing the society

49. All of the following describe a worker EXCEPT
    (A) it is a fertilized egg deposited by the queen
    (B) it is always a diploid female
    (C) it is sometimes an unfertilized egg and a haploid
    (D) it becomes a larva before hatching as an adult bee

50. Look at the word It in the passage. Click on the word or phrase in the **bold** text to which It refers.

51. The word successive in the passage is closest in meaning to
    (A) productive
    (B) exhaustive
    (C) consecutive
    (D) prosperous

52. All of the following describe the work of a female bee EXCEPT
    (A) she enlarges the comb by extracting wax from the drone's abdomen

    (B) she produces wax which she subsequently chews in order to enlarge the comb
    (C) she feeds the larva continuously with honey and pollen that she obtains from storage
    (D) she acts as housewife, cleaning the cells of the comb and guarding the hive entrance

53. The following sentence can be added to paragraph 2 or 3.

    During this period, a houseworking bee begins to make brief trips outside, seemingly to become familiar with the immediate neighborhood.

    Where would it best fit in the paragraph? Click on the square [■] to add the sentence to paragraph 2 or 3. Paragraphs 2 and 3 are marked with an arrow [→].

54. The main purpose of the passage is
    (A) to understand the structure of sociality of insects such as the honey-bee
    (B) to compare the sociality of insects to animals and to humans
    (C) to explain how a honey-bee develops from an egg to an adult worker
    (D) to analyze the social structure of a honey-bee and its different responsibilities

55. Click on the sentence that states how much a larval bee consumes.

    Scroll the entire passage to see all of the paragraphs.

VOCABULARY

solitary: being the only one, or not being with other similar things, often by choice
occasion: a particular time when something happens
fertilize: to spread a natural or chemical substance on land in order to make plants grow well
larva: a young insect that has left its egg but has

not yet developed wings, or the young of some animals
pupate: to develop into a pupa (an insect in the stage of development between a larva and an adult insect)
exude: to produce from the inside and spread out slowly

abdomen: the part of the body that contains the stomach, bowels, and other organs in a person or animal
comrade: a friend or other person that you work with
forage: to go searching, esp. for food

chapter 6 Miscellaneous Overview and Purpose Questions

Frequency of appearance per passage with 11 questions: one or none
Standard Multiple-Choice
Difficulty Range: Medium to Difficult

Overview & Strategies

1. Organization

These questions test your ability to analyze the organization of the passage or to identify the author's logic, reasoning, or tools of persuasion in writing the passage.

Organization questions ask about the overall structure of a passage or a particular paragraph. The organizational structure is the author's structural plan or the persuasive technique used to deliver his or her points.

In sum, the organization of a passage may be understood as the way the author presents the information, ideas, or details.

How is the question worded?

Which of the following best describes the organization of the passage?
Which of the following best describes the development of the passage?
The passage is organized by ...
The author organizes the discussion of _____ in terms of ...
The third paragraph is developed primarily by means of ...
In paragraphs __ and __, the author organizes the discussion of _____ by ...
  Paragraph __ and paragraph __ are marked with arrows [➜].

Examples of Answer Choices				
comparison	contrast	explanation	narrative	cause and effect
definition	summary	process	classification	description
illustration	analysis	instruction	chronological order	

2. Tone/Attitude/Purpose

2-1. Tone

Tone questions ask you to determine the relation of the author to his or her topic. For that purpose, pay attention to the language used in the passage. Scan the passage for possible indications of tone such as humor, admiration, and the like.

How is the question worded?

What tone does the author take in writing this passage?
The tone of the passage could best be described as ...
What is the tone of the passage?

Examples of Answer Choices				
worried	humorous	outraged	favorable	critical
admiring	optimistic	unfavorable	impersonal	amused
angry	pleased	defiant	respectful	positive
negative	neutral	apologetic	accusative	unconcerned

2-2. Attitude

Attitude questions are very similar to tone questions, especially in terms of answer choices. It is crucial to understand the author's opinion about the topic. Moreover, the vocabulary that the author uses in the passage is likely to disclose what his or her attitude is.

Therefore, pay attention to descriptive words that will help you guess the author's attitude toward a particular topic.

Example

The bald ibis lived in Europe for thousands of years. Now there are no bald ibis in Europe. The last ibis visited there in 1989. **Happily**, we can see the bald ibis in other areas, such as Morocco and Turkey, although in small numbers.

[Explanation]

The author thought the bald ibis was in danger because the last bald ibis was seen in Europe in 1989. The use of word "happily" reveals that the author was initially worried, but eventually relieved to see the bald ibis again in Morocco and Turkey.

How is the question worded?

What is the author's attitude toward _____?

The author's attitude toward _____ discussed in the passage is best described as ...

How would the author probably feel about _____?

Examples of Answer Choices				
advisory	complimentary	superior	admiring	approving
concerned	wistful	persuasive	cautionary	critical
indifferent	sarcastic	resentful	conciliatory	worried

2-3. Purpose

The purpose of a passage as a whole is what the author intends to achieve with his writing. The purpose question in a broad sense is related to the main idea of the passage. For example, it is phrased like *"What is the author's main purpose in the passage?"*

On the other hand, the purpose questions in a narrow sense may ask why the author mentions a particular piece of information in the passage.

Some questions may ask what the author mentions by a specific sentence. Others may ask why the author mentions a certain word or phrase. In a general way, these questions involve drawing inferences, and may be phrased in a number of ways. One of them is: *"Why does the author mention _____ in paragraph 1?"*

In sum, CBT reading questions about purpose can be about either a whole passage or part of a passage. Usually, each paragraph in the passage serves a different purpose. For example, a paragraph may give a definition of the concept. It may provide examples to elaborate on the concept. It may also provide comparison, contrast, proof, or classification.

How is the question worded?

What is the purpose of the passage/paragraph 1?

The purpose of the passage/paragraph 2 is to ...

Why does the author claim that _____?

READING

What does the author mention/suggest in paragraph 3?

Why does the author give an example of ____?

The author mentions ____ to indicate that ...

Examples of Answer Choices					
to criticize	to prove	to persuade	to emphasize	to warn	to analyze
to explain	to compare	to classify	to describe	to support	to predict
to praise	to illustrate	to motivate	to direct attention		

3. Preceding/Following Topics

Occasionally, although less frequently on CBT than on PBT, questions involve the topic of the previous or following paragraph. You are supposed to assume that the given passage is part of a longer passage and ask yourself: "What would be the topic of the paragraph that precedes or follows the passage?"

To find the topic of the previous paragraph, look for transitional or structural clues in the first or second sentence of the passage. Usually, there are signal words or connectors indicating what was discussed previously.

For the topic of the following paragraph, pay attention to the last several sentences of the passage. You will find some clues, whether in words or structure, as to what will be discussed in the following section.

How is the question worded?

With what topic would the following/preceding paragraph most likely deal?

The paragraph prior to/after the passage probably discusses ...

The paragraph following the passage most probably discusses ...

It can be inferred from the passage that the previous/next paragraph concerns ...

Which of the following would be most likely to be discussed in the paragraph following the passage?

Skill Building

Skill Building 1: Organization

Each color has its own unique wavelength. Here's why. All the colors of light travel through empty space at the same speed. This means that the length of a wave is determined by just one thing: how fast the photon/wave vibrates. One vibration makes one full wave, and the faster the photon/wave vibrates, the shorter the distance the light travels before a new wave starts. Red light vibrates about 375 trillion times a second, and violet about 750 trillion times a second.

1. How is the information in the passage organized?

(A) Hypothesis
(B) Chronological order
(C) Cause and effect
(D) Argument

[Explanation]
Skim the paragraph to determine its organization. In the above paragraph, the sentence "Here's why" provides a clue. The paragraph presents scientific facts (effects) and proceeds to explain their causes.

Material like water or glass that lets some light pass through unchanged is called "transparent." On the other hand, material like tissue paper or frosted glass that lets some light through but scatters it is called "translucent." Finally, material like metal or wood that does not let light through at all is called "opaque." Certain opaque objects, like the mirror in a bathroom, bounce almost all the light back into the air instead of absorbing it.

2. The author organizes the paragraph by means of

(A) classification
(B) chronological order
(C) response
(D) generalization

[Explanation]
In the above paragraph, the author classifies several materials into three categories such as "transparent," "translucent," and "opaque" depending on whether they block light or let it pass through unchanged. Pay attention to the transitional structure of the paragraph like listing materials one category by another, wrapped up by "finally." This paragraph is organized by means of classification. Listing events in the order in which they happened is called organization in "chronological order," mentioned in choice (B).

VOCABULARY

1. 1. **wavelength**: the distance between two waves of energy
photon: a unit of electromagnetic energy
vibrate: to move from side to side very quickly and with small movements

1. 2. **transparent**: allowing light through so that objects can be clearly seen through it
frosted: (of glass) that has been given a rough surface, so that it is difficult to see through
opaque: preventing light from traveling through,

and therefore not allowing you to see through it
bounce: to move quickly away from a surface
absorb: to take in (a liquid, gas, or chemical) and make a part of itself

Skill Building 2-1: Tone

Melatonin has been getting undue media attention. Some enthusiasts claim that a daily dose can slow aging, combat jet lag, protect against disease, help you sleep. Millions of people have bought melatonin frenetically. Synthetic melatonin is relatively inexpensive. However, according to scientists, most claims are suspicious, although some of melatonin's benefits may be real.

1. What is the tone of the passage about Melatonin?

   (A) Excited
   (B) Positive
   (C) Skeptical
   (D) Sarcastic

[Explanation]

   The expressions the author used in the paragraph, such as "undue," "frenetically," or "suspicious," give some clues about the tone of the passage – whether it is positive, negative, or indifferent. The author felt skeptical about the credibility of claimed effects of "melatonin." To bolster his skeptical position, the author relies on scientists saying that they have doubts about the effects of "melatonin."

In Asia's ailing cities the gap between laws and law enforcement is wide enough to drive a truck through. For example, Taiwan's standards for mobile sources of air pollution are said to match the toughest in the world. However, the problem is limited enforcement or poor laws. In some cities, government transport breaches the rule with impunity while other private vehicles belching smoke would be fined.

2. What tone does the author take in writing this passage?

   (A) Neutral
   (B) Cynical
   (C) Optimistic
   (D) Angry

[Explanation]

   The author does not trust laws and law enforcement as a way of fighting pollution, because of gaps and legal loopholes. (Loopholes mean opportunities to legally avoid an unpleasant duty because of a mistake in the way rules have been written.) The word "cynical" means not trusting or respecting the apparent sincerity of other people and their actions.

VOCABULARY

2-1. 1. **enthusiast**: someone who is very interested in and involved with a particular subject or activity
claim: to state that something is true or is a fact
dose: amount of something
frenetic (adv. frenetically): involving a lot of energy and activity in a way that is not organized

suspicious: feeling that someone has done something wrong, illegal or dishonest, without having any proof
2-1. 2. **ail**: to feel or to cause to feel unhealthy or weak
enforce: to make sure that people obey a

particular law or rule
mobile: able to move freely
impunity: freedom from punishment for something that has been done that is wrong or illegal
belch: to send out large amounts of smoke, flames, etc.

Skill Building 2-2: Attitude

Every day and every year the same: life for the factory workers was an exhausting routine. But you wouldn't dare miss a day or show up late for work. If you did, you might have to pay a fine. For showing up only twenty minutes late, you could lose a quarter of a day's pay. You could also be fined if you were caught talking to another worker or sitting down on the job. And if you complained or talked back to your boss, you would be fired on the spot.

1. How would the author probably feel about the labor conditions of factory workers?

   (A) Indifferent
   (B) Favorable
   (C) Sarcastic
   (D) Outraged

[Explanation]

The word "outraged" here describes an attitude such as "feeling angry, shocked, or upset." Expressions such as *"exhausting, dare, fine, fired on the spot",* disclose what the author's position is. The author is upset about the labor conditions of factory laborers.

Imperialism had long-lasting effects in the African and Asian colonies, even after the colonies gained their independence from Britain. Since the wealth went to the British rulers and a few native people who collaborated with them, the majority of people in these colonies were reduced to living in poverty. In some cases, the imperialists caused huge ecological damage, leaving the landscape scarred and barren. Imperialism denied the right of every country to govern itself: in the African and Asian colonies, native people, no matter how talented, were rarely allowed to serve in the colonial government. Finally, by sending out the degrading message that people of darker complexions were "inferior" to their lighter-skinned rulers, imperialists caused deep anger and resentment that persist to this day.

2. The author's attitude toward imperialism could best be described as

   (A) approving
   (B) amazed
   (C) critical
   (D) uncertain

[Explanation]

Expressions such as "reduced to living in poverty," "ecological damage," "scarred and barren," "degrading message," or "causing deep anger and resentment" tell you what the author's position about imperialism is. The author is critical of the impact of imperialism on the African and Asian colonies.

VOCABULARY

2-2. 1. **exhaust**: to tire (a person or an animal) greatly
routine: a usual set of activities or way of doing things
dare: to be brave enough to do something difficult or dangerous
fine: an amount of money that has to be paid as a punishment for not obeying a rule or law

2-2. 2. **imperialism**: the attempt of one country to control another country, esp. by political and economic methods
colony: a country or area controlled politically by a more powerful country
collaborate: to help an enemy of your own country, esp. one which has taken control of your country

damage: harm
barren: (of land) not producing or unable to produce plants
complexion: the color or appearance of the skin of a person's face
resent (n. resentment): to dislike or be angry at something or someone
persist: to continue to exist past the usual time

Skill Building 2-3: Purpose

Initially, among the first settlers, fathers exercised strong authority over sons through their control of the land. They kept the sons and their families in the town, not letting them set up their own households or get title to their farmland until they reached middle age. In New England, as elsewhere, fathers tended to subdivide their land among all the male children. But by the eighteenth century, with land scarcer, the younger sons were either getting control of property early or moving on. Often they were forced out, with family help and blessings, to seek land elsewhere or new kinds of work in the commercial cities along the coast or inland rivers. With the growing pressure on land in the settled regions, poverty and social tension increased in what had once seemed a country of unlimited opportunity.

1. The author's purpose in writing the passage is

   (A) to introduce the common law method of inheritance regarding land in New England towns
   (B) to present the New Englanders as the most conservative settlers in the U.S.
   (C) to criticize the way land was subdivided among all the male children in New England
   (D) to explain how the inheritance of land in New England towns became the source of social strain

[Explanation]

The purpose of a passage is the reason why the author wrote it. It is also related to the main idea of the passage. The last sentence of the above paragraph is the main point the author tries to make. The focus does not lie on the custom of inheritance in New England, but on what social effect the system of inheritance of land brought about. The author gives an explanation of the cause of poverty and social tension in New England.

Migrants from rural areas often arrive with no money and set up camp-like settlements overnight. These migrants are called parachutists because they appear suddenly, as if they had dropped out of the sky. The constant arrival of parachutists makes existing problems in the city worse. Housing is already in short supply, and over one half of all families sleep in single rooms. Many are adding to the city's unemployment because many young people each year join the search for jobs. Urban crowding, when combined with a natural disaster such as an earthquake, can result in catastrophe.

2. The purpose of the paragraph is

   (A) to encourage the migration of young people from rural areas to the city
   (B) to warn about the ill effects of urban overcrowding
   (C) to solve the existing problems of overcrowded cities
   (D) to prevent natural disasters in urban areas

[Explanation]

Throughout the paragraph, the author mentions the ill effects of overcrowding in cities, caused by migration from rural areas. The author tries to send the warning of a potential catastrophe in case the current migration continues.

Jupiter contains an abundance of hydrogen as well as compounds of hydrogen with relative common elements such as carbon, nitrogen, and oxygen. These compounds – among which ammonia and methane have been observed, and water vapor probably exists also – were present in abundance in the primitive atmosphere of the earth, and are believed to have played a critical role in the events that led to the development of life on our planet. Their importance in evolution on the earth has ended, and they have long since escaped, but their continued presence on Jupiter leads us to wonder whether the initial steps along the path to life have not also occurred on that planet.

3. The author mentions the chemical compounds to answer the question whether

(A) Jupiter plays a critical role in exploring the primitive atmosphere of the Earth
(B) Jupiter has chemical compounds such as ammonia and methane in abundance
(C) Jupiter has a solid atmosphere
(D) life exists on Jupiter

[Explanation]
Refer to the sentences such as " ~ play the critical role ~ that led to the development of life on our planet" and " ~ the initial steps along the path to life have not occurred on the planet."

Skill Building 3: Preceding/Following Topics

Determined himself to practice plain living and high thinking, Thoreau boarded with the Emersons for a time and then embarked on an experiment in self-reliance. On July 4, 1845, he took to the woods to live in a cabin he had built on Emerson's land beside Walden Pond. He wanted to see how far he could free himself from the complexities and hypocrisies of modern commercial life, and to devote his time to observation, reflection, and writing. His purpose was not to lead a hermit's life. He frequently walked the mile or so to town to dine with his friends, and he often welcomed guests at his cabin.

READING

VOCABULARY

2-3. 1. **initially**: at the beginning
settle: to live in a place or to go somewhere to live, esp. permanently
property: a thing or things owned by someone; a possession
commercial: intended to make money, or relating to a business intended to make money
tense (n. tension): tight and stiff
2-3. 2. **migrant**: a person who moves from one place to another; especially in order to find work
rural: of the country
parachutist: a person who jumps from a plane using a parachute

urban: of a city or town
catastrophe: a sudden event that causes great suffering or destruction
2-3. 3. **abundance**: a large quantity that is more than enough
hydrogen: the lightest gas, one of the chemical elements, and having no color, taste, or smell
compound: a mixture of two or more different parts of elements
carbon: a chemical element that is contained in all animals and plants; an important part of other substances such as coal and oil
nitrogen: a gas, one of the chemical elements, that

has no color or taste, is a part of all living things, and forms about 78 percent of the earth's atmosphere
oxygen: a colorless gas, one of the chemical elements, that forms a large part of the air on earth and is needed to keep most living things alive and to create fire
ammonia: a gas or liquid with a strong smell, having various industrial uses such as in cleaning
methane: a gas having no color or smell which is often used as fuel
critical: expressing an opinion about something or someone, especially, a negative opinion

1. With what topic would the preceding paragraph most likely deal?

   (A) Thoreau preached that people should lead a hermit's life.
   (B) Thoreau attracted many followers among the public.
   (C) Thoreau inspired a generation of writers that produced classic American literature.
   (D) Thoreau spread the ideal of plain living in the beauties of nature.

[Explanation]
   The first sentence of the paragraph indicates that Thoreau himself determined to practice the plain living and high thinking that he preached before. He must have showed interest in such a simple lifestyle and preached about it prior to his actual commitment to living in the woods in self-reliance. Therefore, the most likely preceding topic is the answer Choice (D).

Most captive Africans had no choice over their fate and served for life. Slavery evolved in the Chesapeake after 1619, when a Dutch vessel dropped off twenty Africans in Jamestown. Some of the first were treated as indentured servants, with a limited term. Court records indicate that black and white servants occasionally escaped together. A Virginia court, for instance, declared that six white servants and a "Negro Servant" who had run away from their masters be given "thirty-nine lashes well laid on." Those African servants who worked out their term of indenture gained freedom and a fifty-acre parcel of land. They themselves sometimes acquired slaves and white indentured servants. Gradually, however, color difference between whites and blacks served as the basis for justifying the practice of hereditary life service by blacks.

2. What is the most likely topic that follows the above paragraph?

   (A) Slavery became recognized in the colonies of North America.
   (B) Indentured African servants became the custom of the land.
   (C) Voluntary indentured servitude accounted for the most of the servants of the land.
   (D) The demand for slaves decreased as available lands diminished.

[Explanation]
   Since the last sentence of the passage mentions that the practice of hereditary life service became the custom of the land, it may be concluded that the following topic may include the recognition of slavery in the colonies of North America. "Hereditary life service" indicates the practice of "slavery." Choice (B) contradicts the fact in the passage that the practice of "indentured African servants" was replaced by that of slaves burdened with hereditary life service.

VOCABULARY

3. 1. **board**: to arrange to be temporarily taken care of and fed at a place other than one's home
embark: to go on to a ship or an aircraft
hypocrisy: pretending to be what you are not
reflect (n. reflection): to think carefully
hermit: a person who lives alone and apart from society

3. 2. **captive**: a prisoner, esp. a person held by the enemy during a war
indenture: a type of contract in the past that forced a servant or apprentice to work for their employer for a particular period of time
declare: to announce or express something clearly and publicly, esp. officially

rationalize: to provide an explanation, esp. one based on reason
heredity (adj. hereditary): the natural process by which parents pass on to their young through their genes the characteristics that make them related

Intensive Exercises

Exercise 6.1

People can contribute to erosion, too. Sometimes their activities cause severe erosion, as they did in the 1930s in the region of the Great Plains known as the Dust Bowl. From about 1900 through the 1930s, farmers in the south-central United States plowed the soil over and over again, year after year. They left few areas unplowed where prairie grass once grew and held the topsoil in place. They did not grow anything to cover the land when their main crops weren't growing. They also left the soil uncovered once the crops were harvested. These practices led to a disastrous period of drought in which the thousands of acres of uncovered topsoil dried to dust. Strong winds then swept over the plains, picked up the dust and carried it hundreds of miles away. What was once rich farmland became exposed subsoil – cracked, dry, and useless to farmers.

1. Which of the following most likely precedes the passage?
   - (A) There are many ways in which erosion can be caused.
   - (B) There are numerous activities that might affect our environment.
   - (C) Abundant examples of erosion can be presented to show the effect of weather.
   - (D) People in the region of the Great Plains do not tolerate erosion.

2. The author's attitude toward the farming practice of the south-central United States in the early twentieth century is
   - (A) approving
   - (B) poignant
   - (C) diffident
   - (D) criticizing

 Time   **LinguaForum**   **Help** **Prev** **Next**

READING

[Explanation]
1. Always read carefully the first sentence of the passage to guess the preceding topic of the given passage. Several causes of erosion were very likely to be discussed before the passage, because it is stated in the beginning sentence that people can contribute to erosion, too.
2. Refer to expressions such as "They did not grow anything ~ their main crops weren't growing," "They also left the soil uncovered ~ harvested," and "These practices led to a disastrous period of drought ~ dried to dust." The author indicates that farmers are to be blamed for the disaster occurring in the Great Plains.

VOCABULARY

contribute: to help by providing money or support
plow: to turn over growing crops with a plow (= a large piece of farming equipment) and mix them into the soil to improve its quality

prairie: a wide area of flat land, covered with grass
disaster (adj. disastrous): an event causing great harm, damage, or suffering
harvest: to cut and gather a crop

exposed: not protected from the weather
crack: to break without dividing into separate parts

Exercise 6.2

Some say that it is useless to speak of peace or world law or world disarmament – and that it will be useless until the leaders of the Soviet Union adopt an attitude more enlightened than it was, disclosed by the incidents mentioned before. I hope they do. I believe we can help them do it.

But I also believe that we must re-examine our own attitudes – as individuals and as a nation – for our attitude is as essential as theirs. And every graduate of this school, every thoughtful citizen who despairs of war and wishes to bring peace, should begin by looking inward – by examining his own attitude towards the course of the cold war and towards freedom and peace here at home.

First: examine our attitude towards peace itself. Too many of us think it is impossible. Too many think it is unreal. But that is a dangerous, defeatist belief. It leads to the conclusion that war is inevitable – that mankind is doomed – that we are gripped by forces we cannot control.

We need not accept that view. Our problems are man-made. Therefore, they can be solved by man. And man can be as big as he wants. No problem of human destiny is beyond human beings. Man's reason and spirit have often solved the seemingly unsolvable – and we believe they can do it again.

1. What tone does the author take in writing this passage?
   - (A) Sarcastic
   - (B) Resentful
   - (C) Optimistic
   - (D) Desperate

2. What is the most likely topic of the paragraph preceding the passage?
   - (A) History of nuclear bomb production
   - (B) Examples of the Soviet Union's actions
   - (C) Listing of the Soviet Union's problems
   - (D) Explanations of man-made problems

 Time

LinguaForum

Help **Prev** **Next**

[Explanation]
1. The passage includes the sentences such as "I believe we can help them do it" and "Therefore, they can be solved by man."
2. In the first sentence, the passage mentions the undesirable attitude of the Soviet Union revealed by particular incidents, which might have been discussed in the preceding paragraph.

VOCABULARY

disarmament: a reduction in or limitation of the number of weapons in the armed forces of a country
enlighten: to cause someone to understand something by explaining it to them
incident: something that happens, esp. something unusual or unpleasant

despair: to stop having any hope that a situation will change or improve
defeatism (adj. defeatist): a way of thinking or behaving that shows that you expect to fail
doom: to make somebody or something certain to fail, suffer, die, etc.
grip: to have a powerful effect on somebody or

something
destiny: the particular state of a person or thing in the future, considered as resulting from earlier actions
event: a thing that happens, esp. something important

Exercise 6.3

The distance of an electron from the nucleus is determined by the amount of potential energy (often called "energy of position") the electron possesses. The greater the amount of energy possessed by the electron, the farther it will be from the nucleus.

An analogy may be useful. A boulder resting on flat ground neither gains nor loses potential energy. If, however, you change its position by pushing it up a hill, you increase its potential energy. As long as it sits on the peak of the hill, the rock once more neither gains nor loses potential energy. If it rolls down the hill, however, potential energy is converted to energy of motion and released. Similarly, water that has been pumped up to a water tank for storage has potential energy that will be released when the water runs back down.

Thus, an electron with a relatively small amount of energy is found close to the nucleus and is said to be at a low energy level; an electron with more energy is farther from the nucleus, at a higher energy level.

1. How is the information in the passage organized?

- Ⓐ Hypothesis
- Ⓑ Contrast
- Ⓒ Chronological order
- Ⓓ Analogy

2. The passage probably continues with a discussion of

- Ⓐ examples of atoms with electrons close to or far from the nucleus
- Ⓑ the molecular composition of rocks and water
- Ⓒ the use of energy of position in a power station
- Ⓓ how the number of electrons in an atom fluctuates

 LinguaForum

READING

[Explanation]
1. The passage first explains the energy of position, then gives an analogy to show how it works.
2. After explaining "energy of position" by means of an analogy, the passage would probably give an example of atoms with electrons that are either close to, or far from, the nucleus.

$\overline{\text{V}}$OCABULARY

nucleus: the central part of an atom, that contains most of its mass (= weight) and that carries a positive electric charge
potential: possible but not yet achieved

analogy: a comparison of the features or qualities of two things to show their similarities
boulder: a large, rounded rock that has been smoothed by the action of the weather or water

convert: to change from one form to another
release: to drop, or to stop carrying, holding, or containing something

Exercise 6.4

Two important features distinguish wars from feuds. First, warfare is conducted on a level above that of the local community; warring groups are usually either relatively large-scale elements within a single nation (civil war) or whole nations (international war). The second difference lies in the relationship between the antagonistic parties. In a feud, the participating groups are part of the same relatively small-scale social system – for instance, antagonistic lineages within the same tribe. In warfare, although the disputants may be covered by the same broad cultural umbrella, as were the combatants in the American Civil War, at a lower level they represent quite distinct political, social or economic organizations. This may be why they fight.

1. The passage is organized by means of
   - (A) hypothesis
   - (B) argument
   - (C) cause and effect
   - (D) contrast

2. The author mentions the American Civil War for the purpose of
   - (A) illustrating the similarities between feuds and warfare in America
   - (B) emphasizing the historical impact of the American Civil War on political groups
   - (C) exemplifying warfare in which antagonistic parties belonged to the same broad culture
   - (D) classifying warfare according to the levels where it occurs

 Time LinguaForum   **Help** **Prev** **Next**

[Explanation]
1. This passage contrasts "wars" with "feuds." It explains the difference between them point by point.
2. In the American Civil War, the warring parties were both American. Nonetheless, the disputants were involved in warfare because their political interests were so directly opposed.

VOCABULARY

feature: something important about a thing
distinguish: to recognize or understand the difference between two things, or to provide a quality that makes someone or something different or special

feud: an angry and sometimes violent argument that has continued for a long time between two people, families, or groups
antagonistic: expressing strong dislike or opposition

lineage: the series of families that somebody is descended from
tribe: a group of people of the same race, and with the same customs, language, religion, etc.
dispute (disputant): an argument or disagreement

Exercise 6.5

TOEFL CBT - Reading

In a caste system, however polluting the occupation and however inferior the caste, at least people owned their own labor. A slave, however, is in a radically different position. Slaves do not own their labor. On the contrary, they are themselves owned by other people.

Slavery has taken a number of different forms. War captives and their descendants formed a class of slaves in some societies; in others, slaves were a commodity that could be bought and sold. The rights granted to a slave varied, too. In ancient Greece, a slave could marry a free person, but in the stratified society of the southern United States before the Civil War, slaves were not allowed even to marry each other, because they were not permitted to engage in legal contracts. Still, slaves in the South often lived together as husband and wife throughout their adult lives, forming nuclear families that remained tightly knit until they were separated at the auction block.

1. The author's attitude towards slavery of ancient Greece is
   - (A) most critical
   - (B) unbearable
   - (C) sarcastic
   - (D) less indignant

2. What is the author's purpose of mentioning a caste system?
   - (A) To explain how a caste system radically polluted the occupation of the inferior class within the caste system
   - (B) To contrast the labor condition of the inferior caste with slaves in the southern United States
   - (C) To show that the author agrees with the practice of a caste system because people own their labor
   - (D) To elaborate on the marital status of the inferior caste

　LinguaForum　

[Explanation]
1. Refer to the sentence "In ancient Greece, a slave could marry a free person, ~."
2. The author intends to emphasize the difference in terms of ownership of labor between the caste system and the practice of slavery in the southern United States in the first paragraph.

VOCABULARY

caste: a system of dividing society into classes, or any of these classes

captive: a person who is kept as a prisoner, esp. in a war

descendants: a person's children, their children's children, and all the people who live after them who are related to them

commodity: a product or a raw material that can be bought and sold

inferior: worse than average, or not as good as others of the same type

grant: to agree to give somebody what they ask for, esp. formal or legal permission to do something

engage in: to take part in or do something

stratify: to arrange something in layers

legal: connected with or allowed by the law

knit: to join people or things closely together

auction: a usually public sale of goods or property, where people make higher and higher bids for each item, until there are no higher bids and it is sold for the most money offered

Vocabulary Review for Intensive Exercises 6.1-6.5

1. Tourism _____ substantially to the local economy.

   - (A) consists
   - (B) contributes
   - (C) recommends
   - (D) removes

2. In 1837, there was a _____ smallpox epidemic.

   - (A) carnivorous
   - (B) hereditary
   - (C) rambling
   - (D) disastrous

3. We hope the pamphlet will _____ voters about the issues.

   - (A) measure
   - (B) emerge
   - (C) enlighten
   - (D) proliferate

4. You'll never get anywhere with a _____ attitude.

   - (A) defeatist
   - (B) generic
   - (C) antiseptic
   - (D) deductive

5. In arguing against welfare, he used the _____ of feeding a wolf and making it dependent.

   - (A) aspect
   - (B) exchange
   - (C) eulogy
   - (D) analogy

6. He was eager to remove a _____ source of conflict.

   - (A) potential
   - (B) possessive
   - (C) polar
   - (D) picturesque

7. It's important to _____ between scientific fact and fiction.

   - (A) console
   - (B) relinquish
   - (C) distinguish
   - (D) diffuse

8. He's extremely _____ toward critics.

   - (A) anonymous
   - (B) artificial
   - (C) antagonistic
   - (D) authentic

9. The men were _____ in a heated dispute.

   - (A) betrayed
   - (B) engaged
   - (C) boarded
   - (D) avoided

10. A _____ holiday is a day on which government offices and many businesses are closed.

   - (A) legendary
   - (B) legitimate
   - (C) liable
   - (D) legal

Word Files IV: TOEFL Vocabulary with Emphasis on Biography, Literature, Culture, and Business

academic: adj. involving a lot of reading and studying; connected with education

acclaim: v. to praise somebody publicly

achievement: n. a thing that somebody has done successfully

adaptation: n. a film/movie, book or play based on a particular piece of work

aesthetic: adj. concerned with beauty and art; made in an artistic way

afford: v. to have enough money or time to buy or to do something

allegory: n. a story related to morality

alteration: n. a change made to something

ambivalent: adj. having opposing feelings; showing both good and bad feelings

appeal: v. to attract; to make a request

appoint: v. to choose someone officially

appreciate: v. to be grateful for something

arrange: v. to change a piece of music

auction: n. a public sale of goods, where people make higher bids for each item

autograph: n. a signature

award: v. to give a prize

bargain: n. an agreement between two people; v. to try to reach an agreement

capability: n. the ability to do something

chronicle: v. to record events in order

colloquial: adj. conversational; informal

commute: v. to travel regularly a distance from work and home

contemporary: adj. modern

customary: adj. usual, typical

debate: n. a formal discussion of an issue

degree: n. the qualification obtained by students

descendant: n. a person related to someone from an earlier generation

desperate: adj. needing something very much

distinctive: adj. clearly different from others

donation: n. the act of giving something to help

edit: v. to prepare a book to be published by correcting mistakes

efficiency: n. the quality of producing results without waste

embellish: v. to make a story more interesting; embroider

emerge: v. to appear, come out

engrave: v. to cut into a hard substance

execute: v. to do or perform something

executive: n. someone in a high position

exploit: v. to use for your own benefit

factor: n. a fact that influences a result

feature: n. a special article or program about something

fortune: n. luck; a large amount of money

intensity: n. the strength of something

latitude: n. freedom to behave or think

legend: n. an old story from ancient times

legitimate: adj. valid, lawful

motivation: n. willingness to do something

obscure: adj. unknown; difficult to understand

occasion: n. a particular time; a reason

occupation: n. a job or profession

originate: v. to happen for the first time

personnel: n. people working for an organization; employees

pervasive: adj. spreading widely and gradually

playwright: n. a person who writes plays

premier: adj. best or most important

prominent: adj. important or well known

promotion: n. advertising intended to increase the sales

research: n. a detailed study

retain: v. to keep something

retrieve: v. to get something back

revenue: n. income

score: n. a piece of written music (musical text)

script: n. a written text of a play, broadcast, etc.

shift: v. to move or change direction

signature: n. a particular quality that makes something different from other similar things

speculate: v. meditate, guess

spiritual: adj. connected with the human spirit

straightforward: adj. honest and open

substitute: v. to use instead of another person or thing

synonymous: adj. having the same meaning

unequivocal: adj. clear and firm

vanity: n. too much pride in your appearance or achievements

READING

Practice Test 6

Questions 1-11

Over the last 20 years, scientists have realized that anomalous behavior in the eastern Pacific Ocean near the coastlines of Peru and Ecuador can have a dramatic effect on world climate. Toward the end of each year, warm currents raise water temperatures by one to two degrees Celsius in this region. Local fishermen named these currents "El Niño," Spanish for the "Christ child," because they noticed their occurrence around Christmas time. **The fishermen also noted that the occurrence of these warm currents coincided with a sharp decline in fish catches.**

➡ **Traditionally, they take a break from fishing around Christmas time. ■ In most years, the break lasts a few months, by which time the waters become cool again, fish stocks are replenished, and they are able to resume fishing. ■ However, every 2-7 years, a warming of more than six degrees Celsius occurs and the break in the fishing season extends until May or June. ■** In 1982, the warming was so profound that the fishing harvest completely failed due to a decline in anchovies and the migration of sardine stocks southward to escape the warm waters. ■

➡ Scientists now reserve the term El Niño for these exceptionally warm periods which are separated by years of more normal circulation, known as La Niña, meaning "the girl." ■ Although the 1982-3 El Niño was the first to gain the attention of the public, it is clear that there have been at least ten such periods in the last 40 years. ■

How does El Niño occur? In a normal year, two important wind directions influence western South America. The southeasterly winds, known as the trade winds, combined with Ekman transport in the southern hemisphere, cause a net movement of ocean water to the west, that is, away from the coastline. This allows the upwelling of relatively cold nutrient-rich deep waters that contain abundant plankton. Because they lie at the base of the food chain, these microorganisms provide the nutrients to sustain the fish populations.

El Niño occurs when, for some unknown reason, the southeasterly winds diminish. As a consequence, the winds no longer drive the ocean water westward and the blanket of warm water stretches to the South American coast, thereby inhibiting the ascent of cold nutritious waters to the surface.

1. The main purpose of this passage is to
   - (A) describe the disastrous effects of El Niño on the world environment
   - (B) explain the phenomenon of El Niño and its effect on the marine environment
   - (C) offer explanations of the possible causes of El Niño
   - (D) discuss unpredictable weather patterns in certain areas of the world

2. The word anomalous in the passage is closest in meaning to
   - (A) audacious
   - (B) anonymous
   - (C) abnormal
   - (D) predictable

3. All of the following are true about El Niño EXCEPT

   Ⓐ it increases the temperature of the water

   Ⓑ it is named after a Spanish fisherman

   Ⓒ it occurs around the time of Christmas

   Ⓓ it originates along the coastlines of Peru and Ecuador

4. Look at the word they in the passage. Click on the word or phrase in the **bold** text that they refers to.

5. It can be inferred from the passage that fish near the coastlines of Peru and Ecuador prefer

   Ⓐ warm currents

   Ⓑ warm waters

   Ⓒ cold waters

   Ⓓ freezing waters

6. The following sentence can be added to paragraph 2 or 3.

Moreover, the decline in fish stocks resulted in a decline in the seabirds that feed on the fish.

Where would it best fit in the paragraph? Click on the square [■] to add the sentence to paragraph 2 or 3.

Paragraphs 2 and 3 are marked with an arrow [➜].

7. All of the following apply to El Niño EXCEPT

   Ⓐ warm currents that are harmful to the fishing industry

   Ⓑ named after the period in which it occurs

   Ⓒ helps fishermen bring the fishes to the surface

   Ⓓ gained its first attention in 1982-3

8. According to the passage, El Niño

   Ⓐ is a recent discovery with significant implications

   Ⓑ has happened only during the last decade or so

   Ⓒ is a recent discovery made by scientists

   Ⓓ is not a recent occurrence that has happened for the first time

9. The movement of water away from the coastline leads to

   Ⓐ the occurrence of El Niño

   Ⓑ the uprising of the waters

   Ⓒ the surfacing of nutrient-rich deep waters

   Ⓓ the occurrence of La Niña

10. Click on the sentence that mentions the name of the period of normal circulation.

Scroll the passage to see all of the paragraphs.

11. It can be inferred from the passage that the absence of fish during El Niño is due to

   Ⓐ the lack of food that is usually available when the cold nutrient-rich water surfaces upwards

   Ⓑ the diminishing of the southwesterly winds that carry the nutrition for the fishes

   Ⓒ the movement of the water away from the coastline that brings warm water

   Ⓓ the blanket of warm water that stretches throughout the coastlines of South America

VOCABULARY

anomalous: different from what is normal or expected

coincide: to happen at the same time

replenish: to make something full again by replacing what has been used

resume: to begin again or continue after an interruption

profound: very serious

migration: the movement of large numbers of people, birds or animals from one place to another

abundant: existing in large quantities; more than enough

sustain: to make something continue for some time without becoming less

inhibit: to prevent something from happening or make it happen more slowly or less frequently than normal

nutritious: very good for you; containing many of the substances which help the body to grow

Questions 12-22

During the last fifty years a number of important changes in American population patterns have had an economic impact on the nation. The movement of African-Americans from the South to the cities of the east coast and Midwest such as New York and Chicago, which was accelerated by World War I, continued throughout the century.

The growth of population in Florida, California, and the Southwest, called the Sunbelt, made those areas increasingly important both economically and politically. These population changes will be of major significance as the Sun Belt continues to grow and as New England and the Midwest continue to shrink in relative population. The Sun Belt states tend to be politically conservative with their relatively older population of retired persons. As the number of representatives from states is changed after each census, this population shift may have an important impact on the United States House of Representatives and its voting patterns on economic and other issues.

→ ■ After the postwar surge in the birth rate, which aided the economy and produced the Baby Boom generation, the birth rate slowed. ■ Then after a brief increase the birth rate declined in the 1980s, and as the Baby Boomers aged, so did the average age of Americans. ■ Social Security will be affected as there are fewer young workers to pay Social Security taxes to support older, retired workers. ■ The birth rate drop was particularly sharp among middle and upper-class whites, where women, enjoying the liberation gained in the 1960s and early 1970s, followed careers and had fewer children or had children later.

→ ■ On the other hand, the Hispanic population, which increased 61% in the 1970s, continued to grow rapidly through births and immigration, both legal and illegal. ■ By the 21st century, the Hispanic American population will be the largest minority group in the United States. ■ Poor educational background and lack of job opportunities keep many Hispanics in poverty. ■ Their frustrations led to several riots in Miami reminiscent of the African-American ghetto riots of the 1960s.

12. The main purpose of the passage is to
- (A) introduce the population profile across the United States
- (B) analyze the reasons for the population shift in the United States
- (C) describe the impact of the population shift in the US
- (D) criticize the racial make-up of the population in the US

13. The word impact in the passage is closest in meaning to
- (A) stimulus
- (B) collision
- (C) injury
- (D) effect

14. The word accelerated in the passage could best be replaced by
- (A) caused
- (B) stimulated
- (C) hastened
- (D) increased

15. According to the passage, a political situation has been influenced by

    (A) the population shift between the regions

    (B) the decrease in the average age of Americans

    (C) the social status of the Asian population

    (D) the decrease of the Hispanic population

16. The second paragraph suggests that

    (A) the Sun Belt states will become more affluent due to population shift

    (B) the number of retired people will decrease as they are replaced by younger people

    (C) the conservatism of the Sun Belt states will diminish due to the population shift

    (D) the conservatism of the Sun Belt states has had a damaging effect on the economy

17. Look at the word their in the passage. Click on the word or phrase in the **bold** text to which their refers.

18. Social Security is financed by

    (A) private savings

    (B) representatives from states

    (C) taxes

    (D) the Hispanics

19. The most important reason for the decline in birth rate is

    (A) the lack of desire of women to have babies

    (B) the strong rise of the feminist movement in the 60s and 70s

    (C) the government effort to control the population make-up

    (D) the incredible number of babies born after the war

20. Click on the sentence that mentions the states that make up the Sunbelt states.

Scroll the passage to see all of the paragraphs.

21. It can be inferred from paragraph 4 that Hispanics

    (A) have been the target of discrimination, as have African-Americans

    (B) have made great efforts to immigrate illegally into the US

    (C) will take over the US population in the near future

    (D) will make Spanish the official language of the US

22. The following sentence can be added to paragraph 3 or 4.

Illegal immigrants came to escape revolution, poverty or both in Central America.

Where would it best fit in the paragraph? Click on the square [■] to add the sentence to paragraph 3 or 4. Paragraphs 3 and 4 are marked with an arrow [→].

VOCABULARY

accelerate: to happen or to make something happen faster or earlier than expected
conservative: opposed to great or sudden social change; showing that you prefer traditional styles and values
representative: a person who has been chosen to speak or vote for somebody else or on behalf of a

group
census: the process of officially counting something, esp. a country's population, and recording various facts
surge: a sudden increase in the amount or number of something
liberate (n. liberation): to free a country or a

person from the control of somebody else
immigration: the process of coming to live permanently in a country that is not your own
illegal: not allowed by the law
frustration: the feeling of being frustrated
reminiscent: associated in memory with something simillar

Questions 23-33

→ ■ The Moon and its phases are at the center of many myths and legends, and have captured the imagination of musicians and poets for centuries. ■ Although half of it is always lit by the Sun, the part people see from Earth may be totally illuminated (full moon) or completely dark (new moon) as the relative positions of the Moon, the Earth, and the Sun change in the course of the Moon's 27.32-day revolution around the Earth. ■ A cursory glance at the night sky reveals that the Sun is responsible for illuminating the Moon. ■ The light that reaches the Earth from the Moon is simply reflected sunlight. Indeed, on clear nights, a full moon can provide appreciable reflected illumination.

→ Although half of the Moon is always illuminated, one can usually see only a portion of the illuminated half from Earth. This gives rise to what are called the phases of the Moon. ■ Thus, the phase people call the "full moon" occurs when the Moon's entire illuminated half faces towards the Earth. ■ This is achieved when the Moon is on the far side of the Earth relative to the Sun. ■ The phase people call the "new moon," occurs when the illuminated half faces away from the Earth. ■ This is achieved when the Moon is between the Sun and the Earth. Crescent, quarter, and gibbous moons represent conditions in between these two extremes. ■ As the Moon moves from full moon to new, the Moon's illuminated portion becomes smaller, and it is said to be waning. As the Moon moves from new moon to the full, the illuminated portion becomes larger, and it is said to be waxing. ■

The same side of the Moon always faces the Earth; it is just the shadow on the Moon that moves as the phases change. In a similar way, an observer on the Moon would see the earth go through phases as the position of the Earth's shadow changed.

23. The main topic of the passage is
   Ⓐ the solar system
   Ⓑ the origin of the phases of the Moon
   Ⓒ the phases and eclipses of the Sun
   Ⓓ the Moon, Sun and Earth

24. Look at the word it in the passage. Click on the word or phrase in the **bold** text that it refers to.

25. Look at the word lit in the passage. Click on the word or phrase in the **bold** text that is OPPOSITE in meaning to lit.

26. Look at the word totally in the passage. Click on the word or phrase in the **bold** text that is closest in meaning to totally.

27. Which of the following statement is true?

(A) Though the moon is continuously lit, people do not see its complete illuminated phase.

(B) The Sun is the only source of light in the solar system.

(C) The Sun and the Moon are the two sources of light in the Universe.

(D) The Moon filters out much of the damaging ultraviolet rays of the Sun.

28. The word relative in the passage is closest in meaning to

(A) parallel
(B) similar
(C) compared
(D) reliable

29. The following sentence can be added to paragraph 1 or 2.

It thus appears that the origin of the phases of the Moon must be addressd here.

Where would it best fit in the paragraph? Click on the square [■] to add the sentence to paragraph 1 or 2.
Paragraphs 1 and 2 are marked with an arrow [→].

30. The phases of the Moon

(A) are the partial illumination of the Moon by the Sun

(B) are eclipses of the Moon, caused by the alignment of the Sun and the Earth

(C) are the partial view of the illuminated half of the Moon that is seen from Earth

(D) are the gradual illumination of the Sun on the Moon

31. All of the following characterize the full moon EXCEPT

(A) complete view of the illuminated half of the Moon from Earth

(B) total illumination of half of the Moon by the Sun

(C) view exactly opposite to the "new moon" phase

(D) complete view of the shadowed half of the Moon from Earth

32. To wax is to

(A) increase the area of illumination
(B) change the position of the Sun
(C) change the position of the shadow
(D) decrease the area of illumination

33. The phases of the Moon occur due to

(A) the change of the Moon's illuminated portion

(B) the vastness of the space between the Sun and the Earth

(C) the change of the position of the Earth's shadow

(D) the reflected sunlight from the Earth

VOCABULARY

legend: a story from ancient times about people and events, that may or may not be true
capture: to catch a person or an animal to be kept as a prisoner or in an enclosed space
illuminate: to shine light on something
revolution: a complete circular movement around a point

cursory: done quickly and without giving enough attention to details
reflect: to show the image of something on the surface of something, as a mirror, water or glass
appreciable: large enough to be noticed or thought important
gibbous: more than half but less than fully

illuminated (used of the moon or a planet)
wax: (of the moon) to seem to get gradually bigger until its full form is visible
wane: (of the moon) to appear slightly smaller each day after being round and full

Although fruits take many different forms, they are generally classified as simple, aggregate, or multiple, depending on the arrangement of the carpels in the parent flower. Simple fruits develop from one carpel or the fused carpels of a single flower, whereas aggregate fruits, such as the magnolia, raspberry, and strawberry, develop from several separate carpels of a single flower. **Multiple fruits consist of the carpels of more than one flower. A pineapple, for example, is a multiple fruit formed from an inflorescence, or flower cluster.**

➡ **Simple fruits are by far the most diverse. When ripe, they may be soft and fleshy or dry. The three principal types of fleshy fruit are the berry, the drupe and the pome. ■ In berries, such as tomatoes, dates, and grapes, there are one to several carpels, each of which may have one or many ovules. The inner layer of the fruit wall is usually fleshy. ■**

➡ In drupes, there are also one to several carpels, but usually only a single seed develops. The inner wall of the fruit is stony and usually adheres tightly to the seed. ■ Some familiar drupes are peaches, cherries, olives, and plums. ■ The peach is a typical drupe; the skin, the succulent, edible portion of the fruit, and the stone are three distinct layers of the wall of the mature ovary. The almond-shaped structure of the stone is the seed. ■ Pomes are highly specialized fleshy fruits characteristic of the subfamily of roses that produces rose hips. ■ Apples and pears are pomes.

Dry fruits are classified into two groups, dehiscent and indehiscent. Among the most familiar dehiscent fruits are those of legumes, such as the pea family. Indehiscent fruits occur in many plant families. The most common is the achene, a small, single-seeded fruit; some achenes, such as those produced by elms and the ash, are winged. The best known kind of indehiscent fruit is the nut. Examples of nut are acorns and hazelnuts. Note that the word "nut" is used very indiscriminately in common speech: peanuts are seeds of legumes; pine nuts are conifer seeds; almonds and coconuts are drupes.

34. This passage is most likely to appear in

Ⓐ the produce section of a supermarket advertisement

Ⓑ the beginner's guide to planting and growing fruits and vegetables

Ⓒ a pamphlet distributed at a botanical museum, exhibiting fruit plants

Ⓓ a journal explaining the latest technological advancements in farming

35. The main purpose of the passage is to

Ⓐ separate the most familiar fruits from less familiar ones

Ⓑ clarify the public's confusion regarding the classification of some fruits

Ⓒ introduce readers to many types of fruits which they already know and consume

Ⓓ analyze the structure of simple fruits which are the most commonly consumed

36. All of the following describe the strawberry EXCEPT

    Ⓐ is an aggregate fruit

    Ⓑ develops from the fused carpels of a single flower

    Ⓒ belongs to the same group as the magnolia

    Ⓓ develops from several separate carpels of a single flower

37. Look at the word they in the passage. Click on the word or phrase in the **bold** text that they refers to.

38. The passage mentions which of the following two examples of simple fruits?

    Click on 2 answers.

    Ⓐ Grapes

    Ⓑ Raspberries

    Ⓒ Peaches

    Ⓓ Pineapples

39. The word succulent in the passage is closest in meaning to

    Ⓐ dietary

    Ⓑ fibrous

    Ⓒ juicy

    Ⓓ flagrant

40. The following sentence can be added to paragraph 2 or 3.

A pome is derived from an inferior ovary in which the fleshy portion comes largely from the floral tube.

Where would it best fit in the paragraph? Click on the square [■] to add the sentence to paragraph 2 or 3. Paragraphs 2 and 3 are marked with an arrow [➡].

41. All of the following are examples of simple fruits EXCEPT

    Ⓐ almonds

    Ⓑ peanuts

    Ⓒ coconuts

    Ⓓ tomatoes

42. The word indiscriminately in the passage could best be replaced by

    Ⓐ accidentally

    Ⓑ intentionally

    Ⓒ carefully

    Ⓓ carelessly

43. Click on the sentence that describes the peach in detail.

Scroll the passage to see all of the paragraphs.

44. Click on the image that is an example of a drupe.

    Click on a picture.

VOCABULARY

aggregate: (botany) crowded or massed into a dense cluster
carpel: one of the structural units of a pistil, representing a modified, ovule-bearing leaf
inflorescence: a characteristic arrangement of flowers on a stem, a flower cluster
drupe: a fleshy fruit, such as a peach, plum, or

cherry, usually having a single hard stone that encloses a seed, also called stone fruit
pome: (botany) a pulpy pericarp without valves, containing a capsule or core
ovule: (botany) the plant part that contains the embryo sac, which after fertilization develops into a seed

succulent: (of fruit, vegetables and meat) containing a lot of juice and tasting good
ovary: the part of a plant that produces seeds
dehiscent: opening, as the capsule of a plant
conifer: any tree that produces hard dry fruit called cones. Most conifers are evergreen.

WRITING SECTION

Writing

1. Overview of the CBT Writing Section

Writing – previously known as the Test of Written English, or TWE – is a required section of TOEFL. It is also very different from other sections of TOEFL.

In other sections of TOEFL, you have to choose the correct one of several given answers. In Writing, however, you have to create your own essay. That is, you have to write a very short essay on a topic TOEFL provides.

The Writing section requires you to produce an idea and develop it into a brief, written composition. You must support your idea with evidence and a strong argument, and must write the essay in correct, standard English.

You can either write the essay by hand, using pencil and paper, or type it on the computer. You must choose which method you will use – paper or computer – before the topic is given. Either way, you have 30 minutes to complete the Writing section.

To end work on the Writing section when you are finished, click on **Next** and **Confirm Answer**. In any case, the computer will close the section automatically after 30 minutes.

2. Step-by-Step Guide to Writing

Writing an essay will be easier if you follow the guidelines below. Here is a step-by-step guide to the Writing section:

(1) **Read the prompt.** The *prompt* is the topic about which you must write. It is given to you on TOEFL. *You may not write on any other topic!* An essay on any topic other than the assigned one will receive a grade of zero!

The prompt will appear on the computer screen in a manner like this:

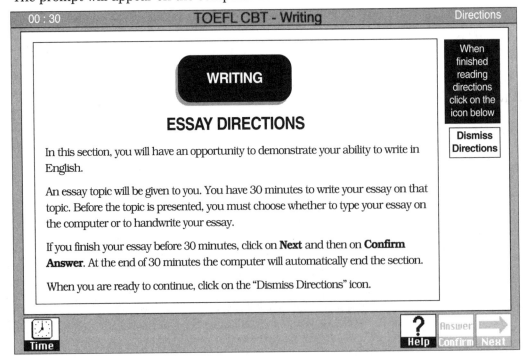

Prompts deal with many different topics, from family life to work and entertainment. You may be asked (for example) to compare or contrast two things, or describe something, or select an opinion and defend it.

Here are the major categories of prompts:

Type 1: Agree / Disagree Question (AD)

You may be asked if you agree or disagree with a certain statement. Then you must decide, and defend your opinion in the essay. For example: "Businesses should hire employees for their entire lives. Do you agree or disagree? Use specific reasons and examples to support your answer." This kind of prompt occurs often on the TOEFL.

Type 2: Choose and Defend a Point of View Question (PR)

You will be asked your opinion on a given topic and asked to write an essay defending your view. For example: "A company is going to give some money either to support the arts or to protect the environment. Which do you think the company should choose? Use specific reasons and examples to support your answer." This kind of prompt also occurs frequently on the TOEFL. *Note: In this case, it is especially important to have a strong thesis.* You cannot support your view if you have no clear view to support!

Type 3: Explain Reasons, Causes, or Results Question (EX)

Here, you may be asked to give reasons for some phenomenon, or to explain how something operates. For example: "Advertising helps to sell products. Describe the qualities of an effective advertisement. Use specific details and examples to support your answer." This is *analytical* writing, and it requires careful thought before you start writing. Take perhaps an extra minute to put your thoughts in order before beginning the essay. This kind of prompt occurs often on the TOEFL.

Type 4: Compare and Contrast Question (CM)

Prompts of this variety require you to describe the differences and/or similarities between two things, or the arguments for and against doing something. For example: "The government has announced that it plans to build a new university. Some people think that your community would be a good place to locate the university. Compare the advantages and disadvantages of establishing a new university in your community. Use specific details in your discussion." This is perhaps the rarest kind of prompt on the TOEFL. It has occurred very seldom on the TOEFL in recent years.

Type 5: If Question (IF)

Prompts in this category ask you to imagine what would happen, or what you would do, in a given situation. For example: "If you could invent something new, what product would you develop? Use specific details to explain why this invention is needed." This question also has appeared only rarely on the TOEFL in recent years.

(2) **Generate ideas and topic sentence.** Take about a minute to think of what you want to say. Then generate a topic sentence. Make it, if possible, the last sentence of the first paragraph. *This will be your thesis! Make it strong and definite!*

Type 1: Agree / Disagree Question (AD) – Sample Essay 1

Read the topic below and then make any notes that will help you plan your response. Begin typing your response in the box at the bottom of the screen, or write your answer on the answer sheet provided to you.

Employees of businesses should be hired for their whole lives when they get jobs. Do you think that policy is justified, or not? Use specific examples and reasons to support your opinion.

Hiring an employee for life is a rare situation in our time. Many years ago, when jobs were less specialized and the character of work changed little from year to year, it was possible for a business to hire someone and keep that person on the job for a lifetime. Now, however, times have changed. Except in very unusual cases, lifetime employment is neither likely nor desirable.

One reason is the ever-changing nature of work. It is constantly changing as new technologies alter it. In our so-called information age, new computers and software products appear every several years. Not everyone is qualified to handle them. Therefore, people without such skills may have to be replaced. Lifetime employment is hardly possible under those circumstances.

Then there is the increasing specialization of work to consider. Almost overnight, a job may change into a new and highly specialized category. It is no longer enough, for example, merely to be a sales representative. Now one must be (to take a hypothetical case) a "canine grooming products representative" or something else equally specialized.

Of course, it would be convenient if everyone could remain employed, for life, in a job that never changed. The problem with such a society would be that it could never change, innovate, or adapt. That is why lifetime employment is rarely feasible, and employment at a series of ever-changing jobs is the price we must accept for our society's adaptability.

Cut

Paste

Undo

        LinguaForum   

[Sample Questions]

1. Some people think attending live performances (of concerts, plays, football games, et cetera) is better than watching those events on television. Do you agree or disagree with that view? Use specific examples and reasons to explain your answer.

2. Literature and history are more important subjects for students than mathematics and science. Do you agree or disagree with that view? Why? Use specific examples and reasons to explain your answer.

3. We learn much about life by playing games. Do you agree or disagree with that statement? Use specific reasons and details to explain your answer.

Type 2: Choose and Defend a Point of View Question (PR) – Sample Essay 2

Read the topic below and then make any notes that will help you plan your response. Begin typing your response in the box at the bottom of the screen, or write your answer on the answer sheet provided to you.

A company plans to give money to either improve the environment or promote the arts. Which plan do you think is the better use for the money? Use specific examples and reasons to explain your answer.

The company in this case should ask: "Which use of money will benefit the greatest number of people over the longest period?" The answer is, I believe, investment in protecting the environment. There are several reasons why protecting the environment will do more good, in the long term, than supporting the arts.

First, investment in the arts is likely to benefit only a few people: namely, artists and those who understand their works. In our time, the number of such people is probably very small. Protecting the environment, on the other hand, benefits everyone, because we all live in the environment.

Second, a seemingly small investment in protecting the environment can have dramatic and far-reaching effects. Preserving even small tracts of land, a few hectares here and there, may provide refuges for hundreds of species that otherwise might be pushed to the brink of extinction. Investment in the arts, by contrast, seems unlikely to have such a desirable outcome.

Finally, there is the record of art in our time to consider. "Subsidized" art, underwritten by corporations or the government, tends to be mediocre at best and repulsive at worst. Moreover, such "art" probably will be forgotten (with good reason) in only a few years. For that reason alone, money is better spent, on the environment than on what some people call the arts.

Cut

Paste

Undo

LinguaForum

WRITING

[Sample Questions]

1. Some people prefer to spend most of their time with friends. Other people prefer to be alone most of the time. Which way of life do you prefer? Use specific reasons to support your answer.

2. Some people prefer to prepare and eat meals at home. Other people would rather eat at a food stand or restaurant. Which place do you think is better? Use specific examples and reasons to explain your answer.

3. Imagine that someone has given you some money as a gift. With the money, you could either buy an attractive piece of jewelry or go to a concert. Which do you think is a better use of the money? Use specific examples and reasons to support your opinion.

Type 3: Explain Reasons, Causes, or Results Question (EX) – Sample Essay 3

Read the topic below and then make any notes that will help you plan your response. Begin typing your response in the box at the bottom of the screen, or write your answer on the answer sheet provided to you.

Advertisements attempt to make people buy products. Which qualities, in your opinion, make advertisements effective? Use specific examples and reasons to explain your opinion.

Two important qualities in an advertisement are a memorable image or slogan, and humor. When these two qualities combine in the right way, the result is an advertisement that can be understood quickly and remembered for a lifetime.

For example, one of the most beloved cartoon characters in American entertainment was a nearsighted old man. A manufacturer of light bulbs used him in an amusing series of advertisements. The images delivered a memorable message: "If our light bulbs can benefit him, then think what they can do for you!"

Also, animals can be used in funny and memorable advertising. An animated stork with a comical New York accent appeared in a famous series of TV advertisements for a brand of pickles, and perplexed cartoon insects helped make a success of a certain insecticide.

An animal's picture combined with a memorable slogan in a series of American advertisements about fire safety. A cartoon bear, dressed in jeans and a forest ranger's hat, advised the public: "Only you can prevent forest fires." The advertisements became classics. In another context, the bear might have looked absurd. Yet, he became the symbol of a serious, important cause: fire prevention.

Of course, presenting a memorable image or slogan in an amusing way is a challenge. It is all too easy to make an amusing image look ridiculous. When everything is done right, however, the result is an advertisement that may be remembered fondly for 50 years or longer.

Cut

Paste

Undo

LinguaForum

[Sample Questions]

1. How do television and motion pictures affect our behavior? Use specific examples and reasons to support your answer.

2. Neighbors are the people who live closest to us. What are the qualities that you think make a person a good neighbor? Use specific examples and reasons to explain your answer.

3. Some young children spend much time playing sports. What are the positive and negative aspects of this practice? Use specific reasons and examples to support your view.

Type 4: Compare and Contrast Question (CM) – Sample Essay 4

Read the topic below and then make any notes that will help you plan your response. Begin typing your response in the box at the bottom of the screen, or write your answer on the answer sheet provided to you.

Imagine that the government intends to build a new university. Would your town be a good place to build the university? Why, or why not? Compare the advantages with the disadvantages of having a new university in your town. Use specific examples and reasons to explain your answer.

Most people think of "college towns" as charming places to live. Colleges and universities bring certain benefits to their communities. Nonetheless, there are also drawbacks to the presence of a new local university. Here are several examples of such benefits and disadvantages.

First, a college brings educational opportunities to a community. Almost everyone in a community probably is eligible for some kind of instruction that the school provides. At the same time, however, a university attracts large amounts of traffic. The resulting congestion can make the community a less desirable place to live.

Second, a university may bring new cultural opportunities, such as concerts and art exhibitions, to a community. Most likely, however, the community already has many such opportunities already through media such as cable television. Thus, the added cultural advantages of a local university may be minimal.

Third, a university may polarize, or divide, a community as almost nothing else can. The students and faculty at a university may consider townspeople inferior and treat them with contempt. This is hardly a desirable situation. In that case, the community probably would have been a better place without the school.

For every apparent advantage, then, a university would appear to present a corresponding disadvantage. The community must decide whether the advantages outweigh the drawbacks.

Cut

Paste

Undo

LinguaForum

Time   ? Help   Answer Confirm   Next

WRITING

[Sample Questions]

1. There is a saying, "Not all knowledge is found in books." Compare and contrast knowledge acquired from books with knowledge acquired from experience. Which do you consider more important, and why?

2. Students at a university may choose to live in dormitories on campus, and in apartments in town. Compare the advantages of each plan. Which do you think is better? Use specific reasons to support your opinion.

3. Imagine that you have to move to another country. Do you think it is better to keep your own customs, or to adopt the new country's customs? Why? Compare these two options. Use specific examples and reasons to explain your answer.

Type 5: If Question (IF) – Sample Essay 5

Read the topic below and then make any notes that will help you plan your response.
Begin typing your response in the box at the bottom of the screen, or write your answer on the answer sheet provided to you.

If you could invent a new device or product, what would you invent? Use specific reasons and examples to explain why this product is important.

There is a need for a highly effective, yet non-addictive, pain reliever that can be administered by injection or by mouth. Extremely effective pain relievers exist already in the form of narcotics, but narcotics are highly addictive and therefore dangerous. If I could invent something new, then it probably would be a pain reliever that combines the effectiveness of narcotics with the non-addictive character of other, less powerful but safer pain relievers.

For centuries, the problem of pain control has preoccupied physicians. Although pain serves an important function by alerting us to problems within the body, pain nonetheless can do as much harm as the original condition that creates it. People can die of pain. If strong anti-pain medications are available, then most patients and doctors would wish to use them. Yet, the most powerful pain-killers present great dangers too, as explained above. Is pain relief worth the risk of addiction?

A safe, non-addictive, powerful pain reliever would resolve this dilemma. Patients with intense, chronic pain would be free of it at last. Narcotic addiction would cease to be a concern. Moreover, the company which developed such a pain reliever would both save humankind from a dreadful burden and earn profits almost beyond imagining.

In short, everyone would benefit from such a product. That is why an optimum pain reliever is one of the greatest inventions one can imagine.

| Cut |
| Paste |
| Undo |

Time   **LinguaForum**   ? Help   Answer Confirm   Next

[Sample Questions]

1. If you were given some land to use as you desire, then how would you use it? Use specific reasons and examples to support your view.
2. Imagine that you could make one big change in a school that you attended. What would that change be? Use specific reasons and examples to support your view.
3. People observe holidays to honor certain events or persons. Imagine you could invent a new holiday. Which event or person would it honor, and how would you like to have people observe the holiday? Use specific reasons to explain your answer.

(3) Think of examples and conclusion. Choose two or three examples that support your thesis. Devote a paragraph to each one. Make your reasons specific! A reason such as "I oppose building a new university in our community because it will lead to overcrowding" is clear and specific. By contrast, a reason such as "I oppose the university because it is a bad idea" is neither clear nor specific. After you have listed your examples, state your conclusion in the last paragraph. Writing a conclusion is easy. Simply rephrase what you wrote in the topic sentence. You may wish to precede the conclusion with a transitional expression such as *Therefore, Thus, or For this reason ...*

(4) Write an outline. Compose a brief outline using all of the above elements. The outline will guide you as you write. Make sure you delete the original outline before you submit the finished essay!

(5) Allocate your time. You have only 30 minutes for the whole essay. In practice, you will have only 3 to 4 minutes for each paragraph. So, do not spend too much time on any one paragraph. Spending a lot of time on an early paragraph will leave you too little time to complete the rest of the essay. If you are dissatisfied with an early paragraph, leave it and finish the remaining paragraphs. Then, if you have time later, go back and look at that early paragraph again.

Remember

Time is important!

Now you are ready to write the essay. Once you have a strong thesis, specific examples, and a good outline, the essay should be easy to finish.

3. How to Write Clearly

The TOEFL essay involves more, however, than just *organization*. It also involves *style* – the way you *choose and use words*.

Your style should as clear and direct as possible. Several simple rules will help you write clearly and effectively:

(1) Keep sentences short. Try to make sentences no longer than 10 or 12 words. In 10 words, you can say almost anything. Also, a short sentence is easier for you to write – and for the grader to read – than a long sentence. Look at the following examples:

> We cannot ignore history.

> It is inadvisable for any individual or group in our time to refuse to acknowledge the influence of past events on present circumstances.

Both sentences have the same meaning. Which is clearer? The first sentence is better, of course. A short, clear sentence is always better than a long, awkward sentence!

This same principle applies to vocabulary. Never use a long word if you can use a short word instead. Here are pairs of long and short words with identical meanings:

Short	Long
sure	indubitable
extra	superfluous
thought	ratiocination
pay	remuneration

Short, simple words are easier to understand. Use them whenever possible!

(2) Keep adjectives to a minimum. In English, adjectives are "heavy" words. They slow down writing and reading. So use them sparingly on your TOEFL essay!
Adjectives in your writing are like fat on your body. A little fat is needed, but not much. Likewise, your essay needs only a few adjectives.

For example, look at the following sentences:

We must act now.

It is debatable whether careful consideration of the current situation will lead to the justifiable conclusion that it deserves indefinite continuation.

Adjectives make that second sentence heavy and hard to understand. By contrast, the first sentence has no adjectives at all. That is why it is so clear. Write the same way!
This does not mean you should avoid all adjectives. Sometimes adjectives are necessary: the *White* House, the *Grand* Canyon, the *binomial* theorem. As a rule, however, the fewer adjectives, the better.

(3) Use the active voice, not the passive voice. In other words, use verbs in active form wherever possible. The active voice is stronger and clearer. It is easier to write and read. It also saves words. Contrast these two sentences:

I mailed a letter. (active)

A letter was mailed by me. (passive)

The active form is clearer, stronger, and shorter. Whenever you can, use the active form instead of the passive form.

Of course, these three rules do not always apply. Sometimes you must use adjectives or the passive voice. Some sentences must be long. Most of the time, however, you will do best with short sentences, few adjectives, and active verbs.

4. Essay Structure

Your essay should have three parts: *thesis, development, and conclusion.* Each part has its own requirements:

(1) Thesis. This is the idea you wish to present. It should occur in the first paragraph, in a topic sentence. The *topic sentence* is usually the last sentence of the first paragraph.

(2) Development. Here, you present information to support your thesis. This is the "body," or middle section, of the essay. Present your arguments and examples one at a time. To begin paragraphs in this section, use "transitional" expressions such as *also, of course,* and *moreover* for a smooth flow of ideas.

(3) Conclusion. This is what you want the reader to remember. The conclusion usually restates the thesis. You may wish to begin this final paragraph with a transitional expression such as *finally, in summary,* or *in conclusion.*

Here is a sample essay to illustrate.

Type 3: Explain Reasons, Causes, or Results Question (EX)

Which custom from your country do you think people in other countries should adopt? Select a custom, and use specific examples and reasons to explain your answer.

It is hard to apply one country's customs to another. Customs from Malaysia or Nepal, for example, would be out of place in Korea. Korean eating customs, however, have many benefits, and I think other countries should adopt them.

To begin with, Koreans eat lots of fresh fruit and vegetables. This kind of diet is healthy. Koreans also eat much less red meat than Westerners do. A diet relatively low in meat cuts fat intake and makes a person feel better.

Also, portion sizes in Korea tend to be small, so one eats less at a single sitting. Small portions discourage overeating – another benefit to health.

Even Korean eating utensils, I believe, are superior. One can use them easily at meals and clean them easily afterward.

In conclusion, Western foods and eating habits dominate much of the world, but I think it is time for a change. People would feel better and enjoy better health if they adopted Korean eating customs.

WRITING

[Explanation]

(1) The first paragraph contains the topic sentence, highlighted here in shaded text:

It is hard to apply one country's customs to another. Customs from Malaysia or Nepal, for example, would be out of place in Korea. Korean eating customs, however, have many benefits, and I think other countries should adopt them.

Look at that thesis carefully. Korean eating customs have many benefits. That is a strong thesis. Always make your thesis strong! Make a definite statement! Otherwise, you cannot support your thesis.

(2) Next, the development begins in the second paragraph. Note the transitional expression, highlighted in shaded text:

To begin with, Koreans eat lots of fresh fruit and vegetables. This kind of diet is healthy. Koreans also eat much less red meat than Westerners do. A diet relatively low in meat cuts fat intake and makes a person feel better.

(3) Another transitional expression introduces the third paragraph:

Also, portion sizes in Korea tend to be small, so one eats less at a single sitting. Small portions discourage overeating – another benefit to health.

(4) This essay uses a third example to support the thesis. Note how starting the paragraph with *even* adds emphasis:

Even Korean eating utensils, I believe, are superior. One can use them easily at meals and clean them easily afterward.

(5) Now, the conclusion, with another transitional expression for smooth flow:

In conclusion, Western foods and eating habits dominate much of the world, but I think it is time for a change. People would feel better and enjoy better health if they adopted Korean eating customs.

Also, the last paragraph restates the thesis from the first paragraph (Korean eating customs, however, have many benefits, and I think other countries should adopt them):

People would feel better and enjoy better health if they adopted Korean eating customs.

Observe how this essay follows the rules of writing mentioned earlier:

1. Most sentences are short.
2. Vocabulary is simple.
3. Adjectives are few, and active verbs predominate.

Follow those rules when writing your TOEFL essay, and your essay will make easier reading.

5. Summary of Transitional Expressions

An essay requires coherence, or a smooth flow of ideas from one sentence or paragraph to another. To provide coherence, use transitional expressions to show how one idea in your essay is related to the next idea. Transitional expressions make your argument easier to follow and your essay easier to read.

Examples of Transitional Expressions		
To Express Conclusion	At last	In summary
	Finally	To sum up
	Eventually	In closing
	In the end	In short
	In conclusion	In brief
	To conclude	Conclusively

To Express Negation or Opposition	Although	On the contrary
	Dissimilarly	On the other hand
	However	Otherwise
	In contrast	Unlike
	Nevertheless	While
To Show Support or Examples	As follows	In this instance
	A is an example of B	To give a specific example
	For example	To illustrate
	For instance	
To Show Additional Support or Examples	Another example is	In addition
	Another reason is that	Moreover
	Furthermore	
To Express Agreement or Similarity	Similar to	Likewise
	Similarly	Correspond to
	Like	Correspondingly
To Show Result or Consequence	As a result	For this reason
	Because	Hence
	Because of	So
	Consequently	Therefore
	Due to	Thus
To Express Personal Opinion	From my point of view	It seems that
	In my opinion	Personally
	In my view	I think
To Show Generality	Generally	In general
	Generally speaking	On the whole
To Show Explanation or Restatement	In other words	To explain
	To clarify	To paraphrase

6. A Few Suggestions

(1) Do not write too little – or too much. An overly long essay is as bad as an incomplete essay! Aim for a length of 250 to 300 words.

(2) Avoid contractions and slang. This is a formal essay, not everyday speech! Use "it is" instead of "it's," and standard English instead of slang expressions.

(3) Stick to the subject. Do not digress onto other topics!

When your essay is finished, reread it. Here is a checklist to follow:

1. Is the thesis clear and strong, and did you stick to it?
2. Are reasons and examples specific?

3. Did you keep sentences short, use the active voice, and avoid excessive use of adjectives?
4. Did you avoid using slang and contractions?
5. Did you use transitional expressions and write a clear conclusion?
6. Is the length appropriate?
7. Did you check for errors in spelling, punctuation, and grammar?

If the answer in all cases is yes, then you probably have a good essay!

7. Essay Ratings

Score 6: An essay at this level
- effectively addresses the writing task
- is well organized and well developed
- uses clearly appropriate details to support a thesis or illustrate ideas
- displays consistent facility in the use of language
- demonstrates syntactic variety and appropriate word choice

Score 5: An essay at this level
- may address some parts of the task more effectively than others
- is generally well organized and developed
- uses details to support a thesis or illustrate an idea
- displays facility in the use of language
- demonstrates some syntactic variety and range of vocabulary, though it will probably have occasional errors

Score 4: An essay at this level
- addresses the writing topic adequately but may slight parts of the task
- is adequately organized and developed
- uses some details to support a thesis or illustrate an idea
- displays adequate but possibly inconsistent facility with syntax and usage
- may contain some errors that occasionally obscure meaning

Score 3: An essay at this level may reveal one or more of the following weaknesses:
- inadequate organization or development
- inappropriate or insufficient details to support or illustrate generalizations
- a noticeably inappropriate choice of words or word forms
- an accumulation of errors in sentence structure and/or usage

Score 2: An essay at this level is seriously flawed by one or more of the following weaknesses:
- serious disorganization or underdevelopment
- little or no detail, or irrelevant specifics
- serious and frequent errors in sentence structure or usage
- serious problems with focus

Score 1: An essay at this level
- may be incoherent
- may be undeveloped
- may contain severe and persistent writing errors

Score 0: An essay will be rated 0 if it
- contains no response
- merely copies the topic
- is off-topic, is written in a foreign language, or consists only of keystroke characters

8. Practice Scoring Writing Essays

The essays below have been written by TOEFL test-takers and scored using the ETS Writing criteria. You will find that these essays contain many errors commonly committed by students when they write essays. The essays have been scored using ETS Writing criteria, and there are 11 essay topics included for each score, 1-6. Also, they are presented in order of their score. All essay samples in the next 11 pages were written as answers to different prompts below. They are as follows:

1. Imagine that there is a plan to build a new motion picture theater in your community. Do you favor or oppose this plan? Why? Use specific examples and reasons to support your opinion.

2. Some people prefer to prepare and eat meals at home. Other people would rather eat at a food stand or restaurant. Which place do you think is better? Use specific examples and reasons to explain your answer.

3. Imagine that there is a plan to build a big shopping center in your community. Do you favor or oppose this plan? Why? Use specific examples and reasons to support your opinion.

4. Should children spend most of their time at play, or should they start going to school as early as possible? Compare these two views. Which do you support, and why? Use specific examples and reasons to explain your answer.

5. The world changed greatly in the 20th century. What do you consider one important change that occurred in the 20th century? Use specific reasons and examples to explain your opinion.

6. Which kind of friend do you prefer: someone who is much like you, or someone who is different from you? Why? Compare the advantages of having these two kinds of friends.

7. Why do you think many students choose to attend schools or universities abroad, outside their own countries? Use specific examples and reasons to explain your opinion.

8. People observe holidays to honor certain events or persons. Imagine you could invent a new holiday. Which event or person would it honor, and how would you like to have people observe the holiday? Use specific reasons to explain your answer.

9. There are many ways to relieve stress. Some people read, others do exercises, and still others work around their homes. Which way would you prefer to relieve stress? Use specific examples and reasons to explain your answer.

10. Some people think attending live performances (of concerts, plays, football games, et cetera) is better than watching those events on television. Do you agree or disagree with that view? Use specific examples and reasons to explain your answer.

11. A gift such as sports equipment or a musical instrument can help a child develop. Which gift would you give a child to help him or her develop? Why? Use specific reasons and examples to support your view.

Score 1.0 – Essay A

Imagine that there is a plan to build a new motion picture theater in your community. Do you favor or oppose this plan? Why? Use specific examples and reasons to support your opinion.

I oppose that plan.
I don't watch movie often, so a new theater in my neighborhood doesn't give me any benefit. And whenever I want to watch it, I can go to the downtown.
Also, Some could say a theater doesn't provide any harm, like noise, unlike a night club, football stadium, but it does provide crowd especially at weekends. I don't want to be blocked by crowd while I'm walking even in my neighborhood. and that is one of the reason why people avoid to live in the downtown.

(handwritten annotations: do not, s, a movie, would not, Also, may, does not, or, living, s, on, do not, s, bothered)

This essay is much too short and is poorly organized. The only way to improve your score is to practice writing complete sentences and paragraphs. Then you will be ready to review the rules of essay structure and practice writing essays. Also, please remember that each new sentence must begin with a capital letter, and that you should avoid using contractions such as "don't" and "I'm" in a formal essay. With practice, I think, you can improve your score.

Score 1.5 – Essay B

Some people prefer to prepare and eat meals at home. Other people would rather eat at a food stand or restaurant. Which place do you think is better? Use specific examples and reasons to explain your answer.

Today time is called "time is money," because people live very busy. at restaurant or home, it spends time much to prepare food. we can another work during preparing it.

in addition, we can see many street deliciouse food stalls and fast food lots of kinds anywhere. but some people can say "the reason of making money is for eating food." Of course, eating is important to live however we have much more important things than eating such as investing ourself, meeting someone in business and necessary studing.

we can often hear from succeed people that we don't have time to eat for working. the time cooking

(There are so many errors that it is impossible to correct them all.)

This essay is too short and is incoherent. It is impossible to tell what you mean to say. Please review the basics of sentence structure, and then practice writing short, simple, correct sentences. Also, please be careful of spelling and remember that every sentence should begin with a capital letter and end with a period. You can improve your score with practice, but much work will be required.

Score 2.0 – Essay C

Imagine that there is a plan to build a big shopping center in your community. Do you favor or oppose this plan? Why? Use specific examples and reasons to support your opinion

It's sensational issue wether a large shopping center may be built in my village. And there are some merits and damage. But I'd like to stand in supprting line because of some reasons.

First of all, It will help my houses value to increase and more sophisticaed atmosphere near my house to establish. I can sell my house more expensive, moreover, my villiage become a centre of the city, so my local communities get wealth. To build a shopping centre is a way of making local econmy vivid.

Another reason is that I can use many center's facilities. And shopping centre offers useful various classes like cooking and violin classes for local people. Thesedays, a shopping centre is not only shopping space but also cultural place.

But there are problems like jams and noise. Maybe I can't take a rest in my house

Handwritten corrections (circled): It is a / (h) / or not / the / (A) / demerits / in / I would / o / for several / establish a / will / for a higher price; / Also, a / can / the / thrive / live / and varied / traffic / a / e / cannot / (?)

Handwritten note:

This essay received a low score because it is incomplete, contains many errors in spelling, and has awkward sentence structure and inappropriate vocabulary.
The only way to improve your score is to review the basics of sentence structure and practice writing simple, clear, correct sentences. When you can do that, you will be ready to practice writing essays.
Please continue practicing.

LinguaForum

Score 2.5 – Essay D

Should children spend most of their time at play, or should they start going to school as early as possible? Compare these two views. Which do you support, and why? Use specific examples and reasons to explain your answer.

A representative institute for early formal education is kindergardens. Youngsteres can learn basic knowledges such as letters and words as well as song and drawing and so on. What is the most valuable thing to learn at kindergarden is to learn the order of community, that is, homoneous communications. Owing to the mediation of teacher, children learn how to consider other people without severe fights.

Children learn to adapt theirselves to society by individual ways, that is, their parents can teach them basic knowledges and rules and they can learn community when they play other children freely. But this way can be not enoughly effective because it is irregular and many parts should be teached are frequently omitted.

Studying and playing are both important to growth of children and they should be done homoneouly. For this purpose, I think formal education is better than individual one because the former is systematic.

[Handwritten annotations around the essay: "harmonious?", "ion", "t", "singing", "t", "the", "respect", "themselves", "in", ";", "5", "rules", "with", "things", "that", "taught", "the", "Nonetheless,", "the", "kind,", "harmoniously?"]

[Handwritten comment:] This essay is unsuccessful for several reasons. It is too short. It does not have a clear thesis, and it does not address the prompt adequately. There are serious misspellings, such as "homoneous." (Did you mean to write "harmonious"?) Much of the vocabulary is poorly chosen, and certain words are without meaning as used. Sentence structure is awkward, and there is confusion about the use of singular versus plural nouns. Please review sentence structure and practice writing simple, complete sentences.

WRITING

Score 3.0 – Essay E

The world changed greatly in the 20th century. What do you consider one important change that occurred in the 20th century? Use specific reasons and examples to explain your opinion.

Before twenties century, we spend many time to find information or to send a letter. However, since twenties century, internet has changed all parts of our life. I think using the internet is the greatest change in the twentieth century because we can find information through this method and communicate with forein friends easily.

Firstly, we can get information on the internet. Only before twenties century, we needed a lot of times to find information. However, now, If we want to find information for a report, we can find them through the internet for short time. The Internet have enormous information, so we can get information easily.

Secondly, we can communicate with our abroad friends very easy. We can send a e-mail to England or America and receive the answer at the same time.

In conclusion, I strongly believe the internet is the greatest change in the twentieth century. Through this method we can find information and communicate with abroad friends easily.

It appears that you understand the basics of essay structure. That is a good beginning. Now, please concentrate on improving spelling, and review the use of the definite and indefinite articles. Also, the essay should have been slightly longer. Next time, please try to write 75 to 100 words more.

Score 3.5 – Essay F

Which kind of friend do you prefer: someone who is much like you, or someone who is different from you? Why? Compare the advantages of having these two kinds of friends.

Some people like spend time with friends who are different from themselves, whereas others prefer being with friends who are similar to themselves. Each type of friends have its own advantages. In this essay I will campare adavantages of those two types of friends.

First of all, friends having different characteristics may show me different aspects of life. By watching their reactions about a single event, my narrow eyesight might be broaden and sometimes the event can give me a lesson of life. Being embarrased or having tons of works to do, I often make things mass up, because I am not good at organizing events. On the contrary, my roommate is very good at doing so. I am learning how to organizing things, taking my time, by looking over her. On the other hand, she is too different from myself, when we are together, usually I can find what to do with her.

Secondly, I can find many things to do with my friends who is much like me. Because my friend and I have same interests and characteristics, we can easily find how we will spend time together. Since my friend, Jina, like me is crazy about outside activities, we play tennis and take a trip frequently. It is very lucky of me that I have friends have same interests. Also, it is fun of us to talk about movies, sports events, and trips what we had done together.

In conclusion, as I mentioned above, having each type friends is advantageous. However, I pursue being friend with someone who are similar to myself, Because the advatages of those friends outweigh the advantages from people who are different from myself.

This essay is a good effort. Please be careful of subject-verb agreement and of spelling; in paragraph 2, for example, "mass" should be "mess". Also, make sure that every sentence is a complete sentence; "Because ... myself" in paragraph 4 should be joined to the preceding sentence. Please keep practicing.

Score 4.0 – Essay G

Why do you think many students choose to attend schools or universities abroad, outside their own countries? Use specific examples and reasons to explain your opinion.

Many students go outside their home countries to study abroad. I also know the person who goes abroad to attend graduate school. The reasons of the international study, I think, are as follows.

First, the education for the expert is more developed in the U.S, Canada, or European countries than other ones in the world. As long as I know, for example, U.S is the most prominent in the electrical and computer engineering field, and Canada is the best in the environmental engineering field. Also, Arts and cultures can be well educated in the several European countries. People who want to study more extensively in these fields are trying to go to these countries and to study harder.

Second, I think relatively bad educational environment in our country is another reason of going abroad. The educational system in our country is out-dated, inefficient, and unreasonal. In this country, for example, the relation of a professor and his students is the same as that of a master and slaves. It seems to give the opportunity of good education only to the person who are tolerant to this unreasonal education system. Thus, the study in a foreign country, which has more reasonable education systerm, is very attractive to people who are not satisfied with this master and slave relationship.

Finally, reasons of international study are the desire for more expert study and better educational environment. It will be very difficult to study abroad due to language problems, strange cultures and racial differentiation. However, people go abroad to satisfy their desire for study.

This essay is a good beginning. Now, please be careful of spelling, and review the correct use of articles, especially the indefinite article.

Score 4.5 – Essay H

People observe holidays to honor certain events or persons. Imagine you could invent a new holiday. Which event or person would it honor, and how would you like to have people observe the holiday? Use specific reasons to explain your answer.

I would like to honor the people who have died on the terrible accident on the 11th of September, 2001. Hence I would like to make a day to honor those who have been killed by the terrorists.

The date of this holiday would be the same day each year, September the 11th, as it was such an horrible memory to many. People or the families involved in this tragedy would take a day off to remember those who lost their lives, And for those who have seen this tragedy on the television or seen it on the radio to thank God for their ongoing lives and pray for the souls who were in that attack.

This day would have numerous purposes other than just remembering the dead. It will be the day to teach our children and youths the consequences of the hatred and stupidity that is present in this world. This memorial day will not only be an American holiday, but also a day for the world to take a moment to think what the life is worth.

This day shouldn't be just a day off from the school or from the work. It was a shocking disaster, which taught us that no men is safe from the terrorism, and for that result, we have lost many loved ones. So It also should be the day to check our attitude towards the evil in this world.

The 11th of September has many different meanings to each person that will be the most important reason to set this date as an international memorial day. Each year, there should be a day for us to cry and moan for the dead, we should not wash away that horrible and sad, but the memory somewhat needed for our awareness. Responsibilities to teach and stop the evil things are ours, so to start, the 11th of September should be set as an holiday.

Here are two suggestions for future essays. Please avoid writing run-on sentences; each complete sentence should be separate. Also, avoid starting sentences with conjunctions such as "And".

WRITING

Score 5.0 – Essay I

There are many ways to relieve stress. Some people read, others do exercises, and still others work around their homes. Which way would you prefer to relieve stress? Use specific examples and reasons to explain your answer.

There are many different ways in which people escape stress and difficulties. Some people excercise; some read; others work in their gardens. The best ways to escape from too much stress are to sleep, meet friends, and eat. In the following paragraphs I will support my opinion.

First, one good way of escaping the stress and difficulties is to sleep. In many cases, people get a lot of stress for not having much time to sleep. Since they are very tired of not having much time to sleep, they cannot do works efficiently and make many problems. Therefore, sleeping is a great way to reduce stress.

Second, meeting friends is also a good way to escape from too much stress. Since they are of the same age as one, they are the ones who understand one best. They can give the person a piece of pratical advice. Moreover, there are many more things to do with friends. For example, one can play sports such as basketball, soccer and so on.

Finally, one can reduce stress by eating nutrient food. Eating nutrient food will obviously make one healthy. When one works or studies too much, one's health will deteriorate. Having a bad health will surely make one tired even more.

There are many ways to reduce stress, such as watching television and playing computer games. On the other hand, these have many side-effects. For instance, doing so makes one even more tired. I think meeting friends, eating, and sleeping are the paramount ways to escape from too much stress for they have many benefits as I have stated above.

[Handwritten annotations throughout the essay: "from", "from", "excessive", "mistakes", "nutritious", "nutritious", "However", "performing them", "excessive", "the reasons"]

[Handwritten comment at bottom:]

This essay is a very good effort. Please remember, however, the difference between countable nouns and non-countable nouns. In paragraph 4, for example, "a bad health" should be "bad health," because "health" is a non-countable noun. Also, please remember the difference between nouns and adjectives; in paragraph 4, "nutrient" (noun) should be "nutritious" (adjective).

Score 5.5 – Essay J

Some people think attending live performances (of concerts, plays, football games, et cetera) is better than watching those events on television. Do you agree or disagree with that view? Use specific examples and reasons to explain your answer.

Everybody likes to be entertained and so do I. People go to concerts, sport games, and movies to have fun and to get entertained. Even though one watches the same event, sitting at home and watching it on TV is less exciting, because usually people don't get excited easily if they are sitting at home. Therefore, attending a live performance is more enjoyable than watching the same event on television.

For example, June was a crazy month for the Koreans because Korea hosted the 2002 FIFA World Cup, and their team played better than ever before. Before the World Cup, I preferred to just stay at home and watch the events on TV, because I thought it was less tiring and it had a better view. However, during the World Cup, my attitude totally changed. I could not just sit at home and watch the games on TV. I had to get up and go out on the streets and cheer, even if I was not able to get a good view. After that, I realized that attending a live performance is more enjoyable than watching the same event of television, because one could cheer with other people.

Also, I once went to a live concert and had a great time screaming and dancing along with other people. It was such a wonderful time and I even bought the concert video tape. However, watching it at home, sitting on the couch, was nowhere near the excitement I had at the concert. At the concert, the sound effect had a higher quality, but at home, the music did not sound good.

In conclusion, I agree that attending a live performance is more enjoyable than watching the same event on television, because it is more exiting when watching it with a whole bunch of other people and cheering along with them. Also, at a live concert, one can get a higher sound effect.

Congratulations: this is one of the best essays that I have seen submitted. Please make sure that spelling is consistent. Also, be careful of words with similar spellings but different meanings; "exiting," in paragraph 4, is a completely different word from "exciting."

Score 6.0 – Essay K

A gift such as sports equipment or a musical instrument can help a child develop. Which gift would you give a child to help him or her develop? Why? Use specific reasons and examples to support your view.

To help a child develop, the most useful gift is probably a book. Literacy is one of the best investments one can make in children, because it yields many benefits in later years. Three benefits in particular come to mind.

One benefit is an overall advantage in one's career. A literate child is likely to be a successful student and therefore to be, in general, a success later in life. This is because education rests on literacy. Success, in turn, depends largely on education. That is the first reason why books are good gifts for children.

The second benefit is the satisfaction that comes with access to a world of learning. A literate person makes the acquaintance of countless authors, from poets like Chaucer to essayists like Samuel Johnson, who have much useful advice for readers in our time. Someone who becomes fond of reading at an early age will have hundreds of distinguished authors for friends and companions throughout life. That is a tremendous benefit.

Third is the benefit of civilization. Here, "civilization" means respect for law, private property, and individual rights within the structure of an ordered society. Civilization, thus defined, is inseparable from literacy. It is worth noting that the most civilized societies, such as Korea and Japan, are also the most literate societies. Less literate societies, by contrast, are less civilized: that is, more violent and lawless. Encouraging literacy in children, then, also prepares them to join and contribute to civilized society.

Of course, the gift of a book does not by itself guarantee a child happiness and success later in life. Nonetheless, it helps direct a child toward literacy and the many benefits that literacy provides. A toy given to a child may be forgotten within days, but books may influence that child for a lifetime.

9. Writing Topics

Below is a list of topics that may appear on the actual test. Before the test, you may wish to become familiar with these topics. On the actual test, you will be assigned a single topic. You must write about the topic, and no other. All of the following essay topics may appear on the actual TOEFL test. They cover a variety of 5 essay types (*Agree or Disagree, Prefer, Explain, Compare and Contrast, If*). These essay topics can be done in class or as a homework assignment, but they should always be practiced within a 30-minute time allotment.

Category

Type 1	**Agree or Disagree** Question **(AD)**
Type 2	**Choose and Defend a Point of View** Question **(PR)**
Type 3	**Explain Reasons, Causes, or Results** Question **(EX)**
Type 4	**Compare and Contrast** Question **(CM)**
Type 5	**If** Question **(IF)**

No.	A List of Essay Topics	Category
1	How do television and motion pictures affect our behavior? Use specific examples and reasons to support your answer.	**Type 3 (EX)**
2	Some people say television has left family members unable to communicate with one another. Do you agree or disagree with that statement? Use specific examples and reasons to explain your opinion.	**Type 1 (AD)**
3	Some people prefer to live in big cities, whereas other people enjoy living in small towns. In which place would you prefer to live? Use specific examples and reasons to explain your answer.	**Type 2 (PR)**
4	Universities should provide as much money for sports programs as for their libraries. Do you agree or disagree with that view? Use specific examples and reasons to explain your answer.	**Type 1 (AD)**
5	Some people prefer to prepare and eat meals at home. Other people would rather eat at a food stand or restaurant. Which place do you think is better? Use specific examples and reasons to explain your answer.	**Type 2 (PR)**
6	Neighbors are the people who live closest to us. What are the qualities that you think make a person a good neighbor? Use specific examples and reasons to explain your answer.	**Type 3 (EX)**
7	The country is a better place for children to grow up than a large city is. Do you agree or disagree with that statement? Use specific examples and reasons to explain your answer.	**Type 1 (AD)**
8	On the job, we work with various kinds of people. These people are our co-workers. What do you think are good qualities for a co-worker to have? Use specific examples and reasons to explain your answer.	**Type 3 (EX)**

WRITING

No.	A List of Essay Topics	Category
9	Imagine that there is a plan to build a big shopping center in your community. Do you favor or oppose this plan? Why? Use specific examples and reasons to support your opinion.	Type 1 (AD)
10	Imagine that there is a plan to build a new motion picture theater in your community. Do you favor or oppose this plan? Why? Use specific examples and reasons to support your opinion.	Type 1 (AD)
11	Imagine that someone has given you some money as a gift. With the money, you could either buy an attractive piece of jewelry or go to a concert. Which do you think is a better use of the money? Use specific examples and reasons to support your opinion.	Type 2 (PR)
12	Employees of businesses should be hired for their whole lives when they get jobs. Do you think that policy is justified, or not? Use specific examples and reasons to support your opinion.	Type 1 (AD)
13	Some people think attending live performances (of concerts, plays, football games, et cetera) is better than watching those events on television. Do you agree or disagree with that view? Use specific examples and reasons to explain your answer.	Type 1 (AD)
14	Some people think governments should spend large amounts of money to explore outer space. Other people think that this money should be used to improve life on Earth instead. Which view do you support? Use specific examples and reasons to explain your answer.	Type 2 (PR)
15	There are many ways to relieve stress. Some people read, others do exercises, and still others work around their homes. Which way would you prefer to relieve stress? Use specific examples and reasons to explain your answer.	Type 2 (PR)
16	Teachers' pay should depend on how successfully their students learn. Do you agree with that view, or not? Use specific examples and reasons to explain your answer.	Type 1 (AD)
17	Some people prefer doing work with machines, whereas other people prefer working with their hands. Which do you think is better? Use specific examples and reasons to explain your answer.	Type 2 (PR)
18	Imagine that you must travel 40 miles (64 km) from your home to another place. Which kinds of transportation could you use, and which would you select? Use specific examples and reasons to explain your answer.	Type 2 (PR)
19	Is it better to learn about life through your own experience, or through advice from friends and family? Use specific examples and reasons to explain your answer.	Type 2 (PR)
20	Some people prefer to spend most of their time with friends. Other people prefer to be alone most of the time. Which way of life do you prefer? Use specific reasons to support your answer.	Type 2 (PR)

No.	A List of Essay Topics	Category
21	Which kind of friend do you prefer: someone who is much like you, or someone who is different from you? Why? Compare the advantages of having these two kinds of friends.	**Type 4 (CM)**
22	People behave in different ways when they wear different clothes. Do you agree or disagree with that viewpoint? Why? Use specific examples and reasons to explain your answer.	**Type 1 (AD)**
23	One can make decisions quickly, or after thinking long and carefully. Some people say it is always wrong to make a decision quickly. Do you agree or disagree with that view? Use specific examples and reasons to support your answer.	**Type 1 (AD)**
24	"People always want more than what they have already, or something new and different. They are never satisfied with what they have already." Do you agree with this statement, or not? Why? Use specific examples and reasons to explain your answer.	**Type 1 (AD)**
25	We should read only books that are about actual persons and events, or proven facts. Do you agree or disagree with that view? Why? Use specific examples and reasons to explain your answer.	**Type 1 (AD)**
26	Literature and history are more important subjects for students than mathematics and science. Do you agree or disagree with that view? Why? Use specific examples and reasons to explain your answer.	**Type 1 (AD)**
27	Some people think students should spend the whole day at school on their studies. Other people think physical exercise should be required for part of each school day. Which view do you favor? Use specific reasons and examples to support your view.	**Type 2 (PR)**
28	Childhood, or the period between birth and age 12, is the most important part of an individual's life. Do you agree or disagree? Use specific reasons and examples to support your view.	**Type 1 (AD)**
29	High schools should let students choose the subjects that they want to study. Do you agree or disagree? Use specific reasons and examples to support your view.	**Type 1 (AD)**
30	A gift such as sports equipment or a musical instrument can help a child develop. Which gift would you give a child to help him or her develop? Why? Use specific reasons and examples to support your view.	**Type 3 (EX)**
31	We learn much about life by playing games. Do you agree or disagree with that statement? Use specific reasons and details to explain your answer.	**Type 1 (AD)**
32	A zoo serves no practical purpose. Do you agree or disagree with that statement? Use specific reasons and examples to support your view.	**Type 1 (AD)**

WRITING

No.	A List of Essay Topics	Category
33	Some countries have banned smoking in public places and office buildings. What is your point of view regarding that policy? Use specific reasons and examples to explain your opinion.	Type 3 (EX)
34	Would you prefer to study at a traditional school, or at home, using computers and television to make your home a "classroom"? Use specific reasons and examples to explain your opinion.	Type 2 (PR)
35	The world changed greatly in the 20th century. What do you consider one important change that occurred in the 20th century? Use specific reasons and examples to explain your opinion.	Type 3 (EX)
36	People who receive special gifts remember them long afterward. Why? Use specific examples and reasons to explain your opinion.	Type 3 (EX)
37	Why do you think many students choose to attend schools or universities abroad, outside their own countries? Use specific examples and reasons to explain your opinion.	Type 3 (EX)
38	Some people believe that it harms a friendship when one borrows money from a friend. Do you agree or disagree with this opinion? Why? Use specific reasons and details to support your view.	Type 1 (AD)
39	People observe holidays to honor certain events or persons. Imagine you could invent a new holiday. Which event or person would it honor, and how would you like to have people observe the holiday? Use specific reasons to explain your answer.	Type 5 (IF)
40	Imagine that a friend of yours has been given a sum of money and plans to spend it all either to buy an automobile, or to take a vacation. If your friend asked you for advice, what would you say? Compare these two options and explain which one you think is better for your friend. Use specific examples and reasons to explain your opinion.	Type 4 (CM)
41	In your opinion, what are some qualities needed to be a good parent? Use specific examples and reasons to explain your opinion.	Type 3 (EX)
42	Which do you think would be the better policy in your country: to develop land for houses and business, or to leave the land undeveloped and natural? Use specific reasons to explain your opinion.	Type 2 (PR)
43	Some people are very fond of their pets and treat their pets almost as family members. Do you approve or disapprove of this kind of relationship with pets? Why? Use specific examples and reasons to explain your opinion.	Type 3 (EX)
44	Motion pictures reveal much about the countries where they were made. What can you learn about a country by watching its motion pictures? Use specific examples to explain your answer.	Type 3 (EX)

No.	A List of Essay Topics	Category
45	Do you prefer to study alone, or as part of a group of students? Why? Use specific examples and reasons to explain your opinion.	**Type 2 (PR)**
46	If you had enough money to buy either a business or a home, which would you prefer to buy? Use specific reasons to explain your preference.	**Type 2 (PR)**
47	Courses in music and art should be required for students in high school. Do you agree or disagree with that idea? Use specific reasons and examples to support your view.	**Type 1 (AD)**
48	Imagine your have chosen to spends several hours each month doing something to benefit your community. What is one thing you would do, and why? Use specific examples and reasons to explain your view.	**Type 3 (EX)**
49	Is literacy, the ability to read and write, more important now than it used to be? Why, or why not? Use specific examples and reasons to explain your opinion.	**Type 3 (EX)**
50	Adults are treated differently from children. Which events, such as ceremonies or customs, make the difference between a child and an adult? Use specific examples and reasons to explain your view.	**Type 3 (EX)**
51	Imagine that you must be away from home for one year on travel. Besides clothing and other essential items, you can take one extra thing with you. What would that thing be? Why? Use specific examples and reasons to explain your choice.	**Type 5 (IF)**
52	Do you prefer classes where teachers do all the talking, or where students are allowed to speak too? Use specific examples and reasons to explain your opinion.	**Type 2 (PR)**

COMPLETE PRACTICE TEST 1

Listening: 60 Minutes (including listening time)
Structure: 15 Minutes
Reading: 70 Minutes
Writing: 30 Minutes

Suggested Total Time: 175 Minutes

ANSWER SHEET

Lingua TOEFL® CBT: Insider
PRACTICE TEST 1

Name		
Sex	☐ male	☐ female
E-mail address		
Telephone No.		

No. of Correct Answers/Converted Score		
Listening		
Structure		
Reading		
Writing		
TOTAL		

Section 1: Listening

1. Ⓐ Ⓑ Ⓒ Ⓓ
2. Ⓐ Ⓑ Ⓒ Ⓓ
3. Ⓐ Ⓑ Ⓒ Ⓓ
4. Ⓐ Ⓑ Ⓒ Ⓓ
5. Ⓐ Ⓑ Ⓒ Ⓓ
6. Ⓐ Ⓑ Ⓒ Ⓓ
7. Ⓐ Ⓑ Ⓒ Ⓓ
8. Ⓐ Ⓑ Ⓒ Ⓓ
9. Ⓐ Ⓑ Ⓒ Ⓓ
10. Ⓐ Ⓑ Ⓒ Ⓓ
11. Ⓐ Ⓑ Ⓒ Ⓓ
12. Ⓐ Ⓑ Ⓒ Ⓓ
13. Ⓐ Ⓑ Ⓒ Ⓓ
14. Ⓐ Ⓑ Ⓒ Ⓓ
15. Ⓐ Ⓑ Ⓒ Ⓓ
16. Ⓐ Ⓑ Ⓒ Ⓓ
17. Ⓐ Ⓑ Ⓒ Ⓓ
18. Ⓐ Ⓑ Ⓒ Ⓓ
19. Ⓐ Ⓑ Ⓒ Ⓓ
20. Ⓐ Ⓑ Ⓒ Ⓓ
21. Mercatorial map -
    T and O map -
    Accurate longitudes -
22. Ⓐ Ⓑ Ⓒ Ⓓ
23. Ⓐ Ⓑ Ⓒ Ⓓ
24. Ⓐ Ⓑ Ⓒ Ⓓ
25. Ⓐ Ⓑ Ⓒ Ⓓ
26. Ⓐ Ⓑ Ⓒ Ⓓ
27. Ⓐ Ⓑ Ⓒ Ⓓ
28. Ⓐ Ⓑ Ⓒ Ⓓ
29. Ⓐ Ⓑ Ⓒ Ⓓ
30.

31. Ⓐ Ⓑ Ⓒ Ⓓ
32. The portrait of a Lady -
    A Passionate Pilgrim -
    The Golden Bowl -
33. Ⓐ Ⓑ Ⓒ Ⓓ
34. Ⓐ Ⓑ Ⓒ Ⓓ
35. Ⓐ Ⓑ Ⓒ Ⓓ
36. Ⓐ Ⓑ Ⓒ Ⓓ
37. Ⓐ Ⓑ Ⓒ Ⓓ

38. Ⓐ Ⓑ Ⓒ Ⓓ
39. Ⓐ Ⓑ Ⓒ Ⓓ
40. Ⓐ Ⓑ Ⓒ Ⓓ
41. Ⓐ Ⓑ Ⓒ Ⓓ
42. Ⓐ Ⓑ Ⓒ Ⓓ
43. Ⓐ Ⓑ Ⓒ Ⓓ
44. Ⓐ Ⓑ Ⓒ Ⓓ
45. Ⓐ Ⓑ Ⓒ Ⓓ
46. Dr. James C. Jackson -
    Will K. Kellogg -
    Ferdinand Schumacher -
47. Ⓐ Ⓑ Ⓒ Ⓓ
48. Ⓐ Ⓑ Ⓒ Ⓓ
49. Ⓐ Ⓑ Ⓒ Ⓓ
50. Ⓐ Ⓑ Ⓒ Ⓓ

Section 2: Structure

1. Ⓐ Ⓑ Ⓒ Ⓓ
2. Ⓐ Ⓑ Ⓒ Ⓓ
3. Ⓐ Ⓑ Ⓒ Ⓓ
4. Ⓐ Ⓑ Ⓒ Ⓓ
5. Ⓐ Ⓑ Ⓒ Ⓓ
6. Ⓐ Ⓑ Ⓒ Ⓓ
7. Ⓐ Ⓑ Ⓒ Ⓓ
8. Ⓐ Ⓑ Ⓒ Ⓓ
9. Ⓐ Ⓑ Ⓒ Ⓓ
10. Ⓐ Ⓑ Ⓒ Ⓓ
11. Ⓐ Ⓑ Ⓒ Ⓓ
12. Ⓐ Ⓑ Ⓒ Ⓓ
13. Ⓐ Ⓑ Ⓒ Ⓓ
14. Ⓐ Ⓑ Ⓒ Ⓓ
15. Ⓐ Ⓑ Ⓒ Ⓓ
16. Ⓐ Ⓑ Ⓒ Ⓓ
17. Ⓐ Ⓑ Ⓒ Ⓓ
18. Ⓐ Ⓑ Ⓒ Ⓓ
19. Ⓐ Ⓑ Ⓒ Ⓓ
20. Ⓐ Ⓑ Ⓒ Ⓓ

Section 3: Reading

1. Ⓐ Ⓑ Ⓒ Ⓓ
2.
3. Ⓐ Ⓑ Ⓒ Ⓓ
4. Ⓐ Ⓑ Ⓒ Ⓓ
5.
6. Ⓐ Ⓑ Ⓒ Ⓓ
7.
8.
9. Ⓐ Ⓑ Ⓒ Ⓓ
10. Ⓐ Ⓑ Ⓒ Ⓓ
11. Ⓐ Ⓑ Ⓒ Ⓓ
12. Ⓐ Ⓑ Ⓒ Ⓓ
13. Ⓐ Ⓑ Ⓒ Ⓓ
14.
15.
16. Ⓐ Ⓑ Ⓒ Ⓓ
17. Ⓐ Ⓑ Ⓒ Ⓓ
18. Ⓐ Ⓑ Ⓒ Ⓓ
19. Ⓐ Ⓑ Ⓒ Ⓓ
20. Ⓐ Ⓑ Ⓒ Ⓓ
21. Ⓐ Ⓑ Ⓒ Ⓓ
22.
23. Ⓐ Ⓑ Ⓒ Ⓓ
24.
25. Ⓐ Ⓑ Ⓒ Ⓓ
26. Ⓐ Ⓑ Ⓒ Ⓓ
27.
28.
29. Ⓐ Ⓑ Ⓒ Ⓓ
30.

31.
32. Ⓐ Ⓑ Ⓒ Ⓓ
33. Ⓐ Ⓑ Ⓒ Ⓓ
34. Ⓐ Ⓑ Ⓒ Ⓓ
35.
36. Ⓐ Ⓑ Ⓒ Ⓓ
37.
38. Ⓐ Ⓑ Ⓒ Ⓓ
39.
40. Ⓐ Ⓑ Ⓒ Ⓓ
41.
42. Ⓐ Ⓑ Ⓒ Ⓓ
43. Ⓐ Ⓑ Ⓒ Ⓓ
44. Ⓐ Ⓑ Ⓒ Ⓓ

■ **Have you taken the official TOEFL Test?**

☐ Yes
☐ No   if any →

PBT Score	
Listening	
Structure	
Reading	
Writing	
TOTAL	

CBT Score	
Listening	
Structure	
Reading	
Writing	
TOTAL	

■ **Educational background**

☐ middle/high school ☐ undergraduate ☐ graduate

SIGNED: _____
(SIGN YOUR NAME AS IF SIGNING A BUSINESS LETTER.)

DATE: ___/___/___
MO.   DAY   YEAR

Cut here

LinguaForum

ANSWER SHEET

Lingua TOEFL® CBT: Insider
PRACTICE TEST 1

Read the topic below and then make any notes that will help you plan your response.
Begin typing your response in the box at the bottom of the screen, or write your answer on the answer sheet provided to you.

Imagine that a friend of yours has been given a sum of money and plans to spend it all either to buy an automobile, or to take a vacation. If your friend asked you for advice, what would you say? Compare these two options and explain which one you think is better for your friend. Use specific examples and reasons to explain your opinion.

Cut

Paste

Undo

Time

LinguaForum

? **Help** **Answer Confirm** ➡ **Next**

SECTION 1
LISTENING

Suggested Time: 60 Minutes (including listening time)

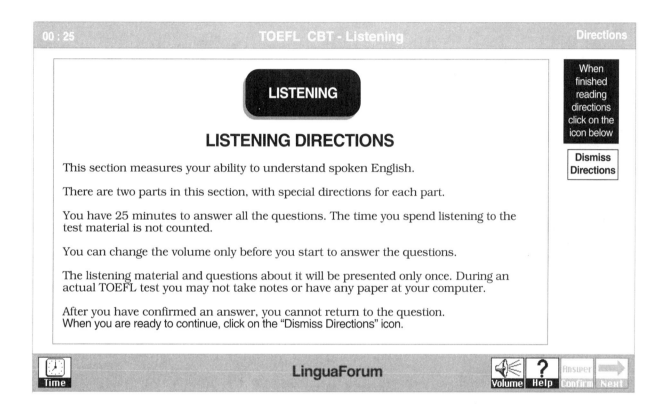

00 : 24 TOEFL CBT - Listening Directions

When finished reading directions click on the icon below

Dismiss Directions

QUESTION DIRECTIONS – PART A

In Part A you will hear short conversations between two people. Each conversation is followed by a question about it.

Each question in this part has four answer choices. Click on the best answer to each question. Answer the questions on the basis of what is stated or implied by the speakers.

Click on the "Volume" icon below to check the sound level NOW. You will not be able to adjust the volume after you dismiss these directions.

When you are ready to continue, click on the "Dismiss Directions" icon.

Time   LinguaForum   Volume Help Answer Confirm Next

PRACTICE TEST 1

Questions 1-17

1. What does the man mean?

  (A) He likes the sound of the woman's idea.
  (B) The woman's idea is interesting.
  (C) There is no controlling her ideas.
  (D) There are strongly divided opinions about her idea.

LinguaForum

2. What is the man implying?

  (A) She can borrow the book from almost anyone in the class.
  (B) Many people asked to borrow the book from him.
  (C) She cannot borrow it because she ran into him.
  (D) She needs the book because she only attended half the classes.

LinguaForum

3. What does the woman mean?

  (A) She is dying from lack of food.
  (B) She does not want anything to eat.
  (C) She is very hungry.
  (D) She is trying to eat something.

LinguaForum

4. What will the woman probably do next?

  (A) Study for the test
  (B) Write her essay
  (C) Do her math problems
  (D) Expand her homework

LinguaForum

5. What does the man imply?

(A) He works for the stadium.
(B) He works for a newspaper.
(C) He pressed the ticket office for extra tickets.
(D) He is a member of the team.

LinguaForum

6. What does the man mean?

(A) He failed that professor's courses.
(B) He never took a class with that professor.
(C) He got a poor grade in those courses.
(D) He did very well in those courses.

LinguaForum

7. What does the woman mean?

(A) The lab on Tuesday was successful.
(B) The experiment went well today.
(C) She found the dates of the experiment successfully.
(D) The lab did not go well that day.

LinguaForum

8. What does the woman suggest the man do?

(A) He should make an appointment.
(B) He should catch the professor in his office.
(C) He should leave the professor alone.
(D) He should use his computer to contact the professor.

LinguaForum

9. What does the woman mean?

(A) She could have gone out last night.
(B) She could have asked for help on her math homework.
(C) She only could have talked to him earlier.
(D) She cannot talk now.

Time LinguaForum Volume Help Confirm Next

10. What will the man probably do?

(A) Go to the department party
(B) Take his son to the department party
(C) Carry his son to the soccer game
(D) Go to his soccer game

Time LinguaForum Volume Help Confirm Next

11. What does the man mean?

(A) His paintings are free.
(B) He cannot go after lunch today.
(C) He wants to go without the woman.
(D) He would like to go to the exhibit after lunch.

Time LinguaForum Volume Help Confirm Next

12. What is the man's most likely relationship with the woman?

(A) Her major advisor
(B) Her boss
(C) Her friend
(D) Her professor

Time LinguaForum Volume Help Confirm Next

13. What is the man suggesting?

(A) The woman should contact him using the computer in the evening.

(B) The woman should telephone him after 10 pm.

(C) The woman should not talk to him any more today.

(D) The woman should get in line to meet him after 10 pm.

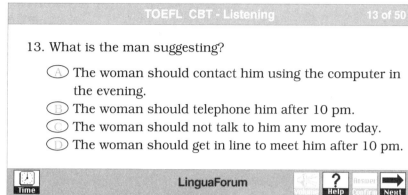

LinguaForum

14. What is the man suggesting?

(A) She should buy the book somewhere else.

(B) She should sign the book out of the library.

(C) She should look in a special, set-aside section of the library.

(D) She should reserve the book, in case it is returned.

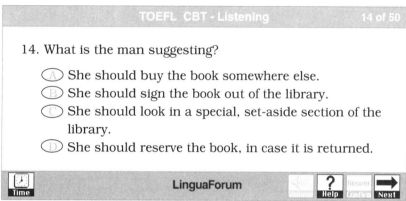

LinguaForum

15. What does the man mean?

(A) He wishes he had more time to do the homework.

(B) He is glad he will miss Mary's party.

(C) He just got the work done, so now he has nothing to do.

(D) He is disappointed that he cannot go to the party.

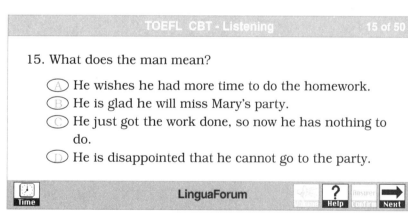

LinguaForum

16. What is the woman implying?

(A) She has seen the movie too many times.

(B) She liked it enough to see it several times.

(C) She would see it if she had the time.

(D) She had not seen it enough, yet.

LinguaForum

PRACTICE TEST 1

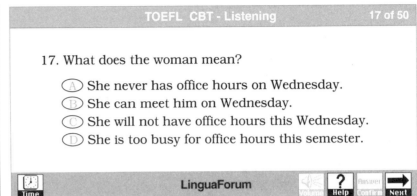

17. What does the woman mean?

    (A) She never has office hours on Wednesday.

    (B) She can meet him on Wednesday.

    (C) She will not have office hours this Wednesday.

    (D) She is too busy for office hours this semester.

LinguaForum

SECTION 1
LISTENING

QUESTION DIRECTIONS – PART B

When finished reading directions click on the icon below

Dismiss Directions

In Part B there are several talks and conversations. Each talk or conversation is followed by several questions.

The conversations and talks are about a variety of topics. You do not need special knowledge of the topics to answer the questions correctly. You should answer each question on the basis of what is stated or implied by the speakers.

Click on the "Volume" icon below to check the sound level NOW. You will not be able to adjust the volume after you dismiss these directions.

When you are ready to continue, click on the "Dismiss Directions" icon.

LinguaForum

PRACTICE TEST 1

Questions 18-22

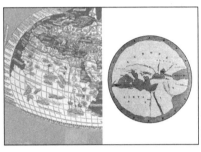

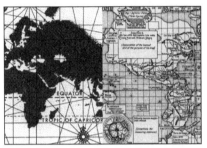

18. What is this discussion about?

    Ⓐ Mapmaking today
    Ⓑ How maps were made in the Renaissance
    Ⓒ How maps have changed over time
    Ⓓ The science of mapmaking

Time   LinguaForum   Volume Help Confirm Next

19. Why have Ptolemy's maps survived?

    Ⓐ They were written on parchment.
    Ⓑ They were recopied many times.
    Ⓒ They were written on clay and tile.
    Ⓓ They were better than other maps.

Time   LinguaForum   Volume Help Confirm Next

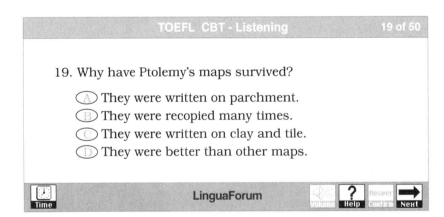

20. Which of the following maps is an example of the maps made by Edward Wright?

Click on a picture.

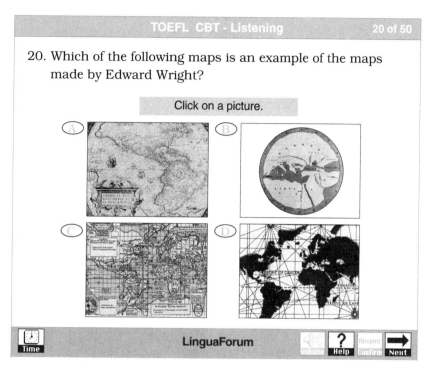

21. The professor is explaining the development of maps over time. Match the time period with the mapping technology.

Click on a term. Then click on the space where it belongs. Use each term only once.

Mercatorial map
T and O map
Accurate longitudes

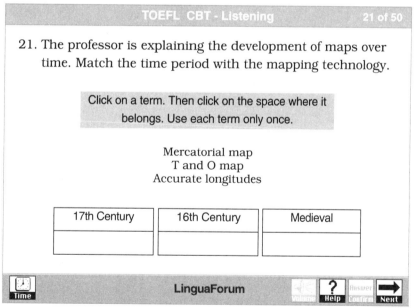

17th Century	16th Century	Medieval

PRACTICE TEST 1

22. What is the major difference between modern maps and pre-modern maps?

  (A) Pre-modern maps were subjective and reflected a religious view.

  (B) Modern maps are made with trigonometry and crisscrossing lines.

  (C) Pre-modern maps were written in ancient languages no one understands today.

  (D) Pre-modern maps were more scientific.

LinguaForum

Time   Volume   Help   Confirm   Next

Questions 23-26

23. What was music for the ancient Greeks?

  (A) Anything that was a higher form of artistic cultivation

  (B) Artworks about the Muses

  (C) Anything related to poetry or literature

  (D) Anything the Greeks found amusing

LinguaForum

Time   Volume   Help   Confirm   Next

24. According to the speaker, what was the main characteristic of ancient Greek music?

    A. The tetrachord
    B. Clear form resulting from precise rhythms
    C. String and flute instruments
    D. Poetic songs

Time   LinguaForum   Volume Help Confirm Next

25. What is Terpander credited with doing?

    A. Creating all ancient music
    B. Inventing the musical chord
    C. Creating the seven note music system
    D. Founding classical Greek music

Time   LinguaForum   Volume Help Confirm Next

26. What is the following diagram an example of?

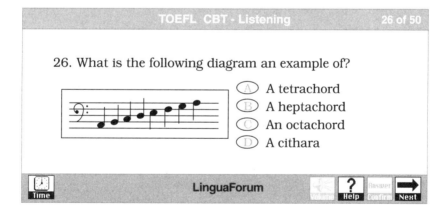

    A. A tetrachord
    B. A heptachord
    C. An octachord
    D. A cithara

Time   LinguaForum   Volume Help Confirm Next

PRACTICE TEST 1

Questions 27-28

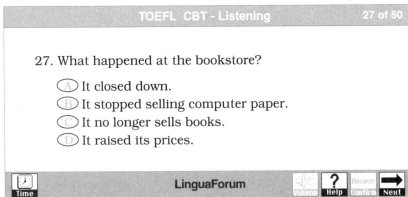

27. What happened at the bookstore?

- (A) It closed down.
- (B) It stopped selling computer paper.
- (C) It no longer sells books.
- (D) It raised its prices.

LinguaForum

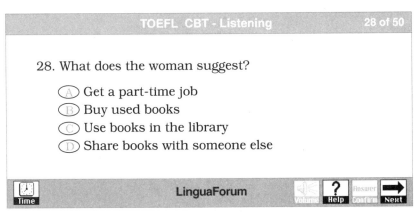

28. What does the woman suggest?

- (A) Get a part-time job
- (B) Buy used books
- (C) Use books in the library
- (D) Share books with someone else

LinguaForum

Four Periods
- the 1860s
- the 1870s
- the 1880s
- the 1890s

29. What is the main idea of this lecture?

    Ⓐ Henry James had limited appeal in his lifetime.
    Ⓑ Henry James was America's greatest author.
    Ⓒ Henry James wrote more than any other American author.
    Ⓓ Henry James is America's biggest selling author ever.

LinguaForum

30. The speaker divided Henry James's work into four periods. Place those four periods into the correct chronological order.

Click on a sentence. Then click on the space where it belongs. Use each sentence only once.

James learned to write theater.
First books were published.
He wrote his greatest novels.
First magazine stories were published.

1. [＿＿＿＿＿]   3. [＿＿＿＿＿]

2. [＿＿＿＿＿]   4. [＿＿＿＿＿]

LinguaForum

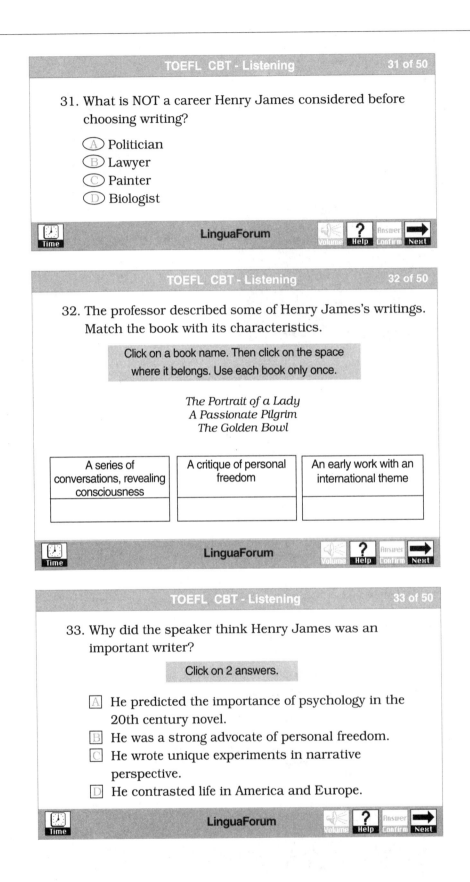

31. What is NOT a career Henry James considered before choosing writing?

   (A) Politician
   (B) Lawyer
   (C) Painter
   (D) Biologist

LinguaForum

32. The professor described some of Henry James's writings. Match the book with its characteristics.

Click on a book name. Then click on the space where it belongs. Use each book only once.

The Portrait of a Lady
A Passionate Pilgrim
The Golden Bowl

A series of conversations, revealing consciousness	A critique of personal freedom	An early work with an international theme

LinguaForum

33. Why did the speaker think Henry James was an important writer?

Click on 2 answers.

   [A] He predicted the importance of psychology in the 20th century novel.
   [B] He was a strong advocate of personal freedom.
   [C] He wrote unique experiments in narrative perspective.
   [D] He contrasted life in America and Europe.

LinguaForum

Questions 34-37

34. What was the compromise reached between the government of Canada and the métis?

(A) Louis Riel was executed.
(B) Their land became a province.
(C) The métis received their own schools.
(D) The métis received guarantees protecting their land and culture.

35. What was the original nickname for Manitoba?

(A) The métis' province
(B) The postage stamp province
(C) The middle province
(D) The prairie province

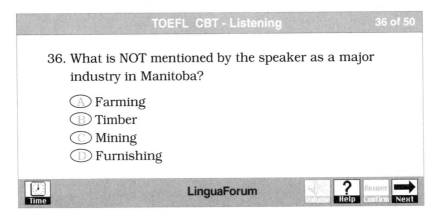

36. What is NOT mentioned by the speaker as a major industry in Manitoba?

   Ⓐ Farming
   Ⓑ Timber
   Ⓒ Mining
   Ⓓ Furnishing

LinguaForum

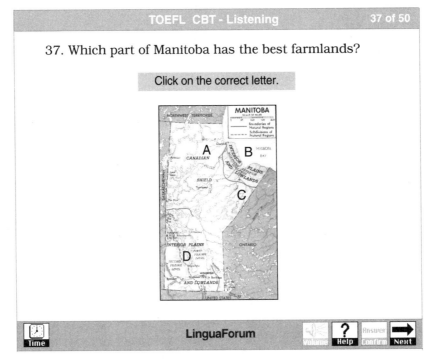

37. Which part of Manitoba has the best farmlands?

Click on the correct letter.

LinguaForum

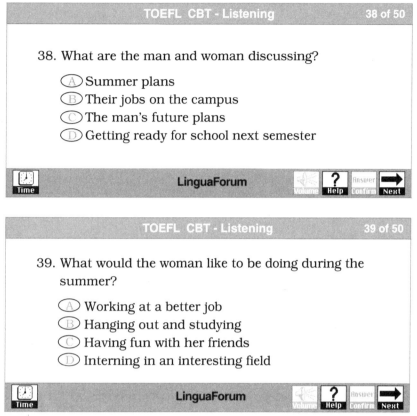

38. What are the man and woman discussing?

    Ⓐ Summer plans
    Ⓑ Their jobs on the campus
    Ⓒ The man's future plans
    Ⓓ Getting ready for school next semester

LinguaForum

39. What would the woman like to be doing during the summer?

    Ⓐ Working at a better job
    Ⓑ Hanging out and studying
    Ⓒ Having fun with her friends
    Ⓓ Interning in an interesting field

LinguaForum

PRACTICE TEST 1

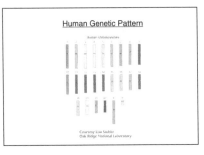

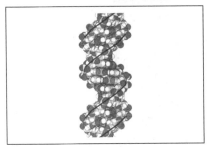

40. What is this discussion about?

- (A) Genetics in modern times
- (B) The Human Genome Project
- (C) Mapping all the genes in the human body
- (D) Problems in gene research

Time   LinguaForum   Volume Help Confirm Next

41. What is the conflict between the Human Genome Project (HGP) and the private biotech companies?

- (A) Private companies produce better data than the HGP.
- (B) Biotech companies want to own the data; HGP wants data freely available.
- (C) HGP works much faster than the private companies.
- (D) Private companies want more data to be available.

Time   LinguaForum   Volume Help Confirm Next

42. Why did the man call the genetic code a "Pandora's box"?

(A) The information creates many new problems.
(B) The information was very difficult to "open," to uncover.
(C) The information does not exist, like the Pandora myth.
(D) The information belongs to a private company called "Pandora."

43. What is NOT a potential problem with this new genetic information?

(A) Genetic discrimination
(B) Designer children
(C) Companies patenting genetic information
(D) How to decipher the human genetic code

Questions 44-47

Nutrition

44. According to the speaker, what is easy to forget
about breakfast cereals?

    (A) How recently they were invented
    (B) How nutritious they are
    (C) That old-style breakfasts were just as good
    (D) How old breakfast cereals are

LinguaForum

45. What did people eat before ready-to-eat breakfast
cereal?

    (A) Coarse whole-meal dough, baked
    (B) Raw cereal grains
    (C) Corn flakes
    (D) Porridge from oats or wheat

LinguaForum

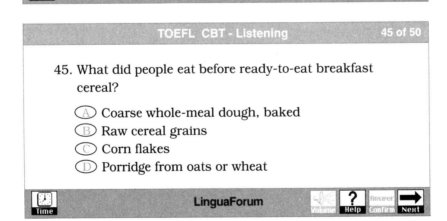

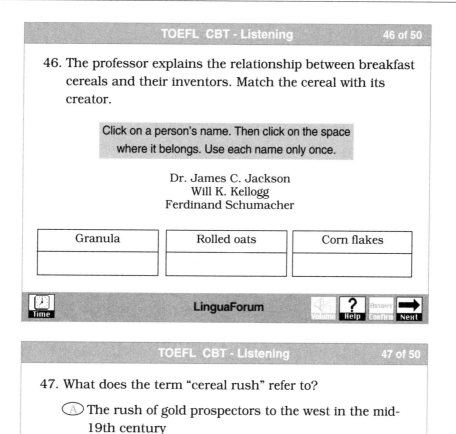

46. The professor explains the relationship between breakfast cereals and their inventors. Match the cereal with its creator.

Click on a person's name. Then click on the space where it belongs. Use each name only once.

Dr. James C. Jackson
Will K. Kellogg
Ferdinand Schumacher

Granula	Rolled oats	Corn flakes

LinguaForum

47. What does the term "cereal rush" refer to?

   (A) The rush of gold prospectors to the west in the mid-19th century
   (B) The feeling of comfort that comes from eating cereal
   (C) The small number of people who got involved in the cereal industry
   (D) The many people who went to Battle Creek to start their own cereal companies

LinguaForum

Questions 48-50

48. What is the major subject of this conversation?

    Ⓐ How poorly the student did on the test

    Ⓑ How to prepare for a test

    Ⓒ How the student can re-take the test

    Ⓓ How the class is divided among different teaching assistants

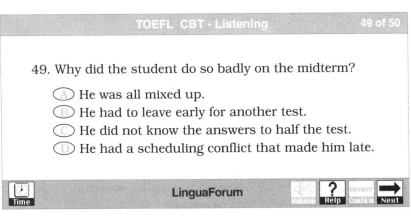

49. Why did the student do so badly on the midterm?

    Ⓐ He was all mixed up.

    Ⓑ He had to leave early for another test.

    Ⓒ He did not know the answers to half the test.

    Ⓓ He had a scheduling conflict that made him late.

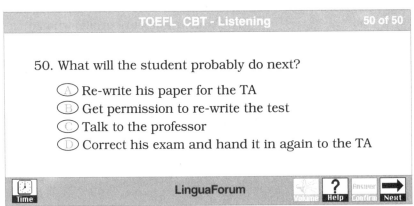

50. What will the student probably do next?

    Ⓐ Re-write his paper for the TA

    Ⓑ Get permission to re-write the test

    Ⓒ Talk to the professor

    Ⓓ Correct his exam and hand it in again to the TA

SECTION 2
STRUCTURE
Suggested Time: 15 Minutes

STRUCTURE

STRUCTURE DIRECTIONS

When finished reading directions click on the icon below

Dismiss Directions

In this section there are two types of test questions.

In one type, you choose the word or phrase that best completes a sentence.

> Example: _____ of igneous rocks results from the two main features of these rocks – the size and the chemistry of their constituent crystals.
>
> ○ Most of the great varieties
> ○ Great varieties
> ○ Greater variation which
> ○ The great variety

In the other type, you look at a sentence with four underlined words or phrases and choose the underlined word or phrase that must be changed for the sentence to be correct.

> Example: The tides <u>caused</u> by the <u>gravitational</u> <u>pull</u> of the moon and sun and
>
> <u>by the rotations</u> of the earth, moon, and sun.

You have 15 minutes to answer all of the questions.

After you have confirmed an answer, you cannot return to the question.

When you are ready to continue, click on the "Dismiss Directions" icon.

Time   LinguaForum   Help   Answer Confirm   Next

1. <u>During</u> the 19th century, global temperature has risen <u>by about</u>
   A   B

1°F <u>in response to</u> <u>increasing concentrations</u> of "greenhouse"
       C   D

gases in the atmosphere.

LinguaForum

2. Blood <u>contained</u> a <u>fresh supply</u> of oxygen <u>leaves</u> the left side of
         A   B   C

the heart in a big arched vessel <u>called</u> the aorta.
                                D

LinguaForum

3. Adolescence is <u>the period</u> of growth and development
                A

<u>during which</u> a boy or girl <u>pass</u> from childhood <u>to adulthood</u>.
   B   C   D

LinguaForum

4. The Coriolis effect is _____ to notice when you're walking
along or driving in a car, so most people are not aware of it.

   Ⓐ so slight
   Ⓑ slightness
   Ⓒ too slight
   Ⓓ very slightly

LinguaForum

5. <u>Because of</u> their high resistance to decay, their widespread
       A

   <u>disperse</u> by wind and water, and their abundant production by
       B

   plants, <u>pollen grains are</u> very <u>common constituents</u> of geologic
             C   D

   sediments.

LinguaForum

6. All societies have regulations that determine _____
   valuable land resources will be allocated.

   (A) the way of
   (B) the way which is
   (C) the way
   (D) the way is

LinguaForum

7. The albatross may <u>stand still</u> in the air, <u>balanced</u> with delicate
                  A   B

   wing motion <u>against</u> the breeze; yet, when taking advantage of
           C

   a favorable wind, its speed may exceed a hundred miles <u>a</u> hour.
                                           D

LinguaForum

8. In the lower vertebrates _____ is tubular and resembles an
   early developmental stage of the brain in higher vertebrates.

   (A) the brain
   (B) of the brain
   (C) in which the brain
   (D) the brain which

LinguaForum

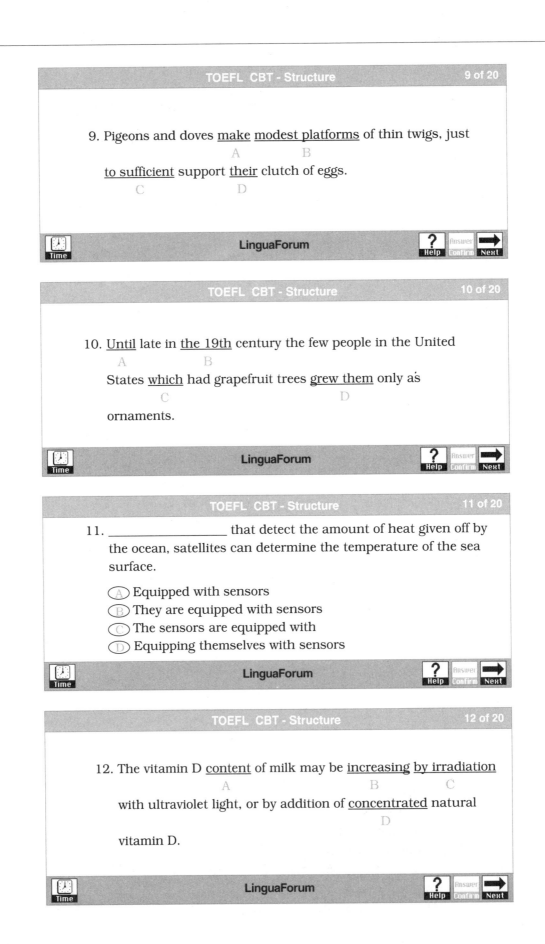

9. Pigeons and doves <u>make</u> <u>modest platforms</u> of thin twigs, just
                 A   B

<u>to sufficient</u> support <u>their</u> clutch of eggs.
   C   D

LinguaForum

10. <u>Until</u> late in <u>the 19th</u> century the few people in the United
     A   B

States <u>which</u> had grapefruit trees <u>grew them</u> only as
       C   D

ornaments.

LinguaForum

11. _____ that detect the amount of heat given off by
the ocean, satellites can determine the temperature of the sea
surface.

(A) Equipped with sensors
(B) They are equipped with sensors
(C) The sensors are equipped with
(D) Equipping themselves with sensors

LinguaForum

12. The vitamin D <u>content</u> of milk may be <u>increasing</u> <u>by irradiation</u>
              A   B   C

with ultraviolet light, or by addition of <u>concentrated</u> natural
                                      D

vitamin D.

LinguaForum

13. Whereas most solids dissolve better in warm water than cold,
       A   B   C

gases are the opposite; they dissolve better in cold water.
            D

14. When pushed by the wind, surface water does not move _____ but moves off at an angle of 45° to the wind's direction.

   (A) in the direction same as the wind
   (B) in the same direction as the wind
   (C) in the same as direction the wind
   (D) in as the wind the same direction

15. Culture is not observable behavior, but rather the shared
                                         A   B

ideals, values, and beliefs that people use them to interpret
                                         C

experience and generate behavior and which are reflected in their
                                      D

behavior.

16. By the time a permanent tooth is ready to replace a primary tooth the root of the primary tooth _____ by the tissue of the jaw.

   (A) absorbs
   (B) has been absorbed
   (C) absorbed
   (D) which has been absorbed

PRACTICE TEST 1

17. Oceanographers use floating instruments and satellites not

only <u>to measure</u> temperature, <u>and</u> also to track ocean currents,
    A   B

tell <u>how much</u> plant life <u>there is</u>, and monitor many other water
     C   D

Characteristics.

18. _____ the internal composition of a cell differs from that on the outside, substances will tend to move in or out of the cell by diffusion.

(A) Whenever
(B) Despite
(C) What
(D) That

19. Insulin affects <u>nearly</u> every <u>cells</u> in the body <u>because</u> it is
              A   B   C

<u>involved</u> in the metabolism of carbohydrates, fats, and proteins.
  D

20. _____ a clear correspondence between the geographical distribution of volcanoes and major earthquakes, particularly in the circum-Pacific earthquake belts and along mid-oceanic ridges.

(A) It is
(B) In
(C) There is
(D) That

SECTION 3
READING
Suggested Time: 70 Minutes

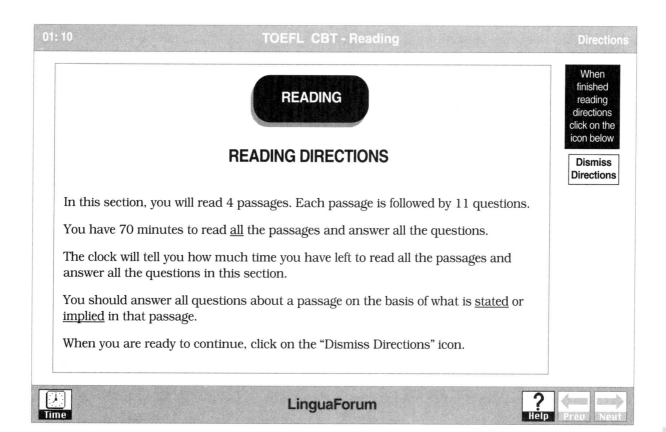

Questions 1-11

As an amateur scientist long before he became president, Thomas Jefferson had nourished an active curiosity about the Louisiana country, its geography, its flora and fauna, and its prospects for trade and agriculture. In 1803, he asked Congress for $2,500 to send an exploring campaign to the Far Northwest, beyond the Mississippi. Although Jefferson was keenly interested in mapping the trans-Mississippi wilderness and collecting scientific information, as well as promoting the fur trade and trade with the Indians of the interior, he explained to Congress that the expedition would be "for the purpose of extending the foreign commerce of the United States." Congress approved, and Jefferson assigned as commanders twenty-nine-year old Meriwether Lewis, who as the president's private secretary had been groomed for the job, and another Virginian, William Clark.

In 1804 the "Corps of Discovery," numbering nearly fifty, set out from St. Louis to ascend the Missouri River. Forced to live off the land, they quickly adapted themselves to a new environment. Local Indians introduced them to new clothes made from deer hides and taught them new hunting techniques. In April 1805, having shipped back to the president more than 30 boxes of plants, minerals, animal skins and bones, and Indian artifacts, they struck out again toward the mountains, accompanied by a native American Indian woman and her French-Canadian husband. They passed the Great Falls of the Missouri and then clambered over the Continental Divide at Lemhi Pass, in southwestern Montana.

After two and half years of exploration, they returned back East and the country greeted the news of their return with delight. Besides locating several passes across the Rockies, Lewis and Clark had established friendly relations with a great many Indian tribes to whom they presented gifts, medals and a sales talk designed to promote peace and the fur trade. They brought back a wealth of data about the country and its resources. The journals kept by members of the group were published and along with their accurate maps, became major sources for scientists, students and future explorers.

1. The main topic of the passage is
   - (A) the scientific interests of Jefferson
   - (B) the expedition of Lewis and Clark
   - (C) the accomplishments of Lewis and Clark
   - (D) the scientific efforts of Lewis and Clark

2. Look at the word campaign in the passage. Click on the word or phrase in the **bold** text that is closest in meaning to campaign.

3. The main purpose behind the expedition of Lewis and Clark was
   - (A) to expand scientific and geographical knowledge of the US
   - (B) to strengthen the fur trade with native Indians
   - (C) to expand the territory of the US
   - (D) to increase America's influence

LinguaForum

4. It can be inferred from the passage that Jefferson described the expedition as a commercial one to Congress because

　Ⓐ he felt strongly that the nation needed to expand its commerce
　Ⓑ he knew that he needed to circumvent the law
　Ⓒ he realized that it would be difficult to lie to Congress
　Ⓓ he realized Congress would not approve a merely scientific expedition

5. Look at the word wilderness in the passage. Click on the word or phrase in the **bold** text that is closest in meaning to wilderness.

6. All of the following describe Lewis EXCEPT

　Ⓐ Virginian
　Ⓑ secretary to Jefferson
　Ⓒ relative of Jefferson
　Ⓓ one of the commanders of the expedition

7. Look at the word they in the passage. Click on the word or phrase in the **bold** text that they refers to.

8. Click on the sentence that describes how Thomas Jefferson obtained support from Congress.

Scroll the passage to see all of the paragraphs.

9. The second paragraph suggests all of the following EXCEPT

　Ⓐ the expedition reached near-starvation
　Ⓑ the expedition had many people to feed
　Ⓒ the expedition was in unfamiliar territory
　Ⓓ the expedition would not have succeeded without the help of the Indians

10. Lewis and Clark helped future explorers mostly through their

　Ⓐ courage
　Ⓑ knowledge
　Ⓒ journals and maps
　Ⓓ fame

11. Lewis and Clark sent all of the following to Jefferson EXCEPT

　Ⓐ Indian artifacts
　Ⓑ gold
　Ⓒ plants
　Ⓓ fur

Questions 12-22

Arthur Eddington, who was three years younger than Einstein, will be remembered for two great achievements. He invented the subject of astrophysics – the study of how physical laws deduced here on Earth, together with observations of the light from stars, can explain how the processes going on inside stars keep them hot, and how the stars must change as they age. **He was also the definitive popularizer of Einstein's theory of relativity in the English language, not just in the sense of communicating these ideas to lay persons, but also as the scientific interpreter who made them clear to experts, and wrote textbooks on the subject which helped spread its message.**

➜ After first presenting in 1915 his general theory at the Berlin Academy of Science, Einstein sent his paper to his friend in Holland, William de Sitter, who in turn mailed it to Eddington. ■ The latter was Secretary of the Royal Astronomical Society at the time, and was the one person who had the intellectual ability and background to fully appreciate the significance of Einstein's work. ■ Fate had several more twists to add to the story before Einstein's new theory was proved correct. ■

➜ The way to test for light bending, as Einstein pointed out, was to look at stars seen near the Sun during an eclipse. ■ Normally, of course, the bright light of the Sun makes it impossible to see stars in that part of the sky, but with the Sun's light temporarily blotted out by the Moon it would be possible to photograph the positions of stars which lie far beyond the Sun but in the same direction in the sky. ■ By comparing such photographs with photographs of the same part of the sky made six months earlier or later, when the Sun was on the other side of the Earth, it would be possible to see any shift in the apparent positions of the stars produced by the light bending effect. ■ What the astronomers needed was an eclipse of the Sun. If they could have chosen the eclipse they wanted, they would have asked for one on May 29 because the Sun is seen passing in front of an exceptionally rich field of bright stars. Eclipses are quite frequently visible from some part of the earth, but to have it occur on such a specific day is very rare. ■ But by a remarkable stroke of good fortune, there was an eclipse due in 1919 on May 20, visible from Brazil and from the island of Principe off the west coast of Africa. ■

12. The author primarily discusses
    (A) the achievements of Arthur Eddington
    (B) the significance of the eclipse in Einstein's general theory
    (C) the reception of Einstein's work in Europe
    (D) the background in proving Einstein's general theory

13. Eddington is known as all of the following EXCEPT
    (A) close friend of Einstein
    (B) translator of Einstein's work into English
    (C) father of astrophysics
    (D) interpreter of Einstein's work

14. Look at the word them in the passage. Click on the word or phrase in the **bold** text that them refers to.

15. Look at the phrase lay persons in the passage. Click on the word or phrase in the **bold** text that is OPPOSITE in meaning to lay persons.

16. It can be inferred that de Sitter sent Einstein's work to Eddington because

    (A) Einstein was not acquainted with Eddington
    (B) due to World War II, Einstein could not send anything to Eddington
    (C) due to World War II, England and Germany were rivals
    (D) Einstein had few friends

17. The word appreciate in the passage is closest in meaning to

    (A) approve
    (B) enjoy
    (C) understand
    (D) judge

18. Einstein's General Theory needed to test

    (A) the eclipse of the Sun
    (B) the visibility of the stars surrounding the moon
    (C) the gravitational force of the Sun
    (D) the bending of light

19. According to the passage, the validity of Einstein's general theory depended mainly on

    (A) the visibility of the Sun
    (B) the eclipse of the moon
    (C) the large numbers of visible stars around the Sun
    (D) the observed or apparent position of the stars

20. Which of the following could best replace the word apparent in the passage?

    (A) Light
    (B) Invisible
    (C) Distinct
    (D) Fixed

21. The successful testing of Einstein's general theory was partially due to

    (A) luck
    (B) collective effort
    (C) Eddington's intelligence
    (D) Eddington's and Sitter's friendship

22. The following sentence can be added to paragraph 2 or 3.

    As Eddington himself commented, "it might have been necessary to wait some thousands of years for a total eclipse of the Sun to happen on the lucky date."

    Where would it best fit in the paragraph? Click on the square [■] to add the sentence to paragraph 2 or 3.
    Paragraphs 2 and 3 are marked with an arrow [➡].

Questions 23-33

The earth's long history is recorded in the rocks that lie at or near its surface, layer piled upon layer. These layers, or strata, are formed as rocks in upland areas, are broken down to pebbles, sand, and clay and are carried to the lowlands and the seas. **Once deposited, they slowly become compacted and cemented into a solid form as new material is accumulated above them. As continents and ocean basins change shape, some strata sink below the surface of an ocean or lake, others are forced upward into mountain ranges, and some are worn away by water, wind or ice or are deformed by heat or pressure.**

➜ Individual strata may be paper-thin or many meters thick. ■ **They can be distinguished from one another by the types of parent material from which they were laid down, the way the material was transported, and the environmental conditions under which the strata were formed.** ■ **They can also be differentiated by the types of fossils they contain. Small marine fossils can be associated with specific period in the earth's history.** ■ **The fossil record is seldom complete, but because of the identifying characteristics of the strata, it is possible to piece together the evidence from many different sources.** ■

➜ The geologic eras – Precambrian, Paleozoic, Mesozoic, and Cenozoic – which are major volumes of the geologic record, were identified and named in the early nineteenth century. ■ They were subdivided into periods, many of which are named for the areas in which the particular strata were first studied or studied most completely: the Devonian for Devonshire in England, the Jurassic for the Jura Mountains between France and Switzerland, etc. ■

Early attempts to date the various eras and periods were based simply on their relative ages compared to the age of the earth. **The first scientific estimate was made in the mid-1800s by the famous British physicist Lord Kelvin. On the basis of his calculations of the time necessary for the earth to have cooled from its original molten state, Kelvin maintained that the planet was about 100 million years old, a calculation that posed difficulties for Darwin.** In the last 40 years, however, new methods for determining the ages of strata have been developed involving measurements of decay of radioactive isotopes.

23. What is the best title for this passage?
    Ⓐ The Geologic Eras
    Ⓑ The Record in the Rocks
    Ⓒ Jurassic Park – Fact or Fiction?
    Ⓓ Dating Mother Earth

24. Look at the word deposited in the passage. Click on the word or phrase in the **bold** text that is closest in meaning to deposited.

25. The first paragraph discusses
    Ⓐ the formation of strata
    Ⓑ the formation of mountains
    Ⓒ the changes in the earth's formation
    Ⓓ the formation of continents

26. All of the following are characteristics of strata EXCEPT

Ⓐ solid form
Ⓑ made of volcanic material
Ⓒ paper-thin
Ⓓ contain fossils

27. Look at the word distinguished in the passage. Click on the word or phrase in the **bold** text that is closest in meaning to distinguished.

28. The following sentence can be added to paragraph 2 or 3.

    It is somewhat like having many copies of the same book, all with chapters missing – but different chapters, so it is possible to reconstruct.

    Where would it best fit in the paragraph? Click on the square [■] to add the sentence to paragraph 2 or 3.
    Paragraphs 2 and 3 are marked with an arrow [➡].

29. The Jurassic era is named after

Ⓐ the movie by Steven Spielberg
Ⓑ the place that the strata were first studied
Ⓒ the fossil records found in the strata
Ⓓ the place in Switzerland where the strata were discovered

30. Click on the sentence which mentions the geologic eras in the passage.

    Scroll the passage to see all of the paragraphs.

31. Look at the word its in the passage. Click on the word or phrase in the **bold** text that its refers to.

32. One can infer that Kelvin's calculation caused problems for Darwin because

Ⓐ the calculation was accurate
Ⓑ he thought that the calculation was incorrect and inaccurate
Ⓒ he had no evidence to refute Kelvin's calculation
Ⓓ many scientists were supporting Kelvin's calculation

33. The new method of measuring the age of the strata assumes that

Ⓐ the strata are relatively recent
Ⓑ the strata lie near the surface of the earth
Ⓒ the strata contain radioactive materials
Ⓓ the strata are relatively thin

The 1830s witnessed the emergence of the first uniquely American form of mass entertainment: the blackface minstrel show. **Rooted in an old tradition of folk theatricals, the minstrel shows featured white performers made up as blacks. "Minstrelsy" drew upon African-American subjects and reinforced prevailing racial stereotypes. It presented banjo and fiddle music, "shuffle" dances, and low-brow humor. Between 1830s and 1870s, the minstrel shows were highly popular throughout the nation, especially among northern working-class ethnics and southern whites, who were eager to flaunt their presumed superiority to blacks.** The shows expanded to include entire troupes of performers who would tour the country, often using riverboats as their means of transportation.

The two most famous minstrel performers were George Washington Dixon, who invented the character named "Zip Coon," and Thomas "Daddy" Rice, who popularized a song-and-dance routine called "Jump Jim Crow." Rice claimed that the inspiration for his act was an old Louisville slave belonging to Jim Crow whom he saw entertaining other workers at a livery stable.

The most popular minstrel songs were written by a young composer named Stephen Foster. Born into a Scotch-Irish family, Foster was a self-taught musician who could pick up any tune by ear. By age fourteen, he was composing songs on the piano. In 1846 he composed a song named "Oh! Susanna." It immediately became a national favorite. The popularity of "Oh! Susanna" catapulted Foster into the national limelight, and he followed it with equally popular tunes such as "Old Folks at Home," better known as "Way Down upon the Swanee River," "Old Black Joe," and "My Old Kentucky Home," all of which perpetuated the sentimental myth of contented slaves, and none of which used actual African-American melodies.

Although antebellum minstrel shows usually portrayed slaves as blissfully contented and caricatured free blacks in the North as superstitious buffoons who preferred slavery to freedom, minstrelsy represented more than an expression of virulent racism and white exploitation of black culture; it also provided a medium for the expression of authentic African-American art forms.

34. What is the best title of the passage?
    (A) Forms of entertainment in nineteenth century America
    (B) Minstrel Show: An American Art Form
    (C) The most popular mass entertainment
    (D) Racism in nineteenth-century America

35. Look at the word featured in the passage. Click on the word or phrase in the **bold** text that best replaces featured.

36. The minstrel shows featured
    (A) slaves from the South
    (B) free slaves living in the North
    (C) white performers acting as blacks
    (D) black actors

37. The word contented in the passage is closest in meaning to
    (A) happy
    (B) moral
    (C) omnifarious
    (D) conceited

38. The minstrel shows were popular among working-class ethnics because

    (A) they could laugh at blacks
    (B) they allowed them to ridicule blacks
    (C) they allowed them to express their hatred towards blacks
    (D) they confirmed their superiority over blacks

39. Click on the sentence that describes the definition of the minstrel shows in the passage.

Scroll the passage to see all of the paragraphs.

40. Rice's performance is supposedly based upon

    (A) a slave called Jim Crow
    (B) original work
    (C) the performance of a slave
    (D) the performances of other minstrel actors

41. Look at the word **it** in the passage. Click on the word or phrase in the **bold** text that **it** refers to.

42. Foster is mentioned for all of the following EXCEPT that

    (A) he incorporated African tunes
    (B) he experienced early success
    (C) he was self-taught
    (D) he wrote music at the age of fourteen

43. Foster's music is described as

    (A) upbeat
    (B) sentimental
    (C) traditional
    (D) African-American melodic

44. The author's attitude towards minstrel shows is

    (A) hostile
    (B) highly critical
    (C) biased and racist
    (D) partly critical but positive

SECTION 4
WRITING
Suggested Time: 30 Minutes

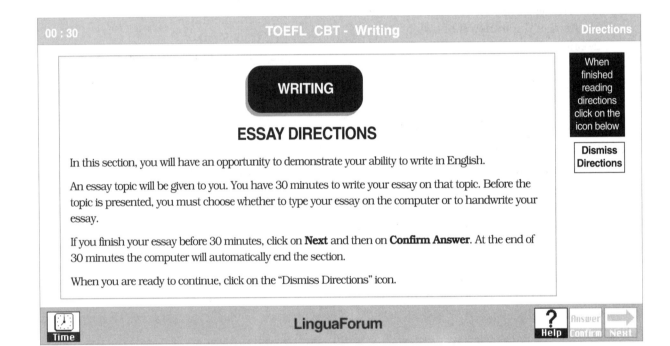

Read the topic below and then make any notes that will help you plan your response.
Begin typing your response in the box at the bottom of the screen, or write your answer on the answer sheet provided to you.

Imagine that a friend of yours has been given a sum of money and plans to spend it all either to buy an automobile, or to take a vacation. If your friend asked you for advice, what would you say? Compare these two options and explain which one you think is better for your friend. Use specific examples and reasons to explain your opinion.

Cut

Paste

Undo

Time

LinguaForum

PRACTICE TEST 1

LISTENING SCRIPT

Listening Script

Diagnostic Test 1

Listening Script Part A

1. (woman) So, are you glad to be back?
   (man) You bet. I had a terrible summer job, but now I really want to get back to work. Why? Aren't you happy to be back?
   (woman) No, I had a great summer. I spend the whole summer on the beach with my friends.
   (man) You can always see your friends again, come Thanksgiving.
   (narrator) When is this conversation probably taking place?

2. (man) If you are still looking for a new printer, the university computer store has a good sale going on.
   (woman) I know about the sale. I went, but they had already sold out of printers.
   (man) There were lots there when I was there around 11 this morning or so.
   (woman) Well, when I got there, there were none left.
   (narrator) What is the woman implying?

3. (woman) Kevin, have you seen my student card? I forgot it at your place last night.
   (man) No, Caery. I gave it Terry. He said he was supposed to meet you this morning. I wonder what happened?
   (narrator) Where is Caery's student card?

4. (man) I have to go meet Bob about something over at the college park.
   (woman) But I just met Bob in the dormitory. He said he was on his way to the student union building.
   (narrator) What will the man probably do next?

5. (man) I'm feeling guilty. I have this big research paper for Dr. Donne's class, but I haven't started it yet.
   (woman) So you're going to get started tonight, I assume.
   (man) Actually, I think I'll go to the movie tonight. There's a film I really wanted to see, and, besides, the paper isn't due yet.
   (woman) You can't put it off forever.
   (narrator) What does the woman suggest to the man?

6. (woman) I know you were really stressed out about your astronomy exam. How'd you do?
   (man) I can't complain.
   (narrator) What does the man mean?

Listening Script Part B

Questions 7-9

Listen to a professor and his students discussing information from a musicology class. The class is on pianos.

(professor) Last time we looked at the invention of the grand piano and how it revolutionized music in the 18th century. But around 1800, an American, John Isaac Hawkins, further altered the piano. Does anyone know how?
(man) Didn't he invent the upright piano?
(professor) That's right. On a regular piano, the strings are horizontal, but Hawkins strung the piano vertically, so it took up much less room. In order to do so, he also had to change the hammer mechanism that strikes the strings and makes the piano sound. On the grand piano, gravity returns the hammer to the resting position. Since this is not possible on the upright, Hawkins invented a spring mechanism to return the hammer.

	This mechanism is what gives the upright piano a distinctly different feel than the grand piano.
(woman)	What about those really small upright pianos I've seen? My family had one when I was young. Are they the same as regular uprights?
(professor)	The shortest of the upright pianos are called "spinets" or consoles. They're generally considered to have an inferior tone and sound quality because their strings are so short and their soundboards are so small.
(woman)	Are there other kinds of upright pianos?
(professor)	Well, before Hawkins' piano, other people tried to design uprights, but they looked very different. Remember, Hawkins' key invention was running the strings and the soundboard up from the floor. Before that, most piano makers tried running the strings from the keyboard upward, making the piano much taller and unwieldy. In Germany, Ernst Friderici designed the "pyramid" piano, pictured here, that peaked in the middle, and in Vienna, Martin Seuffert made the "giraffe-style" piano, that looked more like a grand piano turned on its side. I'm going to give all of you a couple of essays about the development of the piano; I want you to read them for next class. Next class, we're going to have a quiz about the 19th century piano, so be ready.

7. What is the main topic of this discussion?

8. What makes the upright piano different than the grand piano?

9. The professor mentioned several different kinds of upright pianos. Match the name of the piano with the diagram.

Questions 10-13

Listen to part of a lecture in a literature class. The professor is talking about magazines.

Magazines have been an important part of American culture since the 18th century. Benjamin Franklin published the first magazine in America, titled *General Magazine*, in 1741, just 9 years after the first monthly magazine was started in England. But in those early days, printed on cheap paper, most magazines did not last long. The 19th century, however, was a grand age in American publishing, and magazines were instrumental in developing the young American literary scene.

Early in the 19th century, the miscellaneous city magazine, designed for weekend reading, became popular. Nearly every city in America had one of these magazines, and Philadelphia in 1852 had 16 of them. One of the first and most enduring of these sorts of magazines was the *Saturday Evening Post*, founded in 1821 by Charles Alexander, a Philadelphia printer.

Harper's New Monthly Magazine began in 1850 and dominated the magazine industry for its first 20 years, and was for a long time one of the best selling magazines in America. Most popular were its many woodcut illustrations and stories by English novelists. In Boston, *Atlantic Monthly* began in 1857 and was renowned for its high literary standards. Both *Harper's* and *Atlantic Monthly* inspired dozens of imitators, but none of the imitators survive today.

One magazine that did not survive long was *Putnam's Monthly Magazine*, published from 1853 to 1857. But in three short years, *Putnam's* was the best all-round quality magazine ever published in America. Writers like Longfellow, Thoreau, Melville, and Cooper were all frequent contributors. Unfortunately, competition was tight, and the magazine did not last.

In general, the success of the magazine spelled its own demise. With increased competition, each magazine tried to outdo each other. The result was a decline of serious standards and a rise in sensationalism – increasingly shocking or exciting stories at the expense of accuracy. When publishers saw how popular this sort of writing was, it gave birth to the pulp magazine, so-called because of the cheap pulp paper it was printed on. Pulp magazines had few illustrations, and were mostly Westerns, mysteries, love stories, sports and horror stories.

10. What is the main idea of this lecture?

11. The professor mentioned several popular magazines from the 19th century. Match the magazine and its characteristics.

12. The professor described the history of American magazines. Place the following developments into the correct chronological order.

13. What can be inferred from what the speaker said about pulp magazines?

Questions 14-15

Listen to part of a conversation between two speakers.

(man)	Hey, Diane. When is your sister arriving tomorrow?
(woman)	Sarah's flight is supposed to arrive around 1:30 or so. I'm pretty excited about meeting her since we haven't seen each other in so long.
(man)	But I know your car's in the shop right now, so how're you going to pick her up?
(woman)	I was thinking about taking the subway since it's cheap. But then I remembered the airport express bus stops right by my apartment.
(man)	If you need a hand, I'd be happy to come with you.
(woman)	Thanks, but Sarah always travels light, so she should only have a bag or two. I'm sure we can handle it ourselves.
(man)	What are you going to do while she's visiting?
(woman)	Well, she's visited me here before, so I don't need to give her the grand tour of the campus. She already knows where everything is. So, instead, we're planning on taking it easy.
(man)	Maybe take in a movie? Something like that?
(woman)	Something like that, except Sarah doesn't like to go to the movies. I think we'll mostly just talk, so we'll probably spend most of her visit in coffee shops around campus.
(man)	That does sound like a quiet visit. Well, if you change your mind and want to do something fun, feel free to give me a call.

14. Why is Diane excited?

15. What will Diane and Sarah most likely do during her trip?

Chapter 2 – Question Types for Short Conversations

TOEFL Exercise 2.1

Listen to each short dialogue carefully, and then choose the best answer to the question.

1. (man)	Mandy, I was looking for you. Have you gone to lunch yet?
(woman)	No, but I had a late breakfast.
(narrator)	What is the woman implying?

2. (man)	I have a big research assignment to do. I'm hoping if I stay up all night I might get it done by dawn.
(woman)	That's a lot of work. Why don't you take a break and come get some coffee with the rest of us?
(man)	Oh, please. If I listened to talk like that I'd never get this done.
(narrator)	What is the man implying?

3. (woman)	This paper for Professor Schultz's class is really tough.
(man)	I know. I've been working on it all week and I'm barely half done. We could use another week to get it done.
(woman)	I'm going to ask the professor if I can get an extension.
(man)	Don't bother – I already asked him.
(narrator)	What is the man implying?

4. (woman)	Should we go out tonight, maybe do some dancing?
(man)	I certainly have no desire to stay in and study any more.
(narrator)	What is the man implying?

5. (woman)   Our school's next basketball game is against North Carolina. They're a great team, so I bet it'll be an exciting game.
   (man)   Should we watch the game on TV tonight?
   (woman) The game is on Tuesday night.
   (narrator)   What is the woman implying?

6. (man)   I can't believe we have so much work to do for our chemistry class.
   (woman) I know. Homework problems, readings, a test, and a lab – that's just too much.
   (man)   Do you think I should work on the homework questions first?
   (woman) The professor said we shouldn't start the homework problems until we finish the lab.
   (narrator)   What is the woman implying?

7. (woman)   Dr. Williams, you said the test will be on chapters 5 to 7. So do you think it would be a good way to study if I spend my time working on the problems in the textbook from these chapters?
   (man)   That sounds good. But don't spend too long studying chapter 5.
   (narrator)   What is the man implying?

8. (woman)   I'll be over around 3 o'clock to help you move.
   (man)   Thanks a lot, Debbie. I could really use the help.
   (woman) No problem. To be honest, I was hoping you'd have time to return the favor next weekend.
   (narrator)   What is the woman implying?

9. (woman)   Dr. Hensen, could I talk to you about the political science courses you're offering next semester?
   (man)   Sure, what can I do for you?
   (woman) Well, I was really interested in your advanced seminar about political parties.
   (man)   It's an interesting course; unfortunately, it's only for poli sci majors.
   (narrator)   What is the man implying?

TOEFL Exercise 2.2

Listen to each short dialogue carefully, and then choose the best answer to the question.

1. (man)   How did your friend Bill fare in the student council elections?
   (woman) He won by a landslide.
   (narrator)   What does the woman mean?

2. (woman)   Our chemistry experiment just isn't working out right. We need to get some help. I think we should ask Randy for advice.
   (man)   Really? Sandra is a much harder worker than Randy.
   (woman) But Randy knows all the ins and outs of this experiment.
   (narrator)   What does the woman mean?

3. (woman)   This apartment is looking run down these days. I wish our landlord would paint the place and fix it up.
   (man)   You know, if we offered to do the painting ourselves, I bet the landlord would buy us the paint.
   (woman) Do you think it will be very difficult, painting the house?
   (man)   It'll be a breeze.
   (narrator)   What does the man mean?

4. (woman)   I just realized I haven't talked to Jim since he graduated last year.
   (man)   Yeah, I wonder what's become of him.
   (narrator)   What does the man mean?

5. (woman)   Hi, Reggie. I see you're reading yet another new book.

(man)	I finished that other novel last night, so I decided to start a new one.
(woman)	You really are quite the bookworm, aren't you?
(narrator)	What does the woman mean?

6.
(woman)	Dave, have you gotten word back from your professor about that great research proposal?
(man)	Yeah, I just met with him.
(woman)	So, what's going to happen?
(man)	He said no dice, so I had to shelve the idea.
(narrator)	What does the man mean?

7.
(woman)	So are you going to take that research position with Dr. Adams?
(man)	It's an amazing opportunity. But I'm so overloaded with work I think I'll have to give it a pass.
(narrator)	What does the man mean?

8.
(man)	If you are looking for a good place to go for dinner with your parents, I'd recommend eating at that new French restaurant on campus.
(woman)	I know that place. It's a little expensive, but the food is great.
(man)	Just remember to book a seat well ahead of time – it always has a good-sized waiting list.
(narrator)	What does the man mean?

9.
(man)	How long have we been studying now?
(woman)	For hours. It was light out when we first got here. I think it's past midnight now.
(man)	I'm going to stay until I finish all my math problems.
(woman)	I'm beat. I'm going to pack it in.
(narrator)	What does the woman mean?

10.
(woman)	You seem to be having a good semester right now.
(man)	Yeah, I'm just as surprised as you are. I barely passed my classes last semester. Now, I'm acing everything.
(woman)	I remember you said how hard you were finding school last year. But now, look at you.
(man)	Things certainly are looking up.
(narrator)	What does the man mean?

11.
(woman)	Have you seen Dave lately? He looks really exhausted and overworked.
(man)	Yeah, his graduate advisor keeps assigning him more and more work to do. He's even helping his advisor out with the advisor's research.
(woman)	That's not right. Why does he put up with it?
(man)	Oh, Dave never stands up for himself. Until he does, people will keep taking advantage of him.
(narrator)	What does the man mean?

TOEFL Exercise 2.3

Listen to each short dialogue carefully, and then choose the best answer to the question.

1.
(man)	I can't believe I failed my cultural studies essay. I guess I'll have to try harder next time.
(woman)	If I were in your shoes I'd ask my professor if I could rewrite the whole thing.
(narrator)	What does the woman suggest?

2.
(man)	Say, you know Ritchie is looking for you, don't you?
(woman)	I was afraid of that. I was supposed to return this lab manual to him by today, but I've not finished using it yet.
(man)	Brad is a pretty understanding guy. Why don't you ask him for more time?
(narrator)	What does the man suggest to the woman?

3. (man)   I can't decide if I want to take the regular major seminar or the advanced seminar.
   (woman)   Well, I guess it depends on what you want. Certainly the advanced seminar is difficult.
   (man)   I want to graduate with a strong set of transcripts. I'm worried the advanced seminar would pull down my grades.
   (woman)   But you could graduate with honors if you took the seminar. That looks better than just a good GPA.
   (narrator) What does the woman suggest?

4. (woman)   This school is so big, I feel totally lost. I don't even know where the registrar's office is yet.
   (man)   I don't know where that is either. How about I check my campus guide and see what it says?
   (narrator) What does the man suggest?

5. (woman)   Dan, I hear you won the Dean Scholarship! Congratulations!
   (man)   Thanks a lot. I'm so excited, I don't know who to tell first.
   (woman)   You might want to call your parents and let them know.
   (narrator) What does the woman suggest the man do?

6. (man)   I'm thinking of buying a used computer from the student store.
   (woman)   Why would you get a used computer?
   (man)   New ones are too expensive. But I can save a lot of money with a used computer.
   (woman)   In the short term, maybe. But if you want a system that will last, you shouldn't be too stingy.
   (narrator) What does the woman suggest to the man?

7. (man)   My bank balance doesn't seem to be quite right. I can't understand this statement they sent me.
   (woman)   You could always get it explained for you down at the bank; that way you would know for sure what's going on.
   (narrator) What does the woman suggest the man do?

8. (woman)   I have so many papers to grade. I'll never get them all done.
   (man)   I'd just go home and get them finished right now, even if it takes all night.
   (woman)   That's probably a good idea. Doing a little every day would take forever.
   (narrator) What does the man suggest?

9. (woman)   Dave, how is the swim team doing?
   (man)   We're doing all right. But my swim coach wants me to join the gymnastics team, too, just to work on my flexibility.
   (woman)   But you're too short of time to get your schoolwork done as it is. I'd just forget about it if I were you.
   (narrator) What does the woman suggest to the man?

TOEFL Exercise 2.4

Listen to each short dialogue carefully, and then choose the best answer to the question.

1. (woman)   I finally got an "A" on a project in Dr. Page's class.
   (man)   Wow. I don't know anyone who's gotten an "A" with him before.
   (narrator) What can be inferred about Dr. Page?

2. (woman)   I'm so excited about our trip to Washington D.C. It's going to be great.
   (man)   What time is Pat picking us up?
   (woman)   She said she'd be here around 1, as soon as she finished packing her bags.
   (narrator) What can be inferred about their trip?

3. (man)   There's nothing on TV. We need to get out and do something.

	(woman)	What did you have in mind?
	(man)	Let's go to the campus store for a while – maybe check things out in the library.
	(woman)	But it's Sunday. Everything is closed until noon.
	(narrator)	What can be inferred from this conversation?

4.	(man)	If you had more experience, I would definitely hire you.
	(woman)	My last boss will tell you that I learn really quickly.
	(narrator)	What is the relationship of the two speakers?

5.	(woman)	Hi, Dan, how's it going?
	(man)	I'm starving. The lunch today in the cafeteria wasn't very good.
	(woman)	That's why I prefer to eat off-campus.
	(narrator)	What can be inferred about the woman?

6.	(woman)	I'm having trouble choosing my classes for next semester. I just don't know what to take.
	(man)	How about Dr. Silverman? He's famous for his entertaining lectures.
	(woman)	I don't know. I've never taken a philosophy class before.
	(man)	Really, take my word for it – he's a great professor.
	(narrator)	What can be inferred about the professor?

7.	(woman)	Brian, sorry I didn't submit my story yesterday. I needed to get some more quotes before it was ready.
	(man)	I know you wanted to improve your story, but you can't just miss deadlines, especially when you have the university news beat.
	(narrator)	What can be inferred about the woman?

8.	(woman)	Sorry I'm late. Traffic was really awful. It took twice as long as it usually does.
	(man)	That's really annoying when that happens.
	(woman)	And to make matters worse, I missed my stop and had to walk back three blocks.
	(narrator)	How did the woman come to school?

9.	(man)	I have to go see my academic advisor now.
	(woman)	Are you having some kind of problem in school?
	(man)	No, I just want to get more information about some of the majors.
	(woman)	See? I told you if you took some more diverse classes, you'd be more open-minded about what you wanted to study.
	(narrator)	What can be inferred about the man?

10.	(man)	Excuse me, but could you help me find the psychology section?
	(woman)	It's one floor up, at the far end of the stacks.
	(man)	Thanks. And how late are you open tonight?
	(woman)	You can check books out until 11:30, and the study lounge in the basement is open until 3 am.
	(narrator)	What can be inferred about the woman?

TOEFL Exercise 2.5

Listen to each short dialogue carefully, and then choose the best answer to the question.

1.	(man)	If I go to Houston, can you meet me there? We can see that new zoo they've built.
	(woman)	Well, I have to go to Dallas to do some research, but if I have time I'll meet you there during the weekend.
	(narrator)	What will the woman most likely do?

2.	(man)	What're you doing, Sue?
	(woman)	Trying to decide what to tackle next. Should I do my math homework or study for my history midterm?
	(man)	Well, the math homework isn't due for another couple of days.

(narrator)   What will the woman most likely do next?

3. (man)   Hi there. What can I do for you?
   (woman)   I'm trying to decide what classes I want to take next semester, and your Labor Economics course looked really interesting.
   (man)   Thanks for saying so. But since my Labor Economics course is an upper-division class, you'll have to take the major seminar first.
   (woman)   But I already took that class last year.
   (narrator) What will the woman most likely do?

4. (man)   I'll meet you in the library right after I've finished talking to my major advisor.
   (woman)   Actually, I have to go to the student union building for a while to run a couple of errands and get something to eat, but you're welcome to join me there.
   (narrator) What will the man most likely do?

5. (woman)   Aren't you coming with me?
   (man)   I'm going to have to stay here in the lab all night if I'm going to get this experiment finished.
   (woman)   Well I have an exam first thing in the morning. I simply have to study for it and get some decent sleep.
   (narrator) What will the man most likely do next?

6. (man)   Is this our shopping list for this week?
   (woman)   Yes, that's it.
   (man)   Wow, is it ever big this week! I guess I'd better get it done right away. I have a lot of homework to get done for tomorrow.
   (woman)   Oh, I already did the grocery shopping this morning. Sorry, but I forgot to throw out the list.
   (narrator) What will the man most likely do next?

7. (woman)   I can't have lunch with you because I need to hurry and get tickets for this week's basketball game.
   (man)   Actually, I heard they're sold out already.
   (narrator) What will the woman most likely do?

8. (man)   Are you off to see the big soccer game now?
   (woman)   Yes, it should be really exciting. Sorry I couldn't get you a ticket, but the game is sold out. Are you going to watch it on TV tonight instead?
   (man)   No, I think I'm going to watch the news. And then there's a movie on after that I really want to see.
   (narrator) What will the man watch first?

9. (woman)   I can't believe we still don't have a phone in our apartment.
   (man)   Have you talked to anyone at the phone company about it yet?
   (woman)   Yes, I called them this morning. They said they can send someone over tomorrow between 2 and 4, but there'll have to be someone at home to let him in. I have to be at my research job then, so I can't be home.
   (man)   Then I guess I'll have to skip my biology class tomorrow afternoon. We can't go without a telephone any longer.
   (narrator) What will the man most likely do?

TOEFL Exercise 2.6

Listen to each short dialogue carefully, and then choose the best answer to the question.

1. (woman)   The reunion was really interesting. Sixty people showed up, including a couple of people from the class of 1950.
   (man)   Wow. I hope I'll be able to attend a reunion here in 50 years, too.
   (narrator) How many people attended the class reunion?

2. (woman) Hi there. I wanted to talk to Provost Johnson about something.
   (man) I'm sorry, but you have to have an appointment to see the Provost.
   (woman) But I was too busy for the past couple of days. Can't you make an exception?
   (narrator) Why is the woman not allowed to meet the Provost?

3. (man) I just got a form in my mailbox asking me about next year's housing.
   (woman) Where do you think you're going to live?
   (man) Well, the old dorm is conveniently located, but I'd rather walk a bit and stay in the nice, new dorm building across campus.
   (woman) Sounds good. That's why I moved there, too.
   (narrator) What did the woman ask the man?

4. (man) Do you know how I can get in touch with Dr. Kilmer?
   (woman) He's busy in the lab right now. But he has office hours this afternoon.
   (narrator) What does the man want to know?

5. (man) Hi Janet. I got a message you were looking for me.
   (woman) Yes, I was. I just wanted to return the $15 I borrowed from you the other day. Thanks a lot for helping me out.
   (man) No problem, but don't forget, though, you bought me lunch yesterday. So you already paid me $6.50 of that.
   (narrator) How much money does the woman owe the man?

6. (man) Excuse me, I'm a little lost. I'm looking for the music auditorium.
   (woman) That's in the Franklin Building. Just go to the end of this road and turn right. You can't miss it.
   (man) I thought it was in the Reed Building.
   (woman) No, the Reed Building is where the music department is. But the auditorium is in another building.
   (narrator) Where is the music auditorium?

7. (man) The campus computer store is having a two-for-one sale on hard drives.
   (woman) Really? That's a great deal. They're normally around $90 each. Let's split it and each get one.
   (narrator) How much does the woman pay for her hard drive?

8. (woman) Thanks a lot for taking an interest in our creative arts club. You need to fill out this application form so we can learn a little bit about you. And you're going to have to submit an artistic project of some sort within the next two weeks.
   (man) What kind of project?
   (woman) Anything, really. A story, a painting, some poems – even an essay, if you have a good one.
   (narrator) What must the man do to apply to the literary society?

9. (man) Julie, this report you wrote is simply not good enough.
   (woman) I don't understand – I worked on it really hard and I used lots of sources.
   (man) But you almost solely used secondary sources. I specifically said I wanted you to use primary sources. I was interested in your ideas, not other people's.
   (woman) You mean I was supposed to use only original sources?
   (narrator) What's wrong with the woman's report?

TOEFL Exercise 2.7

Listen to each short dialogue carefully, and then choose the best answer to the question.

1. (man) How was the student play last night?
   (woman) I was hoping you could tell me.
   (narrator) What did the woman assume about the man?

2. (woman)   I need to find one more class to take next semester, but I'm having a hard time deciding. I want something outside of what I usually study – I'm tired of science courses. I want to take something more fun.

(man)   You should take Dr. Gould's advanced anthropology seminar. It's really good.

(woman)   I thought non-majors weren't allowed to take it.

(narrator)   What did the woman assume about the class?

3. (woman)   Are you excited about Linda and the play?

(man)   Very much so. I've never had a friend act in anything before.

(woman)   Here you go – Linda gave me a couple of free tickets.

(man)   But I already bought us tickets to the show!

(narrator)   What did the man assume about the woman?

4. (woman)   I'm so happy. I just got into the science and engineering dual-degree program.

(man)   That's great, but I thought you had to have at least an A⁻ average to get accepted.

(narrator)   What did the man assume?

5. (man)   Rachel, what happened to you?

(woman)   I'm so tired. I was at the library all night, studying with Jen.

(man)   So you weren't just sleeping when you didn't answer your phone last night.

(narrator)   What did the man assume about the woman?

6. (woman)   Your proposed schedule of courses for the economics major looks pretty good. Just a couple of questions, though. What concentration are you going to take?

(man)   I'm going to concentrate on international microeconomics.

(woman)   Okay... And will you be taking Calculus 101 or 102?

(man)   You mean there's a math requirement?

(narrator)   What did the man assume about the major?

7. (woman)   Congratulations! I just saw your name on the football team roster.

(man)   Then someone else must have the same name. I've never even tried out for the team.

(narrator)   What had the woman assumed?

8. (woman)   Sam, here's that book I mentioned would be useful for your essay.

(man)   Thanks Janet. This will help out a lot.

(woman)   So I guess I'll see you at Dr. Harrison's office at 3 o'clock so we can discuss our project.

(man)   You mean our meeting wasn't postponed until next week?

(narrator)   What did the man assume about the meeting?

Mini-Test 1

Listening Script Part A

Questions 1-6

1. (woman)   Excuse me. I was in last week's try-outs for the student theater company. Could I ask you a question?

(man)   Sure. What is it?

(woman)   I'm just very nervous about how I did. When do I find out if I made it in?

(man)   We'll be posting the new members list sometime early next week.

(narrator)   What can be inferred about the woman?

2. (man)   I see you're up late studying for Professor Henry's chemistry exam tomorrow.

(woman)   Yeah, it's going to be a difficult test. I'm worried I won't be ready for it.

(man)   Do you want to come join me? A bunch of us are going to be studying all night in the dorm lounge.

(woman)   I don't think I could keep my eyes open another five minutes.

(narrator)	What is the woman implying?

3. (woman)   Have you seen that calculator I was using? First Dan had it, then Janet. Now I can't find it.

   (man)   It's her calculator, so I gave it back.

   (narrator)   To whom does the calculator belong?

4. (man)   I really need to get my laundry done tonight. I have absolutely nothing left to wear tomorrow.

   (woman)   Oh, I'm sorry. I just put my things into the washer.

   (narrator)   What will the man most likely do?

5. (woman)   Oh, no. I think I'm going to have to drop out of this anthropology class.

   (man)   Is something wrong?

   (woman)   I failed the midterm exam. Even if I do well on the final, I can't get a good grade. And I need a good grade in this class.

   (man)   Don't forget that you can always take a make-up test next week.

   (narrator)   What does the man suggest the woman do?

6. (man)   You've been writing here a long time. How's it going?

   (woman)   It was going pretty well, but then I hit a wall.

   (narrator)   What does the woman mean?

Listening Script Part B

Questions 7-9

Listen to a professor and his students discussing information from a business class. The class is on free market economics.

(man)   Professor? We mostly talk about free market economics in this class, but that only started with Adam Smith's book, *The Wealth of Nations*, a couple of hundred years ago. Were there economic theories before then?

(professor)   Of course as long as there has been civilization, there have been people thinking about economic issues. Aristotle and Plato in ancient Greece wrote about problems of wealth, property, and trade. But back there, most aristocrats and intellectuals were prejudiced against commerce, feeling that to live by trade was undesirable. The Romans felt pretty much the same way. During the Middle Ages the economic ideas of the Catholic Church dominated. Usury, that is the taking of interest on money loaned, was condemned, and commerce again was considered inferior to agriculture.

(woman)   So how did this change?

(professor)   Well, with the development of the nation-state in the 16th and 17th centuries, attention shifted to the problem of increasing wealth and power of the various nation-states. The economic policy of that time was known as mercantilism. Under mercantilism, leaders tried to make their nations self-sufficient, frowning on trade. They also viewed gold and silver as an index of national power. Since most nations did not own gold mines, a nation could only accumulate wealth by taking it away from someone else. Nations then just assumed that they would be at war with their neighbors, and gold and silver were needed to pay for their armies.

(man)   Were there any other major theories?

(professor)   For a brief time in 18th century France, there was a movement called "physiocracy." It was a reaction against the narrow and restrictive policies of mercantilism, emphasizing instead free trade and government non-interference. They also believed that agriculture was the foundation of all wealth, and that through trade, wealth is distributed from farmers to other groups.

(woman)   Hmm. No one you mentioned seems to like commerce.

(professor)   That's right. Before Adam Smith, almost everyone agreed that agriculture was the most desirable form of wealth. Smith was the first to emphasis the benefits of trade and commerce to the whole economy.

7. What is the main idea of this discussion?

8. The professor mentioned several different economic theories. Match the economic era with the economic policy.

9. What was the cause of mercantilist economics?

Questions 10-13

Listen to part of a lecture in an agricultural science class. The professor is talking about the diversity and efficiency of farms in the United States.

It is the tremendous diversity and efficiency of farms in the United States that has made America the premier agricultural nation in the world.

American farms do not rely one any single crop. Instead, there is a kind of farming appropriate to almost every climate in the country. In the northeastern United States, from the Atlantic to Wisconsin, farming is overwhelmingly dairy-based. This partially reflects the colder weather in the region, where the growing season for crops is short. Hilly places, where big fields are not possible, are most likely to have fruit farms or other tree-based products. Much of the east coast and California has fruit crops. The Midwestern United States is mostly corn, with wheat more common to the south. West of the prairies and into the Rocky Mountains is livestock country. Immense cattle ranches sweep across large areas, where the soil is too poor and rocky for most crops. Only in the Nevada desert and the most mountainous areas is there no farming at all.

The small, family farm has greatly faded in importance in the United States. Eighty percent of American farms are commercial farms, producing over 98% of the country's agricultural output. These commercial farms have led the productivity increases in American agriculture. Over the past 100 years, per person man hours worked on farms have steadily fallen, while productivity has increased. In the 19th century, increases in production were mostly the result of increasing the amount of land being farmed. But in the first half of the 20th century, efficiency increased. With the increasing help of machines like tractors, productivity per acre doubled.

Because the total output of American farms has increased by an average of 2% a year for over 150 years, but the population has increased by an average of only 1.3%, that has gradually led to a great surplus in the amount of food America produces, allowing America to become the greatest food exporting nation in the world.

10. What is the main idea of this talk?

11. The speaker mentioned many kinds of farming. Match the crop with the area where it is usually grown.

12. What is responsible for the increases in farm yields in this century?

13. What is true of America's agricultural production?

Questions 14-15

Listen to part of a conversation between two people.

(woman)	I heard you just got accepted into the journalism program. Congratulations!
(man)	Thanks. I can't believe I made it.
(woman)	That's right, our university's requirements are pretty stiff. I thought you needed at least a B$^+$ to get in; how'd you make it?
(man)	Getting into the journalism program is about more than just grades. Several people with solid "A" averages didn't get accepted. In my case, most of my grades have been pretty good. It was just that one semester I was sick that brought down my average. I was told the application committee really liked my writing sample, and that's what got me in.
(woman)	That's great. I always liked your writing. So, what happens now?
(man)	Now that I'm accepted, the program begins next semester. The first semester is like an introduction, and then I have to choose a track.
(woman)	What kind of track?
(man)	There's a bunch: news editing, television and media journalism, features writing, news

	administration and a couple of others.
(woman)	What do you think you'll do?
(man)	I'm not much of a beat reporter – I don't like writing lots of short little pieces. And I'm certainly not an administrator. I want to write longer and more involved stories.

14. What happened to the man?

15. Why was he accepted into the journalism program?

Chapter 3 – Diverters for Short Conversations

TOEFL Exercise 3.1

Listen to each short dialogue carefully, and then choose the best answer to the question.

1.	(man)	You know how I've been taking Dr. Stanton's class on zoology? Well, we were supposed to have two weeks to work on this lab about canine behavior; but just yesterday afternoon, the professor tells us that we all have to be finished by tomorrow!
	(woman)	That's no way to run a laboratory.
	(narrator)	What does the woman mean?

2.	(woman)	Have you heard anything about whether or not you made the scholarship?
	(man)	No, nothing's been announced yet.
	(woman)	Well, no news is good news, as they say.
	(narrator)	What does the woman mean?

3.	(woman)	So I'm thinking about changing departments and becoming an English major.
	(man)	An English major? That's quite a change.
	(woman)	Why did you say it like that? Is there something wrong with studying English literature?
	(man)	Frankly, I don't think the department is very good.
	(narrator)	What does the man mean?

4.	(man)	I can't believe how crowded the library is today. There isn't a seat available anywhere.
	(woman)	That's why I always rent a carrel, so I know I have a place to sit and keep my books.
	(man)	Do you mind if I use your carrel for a while?
	(woman)	Go right ahead. I'm not going to be back in the library until around 7 or so this evening.
	(narrator)	What does the woman mean?

5.	(woman)	Hi Steve. How's it going?
	(man)	Pretty well. But you know, I saw your roommate's new dog the other day. It's really cute. Does it have a name?
	(woman)	She calls it Pat – the same name as her mother!
	(narrator)	What is true about the dog?

6.	(man)	Wow, you've really cleaned up this place. You've thrown out a ton of things.
	(woman)	I threw out a lot. But do you know where I can get the rest of this stuff recycled?
	(man)	Actually, there's a pick-up point for recyclables just down the street by the park.
	(woman)	Really? Thanks a lot.
	(narrator)	What did the woman want to know?

| 7. | (man) | The weather is looking pretty bad today. I hear we might get thundershowers and even some hail. |
| | (woman) | No problem – I brought my umbrella with me. And besides, a summer storm can be exciting. |

(man)	But I'm worried the storm might wreak havoc with my garden.
(narrator)	What does the man say about the storm?

8. | (woman) | Your garden really looks great. |
|---|---|
| (man) | Thanks. It's a little time-consuming, but I find it a big release from the stress of studying. Hey, I need to go pick up a few flowers and things – you want to come along? |
| (woman) | Sure, sounds like fun. Maybe we should try out that new gardening store down the street. |
| (man) | Their roses are too expensive. Besides I've got to buy fertilizer, and they don't sell any at that store. |
| (narrator) | What does the man mean? |

9. | (man) | You're back from your trip! You and Stephanie were gone a long time. |
|---|---|
| (woman) | Yes, but we had such a great time, it felt like we were barely gone any time at all. |
| (man) | So where in Africa did you go? What did you think of it all? |
| (woman) | It was amazing. We went all over the place. Monaco was exciting, and Mauritius and Madagascar were gorgeous. |
| (narrator) | Where did the woman and her friend not go on vacation? |

TOEFL Exercise 3.2

Listen to each short dialogue carefully, and then choose the best answer to the question.

1. | (man) | When are you flying to Florida tomorrow? |
|---|---|
| (woman) | I need to take off for the airport around 1 to arrive there in time. |
| (narrator) | What does the woman mean? |

2. | (man) | I'm starving, but there's nothing to eat in the house. We haven't done any shopping for a week. |
|---|---|
| (woman) | Well, then I'm going to go to the supermarket. |
| (man) | It's nearly 10 already. It's probably already closed. |
| (narrator) | What is the man implying? |

3. | (man) | I need to get an extension from Dr. Sanders. I didn't get my paper finished that was due today. |
|---|---|
| (woman) | What happened to it? |
| (man) | I was up late finishing off my paper, when there was a power failure in the dorm. My whole paper got erased before I had a chance to print it. I did my best – I just need a little more time. |
| (woman) | Dr. Sanders said late papers were not acceptable. |
| (narrator) | What does the woman mean? |

4. | (woman) | I can't believe Professor Leonard just sprang a surprise test on us. |
|---|---|
| (man) | I knew there was going to be a test – I have a sort of sixth sense for these things. |
| (narrator) | What does the man mean? |

5. | (man) | Tim and I got into a fight last night. He didn't do his share of a project we're working on yet again. So I got pretty mad. |
|---|---|
| (woman) | I hope you weren't too mean on him. He's rather sensitive. |
| (man) | I just pointed out that he never pulls his own weight. |
| (narrator) | What does the man mean? |

6. | (man) | Did you see that tie Professor Harrington was wearing today? |
|---|---|
| (woman) | Yeah, but his wife bought it for him, so I told him it looked nice. |
| (man) | Nice? It's really ugly. You shouldn't have lied to him. |
| (woman) | It was just a white lie. |
| (narrator) | What does the woman mean? |

7. (man)   Kerry was supposed to meet me 20 minutes ago to give me her biology notes, but she hasn't shown up yet.

(woman)   I'd like to give her a taste of her own medicine for a change.

(narrator)   What does the man mean?

8. (woman)   Can you tell me when my car will be ready?

(man)   Well, it only takes a couple of hours to align the wheels, but your transmission needs to be replaced, and that's a good two-day job.

(narrator)   What does the woman want to know?

9. (woman)   Boy, classes sure are different here as they get more advanced.

(man)   That's right. And they get more interesting. In upper division classes, you can actually interact with your professor, instead of just listening to long lectures all semester.

(woman)   Yeah, especially in the seminar courses. I like how in the upper levels, there are more seminars and fewer lecture courses.

(man)   As a matter of fact, I have 3 seminars this semester alone.

(narrator)   What does the man mean?

TOEFL Exercise 3.3

Listen to each short dialogue carefully, and then choose the best answer to the question.

1. (man)   I like taking an easy class each semester, to help boost my grade and lighten my workload. Like look at this: "Physics for Poets and Other Non-Majors."

(woman)   If I wanted to learn about physics, I'd take a real class.

(narrator)   What is most likely true about the woman?

2. (woman)   So what did you think of your play? How did you do?

(man)   It was pretty hard, but I think we did pretty well. Where were you, though? I looked for you all over the theater, but I couldn't see you.

(woman)   I should have been there for your show, I know, but I couldn't get out of this meeting with my professor.

(narrator)   Which statement is probably true?

3. (woman)   I'm sorry to hear you didn't make the football team. But don't feel bad – our school has a really good team. It's tough to qualify for it.

(man)   I know, but I'm still disappointed. I worked really hard trying to make the team.

(woman)   And you can always try again next year if you want to.

(man)   I don't know if I could stand being disappointed again. The coach told me how close I came this year. I could have made it, too, if I was a little faster.

(narrator)   What is the man implying?

4. (woman)   Tim, where's your new video game system? I was hoping to play for a little while.

(man)   You should go easy on that. You have to study, you know.

(narrator)   What does the man mean?

5. (woman)   We'd better get more data about the science experiments if we want to complete this research properly.

(man)   There should be more information in the reference section of the library.

(narrator)   What does the man mean?

6. (man)   Sorry I can't stay. I have to go to my engineering seminar.

(woman)   You sure seem to put a lot of time into that class.

(man)   I don't have any choice. All the engineering seminars meet for at least 5 hours a week.

(woman)   Five hours every week? There's no way I'd take any course that met that much.

(narrator)   What is the woman implying?

7. (man)   Do you think we should try to do that extra physics problem Professor Spears showed us? He says he's never had any undergraduate solve it.

   (woman)   I think we should give it a go.

   (narrator)   What does the woman recommend?

8. (woman)   Well, it took all night, but I finally got that essay finished for our folklore class that's due today.

   (man)   Didn't you hear? Dr. Thompson is sick and won't be coming in today. We have until Monday to work on the paper now.

   (woman)   Oh, I wish I hadn't stayed up all night.

   (narrator)   What is most likely true?

9. (woman)   Dave, did you hear about the ridiculous decision the university trustees just made? They're going to cut the number of professors at our school and raise tuition rates.

   (man)   Yeah, that's kind of unfair, but I can see the other side, too. The school needs more money to buy better facilities. I guess it's all pretty controversial.

   (woman)   I think it's just wrong. In fact, I was thinking of writing a letter criticizing their decision for my column in the school paper.

   (man)   I wouldn't do that if I were you. Some people might misunderstand what you mean.

   (narrator)   What is most likely true about the man?

10. (man)   What happened to Sam? He looked really upset at something.

   (woman)   Oh, we were up late studying, when he suddenly realized he really needed a book from the library only five minutes before closing time.

   (man)   So I guess Sam didn't get to the library on time.

   (woman)   No, he actually made it to the library before it closed. But he couldn't sign out the book because he forgot his student identification card.

   (narrator)   What does the woman mean?

TOEFL Exercise 3.4

Listen to each short dialogue carefully, and then choose the best answer to the question.

1. (man)   Pam, I need to buy a computer, and the university offers 3 special deals on new computers. Which one do you think I should buy?

   (woman)   I've talked to a lot of other students about that, and no one thinks any of them are any good.

   (narrator)   What does the woman mean?

2. (man)   Hi, Jen. I finally saw that movie last night that you told me about. It was so amazing. I think it's the best action film I've seen all year.

   (woman)   Is it ever!

   (narrator)   What does the woman mean?

3. (man)   I'll be ready in a minute. I just need to finish printing my essay.

   (woman)   Still? Weren't you printing it an hour ago?

   (man)   Yeah, but you know how my printer is – always jamming and having one problem or another.

   (woman)   I don't know why you don't just get a new one.

   (narrator)   What does the woman mean?

4. (woman)   If you don't put some work into your project for Dr. Summers and fix it up a lot, I think it's going to get a really bad grade.

   (man)   Honestly, I couldn't care less.

   (narrator)   What does the man mean?

5. (woman)   Dan, how is your new semester going?

   (man)   Let me tell you, I'm just loving my microeconomics class with Dr. Safely. I think

		he's about the best professor at this school.
	(woman)	Isn't he, though? I can still remember taking that class with him a couple of years ago.
	(narrator)	What does the woman mean?

6. (woman)   Dave has had my notes for three days now and he still hasn't returned them.

    (man)   Yeah, Dave's pretty irresponsible with other people's things.

    (woman)   I don't want to ask him for my notes back; he'll think I don't trust him. I'm sure he'll return them as soon as he's done with them.

    (man)   I wouldn't hold your breath.

    (narrator)   What does the man suggest to the woman?

7. (woman)   I am so tired of all this work in our chemistry class. I really don't want to look at another chemistry problem for the rest of the year.

    (man)   Me neither.

    (narrator)   What does the man mean?

8. (man)   I need to go to the library and find a couple of books for my sociology research.

    (woman)   Would you mind picking up a book for me while you're there?

    (man)   No problem.

    (narrator)   What will the man probably do?

9. (man)   I can't believe it. I was supposed to get a "C" in physics, but for some reason I received a "B$^+$."

    (woman)   There must have been some sort of mistake. Are you going to tell your professor?

    (man)   I don't think so. I think I'll just keep quiet about it.

    (woman)   I could never do that.

    (narrator)   What does the woman mean?

10. (woman)   Hi John. What's wrong with you?

    (man)   My computer's not working properly. These programs I'm running should take just a few seconds. But each one is taking a few minutes.

    (woman)   Do you think your computer would work better if you reformatted the hard drive?

    (man)   It's not impossible. I'll look into it later.

    (narrator)   What does the man mean?

TOEFL Exercise 3.5

Listen to each short dialogue carefully, and then choose the best answer to the question.

1. (man)   I'm so confused by our astronomy assignment. I'm not sure what we're supposed to do.

    (woman)   Don't worry about it. The project was cancelled by Dr. Phillips.

    (narrator)   What does the woman mean?

2. (man)   Are you going to the student orchestra concert tonight?

    (woman)   I wanted to, but I couldn't get any tickets.

    (man)   I actually had two tickets to the show, but my dog ate them.

    (narrator)   What is most likely true?

3. (man)   Only about 10 people showed up at the poetry reading last night.

    (woman)   That's not a bad number, I suppose.

    (man)   Well, I was hoping for a lot more than that.

    (woman)   But the event wasn't announced in the university newspaper, so that must have hurt attendance.

    (narrator)   What does the woman mean?

4. (woman)   I'm sorry, but you're not allowed to put up posters here. You'll have to take those down.

(man)	But the poster was approved by the Provost.
(narrator)	Which statement is most likely true?

5. (woman)   I love how the student art gallery is looking these days. It's much nicer than it used to be, and the exhibits are top-notch.
    (man)   Thanks. You seem to know a lot about the student gallery.
    (woman)   I ran the student art gallery myself for a year when I was an undergraduate.
    (narrator)   What is true about the woman?

6. (woman)   I see you used Dr. Riley's newest book in your sociology essay.
    (man)   It's a great book. But because it's so new, it was really hard to find. Our university's library didn't have it.
    (woman)   So how did you get it?
    (man)   I special-ordered the book from another library.
    (narrator)   What is most likely true?

7. (man)   Did you go to our school's football game on Saturday?
    (woman)   Yes, I did. It was a lot of fun.
    (man)   I was surprised to find our team actually doing well this year.
    (narrator)   What is most likely true?

8. (woman)   Hi Kevin. Did you need to see me about something?
    (man)   Yes, do you think I could borrow your notes from your political science class? My friend Adam wasn't in class today and wants to see what he missed.
    (woman)   I gave my notes to Jonathon already. He said he needed them.
    (narrator)   What is true about the woman's notes?

TOEFL Exercise 3.6

Listen to each short dialogue carefully, and then choose the best answer to the question.

1. (man)   My conditioning is really getting better. Every day I work out, I get a little faster. I'm already faster than Ted, and I'm nearly as fast as Megan.
    (woman)   Wow. I'm not faster than Ted yet, and I've been working out much longer than you.
    (narrator)   What is true about Ted?

2. (woman)   I find studying much easier if I break everything down into sections and tackle each section on its own, rather than study everything all at once. How about you?
    (man)   For the most part, I hardly ever study like that. It's just not my style.
    (narrator)   What is probably true about the man?

3. (woman)   Where should we go for lunch?
    (man)   How about the Abrams Cafeteria?
    (woman)   The food there isn't as good as at the College Cafeteria or Smith Cafeteria.
    (man)   But it's cheaper.
    (narrator)   What is most likely true?

4. (man)   Did you do very well on your chemistry test?
    (woman)   Okay, I guess. It was a tough test, though. I answered fewer questions than I wanted to, but at least enough to pass.
    (narrator)   How well did the woman do on her test?

5. (woman)   I should work out a little and try to get myself into better shape. Do you exercise much?
    (man)   Are you kidding? All the time. I go running or swimming almost every day.
    (woman)   Really? I hardly ever go.
    (narrator)   What is true about the woman?

6. (woman)   I had a great time shopping today. I bought a new bookbag for $9.95, a box of floppy disks for $6, and a great book for only $4.

(man)	So how much did you spend overall?
(woman)	With tax it was less than $22.
(narrator)	How much tax did the woman pay?

7.
(woman)	I'm really annoyed at Sean. He borrows my pencil, and then he loses it.
(man)	Oh, it's only a little pencil. I'm losing them all the time.
(narrator)	What does the man mean?

8.
(woman)	We're going to have to do something about Becky. She keeps coming to our meetings late.
(man)	Oh, that's not so bad. Everyone is late sometimes. Even I was a little late today.
(woman)	But she's late practically every day.
(narrator)	What is true about Becky?

9.
(woman)	So how are you enjoying your new job at the library?
(man)	It's not bad. The work is pretty easy and I can even study sometimes while I work. I just wished it paid better. I'm only making $6 an hour.
(woman)	That isn't very much; you're right. I get paid closer to $10 an hour working over at the cafeteria.
(man)	And I know Diane gets paid nearly twice what I do working over at the university hospital.
(narrator)	What is true about their jobs?

TOEFL Exercise 3.7

Listen to each short dialogue carefully, and then choose the best answer to the question.

1.
(man)	So did you get your security deposit back on your apartment?
(woman)	Yeah, there wasn't anything wrong with it, aside from the usual wear and tear.
(narrator)	What does the woman mean?

2.
(man)	Yes, may I help you with something?
(woman)	I think so. I need to use the microfilm archives.
(man)	I'm sorry, but you need the reference desk. I just take care of signing books out and paying for overdue fines here at the checkout desk.
(narrator)	What can be done at the reference desk?

3.
(man)	So why isn't my ticket ready? I have to go to the airport right away!
(woman)	I'm sorry, but the computer was down all morning, so work got really backed up.
(narrator)	Why was the man's ticket not ready?

4.
(woman)	Yes, please come in. How may I help you?
(man)	My name's Stephen. You asked me to come to the academic advising office to talk about my courses next semester.
(woman)	Yes, Stephen, you haven't fulfilled your graduation requirements yet. Specifically, you haven't taken enough hard science courses. You need to enroll in at least one more this spring if you want to graduate when the semester's over.
(narrator)	What will Stephen most likely do?

5.
(man)	Didn't your friend Mike run in the elections for student council this year?
(woman)	More than that, he ran for council vice-president.
(man)	That's a fairly difficult challenge. How'd he do?
(woman)	He won by a landslide.
(narrator)	What does the woman mean?

6.
(man)	What do you think of that extra computer class you've been taking in the evenings?
(woman)	I've been surprised. It really panned out.
(narrator)	What does the woman mean?

7. (woman)   How was your trip here?
   (man)   Really nice. I had some legroom for once. There weren't too many stops, and we were on time.
   (woman)   That's good. I bet the scenery was amazing.
   (man)   Sometimes it was, but often you can't see much from the interstate.
   (narrator)   How did the woman travel?

8. (man)   Hey, do you know what happened to Cheri in Professor Grant's class last semester?
   (woman)   Cheri had a bad time in his class. She worked hard, but he wouldn't give her a good grade.
   (man)   I met her last night, and she was still complaining about what happened.
   (woman)   She needs to get over it.
   (narrator)   What does the woman mean?

9. (woman)   I heard you applied for the Provost's Research Program.
   (man)   Yes, I did. The school offers financial support to undergraduates doing original research, and since I had an idea I wanted to explore about the genetic characteristics of plants, I applied for the program.
   (woman)   So did you get accepted?
   (man)   My application was turned down, but the Provost told me that I at least got put onto the waiting list.
   (narrator)   What does the man mean?

TOEFL Exercise 3.8

Listen to each short dialogue carefully, and then choose the best answer to the question.

1. (woman)   Rick told me the strangest story about his sister.
   (man)   I knew. She told me the story herself yesterday.
   (narrator)   Who told the woman the strange story?

2. (man)   I'm all set for my party tomorrow night. I think it's going to be a lot of fun and just about everybody is coming.
   (woman)   Is Jason going to come?
   (man)   Actually, I didn't ask him. But I invited his roommate, Terry, and told him to let Jason know about it.
   (narrator)   Who did the man invite to his party?

3. (woman)   Are you excited about Dan coming back to visit?
   (man)   I sure am. It's been quite a while since I've seen Dan.
   (woman)   Are you going to pick him up at the airport?
   (man)   I was supposed to, but a friend of mine needs my help fixing a little emergency, so now Dan's brother is going to do it.
   (narrator)   Who is going to pick up Dan at the airport?

4. (woman)   Why did Peter pick Janice for the lead part in the play? Naomi is a much better actress.
   (man)   That's true, but she doesn't sing nearly as well.
   (narrator)   According to the woman, who is the best actor?

5. (woman)   What do you think of your jogging program?
   (man)   Oh, it's going really well. I'm already nearly as fast as you.
   (woman)   And you're already faster than Dave or Jan. You've really done a great job.
   (narrator)   Who is the fastest runner?

6. (man)   Hi, Betty, how is going?
   (woman)   Pretty good. I'm still getting used to my classes this semester. So, tell me, how are you enjoying taking a psychology class with Sam?
   (man)   Oh, Sam just transferred out of my class with Dr. Richard to a different one taught

by Dr. Kline.

| (woman) | Really? I heard bad things about Dr. Kline from my friend who was in his class last semester. I'd never take his class. |
| (narrator) | Who is in Dr. Richard's class now? |

7. (man) I heard you and your sister went to Erica's place last night.
   (woman) Yeah, we saw a short film Erica's friend Debby made.
   (narrator) Where did the woman go last night?

8. (man) So have you decided what we're going to do tonight?
   (woman) Since it's your friend Phil's birthday today, I thought we could all take him out for dinner.
   (man) Sounds good. I bet his sister would like to come along, too.
   (narrator) Whose birthday is it?

9. (woman) Karen's friend, Sue, is going to be coming with us on our trip, too.
   (man) Is there enough room for her in your sister's car?
   (narrator) Whose car are the speakers going to use?

Mini-Test 2

Listening Script Part A

Questions 1-6

1. (man) Mary, you're back. I haven't seen you in a while.
   (woman) I had to go home because of a family problem, so I missed a few days of work.
   (man) Considering all the work we've had assigned recently, you must be really behind.
   (woman) I'm going to have to free up my schedule for the next week, until I'm all caught up.
   (narrator) What does the woman mean?

2. (woman) Sorry I'm late. I overslept.
   (man) You do look kind of tired. Are you okay?
   (woman) I'm exhausted. I didn't nearly get enough sleep last night, yet again.
   (man) At least you'll be better off when the exam period comes. Then all your late nights will pay off.
   (narrator) What is the man assuming about the woman?

3. (man) I didn't know I had to take a major seminar this semester.
   (woman) All juniors have to take a seminar in their concentration in the fall semester. You're going to have to change your schedule, or else you won't be able to graduate on time next year.
   (narrator) What can be inferred about the man?

4. (woman) I have to go see Dr. Stephens after my math test tomorrow. But that's really inconvenient, because I need to spend that time getting ready for my history presentation later in the day.
   (man) Dr. Stephens can be really difficult that way. He never cares about what's happening in your other subjects. He once tried to make me come talk with him in the middle of exam period.
   (narrator) When does the woman have to meet Dr. Stephens?

5. (man) I want to get my cafeteria meal tickets redeemed for cash. Do you have any idea where I can do that?
   (woman) At the front desk of the dining management office, I believe. What's wrong? Don't you like the cafeteria food?
   (man) It's okay, I guess. But with my schedule, I'm almost never free during the serving times. I figured it would be easier just to cancel my dining service plan and use the money to buy my own meals.
   (woman) That might be more convenient, but you can spend a lot more money eating off-

campus. You should be careful.

(narrator)   Why does the man want a refund for his cafeteria meal tickets?

6. (woman)   I'm really worried about this literature exam. I've been cramming day and night for a week, but I still don't know half the equations we're supposed to know. It's going to be really hard.

(man)   It wouldn't be if you kept up with the homework during the semester.

(narrator)   What is the man implying?

Listening Script Part B

Questions 7-9

Listen to a professor and two students discussing information from an American history class. The class is on great explorers in American history.

(professor)   So, as we've seen over the past couple of weeks, a lot of great explorers in American history did their explorations in pairs. These explorers were instrumental in opening up the unknown lands of the New World to the European settlers. Who can give me some examples of these exploring pairs?

(man)   Lewis and Clark.

(professor)   They're probably two of the most famous. Their most famous expedition across America happened from 1804 to 1806. They got funding from Congress to explore America west of the Mississippi River. So the two of them went up the Mississippi until they came to the Missouri River, then all the way up the Missouri, crossed the continental divide, then went down the Columbia River until they came to the Pacific Ocean. Who else?

(woman)   Jacques Marquette and Louis Joliet.

(professor)   Yes. They were Frenchmen, and were important explorers in the early days of European exploration in North America, around 1673. Joliet and Marquette canoed from Lake Michigan to the Mississippi River, down to the Gulf of Mexico, then back up the Mississippi to the Chicago River, and back to Lake Michigan. It was an amazing journey for those days, going over 2,500 miles less than 5 months.

(man)   Did Daniel Boone explore with anyone?

(professor)   Not really. He was more of a guide, helping settlers move westward in the mid-to-late 18th century. He didn't cross the Mississippi until late in life, and in general was more a guide than a true explorer.

(woman)   How about Radisson and Groseilliers?

(professor)   Very good. They explored North America even before Marquette and Joliet. Both were French-Canadians who spoke several Indian languages well and were very comfortable in the wilderness, having been raised there. They were the first Europeans to find the northern part of the Mississippi, and even made the difficult overland passage from Lake Superior to the Mississippi and Missouri rivers. Eventually, they were so successful they were given a contract by the English king to begin the Hudson's Bay Company – a fur trading company that controlled land and all the rivers that emptied into Hudson's Bay.

7. What is the professor's opinion of these explorers?

8. The speaker mentioned many pairs of explorers. Match the pair with the region they explored.

9. The speaker mentioned many different explorers. Put the following explorers into the correct chronological order.

Questions 10-13

Listen to part of a lecture in an urban planning class. The professor is talking about American highways.

To many, nothing defined America better than the car. But it is the roads and highways that crisscross America that have defined America's car culture. So it is important to remember just how recent America's freeway system is – recent, but of pivotal importance.

The first engineered and planned road in the United States was the Lancaster Turnpike, a privately constructed toll road built that opened in 1795 connecting Philadelphia and Lancaster, Pennsylvania. The 62-mile-long road was first built with broken stone and gravel; however, pavement failures in 1796 led builders to adopt European road-building methods.

More significant was the Cumberland Road, also known as the National Pike. It was the first highway in America paid for with public funds. This road, going from West Virginia to Ohio, was first proposed by George Washington and Thomas Jefferson in order to aid westward expansion and national unity. Work on the Cumberland Road began in 1811 and finally made it to Springfield, Ohio by 1838, but soon afterward the project was abandoned because of a lack of funds.

The rapid development of railroads in America, beginning in the 1840s, greatly hindered the development of roads. For the next 60 years, railroads dominated transportation in America, and road works were basically confined to city streets. In the country, roads declined and were often impassable in wet weather.

The renewal of road building came not from the automobile, but the bicycle. Starting in the 1880s, the bicycle was extremely popular. The new bicycles were much more comfortable on smooth, paved surfaces than on rough dirt roads. When the automobile did come along after 1900, however, it did greatly increase the demand for good roads.

Most early paved surfaces were difficult to maintain or inappropriate for the United States, so it was in the United States that the modern asphalt road was developed. Edward de Smedt created the new, high-density asphalt in the 1860s and 70s.

Most of the first roads were built and maintained locally. In 1893, however, the state of Massachusetts established the first state highway commission. By 1920, all the other states would also have highway commissions of their own. The federal government also got slightly involved in highways, and in 1921 passed the Federal Aid Highway Act to help states pay for their roads.

The first freeway in the United States was the Pennsylvania Turnpike, built in 1937. The Pennsylvania Turnpike was a toll highway built on the route of an abandoned railway, making construction much simpler. Originally built to connect Pittsburgh and Harrisburg, the Pennsylvania Turnpike was later extended to Philadelphia in the east and Ohio in the west, making it 327 miles long.

In 1950s the U.S. Interstate Highway System was developed to provide a national network of high-quality roads. Funded by a gasoline tax, the Interstate System has grown to a total length of more than 45,000 miles, connecting all the major cities in the U.S.

10. What is the main topic of this lecture?

11. The professor talked about the history of highways in the United States. Summarize by placing the following events into the correct chronological order.

12. The speaker mentioned several early roads in American history. Match the highway and its significance.

13. What caused the renewal of road building at the end of the 19th century?

Questions 14-15

Listen to part of a conversation between two people.

(man)	I think I'm going to check out that new action movie this afternoon. You want to come along?
(woman)	I've seen ads for that movie; it looks really good. When're you going to go see it?
(man)	There's a show at 2:00 at the campus cinema.
(woman)	Oh, I really don't like that place at all.
(man)	But it's the closest place around.
(woman)	But it's a terrible theater. The screen is small, the sound is terrible, and the seats are cramped. If I'm going to see a big, exciting movie, I want to see it in a big, nice cinema.
(man)	Did you have some place in mind?
(woman)	Downtown, there's the Pantages Theater. That's my favorite movie theater in the city.
(man)	Isn't it kind of expensive?
(woman)	It's a couple of dollars more, but it's totally worth it. Plus the popcorn there is excellent.
(man)	Well, that sounds like fun, but I have an evening class today that begins around 5. If I went downtown, I don't think I could make it back in time. And personally, I don't care that much about how nice the cinema is. I just want to see an exciting movie this afternoon.

14. What is one reason the woman likes the Pantages movie theater?

15. What will the man most likely do?

Chapter 4 – Reviews for Part A

Type A – 11 Questions for Part A

Questions 1-11

1. (man)   I can't find the history book I need to write my essay. I've looked all over the history section of the library and it's just not there.
   (woman)   Of course you can't find it – I checked it out a week ago.
   (narrator) What does the woman mean?

2. (woman)   I just don't have time for this sociology class I signed up for. It's too much work. But the add/drop deadline's passed, so there's nothing I can do about it.
   (man)   Actually, just the add deadline is over.
   (narrator) What is the man implying?

3. (man)   So did you get a chance to talk to your academic advisor?
   (woman)   No, I didn't. Whenever I go to the advising office, there's always a huge lineup. And I just don't have time to wait around forever to talk to him.
   (man)   Well, you really need to talk to him; you can't put it off any longer. I bet if you got there first thing in the morning, there wouldn't be many students there.
   (narrator) What does the man suggest the woman do?

4. (woman)   If you're looking for a good class to take next semester, you should think about Dr. Robbins' class about modernist literature.
   (man)   Does Dr. Robbins' class satisfy the humanities requirement?
   (woman)   No, it's an upper-level class. But it's really good nonetheless.
   (narrator) What can be inferred from the conversation?

5. (man)   Jen, I heard you took quite a hit in yesterday's field hockey game.
   (woman)   Yeah, I wasn't ready for it and fell really hard. I twisted my ankle pretty bad and I bruised a couple of ribs.
   (man)   Wow. I guess you're lucky you didn't break anything or suffer anything more serious.
   (woman)   I guess so, but I think I'm going to sit out a few games, just in case.
   (narrator) What does the woman mean?

6. (woman)   Excuse me, is there a bus going downtown at this bus stop?
   (man)   Sure is. Buses 9, 11, 15, and 19 all go downtown, via the university, from here.
   (woman)   Oh, good. I really need to get to City Hall before it closes.
   (man)   City Hall isn't downtown, though. If you want to go there, you should take a number 20 bus. It'll only take about 10 minutes, too.
   (narrator) Why does the woman want to take the bus?

7. (man)   Jane, you want to go out with a bunch of us tonight? We're thinking of catching a movie and maybe going dancing.
   (woman)   No. I'm going to be up all night finishing off our report that's due tomorrow.
   (man)   Finishing our report off? But I finished it yesterday. Remember our agreement – you do most of the research, and I would write it up.
   (woman)   I know. But it's going to take hours to re-write it.
   (narrator) What is the woman implying?

8. (man)   This political science class is pretty difficult. I can't believe Dr. Clay is giving us another test this week.
   (woman)   Maybe we could meet tomorrow morning around 10 a.m. to get ready for the test together?
   (man)   I'd like to, but I have to meet my editor then to work on a story.
   (woman)   Oh, so you did join the school paper after all!
   (narrator) What did the woman assume about the man?

9. (woman)   This is so great that we have spring break next week. I was getting so run down and stressed out over my classes, I thought I might be crazy.
   (man)   I think we all felt the same way. That's why I think it's a great idea that your and my friends get together and take a little vacation all together. It could really be a lot of fun. Of course, first we have to think of something to do.
   (woman)   I was thinking we could do something outdoors – enjoy the warm weather. Do you think we should go to the beach or go camping?
   (man)   Oh, whenever I do anything like that I get really sunburned.
   (narrator)   What is the man implying?

10. (man)   Professor Stein said that because people in our class haven't been doing their homework, she's going to start giving weekly quizzes.
   (woman)   She was probably just mad. But there're over 100 people in our class, so I don't think she'll really follow through on it.
   (narrator)   What does the woman mean?

11. (woman)   I think I'm going to get going. I'm feeling really beat.
   (man)   Aren't you going to stay and study some more with me? We both really need to work on this material for the test tomorrow.
   (woman)   No, I need to get some sleep. Besides, Karen said she would be here soon. You can study with her.
   (man)   Karen's coming? That's great. She's smarter than the two of us put together. With help I know I can do well on the test.
   (narrator)   What will the woman most likely do next?

Type B – 17 Questions for Part A

Questions 1-17

1. (man)   Hey, Sue. I heard you got yourself a kitten recently.
   (woman)   I did, and he was really cute, too – but I had to give him away to a friend of mine.
   (man)   You did? What was wrong? Didn't you like him?
   (woman)   No, I liked him a lot, but I'm really busy with my classes and he just demanded too much attention.
   (narrator)   What does the woman mean?

2. (woman)   Allen, you look kind of tired. Is everything going okay?
   (man)   Not really. It's the school paper – we've been having problems, and I've had to do a lot of extra work to make sure the paper gets published on time.
   (woman)   I bet you're having problems getting good features written; it's always hard to think of longer stories that are interesting.
   (man)   Actually, we've been having the biggest problems with the shorter stories – we don't have enough reporters who can write short news summaries well.
   (narrator)   What is the man implying?

3. (man)   Have you seen Derrick around? I was supposed to borrow a disk from him with all the homework solutions for math class.
   (woman)   Derrick's at the library. But I know he lent the disk to his friend Dale.
   (narrator)   Who has Derrick's disk?

4. (woman)   I'm going to the dorm to study for the test tomorrow with Chris. I really need his help.
   (man)   But I just saw Chris at the student union. He said he was waiting for you, too.
   (narrator)   What will the woman most likely do next?

5. (man)   I'm all set to spend the afternoon working on our science experiment. Except that I'm kind of hungry. I'd like to get something to eat before we get started.
   (woman)   That sounds good – I haven't had lunch either.
   (man)   Well, the university cafeteria is right beside here. The food's not great, but it's

		inexpensive.
	(woman)	What do you say we get something to eat off campus? I know a great Italian place near here.
	(narrator)	What did the woman suggest to the man?

6. (woman) I feel like doing something tonight. How about we go see the student theater's version of _Romeo and Juliet_ that's going on these days?

(man) Oh, I know it's sold out all week.

(narrator) What does the man mean?

7. (man) I'm really happy with the grade Professor Lott gave me for my history exam. I was worried I might do poorly.

(woman) Oh, Dr. Lott has finished grading the papers already? I should go pick mine up.

(narrator) What did the woman assume?

8. (woman) How're your plans for housing next semester going?

(man) Pretty well. A couple of friends and I are going to get one of the three-bedroom suites in the north dorm. They're a good price for the size, and they're close to my classes. How about you? Have you made a decision yet?

(woman) I think I'd like to get something to live off-campus for a change. I want more freedom than I have living in the residence here.

(man) I can understand that. But you should start looking for a place as soon as possible; it can be hard finding something affordable.

(narrator) What can be inferred about the woman?

9. (man) Excuse me, but can you tell me how to get to the president's office?

(woman) Sure. Just walk a block and turn right at the statue, then walk another four blocks and it's the red building on your right.

(narrator) How far away is the president's office?

10. (woman) Ryan, have you decided which history class you're going to take next semester?

(man) I think I'm going to take Dr. Fields' seminar on life in colonial America. It looks interesting, plus it meets Monday afternoons, which is good for my schedule.

(narrator) What does the woman want to know?

11. (man) I can't believe how busy I am these days. This morning I have to finish a lab for biology before lunch, then spend the afternoon in the library studying for an economics test. And tonight I'll probably have to stay up all night working on an essay for my anthropology class.

(woman) So when are you going to find time to go with me to the store?

(man) Oh, I nearly forgot I promised to go with you. I guess I could find the time right after lunch.

(woman) Sounds okay. I'll see you then.

(narrator) When will the man study for economics?

12. (woman) So you're back from the used furniture store. What did you think of that antique table you were thinking about buying?

(man) It looked kind of run down, but nothing a little elbow grease couldn't fix.

(narrator) What does the man mean?

13. (man) Hey, Sharon! It's a nice surprise to see you. I was sitting with some friends at the back of the library studying. I just happened to come over here to take a little break.

(woman) That is lucky. Listen, I was about to go to the student union building to get some coffee. Want to come?

(man) Let me just run in to the library first and tell my friends I won't be back.

(narrator) What is the man implying?

14. (woman)   Dr. Brown's class must be the hardest one in my major. There are so many theories and charts to remember! Every unit has 4 or 5 new ones. And now I'm supposed to combine all of them into one big, final paper.

    (man)   And how's that paper going?

    (woman)   Slow. I've built up my models projecting Gross National Product and incomes for five years, but I still haven't figured out the import and export figures.

    (narrator)   What can be inferred about the woman?

15. (man)   So I've completed the first part of the experiment. What comes next?

    (woman)   First, you've got to take the mixture you've made and heat it over a light flame for about 15 minutes.

    (man)   That's in order to boil off the excess water, right?

    (woman)   Yes, and to start a chemical reaction. Once you've done that, take the remaining chemical and add it to 100 milligrams of aluminum oxide, and put that new mixture back over the flame for another 20 minutes.

    (narrator)   What is the total amount of time the man will use the flame?

16. (woman)   Have you read the student newspaper lately? It's really gotten a lot better.

    (man)   I've read it. I guess I've noticed a small difference, but nothing I could put my finger on. How is it better?

    (woman)   Well, the design and organization are both a little better, but most of all, the editing is much better. The writing was always okay, but sloppy editing used to make the paper look worse than it really was.

    (narrator)   What is the main reason the woman thinks the student paper is much better now?

17. (man)   Are you excited about the vacation coming up?

    (woman)   You bet I am. I haven't had a chance to see my family in so long – I really miss them. It will be great to fly back and spend some time with them again.

    (man)   Well, I'm not nearly as excited to see my family again.

    (woman)   Yeah, but you see them all the time, so that's understandable.

    (narrator)   What can be inferred from this conversation?

Chapter 6 – Casual Conversations and Question Types

TOEFL Exercise 6.1

Ex. 1   Listen to part of a conversation between a professor and her student.

(man)   Professor Burton, could you tell me a little about your course "Topics in Environmental Science"?

(woman)   Sure. It's a senior-level course that covers a wide range of topics about environmentalism. It's not so much an in-depth course as it is one that tries to show you the wide range of issues involved in environmentalism these days.

(man)   Is there a lot of work for the class?

(woman)   There's not so much written work to do. There're a couple of essays to do – one in-depth research essay and a bibliographic essay. But that's it – no final exam or weekly homework.

(man)   What's a bibliographic essay?

(woman)   That's an essay where you take one topic and write all about what everyone else has written about it. You need to find all the major books, articles, or whatever.

(man)   That doesn't sound too bad.

(woman)   Well, be careful. There is a lot of reading for this course. Every week you'll have a couple of hundred pages I expect you to go through and know well. In fact, your participation is a major part of your grade for the class.

(man)   I see. Well, thanks a lot, professor.

(woman)   Are you still interested?

(man)   The course sounds tougher than I thought it would be, but I'm interested in environmental issues, so I think I'll take it.

Why is the man meeting with the professor?

Ex. 2   Listen to part of a conversation between two speakers.

(man) Your resume indicates that you studied for a semester in Paris.

(woman) That's right. I got to examine all the architecture in the city up close and personal.

(man) How was that experience?

(woman) Oh, it was amazing. There are so many old and important buildings there that I really learned a lot. I even got to study with Hugo Leiber, one of my favorite architects.

(man) Did you travel anywhere else while you were there?

(woman) To quite a few places – Lyons, Antwerp, even Luxembourg.

(man) Do you think those experiences could help you here at our company?

(woman) Definitely. You do a lot of international work, and someone with that kind of experience could only help.

(man) Very good. If you'd leave me a copy of your portfolio, we'll get back to you as soon as we've made a decision.

What can be inferred about the woman?

Ex. 3   Listen to part of a conversation between two people.

(woman) Hi there. I'm having trouble finding this certain book on Medieval German nobility.

(man) Let me check on the computer... Hmm, it appears that we don't have it.

(woman) Oh, no. It was really important for an essay I'm working on right now.

(man) Well, you could always borrow it from another library.

(woman) Really? How can I do that?

(man) We have a central computer system that is connected to most of the other university libraries in the state. I can search them all to see where your book is, then order it from the nearest university.

(woman) That would be great. How long will it take?

(man) We can usually get a book here in two or three days. But the lending period is shorter than for a normal book – only 10 days instead of two weeks. And if you're late returning books from other libraries, the overdue fine is a lot larger.

(woman) No problem; I won't be late. But does it cost anything to sign out books from other libraries?

(man) Not for up to five books. Any more than that, and you would have to pay a small service charge.

What is the woman's problem?

Ex. 4   Listen to part of a conversation between two students.

(man) Hey, Jen, you look pleased.

(woman) I am. Remember how I lost my laptop computer yesterday? Well, I finally found it.

(man) That's terrific news. What happened to it? Did you just leave it at home?

(woman) No, I actually left it in the study lounge in the student union building.

(man) You did? But I thought we checked there for it.

(woman) We checked the second floor study lounge. But I totally forgot that I was studying up on the third floor lounge.

(man) Really? Are you ever lucky to get your computer back.

(woman) I know. I went to the student union a couple of hours ago to report that I lost my notebook, and the man at the front desk just pulled it out. Turns out someone had turned it in last night, not long after I left it there.

(man) I hope you thanked him.

(woman) I was so happy, I offered to take him to a movie tonight.

Why is the woman happy?

Ex. 5   Listen to part of a conversation between two speakers.

(man) I'm having the hardest time trying to decide on what major to declare.

(woman) Isn't there anything you're interested in?

(man)	No, I have the opposite problem – there's too much. I really like history, but the English department is fascinating, too.
(woman)	Well, you could try a double major – majoring in both fields.
(man)	I thought about that. But I have so much going on, with my extracurricular activities and my computer science minor, that I cannot change. I just don't have time for two majors.
(woman)	In that case, you could become a Humanities major.
(man)	What's that?
(woman)	It's a broader major that covers many different subjects – history, literature, philosophy, religion – almost anything about the culture of humans.
(man)	That sounds like it might be for me. Where can I find out more about it?
(woman)	Since it's an interdisciplinary program and not a normal major department, they don't have a department office of their own. You have to go to the College Office to get more information and apply.

What is the man's problem?

Ex. 6   Listen to part of a conversation between two people.

(woman)	Did you hear about the chemistry building?
(man)	No, what happened?
(woman)	There was a big fire in one of the labs last night.
(man)	Really? I remember hearing fire trucks last night, but I didn't see where they were going. How bad was the fire?
(woman)	Well, the firefighters got there before too much damage happened. But Dr. Solomon's lab was totally gutted by the fire.
(man)	How about the lab you work in?
(woman)	We were lucky – Dr. O'Reilly's lab was at the far end of the hall. It's a little smoky, but there wasn't any damage. Not even any water damage from the firefighters.
(man)	Do they know what caused the fire?
(woman)	They think it was an electrical short in one of the outlets. You know how old the chemistry building is.
(man)	Yeah. Maybe this will finally inspire the university to build a more modern lab building.

What is the woman's news?

Ex. 7   Listen to part of a conversation between two students.

(man)	I'm really excited about next semester.
(woman)	Why's that?
(man)	Because Stephan Kingsley, the famous author, is going to be a guest instructor here.
(woman)	Really? What's he going to teach?
(man)	He's going to be teaching a class on the modern novel and, even better, he's going to be leading a creative writing workshop.
(woman)	Which one do you want to take?
(man)	Both. His opinions of modern literature are really interesting, and when else could I get a chance to learn writing from someone so talented?
(woman)	Won't that class be difficult to get into?
(man)	Yeah, but I talked to the department chairman, and told him all about how I wanted to be a writer one day myself. He seemed impressed, because he assured me I would get in.
(woman)	That is great news.
(man)	Are you going to take his lecture class, too?
(woman)	I'm up to my eyes in field research these days for my thesis; there's no way I'd have time.

Why is the man excited?

Ex. 8   Listen to part of a conversation between two students.

(man)	Sara, you certainly look like you're in a good mood.
(woman)	I'm in a great mood. I just found out I got accepted into the Study Abroad scholarship program.
(man)	What's that?
(woman)	It's a special program the university has where you get to study for a semester at another university overseas.
(man)	That sounds like a great opportunity. Where can you study?
(woman)	At any of the other universities affiliated with this program – Edinburgh, Scotland; London, England; Paris, France; or Florence, Italy.
(man)	Wow. Do you know where you want to study yet? I bet London, right?
(woman)	Actually, I'm planning on majoring in art history, so I was thinking of Florence.
(man)	Really? I didn't know you know Italian.
(woman)	I don't. That's why I'm starting an intensive language program. I have a year before I get to go, so I need to really study hard.
(man)	Well, at least you'll have all that great Italian food to eat.

What happened to the woman?

TOEFL Exercise 6.2

Ex. 1   Listen to part of a conversation between two students.

(man)	Hey Linda. I saw you had a big package outside your place this morning. What was it?
(woman)	Oh, it was some books I ordered last month. They finally arrived.
(man)	What kind of books? For school?
(woman)	Kind of. I'm writing my senior thesis about women's issues in the writing of Virginia Woolf, so I ordered a couple of her books. But I also ordered a couple of new mystery novels, just for fun.
(man)	I see. Why didn't you just buy them at the campus bookstore?
(woman)	Well, I guess the campus bookstore would have been more convenient, and it has an okay selection. But in this case, my parents gave me a gift certificate for an Internet bookstore, so I used it to buy the books.
(man)	That's a nice gift. Was it your birthday?
(woman)	No, that's next month. My parents like to reward me when I get good grades. Last semester, I got straight A's, so they gave me a book certificate.
(man)	Straight A's? I guess you really earned that gift.
(woman)	It was hard work, but it really felt great.

Why did the woman order the books on the Internet?

Ex. 2   Listen to part of a conversation between two speakers.

(man)	Leanne, I heard you just bought a new bike.
(woman)	Yeah, I just got it yesterday.
(man)	But I heard it's supposed to be really nice.
(woman)	It's a racing bike. It's kind of fancy, but I got a great price on it.
(man)	Why'd you get such a special bicycle?
(woman)	Because I'm in a biking club. I've been quite involved in it for a while, and I thought it was about time I got a good bike.
(man)	What do you guys do? Racing?
(woman)	No, we're more about exercise and fun. During the week, we bike in the evenings all over town. And every weekend we go on really long rides through the countryside, sometimes even for two days or more.
(man)	So you're really serious about it?
(woman)	I guess so. I started in middle school. My family would go on these cycling trips through state parks together. It's more fun than being stuck in a car, and it's great exercise.

When does the woman NOT say her club goes biking?

Ex. 3   Listen to part of a conversation between two people.

(man)   Wow, you really have a lot of compact discs, Marianne.
(woman)   Thanks. Is this the first time you've seen my collection?
(man)   Yeah, I've never been over here to your dorm room before. How many CDs do you have?
(woman)   Around five or six hundred, I guess. But I have another couple hundred at home.
(man)   More? That really is a lot. How long did it take you to buy all of them?
(woman)   Quite a few years. My first job in high school was working in a music store, mostly so I could get the employee discount. And all I ever asked for during Christmases or my birthday was music.
(man)   Do you have a favorite kind of music?
(woman)   Actually, I like almost everything – rock, classical, jazz. Everything except country, I guess.
(man)   Really? I like country music.
(woman)   My parents always listened to it while I was growing up. I guess that turned me off of it.

How many compact discs does the woman have in her collection?

Ex. 4   Listen to part of a conversation between two speakers.

(man)   Sandra, you know how Jeff, Doug and I have been trying to start a band?
(woman)   Yeah, I've heard you talk about it.
(man)   Well, our first concert is going to be tonight. We'd love it if you came.
(woman)   That's great. I'd love to come. Where's it going to be?
(man)   We're playing at Smokey Joe's at 8:30.
(woman)   Oh, I have a meeting then, for my poetry group. It goes from 8 to 9 and I promised I'd go. I guess I could cancel ...
(man)   Don't worry. We have a second set that starts at 10:00.
(woman)   Super. And how much are tickets?
(man)   There's a $5 cover charge, but I'll give your name to the doorman so he'll let you in for free.
(woman)   Wow, thanks a lot. What kind of music do you guys play? I think you said it was a rock band.
(man)   Actually, we changed our styles a few times. We tried rock, punk, even country. But in the end, we decided to become a blues band.

1. When will the woman come to the concert?

2. What kind of music does the man's band play?

Ex. 5   Listen to part of a conversation between two students.

(man)   I heard you and Pat have been looking for a new roommate.
(woman)   That's true, and let me tell you, it's really stressful. We need to find someone soon because the rent is too much for Pat and me to pay by ourselves; but we're having trouble finding anyone.
(man)   I can imagine. It's the middle of the semester and most people already have apartments and are all moved in and comfortable. It's usually easier finding someone at the end of a semester.
(woman)   Exactly. And not just that, but Pat and I are looking for the right kind of person, too. If you're going to live with someone, you better live with someone you're compatible with.
(man)   So what kind of person are you looking for?
(woman)   We want someone who'll fit in, who's like us. You know, neat and clean, but who also likes to have fun and keep odd hours.
(man)   I can imagine that's a tough combination.
(woman)   I'll say. It seems like most clean people are really uptight and go to bed early, and most party people are real slobs. I'm worried we might have to choose someone who's not a good fit.
(man)   Well, I'd post an ad at the student housing office first. It's a good way to let a lot of people

know you're looking for a roommate.

| (woman) | I hadn't thought of that. I was just putting up posters around campus and asking people I knew, but I like your idea more. |

What kind of roommate does the woman want?

Ex. 6 Listen to part of a conversation between two students.

(woman)	I'm going to the concert tonight. Do you want to come with me?
(man)	What kind of a concert is it?
(woman)	The university's student orchestra is going to be playing some pre-baroque music in the Jackson auditorium.
(man)	That sounds like it could be really interesting. When is it going to be?
(woman)	At 7:30. But in order to make sure we get good seats, I want to get there a half-hour early at 7. I think it's going to be really crowded.
(man)	Well, I can't get there at 7, but if you save a seat for me, I'll join you around 7:20, if that's okay.
(woman)	No problem. Why are you going to be late?
(man)	Oh, I have to meet with a friend of mine after dinner to discuss a project we're working on together. We're meeting with the professor tomorrow, so we want to be all ready.
(woman)	Good luck with that. And I guess I'll see you soon.
(man)	See you later.

1. When does the concert start?

2. Why is the man going to be late?

Ex. 7 Listen to part of a conversation between two speakers.

(woman)	Hey, Sam, what's wrong?
(man)	Oh, I lost my address book last night. I've been looking all over for it all day, but I can't find it anywhere.
(woman)	Is it important?
(man)	Yes! I kept all my phone numbers in there.
(woman)	You don't have a backup on computer or anything?
(man)	I did, but my computer crashed just last week and I lost the file with my addresses in it. I meant to back it up, but I never got around to it.
(woman)	That's too bad. Well, where have you looked so far?
(man)	Last night, I went to a movie at the student center, so I checked there. Then I went to the library to study for a couple of hours, and I checked there, too. I followed the exact same route I walked last night, just in case I dropped it while walking, but it isn't anywhere.
(woman)	Didn't you go to the movie with Jack last night?
(man)	Yeah, I did. That's right! I picked Jack up at his place – I totally forgot about that. I think I left my address book there. In fact, I can remember putting it down on a counter when I went to make a call. Thanks a lot, Marcy.
(woman)	No problem.

1. Why can the man not use his computer?

2. Where is the man's address book probably?

TOEFL Exercise 6.3

Ex. 1 Listen to part of a conversation between a professor and her student.

(man)	Dr. Davis, I'm sorry, but I won't be able to get my paper finished on time for your cognitive psychology class.
(woman)	And why's that, Dennis?
(man)	Well, I was really sick last weekend. I actually went to the hospital for a couple of days. I'm okay now, but I wasn't able to work on the assignment for a few days.
(woman)	I see. If you were that sick, I guess you can have a little more time to work on the essay. How long do you want?

(man)	Uh ... a week would be great.
(woman)	How long were you in the hospital?
(man)	A couple of days.
(woman)	Then you can have a two-day extension for your paper. You've had over a month to work on it, so you should be nearly finished by now.
(man)	Okay, that's fair. But I'm going to have to work really hard to get it done.
(woman)	And Dennis? Remember to bring me a note or receipt from the hospital that shows you were there for a couple of days.
(man)	Oh, right. Can I just attach it to my paper when I hand it in?
(woman)	That will be fine.
(man)	All right. Thanks a lot, Dr. Davis.

What will Dennis most likely do?

Ex. 2   Listen to part of a conversation between two students.

(man)	Jan, I was hoping you might be able to help me with my computer.
(woman)	Sure, what's the problem?
(man)	I have an Internet connection in my apartment, but I can't get it hooked up right to my computer.
(woman)	I see. Can the computer find the connection?
(man)	I don't think so, but I'm not sure. I'm not very good with these things.
(woman)	Don't worry about it. It's probably just a problem with how your software is configured. I'll come over tonight – it'll probably only take me about ten minutes to fix it.
(man)	Great. That's a big help.
(woman)	No problem. It's what I study; it's a piece of cake.
(man)	Still, I owe you one. How about I buy you lunch tomorrow?
(woman)	That sounds good. Thanks a lot.

What will the man probably do?

Ex. 3   Listen to part of a conversation between two speakers.

(man)	Have you seen Dr. Farber around today?
(woman)	I'm sorry, but he hasn't come in yet.
(man)	I really need to get his help. I'm trying to do some research, but I'm having a hard time finding the right books. Do you know when he's going to be here?
(woman)	I'm not sure. Have you checked to see when his office hours are?
(man)	Yes. He was supposed to be here at 11 o'clock for office hours. I was waiting outside his office for over an hour, but he never came. Maybe he's sick.
(woman)	Dr. Farber has office hours at 11 o'clock on Wednesdays.
(man)	Right. Today's Wednesday.
(woman)	I'm sorry, but today is Tuesday. But he might have office hours this afternoon. I'm not sure.
(man)	It's okay. I have class this afternoon. I'll just come back tomorrow.

What will the man do?

Ex. 4   Listen to part of a conversation between two people.

(man)	This is such a great day!
(woman)	Why? What happened?
(man)	I just got the results back of my law school test – and I aced it!
(woman)	Wow, that is great news. I know how you wanted to be a lawyer, just like your father.
(man)	Yeah, he really inspired me. He's a great corporate lawyer.
(woman)	Is that what you want to do?
(man)	Actually, I'm more interested in constitutional law. In fact, I was thinking about trying to get a Ph.D. in law.
(woman)	What would you do with a doctorate?
(man)	I'd like to be a law professor at a university. I think it would be really interesting.

(woman) It sounds interesting, but really difficult, too.

What does the man want to do?

Ex.5 Listen to part of a conversation between two speakers.

(man) My old computer finally crashed and died last night, in the middle of a paper I was writing.

(woman) That's bad news. What are you going to do?

(man) I was thinking about getting a computer repairman to fix it, but it's such an old computer, it really isn't worth it. So I'm just going to get a new one.

(woman) It can be tough getting the right computer. Would you like some help?

(man) Yeah, I could really use some advice, and you're the best computer person I know.

(woman) Thanks. So, tell me what you're looking for. What do you need to do on your computer?

(man) I don't think I need anything special. I just use it for writing papers for school and using the Internet.

(woman) If you get a laptop, you can carry the computer with you to the library or wherever.

(man) That would be convenient. But aren't portable computers expensive? I don't have a lot of money to spend these days.

(woman) Well, if saving money is most important to you, you should think about buying a used computer. Even if it's only a year or two old, a computer costs a lot less than a new one. I know a store that fixes up people's old computers and resells them. They're honest and a good price; we could go check it out.

(man) Sounds good. Can we go right now?

What will the man probably do next?

Ex. 6 Listen to part of a conversation between a professor and her student.

(man) Hi there, Dr. Maxwell. Do you have a minute?

(woman) Sure. What's on your mind, Sean?

(man) I've really liked your survey class this past semester, so I was thinking about taking some more of your classes.

(woman) Thanks a lot, Sean. It's nice to know someone enjoys my classes. What else are you interested in taking?

(man) Well, I guess I've long been interested in the Civil War. Aren't you teaching a course on that next semester?

(woman) I am, sort of. But that course is the second part of a two-part course on the economic history of the Civil War. You really can't take that course until you take the first half, and I'm not offering that class until next fall.

(man) Oh, that's too bad. I wanted to take a class with you.

(woman) I am offering a seminar next semester on early 19th century American history – it would be a good background to the Civil War.

(man) Really? That sounds about perfect.

What will the man most likely do next semester?

Ex. 7 Listen to part of a conversation between a professor and his student.

(man) Thanks for coming here today, Sabrina.

(woman) No problem, Professor Silverman. What did you want to see me about?

(man) Well, you've done a lot of work for me over the past year. You've done a lot of research and really helped me out. And that's why I've decided to nominate you for the department's annual Undergraduate scholarship.

(woman) The department scholarship? Me? Wow, I don't know what to say. That's incredible.

(man) It is a big honor. But I truly think you've earned it and you deserve it.

(woman) The department scholarship covers the full tuition, doesn't it?

(man) Yes, that's right. It's a lot of money. And more importantly, the scholarship carries a lot of weight. Since you were hoping to get into graduate school, this will greatly help out your application.

(woman) Wow. Since I hope to become a professor myself, one day, this is a real boost to my chances.

(man)	That's true. But everyone on the faculty likes your research, especially your work on how government intervention can affect the economy.

What does the woman want to do in the future?

Ex. 8   Listen to part of a conversation between two speakers.

(man)	Are you ready to go home for vacation?
(woman)	I'm not going home. My family lives too far away. Besides, my parents are busy traveling these days, so they wouldn't be at home.
(man)	That's too bad. So what are you going to do?
(woman)	I thought I'd just stay here.
(man)	But our dorm is closed over the vacation.
(woman)	It is? I didn't know that! Oh no, what am I going to do? I can't afford to stay in a hotel for two weeks.
(man)	Well, you could go to the housing office and sign up for special housing over the break.
(woman)	What's that?
(man)	This main dorm is closing, but the King's Court dormitory stays open over the break, so students like you can have a place to stay if they need it. The dorm's cafeteria is open, too. They even have special events for Christmas.
(woman)	Wow. I didn't know about that. That's just what I need. Do I need anything to sign up for the special housing?
(man)	You'll need to bring a copy of your current residency contract. And you do have to pay for the extra housing, so you'll get a bill, too.
(woman)	Well, it's better than living in a hotel for a couple of weeks. I'll go to the office right away.

What does the man suggest the woman do during the vacation?

Ex. 9   Listen to part of a conversation between two students.

(man)	Jen, you look really upset.
(woman)	I am. I was just finishing off my homework assignment when my computer crashed. All that work, down the drain.
(man)	That's terrible. But don't you have a back-up copy?
(woman)	My only copy was on the hard drive, but it isn't working at all now.
(man)	Isn't your paper due today?
(woman)	Yes, it is – around 4 o'clock. That's why I'm in such a hurry.
(man)	Are you going to try to get an extension from your professor?
(woman)	No, I think the data on the hard drive are recoverable. So I'm taking it to a friend of mine in the computer science department to see if she can help me out.
(man)	Okay. But if she can't help you, I'd be glad to do what I can.
(woman)	Thanks, but my friend is really good. And if she can't help me, I don't think I'd have time for anyone else to help me.

What will the woman most likely do next?

Mini-Test 3

Listening Script Part A

Questions 1-6

1. (woman)	Sam, where're you going? We were supposed to study for another couple of hours.
(man)	I need to go home and sleep for a while.
(woman)	You look like you could use a rest. Are you tired?
(man)	No. I'm getting a really bad migraine.
(narrator)	What does the man mean?

2. (man)	I saw your light on and wondered what you were doing up so late. What's going on?
(woman)	I'm having trouble getting my physics project to work.

(man)	Maybe you should go talk to your professor about it.
(woman)	I don't like to bother him unless the problem is serious.
(narrator)	What is the woman implying?

3.
(woman)	Dave, have you seen John's great new apartment? It's even bigger than yours.
(man)	It is nice, Anne, but it still isn't as big as Tony's, and it's only a little more so than yours.
(narrator)	Who has the smallest apartment?

4.
(man)	I have so much to do still. I have to go to the library and get a book before I go to the department office and do some paperwork. Then I'm meeting some friends for dinner.
(woman)	But the department office is going to close soon, and I know you need to get that paperwork done today.
(narrator)	What will the man probably do next?

5.
(woman)	I can't sleep at night. My annoying neighbors keep playing their music too loud until all hours.
(man)	Have you tried complaining to the student housing office?
(narrator)	What does the man suggest?

6.
(man)	Julie, thanks for telling me about this job. I love working in the library.
(woman)	Yeah, I got a job here by chance last year. But I thought you'd like it.
(man)	It's easy, and I can study while I'm here. It really is a great job.
(woman)	Isn't it, though?
(narrator)	What does the woman mean?

Listening Script Part B

Questions 7-10

Listen to part of a lecture in an English literature class. The professor is talking about Sinclair Lewis.

One of the novelists of this century to best capture the reality and spirit of life in America was Sinclair Lewis. His writing style was rough but insightful, and Lewis had great skill in producing realistic dialogue. The son of a country doctor, Lewis grew up in small-town Minnesota. After a year at Oberlin College in Ohio, he studied at Yale University and graduated in 1908. He spent the next few years in editorial and newspaper work at various places around America while he wrote short stories and poems on the side. It was while living in New York City that he published his first book in 1912, titled *Hike and the Aeroplane*. Several other books followed of varying success. But in 1920, he wrote *Main Street*, a powerful satire about the dullness of small town life. The novel was incredibly successful, smashing many long-held sentimental beliefs about rural villages.

Lewis's favorite book was *Arrowsmith* written in 1925. It told the story of a young doctor and his struggle between his personal desires and his scientific ideals. For *Arrowsmith*, Lewis was awarded a Pulitzer Prize, but he turned it down because he thought the book did not have enough literary merit.

Perhaps Lewis's most famous book was *Elmer Gantry*, written in 1927, a merciless satire about a Midwestern minister. Many people were outraged by Lewis's portrayal of an immoral preacher, but critics and most of America were greatly impressed by the high quality of the book. Lewis was the first American ever to win a Nobel Prize for literature, in part on the strength of that book.

In the 1930s, he turned to the theater, writing plays and sometimes acting in his own works. There, his skills as a mimic and public speaker made him a talented actor. But in general, after the 1930s, the quality of Lewis's work began to decline. In spite of this, he continued writing. By the time of his death in 1951, Lewis had written 22 books and numerous short stories and other works.

7. What is the speaker's main opinion of Sinclair Lewis?

8. The lecturer described Lewis's life. Summarize by putting the following events into the correct chronological order.

9. The speaker mentioned many of Sinclair Lewis's books. Match the book with what the book was about.

10. What made Sinclair Lewis a good actor?

Questions 11-13

Listen to a professor and his students discussing information from an anthropology class. The class is on chimpanzees.

(professor)	So over the past month, we've looked at primate social behavior, looking for clues about our early human ancestors. The philosopher Aristotle once called man a political animal. In fact, many elements of our political behavior are very evident in the social activities of chimpanzees.
(woman)	You mean primates have politics?
(professor)	In a way, yes – they have a constant jostling for power, they form coalitions, and they plot strategies. Take the case I studied of three chimps named Arnold, Bugs, and Chris. Arnold was the traditional alpha male or group leader of his chimp tribe. And as he was alpha male, all the other chimpanzees in the tribe greeted him frequently, a sign of dominance, as you can see in this graph. But after a time, Bugs decided he wanted to be the boss. He stopped greeting Arnold and instead began to harass him. But he did not do so alone. He had help from the tribe's females and from a younger male, Chris. When Bugs became the dominant male, now he received more greetings from the others. This only lasted a short time before Arnold regained control. Eventually, in all this confusion, Chris, with the support of the chimp females, actually won control of the group. But because he was so young, he did not receive a majority of the greetings right away. It took a couple of years, as slowly Arnold lost support and the other chimps began to respect Chris's leadership and give him the signs of respect.
(man)	So the hierarchy of the group becomes formalized through the chimps greeting each other and showing submission?
(woman)	Right, but it's important to remember that an individual chimp's influence does not always correspond to his or her rank. It also depends on age, experience, and connections.
(professor)	Very good. But it's important to remember with our chimpanzee community, that politics are not bad or evil. They give their lives a logical coherence and even a democratic structure, allowing weaker members to participate. Once a balance is reached, the social hierarchy acts as a cohesive factor, putting limits on confrontation and conflict.

11. What is the main topic of this discussion?

12. The professor discussed a struggle for leadership in the chimpanzee tribe. Summarize that struggle by placing the following events into chronological order.

13. What does the professor say about chimpanzee politics?

Questions 14-15

Listen to part of a conversation between two speakers.

(man)	Jan, I really need your help.
(woman)	What for?
(man)	For that creative writing assignment I have to have finished by tomorrow.
(woman)	The one you asked me to read last night?
(man)	Yeah, that one. Did you get it finished?
(woman)	I did.
(man)	And what did you think of it?
(woman)	It's a good beginning, but it certainly needs more work before you hand it in.
(man)	It's the characters, isn't it?
(woman)	No, the characters are fine. It's the pacing – the story doesn't flow very well.
(man)	Really? What do you mean?
(woman)	Well, the flow isn't very good. In the first half of the story, nothing happens. You just describe the characters and their lives and their school and everything. Then you have this really fast bit of action. Then you spend the last 3 or 4 pages describing things again.
(man)	So you think I should add more action and break up the descriptions?
(woman)	That's a good start. The basic plot is okay, and the ideas are really good; I'd just try to make it flow better.

(man)   Thanks a lot. I'm going to get to take your advice and change my story right after dinner.

14. What is the man's problem?

15. What does the woman think is wrong with the man's story?

Chapter 7 – Academic Discussions/Lectures and Question Types

TOEFL Exercise 7.1

Listen to the following excerpts from academic discussions and lectures, then answer the main topic/idea questions.

Ex. 1   Listen to a professor and his students in a literature class discussing information on essay structure.

(professor)   Okay, I'm kind of concerned about the quality of essays I've been receiving lately, so I want to go over what makes a good essay. Now all essays have essentially three parts. What are they?

(man)   The introduction, body, and conclusion.

(professor)   Very good. It's important to have all three sections, fully developed. For an introduction to be complete you need to begin generally and become increasingly specific. This is where your thesis statement will be. The thesis is your original idea, the reason you are writing your essay. A thesis is not just a statement of fact; it is an original idea.

(woman)   Where does the thesis go?

(professor)   It's always the last sentence of the introduction. If it is not there, you've made a major mistake. After the introduction comes the body. This is where you will prove your thesis. The essay usually has three major proofs for the thesis. You should start with your strongest proof first, and weaker ones later. The body is where you will include all your quotes and sources.

What is the main topic of this discussion?

Ex. 2   Listen to part of a lecture in a biology class. The professor is talking about horses.

Horses have a long and interesting history, and the study of their complex evolution is one of the most extensive and intensive searches done by scientists. As a result, the evolutionary story of the horse is perhaps the best documented and most complete of that of any animal.

Whereas people have been around for about 2 million years, the earliest horses were in existence over 60 million years ago, just after the end of the age of dinosaurs. Evidence of those early horses can be found in North America and Europe, with researchers thinking that the horse probably first originated in North America.

The oldest ancestor of the horse is called the *Eohippus*, which means "dawn horse." It looked very different from the modern horse. It was about the size of a fox, and looked a little like a cross between a dog and a rabbit. It ranged from 10 to 20 inches high at the shoulder, with a high, arching back, a long tail, and a long snout. The feet of the *Eohippus* had four toes, like a dog, and simple teeth designed for chewing leaves.

What is the main topic of this lecture?

Ex. 3   Listen to a discussion between a professor and his students in a materials science. The class is on cork.

(professor)   We've been talking a lot lately about versatile materials that can be used in a wide variety of ways, such as plastics and chalk. Today, though, I want to talk about cork. Where does cork come from?

(man)   Cork is the bark of a kind of oak tree that grows mainly in North Africa, Spain, and Portugal.

(professor)   That's right. Virtually all the world's cork comes from this region. A cork tree can usually live about 150 years, with a new layer of cork maturing every nine years.

(man)   Why is cork different than regular bark?

(professor)   It's because of the unique cell structure of cork. Each cell has a tiny amount of air trapped in it, so that more than 50 percent of the volume of a piece of cork is actually trapped air. Because of its structure, cork is one of the lightest of all natural solid substances. It is resistant to moisture, is chemically stable, and does not transmit heat. The most important property of cork is its compressibility.

What is the main subject of this discussion?

Ex. 4 Listen to part of a lecture in a philosophy class. The professor is talking about transcendentalism.

One of the most influential movements in America in the mid-19th century was transcendentalism – a philosophy that both reflected and inspired American individualism and independence. It was a movement of philosophical idealism that reached its height in New England in the 1840s, and inspired the work of Emerson, Margaret Fuller, Thoreau, Bronson Alcott, and many others. Together, the transcendentalists rebelled against the coldness of 18th-century philosophy, with its emphasis on reason and the senses. Instead, the transcendentalists argued for the supremacy of mind over matter and defended intuition as a guide to truth.

The term "transcendental" was used originally for concepts that have no limits. But for those thinkers in New England, "transcendental" was used for ideas that did not come from sense experience, but that were purely from thought. In many ways, this New England transcendentalism was a kind of the new romanticism that came from France and Germany originally. It was inspired by writers such as Kant, Hegel, Goethe, and most notably Coleridge.

What is the main idea of this lecture?

Ex. 5 Listen to a professor and his students in a biology class discussing information on cloning.

(man)	Professor Brundle, we've been talking about the science of cloning for the past couple of weeks; but even if the technology is possible, I was wondering if it is a good idea.
(professor)	That's an interesting question. Lots of people think that cloning is too scary and that scientists should not play around with nature. But in fact, there are some very useful reasons to develop cloning.
(woman)	Like in order to help endangered species?
(professor)	That's one good example. Many people want to use cloning to help save endangered species, especially animals like cheetahs and pandas that are dangerously few in number and that reproduce poorly in captivity.
(man)	How about extinct animals?
(professor)	Now that is a more ambiguous and difficult idea. Not for dinosaurs or anything like that – they have been extinct so long that it would be almost impossible to find any usable DNA. But people are looking into cloning animals that only recently became extinct, so it is possible to get good copies of their DNA. For example, there is a Spanish mountain goat called the "bucardo" that died out just a couple of years ago; scientists managed to save some of the DNA of the last known bucardo female. But even this has complications. Even if the scientists successfully clone this goat, this produces just one single bucardo. And without a member of the opposite sex, they cannot reproduce the species. So now scientists are trying to figure out a way to make a male bucardo from that female bucardo DNA.

What is the main idea of this discussion?

Ex. 6 Listen to part of a lecture in an American history class. The professor is talking about the Mexican War.

The Mexican War represents one of the most dubious events in American history – a shameless land grab of some of the most valuable territory in North America, thinly veiled by the United States as a war of defense. Americans had been streaming into the Mexican territory of Texas for years, resulting in revolution and a sort of independence by 1836. The Mexican War grew out of a border dispute between the two nations. Texas, when part of Mexico, stretched all the way down to the Rio Grande River. When Texas entered into the United States, however, its southeastern boundary was changed to the Nueces River, 100 miles eastward.

On January 13th, 1846, American President James Polk ordered American troops to march to the Rio Grande. When, that May, a Mexican force crossed the river at Palo Alto, Polk used the incident as an excuse to start the war.

On September 14, 1847, American forces entered Mexico City, the capital of Mexico, bringing the fighting to an end. It took until February 1848 for the two countries to sign the Treaty of Guadalupe-Hidalgo. In this treaty, Mexico accepted the Rio Grande River as the border and ceded its northern provinces to America in exchange for $15 million. It was a trivial amount of money for lands with so much mineral wealth, including gold. In addition to California and Texas, this territory would later become the American states of Nevada, Utah, Arizona, Colorado, and Wyoming.

What is the speaker's opinion of the Mexican War?

Ex. 7 **Listen to a discussion between two students in a geography class. The class is on Niagara Falls.**

(man)	I heard you're going to Niagara Falls with your geology class. I bet that's really exciting.
(woman)	Yeah, we've been reading about it in class for a while now. Niagara Falls is definitely the most impressive waterfall in the world. Not because they are the biggest – they're only 167 feet high at the tallest point, and there are lots of waterfalls higher than that. But Niagara Falls is amazing because of the amount of water going over them – 12 million cubic feet every minute, or 380,000 tons. The plunging water also sends out a never-ending roar as it strikes the bottom. In fact, "Niagara" comes from the Iroquois Indian word meaning "thunder of waters."
(man)	That is impressive. Is Niagara Falls American?
(woman)	The falls are divided into two parts by Goat Island. The American side is northeast of Goat Island – it's a straight strip about 1000 feet long. The larger Canadian portion on the southwest side is called the Horseshoe Falls, on account of its shape. It's about 3,000 feet long. Before going over the American side, the water is only about 3½ feet deep, while it's around 20 feet deep on the Canadian side, so in fact the Canadian side accounts for about 95% of the total water going over the falls.

What is the main idea of this discussion?

Ex. 8 **Listen to part of a lecture in a geography class. The professor is talking about settlement patterns.**

The United States was settled in a much different manner than nations in the Old World. In Europe and elsewhere, cities and rural areas grew and developed slowly and relatively densely, in harmony with geography and the landscape. But the pattern of settlement in America was more disordered and random. Although the land that now is the United States was inhabited before any Europeans arrived, those pre-European settlement patterns had virtually no impact on the contemporary nation. When the Europeans and others came to the New World, they quickly and dramatically re-ordered the land. The land was so vast and full of resources, and the population so spread out and mobile, that development came chaotically. Patterns of rural settlement indicate much about the history, economy, society, and minds of those who created them. From the beginning, the prevalent official policy of the British and then the U.S. government was to promote agricultural and other settlement – to push the frontier westward as fast as physical and economic conditions permitted. The federal government administered the nation's lands, most of which were acquired in the Louisiana Purchase of 1803, and later past the Mississippi River to the west coast in 1819. Federal land managers surveyed, numbered, and mapped their territory in advance of settlement, beginning with Ohio in the 1780s.

What is the main idea of this lecture?

Ex. 9 **Listen to a discussion between a professor and his student in an American culture class. The class is on the Beats.**

(professor)	So we're continuing our discussion of American culture in the 50s by talking about the Beats. The Beats never sold like the mainstream literature of the time, but their effects were extremely far-reaching. What can you tell me about the Beat movement?
(woman)	The Beat poets were rebelling against middle class life, embracing alcohol, self-destruction

	and despair instead.
(professor)	It might look that way, but the Beat poets were actually embracing life. It was life on their own terms, shocking to many people, but still it was a quest for a visionary and spontaneous way of life. The Beats began in Greenwich Village, in New York City, where they sought personal rather than social solutions to their anxieties. Their road to enlightenment and freedom lay in street life, jazz, Buddhism, and a vagabond spirit that took them speeding back and forth across the country from New York to San Francisco.
(woman)	So in a way, the crazy anarchy of the Beats played an important role in preparing the way for the more widespread youth revolt of the 1960s.
(professor)	Exactly. Their work led to the images of rebellion, like James Dean and Marlon Brando and others, but they were not about just rebelling themselves; they were chiefly about living and freedom.

What is the professor's attitude toward the Beat poets?

TOEFL Exercise 7.2

Listen to the following excerpts from academic discussions and lectures, then answer the comprehension questions.

Ex. 1   **Listen to a discussion between a professor and his students in an American history class. The class is on William Penn.**

(professor)	We've been talking about some of the early leaders of the American colonies. One of the most famous was certainly William Penn. Why is he famous?
(man)	For founding the state of Pennsylvania – which means "Penn's woods," by the way.
(professor)	That's right. Penn began one of the earliest and largest colonies in America.
(woman)	Why did he do that?
(professor)	Well, William Penn was born in England in 1644, the son of a wealthy man. William was a religious young man, but he rebelled against the Church of England. At about 20 years of age, Penn discovered the Quaker sect and soon became a devout follower. He wrote many pamphlets about his beliefs and even spent time in jail.
(man)	OK. How was England at that time?
(professor)	Then, in 1681, King Charles II repaid a debt to Penn's father by granting Penn the land in America that became known as Pennsylvania. At the time, Quakers were greatly persecuted, in England and in the American colonies, too. So he opened his colony to members of all religious faiths and to those with no religious faith – a radical idea at the time. Penn gave his colonists a popular government, with the right to elect their own assembly and make their own laws.

What does "Pennsylvania" mean?

Ex. 2   **Listen to part of a lecture in a literature class. The professor is talking about science fiction.**

Science fiction is a genre that often gets little respect from academics and "serious" literary critics. But in fact, science fiction is a broad and popular subject that authors have long turned to contemplating our world. By the term "science fiction," we merely mean stories about the effects of science or future events on human beings. Common subjects include the future, time or space travel, life on other planets, and crises created by technology or alien creatures. With such a broad mandate, it is not surprising there is a wide variety of stories over time that can be classified as science fiction.

In its modern form the first true science fiction book is probably Mary Shelley's *Frankenstein*, written in 1818. In that book, Shelley used the story of Frankenstein's monster as a way of exploring the potential of science for both good and evil. The greatest writer of science fiction in the 19th century was the French author Jules Verne. He explored a wide array of subjects, from space travel to underground and undersea exploration, mostly writing about travel to exotic and fantastic locations.

The best English science fiction writer in this period was H.G. Wells. Wells was more interested in biology and evolution and the social consequences of inventions than the exact science of the inventions.

In the 19th century, many American writers tried their hands at science fiction, too, including Edgar Allan Poe, Mark Twain, and Nathaniel Hawthorne. Poe in particular was an important contributor to this genre, with tales that crossed back and forth between fantasy and science fiction.

Who does the speaker call the greatest science fiction author of the 19th century?

Ex. 3 Listen to part of a lecture in a botany class. The professor is talking about corn.

Corn is a member of the grass family and is one of the most popular of all the cereals. There are over 1000 different types of corn, including popcorn, sweet corn and soft corn. Corn even has different names in other parts of the world. Traditionally in Britain, corn referred to other types of cereal grains – usually wheat in England, and oats in Scotland. There, what Americans call corn is called "maize" or "Indian corn."
Corn is also a mysterious crop. Researchers have been unable to find any of its wild ancestors. Wild plants need to be able to take care of themselves. But corn does not grow well in the wild. For example, the way corn reproduces is not very practical. The top of each corn stalk produces pollen, and the corn "ears" receive the pollen. But the ears are completely wrapped with leaves, and only very little bits of pollen-receiving filaments stick out of the end. Therefore the filaments cannot get much pollen unless the plants have a lot of neighbors – no problem in a farmer's field, but uncommon in the wild. Furthermore, there is no evidence of corn ever existing anywhere except in the Americas, nor is there any proof of how corn was first cultivated.

Why does the speaker call corn a mysterious crop?

Ex. 4 Listen to a professor and his students in a zoology class discussing information on hibernation.

(man)	So what kinds of animals hibernate?
(professor)	Actually, many different kinds do. Mammals like squirrels, mice, bats, and bears can hibernate in burrows, caves, or hollow trees. And the most famous is the groundhog, which, according to folklore, is said to come out of its burrow on February 2nd every year, only to go back in for six more weeks if it sees its shadow.
(woman)	I see. How about insects?
(professor)	That's a good question. Most insects do. They hide under dead leaves or burrow in the ground. They can even freeze solid! When the warmer weather comes in spring, the insects crawl out to resume living. Even freshwater fish hibernate, in a way. They become very sluggish and stop eating and even can bury themselves in the mud.
(woman)	If northern animals hibernate when it gets too cold, do animals near the equator hibernate when it gets too hot?
(professor)	Actually, yes. In deserts and dry areas, some animals go into their burrows during the hottest times, only this is called "aestivation" when it is done to escape the heat. And the desert tortoise actually both hibernates and aestivates.

1. What animal, according to folklore, awakens from hibernating every February 2nd?

2. What is significant about the desert tortoise?

Ex. 5 Listen to part of a lecture in a biology class. The professor is talking about farming.

The rise of farming was one of the greatest revolutions in human history. Domestication refers to the evolutionary process where humans, either intentionally or unintentionally, alter the genetic makeup of a population of plants or animals. Sometimes this modification goes so far that the species is unable to survive or reproduce without human assistance.
Why the first people switched to food production from foraging is a mystery. Early people clearly knew about the connection between seeds and plants, so knowledge is not the reason. Nor is farming easier than foraging. In fact, farming is clearly more difficult work, and farmers usually work far longer hours than most foragers. Furthermore, farming produces more undesirable food; that is, of the different food that foragers might eat, the least favored ones were typically the foods that were domesticated. Finally, farming is not more secure than foraging, either. Low species diversity means that farms are very vulnerable to various crises.
In order to understand why farming began, we can look at the first farmers – a people called the "Natufians" in the Jordan River Valley around 10,300 years ago. As the weather warmed, the lands in this area became more seasonal – with warmer and drier summers. This caused the plants in the area to change, with the most successful being annuals, like wild cereals, peas and lentils. The Natufians needed to gather and store seeds more in the plentiful times in order to have enough to eat through the dry season. The need to store

LISTENING SCRIPT

food and relative scarcity of water made the Natufians more sedentary, less mobile. Completely accidentally, these people started to alter the plants in the area simply by the act of harvesting and storing wild grains. Eventually, they began to deliberately try to promote the growth of their plants.

1. How does the speaker define "domestication"?

2. According to the speaker, why did domestication first occur?

Ex. 6   Listen to a professor and a student in a geology class discussing information on ancient continents.

(woman)   Professor, I was reading about some sort of ancient world called "Pangaea" the other day. What is that?

(professor)   Well, Pangaea refers to a time when there was only one large landmass in the world, about 250 million years ago. Because the Earth is made up of several great plates that move about, the shape of the Earth's landmasses changes over time.

(woman)   So what happened to Pangaea?

(professor)   As the Earth's plates moved, gradually Pangaea broke apart. First, around the Jurassic Period 200 million years ago, it broke into a northern and a southern continent, called Laurasia and Gondwana. And by about 100 million years ago, in the Cretaceous Period, Gondwana had broken apart, too. About 50 million years ago, the various landmasses began to collide and rejoin, first with India connecting to Asia, then Europe and Africa, too. Finally, about 5 million years ago, South and North America joined together to give us the world we know today.

(woman)   What was there before Pangaea?

(professor)   We just don't know very well. There is not much ocean crust that is older than 250 million years, so dating further back is very difficult. Some people think there was always Pangaea, but more likely the process I just described was simply happening over and over again.

Why do geologists not know what the world was like before Pangaea?

Ex. 7   Listen to part of a lecture in a physiology class. The professor is talking about bones.

The bones are the part of the body least susceptible to disease. However, bones are liable to injury, particularly from falls, being hit, or traffic accidents. The most frequent injury is the fracture, when a bone breaks.
There are several different kinds of fractures. The most common type is the simple fracture – a broken bone deep beneath the skin. If the skin is pierced by the broken bone, then it is called a "compound fracture." These breaks can be either impacted or comminuted. An impacted fracture is one in which the broken ends have been jammed together. A comminuted fracture, however, is when the broken bone is crushed or splintered into two or more fragments.
The bones of young children and older people are very different. In young children, the fracture is more likely to be what doctors call a "greenstick" fracture. That is, the bone splinters and bends instead of breaking outright, like a green, living stick of wood instead of a dry twig. People's bones become more brittle as they grow older, and more susceptible to serious breaks.

What is a greenstick fracture?

Ex. 8   Listen to part of a lecture in a literature class. The professor is talking about science fiction.

The 20 years, from 1935 to 1955, were a golden age for science fiction, with many new magazines started. In 1937, when John Wood Campbell, Jr. became editor of *Astounding Stories*, he began to showcase a new type of science fiction writing. As a writer himself, Campbell had already started to emphasize mood and characterization. As an editor, he helped to encourage other authors to produce science fiction with serious literary merit. Later magazines, like *The Magazine of Fantasy and Science Fiction* in the 1940s and *Galaxy Science Fiction* in the 1950s, continued this shift in emphasis.
The 60s saw a new concern for humanistic values and experimental techniques. British writers dominated what was called the "New Wave" movement, but it also had prominent American participants, most notably Harlan Ellison. Ellison hated the term "science fiction" and its diminutive, "sci-fi," preferring to call his work "magical realism."

In the 80s, a new type of science fiction emerged called "cyberpunk." Cyberpunk authors portrayed decentralized societies dominated by technology and science, emphasizing technological detail, intricate plots, and a confusing, dazzling style. The first cyberpunk novel was *Neuromancer* by William Gibson.

What did Harlan Ellison prefer to call his stories?

TOEFL Exercise 7.3

Listen to the following excerpts from academic discussions and lectures, then answer inference questions.

Ex. 1   Listen to a professor and a student in an economics class discussing information on the Great Depression.

(man)	Professor, I'm having trouble with my paper for your economics class.
(professor)	What happens to be the problem?
(man)	Well, I'm trying to write about the economics of the Great Depression, but I just don't understand what caused it. Different books give me different answers.
(professor)	I see. There are two major views on the Great Depression. One says that the Depression was caused by the stock market crash. When the stock prices suddenly dropped by 40% in October 1929, that caused people to stop spending, and that caused the Depression. Others say the stock market crash wasn't very serious and the Depression was actually caused by the federal government's reaction to the crash – the government panicked and raised interest rates. They were trying to increase investment, but instead they ended up crippling businesses.
(man)	And I should make my analysis based on those theories?
(professor)	That's right. And don't forget to clearly show how you developed all your formulas.

What can be inferred from this talk?

Ex. 2   Listen to part of a lecture in a geography class. The professor is talking about supercities.

The continual spread and sprawl of cities in America has created some novel patterns of settlement. Most notable is the so-called "megalopolis" or supercity, a combining of two or more sizable cities whose boundaries have grown together. The first examples of this appeared in the 19th century in Europe as well as Japan. But nowhere in the world are there supercities that rival the size or complexity of those in America.

There are several supercities in America. The greatest one runs along the Atlantic coast, from Portland, Maine to Richmond, Virginia. This huge area is almost continuous urban sprawl, featuring many of the oldest cities in America. It includes major cities such as Washington D.C., Baltimore, Philadelphia, New York City, and Boston.

One of the few predictions that seem safe in such a dynamic and rapidly-changing land as the United States, since few people are willing to put up with severe and economically painful controls on the use of land, is that the nation will only continue to become more megametropolitan.

What can be inferred from the speaker's conclusion?

Ex. 3   Listen to a discussion between a professor and his students in an anthropology class. The class is on primates.

(woman)	Professor, we've been studying about how primates evolved into hominids and other human relatives. But I was wondering how primates first evolved.
(professor)	That's an interesting question, Jen. The first primates evolved at a time of great change all over the world. It was just after the age of dinosaurs, about 65 million years ago. Mammals started to undergo an incredible period of adaptive radiation.
(man)	What's adaptive radiation?
(professor)	That's when a species begins to branch out and evolve into other species. The first mammals were mostly small, nocturnal carnivores. But when the dinosaurs died out, all of a sudden there was a huge amount of space in the ecosystem to handle new organisms. The new mild climate of the period and the evolution of new kinds of plants caused the spread of dense, lush tropical and subtropical forests over much of the Earth. With these

forest belts, the stage was set for the evolution of some mammals from a rodent-like ground existence to the trees. Anyhow, by 40 million years ago, some of those primitive mammals had evolved into the "Adapidae," creatures that were active during daylight, ate nuts and leaves, and lived in the trees. Physically, they had slightly larger brains, smaller snouts, and eyes that were more forward.

(man)   So what happened next?

(professor)   Again, a climate change occurred, at about 30 million years ago. The temperature plunged, and for the first time, the poles were covered in ice. There were suddenly many fewer places where the Adapidae could live. This led to the development of the famous ancestor, *Aegyptopithecus*, or "Egyptian ape," named for where the first fossils were discovered.

What can be inferred to be the major force behind the development of the primate ancestors?

Ex 4   Listen to part of a lecture in a physiology class. The professor is talking about the skeleton.

One of the most recognizable parts of our bodies is our skeleton. In human beings, mammals, and many other animals, bones provide a framework for the body. They support the softer tissues by supplying surfaces for the attachment of muscles, tendons, and ligaments. The soft tissues which the bones support also hold the bones together. The entire structure of the soft tissues does so indirectly. At the joints, fibrous bands of tissue, usually in the form of ligaments, supply direct connections to join bones and hold them together. Bones are also responsible for protecting many vital organs, as the chest encloses the heart and lungs, and the skull protects the brain.

Bones, like all living organs, require blood. Large bones have one or more nutrient arteries, usually around the center of the top of the bone. Nerves and veins also enter with the arteries. The veins are especially large and numerous in the spongy bone because they have to carry away all the blood cells formed by the red marrow.

What can be inferred about the skeleton?

Ex. 5   Listen to a professor and a student in an education class discussing information on field research.

(woman)   Professor Harris? I'm sorry but I missed our seminar this morning; I had a doctor's appointment that I couldn't get out of. Did I miss anything?

(professor)   Yes, you did. We assigned teams for the research projects you'll be working on over the next three weeks or so.

(woman)   So do I need to find a group to join?

(professor)   No need – I put you and two other students who weren't there today into one group. Don't worry about not being with your friends; groups were assigned at random.

(woman)   I see. And what is this project going to be about?

(professor)   You're going to be using a local elementary school for your case studies, examining how the students interact with the teacher and with each other.

(woman)   And what are we supposed to be looking for?

(professor)   Actually, I'll be going over that in more detail next class. But basically, you'll be looking to compare the development of social abilities between different age groups.

What subject is this class most likely?

Ex. 6   Listen to part of a lecture in an American history class. The professor is talking about conditions before the Civil War.

In the years before the Civil War, the northern and southern regions were economically very different from each other. The South strongly resisted developing industry, preferring instead to emphasize agriculture, especially cotton. For example, a single factory in Massachusetts had more textile workers than the entire state of South Carolina. Less than 15 percent of all the goods manufactured in the United States in 1860 came from the South; the region did not really develop an industrial society. Its textile manufacturers depended on the North for machinery, for skilled workers, for financing, and for insurance. New Orleans, the biggest city in the South, did not even have a single publisher as late as 1846.

In the North, though, manufacturing expanded in so many directions that it is difficult to summarize it. The discovery of rich coalfields in Pennsylvania allowed access to cheap power to run the factories. Between

1825 and 1850, a huge number of important inventions were first developed – the sewing machine, the lead pencil, matches, and industrial-strength rubber.

What can be inferred from this lecture?

Ex. 7   Listen to a discussion between a professor and his students in an aerospace science class. The class is on space exploration.

(professor)	Although when we think of the space race and space exploration, we usually think of America's NASA, in fact many other countries around the world have space programs. Can you think of some examples?
(woman)	Well, the old Soviet Union's program is the most famous. After all, they were able to put the first man into space.
(professor)	That's true. And until recently the Russians had the Mir space station in orbit around the Earth.
(man)	Western Europe has been really increasing its space presence in recent years.
(professor)	That's right. Several European countries have formed a consortium, working together mostly to launch satellites into orbit.
(woman)	Even the Chinese space program is increasingly active these days. Even though they have not yet put any astronauts into space, they are launching ever more rockets and are making plans to put their first astronauts into orbit in the near future.

What can be inferred from this academic discussion?

TOEFL Exercise 7.4

Listen to the following excerpts from academic discussions and lectures, then answer negative questions.

Ex. 1   Listen to part of a lecture in a biology class. The professor is talking about mammals.

One of the big questions in the most ancient history of our natural world is where mammals came from. After ruling the world for 170 million years, the dinosaurs were suddenly replaced by a completely different class of animals.

It is interesting to note that the evolution of the mammals into all the diverse forms with which we are familiar today was the product of a great evolutionary divide that did not begin until after mammals had been present on the earth for more than 100 million years.

Actually, the story of mammalian evolution starts as long ago as 250 million years ago, before the great age of dinosaurs. In a period geologists call the Permian, we have found the remains of reptiles with features that are beginning to look distinctly mammalian. These slim, flesh-eating reptiles had limbs that were underneath the body, the development of a separation between the mouth and nasal cavity, the development of different kinds of teeth, and a reduction in the number of bones to a more mammal-like number.

And by 180 million years ago, at the end of the Triassic Period, the first true mammals had arrived.

Which is NOT an example of an early mammal feature on some reptiles?

Ex. 2   Listen to a professor and his students in an American history class discussing information on the history of the U.S. government.

(professor)	The United States, as it first emerged from the Revolutionary War, was a very different type of government than we have today. Do you know how it was different?
(man)	I know at first there was no president of the United States.
(professor)	That's is true, but it was even more different than that. The Revolutionary War left America deeply suspicious of centralized government. For the first 10 years or so of independence, most governing went on at the state level. This is where constitutions were drawn up and governing powers divided. At the federal level, the Congress was originally thought of as a collective substitute for the king – that is, it had certain responsibilities, but was not an actual parliament.
(man)	So what could the Congress do?

(professor)	Well, it had full authority over foreign affairs, in questions of peace and war. And it was responsible for arguments between the states. It also had authority over coinage, postal service, and Indian affairs. However, it had no power to raise taxes, no executive authority, no administration, and no courts.
(woman)	Wow. It is amazing the country could run at all.
(professor)	After a while, it became apparent that this system would not work, and that is why a new constitution was drawn up in 1787.

Which was NOT a power of the United States' original Congress?

Ex. 3   Listen to a professor and his students in a geology class discussing information on uranium.

(professor)	So I asked you to read chapter 6 in your textbooks for today so we could talk about uranium. What can you tell me about this element?
(woman)	Well, of course it is radioactive, and it's essential for almost all of our nuclear power.
(professor)	That's good. Anything else?
(man)	It is actually a fairly common mineral. There's more uranium on our planet than gold or silver. And it is nearly as common as lead, zinc, or tin.
(professor)	That's also true. However, most uranium is spread thinly through rocks and it is hard to recover. Large deposits of ore are fairly rare. Usually, uranium is found combined with other elements in a compound mineral. In fact, there are over 150 minerals that contain uranium, with odd names like carnotite and coffinite. Where can we find uranium?
(woman)	The major uranium-producing countries are Canada, the United States, South Africa, France and Australia. And the Congo used to be a major producer, too, before all of its supplies were exhausted in the 1960s.

1. Which is NOT a more plentiful element than uranium?

2. Which is NOT a nation that is a major uranium producer?

Ex. 4   Listen to part of a lecture in an American literature class. The professor is talking about science fiction.

Most early American science fiction was published in magazines. These magazine authors tended to emphasize technical accuracy and plausibility above literary value or character development. The mass magazines that were established in the 1890s published many different sorts of stories besides science fiction, and the pulp fiction magazines at the turn of the century included many stories of romance and wild adventure. One of the most famous of these writers was Edgar Rice Burroughs, who wrote several books about Mars as well as the famous Tarzan series.

A big change started in 1926 when Hugo Gernsback, a Luxembourg emigrant, founded the first science fiction magazine, *Amazing Stories*. He started the magazine with the idea that fiction could be a medium for disseminating scientific information and creating scientists, and he published stories with these goals in mind. He also created a name for this kind of stories – scientifiction. But three years later when he started a second magazine, *Science Wonder Stories*, he changed the genre name to the one we are familiar with today – "science fiction."

What is NOT true about Hugo Gernsback?

Ex. 5   Listen to a discussion between two students in a botany class. The topic is on vines.

(woman)	Hey, Steve. I haven't seen you for a while.
(man)	Oh, I'm working on a project for my plant biology class. We're supposed to examine some of the plants around campus and write a report about them.
(woman)	So what is that plant you are looking at now?
(man)	This is called a Virginia Creeper. Also known as American Ivy because it's found all over the United States.
(woman)	I've always wondered what that was called. I see them growing on the buildings all over campus.
(man)	They're really common. At the end of the vines are these flat tendrils which secrete a

cement-like substance that's really strong; it lets the plant grow up walls and hold on to almost anything.

(woman)   Do they all grow those little berries?

(man)   Yeah, the Creeper is a member of the grape family, so these little blue-black berries are a characteristic of the plant. It also has really small, greenish-yellow flowers there are pretty hard to see.

What is NOT a characteristic of the Virginia Creeper?

TOEFL Exercise 7.5

Listen to the following excerpts from academic discussions and lectures, then answer multiple-answer questions.

Ex. 1   Listen to part of a lecture in an American history class. The professor is talking about manufacturing.

In the mid-18th century in America, manufacturing expanded in so many directions that it is difficult to summarize it. The South was, of course, centered around cotton production. But the north was more diverse and industrial. The discovery of rich coalfields in Pennsylvania allowed access to cheap power to run the factories. Between 1825 and 1850, a huge number of important inventions were first developed – the sewing machine, the lead pencil, matches, and industrial-strength rubber.

By 1850, America led the world in precision instruments, allowing it to mass-produce many items such as clocks, pistols, and locks. But America's vast natural resources were also essential for its economic expansion. Of the top 10 American industries in 1860, 8 of them relied on farm products for their raw materials. By far the biggest industry was flour, followed by cotton and then lumber. Iron also was an important product and was growing very quickly.

What are examples of inventions made in America in the first half of the 19th century?

Ex. 2   Listen to a discussion between a professor and his students in a botany class. The class is on trees.

(professor)   Last week we finished our look at the various grasses. Today I want to move on to trees. Who can tell me what are the basic parts of a tree?

(man)   The most important parts, like most plants, are the roots, trunk, and leaves. The roots hold the tree in place and absorb water and minerals for the tree. The trunk is protected by a layer of bark and contains the transportation columns that carry nutrients up and down the tree.

(woman)   And the center of the trunk is a woody column called the pith, often made up of crushed waste cells. The leaves are where photosynthesis occurs, turning carbon dioxide into oxygen.

(professor)   Very good. And what are the uses of trees? How is their role in the ecosystem?

(man)   Well, besides providing a large amount of the oxygen that we breathe, the most important ecological function of trees is protecting the land against erosion – the wearing away of topsoil due to wind and water.

(professor)   It's good to see you've done your readings this week. Now let's turn to page 192 and go over the interaction between trees and other plants, like flowers or grasses, in a simple ecosystem.

What are the important ecological functions of trees?

Ex. 3   Listen to part of a lecture in an ecology class. The professor is talking about mammals.

By 180 million years ago, the first true mammals appeared. These first mammals were small and flesh eating – feeding mostly on things such as insects, worms, and eggs. They seem to have been nocturnal, which is probably why the senses of smell and hearing became so developed in mammals. In the dark of night, vision is much less useful than scent or sound. This development in the senses improved mammals' ability to process information, and in the process also improved the corresponding part of the brain – the cerebral cortex.

For 100 million years, in spite of being smarter and more energetic, mammals were marginal animals, far less common than dinosaurs. That is because mammals, being warm-blooded, need more energy than reptiles. High-quality foods, such as fruits, nuts, and the seeds of flowering plants evolved only at the end of the Cretaceous Period. The other animals that mammals ate, worms and insects, were limited in number until the rise of flowers and fruits provided new ecological niches for them.

In addition, it was hard for mammals to spread because reptiles already had most of the available ecological niches. With the mass extinction of so many reptiles at the end of the Cretaceous, around 65 million years ago, a number of existing niches became available to the mammals. At the same time, whole new spaces in the ecosystem were opened up as the new grasses provided abundant food in dry places, and flowering plants provided high-quality food elsewhere.

Why did mammals not replace the dinosaurs for so long?

Ex. 4   Listen to a professor and his students in a physics class discussing information on properties of light.

(professor)	So we've been discussing some of the properties associated with light over the past couple of weeks – how it travels, what it's made out of, and how our knowledge of light has changed over the years. Today, though, I'd like to talk about the future of light.
(woman)	Professor, the future of light?
(professor)	Yes, scientists recently made a huge breakthrough when they brought light to a full stop. Usually, light can travel through space at 186,000 miles per second. But when light passes through other media, like water or glass, it slows down a little. That's how lenses and eyeglasses work and why, when you look at something in a swimming pool, it seems all distorted. So what researchers have done is that they've discovered that by passing laser light through different kinds of super-cooled gases, they could slow it down a lot.
(man)	What kind of gases?
(professor)	They tried a lot of different ones, but the gas that worked best is something called rubidium, which is actually a metallic element.
(woman)	And are there any practical applications to stopping light?
(professor)	Many. The biggest areas could be in the development of quantum computers and quantum communications. Quantum computers would be vastly faster than the ones we use now. And quantum communications cannot be eavesdropped on or tapped. Currently, these use electricity to store information and transmit data. But electricity has its drawbacks. Light would be much more efficient, but in order to use light, we need to be able to hold it still and store it.

What are some of the ways still light could be used in technology?

Ex. 5   Listen to part of a lecture in a geography class. The professor is talking about Kansas.

Kansas is called the Sunflower State, and is located in the north-central region of the United States. It is a large state and only moderately populated.

Its chief natural resource is its rich soil. Large, flat plains dominate much of the state, making it ideal for agriculture. In fact, about 90% of Kansas is cropland or pasture. The most important crop by far is wheat, but hay is also quite common. Some smaller crops are corn, soybeans, and barley. Only about 6% of the state's population is involved in manufacturing.

Other natural resources in Kansas include petroleum, natural gas, and even a few salt mines.

What are the major two crops in Kansas?

Ex. 6   Listen to a discussion between two students in a physics class. The class is on plasma.

(man)	I'm having real troubles with our latest unit in physics class.
(woman)	You mean the one on plasma? I understand it pretty well, so you can ask me any questions you want.
(man)	Well, what exactly is plasma? Is it a gas or a liquid or what?
(woman)	That is confusing. We usually talk about three kinds of matter – solids, liquids, and gases. But in fact, there is a fourth state – plasma. Plasma is actually the highest energy state of

all matter.

In a normal gas, atoms just bounce around freely, occasionally bumping into one another. As the gas is heated, the atoms move more quickly and bounce into each other with more energy. But at higher temperatures, they have so much energy that they actually knock away electrons from the atoms during the collisions. When many atoms in a gas lose electrons, the gas becomes just a mixture of electrons and positive particles. And this mixture is called plasma.

(man)   I see. And is plasma very common?

(woman)   It's the most common substance in the universe. 90% of everything is plasma. Most notably, stars are all made of plasma. Auroras and lightning are also plasma. The earth itself is bathed in a plasma called the solar wind, and is surrounded by a dense plasma called the ionosphere. But here on Earth, you're probably more familiar with neon and fluorescent lights – they're plasma, too.

(man)   So why is there so much plasma in the universe?

(woman)   Well, in interstellar space, clouds of hydrogen gas are really spread out, so if an electron escapes from a hydrogen nucleus, there is very little chance that it will meet another nucleus and combine to form a neutral atom. And in the interiors of most stars, the temperatures are so high that atoms break down into electrons and bare nuclei. These nuclei move about at tremendous speeds and often collide with one another so strongly that they merge to form larger nuclei. This process, called a fusion reaction, gives off a great deal of energy.

What are the major causes of plasma in the universe?

Ex. 7   Listen to part of a lecture in an engineering class. The professor is talking about locks.

Locks are special kinds of fastening devices used to prevent unauthorized entry, exit, or use of equipment. Of course, the use of locks is nothing new. Egyptians developed sophisticated locking devices over 4,000 years ago, including the sliding bolt lock. The ancient Greeks invented the key, so that locks could be opened or closed from the outside as well as the inside.

Today, however, two kinds of key-locks are most common – warded locks and tumbler locks. Warded locks are simple and inexpensive, but can be opened easily by skeleton keys. The key for a warded lock resembles a flag on a pole – a long shaft with a specially-designed end, shaped to fit the lock.

Tumbler locks are used where greater precautions are needed. Tumbler locks use a number of small pins, or tumblers, in a row inside the lock. Each of these pins must be raised to a predetermined height before a key can turn to work the bolt. The tumbler lock was developed by a man named Robert Barron in the late 18th century. Most of the keys we use today – car keys, house keys, or whatever – are tumbler locks. Combination locks are used when extreme security is needed. Instead of a key, the lock is operated by a pattern of movements of a knob or handle. Safes usually use combination locks. Time locks are equipped with clockwork devices, making them impossible to open except at specific times.

What are two kinds of key locks?

Ex. 8   Listen to a professor and his student in an astronomy class discussing information on space probes.

(woman)   I was thinking of taking astronomy. Is there much of interest going on in the field these days?

(professor)   Most definitely. New telescopes, like the Hubble, are enabling astronomers on Earth to see more of the universe than ever before.

(woman)   Actually, I was more interested in planetary exploration. For example, is there any work being done these days exploring the planets of our solar system?

(professor)   Well, these days most people are concentrating on Mars. There is some evidence that Mars might contain water or even simple life forms.

(woman)   But didn't NASA's most recent projects to Mars fail?

(professor)   That is true, the last couple of projects were not successful. In 1999, NASA lost a Mars orbiter and a lander, just before they were to begin operating. The Orbiter burned up in the atmosphere because managers did not convert some numbers from Imperial to metric correctly; and the lander crashed into the surface because of a software glitch. But there is a lot of other exciting work going on. In fact, they've scheduled eight more probes over the next two decades. There will be a new orbiter in 2001, two land rovers in 2003, then an even more powerful orbiter in 2005, and a kind of mobile laboratory in 2007. In fact, NASA might even send a return mission – one that collects samples of Martian soil or rock and returns to Earth – starting in 2011.

What happened to NASA's Mars missions in 1999?

Ex. 9   Listen to part of a lecture in a biology class. The professor is talking about insects.

Insects appeared on earth long before man or the earliest mammals. The oldest fossils of insects' ancestors date back some 350 million years ago. The first insects most likely evolved from primitive ringed worms. Since then, they have evolved into perhaps the most successful animals on the land.
Because insects have so many enemies, they have developed many means of self-defense. One of the most common is flight. Many insects like bees, mosquitoes, and butterflies are able to hover high above the earth where many land animals would otherwise eat them.
Other insects are specially adapted for hiding. The flattened bodies of cockroaches and bedbugs enable them to disappear into narrow cracks.
Others hide by means of camouflage, looking like twigs, leaves or other natural phenomena. Butterflies and moths are famous for their elaborate and sometimes beautiful color schemes.
Still other insects have armor or weapons. Beetles have tough, horny shells. Bees can sting potential enemies. And the bombardier beetle can actually eject a smelly vapor explosively from its tail.

Which insects protect themselves by hiding?

Ex. 10   Listen to a discussion between a professor and her student in a physiology class. The class is on the eye.

(man)	Professor, I'm having problems trying to understand how the eye works, and I know it's going to be on the upcoming test, so could you help me out?
(professor)	Sure thing, John. You'll need to know about the cornea; that's the outer layer of the eye. It's a clear protective layer that allows light to pass through. It also acts as a kind of outer lens, refracting the light towards the center of the eye. You'll also need to know the iris and the pupil really well. The iris is the colored part of the eye that light cannot penetrate. The pupil is the hole in the iris where the light does pass through. Depending if you need more or less light, a muscle in the iris can enlarge or contract the pupil.
(man)	And will we need to know about the retina?
(professor)	Definitely. That's where seeing actually takes place. The retina is a soft, transparent membrane at the back of the eye. It has layers of cells called "rods" and "cones" that absorb the light. The rods perceive only light and dark tones. The cones detect details and color.
(man)	And how about non-human eyes, like insects'?
(professor)	Not for this test. For now, we are only talking about human eyes.

What are the functions of "cones" in the eye?

TOEFL Exercise 7.6

Listen to the following excerpts from academic discussions and lectures, then answer ordering questions.

Ex. 1   Listen to part of a lecture in an American history class. The professor is talking about Los Angeles.

Los Angeles was founded in 1781 by the Spanish governor of California, Felipe de Neve, near the site of an Indian village. He named the city "The Town of Our Lady Queen of the Angels of Porciuncula," after a church in Italy. Soon after, people called it by the much shorter name City of Angels – Los Angeles. At the time Los Angeles was a quiet town of 44 people – quite a change from the 10 million who live in the greater Los Angeles area now.
Later control of California was taken over by Mexico, and Los Angeles became the sometime capital of California.

During the Mexican War in 1847, the small town was one of the many southwestern regions taken by the United States.

Soon afterwards, Los Angeles started to grow more rapidly. It incorporated as a full city in 1850. When the San Francisco gold rush started, many more people moved to Los Angeles. Life was so lawless then that the city was nicknamed Los Diablos, or City of Devils.

When the railroad connected here in 1885, it created a population boom. Within five years, the population reached 50,000 people.

Advances in irrigation made the desert region around Los Angeles more livable, also helping to increase the population. The rise of the oil, motion picture, and technology industries also helped Los Angeles grow into the vast, sprawling city we know today.

The speaker mentioned several events in the history of Los Angeles. Summarize by placing the following events into the correct chronological order.

Ex. 2 Listen to part of a lecture in a paleontology class. The professor is talking about ancestors of horses.

The oldest ancestor of the horse is called the *Eohippus*, which means "dawn horse." It looked very different from the modern horse. It was about the size of a fox, and looked a little like a cross between a dog and a rabbit. It ranged from 10 to 20 inches high at the shoulder, with a high, arching back, a long tail, and a long snout. The feet of the *Eohippus* had four toes, like a dog, and it had simple teeth designed for chewing leaves. By about 40 million years ago, the *Mesohippus* appeared. The *Mesohippus* looked much more horse-like than the *Eohippus*. It was slightly bigger and longer, with a back that was less arched, though still not straight. The head looked more like a horse's, too, with larger and stronger teeth. Its legs were longer and more slender, and now it had only three toes instead of four.

Some of the most radical changes took place around 25 million years ago, when the *Mesohippus* gave way to the *Merychippus*. Most important, the teeth had changed enough to allow this early horse ancestor to become a grass eater instead of a leaf eater. These new teeth were stronger than before, good for grinding coarse grasses. The *Merychippus* now stood up to 40 inches high.

Finally, about 5 million years ago, the *Pliohippus* appeared. The *Pliohippus* is very similar to the modern horse. It had a single hoofed toe, just like today's horse. It stood nearly 50 inches high, with a long, straight back.

The professor described the evolution of the horse. Summarize by placing the following steps in the horse's evolution in the correct chronological order.

Ex. 3 Listen to part of a lecture in a geography class. The professor is talking about states of the U.S.

America is comprised of 50 separate states, all of which vary widely in size, climate, culture, and more. For example, Texas is the largest and furthest south of all the states in the contiguous United States. It is more than twice the size of any other state in the "Lower 48," and it is the fourth most populous.

Its great size contrasts with tiny Rhode Island – just one-half of one percent the size of mighty Texas. But although it is so tiny, Rhode Island has 1/10th the population of Texas – a little over a million people packed onto its tiny area.

But while Texas is the largest state of contiguous America, Alaska is even larger. Located far to the north, separated by hundreds of miles from the rest of the country by Canada, lies the immense coldness that is Alaska. Alaska is, in fact, over twice the size of Texas. But although it is so large, it contains only a fraction of Texas's population. Alaska is nearly 1/6th the total size of the entire United States, but it contains only 1/1000th of the population.

One other state is located far from the mainland – Hawaii. Hawaii is also a smaller state, made up of a series of islands situated in the middle of the Pacific Ocean. Hawaii is actually further south than Texas, although the Pacific Ocean serves to give it a vastly different climate than Texas. Hawaii is four times larger than Rhode Island, but its population is actually slightly less than that of the smallest of states.

1. The professor mentioned the sizes of several states. Place the following states in order according to size, from smallest to largest.

2. The professor mentioned the populations of several states. Place the following states in order according to

population, from smallest to largest.

3. The professor mentioned the locations of several states. Place the following states in order from north to south.

Ex. 4   Listen to a discussion between two persons in a geology class. The class is on volcanoes.

(woman)	I've really been enjoying our unit on volcanoes in our geology class.
(man)	Yeah, volcanoes are certainly one of the most exciting parts of geology. I especially liked learning about Mount Vesuvius.
(woman)	Isn't that the volcano in Italy that buried the famous city Pompeii in lava and ash a couple of thousand years ago?
(man)	That's the one. In 79 AD, Vesuvius erupted and completely destroyed that great Roman city. But in the process, the ash preserved a lot of the city – the buildings, pottery and other artifacts – giving historians a great resource for exploring the past.
(woman)	Hasn't Vesuvius continued to erupt over the years?
(man)	It sure has – around 50 more times since then. In 1631 there was an eruption so big it spread ash 150 miles away and killed 18,000 people.
(woman)	That's terrible.
(man)	Fortunately, science has gotten better at predicting eruptions, so ones this century have not killed nearly as many people. But there have been a couple of spectacular eruptions in the past 100 years. In 1906 an eruption blew off the top of the mountain, making the volcano several hundred feet lower. But another eruption in 1944 raised the volcano back up again by about 500 feet. Even now, the mouth of Vesuvius is so hot that scientists think it could erupt again any time.

The speakers mentioned several dates in the history of Mount Vesuvius. Summarize by placing the following events into the correct chronological order.

Ex. 5   Listen to a discussion between a professor and his students in an anthropology class. The class is on Native Americans.

(professor)	The ancestors of the Native Americans, or Indians, first arrived in North America by crossing over the Bering Strait from what is now Russia over 30,000 years ago. They migrated all over North and South America, forming a wealth of different cultures, all very different from one another.
(woman)	I heard there used to be many more Native Americans living here before the Europeans arrived.
(professor)	Very true. In North America, the various tribes living there were not densely populated, but there were probably not many more than about one-and-a-half million Native Americans living in the lands that are now the United States. In the territory that is now Canada, there were about another 400,000 Indians and Inuit peoples.
(man)	How did those numbers compare with South America?
(professor)	By far, there were more people living south of the Rio Grande River. In the areas comprising Mexico and Central America, there was about 4 times the population of all of the U.S. and Canada. And in South America, the native population was more than twice that of Middle and North America combined.
(woman)	I never realized the population was distributed that unevenly.
(professor)	We usually spend most of our time talking about the Native Americans of North America because U.S. history intersects with them so much. But in fact, in order to understand Native American culture, you really do need to know the whole continent.

The professor mentioned the relative Native American populations across the Americas. Put the following groups into order according to population size, from least to greatest.

Ex. 6   Listen to a discussion between two people in a history class. The class is on the Statue of Liberty.

(man)	So how are you enjoying New York City so far?

(woman)	It's great! There is so much to see and do. I'm really happy Dr. Stevens arranged for our history class to take a trip here.
(man)	Where did you go today?
(woman)	A couple of us went to see the Statue of Liberty. It's such an amazing statue, with a really interesting history.
(man)	Like what?
(woman)	Well, although the statue was dedicated on October 28, 1886, planning for it actually began over twenty years before that.
(man)	Really?
(woman)	Yeah. A French historian named Edouard de Laboulaye proposed in 1865 that France create a memorial for the United States for the 100th anniversary of the signing of the Declaration of Independence. But it wasn't for another 10 years that any work got started.
(man)	What happened then?
(woman)	In 1874 a young sculptor, Frederick August Bartholdi, sailed to New York to talk to authorities about what kind of monument to build. As he sailed into the harbor, he imagined a giant goddess of liberty to greet all new arrivals to America. But it wasn't until 1924 that the statue was declared an official national monument.
(man)	Interesting. I didn't know all of that.

The speakers mentioned several events in the history of the Statue of Liberty. Summarize by placing the following events into the correct chronological order.

Ex. 7   Listen to part of a lecture in a geography class. The professor is talking about Kentucky.

Kentucky is a state with fertile soil and plenty of natural resources. About two fifths of the land is forested, with the heaviest stands of timber in the east. Deposits of coal, petroleum, and natural gas provide fuels for manufacturing. The state's rivers are an important means of transportation. Horse farming and horse racing are both major tourist attractions.

About six percent of all the workers in Kentucky are engaged in agriculture. That state has about 100,000 commercial farms. The most valuable crop in Kentucky is tobacco, accounting for two fifths of the total farm income. Corn is the second most valuable crop and is grown throughout the state. Hay is another important crop, and there is even some wheat and barley grown in places around the state.

Coal is by far the most valuable mineral in the state. There are major coal-mining areas around the state, and only West Virginia and Pennsylvania have larger coal industries than Kentucky. Other important minerals include stone, natural gas, and clay.

The speaker mentioned the agricultural products of Kentucky. Summarize by placing the following crops in order, from most valuable to least.

TOEFL Exercise 7.7

Listen to the following excerpts from academic discussions and lectures, then answer matching questions.

Ex. 1   Listen to part of a lecture in a geography class. The professor is talking about American cities.

The rise of the city has greatly changed the character of the United States. Cities have not only grown larger, but they also have significantly altered the rural parts of the nation.

Until at least the beginning of the 20th century, American cities all depended on transportation systems. The inadequacy and high cost of overland traffic meant cities were most often built on sites along ocean bays or rivers with access to the ocean. Boston, New York, and Philadelphia were founded at the same time as the colonies they served and, like nearly all other North American colonial towns of consequence, were ocean ports. As more and more people moved inland, cities that lay on canals and major rivers became more important – cities such as Pittsburgh, Cincinnati, and Buffalo. From about 1850 to 1920, the success of cities was more dependent on railroads, anchoring the rise of cities like Chicago, San Francisco, and Atlanta.

Today the city defines America. Where once cities depended on the country, now, the city dweller is the dominant consumer for most products. During weekends and vacations, city folk stream out to relax in the countryside. In fact, in many rural areas, recreation is the principal source of income and employment.

The speaker mentioned many cities and where they are located. Match the city and the significance of its location.

Ex. 2　Listen to a professor and his students in a zoology class discussing information on reptiles.

(professor)　Last class, I asked you all to read in your zoology textbooks chapter 11 on reptiles for homework. So who can tell me how many different kinds of lizards there are in the world?

(man)　There are over 3,000 different kinds of lizards ... and about 125 different kinds in the United States alone.

(professor)　That's right. What kind of lizards are in the United States?

(woman)　In the east, there are mostly fence lizards – small lizards, about 5 inches long. In the desert southwest, you get some larger and more dangerous ones. For example, there is the Gila monster, one of the few poisonous lizards in the world.

(professor)　And how do they compare to lizards in other parts of the world?

(man)　There are many different kinds of lizards. There are lizards called glass snakes, even though they aren't really snakes at all. They have no arms or legs and really look like snakes, but they are lizards.

(woman)　And the monitor lizard is the largest of all the lizard species. The Komodo dragon is the largest of the monitor lizards, and can grow to be twelve feet long and 250 pounds.

(man)　Geckos are also well known. Their toes have tiny, microscopic hair-like hooks, allowing the Gecko to climb almost any surface.

(professor)　Those are some good examples. But no matter how different they seem, remember all lizards have scales, movable eyelids, and ear openings. And they are all cold-blooded, too.

The speakers discussed several kinds of lizards. Match the lizard with its characteristic.

Ex. 3　Listen to part of a lecture in a U.S. government class. The professor is talking about separation of powers.

One of the central ideas behind the United States government is the separation of powers. All powers of the central government were divided among three co-equal departments – the executive, the legislative, and the judiciary. The idea of dividing the powers of the government like this was that no one body could take control and override the will of the people. For the founding fathers of the United States, protecting America from tyranny was one of their most important goals.

The executive branch is headed by the president of the United States. Today, the president's power has grown much from what it was in George Washington's day when America was first founded. For example, America's first president had only four Cabinet departments – state, treasury, war, and justice. Today, however, there are 12 departments and over 50 major agencies.

The legislative branch of government is the Congress. This is the part of government responsible for making the laws of the land. The American Congress is divided into two parts – the House of Representatives and the Senate. The House of Representatives has 435 members who are elected on the basis of population. The Senate has 100 members, 2 per state regardless of state size. Together, these two bodies balance the will of the majority with the needs of individual states.

The judiciary branch of the United States government is the Supreme Court. There are nine members of the Supreme Court, including the Chief Justice. The Supreme Court is the only one of the three branches that is not directly elected. Instead, the president nominates a person to the court and the Senate confirms the nomination. Once appointed, Supreme Court justices can serve for life.

The speaker mentioned the three branches of government in the United States. Match the name of each branch and its function.

Ex. 4　Listen to part of a lecture in an American literature class. The professor is talking about transcendentalism.

Ralph Waldo Emerson's book *Nature*, published in 1836, was the first significant statement of American transcendentalism. He said that the label "transcendental" was another word for "idealism" – that ideas are more important than the material world or the physical senses. He believed that people interested in the material world cared about facts and history, but that in fact thought, will, miracles and culture were all more important. His other major belief was in self-reliance, thinking that people were all completely capable of taking care of their own needs by themselves. He thought that the individual could be made spiritually better through nature rather than through society.

Henry David Thoreau was the one who put Emerson's ideas into practice. In 1845, when he was just 28 years old, he moved to a small cabin he had made himself by Walden Pond in Massachusetts. There, he grew his own food and for the most part lived in isolation, writing and contemplation. He spent six weeks a year growing enough food to sell at a nearby town in order to earn enough money to pay for clothes and other items he could not make himself. He also spent time in jail in 1848 for not paying his taxes because he objected to how the government was going to use the money. From that experience, he wrote an extremely influential essay on the necessary role of civil disobedience in society.

Margaret Fuller was the founder and was first editor of *The Dial*, the quarterly newsletter of the transcendentalists begun in 1840. She applied their ideas to women's rights, and firmly believed that both men and women have equal potential. She even took up with women's rights groups in Italy and fought over there. Unfortunately, she drowned at sea in 1850.

The speaker mentioned several important figures in the transcendentalist movement. Match the person's name to the significant achievement.

Ex. 5   Listen to a discussion between a professor and his student in an American history class. The class is on Thomas Edison.

(man)	Professor Hamilton, I'm having problems with our current unit on great inventors who worked with electricity. For example, you called Thomas Edison "the greatest inventor in American history." Why is that?
(professor)	Well, Tom, that's because Edison invented both a huge number of inventions and such important ones. Over his career, Edison actually patented over 1,000 inventions, which is a huge number. And he did for such different devices as the phonograph, the electric light bulb, the dynamo, and the movie projector.
(man)	That is impressive, but you mentioned inventors who patented even more than that. I remember you said Alexander Graham Bell had over 3,000 patents.
(professor)	That's true, but almost all of Bell's patents centered around his greatest invention – the telephone. His work was more about improving this one invention than creating a great number of unique inventions. But in any event, because of all his work involving sound and electricity, Bell is certainly an important inventor.
(man)	You said that there were three electrical inventors we should know.
(professor)	Yes, the third is less famous, but he was still quite important. Charles Hall was responsible for discovering that electrolysis can be used to produce aluminum from alumina – the naturally occurring and fairly useless crystalline form of aluminum. Most amazingly, he made this complex discovery when only 22 years old.

The professor described three significant inventors. Match the inventor and his invention.

Ex. 6   Listen to part of a lecture in a geology class. The professor is talking about glaciation.

Over the past 2 million years, North America has been periodically steamrollered by a series of massive Ice Ages. Four major times, thick sheets of ice, thousands of feet thick, spread down from the north to churn up and wrack the land as far south as Kentucky and Kansas. The climate was only about 12 degrees cooler then than now, but that was enough so that the summer heat was no longer enough to melt the snow of the previous winter. So the snow and ice built up year after year until they covered much of the north.

Such massive sheets of ice creeping across the continent had great affects on the land. The ice flow carried boulders and soil southward until it reached a climate warm enough to melt it completely each summer. As it melted, it dropped its rocks and dirt into a kind of heap called a moraine, along the line of melting. When warmer summers drove the glaciers back north, the moraines were left behind. Today they look like broad, gently sloping mounds across the landscape.

As a moving glacier passes over a tough, resistant rock hill, the debris carried in the glacier smooths the shape of the uphill side, while scratching striations in the rock. These upward-pointing mounds are called "roches moutonnées."

Another formation glaciers cause is called a drumlin. Drumlins are mounds of soil deposited by the glacier. Drumlins tend to point downward, unlike the roches moutonnées, and they can be several miles long.

The speaker mentioned several features caused by glaciers. Match the geological feature with its characteristic.

Ex. 7 **Listen to a professor and his students in a linguistics class discussing information on the history of the English language.**

(professor)	English is increasingly becoming the standard language around the world for business. This is striking because it wasn't so long ago that English was a very marginal language. Around 1600, English was only spoken by the people living on the small island of Britain. And even there, the elite often spoke French, the international language of the day.
(man)	Hasn't English been heavily influenced by French?
(professor)	Actually, English is very much a mixture of several languages. At its base, English is a Germanic language, but over half the words in English derive from French or Latin. In fact, English has taken words from many different languages all over the world.
(woman)	I knew about German and French, but you're saying there're more?
(professor)	That's right. A lot of common words come from surprising sources. Some common words like "window" or "to take" are actually Scandinavian. Other words are Dutch or Greek.
(man)	How about non-European languages? Have they influenced English?
(professor)	Certainly. Arabic is a language that has added a lot to English. Many mathematical words, like "algorithm" and "algebra," are Arabic. Even "alcohol" is an Arabic word. And there are lots of words from Hindi, the main language of India, such as "pajamas" and "hammock."

The professor described the origins of many English words. Match the words with the language they come from.

Ex. 8. **Listen to part of a lecture in a biology class. The professor is talking about horses.**

One of humanity's most important partners in the animal kingdom has long been the horse. Since ancient times people have used horses for transportation, riding, and other duties. Over time, selective breeding has allowed people to develop different kinds of horses specially suited for specific tasks.

Today, horses can be divided into three broad groups – ponies, draft horses, and light horses. Large, strong draft horses like Clydesdales were in demand for use in teams to draw carts of bulk merchandise over long distances. In Arabia, people bred small, swift horses. In fact, all thoroughbred horses today can trace their lineage back to one of three Arabian horses imported to England in the early 18th century. Ponies are the smallest of all the horses.

Only now, after 200 years of mechanization, have we begun to replace the horse with cars and other machines. But the legacy of the horse remains an important part of our culture.

The speaker mentioned several breeds of horses. Match the breed with its characteristic.

Ex. 9 **Listen to a discussion between a professor and his students in an American history class. The class is on American monuments.**

(professor)	Even though America is a relatively young country, it already had a large number of significant monuments – giant objects or statues that symbolize ideas or events of great importance. For example, everyone knows the Statue of Liberty in New York. What can you tell me about it?
(woman)	Well, as the name implies, the statue is a symbol of the liberty America so highly values – it is the symbol of freedom for oppressed people everywhere, and it was given to the United States by France to celebrate the alliance between the two countries during the American Revolution.
(professor)	That's right. Designed by the Alsatian sculptor Frédérick Auguste Bartholdi in 1874, the Statue of Liberty has become one of the most famous monuments in the world. So, can you name some other examples for me?
(man)	In St. Louis, Missouri, there is the Gateway Arch.
(professor)	That's a great example. Made by the architect Eero Saarinen, the Gateway Arch is 630 feet high and 630 feet wide. It was designed to symbolize how St. Louis was the historic Gateway to the West.
(woman)	And of course, there's Mount Rushmore.
(professor)	Mount Rushmore in South Dakota is certainly a mammoth monument. Nearly 6,000 feet high, Mount Rushmore was designed by architect Gutzon Borglum in 1924 to represent the best of American presidents – Washington, Jefferson, Lincoln, and Teddy Roosevelt. Mount Rushmore was so huge, it took 14 years to create.

1. The speakers mentioned several significant American monuments. Match the monument with what it symbolizes.

2. The speakers mentioned several significant American monuments. Match the monument with its location.

3. The speakers mentioned several significant American monuments. Match the monument with the architect who designed it.

TOEFL Exercise 7.8

Listen to the following excerpts from academic discussions and lectures, then answer graphic questions.

Ex. 1 Listen to part of a lecture in an astronomy class. The professor is talking about the solar system.

The nine planets in our solar system divide into two groups that are very different in terms of size, mass, and composition. Mercury, Venus, and Mars resemble the earth in being composed almost entirely of rocky materials and iron. They are, along with the earth, collectively known as "terrestrial planets."
Sometimes the earth's moon is included in this group since it is only slightly smaller than Mercury and is composed of similar materials.
Separating the terrestrial planets from those further out is a large gap containing a big asteroid field. After that gap come the giant planets – Jupiter, Saturn, Uranus, and Neptune. All are significantly larger and more massive than the earth, although less dense. They are less dense because they are mostly made of hydrogen and helium, two light gases. Pluto, the furthest planet from the sun, is significantly different from any of the other planets, made primarily of methane and ice.

The speaker described various parts of our solar system. Where in the following diagram would you most likely find an asteroid field?

Ex. 2 Listen to a professor and two students in a music class discussing information on an orchestra.

(professor)	An orchestra is a group of musicians that plays music written for a specific combination of instruments. The exact number and type of instruments in the orchestra has changed a lot over time.
(woman)	Professor, how about today? How many kinds of instruments are in a modern orchestra?
(professor)	Well, the number and type of instruments included in the orchestra depends on the style of music being played. But usually, we say the orchestra has four types of instruments – stringed, woodwind, brass, and percussion.
(man)	And does it matter where the musicians sit?
(professor)	Very much so. The musicians are usually arranged in a semi-circle, with the strings spread out along the front. Woodwinds are in the center, and brass instruments are further back. At the very back is where the percussion instruments are usually located.

The professor discussed where the various instruments in a modern orchestra are usually
located. Where in the following diagram would you most likely find the woodwind instruments?

Ex. 3 Listen to part of a lecture in a zoology class. The professor is talking about chimpanzees.

The facial expressions of chimpanzees can reveal a lot about their mood at a particular time. Of all the great apes, chimpanzees have the most complex social structure, so effective communication between chimps is very important to keeping order.
When simply calling to other chimps, it has a "calling face" – a relaxed look where the chimpanzee hoots playfully. This is used for simple communication.
This contrasts with the "display face." The display face is an aggressive face, particularly used during charging displays or when attacking another chimp. The strong frown and closed mouth is a danger sign.

The closed grin, on the other hand, is a sign of submission or subservience. Even though the chimpanzee is displaying its teeth, it is doing so in a respectful, fearful way. Often a low-ranked chimp when approaching a superior will make this expression as a show of respect.

The speaker mentioned different facial expressions chimpanzees can have. Match the following expressions with the correct picture.

Ex. 4   Listen to a discussion between two students in an anthropology class discussing information on sports.

(man)	I'm really enjoying my class on sports.
(woman)	Sports? What kind of class is that?
(man)	I'm studying it as part of my anthropology major. After all, games involving a ball or played on a field have been going on for thousands of years.
(woman)	So what are you enjoying in this sports anthropology class?
(man)	Right now we are comparing various fields, showing how local conditions produced the different kinds of playing fields that different games use.
(woman)	Do the fields really differ that much from each other?
(man)	Sometimes a lot; other times the differences are subtle. Here, take a look at the pictures in my textbook. This is a soccer field. It's 300 feet long and 150 feet wide. The field is divided into two halves, and in each half there is a goal, surrounded by a rectangular goal area and a larger penalty area.
(woman)	So how is that different than, say, a football field?
(man)	The football field is wider, 160 feet, while it is the same length as the soccer field. However, instead of goals at either end, football merely has fork-like goalposts. And the field is divided much more, every five yards for the entire length of the field.
(woman)	Those are pretty similar, though.
(man)	Yeah, but look at this cricket field. It's totally different. Instead of a rectangle, the cricket field is an oval. The exact size does not matter so much, though in general the cricket field is much larger than football or soccer. The important part is the cricket pitch, in the middle of the field, where the pitcher throws to the batsman, and two wickets are 66 feet apart.
(woman)	How about baseball?
(man)	Baseball's field is more irregular. It is square on two sides, and more rounded in the outfield. It must be at least 325 feet from the batter to the outfield wall. The infield is diamond-shaped, with four bases.

Which of the following fields is a cricket field?

Ex. 5   Listen to part of a lecture in a naval architecture class. The professor is talking about sailing ships.

The classic wooden sailing ships of the British and French in the 18th and 19th centuries were quite a sight. These great boats could hold up to 74 heavy cannons at a time. In order to be so big, much support and reinforcement were needed, and the boats reached 170 feet in length.
The "head" of the ship referred to the very front or bow of the boat. The figurehead was the carving on the front that led the way, symbolically looking out for the ship. The next part of the ship was the forecastle (pronounced "foc's'l"). This is where the ship's kitchen, or galley, could be found, along with the stove chimney. It might seem strange to have the chimney at the front of the ship, but remember, these old ships were powered by the wind, so by putting the chimney at the front, it actually ensured smoke and odors blew away from the rest of the boat.
After the foc's'l came the waist, where the upperdeck was actually open. Then came the quarterdeck, where the main mast was fixed. The stern or back of the ship was called the poop deck. This is where the captain's and other officers' quarters were located.

The speaker described several parts of the classic, wooden battleships. Where on one of these ships would you expect to find the galley stove chimney?

Ex. 6   Listen to two students in a meteorology class discussing information on clouds.

(woman)	This meteorology class is really tough.
(man)	Yeah, I remember taking it last year. It was difficult and a lot of work. What are you having problems with?
(woman)	We're studying clouds right now. I understand that clouds come from all the moisture in the atmosphere, but I don't understand all the different kinds of clouds that can form.
(man)	Well, it takes more than moisture to form clouds – you also need the air to cool. And there are lots of reasons the air can cool down – the atmosphere in general cools down at higher altitudes, but mountains, turbulence or even power stations can cause clouds to form.
(woman)	But what about the different kinds of clouds?
(man)	Cloud names are classified by their height and shape. Low-level clouds that are small and dome-shaped are called "cumulus." These small clouds are usually short-lived, lasting only 15 minutes or so before dispersing. They are usually formed on sunny days, when localized currents lift and cool the air.
(woman)	How about those larger storm clouds?
(man)	The biggest is called cumulonimbus and can reach up to 7 miles in the air. Their high, flattened tops contain a lot of ice, which can suddenly fall to the ground in heavy showers or hail.
(woman)	And what are stratus clouds?
(man)	Stratus clouds are amorphous, very low-level clouds, usually featureless and gray. They can be so low in the sky they obscure hilltops or even extend all the way to the ground, and can occur in huge sheets covering thousands of kilometers. The other major form of clouds is cirrus clouds – those are the highest forming clouds and resemble wisps of hair or feathers.

The speakers discussed several kinds of clouds. Match the name of the cloud to its correct picture.

Ex. 7   Listen to part of a lecture in an architecture class. The professor is talking about domes.

One of the most beautiful forms in classical architecture is the domed roof. Many of the greatest buildings in the world are instantly memorable for their domed roofs – such as St. Paul's Cathedral in London or the Capitol in Washington D.C.

Domes come in several different styles. The most basic type is the hemispherical dome, which has a spherical base and is a half-circle on top. There are many famous examples of this type of roof, such as St. Paul's and the Dome of the Rock in Jerusalem.

The saucer dome also has a circular base, but its top is less than a semi-circle. The Church of Santa Sophia in Turkey is a notable example of the saucer dome.

The polyhedral dome is a dome with square sides instead of being circular. These flat sides form a dome on top that is angular, not circular. The Florence Cathedral in Italy is a polyhedral dome.

Finally, there is also the onion dome. The onion dome looks remarkably different than the other kinds of domes. It can rest on either a circular or a square-sided base, but the dome itself goes outwards before rounding inwards to form a dome. Many Eastern Orthodox churches, such as St. Basil's Cathedral in Moscow, have onion-shaped domes, as do many Muslim mosques.

Which of the following pictures is an onion dome?

Ex. 8   Listen to part of a lecture in a physiology class. The professor is talking about the spine.

The spine of humans has two main functions: it serves as a protective surrounding for the delicate spinal cord and forms the supporting backbone of the skeleton. The spine consists of 24 separate differently shaped bones called vertebrae. There are three types of vertebrae – the cervical vertebrae that go from the base of the skull to about the shoulders, the thoracic vertebrae that go from the shoulders to the lower back, and the lumbar vertebrae in the lower back. After the vertebrae is a triangular bone called the sacrum; it's actually made up of several vertebrae that have fused together. At the very bottom of the spine is the coccyx, a small tail-like structure. Together, this arrangement allows the skull to move about freely up and down and from side to side, while also allowing maximum mobility to the whole body.

The speaker described the human spine. Where on the following diagram would you find the sacrum?

Mini-Test 4

Listening Script Part A

Questions 1-6

1. (man)   What kind of paints did you want to buy for class?
   (woman)   I really want to get one of those nice watercolor paint sets, like our art teacher uses.
   (man)   You like those paints? The art store downtown had a big sale on them, part of their annual fall sale, but it ended last Saturday.
   (woman)   If only I had known, I would have gone before then.
   (narrator)   What does the woman mean?

2. (woman)   Scott, you're looking really healthy these days.
   (man)   Thanks. I feel so much better since I've started running regularly. The longer I run, the better I feel.
   (woman)   I'm not a big fan of running. It's doesn't seem very beneficial to me. There are other ways I'd rather exercise.
   (man)   If you ever tried long distance running, you'd totally know what I mean.
   (narrator)   What is the man assuming about the woman?

3. (man)   I was interested in becoming a philosophy major. Can I fill out the proper forms?
   (woman)   That's great you're interested in philosophy. But you can't officially declare until sophomore year.
   (narrator)   What can be inferred about the man?

4. (woman)   Last night's attendance for the film society meeting was really good. There must have been 25 people there, all told.
   (man)   That is good. That's near our record of 27 people. I wonder if we can break it next week? Since we're starting that short film festival, with a couple dozen of the best short films from all over the world, there should be a great turnout.
   (narrator)   How many people came to their meeting last night?

5. (man)   I'm not going to take another economics class with Dr. Fillmore again. She's too smart – I can't understand a thing she says.
   (woman)   I told you she was difficult. She doesn't give much homework, but it doesn't matter because the questions are so difficult.
   (narrator)   Why does the man not like Dr. Fillmore?

6. (woman)   You seem like you're in a good mood.
   (man)   I found this great jazz bar last night. Good music, relaxing ambiance – it's a real find.
   (woman)   Maybe you could show me where it is tonight.
   (man)   I have a test tomorrow I have to get ready for.
   (narrator)   What is the man implying?

Listening Script Part B

Questions 7-10

Listen to part of a lecture in a history of science class. The professor is talking about alchemy.

When most people think of alchemy, if they think of it at all, they think of superstition, pseudo-science, and frauds trying to turn lead into gold. But in fact, many of the greatest minds in history were believers in alchemy, from the dawn of civilization up until only a couple of hundred years ago. When we look at the many serious and important scientists who have engaged in alchemy over the years, we can see how it was the main way people tried to make sense of nature and the universe before modern science.
Alchemists were a diverse lot, with many different secrets and ideas; but the key to almost all of them was something called "panvitalism" – the idea that the universe and everything in it was alive; plants and animals, but also minerals. Animals had the shortest and most complicated lives, minerals the longest and

simplest. Minerals were believed to grow from seeds, just as plants and animals do. These grew deep in the earth and rose to the surface, maturing as they moved. Depending on the path taken, they developed into different types of rocks. If a young mineral rose quickly along a poor route, it emerged in a bad form, like volcanic lava. If it rose slowly and well, it might emerge as gold.

Most alchemists were not trying to turn lead into gold in order to make money. For most, making gold meant learning how to make a mineral more perfect. The means of making a mineral perfect might then be applicable to plant, animals, or even people.

In their quest, alchemists looked for certain substances. The Philosopher's Stone was the substance that combined with lesser rocks and turned them into gold. The Elixir of Life was a universal medicine, which would cure all sicknesses. And the "alkahest" was a universal solvent, which would dissolve all substances. For centuries, alchemy was based on the works of Aristotle, who proposed that all worldly substances were made up of four elements: air, earth, fire, and water. But alchemy began to turn into modern science with the work of Paracelsus in the 16th century. He did not believe in the science of Aristotle, so he sought to re-invent chemistry using only his own observations, without tradition. A Polish doctor named Sendivogius was inspired by Paracelsus' work. He published a book about alchemy that was the most influential work of its kind for the next 100 years. Most importantly, he was the first to recognize that our air is a chemical mixture – amazing at a time when the very idea of gases was undiscovered.

In the 17th century, alchemy was still the only way of thinking about the world. Even Sir Isaac Newton spent most of his life conducting alchemical experiments. Finally, only with the work of Lavoisier in the late 1770s did alchemy finally end. Lavoisier recognized that what we breathe in the air is oxygen, and modern chemistry was born.

7. What is the main idea of this lecture?

8. What does "panvitalism" mean?

9. Several alchemical ideas were mentioned. Match the idea and what it meant.

10. The speaker mentioned how alchemy turned into modern chemistry. Summarize by placing the following events into the correct order.

Questions 11-13

Listen to a professor and two students discussing information from a sociology class. The class is on human populations.

(professor)	For most of history, human populations have been very stable. In fact, by 1800, total population all over the planet was only 1 billion people. But since then there has been a great explosion in birth rates. Do you know how population has changed according to the demographic transition theory?
(man)	There're three stages – the initial stage, called the "high potential growth" stage; a transitional stage; and the mature stage, with low birth and death rates.
(professor)	That's right. Most of the world for most of history was in the high potential phase, with high birth and death rates. The birth rate was usually at about the maximum humans can biologically accomplish, but death was also common.
(woman)	Is that why women used to give birth to so many children?
(professor)	That's a major reason. One infant in three died before its first birthday, and another died before reaching adulthood. Each woman needed to give birth to an average of 7 babies just to ensure that two children survived to adulthood. But then, around 1750, the death rate started to decline in Europe.
(man)	Why's that?
(professor)	There were two major reasons. For one, advances in science and technology made food much more plentiful. Better food meant healthier populations, better able to resist diseases. And secondly, public health and sanitation greatly improved.
(woman)	What about advances in medical technology?
(professor)	Contrary to popular belief, that had little influence on death rates until the 20th century; it was mostly improvements to nutrition and sanitation. Over about a 100-year period, death rates in Europe declined from 50 per 1000 to below 20 per 1000, and life expectancy increased to over 50 years of age. In this transition stage, high birth rates and low death

rates meant that the population increased dramatically. This led to urbanization, as cities across Europe and America grew dramatically. Finally, around 1880, fertility rates began to decline and the Mature Demographic Stage began. Why this happened is not exactly known and is the cause of a lot of debate.

11. What is the main topic of this lecture?

12. The speaker mentioned three different demographic stages. Match each phase with its characteristic.

13. Why did death rates decline in Europe?

Questions 14-15

Listen to part of a conversation between two speakers.

(woman)	Hi, Steve! You're still here? I thought you would've gone home for break by now.
(man)	No, I'm not going this year. My family is scattered all over the place, either for work or visiting relatives, so there really wasn't anyone for me to visit at home.
(woman)	Oh, that's too bad. You must be lonely.
(man)	Not really. I have a lot of work to do for my senior thesis. Between semesters is a great time to get work done – there's barely anyone around at all to distract me.
(woman)	It certainly is quiet around here these days.
(man)	How about you? What are you doing at school still?
(woman)	My family lives just across town; it's easy for me to go see them anytime. I like the school a lot more when it is cold and quiet like this.
(man)	Are you taking any classes?
(woman)	No, I decided to use my free time to work on that book I've been talking about for a while now.
(man)	That's great. Do you think you'll get it finished?
(woman)	I doubt it, but I am getting a lot done. That's the important thing.

14. When is this conversation probably taking place?

15. Why did the man not go home?

Chapter 8 – Reviews for Part B

Type A – 19 Questions for Part B

Questions 1-4

Listen to part of a lecture in an ecology class. The professor is talking about herons.

Of all the many birds that cover America, one of the largest and most common is the heron. These long-legged birds live in the marshes of saltwater lagoons, freshwater lakes, and rivers. They are expert fishermen, able to walk through shallow water so gently that they produce no ripples. When they see a fish, they jab their beaks into the water, catching their prey.

Herons live all over North and South America, except the extreme polar regions. A hundred or more herons often live in a single nesting site, which is called a heronry. Their nests are crude platforms of sticks, usually placed in trees. The eggs number from three to six and are white or bluish green.

People often confuse herons and cranes. The difference is that herons and egrets fly with their necks curved back so that their head lies between the shoulders – cranes fly with their necks outstretched.

In the U.S., there are several major species of heron. The great blue heron ranges throughout the continental United States. It ranges from 42 to 50 inches long. Most of its body is a dull blue, with a long, black crest on the back of the head.

The green heron is common in the eastern United States and is between 16 and 22 inches long. Unlike most herons, the green heron is a solitary bird and does not live in large heronries.

The largest of all the herons is the great white heron. Reaching up to 55 inches long, with pure white plumage, the great white heron lives in the mangrove swamps of Florida. There are also the yellow heron and the black-crowned night heron.

The "egret" is a kind of heron. It usually refers to herons with extra-long, stylish white plumage, especially noticeable in the males during the breeding season. Egrets are pure white, but not as large as the great white heron. Instead, they range only up to 40 inches long. They live mostly in the west, from Oregon to California. Egrets are some of the most beautiful birds in North American. However, for the egret, its beauty was also a curse. Their feathers became highly prized by people for use on hats, clothes, and other types of decorating. So popular were they that the egret was nearly exterminated. Only protection by wildlife groups has allowed the egret to begin to populate America again.

1. What is the best possible title for this lecture?

2. What is the difference between egrets and herons?

3. Where do you NOT find herons?

4. The speaker mentioned where several species of heron live. Match the species with its region on the map of the United States.

Questions 5-7

Listen to a discussion between a professor and two students in a biology class. The class is on names of species.

(professor)	One of the odd things people do when naming animals is to name some creatures after human objects and inventions. For example, there are several fishes named after tools. Can you think of any examples?
(man)	Do you mean like the hammerhead shark?
(professor)	That's exactly the kind of example I was thinking of. Hammerheads are named for the unusual shape of their heads, which are broad, flattened, and, obviously, hammer-shaped. Scientists don't know why these sharks have such odd-shaped heads, although they do have several theories. Some think the head may act as a rudder, helping the shark to steer or dive. Others think that having their eyes so far apart might help them to see better.
(woman)	So they don't use their heads like a hammer?
(professor)	I'm afraid not, although another oceanic animal, the sawfish, does use its head as the name implies.
(man)	Sawfish?
(professor)	The sawfish is a huge member of the ray family. They can grow up to 20 feet long and weigh over 700 pounds. The "saw" is a flat extension of the snout, covered with tough skin, and with a row of about 25 pairs of sharp teeth on each side. This saw can be 6 feet long and a foot wide at the base. Anyhow, the sawfish usually uses this "saw" by swimming into schools of fish and wielding it in a side-to-side movement.
(woman)	Are sawfish dangerous to people?
(professor)	Not especially, although anything that big can hurt you. If the sawfish has a bad reputation, it is probably because a lot of people confuse it with the swordfish. The swordfish is a kind of marlin, not related at all to the sawfish. But it is much more aggressive and has been known to hurt people with its large, sharp-pointed snout.

5. What is this discussion mainly about?

6. The professor mentioned several types of fishes. Match the name with the kind of fish.

7. Why do researchers think hammerhead sharks have hammer-shaped heads?

Questions 8-9

Listen to part of a conversation between two speakers.

(man)	You know, I've been thinking about joining the student literary society.
(woman)	We have a literary society on campus?
(man)	Yeah. It's on the top floor of the English building. It's for any undergraduate who wants to spend time reading or writing or talking about literature.

(woman)	How long have you been thinking about joining?
(man)	For a while now. I went to a couple of their meetings in my freshman year, and it seemed pretty interesting.
(woman)	Now that you mention it, I do remember this group. My friend Janet joined last year.
(man)	She did? Has she liked it?
(woman)	I think she likes it a lot. I remember her talking about a poetry journal or something like that.
(man)	That's right. They publish a small book of student poetry every spring.
(woman)	Right. Janet said she was interested in helping out on that.
(man)	Does she like to write poetry?
(woman)	Not really. She's more interested in the editing and preparation.

8. What can be inferred about the man?

9. Why did Janet join the literary society?

Questions 10-13

Listen to part of a lecture in a business class. The professor is talking about the Studebaker Company.

One of America's most successful vehicle-manufacturing companies was the Studebaker Brothers Manufacturing Company, or just "Studebaker" for short. Through hard work and a little luck, they managed to lift themselves up from having almost nothing to being one of the most successful vehicle manufacturers of the 19th and 20th centuries.

The Studebaker brothers were children of John and Rebecca Studebaker, and were born between 1826 and 1836. The family lived near Gettysburg, Pennsylvania until 1836 when they moved to Ohio. The boys went to regular, public schools and learned the blacksmith's trade from their father.

The two oldest brothers then moved to Indiana in 1850, where they used their savings to open their own blacksmith and wagon-building shop. That first year, they only made 3 wagons and only sold 2.

It was during this period that the railroad began to make inroads into the Midwest. The resulting agricultural development increased demand for wagons. But the brothers' best bit of luck came in 1858, when they received their first government contract to build wagons. Many other government contracts followed, and soon the Studebaker company was a financial success. Eventually, by the 1870s, they were the biggest horse-drawn vehicle manufacturer in the world.

In 1897, they started to experiment with self-propelled, horseless vehicles. This led to electric and gasoline automobiles. By 1920, Studebaker was so successful in this new field of motorized vehicles that they stopped producing wagons altogether.

10. What is the speaker's attitude towards the Studebakers?

11. Several events were mentioned in the history of the Studebaker Company. Summarize by placing the following events into the correct chronological order.

12. Which did the speaker say was the most fortunate event in the history of Studebaker?

13. Why did Studebaker stop making wagons?

Questions 14-16

Listen to two students in a microbiology class discussing information on viruses.

(man)	I'm worried about our microbiology test on Tuesday. I know that viruses are going to be an important part of the test, but I don't understand them at all.
(woman)	Well, I think I'm fairly well prepared for the test. You can try asking me if you want.
(man)	First of all, what are viruses? I mean, they don't look like or act like any other type of cell we've studied about in class.
(woman)	That's because viruses are not cells. In fact, it is hard to say whether or not they're even alive. Outside a cell, they seem to be nothing but inert chemicals. But once inside a cell, they come to life, taking over the cell's biochemical machinery for their own ends – to make more viruses.

(man)	So what are viruses if they're not cells?
(woman)	An individual virus is called a phage – it's basically a core of genetic material wrapped in protein. The virus DNA is stored in a protein "head" that can be round or multi-sided. It has a hollow tail that ends with a single tail fiber.
(man)	And the protein shell protects the virus?
(woman)	Sort of. It also is needed to get the virus DNA into the cell. All cells need various proteins to live and to carry out their tasks. The protein shell of a virus often resembles the good proteins the cell uses. The cell gets fooled into thinking the virus is one of those good proteins, and lets it in.
(man)	And once inside, the virus takes over, right?
(woman)	That's right. The virus DNA sheds its protein coating and takes over the infected cell's biological machinery, changing it so the cell now works for the virus. The virus makes thousands of copies of itself. Eventually, the cell bursts, and all the thousands of new phages go out in search of cells of their own to infect.
(man)	Hmmm. I think I understand a little better now. Thanks a lot.

14. Why is the man talking to the woman?

15. What part of the virus contains the DNA?

16. What is the purpose of the virus's protein shell?

Questions 17-19

Listen to part of a conversation between a professor and his student.

(woman)	Professor Atkins, could I get some help with my chemistry lab?
(professor)	Certainly, Julie – what happens to be the problem? Have you not been able to understand the experiment?
(woman)	I understand the experiment – no problem; but I have really different results from what the textbook indicated.
(professor)	That certainly is a possibility. Remember, the textbook tends to give you an ideal explanation of the experiments. But in real life, any number of factors can cause you to get different results.
(woman)	So any result is acceptable?
(professor)	No, of course there is a range. For this particular experiment, I'd expect your answer to be within 4 or 5% of the textbook.
(woman)	Really? My answer was nearly 10% off.
(professor)	That would be a problem. If your answer were that far from the proper answer, even if you could explain the difference, I would have to lower your grade significantly.
(woman)	I see. Then I guess I'm going to have to redo it. I want to do well in your class and can't afford to get a bad lab grade.
(professor)	Very good. But you'll have to hurry – the lab is due Friday, and I won't be giving any extensions.

17. What is the woman's problem?

18. How close to the textbook does the professor say is acceptable?

19. What will the woman most likely do?

Type B – 33 Questions for Part B

Questions 1-4

Listen to part of a lecture in an architecture class. The professor is talking about American architecture.

Architecture in America started out as simple imitations of what settlers had known in their home countries. However, America had a different climate and other special characteristics that meant that those buildings were not always appropriate to this new land. Soon America developed unique architectural styles and techniques that were better suited to life there.

For example, the first colonists in New England found that the winter winds there were much colder than in Europe. Therefore, new construction techniques were developed to keep those winds out of the home. Because wood was so plentiful in New England, clapboard became the most common style of building – horizontal wood panels that overlapped the panels beneath them. Windows were small, and the center of the house had a large fireplace for cooking and for warmth.

In the frontier regions, the well-known log cabin was most common. Relatively easy to build and maintain, the log cabin was the best option for the rough and isolated life at the edges of America.

As the colonies grew and prospered, larger and more comfortable houses became more common. The English Georgian style, with its chiefly brick construction, became popular. Georgian homes were especially dominant on the east coast, from Philadelphia to Virginia.

In the southwest, on the other hand, Spanish baroque architecture had a great impact. Large compounds with white adobe and red tile roofs were common from Texas to San Diego and up the Pacific coast, and that style still greatly influences the architecture of the region today.

Many other unique architectural styles exist in various regions of America, from the Greek revivalism of the southern plantations to the ornate ironwork of New Orleans. It is all part of the unique heritage America has grown over the past 400 years.

1. What is the main idea of this lecture?

2. What was NOT a characteristic of early New England homes?

3. The speaker described several architectural traditions in the early United States. Match each architectural style and where it was used.

4. What kind of architecture would you expect to find in New Orleans?

Questions 5-8

Listen to part of a lecture in an American history class. The professor is talking about national parks.

The early settlers who covered the United States found their land so rich in natural resources that they seemed without limit. The forests were cut down for lumber or just to clear the land for farming. Minerals were mined carelessly, and often abandoned with much valuable ore still left in them. The buffalo and other animals were thoughtlessly slaughtered, often for no purpose besides sport. And for several generations, Americans continued in this behavior, as if the land and its resources were endless.

Only towards the end of the 1800s did a number of Americans begin thinking about conservation. They worried about how the loss of wildlife and natural resources might affect future generations. One of the first efforts made to turn this tide of destruction was the creation of Yellowstone Park in 1872. This huge park of 3,500 square miles extends through parts of the states of Wyoming, Montana, and Idaho, across an area with some spectacular scenery. Yellowstone Park has the world's largest concentration of geysers as well as many hot springs.

Since then, many national parks have been established. One of the most famous is Yosemite Park in California. Yosemite contains mountains, lakes, and waterfalls. But most spectacular is its collection of ancient giant sequoia trees. There are trees in the park that are over 200 feet tall and 35 feet in diameter, and estimated to be around 3,000 years old.

Perhaps the most spectacular scenery of all is in the Grand Canyon National Park. This 300-mile-long gorge was cut 3,000 to 4,000 feet deep through the rocks by the Colorado River.

In 1916, all the national parks were consolidated and put under the control of the National Park Service, part of the Department of the Interior. Today, the National Park Service maintains over 30 million acres of public parklands and hundreds of national shrines and recreational areas.

5. What is the main subject of this lecture?

6. What is NOT an example the speaker mentioned of how Americans wasted resources?

7. The speaker mentioned several national parks. Match each park with what makes it notable.

8. How much parkland is controlled by the National Park Service?

Questions 9-11

Listen to part of a conversation between two speakers.

(man)	Dr. Dixon is famous for being such an interesting lecturer, but I never knew his class would be so hard.
(woman)	You're having problems in his class? Why's that? Is the work really tough?
(man)	Well, the level isn't so bad. But he keeps assigning more to do! It's impossible to get everything done.
(woman)	Didn't he tell you about the course at the start of the semester? All teachers are supposed to hand out a syllabus at the start of the semester that gives an overview of requirements, readings, and obligations.
(man)	Professor Dixon did hand out a course syllabus, but it wasn't very accurate. It seems like almost every week he's changing the course – adding a new article to read, or telling us to make a little presentation.
(woman)	That doesn't sound very fair. I mean, you do have other classes besides Dr. Dixon's.
(man)	That's right. Because he keeps giving more work, it's impossible for me to organize my schedule. Not only am I falling behind in Professor Dixon's class, but I'm beginning to have problems in my other classes as well.
(woman)	That's not good at all. Dr. Dixon might be an interesting history teacher, but you can't allow his course to start affecting your major.
(man)	Yeah, my other classes are too important to risk getting poor grades in them.
(woman)	So what are you going to do about it? Are you going to drop the course?
(man)	Luckily, it's not too late for that. Otherwise I would have had to petition the department to change courses or, worse, kept taking it.

9. What is the man's problem?

10. What can be inferred about the man?

11. What will the man most likely do?

Questions 12-16

Listen to a professor and two students in a biology class. The class is on insects.

(professor)	The world's most abundant creatures are insects. In fact, the known species of insects outnumber all the other animals and plants combined. Entomologists, the scientists who study insects, have so far named 800,000 species; and they estimate that that is only one-third the total number out there. Insects thrive almost anyplace where life is possible, from the cold Arctic to the hottest deserts. Some have wings, others swim, some sting and others are parasites. But for all the different kinds of insects in the world, there are also remarkable similarities among all insects. Can you name any?
(woman)	Well, most obvious is that they have 6 legs.
(professor)	Very good. A lot of creatures people think of as insects are not insects at all. Spiders and scorpions have eight legs, and centipedes have dozens of legs. But true insects have only six. In fact, insects are also called "hexapods", from the Greek word for "six-footed."
(man)	Their bodies are similar, too. All insects have bodies that are segmented, right?
(professor)	Yes, and that's where they get their name – "insecta" is Latin, meaning "segmented." All insects have bodies that can be divided into three segments – the head, the thorax in the middle, and then the abdomen. The thorax itself can be further divided into three segments, each having one pair of legs. And in addition, all insects have a pair of sensory antennas.
(woman)	And all insects have exoskeletons, don't they?
(professor)	That's also correct. Instead of having an internal skeleton, like we do, they are covered in a horny shell, called "chitin."
(man)	How about the inside of the insect? Is that the same, too?

(professor)	Pretty much the same. The nervous system includes a brain and two parallel nerve cords which run along the underside of the body. Along the nerve cords are a series of masses called "ganglia." Each ganglion controls certain activities and is more or less independent from the others and even, to a certain extent, from the brain. If an insect loses its head, the rest of the body can actually keep functioning for quite a while.

12. What is the main subject of this discussion?

13. What is true of all insects?

14. What does the Latin word "insecta" mean?

15. What part of an insect is the abdomen?

16. What are the ganglia?

Questions 17-19

Listen to part of a lecture in a mathematics class. The professor is talking about computing devices.

We think of computers as thoroughly modern inventions. But in fact, the first computers and the ideas behind computers are both quite old. I'm not talking about digital, electronic computers, but machines and theories designed to aid in computing and calculations.

At first, counting was done by matching one set of objects to another set – for example, sheep and stones. A farmer counting his sheep might add a pebble for each additional sheep. Early counting tables, like the abacus, not only formalized this way of counting, but introduced the idea of position – ones, tens, hundreds, and so on. Only when counting and arithmetic became more abstract did people need to learn some way of storing numbers, such as by writing them down in clay or on papyrus.

One of the most important people in this numerical evolution was Muhammad ibn Musa Al'Khowarizmi, a Middle Eastern cleric from way back in the 12th century. He invented the idea of a writing process to achieve a specific goal, which he called the "algorithm" – today a well-known mathematical term essential to the functioning of computers.

In 1622, William Oughtred created the slide rule, a familiar calculating device used by engineers ever since. Although this was an analog, not a digital, device, it was precise to 3 decimal places and fast.

Later in the 17th century, philosophers like Blaise Pascal of France and Gottfried Wilhelm Leibnitz of Germany invented mechanical calculating machines. By turning wheels, digits could be added and displayed. But these were mostly used for show by well-to-do hobbyists, and had little practical influence on the scientific world.

But the true father of the calculating devices was Charles Babbage. In 1833, he designed the analytical engine, using a steam engine to power his calculating device. This machine was not designed to work like any computer we would recognize today – there was no monitor or disk drive. Instead, it was designed to produce larger and more accurate charts that could be used by scientists and engineers.

Another important advance was made in 1854 by George Boole. He created a mathematics system that only used 1's and 0's – Boolean algebra – and is the basis for all computer programming even today.

17. What is the main subject of this lecture?

18. The professor mentioned several inventions in the history of calculation. Summarize by placing the following inventions into the correct chronological order.

19. What is significant about Boolean algebra?

Questions 20-22

Listen to part of a conversation between two speakers.

(man)	Professor Greeley? You wanted to see me?
(professor)	Yes, come in, Jake. I was wondering if you were still planning on going to graduate school in the future.
(man)	That's my goal, yes. I guess it sort of depends on how my senior thesis project goes next year.

(professor)	That's a major factor involved in admissions, that's true. But there're a lot of other things you can do to help your application.
(man)	Do you have something in mind?
(professor)	Well, are you still looking for a little work?
(man)	Yeah, I am. Paying for books and everything is kind of expensive.
(professor)	As it turns out, I'm going to need some help putting a book together over the next year. And I just received a grant from the university to hire a research assistant. It's not a lot of money, but it's yours if you want it.
(man)	Really? Wow. What kind of help do you need?
(professor)	I'm looking for a research assistant, someone who can comb through the archives, looking for the materials I need, and who can keep all of my records straight so that nothing gets lost.
(man)	That sounds like something I could do. How much help do you need?
(professor)	I was thinking somewhere between 10 and 15 hours a week, depending on my schedule and yours.

20. What is the main reason the professor wanted to meet the man?

21. What kind of job does the professor suggest to the man?

22. How often will the student help his professor?

Questions 23-26

Listen to a discussion between a professor and his students in a child development class. The class is on communication.

(professor)	Who can tell me something about how babies or young children communicate?
(woman)	Well, long before babies can talk, they can let others know what they want by crying. Their cries take on different tonal qualities so that it is fairly easy to interpret them.
(professor)	Good, Tina. And they also use simple gestures, such as pointing and pushing, to indicate what they want or do not want. Crying and gestures are useful so long as the baby cannot talk. But as the babies slowly learn how to talk, their communication becomes more sophisticated. For example?
(man)	Well, by three or four months, babies have learned how to babble – that is, make those cooing and gurgling sounds.
(professor)	That's right. Babbling is considered "play speech" because it isn't used to convey any meaning. Babies just like to amuse themselves by babbling, even when they are alone. But as the baby spends more time babbling, the combinations of sounds becomes more varied. They're trying to imitate the sounds they hear around them. But what are the tasks the baby must learn in order to talk?
(woman)	They have to learn how to associate meanings with words. And they have to be able to understand the meaning of words other people use.
(professor)	You're talking about vocabulary. At first, children learn the words they use most often – mostly nouns like the names of people around them, toys, or food. Then they learn basic verbs, such as "go" or "give," and the adjectives that describe their feelings, such as "good" and "bad." Next they learn adverbs, prepositions, and conjunctions. Last of all, they learn pronouns. Also, children tend to learn general words, such as "boy" or "dog," before they learn more specific words like colors or the days of the week.
(man)	Children also need to learn pronunciation.
(professor)	Good point. For a children to pronounce words correctly, they must be able to hear them clearly and then coordinate the muscles of their tongue and lips. But communicating your feelings takes more than just the ability to say words and sentences. They also need to learn about emotions. And that will be our discussion next class.

23. What is the main subject of this lecture?

24. Why do babies babble?

25. The speakers discussed how children learn language. Summarize by placing the following kinds of words into the order in which children learn them.

26. What do children need for proper pronunciation?

Questions 27-31

Listen to part of a lecture in an astronomy class. The professor is talking about stars.

As we examined last class, stars are bodies of hot, glowing gas that are born in clouds of hydrogen in space. They vary enormously in size, mass, and temperature – they can have diameters 1/50th the size of our sun, or 1,000 times greater; masses can be 1/20th of our sun, or over 50 times greater; and surface temperatures can range from 5,500 degrees Fahrenheit to over 90,000 degrees. Stars begin to form when a region of higher density gas in space begins to contract under its own gravity. As it contracts, it begins to heat up, forming a protostar. When the temperature reaches 27 million degrees Fahrenheit, nuclear reactions start, where the hydrogen fuses into helium. This process releases energy, which prevents the star from contracting further and causes it to shine.

Today, I want to talk about what happens towards the end of the life of such a star, specifically a red supergiant. The bigger the star, the less time it takes to burn through the main sequence and become a red supergiant. After most of the hydrogen has turned to helium in the core, the helium begins to contract, and a new round of nuclear reactions occurs. Over the next few million years, several heavier elements will be formed. The outer edges of the supergiant remains hydrogen, but there is then a large region of helium. After that comes a layer of carbon, followed by oxygen and then silicon. At the center of the red supergiant is a core of iron.

That iron core eventually collapses in less than a second, causing a massive explosion called a supernova. A shock wave blows away the outer layers of the star, and for a time, a couple of years, the supernova shines brighter than an entire galaxy.

Sometimes the core survives the explosion. If that core is about the size of our star, it contracts to become a tiny, dense neutron star – only about 6 miles across, and so dense a teaspoon of it would weigh a billion tons.

However, if the core is bigger than three times the size of our sun, it contracts to form a black hole – a singularity of infinite density, pressure, and temperature. Black holes are characterized by extremely strong gravity, so powerful not even light can escape.

Now for the rest of this lecture, I'm going to explore the red supergiant in more detail ...

27. What is the main subject of this lecture?

28. The professor talked about the life of a star. Summarize by placing the following steps into the correct chronological order.

29. Where in the following diagram of a red supergiant would you expect to find helium?

30. About how big is a neutron star?

31. What is NOT a characteristic of a black hole?

Questions 32-33

Listen to part of a conversation between two people.

(woman)	So, have you made plans for this weekend yet?
(man)	You bet! Since it's a long weekend, I thought I would try to get away for a couple of days and relax – leave all my work behind me.
(woman)	That sounds really nice. Where're you planning on going?
(man)	A couple of friends and I are going to drive on up to the state park a couple hours north of here and go camping.
(woman)	Really? That sounds like so much fun. I love camping.
(man)	Yeah? Well, you're welcome to come with us if you want to.
(woman)	I want to. But I have a lot of work due early next week – two essays and a book report. I have no time for fun and games. My friends even invited me to go dancing with them

tonight, and I had to turn them down. I'm going to be doing nothing but writing for the next three days.

(man) That's too bad. I know this break is really what I needed. Especially since starting next week, I'm going to have so many tests to write.

32. What is this conversation mostly about?

33. What will the woman most likely do?

Complete Practice Test 1

Listening Script Part A

1. (woman) I was reading something interesting about mythology the other day.
   (man) Really? What was it?
   (woman) It said that myths were actually early people's first attempt at psychology.
   (man) That sounds rather controversial.
   (narrator) What does the man mean?

2. (woman) Oh, I'm glad I ran into you. I really need to borrow your biology book.
   (man) Yeah, you and half the rest of the class.
   (narrator) What is the man implying?

3. (man) The lecture lasted forever. We'll have to hurry before the cafeteria closes.
   (woman) I'm dying for something to eat.
   (narrator) What does the woman mean?

4. (woman) I have so much work to do for tomorrow. A science test, a history essay, and a ton of math homework.
   (man) How are you going to do it all?
   (woman) Well, I can always get an extension on the homework and the paper.
   (narrator) What will the woman probably do next?

5. (man) What's wrong?
   (woman) The big football game is tomorrow and I couldn't get any tickets. The stadium was all sold out.
   (man) I have a couple of extras if you want them.
   (woman) What? How could you get them?
   (man) They had a few extra available for the press. I'm covering the game.
   (narrator) What does the man imply?

6. (woman) I don't know whose classes to take next semester.
   (man) I know most of those people on your list. You can ask me about them.
   (woman) Do you like Professor Chris?
   (man) Do I like her? Professor Chris ONLY gave me two "A"s.
   (narrator) What does the man mean?

7. (man) I haven't gone to the lab in a while. I'm worried my experiment isn't going well.
   (woman) Really? I'm busy these days, but I never miss lab.
   (man) Did you work on the lab experiment last Tuesday?
   (woman) Yeah. I got the best results to date.
   (narrator) What does the woman mean?

8. (man) Have you seen Professor Allen around?
   (woman) I don't think so. The professor is on leave this semester.
   (man) He is? But I need to talk to him about my thesis. Doesn't he ever come to his office?
   (woman) He's out of the office most of the time. If you can't catch him there, you can always email him.

	(narrator)	What does the woman suggest the man do?

9.
(woman)	I can't believe how hard those math problems were.
(man)	You think so? I did them all.
(woman)	Really? What did you get for the first problem?
(man)	17.
(woman)	17? And did you get "2x" for the second?
(man)	No, "x-squared."
(woman)	If only I had talked to you last night.
(narrator)	What does the woman mean?

10.
(woman)	Are you going to the department party later? It looks so important.
(man)	I have to pick my son up and take him to his soccer game.
(narrator)	What will the man probably do?

11.
(man)	I want to go to the student art show in Shipley Hall.
(woman)	Yeah, I heard all the work is for sale, and most of it is actually affordable. When do you want to go?
(man)	Well, I'm free after lunch.
(narrator)	What does the man mean?

12.
(woman)	I need to talk to you about something.
(man)	Sure, what's up?
(woman)	I need some time off. I've been running around and working extra hours lately. I'm beat.
(man)	Well, you know how busy we are these days. If you wanted to take a half-day off, I could let you go this week.
(woman)	I was really hoping for a whole day. Maybe a long weekend.
(man)	Then I think you'll have to wait a week. I might be able to free up some time for you a week from Friday.
(woman)	That would be great ... assuming I can last until then.
(narrator)	What is the man's most likely relationship with the woman?

13.
(man)	I have to get going to class.
(woman)	Oh? That's too bad. I was just enjoying our talk.
(man)	Well, I'll be on the Internet tonight, after ten o'clock. You can try chatting with me online then.
(narrator)	What is the man suggesting?

14.
(woman)	I can't find the book I need for my paper anywhere.
(man)	Where did you look?
(woman)	I tried both the university's major libraries. I tried the city library. I even checked the bookstore.
(man)	Did you try the library reserve?
(woman)	I didn't think of looking there.
(narrator)	What is the man suggesting?

15.
(woman)	Do you want to go with all of us to Mary's party tonight?
(man)	I'd like to, but I have work to do. Why is she having a party?
(woman)	It's her birthday. She really wanted you to come.
(man)	Oh, if only I had done my homework ahead of time.
(narrator)	What does the man mean?

16.
(man)	Will you be going to the movies with us tonight?
(woman)	What are you going to see?
(man)	I think we're planning on seeing that new British comedy.
(woman)	Oh, I've seen that.
(man)	Really? Did you like it?
(woman)	Like it? I've ONLY seen it 4 times already.
(narrator)	What is the woman implying?

17. (man)   Professor? I had some questions about yesterday's lecture.
    (woman)   You need to make an appointment during my office hours. I'm really busy right now.
    (man)   Do you have office hours Wednesday?
    (woman)   Usually, yes, but I've cancelled office hours for the rest of this week.
    (narrator)   What does the woman mean?

Listening Script Part B

Questions 18-22

Listen to a professor and two students discussing information about cartography.

(professor)   So that about wraps up our discussion of mapping today and how technological advances have changed it. Any last questions?
(man)   I have a background question. How old is mapping, anyhow?
(professor)   Well, the oldest surviving maps are from Mesopotamia, made on clay tablets, and maps from the ancient Mediterranean cultures made on mosaic tile. The writings of ancient Greece and Rome refer to other maps, but these were drawn on perishable parchment or paper, and the originals have disappeared.
(woman)   But I've seen maps from the period. Ptolemy, for example.
(professor)   Ptolemy's maps exist because they have been copied and recopied frequently over the centuries.
(woman)   And why were the old maps so strange? Were they just terrible mappers?
(professor)   No, not at all. Some ancient maps, especially Ptolemy's, were quite advanced in their way, like in their use of latitude. But most early maps centered on the mapmakers' world and world-view. Greek maps centered on the Mediterranean. Chinese maps centered on China. Important areas were drawn larger and less important areas were drawn smaller.
              And maps were usually drawn to reflect a people's world and moral view. For example, Medieval maps were a "T" and "O" design – that is, the map was circled by a ring of water, then the land was drawn as a "T" shape. The East was above the T, with Europe on the left and Africa on the right. Jerusalem, the most important city to Medieval Christians, was at the center.
(man)   When did this begin to change?
(professor)   It was a many-stepped process. The Renaissance brought better techniques and the return of many mathematical techniques forgotten in medieval times. In 1569, the first Mercator map was made. And in 1599, Edward Wright used Mercator's system and combined it with crisscrossing diagonal lines and trigonometry to create much more accurate maps. In the 17th century, there was a great improvement in astronomical techniques, and for the first time, longitude could be determined as accurately as latitude. Greater ocean exploration, especially in the 18th century, also helped. The biggest change, though, was about becoming more objective and scientific.

18. What is this discussion about?

19. Why have Ptolemy's maps survived?

20. Which of the following maps is an example of the maps made by Edward Wright?

21. The professor is explaining the development of maps over time. Match the time period with the mapping technology.

22. What is the major difference between modern maps and pre-modern maps?

Listen to part of a lecture in a music class. The professor is talking about the origin of music.

For the ancient Greeks, the term "music" referred to everything that belonged to a higher intellectual and artistic education. Plato himself put literature beneath music in importance. Indeed, the word "music" comes from the Greek "musice," which means the art of the Muses.

More narrowly, music was regarded by the Greeks as more than just enjoyment, but also as one of the most effective means of cultivating the feelings and the character. The great importance they attached to music is also shown by their idea that it was of divine origin.

It was also originally always allied with poetry. The early epic poems were always read with musical accompaniment. It was not until the time of Alexander that poetry and music were separated into two different forms.

The first place among the various kinds of music was assigned to the indigenous cithara, which was connected with the first development of the musical art; and indeed, stringed instruments were always more esteemed than wind instruments, in part on account of the greater technical difficulties which had to be overcome, and which led to musicians giving particular attention to them. The characteristic of ancient music is the great clearness of its form, resulting, above all, from the extreme precision of the rhythmic treatment.

As the basis of every melodic series of sounds, the ancients had the tetrachord. The tetrachord was a series of four notes, to which, according to tradition, the earliest music was limited. From the tetrachord derived the heptachord, which consisted of two tetrachords joined together, with the central note being the highest of the first tetrachord and the lowest of the second tetrachord – 7 notes alogether.

The man called Terpander is credited with founding classical Greek music. He developed the tetrachord notation system further, expanding the heptachord, adding another note. This led to the eight-note octachord, or "octave" as we call it today.

With regard to musical instruments, only stringed instruments – like the cithara and lyre – and the flute – which more resembles our modern clarinet – were considered proper instruments. Of course, the ancient Greeks had many other instruments, but they were considered to be lesser.

The ancient Romans were completely lacking in native musical development. All music referred to in Roman literature is completely derived from Greek sources. The only difference was that Roman native music was mostly flute-based, and even as the Romans began to co-opt other forms of Greek culture, the flute remained dominant for a long time.

23. What was music for the ancient Greeks?

24. According to the speaker, what was the main characteristic of ancient Greek music?

25. What is Terpander credited with doing?

26. What is the following diagram an example of?

Questions 27-28

Listen to part of a conversation between two speakers.

(man)	Have you been to the bookstore lately?
(woman)	No, why? Did something happen?
(man)	They've raised all their prices. It's terrible. A box of computer paper is $5 more than it used to be. Just about everything's gone up in price.
(woman)	I can't afford to spend even more money on textbooks. They're already too expensive.
(man)	That's for sure. Last semester, I couldn't afford to buy all my textbooks. I tried using the library, but books assigned for classes are always being used by other people. So I actually photocopied an entire book. I don't want to do that again.
(woman)	I tried sharing books with my roommate for this one class last year, but that didn't work very well, either. We both wanted to use it at the same time, so it was really inconvenient.
(man)	That might be possible when you're a literature major – you have a lot of books in your classes, so you can take turns reading different books. That's just not an option for me, though. I think these higher prices are totally unfair.
(woman)	Well, the store needs to stay in business. And these days, everything is getting more expensive. Even with the price hike, I bet most things at the store are still cheaper than

	anywhere else around here.
(man)	That's a good point. But it doesn't help me afford all my books. I'm already so busy, I can't get a part-time job.
(woman)	Maybe you should try to buy more used books. Used books might not look as pretty, but they can save you a lot of money.

27. What happened at the bookstore?

28. What does the woman suggest?

Questions 29-33

Listen to part of a lecture in an American literature course. The professor is talking about Henry James.

Henry James, in spite of enjoying limited appeal in his lifetime, is now commonly recognized by literary critics as America's greatest author.

James's work can be broken down into roughly four periods: his work in the 1860s is like his apprenticeship; in the 1870s he wrote solid and enduring, if unspectacular books; in the 1880s, he struggled to learn how to write for the theater; finally, starting in the 1890s, he returned to writing novels, but now combining the lessons he learned in the theater.

Born in New York City in 1843, the grandson of one of America's first millionaires, Henry James was given the best education possible in the period. He was educated all over America and Europe, where he studied a great many subjects, from painting to biology to law, before deciding upon writing.

James's first story appeared in 1864 in the *North American Review,* and soon he was contributing regularly to the leading magazines of his day. His early fiction was too gloomy for popular tastes, but his editors and friends strongly supported him regardless. His earliest stories concentrated on young love and echoed his own lonely emotional state.

In the 70s while in Paris, James met many of the leading authors of the day. His first book, a collection of his magazine stories, came out in 1875, titled *A Passionate Pilgrim and Other Tales.* His writing in this period had an international theme, as James asked what was the proper role of European experience for an American. James's first full-length novel, *Roderick Hudson,* was published in 1877, a decent, if flawed, book.

His themes and ideas grew more complex and sophisticate over time. In *The Portrait of a Lady,* James described the life of the charming Isabel Archer, a young American woman traveling around Europe. At the beginning, she insists on her moral freedom, but by the end of the book she is a virtual slave. By writing this story, James showed how self-centered freedom is not really freedom at all.

After spending several years writing for theater, James wrote his three greatest books, including the difficult but outstanding *The Golden Bowl.* This book is largely a series of conversations. Its distinction lies in how the characters' consciousnesses are presented.

James was a great novelist and unparalleled critic. From his experiments in narrative perspective sprang many of the greatest writers of the next century. His concern for consciousness forshadowed much of the 20th century novel's concern for psychology, and his contrast of freedom and limits is enlightening even today.

29. What is the main idea of this lecture?

30. The speaker divided Henry James's work into four periods. Place those four periods into the correct chronological order.

31. What is NOT a career Henry James considered before choosing writing?

32. The professor described some of Henry James's writings. Match the book with its characteristics.

33. Why did the speaker think Henry James was an important writer?

Questions 34-37

Listen to part of a lecture in a geography class. The professor is talking about Manitoba.

Manitoba was called the "postage stamp province" when it first joined Canada in 1870, on account of its shape. Since then, its boundaries have expanded to the west, east, and north, to create the 250-thousand-square-mile province it is today. The easternmost of the Prairie Provinces, Manitoba links the resources of western Canada with the principal population centers in the east.

Manitoba's early history was associated with the struggle between France and England for control of the North American fur trade. An English navigator, Sir Thomas Button, was the first European to see Manitoba in 1612. But little interest was subsequently shown in this area, then called Rupert's Land, until reports of vast profits to be made in the fur trade led to the formation of the Hudson's Bay Company in England in 1670. The French fur trade competed fiercely, opening a chain of outposts in Manitoba in the 1730s and 40s. Only after the French were decisively routed in 1763 did control over this area firmly belong to the Hudson's Bay Company.

The first farming settlement in Manitoba was begun in 1811 by Thomas Douglas, Earl of Selkirk. The métis, people of mixed Indian and French decent, resented these newcomers and fought unsuccessfully for years to dislodge the colony.

The métis spearheaded another rebellion when the newly founded Dominion of Canada bought the territory from the Hudson's Bay Company in 1869. Louis Riel led the métis in a fight for self-government because Canada would give them no guarantee of rights to their lands or their distinct way of life. A compromise was reached granting the métis their own schools, but Louis Riel was executed for treason against the crown.

On July 15, 1870, Manitoba became a full province in the Dominion of Canada. Although it was a part of Canada, Manitoba long had stronger links to the United States. It was not firmly tied to the Canadian economy until the completion of the Canadian Pacific Railway in 1885. In the following decades, thousands of newcomers poured into the province. The province grew from barely 25,000 in 1870 to 150 thousand in 1891, and 460 thousand by 1911.

Today, the province has a little over one million people, about half of whom live in the capital city of Winnipeg. Manitoba is divided into two natural regions – the interior plains and the Canadian Shield. The interior plains are in the southwest third of the province and in the northeast around Hudson Bay. The southern plains are very fertile farming land. The Canadian Shield is a vast mass of exposed, ancient rock, largely overlain by glacial deposits. The region is covered by dense coniferous forests. Wheat is the major crop of Manitoba. Lumber and the fur trade are also major industries. And since 1960, mining has been a major industry in Manitoba. Nickel ore is the single most valuable mineral, but copper, zinc, gold, and many other substances are also mined in the province.

34. What was the compromise reached between the government of Canada and the métis?

35. What was the original nickname for Manitoba?

36. What is NOT mentioned by the speaker as a major industry in Manitoba?

37. Which part of Manitoba has the best farmlands?

Questions 38-39

Listen to part of a conversation between two students.

(man)	I can't believe summer vacation is here already.
(woman)	It sure is nice. Too bad I won't be able to enjoy it. I have to spend the summer working.
(man)	What are you going to be doing?
(woman)	Oh, my dad found a job for me at his friend's company, working in the warehouse. It's not very interesting, but it pays well, so I should be able to pay for tuition and books come the fall. I know I have to work, but I feel like I'm wasting my whole summer. I'd rather be relaxing on the beach, or hanging out with my friends. What are you planning? Do you have to work?
(man)	Kind of. But I'm going to be interning at a computer company.
(woman)	Interning?
(man)	Yeah. It doesn't pay much of anything, but it looks really interesting. I'll be learning all about the latest technology and innovations.
(woman)	Wow. That'll really give you a leg up when the time comes to look for a real job, after graduating.
(man)	That would be nice. But I'm more interested in getting into a really good graduate program. This internship, with a good recommendation, should do the trick.
(woman)	Wow. I wish I were that ambitious. Sometimes I think I'll be lucky to graduate, let alone find something to do afterwards.

38. What are the man and woman discussing?

39. What would the woman like to be doing during the summer?

Questions 40-43

Listen to a professor and two students discussing information on biological research.

(professor)	It's been a very exciting year for science. I'm referring particularly to the Human Genome Project. Who knows what happened?
(woman)	Well, scientists finally mapped all the genes in the human body.
(professor)	That's right. Two groups of scientists, working separately, basically finished this massive project at the same time. The Human Genome Project was launched 10 years ago by a consortium of public research institutes, seeking to decipher the human genetic matrix and make the data openly available, for unfettered use. But in the last two years, biotech companies have decrypted sections of the code and rushed to file patents over the fragments that they believe contain useful information. Tens of thousands of such applications have already been filed.
	To make things more complicated, Celera, a private company, launched a similar project only four years ago. They reached the finish line at the same time as the Human Genome Project.
(man)	If this is so important, why are some people calling it a Pandora's box?
(professor)	Because knowledge of the human genetic code may create as many legal and moral dilemmas as medical miracles. Think about it. Should private companies have the right to patent the data? Should employers, life insurers or mortgage lenders have access to our gene file? Can you think of other potential problems?
(woman)	How about designer children? Wealthy parents might be able to build their genetically ideal child.
(man)	Can you discriminate on the basis of genetics?
(professor)	American federal law already bars genetic discrimination. But few other countries have such laws on the books. All in all, this is a great discovery, but it also creates many troubling new issues.

40. What is this discussion about?

41. What is the conflict between the Human Genome Project (HGP) and the private biotech companies?

42. Why did the man call the genetic code a "Pandora's box"?

43. What is NOT a potential problem with this new genetic information?

Questions 44-47

Listen to part of a lecture in a nutrition class. The professor is talking about breakfast cereals.

Breakfast cereals are such an established part of the American diet, it is easy to forget how recent they are. This highly nourishing food product is made of one or more processed cereal grains and usually eaten with milk. The most common grains used are oats, wheat, corn, and rice, in that order.

For centuries, porridge made from oats or wheat was eaten in Great Britain and northern Europe. The people who settled in North America during colonial times also ate cornmeal mush or boiled rice. These simple dishes often served as the main course for lunch and dinner as well as breakfast.

The processed breakfast cereals that are enjoyed today did not have their true beginnings until the latter part of the 19th century. Around 1860, Ferdinand Schumacher of Akron, Ohio, observed that cooked oatmeal was less pasty and tasted better if the oat grains were rolled flat rather than ground into flour. Rolled oats and rolled-wheat cereals gradually gained favor with the American public.

Dr. James C. Jackson developed in 1863 what was probably the first ready-to-eat cereal. Called Granula, the new preparation was intended to be a health food. It was made from a coarse, whole-meal dough which was baked into loaves, crumbled, then baked again and ground into small bits.

Charles W. Post of Battle Creek, Michigan, was the first to realize the natural appeal of ready-to-eat cereals on the basis of their convenience and flavor, rather than as health foods. The founder of Post Cereals, he became the first great merchandiser of breakfast cereals. His first ready-to-eat product was Grape Nuts, marketed in

1898. The Battle Creek Toasted Corn Flake Company, founded by Will K. Kellogg in 1906, manufactured the first corn flakes and wheat flakes.

Battle Creek became the home of the ready-to-eat cereal industry at the turn of the 20th century. Dozens of health sanitariums sprang up, and breakfast cereal wannabes flocked to Battle Creek to try their hand in the new and lucrative business. So many people tried that historians coined the term "cereal rush," after the famous gold rush of the mid-1800s.

44. According to the speaker, what is easy to forget about breakfast cereals?

45. What did people eat before ready-to-eat breakfast cereal?

46. The professor explains the relationship between breakfast cereals and their inventors. Match the cereal with its creator.

47. What does the term "cereal rush" refer to?

Questions 48-50

Listen to part of a conversation between two speakers.

(man)	I need to talk to someone about my grade on the midterm in Dr. Morton's class.
(woman)	That's a big class with a lot of teaching assistants. Do you know who your TA is?
(man)	No, I don't. This is my first time coming here.
(woman)	Well, the TAs have divided the class alphabetically based on last name. What is your last name?
(man)	Smith.
(woman)	I graded the "S" names. I probably graded your exam. What's the problem?
(man)	My grade.
(woman)	Let's take a look at your exam .... Right, I remember this. You didn't do half the questions.
(man)	That's because I had another exam that overlapped with this one. This exam was from 10 to 12, but my biology exam was from 9 to 11. There was some kind of scheduling mix-up.
(woman)	You really should have fixed this ahead of time. I'm sure you can re-write this midterm, but first you'll have to get permission from the department chair. You can get the necessary form from the department office, then get the chair to sign off on it. Then bring it to me and we'll find a time that's good for both of us.
(man)	When should I do this?
(woman)	The sooner the better, I guess.
(man)	I'll get right on it.

48. What is the major subject of this conversation?

49. Why did the student do so badly on the midterm?

50. What will the student probably do next?

ANSWER KEY

Diagnostic Test 1

Listening

1. (C)	2. (D)	3. (B)	4. (A)	5. (D)
6. (B)	7. (D)	8. (A), (C)	9. Spinet – C	10. (C)
			Giraffe piano – A	
			Pyramid piano – B	

11. *Saturday Evening Post* – One of the first city magazines
    Harper's New Monthly Magazine – For a long time, the best-selling magazine in America
    Putnam's Monthly Magazine – Best all-round magazine in American history
12. *General Magazine*
    Saturday Evening Post
    Atlantic Monthly
    Pulp magazines

13. (B)   14. (A)   15. (D)

Structure

1. (B) have	2. (B) hardest	3. (D)	4. (A) wears	5. (B)
6. (C) lacked	7. (C)	8. (B) free	9. (A)	10. (D) but

Reading

1. (B)	2. the body	3. (B)	4. (A)	5. (C)
6. (D)	7. First square (South America. ■ A small)			8. (D)
9. (C)	10. (C)	11. (B)		

Writing

Some people believe that it harms a friendship when one borrows money from a friend. Do you agree or disagree with this opinion? Why? Use specific reasons and details to support your view.

"Neither a borrower nor a lender be," one old adage advises. It is widely quoted because it expresses an important truth. Borrowing money can do serious harm to friendships.

Borrowing from a friend is, in many cases, a form of parasitism. The friend from whom one asks to borrow money may see the borrower as an opportunist and leech whose only aim is to be supported at someone else's expense. If a loan is forthcoming, then whether or not the borrower actually gains anything is a matter of opinion. He has money in his pocket but has obtained it at a tremendous cost to his own reputation. At best, he is seen as improvident. More likely, he will be viewed as a failure who must depend on acquaintances for support, in the manner of a tick on a dog.

The respect of others has a certain value in itself, and its loss may outweigh any benefit one might obtain by borrowing from a friend. If one simply admitted poverty and helplessness in a given situation, genuine friends might be moved by sympathy to help. No shame would be involved, because help would be provided voluntarily. Constant begging for handouts, on the other hand, will reduce one in the eyes of others to the status of a child – or, more precisely, someone who is unwilling to accept the responsibilities of an adult.

A person impoverished by circumstances beyond his or her control is one thing. A reasonably able person who asks others constantly for loans, however, is something else again. If someone in that latter situation has any friends at all, they probably will tell him – with justification – to grow up and support himself.

Listening

Chapter 2 – Question Types for Short Conversations

Practice 2.1

i.   Implication: The woman got a higher grade than the man.
ii. Implication: The man cannot go to the movies.
iii. Implication: The woman had not looked outside.

TOEFL Exercise 2.1

1. (D)   2. (C)   3. (A)   4. (C)   5. (D)
6. (B)   7. (C)   8. (B)   9. (A)

Practice 2.2

i.   Meaning: Jason is not dependable.
ii. Meaning: You have an advantage.
iii. Meaning: It was not his fault that he was late.

TOEFL Exercise 2.2

1. (D)   2. (B)   3. (D)   4. (C)   5. (A)   6. (B)
7. (D)   8. (C)   9. (B)   10. (A)   11. (D)

Practice 2.3

i.   Suggestion: Take another class instead.
ii. Suggestion: Ask for more time.
iii. Suggestion: I am hungry.

TOEFL Exercise 2.3

1. (B)   2. (A)   3. (D)   4. (D)   5. (B)
6. (C)   7. (A)   8. (B)   9. (B)

Practice 2.4

i.   Inference: The play is not very good. The man is generous.
ii. Inference: The paper is very important. The woman must finish the paper.
iii. Inference: One cannot sign out books if one owes fines.

TOEFL Exercise 2.4

1. (C)   2. (A)   3. (B)   4. (B)   5. (C)
6. (C)   7. (D)   8. (C)   9. (A)   10. (B)

Practice 2.5

i.   Future Action: The woman will not go to New York.
ii. Future Action: She will give him the book.
iii. Future Action: The woman will not meet the man.

TOEFL Exercise 2.5

1. (C) 2. (D) 3. (C) 4. (B) 5. (A)
6. (B) 7. (C) 8. (D) 9. (A)

Practice 2.6

i.	Comprehension:	What is the problem here?
		How many questions must be answered?
		What did Dr. Smith do?
ii.	Comprehension:	Where is the woman going?
		Which buses go to the university?
		How often does the number 40 bus come by?
iii.	Comprehension:	What is the full price?
		What is unusual about the books?
		Are most books less or more expensive?

TOEFL Exercise 2.6

1. (D) 2. (C) 3. (B) 4. (A) 5. (B)
6. (D) 7. (B) 8. (A) 9. (D)

Practice 2.7

i.	Assumption:	The speaker thought they did not get married.
ii.	Assumption:	The speaker thought the person went to the party.
iii.	Assumption:	The speaker did not expect Brian to make the football team.

TOEFL Exercise 2.7

1. (C) 2. (B) 3. (A) 4. (D)
5. (A) 6. (B) 7. (D) 8. (C)

Mini-Test 1

1. (B)   2. (D)   3. (A)   4. (D)   5. (C)   6. (B)   7. (D)
8. Mercantilism – Gold and silver an index of national power
   Physiocracy – Against government interference
   Catholic Church – Against earning interest on loans
9. (B)   10. (D)
11. Fruit – In hilly areas, not suitable for fields
    Cattle – In large open places with poor soil
    Dairy – In colder areas, with short growing seasons
12. (C)   13. (D)   14. (D)   15. (C)

Chapter 3 – Diverters for Short Conversations

TOEFL Exercise 3.1

1. (C) 2. (B) 3. (D) 4. (A) 5. (D)
6. (A) 7. (C) 8. (C) 9. (B)

Practice 3.1

i. bill – <u>a statement of money owed</u>
   pill – <u>a small medicine with a hard covering</u>
   fill – <u>to occupy to capacity</u>
   till – <u>to cultivate the soil, farm</u>

ii. boy – <u>a young man</u>
   bay – <u>a body of water formed by an indentation in the shoreline</u>
   buy – <u>to purchase</u>
   buoy – <u>to keep afloat</u>

iii. fit – <u>in good physical condition</u>
   fat – <u>overweight</u>
   fate – <u>destiny</u>
   fete – <u>a holiday</u>
   fought – <u>to have battled (past tense)</u>
   feud – <u>hostilities between two families or clans</u>
   fight – <u>battle or combat</u>
   fad – <u>a temporary fashion</u>
   fade – <u>to lose brightness</u>

TOEFL Exercise 3.1

1. (C)   2. (B)   3. (D)   4. (A)   5. (D)
6. (A)   7. (C)   8. (C)   9. (B)

Practice 3.2

i.   Rewrite: <u>Our school's science department needs more money.</u>
ii. Rewrite: <u>You can take 5 classes, not just 4.</u>
iii. Rewrite: <u>That class requires a lot of work.</u>

TOEFL Exercise 3.2

1. (B)   2. (A)   3. (D)   4. (D)   5. (B)
6. (C)   7. (B)   8. (A)   9. (B)

Practice 3.3

i.   Conditional: <u>He did not study hard.</u>
                    <u>He did not get an A.</u>
ii. Conditional: <u>She did not bring her textbook.</u>
iii. Conditional: <u>Playing with scissors is dangerous.</u>
                    <u>The other person is playing with scissors.</u>

TOEFL Exercise 3.3

1. (C)   2. (D)   3. (B)   4. (A)   5. (B)
6. (B)   7. (A)   8. (C)   9. (C)   10. (D)

Practice 3.4

i.   Agreement: <u>Yes</u>
ii. Agreement: <u>No</u>
iii. Agreement: <u>Yes</u>

iv. Agreement: <u>Yes</u>

v. Agreement: <u>No</u>

vi. Agreement: <u>Yes</u>

TOEFL Exercise 3.4

1. (D) 2. (B) 3. (C) 4. (D) 5. (A)

6. (D) 7. (B) 8. (A) 9. (C) 10. (B)

Practice 3.5

i. Change form: <u>My book was borrowed by Doug.</u>

ii. Change form: <u>Spaghetti was eaten by me for dinner.</u>

iii. Change form: <u>David's professor gave him one last chance to improve.</u>

iv. Change form: <u>Your answer surprised me.</u>

TOEFL Exercise 3.5

1. (D) 2. (B) 3. (A) 4. (C)

5. (C) 6. (D) 7. (A) 8. (B)

Practice 3.6.1

i. Degree: <u>Jane weighs more than Susan.</u>

<u>Susan weighs almost as much as Jane.</u>

ii. Degree: <u>There are fewer French majors than English majors.</u>

<u>There are more English majors than French majors.</u>

<u>There are in excess of 50 History majors.</u>

<u>There are almost as many English majors as French majors.</u>

iii. Degree: <u>The number 50 bus runs more often than the number 8 bus.</u>

<u>The number 8 bus runs less often than the number 50 bus.</u>

Practice 3.6.2

i. Frequency: <u>I rarely exercised last month.</u>

ii. Frequency: <u>My biology lab keeps me busy all the time.</u>

iii. Frequency: <u>Everyone said they would help me, but in the end, hardly anyone did.</u>

TOEFL Exercise 3.6

1. (B) 2. (C) 3. (D) 4. (A) 5. (C)

6. (A) 7. (D) 8. (C) 9. (B)

Practice 3.7

i. Meaning: <u>I made good progress on my experiment today.</u>

ii. Meaning: <u>I will be a candidate for student council.</u>

iii. Meaning: <u>Jane is not appreciated.</u>

iv. Meaning: <u>The provost liked my essay.</u>

v. Meaning: <u>Do not let Dale's action bother you.</u>

TOEFL Exercise 3.7

1. (B) 2. (A) 3. (C) 4. (D)

5. (D) 6. (C) 7. (A) 8. (B) 9. (D)

Practice 3.8

i.	What is "them"?	Answers
	Who has "them"?	Eric's friend
ii.	What is "that"?	Doug's arrival
	Who is coming?	Doug
iii.	What is "it"?	The paper
	Who received more time?	Derek

TOEFL Exercise 3.8

1. (A)   2. (B)   3. (D)   4. (D)   5. (C)
6. (A)   7. (A)   8. (C)   9. (B)

Mini-Test 2

1. (C)   2. (A)   3. (B)   4. (D)   5. (C)   6. (B)   7. (D)
8. Radisson and Groseilliers – B
   Lewis and Clark – C
   Marquette and Joliet – A
9. Radisson and Groseilliers
   Marquette and Joliet
   Daniel Boone
   Lewis and Clark
10. (D)
11. The Lancaster Turnpike opens.
    Modern asphalt is invented.
    The first state highway commission started.
    The U.S. Interstate Highway System started.
12. Lancaster Turnpike – The first engineered and paved road
    National Turnpike – The first public paved road
    Pennsylvania Turnpike – The first freeway
13. (B)   14. (D)   15. (C)

Chapter 4 – Reviews for Part A

Type A – 11 Questions for Part A

1. (D)   2. (B)   3. (C)   4. (C)   5. (A)   6. (D)
7. (C)   8. (B)   9. (A)   10. (B)   11. (D)

Type B – 17 Questions for Part A

1. (D)   2. (B)   3. (B)   4. (C)   5. (D)   6. (A)
7. (D)   8. (A)   9. (B)   10. (C)   11. (B)   12. (D)
13. (A)   14. (B)   15. (B)   16. (A)   17. (C)

Chapter 6 – Casual Conversations and Question Types

Practice 6.1

i.   Context: <u>The woman is having trouble with biology labs.</u>
ii. Context: <u>The woman needs to take one more course to graduate.</u>
iii. Context: <u>Jon succeeds through great effort.</u>

TOEFL Exercise 6.1

Ex. 1   (C)   Ex. 2   (B)   Ex. 3   (A)   Ex. 4   (D)
Ex. 5   (B)   Ex. 6   (A)   Ex. 7   (D)   Ex. 8   (C)

Practice 6.2

i.   Details: <u>The woman saw Dave at the library.</u>
              <u>The time is apparently 3:30.</u>
              <u>Dave thought the meeting was earlier.</u>
ii. Details: <u>The honors program is difficult.</u>
              <u>Courses in literature, poetry and theater are required.</u>
              <u>A's are required in courses taken for the program.</u>
iii. Details: <u>The man did not attend class.</u>
              <u>Ten homework questions are due at the next class.</u>
              <u>There will be no class on Wednesday.</u>

TOEFL Exercise 6.2

Ex. 1   (D)   Ex. 2   (B)   Ex. 3   (C)   Ex. 4   1 (D), 2 (A)
Ex. 5   (D)   Ex. 6   1 (C), 2 (B)   Ex. 7   1 (B), 2 (C)

Practice 6.3

i.   Future Action: <u>The woman will go to the student bookstore.</u>
ii. Future Action: <u>The woman will go to the reading room.</u>
iii. Future Action: <u>The woman will visit the professor's office tomorrow.</u>

TOEFL Exercise 6.3

Ex. 1   (D)   Ex. 2   (C)   Ex. 3   (A)   Ex. 4   (A)   Ex. 5   (C)
Ex. 6   (B)   Ex. 7   (D)   Ex. 8   (B)   Ex. 9   (D)

Mini-Test 3

1. (D)   2. (C)   3. (A)   4. (B)   5. (B)   6. (D)   7. (C)
8. He worked for newspapers.
   He won a Pulitzer Prize.
   He won a Nobel Prize for literature.
   He acted and wrote for the theater.
9. *Hike and the Aeroplane* – His first novel
   Elmer Gantry – A satire on a Midwestern minister
   Arrowsmith – The story of a young doctor
10. (A), (B)   11. (C)

12. Arnold received almost all greetings.
    Bugs became alpha male.
    Chris became alpha male.
    Chris got a majority of greetings.
13. (A), (D)   14. (D)   15. (C)

Chapter 7 – Academic Discussions / Lectures and Question Types

Practice 7.1
i.   Main subject: Corn and its characteristics
     Main idea: Corn is the most important American crop.
ii. Main subject: Hibernation
     Main idea: Animals hibernate to conserve resources.

TOEFL Exercise 7.1
Ex. 1   (B)   Ex. 2   (A)   Ex. 3   (C)   Ex. 4   (A)   Ex. 5   (B)
Ex. 6   (C)   Ex. 7   (D)   Ex. 8   (C)   Ex. 9   (B)

Practice 7.2
i.   Detail: The U.S. economy grew rapidly in the 19th century.
               Most of this economic growth occurred in the northeast.
               Little manufacturing occurred in the South.
ii. Detail: Trees differ greatly in size.
               There are two main categories of trees: angiosperms and gymnosperms.
               Some trees are extremely old.

TOEFL Exercise 7.2
Ex. 1   (D)   Ex. 2   (B)   Ex. 3   (B)   Ex. 4   1 (C), 2 (D)
Ex. 5   1 (A), 2 (D)   Ex. 6   (A)   Ex. 7   (C)   Ex. 8   (B)

Practice 7.3
i.   Inference about molasses: Molasses tastes sweet.
      Inference about sugar: It was once rare and expensive. Or it does
                                                   not occur naturally in its familiar form.
ii.   Inference about the Hubble: It is a new and powerful telescope.
      Inference about anti-gravity: It was once an unpopular idea.
iii. Inference about the man: He is very busy.
      Inference about the clinical psychology class: It is very important.

TOEFL Exercise 7.3
Ex. 1   (A)   Ex. 2   (B)   Ex. 3   (D)   Ex. 4   (C)   Ex. 5   (D)
Ex. 6   (C)   Ex. 7   (A)

Practice 7.4
i.   Answer: Purple
ii. Answer: Jazz music

TOEFL Exercise 7.4

Ex. 1 (D)   Ex. 2 (A)   Ex. 3 1 (C), 2 (B)
Ex. 4 (D)   Ex. 5 (B)

Practice 7.5

i.   Answer: <u>Corn</u>
     Answer: <u>Tomato</u>

ii. Answer: <u>Footnotes were incorrect.</u>
     Answer: <u>Paper was not double-spaced.</u>

iii. Answer: <u>Ragtime</u>
     Answer: <u>Work songs</u>
     Answer: <u>Spirituals</u>

     Answer: <u>Piano</u>
     Answer: <u>Horn sections</u>

     Answer: <u>Syncopation</u>
     Answer: <u>Improvisation</u>

TOEFL Exercise 7.5

Ex. 1 (B), (D)   Ex. 2 (A), (C)   Ex. 3 (A), (D)   Ex. 4 (B), (C)   Ex. 5 (C), (D)
Ex. 6 (A), (D)   Ex. 7 (B), (C)   Ex. 8 (C), (D)   Ex. 9 (A), (B)   Ex. 10 (A), (C)

Practice 7.6

i.   <u>*Brachiosaurus*</u>
     <u>*Tyrannosaurus Rex*</u>
     <u>*Ankylosaurus*</u>
     <u>*Velociraptor*</u>

ii. <u>Pergolesi</u>
     <u>Bach</u>
     <u>Mozart</u>
     <u>Beethoven</u>

iii. <u>Hydrogen</u>
     <u>Helium</u>
     <u>Carbon</u>
     <u>Iron</u>

TOEFL Exercise 7.6

Ex. 1
Governed by Spain
Taken by the United States
Gained the nickname "Los Diablos"
Reached 50,000 in its population

Ex. 2
Looked like a cross between a rabbit and a dog
Reduced from 4 to 3 toes
Developed modern teeth, becoming a grass eater
Walked on a single hoofed toe

Ex. 3
1. Rhode Island
   Hawaii
   Texas
   Alaska

2. Alaska
   Hawaii
   Rhode Island
   Texas

3. Alaska
   Rhode Island
   Texas
   Hawaii

Ex. 4
An eruption buries Pompeii.
An eruption kills 18,000 people.
An eruption lowers the volcano several hundred feet.
An eruption raises the volcano 500 feet.

Ex. 5
Canada
United States
Central America
South America

Ex. 6
A memorial is proposed for the 100th anniversary of the Declaration of Independence.
Bartholdi comes to New York to plan a memorial.
The Statue of Liberty is dedicated.
The Statue of Liberty becomes a national monument.

Ex. 7
Tobacco
Corn
Hay
Wheat

Practice 7.7

i. Inuit: <u>Hides and bones</u>
    Pueblo: <u>Rocks</u>
    Yakima: <u>Trees (totem poles)</u>

ii. Jupiter: <u>Gas giant</u>
    Venus: <u>Dense, poisonous atmosphere</u>
    Mercury: <u>No atmosphere</u>

iii. Phase A: <u>Calm, regular brainwaves</u>
     Phase D: <u>Slow, minimal brainwaves</u>
     REM Sleep: <u>Erratic, energetic brainwaves</u>

TOEFL Exercise 7.7

Ex.1
Philadelphia – Access to the ocean
Buffalo – Connected to a river or canal
Chicago – Major railroad connection

Ex. 2
Gecko – Can climb almost any surface
Komodo dragon – Largest lizard in the world
Gila monster – Poisonous

Ex. 3
Judicial branch – One of the three branches that is not directly elected
Legislative branch – Part of government responsible for making the laws
Executive branch – Headed by the chief of state

Ex. 4
Margaret Fuller – Founded *The Dial*, the transcendentalist magazine
Henry David Thoreau – Wrote the important book *Walden*
Ralph Waldo Emerson – Founded the transcendentalist movement

Ex. 5
Thomas Edison – Light bulb
Alexander Graham Bell – Telephone
Charles Hall – Aluminum electrolysis

Ex. 6
Moraine – Broad, gently sloping mounds
Roche moutonnée – Smoothed, upward-pointing hills
Drumlin – Downward-pointing and several miles long

Ex. 7
Alcohol – Arabic
Window – Scandinavian
Hammock – Hindi

Ex. 8

Clydesdale – Good for hauling heavy loads

Thoroughbred – Descended from one of three Arabians

Pony – The smallest type of horse

Ex. 9

1.

Mount Rushmore – The greatest American presidents

The Gateway Arch – The American west

The Statue of Liberty – Freedom

2.

Mount Rushmore – South Dakota

The Gateway Arch – Missouri

The Statue of Liberty – New York

3.

Gutzon Borglum – Mount Rushmore

Eero Saarinen – The Gateway Arch

Frédérick Auguste Bartholdi – The Statue of Liberty

TOEFL Exercise 7.8

Ex. 1   (C)   Ex. 2   (C)

Ex. 3   Subservient face – C

       Calling face – A

       Display face – B

Ex. 4   (A)   Ex. 5   (B)

Ex. 6   Cirrus – C

       Cumulus – B

       Cumulonimbus – A

Ex. 7   (C)   Ex. 8   (D)

Mini-Test 4

  1. (C)   2. (B)   3. (A)   4. (B)   5. (D)

  6. (C)   7. (B)   8. (C)

  9. Elixir of Life – A medicine that could heal all sickness

     Philosopher's Stone – The substance that turns lesser minerals into gold

     Alkahest – A universal solvent that could dissolve anything

10. Paracelsus overturns Aristotle's ideas.

     Sendivogius realizes air is a chemical mixture.

     Isaac Newton conducts alchemy experiments.

     Lavoisier discovers oxygen.

11. (D)

12. Mature Stage – A decline in birth rate

     High Potential Stage – Birth rate at biological maximum

     Transition Stage – A decline in death rate

13. (B), (C)   14. (D)   15. (C)

Chapter 8 – Reviews for Part B

Type A – 19 Questions for Part B

1. (C)   2. (A)   3. (D)
4. Egret – C
   Great white heron – B
   Green heron – A
5. (D)
6. Swordfish – Marlin
   Hammerhead – Shark
   Sawfish – Ray
7. (B), (C)   8. (B)   9. (C)   10. (D)
11. Moved to Indiana
    Received first government contract
    Became the biggest horse-drawn vehicle maker in the world
    Made self-propelled vehicles
12. (A)   13. (A)   14. (C)   15. (A)   16. (B), (D)   17. (D)   18. (B)   19. (C)

Type B – 33 Questions for Part B

1. (C)   2. (D)
3. Log Cabin – Frontier
   Clapboard – New England
   Georgian – East coast
4. (A)   5. (C)   6. (A)
7. Yosemite – Giant trees
   Grand Canyon – Colorado River
   Yellowstone – First national park
8. (D)   9. (B)   10. (D)   11. (D)   12. (B)
13. (A), (B)   14. (D)   15. (A)   16. (C)   17. (C)
18. Abacus
    Algorithms
    Slide rule
    Analytical engine
19. (D)   20. (C)   21. (B)   22. (A)   23. (A)   24. (B), (D)
25. Nouns
    Verbs
    Adverbs
    Pronouns
26. (A)   27. (B)
28. Protostar
    Red supergiant
    Supernova
    Neutron star
29. (C)   30. (A)   31. (D)   32. (B)   33. (D)

Structure

Chapter 1 – Elements of Clauses

Supplementary Exercise

Exercise 1.1

1. <u>To eat too much</u> is not good for your health.
2. During the conference <u>the board of directors</u> considered its decision.
3. Nowadays <u>recycling products such as bottles, plastics, and paper</u> is encouraged.
4. Deep in our minds lie <u>half-forgotten memories</u>.
5. <u>What he had written</u> surprised me.

Exercise 1.2

1. The requirements for the course <u>have changed</u> since last year.
2. Obsolete equipment <u>caused</u> trouble for researchers.
3. The dancers <u>leap</u> into the air, <u>spin</u> rapidly, and <u>race</u> around the stage.
4. A little more evidence <u>might have proven</u> his thesis to be correct.
5. Pets <u>must be fed and groomed</u> by their owners.

Exercise 1.3

1. Bob appeared <u>ill</u> when he was in class today.
2. What we need to know is <u>whether the program will run or not</u>.
3. He appears <u>to have been healthy</u> before he had that accident.
4. "Yesterday" is <u>one of my most famous songs</u>.
5. My only goal is <u>to provide for my family</u>.

Exercise 1.4

1. I wonder <u>if we can visit there this summer</u>.
              O
2. The author's book has <u>both strengths and weaknesses</u>.
              O
3. I really must speak with you when you have <u>an opportunity</u>.
              O
4. We do consider <u>it</u> <u>right</u>.
        O OC
5. Do not leave <u>children</u> <u>unattended</u>.
        O   OC
6. The committee awarded <u>the author</u> <u>a Pulitzer Prize</u>.
           O   O
7. The doctor urged <u>me</u> <u>to avoid alcohol and exercise regularly</u>.
         O   OC
8. The trainer made <u>her dog</u> <u>jump through a hoop</u>.
         O   OC
9. She disregarded <u>what he said</u>.
         O
10. I prefer <u>being outdoors on a beautiful day like this</u>.
          O

Exercise 1.5

1. The road **is** so long that you can't see the end of it.
2. Put the ice cream in the freezer so that **it** won't melt.
3. I think **it** very dangerous to play that sport.
4. Gold looks like pyrite, which **is** a compound of iron.
5. A hundred years ago, travel was much slower than **it** is today.

Pattern Drill for Patterns 1-6

1. (B) See Pattern 4.
2. (C) See Pattern 2.
3. (D) See Pattern 5.
4. (A) See Pattern 3.
5. (D) See Pattern 4.
6. (A) See Pattern 1.
7. (A) See Pattern 5.
8. (B) See Pattern 4.
9. (B) See Pattern 3.
10. (C) See Pattern 2.
11. (C) enable it to, See Pattern 6.
12. (D) See Pattern 5.
13. (C) See Pattern 3.
14. (D) See Pattern 2.
15. (D) See Pattern 3.
16. (C) See Pattern 5.
17. (B) See Pattern 3.
18. (A) See Pattern 2.
19. (B) See Pattern 5.
20. (D) See Pattern 1.

Mini-Test 1

1. (C) analyze, See Pattern 26.
2. (D) who, See Pattern 9.
3. (C) than, See Pattern 33.
4. (B) See Pattern 38.
5. (D) reliability, See Pattern 49.
6. (D) See Pattern 3.
7. (A) Since the late, See Pattern 28.
8. (A) See Pattern 13.
9. (C) drop, See Pattern 42.
10. (B) See Pattern 7.

Chapter 2 – Subordinate Clauses

Supplementary Exercise

Exercise 2.1

1. <u>Although his arm was broken</u>, he made his way home.
2. <u>After the author finished the last chapter</u>, the book was ready for publication.
3. I was surprised <u>when I saw her in a restaurant</u>.
4. He did not stop working <u>until the sun went down</u>.
5. <u>If the problem is not corrected</u>, it will only get worse.
6. Alan thought about the project <u>while he had lunch</u>.
7. I studied English <u>before I studied abroad</u>.
8. <u>Whenever I hear a song</u>, I think of that singer.
9. The ship changed its course <u>because it had to help another ship in trouble nearby</u>.
10. You've lost a lot of weight <u>since we last met</u>, and I didn't recognize you at first.

Exercise 2.2

1. <u>Although Bill was very tired</u>, he finished his work.
2. <u>When I work</u>, I forget about time.
3. <u>While he was a postman</u>, he wrote many poems.
4. Elisabeth worked on the project <u>until she finished it</u>.
5. <u>Before he left for work</u>, he ate breakfast.

Exercise 2.3

1. where	2. which/that	3. which/that	4. which	5. whom
6. whose	7. which/that	8. who/that	9. who	10. whose

Exercise 2.4

1. ➜ William is the man <u>named</u> to replace our former chairman.
2. ➜ The blue car <u>parked</u> outside is Andrew's.
3. ➜ The girl <u>absent</u> today is Lisa.
4. ➜ Martin, <u>fluent</u> in three languages, works as a foreign correspondent.
5. ➜ We bought a house <u>costing</u> 100,000 dollars.

Exercise 2.5

1. The date on <u>which</u> the U.S. Declaration of Independence allegedly was signed was July 4, 1776.
2. An executive <u>who</u> cannot delegate authority will overwork himself.
3. The whale's brain, <u>which</u> is larger than a human's, also must control a vastly greater body than a human's.
4. The Cascade Mountains, <u>which</u> are popular with tourists, include several famous and beautiful volcanoes.
5. The woman <u>whose</u> computer broke down by accident came near crying.
6. The town had a house <u>which</u> was three centuries old.
7. Difficulties <u>which</u> do not kill us usually make us stronger.
8. The American hot dog <u>has</u> been popular for approximately a century.
9. My professor, <u>whose</u> books are known for beautiful illustrations, has never written a bestseller.
10. I have three brothers, all of <u>whom</u> are very tall.

Pattern Drill for Patterns 7-11

1. (B) See Pattern 8.	2. (A) which/that, See Pattern 9.
3. (A) See Pattern 7.	4. (B) See Pattern 8.
5. (C) what, See Pattern 9.	6. (D) See Pattern 7
7. (C) See Pattern 8.	8. (B) researcher who first, See Pattern 10.
9. (B) See Pattern 7.	10. (B) See Pattern 8.
11. (C) which, See Pattern 9.	12. (B) See Pattern 7.
13. (C) who, See Pattern 9.	14. (C) See Pattern 8.
15. (A) is, See Pattern 10.	16. (D) See Pattern 7.
17. (C) which/that, See Pattern 9.	18. (D) See Pattern 8.
19. (C) which, See Pattern 9.	20. (B) See Pattern 7.
21. (B) whom, See Pattern 9.	22. (C) See Pattern 7.
23. (B) whose, See Pattern 9.	24. (C) which/that, See Pattern 9.
25. (B) See Pattern 7.	26. (C) which, See Pattern 11.
27. (B) See Pattern 8.	28. (C) See Pattern 7.
29. (B) which, See Pattern 9.	30. (A) See Pattern 8.

Mini-Test 2

1. (B) considerable, See Pattern 48.	2. (A) knowing, See Pattern 17.
3. (A) suggests, See Pattern 43.	4. (B) See Pattern 45.

5. (D) other, See Pattern 54.   6. (D) See Pattern 8.

7. (B) is a, See Pattern 6.   8. (C) See Pattern 38.

9. (A) it, See Pattern 21.   10. (B) See Pattern 41.

Chapter 3 – Verbals

Supplementary Exercise

Exercise 3.1

1. wearing   2. composed   3. exhausted   4. Enraged   5. closed

Exercise 3.2

1. receiving   2. to repeat   3. to apply   4. making   5. going

Exercise 3.3

1. bored   2. entering   3. made   4. lost   5. overlooking

Exercise 3.4

1. An <u>encouraging</u> letter from a friend gave her new hope.
2. Who is responsible for <u>washing</u> the dishes after the party?
3. The man <u>asked/who was asked</u> to serve as president accepted.
4. After <u>putting</u> away their tools, the workers went home.
5. The rain looked like a curtain <u>moving</u> across the field.

Pattern Drill for Patterns 12-17

1. (A) See Pattern 12.
2. (C) produced/which are produced, See Pattern 17.
3. (D) featuring/which featured, See Pattern 15.
4. (C) organize, See Pattern 14.
5. (A) falling/which falls, See Pattern 17.
6. (C) See Pattern 13.
7. (C) involved, See Pattern 17.
8. (C) See Pattern 12.
9. (A) founded/which was founded, See Pattern 17.
10. (C) drifting, See Pattern 17.
11. (C) mixing, See Pattern 17.
12. (A) to wear, See Pattern 17.
13. (D) See Pattern 12.
14. (A) to reconstruct, See Pattern 14.
15. (D) supporting, See Pattern 17.
16. (B) See Pattern 13.
17. (D) drying, See Pattern 17.
18. (D) living, See Pattern 15.
19. (B) held, See Pattern 17.
20. (C) See Pattern 12.
21. (A) Restored, See Pattern 17.
22. (D) See Pattern 12.
23. (C) known/which is known, See Pattern 17.

24. (B) See Pattern 12.
25. (B) containing, See Pattern 15.
26. (C) to be, See Pattern 16.
27. (B) going, See Pattern 17.
28. (C) See Pattern 12.
29. (B) to estimate, See Pattern 14.
30. (D) being, See Pattern 14.

Mini-Test 3

1. (D) interested, See Pattern 15.
2. (A) accuracy, See Pattern 52.
3. (A) anger, See Pattern 42.
4. (B) See Pattern 3.
5. (D) an, See Pattern 27.
6. (D) See Pattern 8.
7. (D) substances, See Pattern 22.
8. (B) See Pattern 2.
9. (A) are, See Pattern 43.
10. (B) See Pattern 18.

Chapter 4 – Prepositional Phrases

Supplementary Exercise

Exercise 4.1

1. from, to
2. on
3. for
4. for
5. of
6. in
7. with
8. in
9. with
10. between

Exercise 4.2

1. We did not attend the debate <u>between</u> Miller and Brown.
2. A typical house cat may weigh <u>from</u> 3 to 6 kilograms.
3. There was no one from our company <u>among</u> the many people at the trade fair.
4. Humorist Will Rogers was known <u>for</u> his comic tales about life in the American West.
5. Modern civilization relies heavily <u>on</u> petroleum for energy.
6. (correct)
7. (correct)
8. He weighs <u>about</u> 70 kilograms.
9. (correct)
10. The original story, <u>on</u> which the film is based, has a happy ending.

Exercise 4.3

1. An award was presented <u>to the player</u> who scored the most points.
2. A skilled artist can produce many different <u>kinds of effects</u> with a brush.
3. The rate <u>at which</u> a chemical reaction proceeds depends partly on temperature.
4. We are <u>planning of a</u> visit to France next month.
5. Four rocky planets, Mercury, Venus, Earth and Mars, orbit relatively <u>close to</u> the sun.
6. There were fewer than <u>50 of tigers</u> in the whole country.
7. She has many faults, but we're all very fond <u>of her</u>.
8. His hard work accounts <u>for his</u> success.
9. We are dependent <u>on the</u> sun for energy.
10. The town <u>in which</u> the college is located is very pretty.

Pattern Drill for Patterns 18-21

1. (A) About, See Pattern 19.
2. (B) in which, See Pattern 20.
3. (C) See Pattern 18.
4. (B) the, See Pattern 21.
5. (D) amounts of different, See Pattern 20.
6. (A) From, See Pattern 19.
7. (A) lived in America, See Pattern 20.
8. (B) See Pattern 18.
9. (A) from, See Pattern 19.
10. (C) by, See Pattern 19.
11. (D) See Pattern 18.
12. (D) few minutes, See Pattern 21.
13. (C) of, See Pattern 19.
14. (A) for, See Pattern 19.
15. (D) on which, See Pattern 19.
16. (A) applied to any, See Pattern 20.
17. (A) See Pattern 18.
18. (C) between, See Pattern 19.
19. (B) on, See Pattern 19.
20. (B) unaware of the, See Pattern 20.

Mini-Test 4

1. (A) was, See Pattern 36.
2. (C) orderly, See Pattern 42.
3. (A) is, See Pattern 43.
4. (D) See Pattern 32.
5. (C) fourths, See Pattern 22.
6. (B) See Pattern 7.
7. (B) who, See Pattern 9.
8. (A) See Pattern 12.
9. (C) which, See Pattern 26.
10. (B) See Pattern 18.

Chapter 5 – Noun Phrases

Supplementary Exercise

Exercise 5.1

1. nations	2. brothers	3. minutes	4. exhibitions	5. problems
6. minerals	7. breeds	8. item	9. each family, children	10. pill

Exercise 5.2

1. his	2. (correct)	3. her	4. mine	5. his
6. their	7. they	8. those	9. (correct)	10. (correct)

Exercise 5.3

1. Crowded on the window ledge, the birds <u>they</u> cheeped for food.
2. Any famous person who expects <u>it</u> privacy will probably be disappointed.
3. Bill and Sue <u>they</u> have both applied to the same university.
4. This plan <u>it</u> is sure to succeed.
5. Mr. Anderson, the housing director, <u>he</u> said there was one room left vacant.
6. The paper you wrote <u>it</u> is too short.
7. The woman who <u>she</u> wrote the novel is giving a talk tonight.
8. Sinclair Lewis, who wrote the novel *Main Street*, <u>he</u> also wrote *Babbitt*.
9. The most important thing right now <u>it</u> is to get well.
10. He talks too much, which <u>it</u> annoys me.

Exercise 5.4

1. <u>The</u> state of Virginia, in the United States, is called the "Old Dominion."
2. <u>A</u> university education is one of the necessities for the position these days.
3. The Wright Brothers made their famous flight in <u>the</u> early twentieth century.
4. <u>An</u> hour passed before we received his reply.

5. <u>The</u> tallest building in Manhattan is the Empire State Building.

6. Newfoundland is <u>a</u> large island in eastern Canada.

7. He spent many years in <u>an</u> unpleasant job.

8. <u>An</u> egg is said to provide a complete diet.

9. <u>The</u> first lesson is about author Harold Wright.

10. Be sure to wear <u>an</u> overcoat.

Exercise 5.5

1. The secretary finished her ~~the~~ work for the day.

2. His most famous book <u>was the first</u> that he wrote.

3. Tokyo has one <u>of the highest</u> population densities in the world.

4. It <u>is a reward</u> for your effort.

5. I put ~~a~~ new cartridges in the printers.

6. A juggler must keep several objects in the air <u>at a time</u>.

7. Don Quixote <u>is a character</u> in a novel by Cervantes.

8. He arrived at the theater <u>in the middle</u> of the performance.

9. Few <u>of the people</u> who can draw actually do so.

10. The borough of Manhattan, in New York City, is built <u>on a large</u> island.

Pattern Drill for Patterns 22-30

1. (C) games, See Pattern 22.
2. (C) his, See Pattern 24.
3. (B) over the surface, See Pattern 28.
4. (C) an, See Pattern 27.
5. (B) ventures, See Pattern 22.
6. (D) their, See Pattern 24.
7. (D) those, See Pattern 25.
8. (B) countries, See Pattern 22.
9. (D) its, See Pattern 24.
10. (C) the second, See Pattern 27.
11. (B) farm, See Pattern 29.
12. (C) an, See Pattern 27.
13. (D) in the rest, See Pattern 28.
14. (D) their, See Pattern 24.
15. (D) See Pattern 30.
16. (D) in the midst, See Pattern 28.
17. (A) A balloon, See Pattern 28.
18. (C) stripes, See Pattern 22.
19. (A) the familiar, See Pattern 28.
20. (A) a, See Pattern 27.
21. (D) one, See Pattern 22.
22. (D) their, See Pattern 24.
23. (D) theirs, See Pattern 24.
24. (D) those, See Pattern 25.
25. (C) they, See Pattern 24.
26. (C) her, See Pattern 24.
27. (B) naturalist, See Pattern 29.
28. (D) characters, See Pattern 22.
29. (C) to use, See Pattern 26.
30. (B) temperature, See Pattern 29.
31. (B) pictures, See Pattern 22.
32. (D) arms, See Pattern 22.
33. (D) nation, See Pattern 22.
34. (C) books, See Pattern 22.
35. (D) furniture, See Pattern 23.
36. (B) smokestack, See Pattern 29.
37. (C) reflects, See Pattern 26.
38. (A) types, See Pattern 22.
39. (D) feet, See Pattern 22.
40. (A) See Pattern 30.
41. (B) has a movable, See Pattern 28.
42. (B) in the 16th, See Pattern 28.
43. (C) which, See Pattern 26.
44. (B) writers, See Pattern 22.
45. (D) changes, See Pattern 22.
46. (C) artists, See Pattern 22.
47. (D) See Pattern 30.
48. (A) his, See Pattern 24.
49. (B) its, See Pattern 24.
50. (C) have, See Pattern 26.

Mini-Test 5

1. (B) when, See Pattern 39.
2. (A) their, See Pattern 44.
3. (D) extends, See Pattern 52.
4. (C) See Pattern 12.
5. (C) some, See Pattern 40.
6. (B) See Pattern 1.
7. (B) began, See Pattern 36.
8. (C) See Pattern 4.
9. (D) public interest, See Pattern 46.
10. (D) See Pattern 32.

Chapter 6 – Adjective Phrases and Comparisons

Supplementary Exercise

Exercise 6.1

1. worse	2. as well	3. more	4. tallest	5. more powerful
6. smarter	7. more easily	8. as few	9. as rainy	10. farther

Exercise 6.2

1. The shorter the book, the quicker it is to read.
2. Toni runs faster than any other girl on the team.
3. This new computer is less expensive than the previous model.
4. Their new apartment is larger than any other apartment in the building.
5. New Jersey is the most densely populated state in the United States.
6. The weather today is better than yesterday.
7. This diamond is probably the most famous in the world.
8. This summer will certainly be much hotter than last summer.
9. The longer we stayed, the better the concert became.
10. Heather's grades are no higher this year than they were last year.

Pattern Drill for Patterns 31-34

1. (C) See Pattern 32.
2. (D) larger, See Pattern 34.
3. (B) See Pattern 32.
4. (B) more, See Pattern 33.
5. (B) See Pattern 32.
6. (C) warmer, See Pattern 33.
7. (D) See Pattern 32.
8. (C) less, See Pattern 33.
9. (D) See Pattern 32.
10. (C) See Pattern 32.
11. (A) See Pattern 32.
12. (B) See Pattern 32.
13. (C) See Pattern 31.
14. (C) See Pattern 32.
15. (D) as, See Pattern 33.
16. (C) more, See Pattern 33.
17. (B) See Pattern 32.
18. (A) See Pattern 32.
19. (B) youngest, See Pattern 34.
20. (C) larger, See Pattern 33.

Mini-Test 6

1. (C) in highly, See Pattern 20.
2. (C) animals, See Pattern 22.
3. (D) consistently, See Pattern 48.
4. (B) See Pattern 1.
5. (B) left/that were left, See Pattern 17.
6. (B) See Pattern 4.
7. (C) which, See Pattern 9.
8. (C) See Pattern 5.
9. (A) pitcher, See Pattern 51.
10. (D) See Pattern 7.

Chapter 7 – Verb Phrases

Supplementary Exercise

Exercise 7.1

1. (correct)	2. granted	3. will reach	4. (correct)	5. (correct)
6. met	7. look	8. misunderstood	9. require	10. listening

Exercise 7.2

1. have owned	2. called	3. managed	4. had	5. visited

Exercise 7.3

1. went	2. (correct)	3. puzzled	4. worked	5. (correct)

Exercise 7.4

1. (correct)	2. be printed	3. delivered	4. (correct)	5. to be caught
6. were sent	7. allowed	8. is extracted	9. (correct)	10. carry

Pattern Drill for Patterns 35-37

1. (A) been reported, See Pattern 37.   2. (A) used, See Pattern 35.
3. (B) cut, See Pattern 37.   4. (C) grown, See Pattern 35.
5. (C) drew, See Pattern 36.   6. (C) made, See Pattern 37.
7. (B) broke out, See Pattern 35.   8. (C) faced, See Pattern 35.
9. (B) changes, See Pattern 37.   10. (B) entrusted, See Pattern 35.
11. (A) emerged, See Pattern 36.   12. (C) pass, See Pattern 35.
13. (D) arrived, See Pattern 35.   14. (D) were, See Pattern 36.
15. (C) make, See Pattern 35.   16. (C) discovered, See Pattern 36.
17. (B) appeared, See Pattern 35.   18. (B) divided, See Pattern 35.
19. (C) have been, See Pattern 36.   20. (D) was, See Pattern 36.

Mini-Test 7

1. (A) maintenance, See Pattern 50.   2. (A) been, See Pattern 35.
3. (B) to organize, See Pattern 16.   4. (A) See Pattern 8.
5. (D) home runs, See Pattern 22.   6. (B) See Pattern 12.
7. (A) scatter, See Pattern 43.   8. (B) See Pattern 3.
9. (A) great, See Pattern 29.   10. (C) See Pattern 30.

Chapter 8 – Conjunctions and Parallelism

Supplementary Exercise

Exercise 8.1

1. but/and	2. not only	3. Neither	4. both	5. and

Exercise 8.2

1. and	2. but also	3. or	4. but	5. that

Exercise 8.3

1. He sent her a book in the mail, <u>but it</u> never arrived.
2. Whoever can solve this <u>problem ~~and~~ will</u> get an award.
3. Although the job paid well, ~~but~~ it was also difficult.
4. (correct)
5. To forecast economic trends, ~~and~~ <u>economists</u> use sophisticated computer models.

Exercise 8.4

1. to borrow/borrow   2. attending   3. trembled   4. planting   5. looked

Exercise 8.5

1. careful → carefully
2. fencing → fence
3. dead → death
4. efficient → efficiently
5. to spread → spread
6. patience → patient
7. boredom → boring
8. equipment → equipped
9. beneficial → benefit
10. watch → watching

Pattern Drill for Patterns 38-42

1. (C) and, See Pattern 39.
2. (C) information, See Pattern 42.
3. (B) biology, See Pattern 42.
4. (D) ability, See Pattern 42.
5. (B) Mary M. Bethune, See Pattern 40.
6. (D) adjust, See Pattern 42.
7. (C) See Pattern 38.
8. (D) perfected, See Pattern 42.
9. (C) See Pattern 41.
10. (B) hilly, See Pattern 42.
11. (C) moisture, See Pattern 42.
12. (B) but also, See Pattern 39.
13. (B) See Pattern 38.
14. (D) check, See Pattern 42.
15. (B) emotions, See Pattern 42.
16. (C) either, See Pattern 39.
17. (C) easy, See Pattern 42.
18. (D) grace, See Pattern 42.
19. (A) See Pattern 38.
20. (B) imprisonment, See Pattern 42.

Mini-Test 8

1. (C) was the first, See Pattern 28.
2. (A) transmitted, See Pattern 35.
3. (C) to determine, See Pattern 42.
4. (C) See Pattern 45.
5. (D) virtually, See Pattern 48.
6. (D) See Pattern 30.
7. (A) their, See Pattern 24.
8. (A) See Pattern 2.
9. (D) with, See Pattern 19.
10. (A) See Pattern 5.

Chapter 9 – Dangling Modifiers

Supplementary Exercise

Exercise 9

1. (correct)
2. → Ignoring all objections, the committee made its decision.
3. (correct)
4. → Landing on the moon was the goal of a manned mission launched from Earth in 1969.
5. (correct)
6. → The composition was difficult for the violinist struggling with an unfamiliar instrument.

7. (correct)
8. → The young man's behavior became very strange, because he was deeply in love with a young woman.
9. → Long and narrow, the nation of Chile is often rocked by earthquakes.
10. (correct)

Pattern Drill for Patterns 3 and 1

1. (B) See Pattern 3.
2. (C) See Pattern 3.
3. (B) See Pattern 3.
4. (D) See Pattern 3.
5. (C) See Pattern 3.
6. (A) See Pattern 3.
7. (B) See Pattern 1.
8. (C) See Pattern 3.
9. (B) See Pattern 3.
10. (C) See Pattern 3.

Mini-Test 9

1. (C) to, See Pattern 19.
2. (B) eggs, See Pattern 44.
3. (B) dominant, See Pattern 49.
4. (A) See Pattern 3.
5. (D) a critically, See Pattern 28.
6. (C) See Pattern 32.
7. (D) reaction, See Pattern 22.
8. (D) See Pattern 1.
9. (B) prevent, See Pattern 42.
10. (D) See Pattern 45.

Chapter 10 – Agreement and Word Order

Supplementary Exercise

Exercise 10.1

1. A biologist <u>gets</u> information about the migration of birds by tracking them on radar.
2. The house which <u>faces</u> the sea has a beautiful view.
3. Qualifications for this job <u>become</u> more restrictive every year.
4. There <u>were</u> too many wild animals for the forest to support.
5. The origin of words <u>is</u> often fascinating.
6. Each of the stories <u>requires</u> 20 minutes to read.
7. The console for the CD player and CDs <u>is</u> made of hickory wood.
8. A laser beam, which engineers use for precise work, <u>guides</u> the digging of tunnels.
9. None of our software can help people who <u>lack</u> computer skills.
10. Very broad, colorful ties <u>were</u> popular in the United States 30 years ago.

Exercise 10.2

1. Apartment owners in this neighborhood seldom charge <u>high rents</u>.
2. (correct)
3. It is not <u>warm enough</u> for trees to bloom.
4. Not until next week <u>will the new rules</u> go into effect.
5. Pain can make an illness seem <u>worse than</u> it really is.
6. Microchips are a <u>very recent</u> development.
7. Rarely <u>does Bill drink</u> alcohol.
8. The town <u>in which</u> we live is very small.
9. (correct)
10. Not until you've taken Biology 101 <u>should you</u> try to take higher courses.

Pattern Drill for Patterns 43-47

1. (C) See Pattern 47.
2. (B) were, See Pattern 43.
3. (B) became popular, See Pattern 46.
4. (D) short time, See Pattern 46.
5. (C) excess amount, See Pattern 46.
6. (A) tries to, See Pattern 43.
7. (A) them, See Pattern 44.
8. (A) Long before, See Pattern 46.
9. (B) are, See Pattern 43.
10. (D) See Pattern 47.
11. (D) has been, See Pattern 43.
12. (C) See Pattern 45.
13. (A) native to, See Pattern 46.
14. (C) reflects, See Pattern 43.
15. (B) in which, See Pattern 46.
16. (D) See Pattern 45.
17. (A) early growth, See Pattern 46.
18. (B) such a, See Pattern 46.
19. (B) excessively small, See Pattern 46.
20. (D) they, See Pattern 44.

Mini-Test 10

1. (C) elected, See Pattern 52.
2. (D) the early, See Pattern 27.
3. (A) worst, See Pattern 34.
4. (B) See Pattern 8.
5. (C) their, See Pattern 24.
6. (D) See Pattern 3.
7. (A) produced, See Pattern 10.
8. (B) See Pattern 38.
9. (C) many, See Pattern 54.
10. (B) See Pattern 18.

Chapter 11 – Word Form

Supplementary Exercise

Exercise 11.1

1. adorns/adorned
2. quickly
3. danger
4. candidate
5. represent
6. unexpectedly
7. tasty
8. guard, hazardous
9. vital, involves
10. usually

Exercise 11.2

1. heavily
2. differ, scholars
3. loss
4. literature, philosopher
5. satisfaction
6. appointment, intensely
7. years, labor
8. bland
9. completed/completes
10. different

Exercise 11.3

1. replace
2. selection
3. previous
4. vulnerable
5. constructed
6. sufficient
7. divided
8. tremendous
9. establishing
10. person

Exercise 11.4

1. Puppies and kittens <u>please</u> people.
2. <u>Regular</u>, well-balanced meals and a low-fat diet help to keep one <u>healthy</u>.
3. Johann Sebastian Bach is the most <u>famous</u> of all European <u>musicians</u>.
4. We have a <u>solemn</u> obligation to preserve resources for future generations.
5. Countries ruled tightly by authoritarian governments are sometimes called <u>dictatorships</u>.
6. Downloading is the transfer of a <u>file</u> from the Internet to an individual computer.
7. The American War Between the States represented a <u>bold</u> attempt at Southern independence.
8. One founder of modern <u>physics</u> was the German scientist Ernst Mach.

9. Computers did much to relieve the <u>difficulty</u> of calculation.

10. We could not understand the <u>instruction</u> for the camera.

Pattern Drill for Patterns 48-52

1. (B) requirement, See Pattern 50.
2. (B) annual, See Pattern 48.
3. (B) vary, See Pattern 52.
4. (A) inhabitants, See Pattern 51.
5. (B) fully, See Pattern 48.
6. (C) expense, See Pattern 49.
7. (B) conquest, See Pattern 50.
8. (C) natural, See Pattern 48.
9. (D) permanently, See Pattern 48.
10. (C) abundant, See Pattern 49.
11. (C) distribution, See Pattern 50.
12. (C) portraying, See Pattern 52.
13. (A) notoriety, See Pattern 49.
14. (B) philosophy, See Pattern 51.
15. (D) proper, See Pattern 48.
16. (A) fame, See Pattern 49.
17. (C) settled, See Pattern 52.
18. (D) successful, See Pattern 48.
19. (C) year, See Pattern 49.
20. (C) depends on, See Pattern 52.

Mini-Test 11

1. (B) most, See Pattern 54.
2. (A) by which, See Pattern 46.
3. (A) acquired, See Pattern 35.
4. (B) See Pattern 13.
5. (D) to, See Pattern 19.
6. (B) See Pattern 8.
7. (B) individuals, See Pattern 44.
8. (C) See Pattern 45.
9. (D) ecology, See Pattern 51.
10. (B) See Pattern 57.

Chapter 12 – Word Choice

Supplementary Exercise

Exercise 12.1

1. Bill was <u>too</u> small to play football, so he played baseball instead.
2. The tool had <u>so</u> many applications that it became very popular.
3. Ecosystems involve <u>such</u> different animals as bears, sharks, and bees.
4. Earth's gravitation is <u>so</u> strong that only fast-moving objects can escape it.
5. This food is <u>so</u> fattening that I have to avoid it.

Exercise 12.2

1. (correct)	2. like	3. (correct)	4. a little	5. (correct)
6. other	7. nearly	8. much	9. no	10. Most

Exercise 12.3

1. despite/in spite of
2. during
3. while
4. Because of/Due to/Owing to
5. (correct)

Pattern Drill for Patterns 53-56

1. (B) so, See Pattern 53.
2. (C) all, See Pattern 54.
3. (C) other, See Pattern 54.
4. (A) few, See Pattern 54.
5. (B) another, See Pattern 54.
6. (C) many, See Pattern 54.
7. (A) Despite, See Pattern 56.
8. (C) so, See Pattern 53.
9. (B) little, See Pattern 54.
10. (C) like, See Pattern 54.
11. (D) when, See Pattern 56.
12. (A) No, See Pattern 54.

13. (D) other, See Pattern 54.   14. (A) like, See Pattern 54.
15. (C) many, See Pattern 54.   16. (C) nearly, See Pattern 54.
17. (A) None, See Pattern 54.   18. (A) During, See Pattern 56.
19. (B) so, See Pattern 53.   20. (A) many, See Pattern 54.

Mini-Test 12

1. (A) almost invisible, See Pattern 46.   2. (D) degree of social, See Pattern 20.
3. (C) his pupil, See Pattern 44.   4. (C) See Pattern 18.
5. (A) During, See Pattern 56.   6. (C) See Pattern 5.
7. (B) to identify, See Pattern 14.   8. (A) See Pattern 3.
9. (C) tendency, See Pattern 50.   10. (C) See Pattern 2.

Chapter 13 – Miscellaneous

Supplementary Exercise

Exercise 13

1. No 2. None 3. no 4. not 5. no, not

Mini-Test 13

1. (C) land-dwelling, See Pattern 15.   2. (B) historians, See Pattern 22.
3. (C) became, See Pattern 36.   4. (C) See Pattern 4.
5. (A) so, See Pattern 53.   6. (D) See Pattern 8.
7. (B) spreads, See Pattern 43.   8. (D) See Pattern 47.
9. (C) quick, See Pattern 48.   10. (C) See Pattern 7.

Reading

Chapter 1 – Main Idea

Skill Building

Skill Building: Selecting a topic sentence
1. Animals learn not only by trial and error, but also by conditioning, which involves a system of rewards or punishments.
2. All the hot deserts are found about the same distance north or south of the equator.
3. His great popularity helped get him elected president in 1828, and President Jackson brought his frontier ways to Washington, D.C.
4. The Progressives of the early decades of the 20th century wanted to clean up and reform government and to use government to advance human welfare.
5. No enforcement provisions were included, however, and without federal enforcement provisions, the Act was a failure.

Intensive Exercises

Exercise 1.1	1. (B)	**Exercise 1.2**	1. (B)
Exercise 1.3	1. (D)	**Exercise 1.4**	1. (C)
Exercise 1.5	1. (C)	**Exercise 1.6**	1. (D)
Exercise 1.7	1. (A)	**Exercise 1.8**	1. (B)

Vocabulary Review for Intensive Exercises 1.1-1.8
1. (A) 2. (C) 3. (C) 4. (A) 5. (D) 6. (B)
7. (C) 8. (A) 9. (A) 10. (B) 11. (D) 12. (C)

Practice Test 1

Questions 1-11

1. (D); Read the first sentence of each paragraph. The first sentence of the 2nd paragraph mentions specifically the word "acceptance," which appears in the answer Choice (D).
2. native painters; Check all of the plural nouns within the identical sentence or in the preceding sentence. Replace "their" with "native painters" in the possessive case and verify the meaning to see whether the restated sentence makes sense.
3. (C); Scan the passage to locate "John Sloan," "Max Ernst," "African art," and "modern European art." You will find "John Sloan," "Max Ernst," and "modern European art" in paragraph 1 or 2. African objects influenced Cubist art circles.
4. (A); Refer to sentence 2 in paragraph 1. European Surrealists saw native North American art as the source of their vision.
5. (B); Refer to sentence 2 in paragraph 2, and sentences 2 and 3 in paragraph 3.
6. (C); Scan the passage looking for "San Francisco" or the specific year. It is in sentence 3 in paragraph 3.
7. (B); Refer to the expression "representative of the 'primeval' world" in sentence 2 of paragraph 1 where European artists are mentioned.

8. (D); "To foster" means "to encourage to develop." Among the four choices, "stimulate" is closest in meaning to "foster." Pay attention to the similar structures of the phrases such as "foster interest" and "stimulating the public's interest."

9. (A); Scan the passage for sentence 3 in paragraph 1, "These artists ~ aesthetic principles."

10. revival; "Revival" is most similar in meaning to "renaissance."

11. Third square (anthropological specimens. ■ Other milestones); The number "1931" in the excerpted sentence indicates a place to add the sentence. It should be placed between "1925" and "1939."

Questions 12-22

12. (B); Always read the first sentence in each paragraph. The first sentence in paragraph 4 makes it clear that this passage is about technological advances. Choices (A) and (C) are too broad. Choice (D) is too specific.

13. (D); The verb "note" means "to take notice of." Choice (D) is most similar in meaning to "noted." No other choices are accepted meanings of "noted."

14. busy; You will find a clue in the parallel structures such as "occupy themselves with" and "busy themselves with."

15. (C); Refer to sentence 2 in paragraph 2. The sentence "His research ~ later on." is the clue.

16. Joseph Henry; Look for a singular masculine noun in the surrounding sentences. Always verify the meaning of the sentence with the replaced word.

17. (A); Look at sentence 4 in paragraph 3 and sentence 2 in paragraph 4. To answer factual questions, scan the passage looking for the identical meaning given in the question.

18. First square (people live. ■ To cite); The excerpted sentence reads more like a topic sentence than a supporting sentence. Thus, we may assume that the insertion spot is close to the beginning of paragraph 3. The word "it" in the excerpted sentence refers to the "importance of science and technology" in the preceding sentence.

19. (B); Look at sentence 2 in paragraph 4. The author mentions that working-class residences had fewer "creature comforts." It implies that one has to have means to afford innovative appliances.

20. the affluent; "Working-class" and the subject of the following sentence "the affluent" are used to show the contrast between "haves" and "have-nots."

21. (D); In the context of the passage, "creature comforts" means "improved living conditions."

22. (C); Look at sentence 3 in paragraph 4, which states that "Even the lower classes were able to afford new coal-burning cast-iron cooking stoves that facilitated the preparation of more varied meals and improved heating."

Questions 23-33

23. (C); In this passage, we need to read more than one or two sentences from the beginning of paragraph 1 before figuring out the main topic of the passage. The first sentence in paragraph 2 indicates what the main topic of the passage is going to be. Choice (A), (B), or (D) is too partial.

24. people; Only two plural nouns appear in the preceding part of the sentence. "They" in "they have manipulated ~ " must be the subject of an action. Therefore, "they" refers to "people."

25. (A); See sentence 2 in paragraph 1.

26. (D); See sentence 4 in paragraph 1. Scan the passage for the key words "oral art."

27. (B); Pay attention to the structure of the sentence "Often, the verbal expressions of disparate cultures exhibit remarkable similarities." Here "disparate" and "similarities" are opposite in meanings. Therefore, Choice (B) is the best answer.

28. Eighth square (European peasants. ■ The audience); The expression "The formal study of folklore grew out of ~ European peasants" connects the preceding sentence with the excerpted sentence, which has the expression "Later, when ~ as well."

29. (C); See sentence 3 in paragraph 2. Scan the passage for "trickster."

30. unrelated; "The audience ~ never met" provides a clue about the meaning of "unrelated." It is opposite in meaning to "linked," which means "related."

31. The formal study ~ of European peasants. Scan the passage for "folklore." The last sentence of paragraph 2 mentions the origin of the study of folklore.

32. (D); Choices (A), (B) and (C) share the identical meaning, which is "subject to change." Choice (D) should be "unpredictable" instead of "predictable" to be a correct description of an oral narrative.

33. (B); The last three sentences in paragraph 3 suggest that Choice (B) is the best answer.

Questions 34-44

34. (C); The passage is mainly concerned with seabirds, although the first paragraph mostly deals with birds in general. The first sentences in paragraphs 2 and 3 mention seabirds and their characteristics. Choices (B) and (D) are partial, although they are about seabirds.

35. (A); Refer to the last sentence in paragraph 1. Because birds' eggs are more resistant to water loss, they have a better chance of survival than those of reptiles.

36. birds; "Their feathers" is a clue to find the referent of "their."

37. (C); See sentence 3 in the second paragraph. "Descend from" means "be developed from."

38. (D); The sentence means that seabirds are about 3% of the total species of birds. "Constituting" is most similar in meaning to "comprising."

39. Third square (on plankton. ■ They need); The phrase "feed on" is the reference word connecting the two sentences.

40. awkward; In the context of the passage, "clumsy" is similar in meaning to "awkward." This sentence gives a structural clue by coordinating words with similar meanings to emphasize what the author intends.

41. hooked; "Hooked" is most similar in meaning to "curved." No other words in the bold text have similar meanings to "curved."

42. (A); In the third paragraph, the beaks of the seabirds are classified according to their shapes and main functions. The author explains their shapes in relation to their functions. The form of beak is adapted to catch and hold prey of each seabird's choice easily. Thus, the discussion is an example of the dictum "form follows function."

43. Most are predators ~ feed on plankton; Scan the passage looking for the phrase "feed on." See the sixth sentence in paragraph 2.

44. (B); In the context of this passage, "interfere with" means "hinder." As a whole, Choice (B) is the only restatement that correctly paraphrases the given sentence.

Questions 45-55

45. (B); "The author" in sentence 1 in paragraph 1 gives a clue as to the subject of the passage. Only Choice (B) contains the word, "literature," that relates to "the author."

46. Paine; "He" refers to the subject of the preceding clause. Check the meaning of the whole sentence to verify whether you have chosen the correct referent.

47. (B); Refer to sentence 3 in paragraph 2. The term is defined by its appositive.

48. (C); Refer to the last sentence in paragraph 1.

49. remarkable; Pay attention to adjectives in the bold text. "Remarkable" is closest in meaning to "outstanding."

50. (D); See sentences 4 to 6 in paragraph 2. Paine opposed the status quo in eighteenth-century America.

51. Sixth square (in income. ■ Franklin was); Words such as "organize" and "excisemen" are devices to find the spot to add the excerpted sentence.

52. (C); See sentence 1 in paragraph 3. "Anonymous" is restated as "unknown" in the answer choice.

53. boosted; Pay attention to similar patterns such as "boosted the spirits" and "raised the morale."

54. (B); See sentence 1 in paragraph 3, especially the expression "the first pamphlet published in America."

55. In Philadelphia, ~ from Britain; Scan the passage looking for the word "abolitionist."

Chapter 2 – Reference and Vocabulary

Skill Building

Skill Building 1: Reference
1. (A) 2. (C) 3. (A) 4. (C) 5. (B)
6. (C) 7. (B) 8. (A) 9. (B) 10. (A)

Skill Building 2: Vocabulary
1. (A) 2. (B) 3. (C) 4. (B)
5. (A) 6. (C) 7. (C) 8. (A)

Intensive Exercises

Exercise 2.1
1. reproduce 2. (D) 3. (A)

Exercise 2.2
1. (C) 2. hospitals and clinics
3. The survival rate of infants in the region is high – 990 out of 1,000 live births.

Exercise 2.3
1. evidence 2. (D) 3. figurines 4. (C)

Exercise 2.4
1. responsible 2. accompanying 3. (C)
4. Crop and livestock losses 5. (C)

Exercise 2.5
1. Accidents 2. damaging 3. (D) 4. oil

Vocabulary Review for Intensive Exercises 2.1-2.5
1. (B) 2. (C) 3. (A) 4. (C) 5. (D)
6. (A) 7. (C) 8. (B) 9. (B) 10. (A)

Practice Test 2

Questions 1-11

1. (D); In this type of passage, you have to skim the entire passage to get an idea what the passage is about. However, the first sentence of each paragraph is organized in the order of events. You can guess that the passage discusses the cycle. Choice (A), (B) or (C) is too narrow and paragraph-specific.

2. eusocial honey bees; "The latter" refers to the second one of the two stated one after another.

3. (B); Scan the passage for the key words "subsocial bees." Look at the last sentence of paragraph 1.

4. (A); The first sentence in paragraph 1 mentions that the latter (eusocial honey bees) survive the winter, meaning "permanent."

5. (C); In the context of the sentence "The new colony ~ founded by the old queen ~ the workers with her", the word most similar in meaning is "established."

6. (B); Scan the passage for the expression "As the old queen ~ leave ~." Look at the last three sentences in paragraph 2. The most crucial thing in fact questions is to locate the relevant information.

7. Third square (to emerge. ■ As these); "Sound signals" is the phrase connecting the excerpted sentence with the following sentence where the word "signal" is described in detail.

8. (D); Throughout the entire passage, the author indicates that queen bees are not supposed to work.

9. (A); In the context of "The young queen ~ entices ~ neighboring colonies", "entice" is most similar in meaning to "attract." Other choices are not accepted meanings of "entice."

10. (D); In the passage, "responsibility" is stated as "contribution." Look at sentence 2 in the last paragraph. Choice (D) is inferred from the phrase "their participation in the nuptial flight."

11. (C); Refer to sentence 3 in the last paragraph, which is "Since they are unable to feed ~ an increasing liability to the social group."

Questions 12-22

12. (C); The passage mentions the origin of the food-producing way of life in the first sentence of paragraph 1. The first sentence of paragraph 2 discusses the effects of domestication. Altogether, the passage discusses the development of farming and its effects. Choice (A) or (B) is too broad. Choice (D) is partial.

13. the food-producing way of life; Pay attention to the phrase "its subsequent spread." We can guess that the food-producing way of life had been spreading.

14. (D); Refer to the first sentence in paragraph 1. The author cannot provide one direct cause triggering the food-producing lifestyle.

15. (A); The author explains the cause of spread of the food-producing way of life in paragraph 1.

16. (B); The stem of the word "prolonged" contains "long." We can guess that the meaning is related to something made longer. Choice (B) is most similar in meaning to "prolonged." "Extended" is more closely related to "a period of time." On the other hand, "increased" is more likely to be about "quantity."

17. (A); Refer to sentence 6 in paragraph 1. Choice (A) contradicts the fact in the passage.

18. (B); In the context of the passage, "assets" are described as something that helps out with many household chores.

19. (D); Refer to sentences 3, 4, and 5 in paragraph 2. As a result of increased productivity, farmers have a tendency to rely on a narrow range of resources. It often leads to a shortage of food in

case of crop failure.

20. Third square (food forager. ■ The dependence); The excerpted sentence is an example of the range of crop varieties in modern agriculture compared with those utilized by food-foragers. The excerpted sentence should be added at the spot following the sentence comparing modern agriculture and food-foraging.

21. In humans, prolonged ~ effect on ovulation; Scan the passage looking for the phrase "prolonged nursing." See sentence 5 in paragraph 1.

22. (B); Look at the last sentence in paragraph 2. The fact that the Irish emigrated to the U.S. because of a potato famine suggests that the Irish depended on potatoes as their main staple.

Questions 23-33

23. (A); The first sentence of paragraph 1 mentions the warming effect. The first sentence of paragraph 3 states that the planet may be warming up. Choice (C) or (D) is too broad. Choice (B) is too narrow.

24. (B); Choice (B) is a restatement of sentence 1 in paragraph 1.

25. (D); Scan the passage for key words in each answer choice. Refer to sentences 3 and 4 in paragraph 1 to verify choice (D).

26. (C); The expression " ~ traps ~ like glass" gives a clue as to the meaning of "traps." "Catches" is most similar in meaning to "traps."

27. carbon dioxide; The parallel structures are "remove carbon dioxide" and "return it." "It" refers to "carbon dioxide."

28. (C); Scan the passage for key words in answer choices. Look at sentences 3, 4, 5 and 6 in paragraph 2.

29. These fuels, oil and coal, ~ of ancient forests; Scan the passage for "fossil fuels." Examples are listed by means of commas.

30. (A); "Running power plants" is closest in meaning to "operating power plants." Other choices are not accepted meanings of "running."

31. (C); The direct cause of global warming is mentioned in sentence 3 of paragraph 1.

32. Second square (highly debatable. ■ Warming will); "But" is the transitional device that connects the excerpted sentence with the previous sentence. The question "how warm it will get" is answered in the excerpted sentence.

33. (B); The last paragraph is the relevant part of the passage to pick up the incorrect inference among the answer choices. Choice (B) is a far-fetched conclusion, unjustifiable by the statements in paragraph 3.

Questions 34-44

34. (C); Choice (A) or (D) is too broad. Choice (B) is irrelevant. Only Choice (C) covers the whole passage, because the last paragraph mentions the economic impact as well.

35. (B); Refer to sentences 2 and 3 in paragraph 1.

36. (B); Look at sentences 3, 4, and 5 in paragraph 1, especially sentence 5.

37. Fifth square (airmail contract. ■ A psychological); The specific year is the clue. The year 1925 precedes the year 1926 mentioned in the excerpted sentence.

38. (B); In the context of the last two sentences in paragraph 1, "subsidize" is most similar in meaning to "support."

39. Charles A. Lindbergh, Jr.; Pay attention to the structure of the phrase "the deed, which won him a prize." The person who won the prize is Charles A. Lindbergh, Jr.

40. (C); Scan the passage for the solo flight of Charles A. Lindbergh, Jr. Look at the first sentence in paragraph 2. The solo flight was from New York to Paris.

41. (B); In the context of the phrase "the deed, which won him a prize," we can guess it is an achievement.

42. (D); Look at the last two sentences in paragraph 3. Scan the passage for "democratize the automobile."

43. The first motor car ~ revolutionized the industry; Scan the passage for "the first car" and the year. See sentence 2 in paragraph 3.

44. (A); For the economic impact of the mass production of automobiles, refer to the last paragraph. Choice (A) is not mentioned in the last paragraph.

Chapter 3 – Fact, Negative, Scanning, and Restatement Questions

Skill Building

Skill Building: Restatement
1. (A) 2. (B) 3. (A) 4. (B) 5. (A)
6. (A) 7. (B) 8. (C) 9. (B) 10. (A)

Intensive Exercises

Exercise 3.1
1. (D) 2. (B)

Exercise 3.2
1. (C)

2. Once lured inside the mouth of the trap, insects lose their footing on the slippery surface, fall into the liquid, and either decompose or are digested.

Exercise 3.3
1. (C) 2. (D) 3. (A)

Exercise 3.4
1. (B) 2. (D) 3. (C)

Exercise 3.5
1. (D) 2. (C) 3. (B)

Vocabulary Review for Intensive Exercises 3.1-3.5
1. (A) 2. (D) 3. (B) 4. (A) 5. (D)
6. (B) 7. (A) 8. (B) 9. (C) 10. (A)

Practice Test 3

Questions 1-11

1. (C); Paragraph 1 summarizes the role of radio and movies. Choice (A) is too broad. Choice (B) or (D) is too narrow.

2. radio; In the context of "owned it," "radio" is the most proper candidate for the referent of "it." Verify the meaning of the sentence with "radio" in place of "it" to see whether the replaced sentence has the same meaning as before.

3. (C); Scan the passage looking for "soap opera." See sentence 4 in paragraph 2 for "derived their name from their sponsors, soap manufacturers."

4. season; Compare the parallel structures "season with organ ~" and "flavor with a rich announcer ~."

5. (D); Refer to the last sentence in paragraph 2.

6. (C); Scan the passage looking for the titles of radio programs. Look at the sentences in paragraph 3.

7. sought-after; Check all the adjectives in the surrounding sentences. "Sought-after" is closest in meaning to "popular."

8. Seventh square (musical programs. ■ Franklin Roosevelt); Additional programs are listed in the excerpted sentence. Therefore, the best spot for the excerpted sentence is after the sentence listing several radio programs.

9. (C); Scan the passage to find where the needed information is located. The key word is "talkies."

10. 4th paragraph; Scan the passage for "1920s," "popular," and "1930s."

11. (C); The last paragraph discusses the topics of the films of the 1930s. The last sentence directly mentions the topics.

Questions 12-22

12. (C); In the context of this passage, the best title should mention either "red tides" or "algal blooms," which cause the phenomenon of "red tides." The first sentences of paragraphs 1 and 2 discuss "red tides." Choice (A) or (D) is too broad. Choice (B) is irrelevant.

13. (D); "Literally" is used to emphasize a statement. No other choices are accepted meanings of "literally."

14. (A); Scan the passage looking for "reference" or "earliest." You can find them in sentence 3 of paragraph 1.

15. (C) and (D); For factual questions, scan the passage to locate relevant information using key words from the question. Look at sentences 7 and 10 in paragraph 1.

16. phytoplankton blooms; In the context of "they discolor the water only slightly," "they" should be something that was supposed to change the color of water. The word "they" refers to the object of the preceding sentence.

17. (B); It is specifically mentioned that red tides are not always red in sentence 9 of the first paragraph. It implies that the term "red tide" has been customarily used to describe a certain phenomenon.

18. (C); Scan the passage looking for "nuisance." The reason why it is more than a nuisance is stated in sentence 9 of paragraph 2.

19. Third square (vacation short. ■ Some blooms); The excerpted sentence and the preceding sentence are connected by the words "you" and "your" or "vacation" and "motel owner ~ business ~."

20. fatal; In the context of surrounding sentences, you can guess the meaning of the word "deadly." The sentence "the most severe cases are fatal" contains the word most similar in meaning to "deadly."

21. (B); Scan the passage for a list of marine organisms. The answer to the question can be found in "Mussels, clams, ~ tolerate the toxins by storing them away ~" in the second paragraph.

22. (D); The last sentence of paragraph 2 states that some of the toxins produced by the algal blooms are even carcinogenic. Choice (A) is not specific enough to explain the reason why the toxins are fatal.

Questions 23-33

23. (B); The passage is about the history of dry painting, including its origin, purpose and recent studies about it. Only Choice (B) is related to all three paragraphs of the passage. Choices (A), (C), and (D) are too specific.

24. (C); The very first sentence of the passage usually contains a clue about what was discussed in the preceding sentence or paragraph. Both "painting" and "mosaic" are mentioned in sentence 1 of paragraph 1.

25. (A); Scan the passage looking for a list of materials used for dry painting. See sentence 2 in paragraph 1.

26. (C); Look at sentence 2 of paragraph 2. It mentions Navajo dry painting that deals with traditional designs.

27. (B); The fact that white observers copied the original dry paintings suggests that there was contact between whites and Indians.

28. (D); It is stated in paragraph 3 that none of the sources available for inspection is original. Therefore, studies of dry painting do not conduct research into the original art form.

29. fixed; In the context of the passage, "fixed" is most similar in meaning to "permanent." No other adjectives in the bold text are close to the meaning of "permanent."

30. (D); Scan the passage looking for "impermanent." Look at the last sentence of paragraph 1 to find the reason why dry painting is described as impermanent.

31. display; Compare " ~ exhibit color changes ~" in the main clause with "while copies ~ display many conventionalizations ~" in the adverb clause. Parallel structures often provide clues as to synonyms.

32. (B); Check all of the plural nouns in the surrounding sentences. "They" refers to something made by Navajo men and women. Thus, Choice (A) or (C) cannot be a correct choice. Choice (D) is not specific enough to replace "they."

33. (A); In the middle of the last paragraph, it is stated that copies by Navajos often exhibit color changes. It implies that reproducing the exact color of natural materials is difficult.

Questions 34-44

34. (C); The passage discusses deductive reasoning and induction. Those are two ways of doing science. Choice (A) or (D) is too broad. Choice (B) is too partial.

35. (C); Look at the last sentence in paragraph 1. "Indispensable" means "necessary." Choices (A), (B), and (D) all have negative meanings in common.

36. (A); In paragraph 2, the author gives several examples of inductive reasoning resulting in false conclusions.

37. (B); "Hopefully" is most similar in meaning to "ideally," which means "most desirably, but not realistically." No other words are accepted meanings of "ideally."

38. biologist; In the context of "he might ~," "he" refers to a noun which is used for males in the preceding sentence. In surrounding sentences, "he" refers to "a particular marine biologist."

39. (D); The author's attitude towards "induction" can be seen from the word "ideally." The use of "ideally" implies that the author considers induction as a limited way of reasoning because expecting complete accuracy is not realistic.

40. Third square (of induction. ■ The step); The connecting word is "inductions" in the excerpted sentence and the preceding sentence.

41. (D); Look at sentences 1 and 2 of paragraph 3, where it is stated that "In deductive reasoning, scientists ~ is true. They arrive ~ hunch or intuition." For Choices (A), (B), or (C), refer to paragraph 2.

42. (B); In the context of the passage, "isolated" is closest in meaning to "separated."
43. (C); Induction requires that a statement be generalized from several isolated observations.
44. In deductive reasoning, scientists ~ statement is true; Scan the passage for "deductive reasoning." The answer is the first sentence of the last paragraph.

Questions 45-55

45. (C); Paragraph 1 discusses the nature of rituals. Paragraph 2 is about the non-religious rituals.
46. (A); "Approach" is closest in meaning to "relate to" in the context of the whole sentence.
47. (C); See sentences 2 and 3 in paragraph 1.
48. (B); Refer to paragraph 2, which discusses the "initiation" as an example of the rites of passage.
49. (D); "Disastrous" is closest in meaning to "disruptive."
50. initiates; In the context of "they are dead," "they" refers to "initiates" in the surrounding sentence.
51. (A); See sentence 4 in paragraph 1 and sentences 1 and 2 in paragraph 2. Choice (A) is not suggested in the passage.
52. Second square (and incorporation. ■ Van Gennep); "Separation," "transition," and "incorporation" in the preceding sentence are restated as "~ removed," "isolated," and "incorporated" in the excerpted sentence.
53. (C); Refer to sentences 4 and 5 in paragraph 2.
54. When the time for the initiation ~ as though they are dead; See sentences 3 and 4 in paragraph 2. Scan the passage for the name of a primitive tribe.
55. (D); See paragraph 3. Choice (D) mentions "transition," which is the subject of the rite of passage.

Chapter 4 – Insertion

Skill Building

Skill Building: Rearranging sentences

1. (4)-(1)-(3)-(2) 2. (3)-(2)-(4)-(1) 3. (2)-(1)-(3)-(4) 4. (3)-(1)-(2)-(4)
5. (3)-(1)-(4)-(2) 6. (3)-(2)-(4)-(1) 7. (1)-(3)-(4)-(2) 8. (2)-(1)-(3)-(4)

Intensive Exercises

Exercise 4.1
1. Second square (energy level. ■ The chemical)

Exercise 4.2
1. Fifth square (a mold. ■ The study)

Exercise 4.3
1. Fourth square (especially large. ■ The sheer)

Exercise 4.4
1. Second square (the 1960s. ■ At the)

Exercise 4.5
1. Second square (attached inhabitants. ■ Rocky shore)

Exercise 4.6
1. Fourth square (the energy. ■ The wave)

Exercise 4.7
1. Third square (brain case. ■ Mammals must)
2. Ninth square (more agility. ■)

Exercise 4.8
1. Sixth square (their culture. ■ To become)

Vocabulary Review for Intensive Exercises 4.1-4.8
1. (D) 2. (B) 3. (A) 4. (D) 5. (D) 6. (C)
7. (B) 8. (B) 9. (A) 10. (D) 11. (B) 12. (D)

Practice Test 4

Questions 1-11

1. (B); Choices (A), (C) and (D) are not suitable as topics of the passage as a whole. They are either paragraph-specific or related to several sentences. The first sentence of each paragraph and the last sentence of the last paragraph give clues to the main topic of the entire passage, which is the life and career of Frank Lloyd Wright.
2. motto; In the context of the passage, "dictum" means "motto." The phrase "That motto" refers to the preceding dictum "Form follows function."
3. (D); Refer to the sentence in paragraph 1 that "That motto is the basis of functionalism."
4. (B); "Helical ramp" is the key word of the question. You can find the same key words in the latter half of paragraph 1, which describes the Guggenheim Museum in detail.
5. (B); Look for "Sullivan" and "conflict" in paragraph 2.
6. (D); The answer Choice (D) is not mentioned in the passage.
7. Sixth square (Bear Run, Pennsylvania. ■ Wright designed); Two sentences are related by the reference to "Falling Water."
8. (D); Look at the whole sentence. Because the word "it" refers to something that survived the earthquake in Tokyo, it points to the Imperial Hotel.
9. (A); Choices (B) and (D) contradict the facts given in the passage. Choice (C) is not mentioned in the passage. Look at sentence 7 in paragraph 2.
10. (B); The passage is about an architect. Therefore, it most likely comes from a biographical directory of architects.
11. The name Taliesin is Welsh and means "shining brow."; Scan for the key word "Taliesin."

Questions 12-22

12. (A); The main topic is located at the introductory part of the passage. Refer to the first sentences of each paragraph that mention "benthic environment."
13. compiled; The word "accumulated" is similar in meaning to "compiled" in the bold text.
14. (A); Refer to sentence 3 in paragraph 1.
15. (A); Choice (A) contradicts the fact in sentence 2 of paragraph 2. The Hatteras Abyssal Plain lies off the eastern coast of the United States.
16. benthic; The word "benthic" is most similar in meaning to "abyssal." No other words in the bold text are close in meaning to the word "abyssal."
17. (D); Refer to the list of rivers mentioned in sentence 3 of paragraph 2.

18. First square (abyssal plains. ■ The deep); The excerpted sentence qualifies as the topic sentence. The best place for the excerpted sentence is at the beginning of paragraph 3.
19. (B); Refer to sentence 4 in paragraph 3.
20. (A); The word "intact" is similar in meaning to "untouched."
21. (A); The word "it" refers to the subject of the sentence.
22. Because the benthic environment is the site ~ profoundly interested in it: Scan the passage for words "archeologists" and "historians." See the first sentence of the last paragraph.

Questions 23-33

23. (C); Choices (A) and (B) are too narrow. Choice (D) is irrelevant. Sentence 1 in paragraph 2 supports Choice (C).
24. (B); Refer to sentence 2 in paragraph 1.
25. soil; This sentence defines "soil." The word "it" points to the subject of the preceding sentence.
26. (D); Organic matter, microorganisms, and clays are mentioned in paragraph 4.
27. (C); "Supporting (maintaining) life" is mentioned in sentences 2 and 3 in paragraph 2.
28. (B); In the context of this passage, the word "dictate" is most similar in meaning to "determine."
29. (D); Sentence 3 in paragraph 2 supports Choice (D). "Agricultural purposes" means "farming."
30. (B); Choices (A), (C) and (D) are all mentioned in paragraph 3.
31. (A); "Decaying" is most similar in meaning to "decomposing."
32. (B); Scan the characteristics of topsoil that is named as the A horizon. Choice (B) is about the O horizon. Classifications of layers are mentioned in the last paragraph.
33. Third square (of time. ■ The uppermost); Two sentences are related by the reference to "mature soil." "Layers" in the excerpted sentence is related to "the uppermost layer" in the following sentence.

Questions 34-44

34. (C); Choices (A) and (D) are related to paragraph 1. Choice (B) is related to paragraphs 2 and 3. The last sentence in paragraph 1 mentions that Americans' attitude towards romanticism originated in Europe.
35. (B); "Accentuate" means "to emphasize a particular feature of something." No other choices are close to the meaning of the word "accentuate."
36. stasis; In the context of this passage, the word "stirring" means "a feeling or a mood that begins to be felt." "Stasis" means here "the state of equilibrium." No other words in the bold text are opposite to the meaning of the word "stirring."
37. First square (material gain. ■ By the); The clue can be found in the phrase "another great victory of heart over head." One victory of heart over head should be found in the preceding sentence. It is "the stirrings of the spirit over the dry logic of reason and the allure of material gain." Therefore, the best place to add the excerpted sentence is the first black square (■).
38. (D); "Brewing" means "likely to happen soon." Choice (D) is most similar to "brewing" in the context of this passage.
39. (A); Refer to sentence 2 in paragraph 1 and the last sentence in paragraph 2. The Enlightened thinkers wish a well-ordered world.
40. (C); In the context of this passage, "head" represents "reason and logic," against which the movement of romanticism has been triggered. Choice (C) is the only choice not related to romanticism.
41. Where the Enlightened thinkers of the eighteenth century had scorned the Middle Ages, the romantics ~ to the period with fascination; Sentence 1 in paragraph 2 is the best answer.

42. (C); Sentences 1 and 2 in paragraph 2 give clues to the answer. The Enlightened thinkers scorned the Middle Ages. Therefore, we can conclude that they did not think highly of the Gothic style. On the other hand, America copied the Gothic style in architecture.

43. (C); "Innate" is similar in meaning to "inborn." Other choices are not the accepted meanings of the word "innate."

44. In those areas in which science could neither ~ justified in having faith; "Such ideas" refers to the preceding sentence as a whole. It is in your best interest to verify the flow of ideas by replacing "such ideas" with the preceding sentence.

Chapter 5 – Inference

Skill Building

Skill Building: Drawing inferences
1. (A) 2. (C) 3. (B) 4. (B) 5. (C)
6. (B) 7. (C) 8. (A) 9. (C)

Intensive Exercises

Exercise 5.1	1. (A) 2. (D)	**Exercise 5.2**	1. (A) 2. (C)
Exercise 5.3	1. (C) 2. (A)	**Exercise 5.4**	1. (B) 2. (B)
Exercise 5.5	1. (C) 2. (D)		

Vocabulary Review for Intensive Exercises 5.1-5.5
1. (B) 2. (D) 3. (A) 4. (C) 5. (B)
6. (D) 7. (C) 8. (D) 9. (A) 10. (C)

Practice Test 5

Questions 1-11

1. (A); Choices (B) and (C) are too narrow. Choice (D) is too general. The best answer is Choice (A).

2. stirring; "Exciting" means "stirring" here. No other words in the bold text are close to the meaning of the word "exciting."

3. (C); Choices (B) and (D) are irrelevant to the passage. Choice (A) is an unverifiable statement. Choice (C) can be inferred based on sentence 1 in paragraph 1.

4. (D); Refer to sentence 1 in paragraph 1.

5. Second square (a clergyman. ■ Thus he); Two sentences are related by the reference to "Emerson began ~. He came ~." Emerson started as a clergyman but changed his career to essayist and lecturer.

6. (C); "Lay" is similar in meaning to "untrained." Other choices are not accepted meanings of the word "lay."

7. (D); Choice (D) contradicts the facts in the passage. Refer to sentences 1 and 2 in paragraph 3. Thoreau was influenced by Emerson's teaching.

8. (A); "Sojourn" is similar in meaning to "stay." Other choices are not accepted meanings of the word "sojourn."

9. (B); In the context of this passage, "appeal" means "attraction." Other choices are not accepted meanings of the word "appeal." The first sentence of the last paragraph can be rephrased as "The modern readers are strongly attracted to the simplicity of Thoreau's life."

10. Mahatma Gandhi; Pay attention to the phrase following "his." The phrase "fight to free India from British rule" shows that "his" is the possessive pronoun of Mahatma Gandhi.

11. (C); Choice (B) is not mentioned in the passage. Choices (A) and (D) contradict the facts of the passage. Look at sentence 5 in paragraph 3 and sentence 2 in paragraph 4.

Questions 12-22

12. (C); Read the first sentence of each paragraph. Choices (A), (B), and (D) are too narrow.

13. (C); Choice (C) contradicts the fact that sharks should not be provoked in any way. See the sentence 6 in paragraph 4.

14. (C); The word "killed" in the second paragraph indirectly gives the clue to the meaning of the word "mortally."

15. (B); "White shark attacks ~ cases of mistaken identity" is paraphrased as "perhaps, ~ by accident."

16. people; Look for plural nouns in the identical or adjacent sentences. Always verify the meaning of the sentence with the replacing word.

17. Fifth square (by lightning. ■ A U.S.); The relationship of the excerpted sentence to the previous sentence is that of contrast. You may recognize this by the signal word "however" and the contrasting relationship between the preceding paragraph and the excerpted sentence. Also, the excerpted sentence qualifies as the topic sentence for the second paragraph that lists the examples of shark attacks.

18. (D); "Erratically" means "suddenly" or "unpredictably."

19. exterminated; Pay attention to the parallel structures such as "depleted by" and "exterminated by."

20. (C); Scan the passage for "small sharks" and "blue fish" in order to find the information to draw a valid inference. Refer to "When large sharks were netted off South Africa, for example, the number of species of small sharks, which are eaten by large sharks, increased. As an apparent result, the number of bluefish, a commercially important species, decreased" in the last paragraph.

21. (D); Scan the last paragraph for " Actually, we threaten the survival of sharks ~ the bloodiest predators of them all." Choice (D) contradicts the facts given in the last paragraph.

22. (D); Choice (D) can be inferred from the first sentence of each paragraph.

Questions 23-33

23. (C); Choices (A) and (D) are too narrow. Choice (B) is too broad. The right answer should mention not only jazz music but also its impact. Choice (C) involves the impact of jazz music, which is the cultural change inspired by jazz music.

24. (B); Choices (C) and (D) are mentioned in sentence 3 of paragraph 1 and sentence 1 of paragraph 2. Refer to paragraphs 3 and 5 for Choice (A). Choice (B) is unrelated to the passage.

25. (A); "Spawn" means "lay eggs." In the context of this passage, "create" is most similar in meaning to "spawn."

26. Fifth square (the "petting party." ■ From such); "The petting party" is the connecting word indicating the proper spot to add the excerpted sentence. The excerpted sentence describes what "the petting party" mentioned in the preceding sentence may involve.

27. (C); Choices (A), (B) and (D) contradict the facts given in the passage. In Choice (B), not the jazz age, but Dr. Freud is responsible for the moral degeneration of the 1920s in America. In Choice (D), it is wrong to see a cause and effect relationship between new dance forms and rebellion among young people.

28. (B); "Defy" means "refuse to obey." In the context of this passage, Choice (A) is not a good substitute for "defied" when connected to the following phrase about " ~ expectations for womanly behavior." Choice (B) is the best substitute for "defied."

29. females; "They" refers to the subject of the preceding sentence.

30. (D); Paragraphs 3 and 5 mention the changed lifestyle of the "new woman." Look at the sentences "These independent females ~ skirts above the ankle" and "Fashion also reflected the rebellion against ~."

31. The new jazz ~ and polyrhythms; Scan the entire passage to find the sentence where the names of cities are mentioned.

32. (C); The clue to the best answer lies in sentence 3 of paragraph 4. The attitude of Dr. Freud toward Americans can be found in the phrase "even in prudish America" in sentence 3 of paragraph 4.

33. (A); Choices (B), (C) and (D) contradict the facts of the passage. See sentence 2 in paragraph 3.

Questions 34-44

34. (D); If you see several dates or years scattered through the entire passage, the passage may discuss the historical development of the main topic. This passage is about the history of the Mormons and their religious belief. Choices (A), (B) and (C) are irrelevant to the passage as a whole.

35. Israelites; "Their destruction" means that Israelites were destroyed. Therefore, "their" points to "Israelites."

36. (C); Choices (A) and (B) are irrelevant to the passage. Choice (D) is too broad. In view of sentence 1 in paragraph 1, Choice (C) is the most likely preceding topic.

37. (B); Choices (A), (C) and (D) are not based on the facts in the passage. Using information in paragraph 1, one can choose answer Choice (B).

38. (C); Refer to sentence 2 in paragraph 2 as the basis for selecting Choice (C), especially the phrase " ~ a product of their sense of being a chosen people, ~."

39. (D); "Militant" means "determined or willing to use force." The passage does not mention any militant tendency of the Mormons.

40. (D); In the context of this passage, "circulated" is the best substitute for "spread" because of the subject of the sentence, "rumors."

41. (B); Choices (A), (C) and (D) are not based on the facts in the passage. Choice (B) is based on sentence 5 in paragraph 2.

42. (C); "Asset" is most similar in meaning to "something having value, such as a property or possession." Therefore, "wealth" is the best substitute for "asset."

43. Sixth square (Great Salt Lake. ■ At last); The excerpted sentence is about the Mormons marching westward to Salt Lake City. The sentence after the excerpted sentence has the connecting phrase in "At last, they established ~."

44. (C); The state of Vermont was the home of Joseph Smith, the founder of the Mormons. It is not the place where the Mormons settled. Refer to paragraph 2 for the states where the Mormons settled.

Questions 45-55

45. (C); Refer to sentence 3 in paragraph 1.

46. (A); See paragraph 1. Choice (A) contradicts the fact stated in sentence 4 of paragraph 1. Bees might have needed more time than wasps to evolve into social insects because they underwent change on eight different occasions, while wasps did so four times.

47. (B); "Distinct" in the context of this passage is closest in meaning to "separate."

48. (D); Worker bees are female according to paragraph 2.

49. (C); See paragraph 2. Choice (C) applies to drones, male bees.

50. larva; Possible referents include "larva," "cell," or "wax lid." The phrase "sealing it in" provides a determinative clue that "it" refers to "larva."

51. (C); "Successive" in the context of this passage is closest in meaning to "consecutive."

52. (A); See paragraph 3. Choice (A) contradicts sentence 4 in paragraph 3.

53. Eighth square (hive entrance. ■ It is); "A house working bee" is the device that connects the excerpted sentence with the preceding sentence.

54. (D); Choice (D) mentions both the social structure and the responsibilities. Choice (A) or (C) is partial. Choice (B) is irrelevant.

55. The fertilized egg hatches ~ 1300 meals a day; Scan the passage for "larva." Refer to sentence 4 in paragraph 2.

Chapter 6 – Miscellaneous Overview and Purpose Questions

Skill Building

Skill Building 1: Organization
1. (C) 2. (A)

Skill Building 2-1: Tone
1. (C) 2. (B)

Skill Building 2-2: Attitude
1. (D) 2. (C)

Skill Building 2-3: Purpose
1. (D) 2. (B) 3. (D)

Skill Building 3: Preceding/Following Topics
1. (D) 2. (A)

Intensive Exercises

Exercise 6.1	1. (A) 2. (D)	**Exercise 6.2**	1. (C) 2. (B)
Exercise 6.3	1. (D) 2. (A)	**Exercise 6.4**	1. (D) 2. (C)
Exercise 6.5	1. (D) 2. (B)		

Vocabulary Review for Intensive Exercises 6.1-6.5
1. (B) 2. (D) 3. (C) 4. (A) 5. (D)
6. (A) 7. (C) 8. (C) 9. (B) 10. (D)

Practice Test 6

Questions 1-11

1. (B); Choices (A), (C) and (D) are too narrow. Refer to the first paragraph for the best answer, Choice (B). Other paragraphs detail the main topic of El Niño and its impact on the oceanic

environment.

2. (C); "Anomalous" describes something not normal, which is "abnormal." Other choices are not the accepted meanings of the word "anomalous."
3. (B); Choice (B) contradicts the facts in sentence 3 in paragraph 1.
4. fishermen; The referring word "they" is followed by "take a break." It points to the subject of the preceding sentence.
5. (C); Look at sentence 2 in paragraph 2. It is said that " ~ the waters become cool again, fish stocks are replenished."
6. Fourth square (warm waters. ■ Scientists now); The excerpted sentence explains further the effect of declining fish stocks in paragraph 2.
7. (C); Choices (B) and (D) are based on sentence 3 in paragraph 1 and sentence 2 in paragraph 3. Choice (A) is based on the last sentence of paragraph 1.
8. (D); Refer to sentence 2 in paragraph 3. El Niño has been observed in the last 40 years. Choices (A), (B) and (C) contradict the facts in the passage.
9. (C); Scan the passage looking for the key word "coastline." Sentence 3 in paragraph 4 presents details about a movement of ocean water away from the coastline. Choice (C) is from sentence 3 in paragraph 4.
10. Scientists now reserve the term El Niño ~ meaning "the girl"; Scan the passage for the key expression "normal circulation." Look at sentence 1 in paragraph 3.
11. (A); Refer to the last sentence of the passage.

Questions 12-22

12. (C); Choice (A) is too broad. Choices (B) and (D) are too specific. Choice (C) has the key word "population shift."
13. (D); In the context of the passage, "impact" is most similar in meaning to "effect." "Economic impact" means "economic effect." No other answer choices are accepted meanings of the word "impact."
14. (C); In the sentence "The movement ~, which was accelerated by ~" in paragraph 1, "accelerated" can be best replaced by "hastened." "Stimulate" in Choice (B) does not necessarily mean "go faster" in the sense of "accelerate" or "hasten."
15. (A); Refer to the last sentence of paragraph 2. "The voting patterns in the House of Representatives" is related to a political situation. Choices (B), (C) and (D) contradict the facts in the passage; "Decrease" in Choice (B), "Asian" in Choice (C), and "decrease" in Choice (D) should be changed to "increase," "Hispanic," and "increase" respectively according to the facts in the passage.
16. (C); The last sentence of paragraph 2 is the basis from which Choice (C) can be inferred. The conservatism of the Sunbelt states will diminish because of the population shift toward more young people in the Sunbelt area.
17. Sun Belt states; "Their" refers to the subject of the sentence. Remember to verify the meaning after replacing "their" by "Sun Belt states."
18. (C); The clue is in sentence 3 of paragraph 3, which is "Social Security will be affected ~ young workers to pay Social Security taxes to support ~."
19. (B); Look at sentence 4 in paragraph 3. Scan for the key words "1960s" and "1970s" in the passage.
20. The growth of population ~ economically and politically; Scan the passage for the list of states. Sentence 1 in paragraph 2 has the list of states called the Sunbelt.

21. (A); Refer to the last paragraph, especially the last sentence. Riots of Hispanics are compared to African-American ghetto riots of the 1960s. Choice (B) has no basis in the passage. Choices (C) and (D) are inaccurate statements.

22. Sixth square (and illegal. ■ By the); The word "illegal" connects the preceding sentence with the excerpted sentence. The most proper spot is (B).

Questions 23-33

23. (B); Sentences 2 and 3 in paragraph 1 are clues to the main topic. Choices (A) and (D) are too broadly stated. Choice (C) is irrelevant.

24. Moon; "It" refers to the subject of the preceding sentence.

25. dark; From the phrase "totally illuminated" or "completely dark" in sentence 2 of paragraph 1, we can guess that "illuminated (lit)" and "dark" have opposite meanings.

26. completely; From the phrase "totally illuminated" or "completely dark" in sentence 2 of paragraph 1, we can guess that "totally" and "completely" are similar in meaning.

27. (B); Refer to sentence 4 in paragraph 1 that "the light that reaches the Earth from the Moon is simply reflected sunlight."

28. (C); "Relative" is most similar in meaning to "compared." No other choices are accepted meanings of the word "relative."

29. Second square (for centuries. ■ Although the half); The word "phase" connects the preceding sentence with the excerpted sentence.

30. (C); Sentences 1 and 2 in paragraph 2 give a definition of "the phases of the Moon." The expression " ~ see only a portion of the illuminated half from Earth" is restated as "the partial view of the illuminated half of the Moon."

31. (D); Look at sentences 2 and 3 in paragraph 1 and sentence 1 in paragraph 2 as well as paragraph 3. The full moon is not the shadowed half of the Moon, but the illuminated half of the Moon.

32. (A); Scan the whole passage to find the word "wax." The last two sentences of paragraph 2 mention that " As the Moon moves from new moon to the full, the illuminated portion becomes larger, and it is said to be waxing."

33. (A); Look at sentence 1 in the last paragraph. The phase of the Moon is just the shadow on the Moon as observed from Earth.

Questions 34-44

34. (C); The passage deals with the kinds of various fruits by means of classification and explanation. It is most likely to be prepared by someone specializing in botanicals. Choice (D) is too broad. Choice (B) is irrelevant because the passage is not about the planting and growing of fruits.

35. (C); To figure out the purpose of the passage, the flow of the idea has to be grasped as a whole. Choices (B) and (D) are narrow and specific to the part of the passage. Choice (A) is irrelevant to the passage.

36. (B); Choices (A), (C) and (D) are related to aggregate fruits such as "strawberry." Choice (B) is related to "simple fruits." Refer to sentence 3 in paragraph 1.

37. Simple fruits; In the bold text, "simple fruits" is the plural noun phrase that "they" refers to in this context.

38. (A), (C); Some questions on the TOEFL, although not many, ask you to choose two answers. Look at sentences 3 and 4 in paragraph 2 for grapes. Grapes are simple fruits. Refer to

sentences 3 and 4 in paragraph 3 for peaches. The peach is a typical drupe.

39. (C); "Succulent" describes one aspect of a peach. The most probable synonym is "juicy."

40. Sixth square (rose hips. ■ Apples and); The word "pomes" connects the preceding and the excerpted sentence.

41. (B); Look at the last sentence of the passage. Almonds and coconuts are drupes, which belong to simple fruits. According to paragraph 2, tomatoes are classified as simple fruits.

42. (D); In the context of the last sentence, "nut" is a confusing term because nuts belong to diverse classes of fruits. One can guess that the term "nut" is used carelessly.

43. The peach is a typical drupe; ~ of the mature ovary; Scan the passage for the term "peach." Then decide which sentence describes the peach in detail. Click anywhere on sentence 4 in paragraph 3.

44. (A); Sometimes on the TOEFL, answer choices are given in pictures. The peach is a typical drupe. Therefore, you may safely choose the picture resembling the shape of a peach.

Complete Practice Test 1

Listening

1. (D)	2. (B)	3. (C)	4. (A)	5. (B)
6. (D)	7. (A)	8. (D)	9. (B)	10. (C)
11. (D)	12. (B)	13. (A)	14. (C)	15. (D)
16. (B)	17. (C)	18. (C)	19. (B)	20. (D)

21. Mercatorial map – 16th Century
    T and O map – Medieval
    Accurate longitudes – 17th Century

22. (A)	23. (A)	24. (B)	25. (D)
26. (C)	27. (D)	28. (B)	29. (B)

30. First magazine stories were published.
    First books were published.
    James learned to write theater.
    He wrote his greatest novels.

31. (A)

32. *The Portrait of a Lady* – A critique of personal freedom
    A Passionate Pilgrim – An early work with an international theme
    The Golden Bowl – A series of conversations, revealing consciousness

33. (A), (C)	34. (C)	35. (B)	36. (D)
37. (D)	38. (A)	39. (C)	40. (C)
41. (B)	42. (A)	43. (D)	44. (A)

45. (D)

46. Dr. James C. Jackson – Granula
    Will K. Kellogg – Corn flakes
    Ferdinand Schumacher – Rolled oats

47. (D)	48. (C)	49. (D)	50. (B)

Structure

1. (A) Since	2. (A) containing
3. (C) passes	4. (C)
5. (B) dispersal	6. (C)
7. (D) an	8. (A)
9. (C) sufficient to	10. (C) who
11. (A)	12. (B) increased
13. (C) in cold	14. (B)
15. (C) use	16. (B)
17. (B) but	18. (A)
19. (B) cell	20. (C)

Reading

1. (B)	2. expedition	3. (A)	4. (D)	5. interior
6. (C)	7. Lewis and Clark	8. Although Jefferson ... United States."	9. (A)	10. (C)
11. (B)	12. (D)	13. (A)	14. these ideas	15. experts
16. (A)	17. (C)	18. (D)	19. (D)	20. (C)
21. (A)	22. Seventh square (very rare. ■ But by)		23. (B)	24. accumulated
25. (A)	26. (B)	27. differentiated		

28. Fourth square (different sources. ■ The geologic)   29. (B)

30. The geologic ... nineteenth century.

31. the earth	32. (B)	33. (C)	34. (B)	35. presented
36. (C)	37. (A)	38. (D)	39. Rooted in ... as blacks.	
40. (C)	41. minstrelsy	42. (A)	43. (B)	44. (D)

Writing

Imagine that a friend of yours has been given a sum of money and plans to spend it all either to buy an automobile, or to take a vacation. If your friend asked you for advice, what would you say? Compare these two options and explain which one you think is better for your friend. Use specific examples and reasons to explain your opinion.

My own decision would most likely be to take the vacation. A vacation could have both short-term and long-term benefits. Its immediate benefits include relaxation and relief from stress. There are interesting places to visit and beautiful things to be seen, both in one's own country and abroad. Tour packages offered by travel companies can make foreign travel inexpensive, safe, and enjoyable. Moreover, while abroad, one can gather information and obtain perspectives which may be available nowhere else.

For example, my own travels to other countries have shown me what a pleasant change life in another country can provide. Seoul is safer than Washington, D.C. – so much safer, indeed, that I have chosen to remain in Seoul for the time being. One American writer I know visited the Canary Islands, found that environment much more agreeable than America, and stayed in the islands for an extended visit.

On the other hand, the car could be used for years and would provide convenience of movement over a wide area, but the advantages of a private car would be limited. Also, driving is one of the most stressful activities in daily life. Add to these considerations the long-term expenses of owning and operating a car, from insurance and fuel to repairs and parking fees, and to buy a car does not appear the more attractive option.

Therefore, I would recommend investing in a vacation rather than in a new car. A trip to another country might reveal opportunities one has never even imagined. Such discoveries would supply a better return on investment than a car, and the travel itself would be enjoyable.